American Women's Track and Field,
1981–2000

American Women's Track and Field, 1981–2000

A History

LOUISE MEAD TRICARD

McFarland & Company, Inc., Publishers

Jefferson, North Carolina, and London

All quotations from *The New York Times* are
© The New York Times Co. and are reprinted with permission

LIBRARY OF CONGRESS CATALOGUING-IN-PUBLICATION DATA

Tricard, Louise Mead, 1936–
American women's track and field, 1981–2000 : a history /
Louise M. Tricard.
p.   cm.
Includes bibliographical references and index.
ISBN-13: 978-0-7864-2973-8
(illustrated case binding: 50# alkaline paper) ∞

1. Track and field for women — United States — History.   2. Women
track and field athletes — United States — History.   I. Title.
GV1060.8.T752   2008
796.42082 — dc22   2007041736

British Library cataloguing data are available

Cover photograph ©2007 Brand X Pictures

Manufactured in the United States of America

*McFarland & Company, Inc., Publishers
Box 611, Jefferson, North Carolina 28640
www.mcfarlandpub.com*

To my mom
and to the women who made this history
and to the present and future athletes
who continue to carry the torch

Acknowledgments

Firstly, I would like to thank Hal Bateman for the statistical support he provided for the many chapters of this book. And a special thank you to George Dales for providing the opportunity to be part of the 1996 and 2004 Olympic Games. The memories of those two events are wonderfully heartwarming.

Many other people played significant parts: Allan Steinfeld, Bill Monovan, Jim Dunaway, Amy Acuff, Ceci Hopp St. Geme, Danny Williams, Cynthia E. Stinger, USOC, Cindy Slater, USOC, Elliott Denman, Pam Spencer, Jill Geer, USATF, Dorothy Jennings, Karen D'Aprix, Susan Puretz, Walter Murphy, Willie Banks, Dr. Bert Lyle, Dr. Ernie Gregoire, Jean Gregoire, Lynn Cannon, Bruce Tenen, Gary Westerfield, Howard Schmertz, Dr. Harmon Brown, Marjorie Larney, Ray Flynn, Melissa Beasley, USATF, Ken Stone, Darrell Smith, Mike Rohl, Roger Ruth, Phil Raschker, Cedric Walker, Dr. Lillian Greene-Chamberlain, Benita Fitzgerald-Mosley, Karen Simpson, Brevard Community College Librarian, Heliodoro Rico, Pat Rico, Len Olson, Diana Sucich, Karen Mendyka Huff Pawlik, Krista Austin, Stephanie Brown, Rose Monday, Connie Price-Smith, LaTanya Sheffield, Terry Crawford, Bruce Mac Donald, Fran Rizzi, Jocelyn Lowther, Jackie Archis, Berny Wagner, Ben and Marge Carinci, Jane Mead Peter, Al Puma, Jack Pfiffer, Kari Pinnock, Arlene and Joanne Eneman, Sharrieffa Barksdale, Joe Douglas, Wayne Wilson, Darrell Jones, Eric Pelle, Garry Hill, Dave Johnson, Emanuel Hudson, Mike Roth and The Armory Foundation.

I have to thank Dr. William R. Grace, Ann Makoske, Bob Makoske, Pat Davis, John Tricard and Ruth Fountain for their contributions as I drew close to finishing the manuscript. Without them, I could not have finished in a timely fashion.

Contents

Contents

Contents

Abbreviations

AAU	Amateur Athletic Union
AIAW	Association for Intercollegiate Athletics for Women
AJR	American Junior Record
AR	American Record
DNC	Did not compete
DNF	Did not finish
DNQ	Did not qualify
DQ	Disqualified
Dis Med	Distance Medley Relay
EOR	Establishes Olympic Record
H	Heat
HT	Hand Timed
HWR	Heptathlon World Record
IAAF	International Amateur Athletic Federation
IOC	International Olympic Committee
Lp	Lap
MR	Meet Record
NCAA	National Collegiate Athletic Association
OR	Olympic Record
QF	Quarterfinal
Pac 10	Pacific 10 Conference Championships
PR	Personal Record
PTP	Point to Point
S	Semifinal
SEC	Southeastern Conference Championships
SpMed	Sprint Medley Relay
TAC	The Athletic Congress
USATF	USA Track and Field
USOC	United States Olympic Committee
W	Wind Aided
WJR	World Junior Record
WR	World Record

Preface

My first book on this subject, *American Women's Track and Field: A History* (1996), ended in 1980. The women athletes who were members of the 1980 Olympic Team did not get to compete in Moscow because the United States boycotted the games. But there were many other women in the first book who not only did not get to compete in Olympic Games, but were also excluded from the varied events of the track and field program that men competed in; from athletic scholarships which the men got; from recognition; from coaching positions; and from the many track meets open to men only.

Wilma Rudolph was the catalyst for change in the sport after the Olympic games in 1960. After 1972, Title IX was the force behind additional changes necessary for women to stay in the sport through their college years. Because of Title IX, talented high school women athletes could now claim their share of college scholarships.

This second book, which documents events in the years 1981 through 2000, celebrates the reversal of the negative aspects of the sport that women were subjected to in the earlier years.

Slowly but surely, track and field programs have developed in colleges around the country. A full program of distance events was added to the Olympic schedule, culminating in the 1984 Olympic marathon. By the year 2000, women were throwing the hammer, running the steeple-chase, triple jumping and, in the 2000 Olympic games, pole vaulting. Today, we are waiting for the decathlon to replace the heptathlon. When this happens, the men's and women's programs will finally be equal.

National championships and major meets now include women. Women share in the meet publicity. A few meets continued through the years with a disparity of number of events. This is illustrated in the book chapters. The Sunkist Invitational, a major indoor meet in Los Angeles, has had a limited number of events for women throughout the years.

The years 1981–2000 saw prize money awarded to women and major sponsorships allowing them to stay in the sport after college and make a living in track and field. American women began to make their mark on the world stage by establishing world records and winning Olympic gold medals and world championship titles. Athletes like Mary Decker Slaney, Madeline Manning, Evelyn Ashford, Jackie Joyner Kersee, Florence Griffith Joyner, and Stacy Dragila became role models for young girls.

Research for this book involved many hours in the Brevard Community College library and the Merritt Island public library collecting twenty years' worth of articles from the *New York Times*. The author's collection of books, magazines, and articles and statistical material sent from Hal Bateman, USA Track and Field, completed the rest of the research. Several books, which were always close at hand, provided a continuous source of data checking: Hal Bateman's *A Century of Stars: USA International Athletes 1896–1998*; yearly volumes of *FAST—Track and Field Athletics Annual* (Scott S. Davis, General Editor); and Mel Watman's *Olympic Track & Field History.*

With the two volumes of *American Women's Track and Field,* women's track and field history has now been documented with coverage of all indoor and outdoor national championships, Olympic trials, Olympic teams, Pan American teams, world and United States rankings and other meets from 1895 to 2000.

I wrote these books because of my profound love for the sport, which includes a lifetime of competing, coaching, officiating and contributing to the many aspects of track and field. I have also been inspired by my great respect for the unique American women who made a commitment to track and field for a significant part of their lives. I hope their stories and their achievements will inspire young women to follow in their dedicated footsteps.

1

1981

The 93rd USA/Mobil National Outdoor Track and Field Championships were held in Hughes Stadium, Sacramento, California, June 19–21. After a disappointing Olympic boycott year in 1980, athletes this year were selected for the World Cup meet in Rome, Italy, on September 4–6, and for the dual meet in Leningrad, with the Soviet Union, on July 10–11.

The Outdoor Nationals

Two pre–meet articles appeared in the *New York Times* on June 19 and 20, featuring miler Steve Scott and high jumper Benn Fields. A short reference was made to the women's finals held on the 19th, the women's 5,000 meter walk, won by Susan Liers-Westerfield, the 10,000 meter run, won by Joan Benoit, and the women's team of SportsWest that captured the 3200 meter relay. Additionally, the article reported that Evelyn Ashford and Jeanette Bolden advanced in the 100 meters.

Frank Litsky's article in the *New York Times* on Sunday, June 21, featured Carl Lewis' wins in the long jump and 100 meters. It included a brief report of Evelyn Ashford winning the 100 meters, for the third time, in 11.07 and Stephanie Hightower repeating her victory in the 100 meter hurdles in 13.09. Monday and Tuesday's *New York Times* featured stories on Sydney Maree and Carl Lewis respectively. None of the women's winners were mentioned.

100 meters	
1. Evelyn Ashford, Medalist Track Club	11.07
2. Jeanette Bolden, Shaklee Track Club	11.27
3. Alice Brown, Shaklee Track Club	11.28
4. Florence Griffith, Shaklee Track Club	11.29
5. Brenda Morehead, Police Athletic League	11.42
6. Esmeralda Garcia, Florida State Track Club/Brazil	11.58
200 meters	
1. Evelyn Ashford, Medalist Track Club	22.30 MR
(betters meet record of 22.60 by Brenda Morehead, Tennessee State University, 1978)	
2. Florence Griffith, Shaklee Track Club	23.09
3. Jackie Pusey, Los Angeles Naturite Track Club/Jamaica	23.14

Left to right: Sharon Warren, Madeline Manning-Mims, Louise Mead Tricard, 1999.

4. Chandra Cheeseborough, Tigerbelle Track Club	23.17
5. Randy Givens, Florida State Track Club	23.84
6. Michelle Matthias, University of New Mexico	24.21

400 meters
1. Denean Howard, Shaklee Track Club	51.79
2. Rosalyn Bryant, Los Angeles Naturite Track Club	52.53
3. Lorna Forde, Atoms Track Club	52.87
4. Arlise Emerson, Shaklee Track Club	53.37
5. Kelia Bolton, Stanford Track Club	53.56
6. Lori McCauley, Ambler Olympic Club	54.09

800 meters
1. Madeline Manning, Oral Roberts Track Club	1:58.50 MR
(betters meet record of 1:58.75 by Manning, 1980)	
2. Leann Warren, Oregon Track Club	2:00.08
3. Robin Campbell, Stanford Track Club	2:01.02
4. Delisa Walton, Knoxville Track Club	2:01.39
5. Kim Gallagher, Willingboro Track Club	2:01.82
6. Lee Ballenger, Athletics West	2:03.21

1500 meters
1. Jan Merrill, Age Group Athletic Association	4:14.62
2. Cindy Bremser, Wisconsin United Track Club	4:15.34
3. Maggie Keyes, Athletics West	4:15.84
4. Linda Goen, Shaklee Track Club	4:16.14

5. Regina Joyce, SportsWest/Great Britain — 4:16.61
6. Rose Thomson, Wisconsin United Track Club/Kenya — 4:20.2 ht

3000 meters
1. Brenda Webb, Athletics West — 9:04.54
2. Joan Hansen, unattached — 9:07.57
3. Carol Urish, Houston Harriers — 9:19.50
4. Margaret Groos, Charlottesville Track Club — 9:20.28
5. Jan Merrill, Age Group Athletic Association — 9:21.60
6. Debbie Eide, Oregon Track Club — 9:21.90

10,000 meters
1. Joan Benoit, Athletics West — 33:37.5 ht
2. Patsy Sharples, University of Idaho/South Africa — 34:10.2
3. Julie Shea, Athletics West — 34:30.6
4. Glenys Quick, Texas Woman's University Track Club/New Zealand — 34:38.8
5. Kim Schnurpfeil, Stanford Track Club — 34:39.3
6. Jan Oehm, unattached — 34:42.9

100 meter hurdles
1. Stephanie Hightower, Los Angeles Naturite Track Club — 13.09
2. Benita Fitzgerald, Knoxville Track Club — 13.10
3. Jackie Washington, Shaklee Track Club — 13.18
4. Carol Lewis, Willingboro Track Club — 13.73
5. Gayle Watkins, DC International — 13.02
6. Tonja Brown, Florida State Track Club — 13.94

400 meter hurdles
1. Sandy Myers, Los Angeles Naturite Track Club — 56.43 MR
    (betters meet record of 56.61 by Mary Ayers, Prairie View A&M,
        1977)
2. Tammy Etienne, University of Texas — 57.14
3. Edna Brown, Temple University — 57.82
4. Lexie Miller, Oregon Track Club — 57.82
5. Karen Taylor, Shaklee Track Club — 58.98
6. Rachel Clary, University of Houston — 59.06

5000 meter walk
1. Susan Liers-Westerfield, Island Track Club — 24:26.7
2. Bonnie Dillon, Cupertino Yearlings — 25:39.6
3. Vicki Jones, California Walkers — 25:49.1
4. Paula Kash, California Walkers — 26:05.2
5. Barbara Carroll, unattached — 26:08.5
6. Aimee Burr, Mesa Sun Angels Track Club — 26:31.3

4 × 100 meter relay
1. Shaklee Track Club — 43.39 MR
    (Alice Brown, Florence Griffith, Valerie Brisco, Jeanette Bolden)
    (betters meet record of 43.68 by Tennessee State University, 1979)
2. Los Angeles Naturite Track Club — 44.04
3. Los Angeles Mercurettes "B" — 45.02

800 meter sprint medley relay
1. Los Angeles Naturite Track Club — 1:37.86
    (Aeda Hay, Jennifer Inniss, Yolanda Rich, Jackie Pusey)

2. Shaklee Track Club "A"	1:38.38
3. Shaklee Track Club "B"	1:38.85

4 × 400 meter relay
1. Los Angeles Naturite Track Club	3:27.90 MR
(Rosalyn Bryant, Jackie Pusey, Yolanda Rich, Sandy Myers)	
(betters meet record of 3:32.80 by Prairie View A&M, 1979)	
2. Shaklee Track Club	3:29.34
3. Los Angeles Mercurettes	3:33.43

4 × 800 meter relay
1. SportsWest	8:36.94
(Sue Gregg, Theresa Smith, Regina Joyce, Sandra Gregg)	
2. San Jose Cindergals	8:41.87
3. Los Angeles Naturite Track Club	8:44.21

High jump
1. Pam Spencer, Los Angeles Naturite Track Club	6' 4¾" MR
(betters meet record of 6' 4" by Debbie Brill, Pacific	
Coast Club, 1979, and Coleen Rienstra, Sun Devil Sports, 1980)	
2. Louise Ritter, Pacific Coast Club	6' 3½"
3. Coleen Rienstra, Sun Devil Sports	6' 3"
4. Phyllis Blunston, Los Angeles Mercurettes	6' 1¼"
5. Hisayo Fukumitsu, Japan	6' 1¼"
6. Joni Huntley, Pacific Coast Club	6'

Long jump
1. Jodi Anderson, Los Angeles Naturite Track Club	22' ¼"
2. Kathy McMillan, Shaklee Track Club	21' 7½"
3. Carol Lewis, Willingboro Track Club	21' 5½"
4. Pat Johnson, Wisconsin United Track Club	21' 5¼"
5. Lorraine Ray, Florida Track Club	21' 4"
6. Sandy Myers, Los Angeles Naturite Track Club	20' 9¼"

Shot put
1. Denise Wood, Knoxville Track Club	55' 5¾"
2. Lorna Griffin, Athletics West	53' 4¼"
3. Sandy Burke, Northeastern University	52' 5½"
4. Mariette van Heerden, Los Angeles Naturite Track Club/Zimbabwe	51' 9¾"
5. Oneithea Davis, Police Athletic League	51' 6¼"
6. Carol VanPelt, SportsWest	50' 9½"

Discus
1. Leslie Deniz, Sun Devil Sports	182' 9"
2. Denise Wood, Knoxville Track Club	181' 9"
3. Mariette van Heerden, Los Angeles Naturite Track Club/Zimbabwe	179' 9"
4. Lorna Griffin, Athletics West	179' 5"
5. Julia Hansen, SportsWest	174'
6. Jan Svendsen, Shaklee Track Club	169' 11"

Javelin
1. Karin Smith, Medalist Track Club	208' 2"
2. Kate Schmidt, Pacific Coast Club	199' 5"
3. Lynda Hughes, unattached	176'
4. Mary Osbourne, Stanford Track Club	169' 10"

5. Sally Harmon, Oregon Track Club	164' 9"
6. Barbara Moro, Shaklee Track Club	164' 8"

Team scores:

1. Los Angeles Naturite Track Club	99
2. Shaklee Track Club	94
3. Athletics West	45

Outstanding Female Athlete
Evelyn Ashford, Medalist Track Club

Denise Wood, ca. 1981.

The Indoor Nationals

The 1981 TAC Indoor National Championships were held in Madison Square Garden, New York, on February 27, before a crowd of almost 16,000 fans.

The *New York Times*, the day of the meet, featured an article and photograph of high jumper Joni Huntley. Joni was jumping with an injured foot.

Hurt or not, Miss Huntley will seek her sixth national indoor high-jump title in eight years tonight in the USA/ Mobil track and field championships at Madison Square Garden.

...Three weeks ago, in the Wanamaker Millrose Games at the Garden, Miss Huntley won and raised her American indoor record to 6 feet 4¾ inches, 2 inches higher than her outdoor best. A 6–4¾ jump by a 5-foot-8-inch woman was a notable achievement. For someone with Miss Huntley's foot problems, it was remarkable.

With her sparkling green eyes and radiant smile, 24-year-old Joni Huntley hardly looks like a physical wreck. And she is not, except for those feet. The last time they were sound was in 1976, when she finished fifth at the Olympics in Montreal.

...Miss Huntley has been high jumping since she was 9. How long will she continue?

"I take each meet as it comes," she said, "I'd like to jump as long as I'm healthy and performing well. I'm the assistant women's coach at Oregon State and I love the job, so high jumping isn't my entire life. But it's still a big part, even with my feet."

Saturday's *New York Times* headlines proclaimed, "Coghlan Wins 3-Mile Run In 2d Fastest Indoor Time," although photographs of Francie Larrieu, winning the two mile run, and Benita Fitzgerald, winning the 60 yard hurdles, graced the sports page.

Three paragraphs talked about the women's accomplishments:

Other strong women's performances came from Chandra Cheeseborough of Tennessee State University, who ran the fastest indoor 220 yards ever (23.27) and was voted the meet's outstanding woman athlete, and Evelyn Ashford, who beat the season's best sprint field with a 6.63 in the 60-yard dash.

Two years ago, Miss Ashford was the world's dominant sprinter, overwhelming the best from East Germany and the Soviet Union. A knee injury and the United States boycott side-tracked her in 1980, but after overhauling Jeannette Bolden in the final few strides last night, she said, "Everything's fine, I'm where I want to be. I think I'm better than I was."

Besides her speed, Miss Ashford dazzled the crowd with her sleek beige speed-skating suit. She said she began wearing the racing suit at indoor meets as a precaution against muscle pulls. Now she says she feels so comfortable in the outfit ("it feels like a second skin") that she is considering wearing the suit outdoors.

60 yard dash
1. Evelyn Ashford, unattached — 6.63
2. Jeanette Bolden, Shaklee Track Club — 6.69
3. Chandra Cheeseborough, Tennessee State University — 6.72

220 yard dash
1. Chandra Cheeseborough, Tennessee State University — 23.27 — AR, MR
2. Florence Griffith, Shaklee Track Club — 23.86
3. Sheryl Pernell, Tennessee State University — 24.49

440 yard run
1. Diane Dixon, Atoms Track Club — 55.38
2. Stephanie Vega, Atoms Track Club — 57.15
3. Ella Willis, Concerned Athletes-In-Action — 57.6

880 yard run
1. Delisa Walton, University of Tennessee — 2:05.1
2. Robin Campbell, Stanford Track Club — 2:05.7
3. Lorna Forde, Atoms Track Club — 2:07.9

Mile run
1. Jan Merrill, Age Group Athletic Association — 4:34.00
2. Maggie Keyes, Athletics West — 4:35.47
3. Cindy Bremser, Wisconsin United Track Club — 4:41.75

Two mile run
1. Francie Larrieu, Pacific Coast Club — 9:38.1 — WR, AR
2. Margaret Groos, University of Virginia — 9:38.3
3. Brenda Webb, Athletics West — 9:45.6

60 yard hurdles
1. Benita Fitzgerald, University of Tennessee — 7.72
2. Sharon Colyear, Boston University/Great Britain — 7.76
3. Karen Wechsler, Indiana University — 7.78

Mile walk
1. Susan Liers-Westerfield, Island Track Club — 7:05.0
2. Susan Brodock, Southern California Road Runners — 7:30.0
3. Paula Kash, California Walkers — 7:39.0

640 yard relay
1. Tennessee State University — 1:08.99 AR
   (Chandra Cheeseborough, Ernestine Davis, Judy Pollion, Sheryl Pernell)
2. Shaklee Track Club — 1:10.23
3. DC International — 1:10.5

Mile relay
1. Los Angeles Mercurettes — 3:40.46 WR, AR
   (Deanne Gutowski, Paulette Clagon, Cindy Cumbess, Brenda Peterson)
2. Atoms Track Club — 3:41.64
3. Shaklee Track Club — 3:45.76

880 yard medley relay (440, 110, 110, 220)
1. Tennessee State University — 1:42.17
   (Ernestine Davis, Judy Pollion, Sheryl Pernell, Chandra Cheeseborough)

2. Gazelle International   1:46.81
3. Los Angeles Mercurettes   1:47.06

High jump
1. Joni Huntley, Pacific Coast Club   6' 1¼"
2. Yvonne Heinrich, North Carolina State University   5' 11¼"
3. Yolanda Gibson, Atoms Track Club   5' 11¼"

Long jump
1. Ana Alexander, Cuba   20' 9¾"
2. Carol Lewis, Willingboro Track Club   20' 9¼"
3. Evalene Hatcher, Morgan State University   20' 7¾"

Shot put
1. Marita Walton, University of Maryland   52' 11"
2. Denise Wood, Knoxville Track Club   52' 7"
3. Oneithea Davis, St. John's University   49' 4"

Team Champion:
Tennessee State University 19.2 points

Sunkist Invitational (5 women's events): Los Angeles, January 30

60 yards
1. Evelyn Ashford, unattached   6.66 MR

500 yards
1. Denean Howard, Kennedy High School, Granada Hills   1:04.1 MR

800 meters
1. Robin Campbell, Stanford Track Club   2:11.7

Mile
1. Ellen Wessinghage, West Germany   4:36.1

60 meter hurdles
1. Renee Felton, Santa Monica Track Club   8.06

TAC Pentathlon (60 meter hurdles, shot put, high jump, long jump, 800 meters): Pocatello, Idaho, February 15

1. Marlene Harmon, Los Angeles Naturite Track Club   4064
2. Susan Brownell, University of Virginia   4043
3. Mary Harrington, Fort Collins Track Club   3916

1st U.S. Women's Heptathlon Championships: Spokane Community College, Spokane, Washington, June 26–27

1. Jane Frederick, Athletics West   6011 w
2. Jackie Joyner, University of California, Los Angeles/Shaklee Track Club   5827 w
3. Patsy Walker, University of Houston   5704 w

4. Mary Harrington, Pocatello Track Club   5698
5. Theresa Smith, SportsWest   5618
6. Jenny Stary, Metroplex Striders   5583

> Bob Seaman reported that the heptathlon replaced the pentathlon this year.

3rd IAAF World Cup: Rome, Italy, September 4–6

While Evelyn Ashford was racing to an "impressive" victory in the 200 meters, the headlines in the *New York Times* read, "Coe and Moses Win In World Cup Track."

Miss Ashford also beat the Olympic champion in her event, the women's 200 meters. Running in the first lane, Miss Ashford hit the top of the straightaway a foot ahead of Barbel Wockel of East Germany, who won the 1980 Olympic 200 in Moscow, and Jarmila Kratochvilova of Czechoslovakia, running for the European team.

Miss Ashford poured it on down the finishing straight and pulled away to a two-meter victory in 22.13 seconds. Miss Wockel faded to third.

The following day, after Evelyn won her second sprint race, the 100 meters, the *New York Times* headlines read, "2 Sprint Races won By Evelyn Ashford."

Evelyn Ashford, a sprinter for the United States, won the 100-meter dash in 11.02 seconds tonight and became the first double champion in the World Cup track and field competition.

...For Miss Ashford, who won the 200 meters last night, it was her second sprint double in a row in World Cup competition. She also won the 100 and 200 at the second World Cup, in 1979 at Montreal.

Left to right: **Willye White, Pat Connolly at the 1996 Atlanta Olympic Games.**

Pat Connolly wrote in her book *Coaching Evelyn*, "Evelyn was adored by European track fans that summer of '81. They gazed at her. They smiled. Their remarks were kind and flattering, and in English so Evelyn could understand. They gave her flowers, candy, T-shirts, sport pins to trade, and expensive souvenirs like crystal vases or picture books. A young German girl gave us both some beautiful glossy photos of Evelyn wearing her black racing suit, which was a sensation in Europe."

100 meters	
1. Evelyn Ashford	11.02 MR (old MR 11.06, Ashford '79)
200 meters	
1. Evelyn Ashford	22.18
400 meters	
4. Denean Howard	51.76
800 meters	
6. Madeline Manning	2:01.79
1500 meters	
5. Jan Merrill	4:08.98
3000 meters	
5. Brenda Webb	9:13.10
100 meter hurdles	
5. Stephanie Hightower	13.09
400 meter hurdles	
7. Sandy Myers	59.95
4 × 100 meter relay	
2. USA	42.82 AR (old AR 42.87, '68)
(Alice Brown, Jeanette Bolden, Florence Griffith, Evelyn Ashford)	
4 × 400 meter relay	
5. USA	3:30.72
(Delisa Walton, Lorna Forde, Arlise Emerson, Denean Howard)	
High jump	
3. Pam Spencer	6' 3½"
Long jump	
2. Jodi Anderson	21' 8¼"
Shot put	
7. Denise Wood	52' 6"
Discus	
6. Leslie Deniz	174' 6"
Javelin	
3. Karin Smith	206' 10"
Score:	
4. United States	89

USA vs. USSR: Leningrad, USSR, July 10, 11

Prior to the meet, the *New York Times* headlines stated, "Boycott Aura Persists In U.S.-Soviet Track."

American athletes are back in the Soviet Union this week to resume a series of track and field meets that began in 1958.

Just how bruised feelings were by the American-led boycott of the 1980 Moscow Olympic Games was evident today when the teams held an eve-of-competition news conference. The Americans who addressed the issue spoke cautiously, but the Soviets were characteristically blunt.

Dr. Harmon Brown of the University of California-Hayward, the head coach, set the tone for the Americans this morning. He told the 70 athletes on the men's and women's teams that it was up to them what they said to the press, but he urged them to weigh their words.

"We're not politicians; we're athletes," Dr. Brown, a 50-year-old physician, told the athletes. "We're here to talk with our feet, so let's let them talk loudly."

...Denise Wood, a 31-year-old American shot-putter, confirmed the Soviet view that the boycott was unpopular among American Olympians.

And Dr. Brown spoke in a similar vein: "Of course I think American athletes and American amateur sportsmen were very disappointed by having several years of preparations frustrated by not being able to compete in the Olympic Games.

"But I think it must be kept in mind that the decision of the government was supported by a good majority of the American public. The athletic community is heavily supported by the American public, so that although we don't always agree with the decisions we have to go along with the principle that the majority does rule."

Two years ago in Berkeley, the last time the teams met, the American women won handily and the men lost, a reversal of the prevailing pattern over the years, giving the Americans an overall 119–102 victory. But in the history of the event the Russians lead in victories, 12–3 with 1 tie, and the odds this time point to another Soviet victory.

After day one of the two-day meet:

...two stirring sprints by a 17-year-old New Jersey girl, Michele Glover, were not enough to counter Soviet dominance of the women's events today as the national teams met for the first time since 1978.

...Still, for the Americans, the star of the first day's competition was Miss Glover, recently graduated from high school in Willingboro, N. J. and headed this fall for the University of Houston. She had been ninth in the Sacramento meet, but she pulled off an unexpected victory in the 100-meter dash (11.45 seconds) and went on to snatch victory from the favored Russians at the tape by overcoming a 5-yard deficit on the anchor leg of the 400-meter relay (43.65).

The outcome of the final day of competition was reported in the *New York Times* on July 12. "Bolstered by a strong showing in the women's events, the Soviet Union rolled to victory over the United States today...." The Soviet Union named 23 year old Louise Ritter, who won the high jump with a meet record of 6 feet 4 ½ inches, one of the outstanding performers.

"...One crowd favorite was Karin Smith, a 25-year-old javelin thrower from Venice, Calif. whose victory, following Miss Ritter's in the high jump, prevented a Soviet sweep of the women's field events."

100 meters	
1. Michelle Glover	11.45
4. Jackie Washington	11.65

200 meters	
3. Tara Mastin	24.15
4. Jeanette Bolden	24.25

400 meters	
2. Denean Howard	51.65
4. Lorna Forde	55.26

800 meters	
2. Madeline Manning	1:59.62
4. Leann Warren	2:00.51

1500 meters
3. Maggie Keyes	4:15.33	
4. Linda Goen	4:16.92	

3000 meters
3. Joan Hansen	9:20.51	
4. Brenda Webb	9:28.32	

100 meter hurdles
2. Stephanie Hightower	13.09	
3. Benita Fitzgerald	13.24	

400 meter hurdles
3. Edna Brown	57.97	
4. Tami Etienne	58.82	

4 × 100 meter relay
1. United States	46.63

(Tara Mastin, Jackie Washington, Benita Fitzgerald, Michelle Glover)

4 × 400 meter relay
2. United States	3:30.12

(Arlise Emerson, Lorna Forde, Robin Campbell, Denean Howard)

High jump
1. Louise Ritter	6' 4½"
4. Phyllis Blunston	6' ¾"

Long jump
3. Kathy McMillan	21' 7¼"
4. Carol Lewis	21' ½"

Shot put
3. Denise Wood	52' 3¼"
4. Sandy Burke	50' 4¼"

Discus
3. Denise Wood	173' 11"
4. Leslie Deniz	168' 11"

Javelin
1. Karin Smith	207' 3"
4. Kate Schmidt	190' 2"

Score:
Soviet Union	99	USA	60

TAC Cross Country Championships: November 29, Pocatello, Idaho

1. Mary Shea, North Carolina State University	18:18.7
2. Julie Shea, North Carolina State University	18:31.1
3. Jan Merrill, Age Group Athletic Association	18:39.1

Grand Prix Winners

(Amount of money won for club)

200 meters	
1. Evelyn Ashford, Medalist Track Club	$2500.
2. Florence Griffith, Shaklee Track Club	$1000.
3. Chandra Cheeseborough, Tigerbelle Track Club	$ 500.

800 meters	
1. Madeline Manning, Oral Roberts Track Club	$2500.
2. Robin Campbell, Stanford Track Club	$1000.
3. Leann Warren, Oregon Track Club	$ 500.

3000 meters	
1. Brenda Webb, Athletics West	$2500.
2. Joan Hansen, unattached	$1000.
3. Jan Merrill, Age Group Athletic Association	$ 500.

High jump	
1. Pam Spencer, Los Angeles Naturite Track Club	$2500.
2. Louise Ritter, Pacific Coast Club	$1000.
3. Coleen Rienstra, Sun Devil Sports	$ 500.

Long jump	
1. Jodi Anderson, Los Angeles Naturite Track Club	$2500.
2. Kathy McMillan, Shaklee Track Club	$1000.
3. Carol Lewis, Willingboro Track Club	$ 500.

Discus	
1. Leslie Deniz, Sun Devil Sports	$2500.
2. Denise Wood, Knoxville Track Club	$1000.
3. Mariette van Heerden, Los Angeles Naturite Track Club/Zimbabwe	$ 500.

Other News and Honors

Women's Track and Field World USA List
(top five Americans and non–wind aided times/heights distances in event)

100 meters		800 meters	
10.90	Evelyn Ashford	1:58.50	Madeline Manning
11.18	Jeanette Bolden	1:59.63	Leann Warren
11.23	Alice Brown	2:01.02	Robin Campbell
11.23	Florence Griffith	2:01.39	Delisa Walton
11.29	Chandra Cheeseborough	2:01.82	Kim Gallagher

200 meters		1500 meters	
21.84	Evelyn Ashford	4:08.98	Jan Merrill
22.65	Chandra Cheeseborough	4:09.32	Leann Warren
22.81	Florence Griffith	4:09.58	Cindy Bremser
23.22	Benita Fitzgerald	4:11.96	Cathie Twomey
23.24	LaShon Nedd	4:12.09	Joan Hansen

400 meters		Mile	
51.45	Ericka Harris	4:30.36	Leann Warren
51.65	Denean Howard	4:31.69	Jan Merrill
51.80	Evelyn Ashford	4:32.27	Brenda Webb
52.34	Robin Coleman	4:32.61	Joan Hansen
52.49	Arlise Emerson	4:33.12	Maggie Keyes

3000 meters		High jump		
8:51.99	Jan Merrill	6' 5½"	Pam Spencer
8:55.39	Cindy Bremser	6' 4¼"	Louise Ritter
9:02.04	Francie Larrieu	6' 3½"	Coleen Rienstra
9:02.74	Brenda Webb	6' 2¼"	Paula Girvin
9:03.64	Joan Hansen	6' 2"	Phyllis Bluntson

5000 meters		Long jump	
15:39.49	Cathie Twomey	22' 10"	Jodi Anderson
15:42.61	Brenda Webb	21' 8"	Kathy McMillan
15:49.37	Kathie Mintie	21' 6"	Carol Lewis
15:40.64	Mary Shea	21' 5¼"	Pat Johnson
15:52.64	Betty Springs	21' 4"	Lorraine Ray

10,000 meters		Shot put	
33:11.54	Patty Catalano	55' 5¾"	Denise Wood
33:15.74	Nancy Conz	53' 4½"	Lorna Griffin
33:17.94	Judi St. Hilaire	53' 4¼"	Elaine Sobansky
33:28.20	Aileen O'Connor	52' 11½"	Sandy Burke
33:29.00	Joan Benoit	52' 4½"	Natalie Kaaiawahia

Marathon		Discus	
2:27:51	Patty Catalano	187' 9"	Denise Wood
2:30:12	Julie Shea	186' 11"	Lorna Griffin
2:30:16	Joan Benoit	182' 9"	Leslie Deniz
2:33:40	Julie Brown	179' 1"	Jan Svendsen
2:34:48	Nancy Conz	178' 9"	Kathy Picknell

100 meter hurdles		Javelin	
13.03	Stephanie Hightower	211' 5"	Karin Smith
13.10	Benita Fitzgerald	200' 1"	Kate Schmidt
13.18	Jackie Washington	189' 4"	Patty Kearney
13.32	Candy Young	182' 4"	Lynda Hughes
13.34	Linda Weekly	179' 8"	Dana Olson

400 meter hurdles		Heptathlon	
56.38	Sandy Myers	6308	Jane Frederick
57.10	Tammy Etienne	5839	Nancy Kindig
57.24	Robin Marks	5827	Jackie Joyner
57.28	Edna Brown	5752	Patsy Walker
57.53	Tonja Brown	5704	Marlene Harmon

Track & Field News: Athlete of the Year

Evelyn Ashford

World Rankings — *Track & Field News*

100 meters
1. Evelyn Ashford
9. Jeanette Bolden

200 meters
1. Evelyn Ashford

400 meters
9. Denean Howard

800 meters
7. Madeline Manning

5000 meters
5. Cathie Twomey

100 meter hurdles
4. Stephanie Hightower

400 meter hurdles
9. Sandy Myers

High jump
3. Pam Spencer
7. Louise Ritter

Long jump
3. Jodi Anderson

Javelin
4. Karin Smith

Heptathlon
4. Jane Frederick

Marathon
3. Patti Catalano
6. Joan Benoit
8. Julie Shea
9. Nancy Conz
10. Laurie Binder

The Bislett Games were on June 27, in Oslo, Norway. Madeline Manning placed first in the 800 meter run in 2:00.09 and Jan Merrill was seventh in the 3000 meter run in 9:03.90.

Evelyn Ashford set an American record of 10.90 in the 100 meters in Colorado Springs in July and won the 100 meters in the National Sports Festival in Syracuse, New York on July 25 in a wind-aided 11.01.

Two world junior records were held by American women:

100 meters	11.13	Chandra Cheeseborough	June 21, 1976
100 meter hurdles	12.95	Candy Young	June 16, 1979

At the end of 1981, no individual world records were held by American women. Both Mary Decker's mile record of 4:21.68 set on January 26, 1980 in Auckland, New Zealand and Jan Merrill's 5000 meter record of 15:30.6 set in Palo Alto, California on March 22, 1980 were broken.

The development of track and field for women in the nation's colleges is illustrated by the following article from *Women's Track and Field World:*

From left: Julia Dyer, Patty Van Wolvelaere, Mamie Rallins, the three 1968 U.S. Olympic hurdlers, at the 1996 Olympic Games.

Left: Carol Thompson, ca. 1981. *Right:* Doris Brown Heritage, 1999.

SU Expands Women's Sports

Syracuse University will add two women's sports — cross country and track — to its intercollegiate program next fall, the university revealed. To help establish those teams, SU will award eight tuition grant-in-aids during the next four years for student athletes, and a full time coach will be hired.

It was reported in the June issue of *Women's Track and Field World* that the following former athletes are now coaches:

Mamie Rallins, Ohio State University
Jarvis Scott, Texas Tech University
Sherry Calvert, University of Southern California
Terry Crawford, University of Tennessee
Carol Thompson, University of Florida
Cherrie Sherrard, Chico State University
Doris Heritage, Seattle Pacific University
Carla Coffey, University of Kansas
Joni Huntley, Oregon State University

New York State held the first combined (boys and girls) high school state championships this year. The girls' events were: 100 meters, 200 meters, 400 meters, 800 meters, 1500 meters, 3000 meters, 1500 meter walk, 100 meter hurdles, 400 meter hurdles, high jump, long jump, discus, shot put, pentathlon, 4 × 100 meter relay, 4 × 400 meter relay and 4 × 800 meter relay.

Julie Brown, Athletics West, won the USA Cross Country Championships.
Jan Merrill finished second in the World Cross Country Championships in Madrid.

Willye White was inducted into the National Track and Field Hall of Fame. The following biography is on the National Track and Field Hall of Fame website:

WILLYE WHITE   SPRINTS-LONG JUMP

Born January 1, 1939, Money, Miss.

Another track great from Tennessee State University, Willye White was the top U.S. woman long jumper in the 1960s and was the first woman to compete for the U.S. in five Olympics.

She first appeared in Olympic competition at Melbourne in 1956, taking the silver medal. In 1960, she failed to qualify for the final but four years later got another silver medal in the 4 × 100 relay after a 12th in the long jump. She was 11th in the long jump in both 1968 and 1972 in her other two Olympic appearances. She sandwiched a Pan American Games championship in 1963 around a pair of third places in that meet in 1959 and 1967. A veteran of numerous other international competitions, White won a dozen National AAU long jump titles, 11 outdoors. She also lengthened the national long jump record seven times.

Willye White, 1996.

American Records

100m	10.90	Evelyn Ashford	July 22, 1981
200m	21.83	Evelyn Ashford	August 24, 1979
400m	50.62	Rosalyn Bryant	July 28, 1976
800m	1:57.9	Madeline Manning	August 7, 1976
1000m	2:37.3	Madeline Manning	July 12, 1976
1500m	3:59.43	Mary Decker	August 13, 1980
Mile	4:21.68	Mary Decker	January 26, 1980
3000m	8:38.73	Mary Decker	July 15, 1980
5000m	15:30.6	Jan Merrill	March 22, 1980
10,000m	32:52.5	Mary Shea	June 15, 1979
100mh	12.86	Deby LaPlante	June 16, 1979
400mh	56.16	Esther Mahr	August 15, 1980
4 × 100mr	42.82	National Team	September 6, 1981
4 × 200mr	1:32.6	National Team	June 24, 1979
4 × 400mr	3:22.81	National Team	July 31, 1976
4 × 800mr	8:19.9	National Team	June 24, 1979
SpMed	1:37.29	Cal State Los Angeles	May 26, 1978
DisMed	11:08.7	University of Virginia	April 23, 1981
HJ	6' 5½"	Pam Spencer	August 28, 1981
LJ	22' 11¾"	Jodi Anderson	June 28, 1980
SP	62' 7¾"	Maren Seidler	June 16, 1979
DT	207' 5"	Lorna Griffin	May 24, 1980

JT	227' 5"	Kate Schmidt	September 10, 1977
Pentathlon	4708	Jane Frederick	May 27, 1979
Heptathlon	6308	Jane Frederick	May 23–24, 1981

INTERVIEW: ONEITHEA "NENI" DAVIS LEWIS

(December 28, 2005) My interest in track and field started early. My father used to make bets with other people and he had me race against the boys. I would beat them every time. By the time I reached junior high school I joined the track team as a sprinter. I ran the 50, 100 and 200 yard dashes and relays and held the school records. In a few of the meets I was the only girl so I would be put in races with the boys. Needless to say, I upset many boys along the way. Although I was on the varsity team in volleyball and basketball, track and field was my favorite. One day in my senior year in high school [1977], I was playing soccer in gym class and my best friend and I went for the ball at the same time. She tried to kick the ball as hard as she could to get it away from me. Unfortunately, she kicked my ankle. My ankle twisted around. I felt a pop and I ended up with a broken ankle. Little did I know that it would be a blessing in disguise. At the time I broke my ankle, I was looking forward to the indoor track season because a lot of schools wanted to come and look at me to recruit me for their programs. I thought that would be the end of it.

Although I was excused from participating in gym class, I decided to go anyway and do some weightlifting to keep my body in shape. One day Bruce MacDonald, an Olympic racewalker, came along and saw me hobbling in the hallway on crutches. He commented on how big and muscular I had gotten. I was busting out of all my clothes from the weightlifting. He made a comment that I was getting so big that I could become a shot putter. Little did he know that he planted a seed in my head.

When I got the cast off, Mr. Mac started me off racewalking to get me in shape until I was able to get some strength back in my leg. In December of 1977, I mentioned to him that I would like to try the shot put in case I didn't recuperate enough in the sprints to get a scholarship. Mr. Mac knew nothing about the shot put, but one day he handed me a black rubber ball about the size of a shot. Neither of us knew what to do with it, but with him being around track for so long he had an idea. He started me off by throwing the rubber ball against a classroom wall. I left these little black dots all over the place. The poor janitor was trying to figure out where they were coming from and who was doing this. But we never got caught. As a matter of fact, we threw in the gym one day and from what I understand there is still a black spot up on the backboard of the basketball net. That's basically how I got started throwing the shot.

In January 1978, I came in second at the New York State Championships. From there, each meet that I went to, I improved. My first meet I threw 32 feet with the eight pound shot. By June, I was participating in the Junior Olympics and I threw 48 feet in the finals in Lincoln, Nebraska. I came in fourth place in that meet. I was thrilled to be considered the fourth best shot putter in the country at that time after only throwing the shot for six months. My rapid improvement at the time was due to Mr. Mac bringing me over to Al Dawson who was the throws coach at C.W. Post College. Al was well regarded for his knowledge in the throws. I very much appreciated him taking the time to show me the proper technique in the shot. Mr. Mac learned very quickly from him so that he could coach me and we took it from there.

Mr. Mac always seemed full of surprises. One day at an outdoor meet on Long Island he handed me a discus and told me he entered me in the event. I asked him how to throw it. He said just watch what the other girls were doing and imitate them. After observing a few throws I asked one young girl who seemed to have the best form to show me how to throw it. Needless to say I upset several people when I broke the Nassau County record with a standing throw. No one believed that I never threw the discus before. I was told last summer that they believe that I still hold the record.

After one meet Mr. Mac had me conduct a clinic on the shot put. I thought he absolutely lost his mind since I was still learning how to throw it myself. He felt it would be a good way of reinforcing what I had learned. Mr. Mac did the same thing with the javelin. He handed it to me and told me to throw.

Since my Mom bribed me with a car if I went to a college close by, Mr. Mac felt St. John's University would be the best school not only for its business program but because of the throws

Oneithea "Neni" Davis Lewis at National Master's Meet, Hawaii, 2005. (Courtesy Suzy Hess/National Masters News.)

coach. Mr. Mac knew Kenny Bantum, a shot putter with him on the 1956 Olympic team, would be coaching there. Of course, when I first met Ken Bantum, he looked at me and said, "This is the shot putter everybody's been talking about?" I was 5' 2½" and 115 pounds. That's relatively small compared to most shot putters. He said, "Well, if she wants to throw, I'll be happy to work with her." He was surprised at the speed I had coming across the circle. He said, "I am going to have to film you to see what you are doing." He certainly was a tremendous coach who really helped me to climb to the elite ranks. The first meet that I went to I broke the school record in the shot put as well as the 55 meter dash. I was busy running and throwing for St. John's. I was All-America in the shot put in college. I also qualified for the numerous open as well as college nationals.

I did qualify for the 1980 Olympic trials. Unfortunately I did not go because both my club coach and my college coach did not put an entry in for me. When they realized this, it was too late to submit an entry. I took solace in knowing that I did qualify.

In 1981, I went out to the open nationals in California and I came in as the second best college thrower and qualified for the World University Games. I think that was one of the highlights of my track career because it was the first international team that I made and it was a great honor to represent the United States in Romania. Unfortunately, before I got over there, I tore some ligaments in my throwing hand. Several people encouraged me to go just to get the experience of competing internationally. When I got over there, I got terribly sick from the food. Most people on the team got sick. I lost about ten pounds before I competed. Despite being sick and injured it was a good experience for me even if I did not make the finals.

I had never seen the Eastern bloc "girls" up close; they were very scary looking. I remember the U.S. team went to the track to practice and because of the injury to my hand I threw a ball made up of a sock and black tape. When the Eastern bloc girls saw that, they along with their coaches came over to watch me. They were shocked to see me throwing so far. When they realized that I was not throwing a real shot, they seemed relieved and walked away. I had a good laugh at that.

While at St. John's, I had the records in the 55 meters, javelin, discus, shot put and a few relay teams. I currently still have the shot put record at 52' 7".

I did qualify for the 1984 Olympic trials. This time I made sure that an entry was put in. I went but unfortunately I tore some ligaments again in my throwing hand at a meet prior to the trials. I went anyway since I missed out in 1980 and wanted the experience.

In 1985, but I'm not sure of the year, I was selected for the East team for the National Sports Festival in Colorado Springs. That was fun, another highlight meet for me. I was selected for a second National Sports Festival team in 1986, which was renamed Olympic Sports Festival. Unfortunately, I was not able to compete in that since I broke three toes in a meet about two weeks prior to that. But still, I was very proud that I was able to make a couple of national teams during my career. Unfortunately, I pushed myself too much since I was very small and did incur a lot of injuries. The injuries obviously hindered me a lot.

In 1986, I was throwing 58 feet consistently in practice and Kenny Bantum said, "If you don't get hurt you could throw over 60 feet." I told him not to say anything else before I got jinxed. Needless to say I was jinxed. I was going to try for the 1988 Olympic trials but I had a car accident and a couple of injuries which pretty much made me go into retirement along with some other problems. The hip injury from the car accident still bothers me to this day.

In 1988, I was inducted into the Hall of Fame at St. John's University and in 1990, I was inducted at my Schreiber High School.

I laid off for sixteen years and ended up getting involved in master's track when I was diagnosed with Epstein-Barr virus in 1997. My doctor suggested that the best way to combat the fatigue was to exercise. Trust me, the last thing you want to do is exercise. As a result from the exercise, I lost 30 pounds, but the motivation to continue was not there.

In 1998, I received a flyer about an upcoming meet at St. John's University and I decided to pick up the good old shot and give it a try again. I don't know what made me think I could pick up where I left off. When I first picked up the shot, I had to double check that I was not holding a 16 pound shot. I asked myself, "How did I throw this 58 feet?" It was a shocker.

While at the meet, I was recruited into competing as a master athlete. For a 38-year-old, masters track made sense at least until I could get back up to speed. My first meet I threw about 36 feet. I knew I had a long way to go.

Each year I started to improve and break records. I have the American records in the shot and weight throws in the 40–44 and 45–49 age groups. I have world records in the hammer, the weight throw and weight

Bruce MacDonald, three time Olympic race walker, ca. 1981.

pentathlon in the 40–44 and 45–49 age group. I never threw the hammer or 20 pound weight in my younger years so I am still learning how to throw them. I competed in the 2002 Empire State Games in Syracuse and Marty Engel, who is a former Olympian in the hammer, saw me break the Games record with a throw of 58.30 meters and was shocked that I threw it with only two turns. He said if I can ever get the technique down, I could be the best in the world among the young open competitors. I have received comments from several people along the same lines. I don't know if that day will ever come. All I know is that I am having fun now.

Another highlight in my throwing career was winning the shot put at the 2003 Millrose Games. I never competed at Millrose in my younger years so at 43 years old that was fun.

At the 2005 National Master's Championships in Honolulu, I was competing in the 45–49 age group and broke the American record in the shot put four times, and I broke the world record in the hammer, all despite being injured. I actually had a couple of tears in my Achilles tendon most of 2005 but somehow I managed to break records and do well in most of the meets I competed in. I look forward to breaking more records as my health gets better and my technique improves. I look forward to breaking the indoor records in the shot put, 20 pound weight and 35 pound weight for the 45–49 age group in Boston in 2006, since it will be the first time I will be competing in that age group.

The last competition I had this year was the National Masters Weight Pentathlon Championships in Arlington, Texas. I ended up breaking the world record in that with 5414 points and the American record in the 20 pound weight throw. I was voted as the Female Outstanding Single Performance for the weight pentathlon at the annual meeting in Florida this year.

As a master athlete I have won numerous awards such as Female Outstanding Single Performance awards, Female Athlete of the Year for Combined Events and Female High Scorer at the Weight Pentathlons. I have also won numerous national championships in the shot, hammer, discus and javelin.

Every once in a while I run into the person who broke my ankle (she still feels bad about it). I thank her because I never would have become a thrower and never would have had the wonderful experiences that I've encountered down to this day.

2

1982

The Outdoor Nationals

The USA/Mobil Outdoor Track and Field Championships were held at the Tom Black Track at the University of Tennessee in Knoxville, Tennessee, from June 18 to June 20. The first two finishers represented the United States in the USA–USSR Dual Meet in Indianapolis on July 2–3, and two other international meets, West Germany and Africa and East Germany.

Carl Lewis' repeat double wins in the 100 meters and long jump captured headlines on page one of the *New York Times* on Sunday, June 20. Frank Litsky, in a two page story, highlighted Stephanie Hightower's performances in the 100 meter hurdles, writing, "For Matt Centrowitz of the Bronx and Stephanie Hightower of Los Angeles, winning national titles has become routine. Centrowitz took the men's 5,000-meter run for the fourth straight year and Miss Hightower the women's 100-meter hurdles for the third straight year.... Miss Hightower beat Benita Fitzgerald by four feet in 12.86 seconds, equaling Deby LaPlante's 1979 American record. Candy Young of Fairleigh Dickinson ran third in 13.14 seconds."

Litsky continued, "Miss Ashford, wearing a crimson body suit, ran impressively to the fifth fastest time in history for 100 meters. She was close to her 1981 American record of 10.90 and the 1977 world record by Marlies Goehr of East Germany. 'I had a faster-than-usual start,' Miss Ashford said, 'and that threw me off a little at the end. I'm not ready yet. I can improve my start, my acceleration and my head. I need to be stronger.' 'She has no real training background this year,' said her coach Pat Bank, before the race. 'She won't be ready until August. But I wouldn't bet against her.'"

The *New York Times* on June 21 reported victories by Mary Decker-Tabb, Francie Larrieu and Carol Lewis:

Francie Larrieu Smith's victory in the women's 3,000 meters provided her ninth national outdoor title at three distances, dating back to 1970.

Mrs. Tabb won her first national outdoor title in 1974 as a 15-year-old in pigtails. Here she won her second as she ran away at the start and finished 40 meters ahead of the field.

Her time of 4 minutes 3.37 seconds was a meet record and the eighth fastest by an American. She holds the five fastest American times and 10 of the 11 fastest. She thought she should have run faster here.

The most successful family here was the Lewises of Willingboro, N.J., and the University of Houston. On Saturday, 20-year-old Carl retained his titles in the 100 meter dash (10.11) and long jump (27 feet 10 inches). Today, 18-year-old Carol won the women's long jump with 22–4½. Jodi Anderson, the runner-up at 21–10¾, is the only American woman who has jumped farther.

22

Left to right: The author with Denean Howard, 1982.

100 meters
1. Evelyn Ashford, Medalist Track Club   10.96 MR
   (betters meet record of 10.97 by Ashford, 1979)
2. Merlene Ottey, Los Angeles Naturite Track Club/Jamaica   11.06
3. Florence Griffith, Wilt's Athletic Club   11.15
4. Diane Williams, Los Angeles Naturite Track Club   11.18
5. Alice Brown, Wilt's Athletic Club   11.39
6. Jeanette Bolden, Wilt's Athletic Club   11.42
7. Chandra Cheeseborough, Tennessee State University Track Club   11.43
8. Brenda Morehead, Wilt's Athletic Club   11.50

200 meters
1. Merlene Ottey, Los Angeles Naturite Track Club/Jamaica   22.17 MR
2. Florence Griffith, Wilt's Athletic Club   22.58
3. Randy Givens, Florida State University Track Club   23.05
4. Chandra Cheeseborough, Tennessee State University Track Club   23.05
5. Grace Jackson, Atoms Track Club/Jamaica   23.24
6. Janet Davis, Indiana Track Club   23.73
7. Brenda Cliette, Florida State University Track Club   24.01
8. Sherry Funn, DC International   24.12

400 meters
1. Denean Howard, Los Angeles Naturite Track Club   50.87 MR
   (betters AJR of 51.09 by Sherri Howard, 1979 and meet
   record 51.04 by Lorna Forde, 1978)

Delisa Walton Floyd, 2005.

2. Rosalyn Bryant, Los Angeles Naturite Track Club	51.34
3. Arlise Emerson, Wilt's Athletic Club	51.89
4. Diane Dixon, Atoms Track Club	51.98
5. Charmaine Crooks, Atoms Track Club/Canada	52.01
6. Easter Gabriel, Prairie View A&M	52.14
7. Cathy Rattray, Los Angeles Naturite Track Club	52.28
8. LaShon Nedd, Wilt's Athletic Club	52.95

800 meters
1. Delisa Walton, Los Angeles Naturite Track Club	2:00.91
2. Yvonne Hannus, Stanford Track Club/Finland	2:01.73
3. Joetta Clark, Atoms Track Club	2:02.09
4. Sue Addison, Oregon Track Club	2:02.14
5. Kim Gallagher, Wilt's Athletic Club	2:02.83
6. Louise Romo, Golden Bear Track Club	2:04.16
7. Deanne Gutowski, Los Angeles Mercurettes	2:04.62
8. Regina Jacobs, Stanford Track Club	2:06.12

1500 meters
1. Mary Decker-Tabb, Athletics West	4:03.37 MR
(betters meet record of 4:06.53 by Francie Larrieu, 1979)	
2. Leann Warren, Oregon Track Club	4:10.23
3. Cindy Bremser, Wisconsin United Track Club	4:11.29
4. Darlene Beckford, Liberty Athletic Club	4:13.88
5. Michele Bush, Wilt's Athletic Club	4:14.00
6. Kathy Hayes, Oregon Track Club	4:14.94
7. Linda Goen, Wilt's Athletic Club	4:16.07
8. Sue Frederick, Ann Arbor Track Club	4:17.03

3000 meters
1. Francie Larrieu-Smith, New Balance Track Club   8:58.66
2. Jan Merrill, Age Group Athletic Association   8:59.07
3. Cindy Bremser, Wisconsin United Track Club   9:00.38
4. Brenda Webb, Athletics West   9:03.12
5. PattiSue Plumer, Stanford Track Club   9:03.14
6. Ceci Hopp, Stanford Track Club   9:04.18
7. Lesley Welch, University of Virginia   9:09.54
8. Debbie Eide, Oregon Track Club   9:09.58

10,000 meters
1. Kim Schnurpfeil, Stanford Track Club   33:25.88
2. Julie Shea, Athletics West   33:38.74
3. Michelle Mason, Stanford Track Club   33:48.11
4. Carol Urish, Houston Harriers   34:00.59
5. Sue King, New Balance Track Club   34:12.97
6. Lisa Larsen, Ann Arbor Track Club   34:25.70
7. Marty Cooksey, Athletics West   34:27.30
8. Liz Hjalmarsson, Team Kangaroo/Sweden   34:28.9 ht

100 meter hurdles
1. Stephanie Hightower, Los Angeles Naturite Track Club   12.86 equals
        (equals American and meet record by Deby LaPlante, 1979)   AR, MR
2. Benita Fitzgerald, Los Angeles Naturite Track Club   13.01
3. Candy Young, Fairleigh Dickinson University   13.14
4. Kim Turner, Atoms Track Club   13.15
5. Pam Page, Los Angeles Naturite Track Club   13.40
6. Linda Weekly, Atoms Track Club   13.69
7. Gayle Watkins, Coast Athletics   13.78
8. Rhonda Blanford, Los Angeles Naturite Track Club   13.86

400 meter hurdles
1. Tammy Etienne, Metroplex Striders   56.55
2. Tonja Brown, Florida State Track Club   57.43
3. Edna Brown, Temple University   57.49
4. Sandra Farmer, Los Angeles Naturite Track Club/Jamaica   57.85
5. Sharrieffa Barksdale, Knoxville Track Club   58.67
6. Colleen Williams, Los Angeles Mercurettes   58.68
7. Kim Whitehead, Atoms Track Club   59.26
8. Patricia Melton, Liberty Athletic Club   59.30

5000 meter walk
1. Susan Liers-Westerfield, Island Track Club   24:56.6 ht
2. Bonnie Dillon, West Valley Track Club   25:16.2
3. Teresa Vaill, Island Track Club   26:04.4
4. Norma Arnesen, Shore Athletic Club   26:40.7
5. Debbi Spino, Team Kangaroo   27:19.6
6. Carol Brown, Island Track Club   27:24.8
7. Karen Stoyanowski, West Valley Track Club   27:33.5
8. Chris Anderson, Liberty Athletic Club   27:36.8

4 × 100 meter relay
1. Wilt's Athletic Club   43.45
        (Brenda Morehead, Jeanette Bolden, Alice Brown, Florence Griffith)

2. Los Angeles Naturite Track Club "B"	43.73
3. Los Angeles Naturite Track Club "A"	43.91

800 meter medley relay
1. Wilt's Athletic Club	1:36.79
	WR, AR, MR

(betters world and American record of 1:37.29 by Los Angeles
State, 1978; and meet record of 1:37.40 by Ali Track Club, 1980)
(Brenda Morehead, Jeanette Bolden, Alice Brown, Arlise Emerson)
2. Los Angeles Naturite Track Club "B"	1:37.57
3. Southern California Cheetahs	1:38.28

4 × 400 meter relay
1. Los Angeles Naturite Track Club	3:28.68

(Sharon Dabney, Denean Howard, Sherri Howard, Rosalyn Bryant)
2. Atoms Track Club	3:31.62
3. Wilt's Athletic Club	3:31.83

4 × 400 meter relay
1. Stanford Track Club	8:22.26 MR

(betters meet record of 8:31.4 by Oral Roberts Track Club, 1979)
(Yvonne Hannus, Regina Jacobs, June Griffith, Tami Essington)
2. Los Angeles Mercurettes	8:26.58
3. Los Angeles Naturite Track Club	8:42.59

High jump
1. Debbie Brill, Pacific Coast Club/Canada	6' 4¾"
(equals meet record by Pam Spencer, 1981)	equals MR
2. Phyllis Blunston, Los Angeles Naturite Track Club	6' 3½"
3. Coleen Sommer, Wilt's Athletic Club	6' 2¼"
4. Joni Huntley, Pacific Coast Club	6' 1¼"
5. Hisayo Fukumitsu, Stars and Stripes Track Club/Japan	6'
6. Mary Moore, Issaquah Gliders	6'
7. Maggie Garrison, SportsWest	6'
8. Wendy Markham, Florida State University	5' 10¾"

Long jump
1. Carol Lewis, Santa Monica Track Club	22' 4¼"
2. Jodi Anderson, Los Angeles Naturite Track Club	21' 10¾"
3. Shonel Ferguson, DC International/Bahamas	21' 10"
4. Jennifer Inniss, Southern California Cheetahs/Guyana	21' 8¼"
5. Halcyon McKnight, Los Angeles Mercurettes	21' 6¾"
6. Kathy McMillan-Ray, Coast Athletics	21' 5½"
7. Gwen Loud, Coast Athletics	21' 2¾"
8. Veronica Bell, Southern California Cheetahs	21' 2" w

Shot put
1. Maria Sarria, Cuba	61' 8¼"
2. Rosemarie Hauch, Knoxville Track Club/Canada	55' 7¾"
3. Denise Wood, Knoxville Track Club	54' ¾"
4. Sandy Burke, Northeastern University	53' 1¾"
5. Lorna Griffin, Athletics West	52' 10¾"
6. Annette Bohach, Indiana Track Club	52' 9½"

| 7. Ramona Pagel, Vitamins Plus Track Club | 52' 6½" |
| 8. Annie McElroy, Wilt's Athletic Club | 52' 2¾" |

Discus

1. Ria Stalman, Los Angeles Naturite Track Club/Holland	203' 10" MR
(betters meet record of 192' 5" by Stalman in qualifying round)	
2. Leslie Deniz, Los Angeles Naturite Track Club	191'
3. Kathy Picknell, Oregon Track Club	186' 4"
4. Lorna Griffin, Athletics West	184' 1"
5. Denise Wood, Knoxville Track Club	182' 11"
6. Jan Svendsen, Wilt's Athletic Club	177' 1"
7. Lynne Anderson, Oregon Track Club	177'
8. Julie Hansen, SportsWest	175' 8"

Javelin

1. Lynda Hughes, Oregon Track Club	202' 3"
2. Karin Smith, Athletics West	199' 7"
3. Mayra Vila, Cuba	196' 10"
4. Kate Schmidt, Pacific Coast Club	195' 10"
5. Sally Harmon, Oregon Track Club	190' 4"
6. Deanna Carr, SportsWest	173' 11"
7. Jacque Nelson, Wilt's Athletic Club	167' 8"
8. Liz Mueller, Vitamins Plus Track Club	163' 2"

Team scores:

1. Los Angeles Track Club	146
2. Wilt's Athletic Club	62
3. Stanford Track Club	37

Outstanding Female Athlete: Stephanie Hightower, winner of the 100 meter hurdles equaling the American record.

The Indoor Nationals

The Athletics Congress of the USA/Mobil Indoor Track and Field Championships were on Friday, February 26, in Madison Square Garden, New York City. A crowd of almost 14,000 was in attendance.

"Hurdle Duel Spices National Title Meet" was the headline that captured one's attention in the sports section of the *New York Times* on the day of the meet, February 26. The article explained that Stephanie Hightower and Candy Young

expect to race against each other tonight for the seventh time this season, in the final of the 60-yard hurdles. In two previous meetings, they set records simultaneously. The last time was in the Wanamaker Millrose Games, two weeks ago on the Garden track, and the result was one of those rarities, a declared dead heat that satisfied neither runner. Each was convinced that she had won. The debate has not stilled, and the time, 7.38 seconds, continues unsurpassed for the event.

The rivalry between the two is better described as keen than bitter. "It's always keen," Miss Young said the other day. "Lately, the one that wins has been breaking world records. It could hardly be any keener than that."

Miss Young is 19 years old and is from Beaver Falls, Pa. She is a sophomore at Farleigh Dickinson University on an athletic scholarship.

Miss Hightower, 24, and an alumna of Ohio State, says that she and Miss Young are definitely on speaking terms. "We're friends," she said. "It's just not my habit to talk a lot when I'm competing. I don't hug, kiss, that whole bit."

They have been extremely close at the finish line. In the national championships at the Garden two years ago, Miss Hightower was placed first and Miss Young second, with identical times, an unofficial 7.4 seconds. In the Dallas Times Herald meet last month, it was Miss Young first, Miss Hightower second and the times again the same, 7.47 seconds. That was an unofficial American and a world-best standard.

...Miss Hightower is in training in Columbus, Ohio, under the direction of her coach, Mamie Rollins [sic]. She began track competition eight years ago in high school in her home city of Louisville, Ky. Miss Hightower is short for a hurdler, 5 feet 4½ inches tall. She weighs 118 pounds. So, she is asked, why that event?

"In high school," she said, "they didn't have a hurdler, so I was elected."

In Beaver Falls, Miss Young's high school coach similarly designated her a hurdler. She became a Pennsylvania state champion and competed in national events before high school ended.

"Miss Ashford Captures 60-Yard Dash Title at Garden," trumpeted the headlines in the *New York Times* on Saturday.

Along with a finish line photograph, the story read:

Evelyn Ashford, who can run 60 yards faster than any other woman in the world, took 6.54 seconds to cover that distance last night in the USA/Mobil track and field championships at Madison Square Garden. Then she announced that she was going on vacation.

Her time last night has been bettered only once in the history of women's track, by Miss Ashford herself a week ago in San Diego, although that time of 6.48 still has not been acknowledged because of the malfunctioning of timing equipment.

Miss Ashford has had what she describes as a "rough season," losing indoor meets at Toronto and Dallas, in the Millrose Games here and at the Olympic Invitational.

But last night's achievement made the world right. "This was most important for me," said the athlete from Los Angeles. "I was hyped up. I always like to win the big ones. Now I'm going to stop running until August. I've got to rest my body and my psyche."

...A world-best mark was set in a 220-yard dash semifinal heat in the afternoon by Miss Cheeseborough, of Tennessee State. The distance is seldom run indoors. Miss Cheeseborough lowered her mark of 23.27 seconds to 23.25.

Veronica Bell of Los Angeles surprised herself when she won the long jump at 21–11¾, which bettered the nine-year American indoor record by 7 inches.

Miss Bell, who is 21, 6 feet tall and weighs 147 pounds, said she was "shocked" and for good reason. Her winning jump was two feet longer than her previous best effort.

Joan Hansen turned in an indoor world best performance in the two mile run. After setting a blistering pace for the entire run, she increased her lead over Margaret Groos and Brenda Webb in the final yards and won in 9:37.03, breaking the record set by Francie Larrieu in 1981.

Chandra Cheeseborough's outstanding time in the 220 heat led to Sunday's story in the *New York Times*, entitled, "Miss Cheeseborough's Night":

...She had finished third behind Evelyn Ashford and Jeanette Bolden in the 60-yard dash final before winning the 220. Miss Cheeseborough also opened a big lead for the winning Tennessee State quartet in the sprint medley relay and assured first place for the school by running the anchor leg in the 880-yard relay.

So this athlete, who made the 1976 Olympic team as a 16-year-old junior from Ribault High School of Jacksonville, Fla., completed the evening with three firsts, a third, and a world best, albeit in an event seldom run indoors.

Chandra Cheeseborough was selected the outstanding female athlete of the meet.

---

60 yard dash
1. Evelyn Ashford, Medalist Track Club   6.54   WR, AR, MR
2. Jeanette Bolden, Wilt's Athletic Club   6.59
3. Chandra Cheeseborough, Tennessee State University   6.62

220 yard dash
1. Chandra Cheeseborough, Tennessee State University   23.46
2. LaShon Nedd, Wilt's Athletic Club   23.81
3. Florence Griffith, Wilt's Athletic Club   24.49

440 yard run
1. Maxine Underwood, Boston International Athletic Club   54.55
2. Gwen Gardner, Los Angeles Mercurettes   54.78
3. Edna Brown, Temple University   54.06

880 yard run
1. Leann Warren, University of Oregon   2:04.61
2. Delisa Walton, University of Tennessee   2:04.83
3. Joetta Clark, University of Tennessee   2:05.85

Mobil Mile
1. Cathie Twomey, Athletics West   4:32.92   MR
2. Cindy Bremser, Wisconsin United Track Club   4:33.25
3. Jan Merrill, Age Group Athletic Association   4:36.17

Two mile run
1. Joan Hansen, Athletics West   9:37.03   WR, AR, MR
2. Brenda Webb, Athletics West   9:37.64
3. Margaret Groos, Athletics West   9:37.65

60 yard hurdles
1. Stephanie Hightower, Los Angeles Naturite Track Club   7.38   MR
2. Candy Young, Fairleigh Dickinson University   7.39
3. Kim Turner, University of Texas, El Paso   7.67

One mile walk
1. Susan Brodock, Southern California Road Runners   7:07.14
2. Susan Liers-Westerfield, Island Track Club   7:12.02
3. Jeanne Bocci, Motor City Striders   7:39.05

640 yard relay
1. Tennessee State University   1:09.36
    (Chandra Cheeseborough, Wanda Kort, Sheryl Pernell,
     Ernestine Davis)
2. Wilt's Athletic Club   1:11.23
3. Los Angeles Mercurettes   1:11.66

Sprint medley relay (440-110-110-220)
1. Tennessee State University   1:44.26
    (Judy Pollion, Wanda Kort, Sheryl Pernell, Chandra Cheeseborough)
2. DC International   1:46.96
3. Southern California Cheetahs   1:48.19

Mile relay
1. Atoms Track Club   3:40.54
    (Stephanie Vega, Doriane McClure, Lorna Forde, Diane Dixon)
2. DC International   3:41.94
3. Brooklyn Over the Hill Athletic Association   3:46.70

Shot put
1. Marita Walton, University of Maryland   55' 11¾"
2. Denise Wood, Knoxville Track Club   53' 5"
3. Elaine Sobansky, Pennsylvania State University   52' 6½"

Long jump
1. Veronica Bell, Southern California Cheetahs   21' 11¾"
   (possible measuring error)
2. Kathy McMillan-Ray, Coast Athletics   21' 2½"
3. Evalene Hatcher, Morgan State University   20' 10¾"

High jump
1. Coleen Sommer, Wilt's Athletic Club   6' 3¼" MR
2. Louise Ritter, Pacific Coast Club   6' ¾"
3. Joni Huntley, Pacific Coast Club   5' 10"

Team Champion:
Tennessee State University (Their 16th Indoor Team Championship)
    and Wilt's Athletic Club 17 points

Sunkist Invitational (5 events for women): Los Angeles, January 22

60 yard dash		Mile	
Evelyn Ashford, Medalist Track Club	6.78	Mary Decker, Athletics West	4:24.6 MR
500 yard run		50 meter hurdles	
Arlise Emerson, Wilt's Athletic Club	1:04.6	Emi Akimoto, Japan	7.76
800 meter run			
Robin Campbell, Stanford Track Club	2:10.5		

Left to right: The author with Arlise Emerson, 2000.

USA vs. USSR: Lite Summer Games II, Indiana University Track Stadium, Indianapolis, Indiana, July 2–3

The *New York Times* reported that two fouls occurred in the women's running events. Jan Merrill was bumped 20 meters before the finish of her race. Despite being disqualified, the Russian runner was reinstated to second place after it had been determined that she did not interfere with Jan.

"'She cut me off,' said Miss Merrill. 'This happened to me before competing with the Russians. They are physically strong, unlike the soft touch of the U.S. women runners.'"

The second disqualification occurred in the 1500 meters. A Russian runner was disqualified for cutting in on Leann Warren on the final lap. "As a result, Miss Warren, with a career best of 4:05.88, was moved up to second place."

100 meters		
1. Evelyn Ashford	11.18	
2. Florence Griffith	11.35	

200 meters		
1. Florence Griffith	22.23 w	
3. Randy Givens	22.97	

400 meters		
3. Rosalyn Bryant	51.33	
4. Arlise Emerson	51.79	

800 meters		
2. Delisa Walton	2:02.51	
3. Sue Addison	2:02.60	

1500 meters		
2. Leann Warren	4:05.88	
3. Cindy Bremser	4:10.98	

3000 meters		
3. Jan Merrill	8:47.95	
4. Francie Larrieu	8:52.03	

100 meter hurdles		
2. Stephanie Hightower	13.06	
4. Benita Fitzgerald	13.11	

400 meter hurdles		
3. Tammy Etienne	56.56	
4. Tonja Brown	58.86	

4 × 100 meter relay
1. USA   42.47
(Alice Brown, Florence Griffith, Randy Givens, Diane Williams)

4 × 400 meter relay
2. USA   3:28.07
(Rosalyn Bryant, LaShon Nedd, Easter Gabriel, Arlise Emerson)

High jump	
1. Coleen Sommer	6' 2¾"
3. Phyllis Blunston	6' ½"

Long jump	
1. Carol Lewis	21' 8¼"
4. Kathy McMillan Ray	20' 10½"

Shot put	
3. Lorna Griffin	53' ¼"
4. Denise Wood	51' 4½"

Discus	
3. Lorna Griffin	188' 3"
4. Kathy Picknell	167' 6"

Javelin	
3. Lynda Hughes	192' 8"
4. Sally Harmon	185' 7"

Team score:	
USSR 89	USA 67

USA Senior Heptathlon Championships (USA–West Germany Senior Heptathlon Dual Meet): University of Southern California, Los Angeles, California, June 25–27

1. Jackie Joyner, Wilt's Athletic Club	6041
2. Cindy Greiner, Oregon Track Club	5950
3. Marlene Harmon, Los Angeles Naturite Track Club	5902
4. Patsy Walker, University of Houston Track Club	5720
5. Sue Brownell, University of Virginia	5478
6. Renee Nickles, Team Kangaroo	5422

USA–West Germany Dual Meet: June 26–27

1. Jackie Joyner	Team scores:	
3. Cindy Greiner	USA	17,893
5. Marlene Harmon	West Germany	17,841
8. Patsy Walker		

USA–East Germany Dual Meet: July 9–10

100 meters			4 × 100 meter relay		
3. Florence Griffith	11.12		2. USA	42.29 AR	
4. Diane Williams	11.14		(Alice Brown, Florence Griffith, Randy Givens, Diane Williams)		
200 meters			4 × 400 meter relay		
2. Florence Griffith	22.34		2. USA	3:23.13	
4. Randy Givens	23.07		(Rosalyn Bryant, Arlise Emerson, Diane Dixon, Denean Howard)		
400 meters			High jump		
3. Sherri Howard	51.17		3. Coleen Sommer	6' 2"	
4. Rosalyn Bryant	51.85		4. Phyllis Blunston	5' 10¾"	
800 meters			Long jump		
3. Delisa Walton	2:00.67		1. Carol Lewis	22' 4¼"	
4. Joetta Clark	2:01.32		4. Kathy McMillan-Ray	21' 8¼"	
1500 meters			Shot put		
2. Leann Warren	4:06.71		3. Denise Wood	52' 4"	
4. Sue Addison	4:12.51		4. Sandy Burke	51' 2¾"	
3000 meters			Discus		
1. Jan Merrill	9:00.63		3. Lorna Griffin	187' 8"	
3. Francie Larrieu	9:20.30		4. Kathy Picknell	178' 1"	
100 meter hurdles			Javelin		
3. Stephanie Hightower	12.79 AR		3. Karin Smith	199' 10"	
4. Benita Fitzgerald	12.92		4. Lynda Hughes	190' 1"	
400 meter hurdles			Team score:		
3. Tammy Etienne	56.33		GDR 105	USA 52	
4. Tonja Brown	57.78				

United States Cross Country Championships: The Meadowlands, New Jersey, November 28

The *New York Times* reported:

Lesley Welch of the University of Virginia, the women's N.C.A.A. cross country champion, won the senior women's five-kilometer championships in decisive fashion as well. Miss Welch, a 19-year-old sophomore from Peabody, Mass., finished first in 15:52. She was 18 seconds in front of Jan Merrill, the two-time national champion, and Julie Brown, who won last year's race.

...Miss Welch went out to the lead almost immediately in the women's race, opening with a 4:55 first mile and leaving Miss Merrill, Miss Brown, Margaret Groos and Joan Benoit, the American women's record-holder for the marathon, to contend for second. Miss Merrill ended up holding off a late charge from Miss Brown for the runner-up spot.

5000 meters	
1. Lesley Welch, University of Virginia	15:52
2. Jan Merrill, Age Group Athletic Association	16:10
3. Julie Brown, Los Angeles Naturite Track Club	16:10
4. Joan Benoit, Athletics West	16:12
5. Margaret Groos, unattached	16:13

6. Betty Springs, Wolftrack Club	16:13
7. Brenda Webb, Athletics West	16:13
8. Midde Hamrin, Houston Harriers/Sweden	16:14
9. Kathy Hadler, Santa Monica Track Club	16:18
10. Nan Doak, University of Iowa	16:23

143 women finished

Team scores:

1. University of Virginia	75
2. Athletics West	89
3. Team Kangaroo	169
4. Wolftrack Club	205
5. University of Iowa	230
6. University of Western Ontario	263

Grand Prix Winners

400 meters

1. Rosalyn Bryant	$2500.
2. Denean Howard	$1000.
3. Sharon Dabney	$ 500.

1500 meters

1. Cindy Bremser	$2500.
2. Mary Decker	$1000.
3. Brenda Webb	$ 500.

100 meter hurdles

1. Stephanie Hightower	$2500.
2. Benita Fitzgerald	$1000.
3. Candy Young	$ 500.

400 meter hurdles

1. Tammy Etienne	$2500.
2. Sandra Farmer	$1000.
3. Tonja Brown	$ 500.

5 kilometer walk

1. Susan Liers-Westerfield	$2500.
2. Bonnie Dillon	$1000.
3. Teresa Vaill	$ 500.

Shot put

1. Rosemarie Hauch	$2500.
2. Denise Wood	$1000.
3. Maria Sarria	$ 500.

Javelin

1. Lynda Hughes	$2500.
2. Karin Smith	$1000.
3. Mayra Vila	$ 500.

Other News and Honors

Track & Field News: U.S. Athlete of the Year

Mary Decker Tabb

USA Rankings — Track & Field News

1. Mary Decker Tabb	6. Carol Lewis
2. Evelyn Ashford	7. Coleen Sommer
3. Jane Frederick	8. Tammy Etinne
4. Joan Benoit	9. Leslie Deniz
5. Stephanie Hightower	10. Kim Schnurpfeil and Karin Smith

World Rankings — *Track & Field News*

9. Mary Decker-Tabb
10. Evelyn Ashford

The following American women were ranked in the top five in the world in their event:

100 meters		10,000 meters	
2. Evelyn Ashford	10.93	1. Mary Decker-Tabb	31:35.3
200 meters		Marathon	
3. Evelyn Ashford	22.10	1. Joan Benoit	2:26:11
Mile		High jump	
2. Mary Decker-Tabb	4:18.08	2. Coleen Sommer	6' 6¾"
3000 meters		Long jump	
3. Mary Decker-Tabb	8:29.71	4. Jodi Anderson	22' 8"
5000 meters			
1. Mary Decker-Tabb	15:08.26		

The TAC Women's Decathlon was held in Ventura, California, July 31–August 1. There were three previous meets but this one was officially designated the National Women's Decathlon Championships. These decathlon meets may be the first women's decathlon competitions in the United States. Sharon Hanson won the national event (6198) with performances of: 13.17, 16' 5½", 33' 1", 4' 6¾", 61.89, 15.29, 98' 1", 7' 3¼", 115' 7", and 5:47.2.

The only individual winner from the United States at the World University Games was Randy Givens, Florida State University. She won the 200 meters in 22.47.

In a section chronicling the history of the International Amateur Athletic Association, the 1982 handbook states: "Women's athletics has continued to produce ever improving performances in ever greater depth. The 3000m and 400m Hurdles are the latest World Championship events, and the 5000m and 10,000m the latest world record events. In addition, the marathon is proving ever more popular as a race for women and is included in the 1983 World Championships programme."

Pat Rico was the representative of the United States to the eleven member IAAF Women's Committee.

The Chairman of Women's Track and Field was Dr. Evie Dennis. Nina Kuscsik was the Chairman of Women's Long Distance Running and Dr. Harmon Brown, the Chairman of Women's Development.

No American women held Olympic records.

Mary Decker Tabb lowered two world indoor best times in one race at the Los Angeles Times Games in February. "Her time for the 3,000 was 8 minutes 47.3 seconds, which bettered the previous best of 8:50.8 set in 1980 by Norway's Grete Waitz. At 2,000 meters Miss Decker was clocked in 5:53.4, lowering the mark of 5:55.2 set last year by Francie Larrieu," reported the *New York Times*.

On February 19 at the San Diego Invitational indoor track meet, Mary Decker-Tabb ran the fastest mile ever in 4:20.5. "Mrs. Tabb's time was 1.2 seconds lower than her previous world indoor best, set last Friday at the Millrose Games in Madison Square Garden. She also was faster than the outdoor world record of 4:20.89 set by Lyudmila Veselkova of the Soviet Union in 1981," reported the *New York Times*.

On June 5, Mary Decker-Tabb set a world record of 15:08.26 in the 5000 meter run in Eugene, Oregon at the Prefontaine Classic.

On June 26, in Oslo, Norway, in the Bislett Games, Mary Decker-Tabb set a new American record of 4:21.46 in the mile.

On July 7, in Oslo, Norway, Mary Decker-Tabb won the 3000 meter race with a new American record of 8:29.71.

In Paris, France on July 9, Mary Decker-Tabb set a world record of 4:18.08 for the mile. The *New York Times* reported that, Mary Decker Tabb of the United States ran the mile in 4 minutes 18.08 seconds today and broke the women's world record by almost three seconds at the Paris International track and field meet. "Mrs. Tabb, who just two days ago set an American women's record of 8:29.71 in the 3,000 meters during a meet in Oslo, jumped into the lead today at the start and never looked back. She won by about 13 seconds...."

On July 16, Decker-Tabb set a 10,000 meter world record of 31:35.3, in Eugene, Oregon.

On September 12, Joan Benoit set a world record of 2:26:11 in the marathon in Eugene, Oregon.

The Indoor Grand Prix became a reality in 1982.

Hal Bateman reported that this year was the first year that the women participated in the NCAA women's outdoor championships and it was the last year that the AIAW track championships were held.

Will Stephens, the women's track coach at Oregon State University and founder of Will's Spikettes died on August 3.

Mary Decker-Tabb won the Sullivan Award.

INTERVIEW: SUSAN LIERS-WESTERFIELD-REINA

(June 29, 2005) [I got started in track] in 10th grade when they were recruiting for the boys' cross country team. I went to one practice with no preparation, never having really run anything before, and realized that was a bit much [laughter]. The whole team had been practicing over the summer. They were doing a lot of distance. But when wintertime came, I quit the girl's volleyball team to go out for the winter track team. It was called winter track because we ran outside in the snow. I ended up on the boys' team, but whenever the other team had a girl, I would run the event they did. It was usually a short dash. Occasionally I would run the mile. I think I got down to close to six minutes, at the time.

I ran cross country the following year and stuck with track. I ended up being a co-captain on one of the boys' teams. It was either cross country or outdoor track. Eventually we had a bunch of girls running on the track team.

In my senior year, I ran into Gary Westerfield during a cross country practice. He was race walking. I was very interested in that because I used to race walk through the halls of the school. The aids would always yell, "Don't run," but they didn't know what to say when you walked. I would go flying through the halls as fast as I could walking and by the time they figured out what to say, I was gone.

So, Gary got me started. I tried it and he thought that I had some talent. He convinced me to enter a track meet at the Nassau Coliseum. I came in last. I think I walked a mile in 9:23. I just couldn't figure out how to go faster. I think the next track meet I walked in under eight minutes. I came in second to one of the best boys in the county. Gary said, "Do you know, you would have placed in the top three in the indoor national championships?" [laughter]. Ok, this sounds good. From that point I started doing more race walking and getting into some of the national level meets and figuring out what that world was all about.

I went up to Cortlandt. I ran cross country on the men's team because they didn't have a woman's cross country team, basically running by myself. I came back to Stony Brook because it was difficult trying to get to race walking races when I was upstate. I finished out college at Stony Brook University running with the track team there. Eventually they had a woman's cross country team.

I was race walking all during this time and that became more and more important. I never ran faster than 5:40 for a mile but I ended up walking a mile under seven minutes — which was more impressive.

The Empire State Games was a big thing in my life. I guess they wanted to get the race walk out of the way and they put it on the program so early that it ended up being the first event of the Games. It ended up being a big deal; in the dark, I won the first gold medal [laughter].

It ended up being a very good thing. I think I won the first gold medal maybe five years in a row. Then one year they selected an outstanding athlete of the Games, 1979. In January, someone called me and asked if I'd like to go to Greece to get the Olympic flame in Air Force One and I said, let me think about that! [laughter].

I've really gotten a lot of wonderful things out of my race walking. I always tell my son that. I got laughed at a lot but you can't let that bother you. People don't know the hard work that you put in and what you are doing.

I did go to Greece on Air Force One. I ran the Olympic torch into the New York State welcoming ceremony for the 1980 winter Olympics; I competed all over the world.

Unfortunately it was towards the end of my career that they did add it to the Olympics and I had a hard time keeping up with everyone at that point. I competed in everything from 1500 meters to the New York City Marathon, which I really enjoyed.

One year I almost didn't go to the outdoor nationals because I was not able to train. I had some kind of pain in my right side. I didn't know if it was a torn muscle or what it was. I insisted on going. My mother was worried I was going to come in last [laughter]. Apparently nobody knew that I had been injured and they thought that I was going to win; so they let me win [laughter]. That was the first time that I won like that. I had been doing very well before that. It was very unusual. It was pretty exciting to call my parents and say, "I won."

There was a race in Bergen, Norway. I think it was referred to as a world meeting. It was before they started the Eschborn Cup. Probably the one that I am most proud of was when the competition was getting pretty tough and I really, really toughed it out and ended up third in Bergen, Norway. It was sometime before 1983 because at that point I think it was called the Eschborn Cup.

The first one that we went to we had raise the money to pay our own way; we had to make our own USA uniforms. I placed third. It was my first year walking.

I won the race walking division in the New York City Marathon. I beat Teresa Vaill towards the end. I was happy with myself for that one, for hanging in there.

The first Goodwill Games in 1986 was exciting to go too. Although I don't think any of us really performed our best there. I don't know if it was the jet lag or what, but it was exciting to be part of that.

I loved walking in the Garden. It was so much fun. It was difficult to race walk on that track. You're kind of limping around there and trying to go as fast as you can. But, it was very exciting to be in there and be down on the floor. There were usually good crowds. The *Los Angeles Times* meet was similar.

Susan Liers-Westerfield (#599), 1982 National Indoor Championships, Madison Square Garden. (Courtesy of Arthur H. Liers.)

If I had everything to do over, I'd do it all over again. I would tell young athletes to find what they are good at, try everything and if it's something that's unusual like race walking, don't let other people stop you from doing that just because they think it looks funny. I think that was one of the most important things and I tell my son that all the time. I had kids in the street that fell off their bicycles onto the road laughing at me. I just smiled at them. If I had let that bother me I never would have experienced all these wonderful things. I was hoping no one would drive off the road when they saw me race walking. It's a little bit more acceptable now but even at the high school level, you might get people saying, why don't you run? If they see the athletes we have now, like Teresa Vaill walking 20k in an hour and 33 minutes, they have to respect that.

3

1983

The Outdoor Nationals

The 108th Annual USA/Mobil Outdoor Track and Field Championships were held at Indiana University Track Stadium in Indianapolis, Indiana, June 17–19.

The first story in the *New York Times* stated that Diane Williams advanced in the 100 meters with the time of 11.00, making "her the second fastest American to run the event, behind the 10.90 of Evelyn Ashford in 1981." Additionally, "In the only finals today, Katie Ishmael of Wisconsin won the women's 10,000-meter run in 33 minutes 24.71 seconds and Ms. International of Washington, D.C., the 3,200-meter relay in 8:38.04."

On June 19, the four column write-up in the *New York Times* featured nearly half of the space extolling the women winners:

Carol Lewis, the 19-year-old sister of 21-year-old Carl, produced the best long-jump series ever by an American woman. She set a meet record of 22 feet 8 inches on her second jump and equaled it on her sixth. All six of her jumps exceeded 22 feet, and none was wind-aided.

The victories qualified both Lewises for the United States teams for the East German meet next Saturday and Sunday in Los Angeles and the first world championships Aug. 7 through 14 in Helsinki, Finland. In most cases, the first two Americans here win berths against the East Germans and the first three qualify for the world championships.

Not all the qualifiers will take advantage. For example, Louise Ritter (6 feet 4 inches) finished first, Pam Spencer (6–4) second and Joni Huntley (6–2¾) third in the women's high jump. Miss Huntley will pass up the world championships because she will be married Aug. 6, the day before the women's high jump qualifying in Helsinki.

Stephanie Hightower, winner of the women's 100-meter hurdles the last three years, failed to qualify for the major meets. She was bumped early in the race, hit the last hurdle hard and finished seventh in a field of nine finalists in 13.47. Benita Fitzgerald won in 12.97.

Evelyn Ashford won the women's 100 meters for the third straight year and the fifth time in seven years, giving her more national 100-meter titles than anyone else in history. She beat Diane Williams by a foot in 11.24 seconds, running into a wind of 6 miles an hour.

"I thought my time was slow," said Miss Ashford. "There's always a lot of pressure for me to win, but not as much pressure as I put on myself to win."

Meet records were broken by Greg Foster in the men's 110-hurdles final (13.15 seconds), Miss Lewis in the women's long jump, Leslie Deniz in the women's discus-throw final (206 feet 3 inches) and Sharrieffa Barksdale in the women's 400-meter hurdles semifinals (56.09 seconds).

The *New York Times*, a day after the championships ended, reported that "Mary Decker won two titles 50 minutes apart" and Evelyn Ashford captured the 200 meters.

Miss Decker retained her title in the women's 1,500 meters, by winning by 30 meters in 4:03.50. Then she took the 3,000 meters by 45 meters in 8:38.36, a meet record.

On Saturday night, Miss Ashford won the women's 100 meters for the fifth time in seven years. Today she won the 200 meters for the fifth time in seven years, beating Chandra Cheeseborough by 2 feet in 21.99 seconds, a meet record.

It was also noted that Denean Howard won her third 400 meter title in as many years.

100 meters
1. Evelyn Ashford, Medalist Track Club   11.24
2. Diane Williams, Puma and Energizer Track Club   11.28
3. Chandra Cheeseborough, Athletics West   11.31
4. Alice Brown, Wilt's Athletic Club   11.41
5. Randy Givens, Team adidas   11.53
6. Jackie Washington, University of Houston   11.64

200 meters
1. Evelyn Ashford, Medalist Track Club   21.88 MR
    (betters meet record of 22.17 by Merlene Ottey, 1982)
2. Chandra Cheeseborough, Athletics West   21.99
3. Florence Griffith, Wilt's Athletic Club   22.23
4. Randy Givens, Team adidas   22.31
5. Alice Brown, Wilt's Athletic Club   22.41
6. Grace Jackson, Atoms Track Club/Jamaica   22.47

400 meters
1. Denean Howard, California State University, Los Angeles   50.99
2. Rosalyn Bryant, Puma and Energizer Track Club   51.58
3. Roberta Belle, Puma and Energizer Track Club   51.72
4. Sharon Dabney, Puma and Energizer Track Club   51.79
5. Charmaine Crooks, Los Angeles Mercurettes/Canada   51.81
6. Easter Gabriel, Team Kangaroo   51.89

800 meters
1. Robin Campbell, Puma and Energizer Track Club   1:59.00
2. Diana Richberg, Gazelle International   2:00.82
3. Lee Arbogast, Athletics West   2:01.07
4. Essie Kelly-Washington, unattached   2:01.29
5. Joetta Clark, Atoms Track Club   2:01.34
6. Annette Campbell, Tiger International   2:02.02

1500 meters
1. Mary Decker, Athletics West   4:03.50
2. Cindy Bremser, Wisconsin United Track Club   4:09.62
3. Missy Kane, Team adidas   4:10.92
4. Sue Foster, Ann Arbor Track Club   4:11.23
5. Sue Addison, Athletics West   4:12.02
6. Regina Jacobs, Puma and Energizer Track Club   4:13.09

3000 meters
1. Mary Decker, Athletics West   8:38.36 MR
    (betters meet record of 8:53.79 by Francie Larrieu, 1979)
2. Brenda Webb, Athletics West   8:48.09
3. Maggie Keyes, Athletics West   8:49.96

4. Kathy Hayes, University of Oregon   8:50.79
5. Francie Larrieu-Smith, New Balance Track Club   8:53.47
6. Joan Benoit, Athletics West   8:53.49

5000 meters
1. Judi St. Hilaire, Athletics West   16:02.16   MR
   (new event — establishes meet record)
2. Amy Harper, 4 Corners Track Club   16:08.17
3. Tori Neubauer, University of Wisconsin, LaCrosse   16:08.73
4. Connie Jo Robinson, North Carolina State University   16:13.08
5. Sabrina Dornhoefer, Team Kangaroo   16:27.65
6. Leslie White, Southern California Cheetahs   16:28.87

10,000 meters
1. Katie Ishmael, Wisconsin United Track Club   33:24.71
2. Beth Farmer, Athletics International   33:30.44
3. Jill Molen, University of Utah   33:35.19
4. Patti Gray, University of California, Davis   33:42.33
5. Carol Urish, Houston Harriers   33:42.38
6. Linda McLennan, Athletics International   34:04.81

100 meter hurdles
1. Benita Fitzgerald, Team adidas   12.97
2. Pam Page, Puma & Energizer Track Club   13.14
3. Candy Young, Puma & Energizer Track Club   13.16
4. Kim Turner, Los Angeles Mercurettes   13.18
5. Jackie Washington, Puma & Energizer Track Club   13.44
6. Marlene Harmon, Puma & Energizer Track Club   13.45

400 meter hurdles
1. Sharrieffa Barksdale, Team adidas   56.07   MR
   (betters meet record of 56.43 by Sandra Myers, 1981)
2. Judi Brown, Michigan State University   56.51
3. Tonja Brown, Gulf Coast Club   56.64
4. Patty Bradley, Villanova University   56.92
5. Angie Wright, Team adidas   57.33
6. Lexie Beck, University of Oregon   57.88

10 kilometer walk
1. Susan Liers-Westerfield, Island Track Club   50:51.91
2. Deborah Spino-Lawrence, Team Kangaroo   51:39.76
3. Susan Miller, Seattle Track Club   52:49.29
4. Maryanne Torrellas, Abraxas Track Club   52:51.31
5. Gwen Robertson, Team Kangaroo   53:19.58
6. Teresa Vaill, Island Track Club   53:25.40

4 × 100 meter relay
1. Puma & Energizer Track Club   43.61
   (Faye Paige, Denean Howard, Angela Thacker, Diane Williams)
2. Puma & Energizer Track Club   44.65
3. Ms. International   45.00

Sprint medley relay
1. Puma & Energizer Track Club   1:37.46
   (Pam Page, Sandra Howard, Lisa Hopkins, Rosalyn Bryant)

Carol Lewis.   **Robin Campbell.**

2. Ms. International	1:37.96
3. Southern California Cheetahs	1:39.79

4 × 400 meter relay
1. Puma & Energizer Track Club	3:34.18
(Delphina Banks, Sandra Farmer, Rosalyn Bryant, Roberta Belle)	
2. Police Athletic League	3:35.22
3. Boston International Athletic Club	3:37.91

4 × 800 meter relay
1. Ms. International	8:38.04
(Wanda Trent, Cynthia Colquitt, Kim Kelly, Debbie Roberson)	
2. University of Minnesota	8:46.30
3. Liberty Athletic Club	8:46.88

High jump
1. Louise Ritter, Pacific Coast Club	6' 4"
2. Pam Spencer, Puma & Energizer Track Club	6' 4"
3. Joni Huntley, Pacific Coast Club	6' 2¾"
4. Coleen Sommer, Team adidas	6' 2¾"
5. Ann Bair, University of Virginia	6' 1½"
6. Katrena Johnson, University of Arizona	6' 1½"

Long jump
1. Carol Lewis, Santa Monica Track Club	22' 8" MR
(betters meet record of 22' 7½" by Jodi Anderson, 1978)	
2. Jennifer Inniss, Southern California Cheetahs/Guyana	22' 5¾" w
3. Gwen Loud, Coast Athletics	21' 10" w

4. Jackie Joyner, Wilt's Athletic Club   21' 9"
5. Angela Thacker, Los Angeles Track Club   21' 3½" w
6. Dorothy Scott, Atoms Track Club/Jamaica   21' 2½" w

Shot put
1. Denise Wood, Knoxville Track Club   56' 8½"
2. Lorna Griffin, Athletics West   56' 4¾"
3. Regina Cavanaugh, Rice University   55' 5½"
4. Bonnie Dasse, Coast Athletics   54' 7¼"
5. Ramona Pagel, Converse West   54' 5¼"
6. Peggy Pollock, Coast Athletics   54' 3¾"

Discus
1. Leslie Deniz, unattached   206' 3"   MR
    (betters meet record of 203' 10" by Ria Stalman, 1982)
2. Meg Ritchie, Team adidas/Great Britain   202' 11"
3. Carol Cady, Puma & Energizer Track Club   197'
4. Lorna Griffin, Athletics West   195' 5"
5. Penny Neer, Ann Arbor Track Club   190' 3"
6. Kathy Picknell, Oregon International Track Club   188' 1"

Javelin
1. Karin Smith, Athletics West   187' 8"
2. Kate Schmidt, Pacific Coast Club   187' 6"
3. Deanna Carr, Club Northwest   184' 11"
4. Patty Kearney, Oregon Track Club   179' 8"
5. Mary Osbourne, Puma & Energizer Track Club   179' 4"
6. Susie Ray, Wilt's Athletic Club   178' 6"

Team scores:
1. Puma & Energizer Track Club   108
2. Athletics West   89
3. Team adidas   46

The Indoor Nationals

The indoor national championships were held in Madison Square Garden on Friday, February 25.

Prior to the meet, a feature article entitled "The Grueling Road of Evelyn Ashford" appeared in Wednesday's *New York Times*:

On a glaringly bright Sunday morning, three tiring joggers chugged slowly round the quarter-mile track at Santa Monica High School. Pat Connolly checked her watch. It read 10:20, and it was quite clear that the small lithe figure of Evelyn Ashford was not where it was supposed to be.

"She should have been here by 10," Miss Connolly said. Minutes later, a shiny brown car slammed to a stop, and America's fastest woman sprinter popped out of the passenger seat. She was barefoot. "I forgot my shoes and had to go back for them," Miss Ashford said, laughing. She bent over and quickly slipped them on.

And so it began, one more time, one more grueling workout in a regimen that has been ceaselessly adhered to for seven years.

It was seven years ago that Miss Connolly, the track coach, and Miss Ashford, the U.C.L.A. freshman, joined forces in a campaign they pledged would one day end up on the medalist's stand at an Olympics. Twice since then, Miss Ashford has been ranked as the world's fastest woman;

Left to right: **Allyson Felix and Pat Connolly (and unidentified woman) at the 2004 Olympic Games, Athens.**

but she has yet to climb onto that Olympic stand. Now, at 25, she sounds more determined than ever. "I feel I can only go as fast as this body can take me," Miss Ashford says. "But I think it will be fast enough so that if I set a world record, it won't be broken for many years."

...It is the 100- and 200-meter events that the seven years of hard labor have been geared toward, and currently those records are held by East Germans....

...Miss Ashford's training regimen looks like the kind of torture that only a masochist would attempt. First comes a slow mile round the track. Next she ducks behind a couple of school buildings and winds up at the bottom of an outdoor amphitheater. Miss Connolly climbs 25 very steep, very wide concrete steps and perches near the top. In her red sweat pants and white T-shirt, her pony tail bobbing, Miss Ashford plows up the steps full speed ahead. Then she walks slowly down. Then, presto, she's back up.

"Four point 47," Miss Connolly calls out at one point.

Not even visibly panting, Miss Ashford brightens. "All right," she says.

...After completing her eighth sprint up the stairs, Miss Ashford proceeds to jump up the steps, legs wide apart, 10 times.

"After that, your legs don't feel like a part of your body," she says. "They don't want to do what you tell them to."

"...I don't feel like I'm ever going to stop competing. I want to win a gold medal and I want to set a world record. I guess you could say I want to have it all."

While Carol Lewis, Stephanie Hightower and Diane Dixon set records during Friday's meet, the headlines in the *New York Times* on Saturday read, "Lewis Captures 2 Events":

Earlier in the day, Lewis's 19-year-old sister, Carol, won the women's long jump with a leap of 21 feet 5¼ inches, an American indoor best.

Miss Hightower's 7.36 in the 60-yard hurdles broke the mark of 7.37 she had shared with Candy Young. Miss Dixon, a freshman at Ohio State, set her world-indoor best in a trial heat of the 440 (53.52) before winning the final in 53.78.

There were a number of other outstanding performances including Evelyn Ashford's fifth consecutive victory in the 60-yard dash.

The sprint victory by Miss Ashford reaffirmed her place as America's best.

Miss Ashford finished second to Chandra Cheeseborough in the semifinals (6.63 to 6.64) but said she was not worried.

"I'm having some problems with the injury," she said, referring to a pulled left hamstring muscle that she suffered at a meet in Dallas recently. "It takes some time to get it warmed up. I was using the heats and semis to get warm."

In the final, Miss Cheeseborough led at the start, and the two were even at 40 yards. But then Miss Ashford accelerated and drove to the tape, arms raised. Her time was 6.58 seconds, and her victory was her eighth in a row this season.

"I set a world record at this meet last year," she said, referring to her 6.54, "and I wanted to run faster this time, but my injury kept me from doing it."

Nothing seemed to bother Miss Hightower, who has shown consistent improvement under Mamie Rallins, her coach and former world-class hurdler.

To provide practice incentive for Miss Hightower, Miss Rallins spots rival hurdlers five-meter leads and then tells Miss Hightower to play catch-up.

"If I don't catch them, I have to run quarters," Miss Hightower said, "and I hate running quarters."

Miss Rallins said that last Tuesday she could sense that Miss Hightower was ready for a record performance. "I can tell, but she can't," Miss Rallins said.

---

60 yard dash
1. Evelyn Ashford, Medalist Track Club   6.58
2. Chandra Cheeseborough, Athletics West   6.63
3. Alice Brown, Wilt's Athletic Club   6.74

220 yard dash
1. Chandra Cheeseborough, Athletics West   23.52
2. Angela Williams, Flashette Track Club   24.10
3. Gervaise McCraw, Southern California Cheetahs   24.40

440 yard dash
1. Diane Dixon, Ohio State University   53.78
2. Gwen Gardner, Los Angeles Mercurettes   54.42
3. Charmaine Crooks, Los Angeles Mercurettes   54.51

880 yard run
1. Delisa Walton, University of Tennessee   2:03.10
2. Robin Campbell, Stanford Track Club   2:03.54
3. Lee Arbogast, Athletics West   2:04.17

Mile run
1. Darlene Beckford, Liberty Athletic Club   4:33.29
2. Cindy Bremser, Wisconsin United Track Club   4:34.81
3. Monica Joyce, Converse West   4:37.12

Two mile run
1. Jan Merrill, Age Group Athletic Association   9:40.46
2. Brenda Webb, Athletics West   9:42.66
3. Maggie Keyes, Athletics West   9:55.01

60 yard hurdles
1. Stephanie Hightower, unattached   7.36   WR, AR
2. Kim Turner, Los Angeles Mercurettes   7.57
3. Candy Young, Fairleigh Dickinson University   7.61

Mile walk
1. Susan Brodock, Southern California Road Runners   7:14.67
2. Teresa Vaill, Island Track Club   7:17.32
3. Susan Liers-Westerfield, Island Track Club   7:33.93

640 yard relay
1. University of Nevada, Las Vegas   1:10.55
    (Lisa Thompson, Inger Peterson, Vernecia Smith, LaTanya Dawkins)
2. Southern California Cheetahs   1:11.24
3. Tennessee State University   1:11.34

Mile relay
1. Ms. International   3:42.35
    (Alice Jackson, Michelle Collins, Wanda Trent, Deborah Roberson)
2. Atoms Track Club   3:45.24
3. University of Nevada, Las Vegas   3:52.42

880 yard medley relay
1. Southern California Cheetahs   1:45.38
    (Gayle Kellon, Jennifer Inniss, Zelda Johnson, Gervaise McCraw)
2. Tennessee State University   1:45.44
3. Club New York   1:46.21

High jump
1. Louise Ritter, Pacific Coast Club   6' 3½"
2. Silvia Costa, Cuba   6' 1¼"
3. Joni Huntley, Pacific Coast Club   5' 10¾"

Long jump
1. Carol Lewis, University of Houston   21' 5¼"
2. Jennifer Inniss, Southern California Cheetahs/Guyana   21' 2½"
3. Donna Thomas, North Texas State University   20' 11¾"

Shot put
1. Ria Stalman, Los Angeles Track Club   55' 2¾"
2. Denise Wood, Knoxville Track Club   54' 1¼"
3. Elaine Sobansky, Pennsylvania State University   53' 5¾"

Team scores:
1. Athletics West   16
2. Southern California Cheetahs   13
3. Pacific Coast Club, University of
    Nevada, Las Vegas, Tennessee State University   7

The national meet program contained a listing and sketches of the USA/Mobil All Time Indoor Track and Field Team. The women selected for that team were: Wyomia Tyus, 60 yard dash; Patty Van Wolvelaere, 60 yard hurdles; Mae Faggs, 220 yard dash; Rosalyn Bryant, 440 yard run; Madeline Manning-Mims, 880 yard run; Mary Decker Tabb, Mile; Francie Larrieu-Smith, Two mile run; Susan Brodock, Walk; Joni Huntley, High Jump; Martha Watson, Long Jump and, Maren Seidler, Shot Put.

Left: Patty Van Wolvelaere, 1996. *Right:* Maren Seidler at her induction into the National Track and Field Hall of Fame, 2003.

Sunkist Invitational (5 women's events): Los Angeles, January 21

60 yard dash	
Evelyn Ashford	6.70
500 yards	
Gwen Gardner	1:05.7
800 meters	
Louise Romo	2:09.9
2 mile run	
Mary Decker	9:31.72
60 yard hurdles	
Stephanie Hightower	7.48

9th Pan American Games: Caracas, Venezuela, August 23–28

On August 25, the *New York Times* reported:

...Of the track favorites, only one could come up with a victory. Judi Brown of East Lansing, Mich., took the first woman's 400-meter hurdles race ever held at the Games. She was timed at 56.03 seconds.

...The Americans lost two of their top women hopefuls when the hepthathlete Marlene Harmon of Canoga Park, Calif., suffered an ankle injury in the first event and Lisa Hopkins aggravated a groin injury and could not compete in the 100-meter final.

On the 28 of August, the *New York Times* reported that the United States won two bronze medals: Lorna Griffin in the discus and Easter Gabriel in the 400 meters.

On the final day of competition the "United States speedsters ruled the track and gained six more gold medals ... as the IX Pan American Games drew to a close.... Randy Givens ran the anchor behind Jackie Washington, Alice Jackson and Brenda Cliette for the victory in the women's 400-meter relay in 43.21."

Name	Event	Place	Performance
Arbogast, Lee	800m	8	2:07.83
Barksdale, Sharrieffa	400mh	2	56.09
Benoit, Joan	3000m	1	9:14.19
Bolton, Kelia	Mile relay	1	3:29.97
Bremser, Cindy	1500m	2	4:17.67
Brown-King, Judi	400mh	1	56.03
	Mile relay	1	3:29.97
Carr, Deanna	Javelin	7	151' 5"
Cliette, Brenda	400mr	1	43.21
Dabney, Sharon	400m	DNC-injured	
Fitzgerald, Benita	100mh	1	13.16
Gabriel, Easter	400m	3	52.45
	Mile relay	1	3:29.97
Givens, Randy	200m	1	23.14
	400m relay	1	43.21
Greiner, Cindy	Heptathlon	2	6069
Griffin, Lorna	Shot put	3	54' 6"
	Discus	3	185' 5"
Harmon, Marlene	Heptathlon	DNC-injured	
Hopkins, Lisa	100m	DNC-injured	
Huntley, Joni	High jump	3	5' 11½"
Jackson, Alice	400mr	1	43.21
	Mile relay	1	3:29.97
Johnson, Patricia	Long jump	3	20' 9¼"
Kane, Missy	1500m	3	4:21.39
Kearney, Patty	Javelin	5	170' 7"
McMillan, Kathy	Long jump	1	21' 11¾"
Nedd, LaShon	200m	2	23.39
Neer, Penny	Discus	4	174' 11"
Richburg, Diana	800m	6	2:05.29
Sommer, Coleen	High jump	1	6' 3¼"
Turner, Kim	100mh	2	13.39
Washington, Jackie	100m	2	11.33
	400mr	1	43.21
Webb, Brenda	3000m	2	9:28.89
Wood, Denise	Shot put	5	48' 11½"

Dr. Harmon Brown, Head Coach
Roxanne Anderson, Assistant Coach
Terry Crawford, Assistant Coach
Conrad Ford, Assistant Coach
Charles Ruter, Head Manager

U.S. Women's Marathon Championships: Avon International Marathon, Los Angeles, California, June 5

1. Julie Brown	2:26:24	
3. Marianne Dickerson	2:33:44	

6. Debbie Eide	2:35:15
7. Margaret Groos	2:37:02
8. Nancy Ditz	2:37:56
9. Karen Dunn	2:38:46
10. Laura Dewald	2:38:56

250 women completed the race

U.S. Heptathlon Championships: UCLA Drake Stadium, Los Angeles, California, June 21–22

1. Jane Frederick, Athletics West	6493
(13.6, 6'2¼", 49'¼", 24.5, 19'8¾", 150'5", 2:10.5)	
2. Jackie Joyner, Wilt's Athletic Club	6418
3. Marlene Harmon, Puma & Energizer Track Club	6198
4. Cindy Greiner, Athletics West	6051
5. Patsy Walker, unattached	6020
6. Mary Harrington, 4 Corners Track Club	5770

1st IAAF World Outdoor Track and Field Championships: Olympic Stadium, Helsinki, Finland, August 7–14

Neil Amdur's story in the *New York Times* on August 7, "Top Marathoners Ready in Helsinki," provided insight into the development of marathoning in the world for women:

At age 17, Grete Waitz of Norway competed here in the 800- and 1,500-meter runs at the European track and field championships. She did not survive the opening heats.

"Could you imagine ever running a marathon back then?" the 29-year-old Mrs. Waitz was asked the other day.

"No, not at all," the former school teacher and three time New York City Marathon champion replied.

But Sunday Mrs. Waitz and 63 other women will run the marathon in the first World Track and Field Championships. Although thousands of women have covered the 26.2-mile distance in hundreds of marathons in recent years, some of them for women only, the race will have special significance on the international scene.

"It's exciting, it's different," Jacqueline Gareau of Canada, a former Boston Marathon winner, said today at the Athlete's Village on the outskirts of this city. "You can feel the challenge."

Primo Nebiolo of Italy, the president of the International Amateur Athletic Federation, used the occasion of the women's marathon to announce today that the federation had requested a 10,000-meter race for women to be added to the international calendar, along with the 3,000 and marathon, for the 1985 World Cup and 1988 Olympics in Seoul, Korea. As late as 1976, the longest Olympic race for women was only 1,500 meters.

"We must be careful with the ladies," Nebiolo told a news conference at the Finlandia Concert Hall. Among those in attendance was Kathy Switzer, who first crashed the Boston Marathon in 1967, when women were persona non grata, and who helped lobby for a women's marathon in the 1984 Los Angeles Olympics.

Besides Miss Gareau and Mrs. Waitz, the field will include Julie Brown. Miss Brown's time of 2 hours 26 minutes 24 seconds last June in the Avon Marathon was the fastest ever in a women's-only event.

"I'll run with whoever is there until 20 miles, and then I'll make up my mind what to do, depending on the situation," said the 28-year-old Miss Brown. Joan Benoit, who set a world best of 2:22:43 in Boston last April, chose to bypass these championships.

"Mrs. Waitz Takes World Marathon Title" proclaimed the front page of the sports section of the *New York Times* on Monday, August 8. But:

...the most surprising element of the race, which drew 62 starters, was a kick in the last 200 meters that lifted a relatively unknown 22-year-old American, Marianne Dickerson of St. Joseph, Ill., past Raisa Smekhnova of the Soviet Union for the silver medal.

Running in only her third marathon and at one time mistaken on the course for a more prominent American, Julie Brown, who dropped out with three miles left because of Achilles' tendon problems, Miss Dickerson entered the Olympic stadium for the final 300 meters trailing Miss Smekhnova by 1.3 seconds.

"I had a lot of confidence going on the backstretch that I could catch her," said Miss Dickerson, a graduate student in industrial engineering at Purdue University, who began training seriously for the marathon only nine months ago.

The fact that her red-shirted rival was from the Soviet Union was an "incentive," Miss Dickerson later admitted. But it was not until the final turn that she accelerated and moved ahead, finishing in 2:31:09 to Miss Smekhnova's 2:31:13.

...At 5 feet 4 inches and 98 pounds, Miss Dickerson was a modestly successful distance runner at the University of Illinois who says that her strongest attribute may be "guts" and a lack of fear. Ironically, during the American training camp in Sweden before these championships Miss Dickerson said she stressed shorter interval workouts and even teased the head women's coach, Dr. Ken Foreman, about how her speed work might help her in a 26.2-mile event.

U.S. hopes in the 100 meters were dashed when, according to the *New York Times* on August 9, a torn hamstring muscle sent Evelyn Ashford "sprawling to the ground halfway through the women's 100 final." The story went on:

At a time when she needed to accelerate to stay with Marlies Gohr and Marita Koch of East Germany, Miss Ashford broke down, victimized by an old injury that she aggravated Sunday and tried to ignore in her 10.99 semifinal tonight.

...Miss Ashford had beaten Mrs. Gohr in quarterfinal heats Sunday. Today, Mrs. Gohr suggested that she had let her American rival win to build a comfort zone for later confrontations.

"We knew and noticed in the heat and semifinal that she seemed to have problems," Edwin Tepper, the East German national sprint coach, said of Miss Ashford. "But still, she was fighting ahead."

The extent of Miss Ashford's problems became clearer when the new world-record holder (10.79) won her semifinal and then immediately asked for three bags of ice and bandage-wrap from an official on the track at the finish line.

...Miss Ashford was in a position to challenge the East Germans when her leg gave way between 40 and 50 meters. She hopped another 10 meters, wincing in pain and dragging her injured right leg, before falling on her back, clutching the area around her hamstring muscle.

"I'm very disappointed," Miss Ashford said, "but I will be back next year. I have a few scores to settle yet."

Pat Connolly wrote in her book *Coaching Evelyn*:

...At her last workout before we left for the World Championships in Finland, Evelyn ran four fifty-meter sprints against one of Coach Bush's male quarter milers. She won all of them with her fastest times ever. Just as she was slowing down from her final sprint of the day, several children wandered onto the track in front of her, and she had to swerve abruptly to avoid crashing into them. At top speed her muscles weren't ready for a sudden change of direction, and she felt a searing pain in her bootie. Ice, I thought, and hurried to get it.

The tear in Evelyn's gluteus maximus did not heal.

Wrote the *New York Times* on August 11:

Mary Decker led from the start and survived a thrilling stretch duel in the 3,000-meter run at the world track and field championships today.

...There was equal satisfaction in Miss Decker's conquest of Tatyana Kazankina and Svetlana Ulmasova of the Soviet Union. In 1973 and 1974, as a teen-ager, Miss Decker burst onto the international scene with dramatic middle-distance victories over Soviet runners. Bothered by injuries and other personal setbacks, however, Miss Decker had lost all subsequent races to Soviet rivals, including a 1980 defeat to Miss Kazankina, a two-time Olympic champion, that was her last loss on the track. The notion that Miss Decker could run fast but was less adept at racing, especially at the international level, began to follow her.

"I thought I would have the best chance of winning if I led, simply because I've always been a front-runner and don't mind leading," Miss Decker said, explaining her strategy. She had finished in a virtual dead heat with Miss Kazankina in the semifinals.

Miss Decker took the 15-runner field through an opening 1,000 in 2:50.96, with Miss Kazankina never more than a stride or two behind. Reaching the 2,000 in 5:48.89, Miss Decker said she still felt confident and comfortable with the pace. With two laps left, five rivals were within 10 yards, before Miss Kazankina challenged on the backstretch of the last lap and drew alongside Miss Decker on the turn and into the final straightaway.

With 50 meters left, and both runners side by side and stride for stride, Miss Kazankina appeared to inch ahead ever so slightly until Miss Decker suddenly gritted her teeth, pumped her arms determinedly and pulled away. The move so startled Miss Kazankina that she faded to third behind Brigitte Kraus of West Germany.

"I felt strong and in control," Miss Decker said, of her 8:34.62 time. "The most important thing was feeling in control, while I was trying to sprint."

On the front page of the *New York Times* of August 15, above the headline, "U.S. Athletes Stand Out In World Track Events," is a photograph of Mary Decker crossing the finish line to win her second gold medal in the 1,500 meter run. The article reads:

For the second time in five days, Mary Decker outkicked a rival runner from the Soviet Union and won a gold medal today at the world track and field championships.

This time, after being cut off on the final curve by Zamira Zaitseva in the 1,500-meter run, Miss Decker fought back into contention and powered through the stretch to victory as Mrs. Zaitseva tumbled over the finish line.

...Just as she had done in the 3,000, Miss Decker chose to run from the front in the 1,500. In fact, her first 400 of 1:04.06 was faster than the almost embarrassing 1:05.02 pace in the men's 1,500 that drew whistles and boos from many spectators in the capacity crowd of 53,000.

...In contrast to the pushing and shoving among the men, there was no shift of position among the leading women until Mrs. Zaitseva drew alongside Miss Decker 300 meters from the finish, surged slightly ahead on the outside of the top of the last turn and then cut to the inside.

"I lost a lot of momentum off the turn," Miss Decker said. She recalled how she had fallen behind off the turn by three meters, continuing "because I was cut off and had to back off a bit."

"...Today, I felt I wasn't aggressive enough," said the 25-year-old Miss Decker of Eugene, Ore., who has had her share of physical races with Soviet rivals since she first burst onto the scene 10 years ago. "You have to learn to deal with it. But I felt like if I did, maybe we would have been punching it out on the track."

Miss Decker settled the score with a devastating 29.4 last 200. She caught Mrs. Zaitseva 10 meters from the finish and won by 2 meters in 4:00.90, as her Soviet rival lunged in vain, lost her balance five meters from the finish and then went sprawling across the line.

"I had to dig down, and I did all the way through the finish," Miss Decker said.

---

100 meters
3. Diane Williams   11.06
   Evelyn Ashford, dnf

200 meters
4. Florence Griffith   22.46

400 meters
8. Rosalyn Bryant   50.66

800 meters
5. Robin Campbell   2:00.03

1500 meters
1. Mary Decker   4:00.90

3000 meters
1. Mary Decker   8:34.62

100 meter hurdles
8. Benita Fitzgerald   12.99

There were no American women in the final of the 400
meter hurdles

Marathon
2. Marianne Dickerson   2:31:09
12. Debbie Eide   2:36:17

4 × 400 meter relay
5. USA   3:27.57

(Roberta Belle, Easter Gabriel, Rosalyn Bryant, Denean Howard-Hill)

Heptathlon
11. Marlene Harmon   5925

High jump
3. Louise Ritter   6' 4¾"
4. Coleen Sommer   6' 4¾"

Long jump
3. Carol Lewis   23' 1¼" w

There were no American women in the final of the shot put or discus

Javelin
10. Karin Smith   196' 1"

Mary Decker Slaney at her induction into the National Track and Field Hall of Fame, 2003.

USA vs. GDR Dual Meet: Los Angeles Coliseum, June 25–26

The *New York Times* reported:

A year ago, the United States women's track and field team won only two events in two days against East Germany. Today, when this year's meet began, the American women won three of their nine events and broke two American records and one American all-comers record.

The East Germans had a chance in the women's 1,500 meters, though Mary Decker led from the start. But when Miss Decker shifted gears on the last lap, she ran off to an 8-meter victory. She covered the last 400 meters in 60.3 seconds, exceptionally fast, and her time of 3 minutes 59.93 seconds was the fastest ever on American soil.

Women's Track & Field World reported that the highlight of the meet for the USA women "came in the high jump which not only saw the Americans finish 1–2, but had Louise Ritter produce a new American record at 6' 6¾". Best US showing on the track came in the 1500 with Mary Decker winning and the home team outscoring the visitors 6–5."

The second American record was set by the 4 × 100 meter relay team.

100 meters
2. Evelyn Ashford   11.53
4. Diane Williams   11.57

200 meters
2. Chandra Cheeseborough   22.56
3. Randy Givens   22.92

400 meters
3. Denean Howard   51.90
4. Rosalyn Bryant   52.47

800 meters
3. Robin Campbell   1:59.72
4. Diana Richburg   2:03.39

1500 meters
1. Mary Decker   3:59.93
4. Cindy Bremser   4:14.10

3000 meters
3. Maggie Keyes   9:01.27
4. Brenda Webb   9:15.43

100 meter hurdles
3. Pam Page   13.07
4. Benita Fitzgerald   13.30

400 meter hurdles
3. Sharrieffa Barksdale   55.90
Judi Brown, dq

4 × 100 meter relay
1. USA   41.63 AR
    (Alice Brown, Diane Williams, Chandra Cheeseborough, Evelyn Ashford)

4 × 400 meter relay
2. USA   3:28.12
    (Rosalyn Bryant, Roberta Belle, Sharrieffa Barksdale, Easter Gabriel)

High jump
1. Louise Ritter   6' 6¾" AR
2. Pam Spencer   6' 2¾"

Long jump
3. Jackie Joyner   22' 8¼"
4. Gwen Loud   20' 5"

Shot put
3. Lorna Griffin   56' 9¼"
4. Denise Wood   52' 11"

Discus
3. Leslie Deniz   208' 2"
4. Carol Cady   200' 1"

Javelin
3. Deanna Carr   191' 2"
4. Patty Kearney   177' 5"

Team score:
USA 56 GDR 100

Other News and Honors

Track & Field News: Athlete of the Year

Mary Decker

USA Rankings — *Track & Field News*

1. Mary Decker
2. Evelyn Ashford
3. Louise Ritter
4. Joan Benoit
5. Carol Lewis

World Rankings — *Track & Field News*

2. Mary Decker

A significant event promoting the growth of women's running took place when a group of female runners filed a lawsuit. The *New York Times* on August 12 featured the following story:

Mary Decker and Grete Waitz, each of whom has won a gold medal at the current world track and field championships in Helsinki, joined about 50 other leading female runners from 20 countries today in a sex-discrimination suit against international track authorities, the International Olympic Committee and the Los Angeles Olympic Organizing Committee.

The suit, filed in Los Angeles Superior Court, seeks an order that would force the sports authorities to include 5,000 and 10,000 meter runs for women at the 1984 Games in Los Angeles. Those are traditional events on the men's program but not on the women's, a result of the international authorities' longtime sentiment that women could not handle such stamina-testing races.

Among distance events for women, only a marathon and a 3,000-meter race are planned for the 1984 Games, marking the first time that women have been allowed to compete in an event of more than 1,500 meters at the Olympics. But some women, including Miss Decker and Mrs. Waitz, call the 3,000 more a middle-distance event than long-distance, and so they are pressing for both the 5,000 and the 10,000.

The suit was filed on behalf of the female athletes by the American Civil Liberties Union. The defendants, in addition to the I.O.C. and the Los Angeles organizers, are the International Amateur Athletic Federation, the world governing body of track and field; the Los Angeles Coliseum Commission; the United States Olympic Committee; The Athletics Congress, which governs track and field in the United States; the Standing and Joint Programs Commission of the I.O.C., and a member of the Women's Committee for the IAAF.

...Carol Sobel, a spokesman for the American Civil Liberties Union, said that Mrs. Waitz's record-breaking times in several marathons, as well as her triumph in the marathon at the world championships last Sunday, were proof that women were capable of competing in long-distance events.

Evelyn Ashford broke the world record running 10.79 at the National Sports Festival in Colorado Springs on July 3. The 400 meter relay team of Alice Brown, Diane Williams, Chandra Cheeseborough and Evelyn Ashford lowered the American record of 41.63 they set a week ago to 41.61.

Bob Seaman noted that this year was a first for the combined Men's and Women's Senior TAC Multi-events Championships (June 23–24) and the first time that the 10 kilometer walk and 5000 meter run were held in the Senior National Championships.

Betty Springs, Athletics West, won the USA cross country championships.

In the April issue of *Women's Track & Field World*, Vince Reel, the editor and publisher wrote, "As you know, WTFW is sent gratis to every women's track team at every college, university and junior college in the United States. The objective is to give those in the sport something to pull them together, a means of communication, for heaven knows, trying to get publicity in the newspapers for women's sports is, for the most part, impossible. Only through WTFW will you know the performances of opponents. We publish whatever we receive, from Olympics down to the weakest of the Division III teams."

Mildred McDaniel was inducted into the National Track and Field Hall of Fame. The information below is from the National Track and Field Hall of Fame website:

MILDRED McDANIEL (Singleton)   HIGH JUMP
Born Nov. 3, 1933, Atlanta, Ga.

One of the world's top women athletes of the 1950s, Mildred McDaniel excelled both in track and field and basketball and acquired her nickname of "Tex" on the basketball floor because her teammates said she dribbled like a Texan. The world's dominant women's high jumper during that period, she was the Olympic champion in 1956 with a world record 5–9¼.

A 1957 graduate of Tuskegee Institute in Alabama where she was coached by Hall of Fame coach Cleve Abbott, she was the U.S. women's high jump champion in 1953, 1955 and 1956 and was the U.S. indoor champion the latter two years. She also was the 1955 Pan American Games winner with a leap of 5–6¼, a meet mark which stood until 1967. She later became a physical education teacher in California.

Mildred McDaniel Singleton died in October 2004.

INTERVIEW: CHANDRA CHEESEBOROUGH

(December 3, 2000, following Cheeseborough's induction into the National Track and Field Hall of Fame) I began my track career in Jacksonville, Florida, in the sixth grade and continued through middle school and high school. I really started running in the neighborhood, always racing the guys. When my sister ran track, I would always follow her to the meets. She was the high jump champion in the state of Florida in 1970. So, I saw track all of the time. My father took me to all the meets following my sister's track career. I'd be at the meet racing other little kids behind the bleachers. So, it got started like that.

One summer my sister was offered a track scholarship to Tennessee State University. She didn't want to go that far away from home so she declined the scholarship. I told my mom that I'd go to Tennessee State University and run track — and I was still in the sixth grade!

In 1974, I met Coach Temple again at the Junior Olympics. He invited me down to Tennessee State the following summer (1975). I made the 1975 Pan American team then when I was sixteen years old. I won two golds at the Pan Ams. That was the beginning of my track career on the national level — it happened just by speaking something as a child and having it come to actuality.

After the Pan Ams, I went back home. I was going into my junior year of high school. I was a normal kid and did all of the normal things.

In 1976, I tried out for the Olympic team. I was seventeen years old. I made the team in the 100 and 200 and also ran the 4 × 1 relay. I took sixth place in the 100 meter final in the Montreal Olympics.

I graduated from high school in 1977 and made a couple of national teams. One was to Russia. I set my first American record. That year, 1977, was my high school graduation year. I did not walk across the stage. My mother accepted my diploma because I had a choice of either going to Russia or walking across the stage — and I chose Russia. That was a lifetime opportunity.

I went on to Tennessee State University. I didn't get any track scholarships, but I got about fourteen basketball scholarships. I played basketball, All-American basketball. I love basketball but I decided, at the time, that track would take me much further. If I graduated in 2002, I'd probably play basketball. Basketball is really great now.

Chandra Cheeseborough at her induction into the National Track and Field Hall of Fame, 2000.

At Tennessee State I had a lot of good races but ran a lot of times behind Brenda Morehead. She was really quick too. Coach Temple used to divide us — sometimes I ran the 100 and sometimes she'd run the 100. But, I really had a good career. I made the Pan American Games in 1979. I went on to make the 1980 Olympic team, the boycotted Games.

I graduated in 1982. I was still training. I was training then with Ralph Boston in Knoxville, Tennessee.

I made one more move before the 1984 Olympics. I went to Gainesville, Florida, and trained with Jerry Long. In the 1984 Olympics, I medaled with 2 golds and a silver.

My highlights: In 1980 I was voted the Female Athlete of the Year indoors. I had a really good year and in 1983 I had another really good year. I only lost one race indoors. I went over to Australia and did an Australian tour and New Zealand tour back in 1983, and really had a good, super year.

Being the first woman to run the two relays, and being successful at that, was another highlight.

My favorite event is the 200 meters. I love the 200. There is something about going around curves. I love going around curves. I still do. I drive fast around curves, which is not good, but sometimes I even find myself just even leaning into the curve — not going fast all the time but just leaning into the curve. I love the 200.

I have an eleven year old daughter and she is running now. She made it to the Junior Olympics. This is her second time making it to the junior Olympics. She made it at eight. She didn't run at ten and then she came back and made it at eleven. She didn't make it to the finals but she improved her time. She is running 27 in the 200 meters. That is not bad for an eleven year old. We are excited about her running. But I don't want to push her. She is playing basketball, softball and a number of things including playing the flute. So we are just keeping her involved. One thing I can look back on is I'm glad I really didn't bring her into track at an early age — bringing her on the tour and the circuit. I think she can really appreciate track now and she is not pressured because her mother was a great runner. Now she can do her own thing and not be pressured by track and field.

Another memorable moment happened in high school. Title IX had just come into place and they asked me to run on the 4 × 1 relay — the men's 4 × 1 relay. I anchored the boys' 4 × 1 relay and we won the county meet that year. That was another highlight that sticks out in my mind during my track and field career.

Thank God for my career and thank God for everything that has happened to me at this point. It's been a good career.

Chandra is currently coaching at Tennessee State University.

PROFILE: EASTER GABRIEL-YOUNG

(Information provided by Easter Gabriel-Young) Easter Gabriel-Young was born on June 15, 1960, in New Orleans, Louisiana, and migrated to Houston, Texas in 1969. Her move to Houston gave her the opportunity to run for the Houston Astrobells. Easter graduated from Houston Sterling High School and Prairie View A&M University.

Easter Gabriel Young.

While at PVU, Easter had a tremendous career in track and field. She won the 400 meter and the triple jump state championship; she was a member of the state 1600 meter relay team. Easter achieved success through college and beyond, she was a SWAC champion (Outstanding Athletic Conference Championships) in various events: 400 meters, 200 meters, 100 meters, triple jump, long jump, and numerous relays.

After college she participated on a number of USA teams in the 400 meters and relays. She was the 1983 Pan American Games 400 meter bronze medalist and a member of the winning 1600 meter relay team.

Easter's many accomplishments include Drake Relays Hall of Fame, Texas Black African American Hall of Fame, and Prairie View Hall of Fame.

Easter ran in many places in the world such as Germany in 1981 when the mile relay team were World Champions. In 1982, in Canada she ran on the 1600 meter relay and placed third. In Helsinki in 1983, the U.S.A. mile relay team placed fifth; and in Venezuela 1983, the Pan Am 1600 meter relay placed first and she finished third in the 400 meters.

After life in track and field, Easter taught and coached in elementary and high school. She has coached a number of state champions and Olympic hopefuls. She made Dallas, Texas, her home where she resides with her husband and daughter, Charné.

INTERVIEW: EVELYN LAWLER LEWIS

(February 28, 2003) I am living alone in Houston. I have many friends and family in Houston. Carol and my oldest son are there. I play a little tennis and golf. I love golf.

Back in the early '90s I competed in track and field but I kept getting injured because my mind did not connect with my body. I was competing a lot harder than I should have. I was at the long jump in Arizona and broke my back. I decided to leave track but I did win nine gold medals while I was competing in masters. I like to tell Carl I have nine gold medals also.

I got started when I was a sophomore in high school. They started a track and field team for girls at my high school. They selected about six or seven girls. I wasn't one of those selected, but they caught my eye and I would go and watch them practice. One day they were doing the high jump. They were trying out to see who could high jump. They really didn't clear that much of a height. I asked the coach if I could try. I out–jumped all of the girls that he had chosen. I also went over to the long jump, broad jump it was called then, and again I exceeded in the jumping of the girls that he had out there. That's how I got started in track and field.

The next good thing that happened to me was that Major Cleve Abbott of Tuskegee saw me when we were at the Tuskegee Relays. He asked my parents if I could come and be a part of his summer program. They didn't know what they were doing but they let me. Track and field has been good to me because it provided me with a college education and something to interest my children in.

The biggest highlight of my career was making the Pan American Games in 1951. There were so many firsts: my first plane ride; my first trip out of the country abroad; my first team of this nature. I mean, I could just go on with all of the firsts that happened to me at that time. I did not do as well as I would have liked. In fact, I did not do as well as I had been competing. But it was a wonderful experience. I was about nineteen then. Unfortunately, injuries kept me from making the '52 Olympic team because I was one of the top three hurdlers in the world. There's no certainty that I would have made it but the injury took away all opportunity to do so. I never have any regrets.

Of the events that I did I liked hurdles the best. It was very strange how I got into hurdling. Some people will remember the names Teresa Manuel and Lillie Purifoy. They were both hurdlers. After they finished at Tuskegee sometimes they would come back for a couple of years. But Teresa and Lillie were gone and there were never any hurdlers developed. Major looked at me and told me that I was hurdling [laughter]. So here I am getting up at six o'clock in the morning going out and learning how to hurdle and of course, I had my regular practice. With all the reading materials I could get, I learned to hurdle. I learned to hurdle within a season. I probably started in January and that season I was hurdling—just that quick. I hurdled in 1950. It was kind of a natural thing for me because I grew up in the country and we were jumping over things and over streams. It was not a strange thing but I didn't know I would be doing it until he looked around over the group and said, "You're the hurdler" [laughter]. But that was the way our coach was. He was a dynamic person well ahead of his time.

There were many other great times—national championships, All-American teams and we had some great trips especially as a group of about four or five. One of the most memorable trips was from Tuskegee to California. It took us about five days to make the trip out there. We competed and then took five days to make the trip back. Major was always a believer in education. He would take that time off and we would stop in historical places. We would get to see like Carlsbad Caverns, Yellowstone and all that.

When we had the whole college team the boys and the girls would travel on a bus that we called the Blue Goose. It was an old school bus painted blue and we always had to have a mechanic because it never got to where it was going without a break down. It would break down going and break down coming.

There were four of us that traveled all the time and we rotated. One would lie on the floor. We were in the back seat of the car because Major's wife always went with us and the two of them were in the front seat. The three would sit in the seat and then we'd rotate. But we were happy and excited about being able to go places and do things. Every once in a while we might have two cars. You understand about the car situation. That's how we traveled. We were in Chicago, we were in California, a lot of meets were in Texas, we were up in New York, Connecticut, Rhode Island.

In that day and time, of course, track got me to Tuskegee. My parents were not able to provide me with a college education. I went into Tuskegee when I was seventeen years old. That was one of the best things in my life even though my mother and father didn't know exactly what it was about but with the help of the principal they were persuaded to let me go. That is how I got to get into college.

Track and field provided me with so much that we, my late husband and I, exposed our young offspring to it. It wasn't the only thing; they had a lot of opportunities to do other things. In fact, Carl might have been a soccer player because his older brother, Cleveland, who was named for Major Abbott, developed into a soccer player and got a college scholarship for it and then he was drafted and played in a soccer league. He played professional soccer. Right now, my oldest son,

Carl's oldest brother, still has a record that Carl never broke [laughter]. They could not break it because it was yards. Then Carl and Carol came along and Carl might have been a soccer player who followed in his brother's foot steps. But, he felt that the soccer coach did not do him fairly in promotion from the junior team to the senior team. It was the same coach that coached Cleve. Carl was very outstanding. In fact, they were calling him little Cleve. He thought that he should have been moved up. Carl was a leading scorer on the team. There were four of them and they were all outstanding. Three of them moved up and left him there and he was very upset about it. He talked to us about it. He said that he didn't want to play soccer anymore. We agreed with him and that's how track and field began [laughter]. Now Carl was not very good as he was growing up, but he was determined. So he made it. Carol was good and determined and she beat up on Carl as they were growing up. She was always ahead of him. She out–jumped him, she outran him, she did everything. She made junior teams and things like that before he did.

We started the Willingboro Track Club in 1969. We worked until 1985. We started it because of girls. They just did not have anything. They didn't even have a girl's track team at the high school where I taught. We started the track club so we could provide an opportunity for girls. It gave me so much and I wanted the girls to have what I had. I was teaching physical education at the high school. When we started the track club we also started petitioning for girls to get a track team in school. We did not get a team until 1978. It took us a long time to get it. That was Carol's freshman year when we finally got a team. The thing about it is that we went into this league, just this group of girls, there were about nine teams in the league. We were the starting team, the baby team. We came out undefeated that year — and the next year and on and on. We went undefeated for a long time before we lost.

My first four years of teaching was at Alabama State College and then I moved from there to Miles College in Birmingham, Alabama. I taught there for four years and I started the boys' track team and coached at Miles College. They needed another sport so that they could qualify for a league. I left Miles to develop a new physical education program for the new high school that was opening. That school was called Carver High School. It was opening in Birmingham. I developed the physical education program. I stayed there two years and then went back to Miles for a year and then moved to New Jersey. I finished my career in New Jersey. I was in the school for twenty three years for a total of thirty three years.

That was a very good experience. We happened to find this community that was the most progressive community to raise children. They had all types of programs: music, sports, academic programs, everything. It was just a very progressive community to live in. I think that was one of the things that contributed to the upbringing of all of our children. We were able to expose them to so many different facets of life.

I moved to Houston in 1987 and in 1998 I finally gave up and called it home. I sold my house in New Jersey. It took me over ten years to say that. I did not like Houston. The heat was not the problem because I grew up in the heat in Alabama. Somehow I always wanted to go back and I finally gave up. So, Houston is home now and I like it. I learned to like it.

The best part about sports was that not only were Carl and Carol successful but it provided a college education for all four of our children and Cleve was able to play professional soccer. One of the things that was wonderful is that they were supportive of their younger brother and sister. Cleve got his degree in economics from Brandeis and Mack got his degree in political science at Rutgers and finished at Houston. We had no idea what would happen but we just tried to do things that were right. When we started our track club we started it for girls but by the end of the first year boys wanted to become a part and we said ok. The Lord just blessed us. He just blessed us.

INTERVIEW: CAROL LEWIS

(September 15, 2005, and January 25, 2006) How I got started? Well I think the story obviously has been gone over many, many times. Basically, my parents, who went to Tuskegee Institute in Alabama, moved to New Jersey. My mother was a phys ed teacher and my father was also a teacher. At the high school where my mother taught, John F. Kennedy High School, a lot of the people knew my mother was an athlete and as a physical education teacher it was kind of obvious.

From left to right: Carol Lewis, Carl Lewis and Evelyn Lawler-Lewis, 1991.

One spring, they asked my mom to start a track program for women because they really didn't have any sports going on at all for women. They figured, hey, since we've got someone who actually did the sport, it would be great to see if she could come out and organize something for women. So, she started a track program at the high school. It wasn't a real organized team like the boys had. It was just sort of an extracurricular activity.

So, she started the program there and then they started a kind of P.A.L. (Police Athletic League) type of track and field program. At the time, Carl and I were five and seven. You know, back then it was a kind of thing where you take your kids with you and of course, in terms of sports, for them it was a no brainer. Carl and I would go out there everyday and all the kids would be practicing and stuff like that. We'd run along behind them. Whatever they were doing we'd try to do the same thing. So, that's kind of how we got introduced to the sport. At the beginning we did everything.

They moved into holding age-group track and field events in the area and started a team through the P.A.L. for young kids. That's how we started running. We competed with the track club. I did not run on a school team until I was in junior high school in the ninth grade. They didn't have anything. Everything I did as an age-grouper was with the Willingboro Track Club, the club that my parents started in 1969. Basically, we would run track in the summer time. But we started getting better so we started running more year round. We started doing winter track.

We grew up in a community that was really focused on kids. It was focused on raising really healthy children. There were all different types of sports. I was on the diving team when I was a kid; we were on the swimming team. We did not just do track and field as we grew up. We did jazz classes. My mom and her sisters were all physical education teachers. They came from a very physical background. I think all three of them, I know at least two of them, ran track in college at Tuskegee. They had a jazz-type studio for dance. We would do that. Both Carl and I would do everything. It didn't matter that it was jazz — it was one of those things: your parents were doing it, hey, you did it. We have a very well rounded background. I played soccer as a kid. I played softball as a kid. I was on the diving team. I was the best diver in my community when I was ten years old. I was on the swim team and the track team at the same time. We weren't raised "you're going to run track and don't do anything else." We did everything. Carl played some baseball.

Carl played football. Carl played soccer. We both played musical instruments. I played the violin, oboe and French horn. Carl played the cello and we both played the piano.

We lived in a community where there were thirteen parks. What they did was, in every park, there was an elementary school with a big pool and all these recreation facilities. So, they decided that this is a perfect opportunity to have thirteen teams. When you have thirteen teams what would go on is, you would have a season where your team would play all the other teams. At the end of the year you would have play-offs and championships. That would go on all year around depending on the sport. That went on every single year with every single sport that they had. I was on the swimming team for my community and we competed against all the other little areas and towns. In the end they'd have district championships. They never did that in track. There were not enough good coaches in the whole community to do that in track. So, they just had the Willingboro Track Club. But in football, basketball, baseball, swimming, soccer and softball they did that. Every park had their own team. You'd come up and sign up. Everybody competed. Kids did sports. We had a town, maybe at its largest, with about 60,000 people in it and we had four Olympians: Cindy Stinger (who works for the USOC now, team handball), me, Carl and La-Mont Smith — all from a very small community. Everybody did stuff. It was a very encouraging, athletic community. It was very unique. There was no alcohol. It was a dry town. There were no hotels. There were no apartments. It was a planned community to raise a family in. That's what the goal of that community was.

Our parents were college educated. They both graduated from Tuskegee. My mother could have her doctorate degree if she had wanted to write a thesis. My father was well educated. Education was very important to my family. We were raised speaking correctly. This is how we were raised.

That's how we got our start. You almost can't really say that we would have ended up in track. Carl might have ended up playing soccer if it hadn't been for a few unfortunate coaches. He was a great soccer player. My brother Cleve had gone through beforehand. They expected Carl to just go out on the soccer field and as soon as he kicked the ball, be really good. He had some developing to do because he did not grow up only playing soccer like my brother Cleve. Cleve played soccer from day one. He ran a little bit of track but he was always more interested in soccer. So, Carl did not develop at the same pace as Cleve. By the time Carl got to junior high he played a little bit of soccer too, but he liked running more. They expected him to be this great soccer player, and I think he could have been a great soccer player, but they penalized him for things that they thought he should be doing at certain times when he just wasn't at that spot.

We didn't have any junior high school teams in Willingboro. The first time that you could compete on a team was when you were in ninth grade. Our ninth grade was not in the same building as our senior high. I would get in the car and get driven over to the practice at the high school. I competed as a freshman. I was fourteen. My first big crown in high school was winning the Penn Relays long jump in '78 as a freshman. At this point, my parents already had been around the sport so they knew that the big goal at our age was to qualify for junior nationals. That was how you progressed to seniors, which was how you got to the trials. That was the progression that was hammered into your head. I had never jumped nineteen feet before. The qualifying mark for juniors that year, I believe, was nineteen feet. At that point I didn't have the qualifier.

So I went to the Penn Relays that year and jumped nineteen feet one quarter inch and I qualified to go to the junior nationals. Carl also went to junior nationals that year. Michelle Glover went too. I went to juniors that year and I felt, wow, I jumped nineteen feet and a quarter, I'm going to juniors and I'm going to kick butt. I didn't think I was going to kick butt but, I figured you know, I'd be right in there. So, I'll never forget getting to junior nationals, it was in Bloomington, Indiana, and opening up the program. It was one of the first big juniors. I swear there were twenty-four people on the list; I was twenty-three. And I thought I had jumped so far by jumping nineteen feet. I thought I was the cat's meow. Anyway, I get there and there were so many other people: Gwen Loud, Roxanne Keating, Robyn Jackson. There were a lot of really big names on the list and I'm thinking, "Oh my gosh, what am I even doing here?" So my mom said, "It's your first time here and you're only fourteen. I doesn't really matter how you do. Just go out there and do your best." You know, they gave us that story.

And so, I go out there, standing up there, run down and on my first jump — twenty feet five, and I win. The first jump. It's funny because I got out of the pit and I'm walking back. It was the first time too, that I was at a track meet where they had that board up — where you can see what you jumped, because usually in high school, you go back to look at the tape measure or they call it out. They put up on the board "twenty feet five" and I go up to the guy and say, "Excuse me, when are they going to put my jump up? Are they going to put my jump up?" And he goes, "That is your jump." I went to my mom: "That's mine." And she said, "Way to go." That was my big, huge jump into the scene. It was pretty funny though. I remember that because it was so funny.

So I won the juniors that year; the next year I went back and won the Penn Relays again and I won juniors again the next year. The big thing that year was that Carl was in the juniors too. He didn't make it. He was in the finals but he was third in the long jump and they only took the top two. So, of course, by winning the junior long jump I got a chance to go on the team. We called my dad and said, "Oh my gosh, I won. I get to go to Russia. I can go to Russia can't I?" And he said, "Yeah, you can go to Russia, congratulations." My dad didn't go on that trip. He stayed home. I don't remember why. So, anyway, he said, "Let me speak to your mother." He gets on the phone with my mom, talking to my mom, and I get back on the phone and all of a sudden I'm not going to Russia — because my brother didn't make the team. She didn't want me to go by myself, which obviously did not go over very big with me. So, I was very angry with her because she burst my bubble. My dad said I could go. I didn't speak to her for a long time. I was so mad at her.

The next year, I won juniors again. In 1978, I was invited to the first Olympic Festival. I also got invited to a seminar for the best long jumpers in the country. I went to the seminar. Carl didn't get invited, because they probably invited the first two juniors. I told them that since he didn't get invited, that was O.K. and that I would make sure I wrote everything down and I would bring it home and we would practice everything that I was taught.

The next year I competed against the Russians in California and Boston. I did well; I know I won one of them. Galina Chistyakova was there. That was interesting — my first competition against a foreign athlete.

The next year was 1980. I got third at the Olympic Trials. That was kind of a cool situation. Before that I had not done track and field all year round. I was still doing gymnastics and I was diving. I was doing gymnastics in the fall, diving in the winter and track in the spring. I was fifteen. So, my mom came to me and she said, "This is an Olympic year. This is a different year from all the other years that you have been doing sports." She said, "If you are really serious and you want to try to make the Olympic trials, you're going to have to concentrate on the long jump and track. You're not going to be able to do diving and gymnastics and all these other sports at the same time. You're going to have to concentrate one hundred per cent on track and if you do, you need to make a decision, and we need to start working on it right now. You take some time off from the summer before and then we need to start getting to work. You can't think that you're just going to pick it up during the winter, do it a little and then go and make the trials. So," she said, "make your decision and come back and tell me." I made my decision. I said I wanted to give it a try. She said, "Ok, fine." Then we started working out, at night over at the school. We'd do some extra practice on technique. The way we'd practice our technique was, using a beat board that you'd use for the vault in gymnastics, we would run and hit the board and long jump off of that into a pole vault pit so that we could work on perfect technique. We were outside to do our base running. But that's all. How else are you going to train when you live in New Jersey in the wintertime? You're not outside — even in the fall you're not outside. We would do that and that is how we worked on our technique. That's how we got our technique. We did all of our running with the regular kids, but we would always go back over at night by ourselves and work on technique. And you know, some other kids came over, but basically it was for us. Michelle Glover would come over and work on starts. It was just the kids who were trying to go to the trials. It was my mom pretty much. My dad coached at the other school. My dad wasn't a long jumper. He was more a sprinter. So, my mom was the one who really did the technical stuff for the long jump. My dad did mostly starts. My mom did most of the stuff for jumping. We'd go back over there at night and we'd work on technique. What that did was it gave you enough height so that you could actually finish your jump and actually work on your landing by jumping off of that. You'd have enough height and enough time in the air to actually do the whole technique that you were trying to accomplish.

By 1980, Carl was already in the University of Houston. Michelle Glover and I would fly down to Houston for spring break and train with the University of Houston team and Coach Tellez. We'd stay in a hotel for a week. I still hadn't qualified. They had this meet at the University of Houston. That was going to be the big weekend that I was going to try to qualify. It was me, Kim Gallagher and Michelle Glover. Kim was on our team at that time. Her dad was really looking for a team for her that had athletes that were her caliber, so that when she went to juniors or invitational meets, she had someone to go with. Her coach, Mr. Wilson from Ambler, recommended our club because Michelle and I were already doing the same stuff and so was Carl. My mother was traveling with us. It was a perfect situation. So we went down to Houston and that weekend I qualified, Kim qualified and if Michelle hadn't qualified before, Michelle qualified. It was a big weekend. It was a huge meet. Some big company sponsored it. There were a lot of really good athletes there. That was our first opportunity to compete against real seniors. We all qualified for the trials.

The trials came around. We all went and stayed in the dorms, including Carl. It was our first Olympic trials. Our whole goal was to do the best we could and hope to make the finals. From those trials, Carl made the team, I made the team and Kim and Michelle both made the finals. We basically took, in 1980, four teenagers to the trials and we put two on the team. Michelle was in the final and in these days would have been on the team because of the relay. All four of our little high school kids, teenagers, went and two were legitimately on the team and Michelle would have been in the relay pool. So we were just really happy.

"I think I won Penn Relays again for the fourth year. I think in juniors I lost the long jump but won the hurdles. Remember, at juniors we couldn't compete at nineteen like the boys could. We didn't get as many years in juniors as the boys did. I won three junior long jump titles and one hurdle title.

Then it was on to the University of Houston. I guess I always kind of always knew that I was going to the University of Houston because of Coach Tellez. I had worked with him in 1980 a little bit and during spring breaks at school. I did want to go on some college visits, but that was the time when you had to pay for your college visits. I went to California and I went to Florida. I wanted to see what else was out there, but I always truly knew that I wanted to go to U of H.

When I got there it was really not such a big transition for me. I was already doing some of the workouts. The only thing that was different for me was that I never did a lot of weight training. My mom never had us do a lot of weight training in high school. She wasn't that experienced with it, number one, but also we were still growing and the doctor said it's not exactly the wisest thing to do a lot of weight training. So, when I got to the University of Houston, it was the first time I really started weight training. That was different. It was a real transition for me. Since I had already been working with Coach T, I just went there and got started. I think in terms of going to a new place and starting with a new coach, it wasn't that big change for me. I already knew him well.

U of H was fun. I stayed in the dorms the first year. I roomed with some other track and field girls. I remember my first year I went to NC's (National Championships). I was running the relay and the long jump. I remember the outdoor nationals because I did a long jump and ran over to do a relay. When I landed in the pit I felt that I had won the event with the jump. When I looked at it afterwards they were measuring a different jump that was already in the pit. It wasn't my mark. Instead of it being about 21' 11" it was 21' 6". I ended up losing the NC's that year and I was pretty miffed. It was up in Provo, Utah. I was trying to juggle both the long jump and the relay.

Another thing I definitely decided not to do was to room with Michelle. I wanted to meet new people. She had a different roommate. It was fun. I never did a lot of parties in college. I never did that in high school either. I would go to a couple of parties here or there but I wasn't a huge party person.

The first year, we had a great team. Some of the best juniors ended up in Houston including Michelle Glover, Jackie Washington and me. We were all at one school. It was the Southwest Conference and we just killed everybody. We had so much talent in the sprints. I was hurdling, high jumping, and long jumping. We were killing everybody. I might have won indoor NC's. I just haven't totally kept track of everything. One of my indoor NC's, I remember, was in Detroit and they had one of the old cloth tape measures. I told them that they needed to get a metal tape measure. I said, "I truly plan on breaking the American record here and if you don't get a metal tape measure, it won't count." Of course, I broke the American record and I don't think it got ratified because there was no metal tape measure. I was miffed about that because I lost the record and bonus.

Back then we weren't supposed to be making money. I started receiving equipment in, like, 1979. I started receiving money when I was sixteen. So, I was bad. I was just wrong. I was so illegal. I might have even gotten money when I was fifteen. I'm thinking, I'm wrecking my bonus for an American record.

I remember running in an indoor meet in Syracuse. I think we had NC's in Syracuse a couple of times. One year I had qualified for the high jump, long jump and hurdles. Like a fool I tried to do all three of them. I think I made the semis of the hurdles; I didn't do well in the high jump and I might have won or got second in the long jump. But, for me it was too much. I tried to do too much. It was funny; we went to NC's in '84. We had a very talented team at U of H. I had qualified in the high jump, long jump and hurdles again plus the 4 × 1. We were looking at a lot of the other universities and the girls were doubling and tripling to win the championship. Coach Tellez came up to me and said, "You know, forget the championships, we have an Olympics to prepare for." So I only did one event there. I'll never forget that Vince Reel, the editor of the women's track magazine, said how selfish I was because I was only doing one event. Coach Tellez said we had an Olympics to prepare for and that was why I was just doing one event. That's the most important thing.

I did high jump, long jump, hurdles, shot put and javelin at the conference meet in my senior year. I was second in the javelin. A lot of times when I did all of those events, I wanted to. Coach Tellez never asked me to double and triple. Most of the times when I did we had a shot at the championships and we all had said to ourselves, "We are going to go for it."

I high jumped after college in some European meets. I jumped six feet. Not that that's so great. I was ranked fourth in the United States in the hurdles one year and also fourth in the heptathlon one year. The year Jolanda Jones won her first or second NC title, I beat her twice. I went to NC's and I long jumped and she went to NC's and won the heptathlon. But I had beaten her twice that year, with a 2:52 half mile. I did the workouts but could never get better in the half.

In 1991, the year I broke my foot, I was limping around in Randall's Island and I was exhausted one day. There was a seat. I asked the guy if I could sit in the seat. He said, "You can sit in this seat if you let us do an exercise-induced asthma test on you. We are here from the USOC and we are trying to do these tests but no athlete will come over and do them." At that point I would do anything to sit down. My hands were so bruised that I could hardly hold the crutches. Anyway, they said, "You have exercise-induced asthma." I was like, this is perfect. I was doing all the training for the half but when I got to a certain point, all of a sudden I could not breathe. It was because I had exercise-induced asthma. I would have never found that out if I hadn't been gimping around the field that day.

At that point, my foot was pinned and a lot of the doctors that looked at my x-rays thought that I would not be able to walk normally again, let alone compete. I did it on the long jump board in Spain. It was weird. I hit the board and my foot did something funny. I landed in the pit and thought, something's not right. I don't recall it being a strange take-off but for whatever reason my foot just folded in half and broke. Indoors one year, I was jumping in New Jersey, I went down the runway, hit the board and my foot went straight through the board. I stepped straight through the track. But I didn't get hurt. I guess I was lucky because I was behind the board. If I had hit the edge with my toe on the real board and then my heel had gone straight to the ground, I probably would have ripped my Achilles out.

In my sophomore year, 1983, I went to the first World Championships and got a medal. That was the year I truly buckled down and started lifting weights. Also I finally had a base of weight-lifting because before that I had never lifted anything. I think it took a little while for my body to say, OK, this is what weight lifting is all about and to change a little. That was the year that I truly decided that I was going to work 100 per cent at doing this lifting thing.

All of a sudden there was something to train for in track and field besides the Olympic Games. They had had the World Cup, but this was like a true world championship with multiple days. It was an opportunity to go to a big meet and compete over multiple days and see what it was like to compete on a world level. I had gone over to Europe but had not broken 22' 8". A couple of weeks before we were training in Malmo, I had jumped 22' 10½" in a meet in Luxembourg. I think that was the first time I got past 22' 3¾", so, of course, I'm ready for the World Championships. Going in you get *Track & Field News* and they said, "Lewis does compete well internationally but she's not good enough to get better than fifth." I was so happy they said that. *We'll see about that!* I led the qualifying round. I think I jumped 22' 7¾" in the qualifying round. It was a great experience being in Helsinki. My mom was there; my dad was there; a lot of family and friends were there. A lot of people were there from Houston. That was our first meet where Carl and I competed at that level together with my parents there. It was a great meet for the entire family. We ended up with three golds and a bronze. Not bad for a week's work. I remember jumping. Amadeo Francis was the referee on the field for the long jump. I was about the only one who was not European in the final except for an Australian girl. When I did the big jump he walked by and kind of gave me a smile and gave me a high five. I thought it was a good jump. I walked back and looked at the board and wow! That's the first time an American woman had ever jumped over 23 feet. Jodi Anderson jumped 7 meters flat in the Olympic trials in 1980 but that's 22' 11¾". I jumped 23' 1¼" four times in my career. It's weird. How could you long jump, run all the way down the runway, hit the board, land in the pit and have the exact same granules fall away? I jumped 23' 1¼" in Zurich and at a meet in San Jose maybe Olympic year.

What happened Olympic year was they had that mandatory training camp for relays in Santa Barbara. Coach Tellez was going with Carl and I decided to go. I really didn't want to go. We were doing training. The pit was not good and was not dug out. I was long jumping and totally turned my ankle over and almost broke it. In fact, the doctor told me afterwards that it would have been better if I broken it. It heals a lot better. I severely sprained my ankle. Between the trials and the games I did one or two days of long jump run–up training. I couldn't run on it at all. Nothing. I can remember one of the coaches saying, "Oh, a little bad luck." The pit was not even of a caliber that Olympic athletes should be jumping in. By the time I got to the games, Nike had made me these high-top jumping shoes. I had maybe jumped once. I had Dr. Baxter, he's one of the best foot and ankle doctors in the country. He's the one who put my foot back together when I broke it. What I needed was a competition. I needed one competition. I had a crummy Olympic games. After the Olympics I went over to London and jumped 22 feet. So, it was one of those things where I needed one competition to get the kinks out.

I finished my college career in '85. I had a really good year in '85. I jumped the American record twice in the Zurich meet. That was the meet where Jackie upped her PR in the long jump from 22' 4" to 23' 9" in one day. So, all of a sudden I had the American record. In fact, I jumped 7 meters and 4 centimeters again and got fifth place in the long jump in the Zurich meet. It was a good year for me but it was also very frustrating. That was the year when Jackie all of a sudden changed everything. I was third at the Goodwill Games. I was third at the World Cup. Russia and Germany were always ahead of me.

One of the years after that, I was competing in some meets and I was exhausted all the time. I was gaining weight and I couldn't figure out why. So finally, Coach Tellez's wife, who is diabetic and has a really good doctor, sent me to this doctor, Dr. Brown. I found out that I had a hormone imbalance. I'll never forget, I was in Paris and I had finished long jumping. I did my warm-down and I was sitting in the stands. I said to Joe, there is something definitely wrong with me. I'm exhausted. I did my warm-down and I've been sitting here for an hour. My heart was just racing as if I had just been competing. I would start out my long run and I'd get halfway down the runway and I'd be exhausted. In fact, I shortened my run because I was always exhausted. I started taking medicine for hyperprolactemia and also found out that it makes you retain a lot of water.

In '87, I didn't have a good year. That was the year I didn't make the world championship team. In the fall I decided to go out and train a little bit with Pat Connolly just to do something a little different. So, I packed up my car and drove out and I only trained with her until April because obviously Coach Tellez was going to be my jump coach. So, I went out there and did a lot of fun and different things with Pat and then I went back to Houston. I started jumping again and was jumping 22 feet again. That was an interesting Olympic trials. Three people jumped the same jump. Jackie jumped 23 feet; Sheila Echols jumped 22' 7"; then I jumped 22' 7"; then Yvette Bates, from out of nowhere, jumped 22' 7". Sheila had a better second jump. It was very strange. After that Yvette Bates jumped the same thing. Then it came down to the next jump. I came down later and I had one jump left and it was my sixth jump. I can't remember where I was in the order. I was in second place with the 22' 5¾". We keep going. Then Sheila goes into second place with 21' 11". Then we keep going with the 22' 5¾" and then we come down to the second to the last jump and Yvette Bates jumps 22' 7". That moved her into a tie with Sheila in second but third place on the count back. I was in fourth. My last jump I jumped 22' 7". I don't remember if Yvette was before me or after me but I remember running down the runway, I remember jumping, I remember landing in the pit and I remember standing up and just walking out of the pit. I didn't look back because I said, "I either freakin' did it or I didn't and there's absolutely nothing I can do at this point." They measured it and it was 22' 7". I had a 22' 7" and a 22' 5¾" so I was third. How do you get four jumps at 22' 7" in one competition? It was really great for me because I had kind of come back after figuring out that I had this hormone imbalance. It was really a great time for me because I worked really hard to get back in shape and to get back into jumping. I was just really happy to make the team.

I go to the Olympic games. Everything is going really great. One day I'm running and doing training and I tell Coach Tellez, "I don't know what it is but my ankle hurts right here, right above my ankle bone." I go back out the next day and I'm training again and it still hurts. He said, "Why don't we go and have it x-rayed?" I had a stress fracture. The doctor said one of two things can happen: you'll either jump and land in the pit or you'll jump and the ankle will actually explode. I wish I would have never even found out that there was something wrong with it. You don't really want to go down and break the foot any more. So, I did not have a good '88 games. The Olympic games just haven't been good to me. Maybe it was meant to be that way because Carl needed my extra energy for what he did.

In '89–'90 there was a lot of different stuff going on. I gained a lot of weight. I was just a little burned out. You feel that you got there and everything's going well and then wham, second Olympic games and you just get kicked in the teeth after thinking you have everything going really well.

Going into '91, I made my big comeback. I was jumping really well. I went to Spain and competed in Seville. That's when I broke my foot. It's so strange because had I stayed home, maybe I wouldn't have broken it. I jumped 21' 6" when I broke my foot and I ended up getting like fourth in the meet. I had really worked hard to get back in shape; I was fit; I was thin. I was so ready and prepared to compete and then I break my foot and that ruins my world championships. Then, it was my right foot again. First Olympic games, sprained ankle, right foot; second Olympic games, stress fracture, right foot; then I break my right foot. The bad thing was that I could not drive because it was my right foot. I could not go to rehab. We called the USOC and USATF and they set it up so that I could do my rehab at Colorado Springs at the Olympic Training Center. I could sleep there and I could walk down the hill to go to the training. It's great for rehabbing but the worst thing that could happen for anything else. It's so boring there I ate like a pig. Your whole world is in the dining hall. But I did get back in shape and competed outdoors. I did OK. I think I jumped 21' 4". Doctor Baxter, who was my doctor, was the president of the Foot and Ankle Society of America. He took my x-rays to the Foot and Ankle Society and people looking at them said that this person will never even be able to walk normally again. For me, at that point, it was just trying to get back in shape just to get to the trials. I had already qualified for the trials because of the jumps the year before. It was just a matter of me getting in shape to go. I knew when I went that there was not much chance for me to make the team. But, for me, I was just really excited that I made it. I actually made it to the trials and I actually competed. I got tenth and just missed out in competing in the finals at the trials. For me, it was a really huge accomplishment. I've had a lot of ups and downs over my career. It's one of those things I kind of think about sometimes that maybe I needed all those ups and downs so Carl could have smooth sailing.

I trained a little more after that just to stay in shape but had made the transition into television. I was happy doing that. Actually I did my first track and field meet in either 1987 or 1988. I did the Pepsi meet. I did a lot of shows for Turner broadcasting. I wanted to do the '92 Olympics but I only did the long jump for the triple cast. As a result of the triple cast, I was asked to do a couple of events for Entertainment Tonight. In Stuttgart, in '93, I was hired by ABC to be one of the lead analysts. That was really my big break into network television. I did the world championships there and the next ones in Gothenburg in '95. I got the job for '96. It was weird because

I was calling races in the middle of Carl's long jump. I had one eye watching what he was doing and another on my events. From then on I've done all the meets for NBC.

I finished a radio-television degree in '89 and I spent a semester in Paris. I went back to school and finished my journalism degree.

I'm heading to Torino for the winter Olympics. I am an analyst for NBC covering bobsled, skeleton and luge. I will be the first African American woman to cover both the summer and winter Olympics in the capacity of NBC sports analyst.

4

1984: The Los Angeles Olympic Year

The Olympic Games were held in Los Angeles, California from July 28 through August 12.

	Olympic Event	Olympic Place	Olympic Performance	
Anderson, Jodi	Heptathlon	DNF (23)		
Ashford, Evelyn	100m	1	10.97	OR
	4 × 100mr	1	41.65	
Barksdale, Sharrieffa	400mh	DNQ	56.19	
Belle, Roberta	Reserve			
Benoit, Joan	Marathon	1	2:24:52	EOR
Bolden, Jeanette	100m	4	11.25	
	4 × 100mr	1	41.65	
Bremser, Cindy	3000m	4	8:42.78	
Brisco-Hooks, Valerie	200m	1	21.81	OR
	400m	1	48.83	OR
	4 × 400mr	1	3:18.29	OR
Brown, Alice	100m	2	11.13	
	4 × 100mr	1	41.65	
Brown, Judi	400mh	2	55.20	
Brown, Julie	Marathon	36	2:47:33	
Cady, Carol	SP	7	56' 6½"	
Campbell, Robin	800m	DNQ	2:01.21	
Cheeseborough, Chandra	400m	2	49.05	
	4 × 100mr	1	41.65	
	4 × 400mr	1	3:18.29	OR
Cliette, Brenda	Reserve			
Decker, Mary	3000m	DNF	8:44.38	h
Deniz, Leslie	DT	2	212' 9"	
DeSnoo, Laura	DT	10	179' 11"	
Dixon, Diane	4 × 400mr	1	3:22.82	h
Fitzgerald-Brown, Benita	100mh	1	12.84	

67

Gallagher, Kim	800m	2	1:58.63	
Givens, Randy	200m	6	22.36	
Greiner, Cindy	Heptathlon	4	6281	
Griffin, Lorna	DT	12	164' 7"	
	SP	9	55' 9¼"	
Griffith, Florence	200m	2	22.04	
Hansen, Joan	3000m	8	8:51.53	
Howard, Denean	4 × 400mr	1	3:22.82	h
Howard, Sherri	4 × 400mr	1	3:18.29	OR
Huntley, Joni	HJ	3	6' 5½"	
Isphording, Julie	Marathon	DNF		
Joyner, Jackie	Heptathlon	2	6385	
	LJ	5	22' 2½"	
Kane, Missy	1500m	DNQ	4:11.86	
Leatherwood, Lillie	400m	5	50.25	
	4 × 400mr	1	3:18.29	OR
Lewis, Carol	LJ	9	21' 1¼"	
Page, Pamela	100mh	8	13.40	
Pagel, Ramona	SP	11	52' 8¼"	
Richburg, Diana	1500m	DNQ	4:13.35	
Ritter, Louise	HJ	8	6' 3¼"	
Smith, Karin	Javelin	8	203' 7"	
Spencer, Pamela	HJ	11	6' ¾"	
Sulinski, Cathy	JT	10	191' 6"	
Sutfin, Lynda	JT	DNQ	183' 5"	
Thacker, Angela	LJ	4	22' 3"	
Turner, Kim	100mh	3	13.06	
Vereen, Wendy	Reserve			
Washington, Jackie	Reserve			
Williams, Diane	Reserve			
Wright, Angela	400mh	DNQ	59.77	
Wysocki, Ruth	1500m	8	4:08.92	
	800m	6	2:00.34	

Brooks Johnson, Head coach
John Griffin, Assistant coach
Doris Heritage, Assistant coach
Patricia Rico, Manager
Bob Seaman, Assistant manager

"The Games of the XXIIIrd Olympiad of the Modern Era, Los Angeles, California were hype and hoopla, ceremony and celebration, anticipation and achievement. For those who were there as participants or witnesses, the feeling and images of that summer's fortnight will forever tarry in memory," writes Harvey Frommer in his article "Impressions: An Olympic Montage."
He continues:

The Soviet Union did not show and neither did most of its allies. But the People's Republic of China was there for the first time since 1952.... Contestants from 139 nations representing all the continents of the globe were in Los Angeles to partake in the most dazzling, most human Olympics.
Until the 1960 Games, women were apparently thought physically incapable of racing distances as long even as 800 meters in the Olympics, stated Cliff Temple, in his article "Athletics: Great

Leap Forward." Yet the Los Angeles Games will be remembered for opening a whole new dimension in women's running. Each of the three new categories — the 3000 meters, the 400 meter hurdles and the marathon — provided its own historic and dramatic chapter to the history of the Games.

The sight of the diminutive marathoner Joan Benoit running into Olympic immortality will surely help to inspire women the world over to take up running themselves. Benoit, a shy but determined 27-year-old from Maine, was the world record holder for the distance with her 2:22:43 set at Boston in 1983. On paper, this made her two minutes faster than anyone else in the field.

...So Benoit went into the race shouldering enormous pressure from an American public which practically demanded success.... Benoit had just scraped into the USA team, winning the trial marathon in May after having undergone emergency arthroscopic surgery on her knee just 17 days before that race.

...Then there was the fear of the heat and the smog. The 8 A.M. start at the Santa Monica City College was held beneath low gray clouds with even a chill in the air. And as the 50 women lapped the track two and a half times before heading off along their hard route to the Coliseum, conditions were practically perfect.

After only three miles, Benoit, in a white peaked cap to ward off the effects of the sun, was leaving the pack behind.

"I didn't want to take the lead that early, but I promised myself I would run my own race," said Benoit, "and that's exactly what I did." Joan never saw another runner.

In the Coliseum, the spectators could see Benoit's progress on the huge visual scoreboards. And when the little figure entered the arena through the traditional tunnel and ran into the sunlight, it was like a TV character bursting forth from the screen. She won in 2:24:52, some 500 meters ahead of Waitz....

Mary Decker decided to concentrate on just one event, despite also qualifying in the 1500 meters at the USA trials, because she felt that the schedule of heats and finals might be too much for her fragile legs.

...While Puica loomed as the main threat in the Decker camp, the match-up with Budd caught the public's imagination. So when the final found them side by side in the early stages, leading the field, the tension was growing. Just after completing the fourth lap of the seven and a half laps, Budd made a move to get rid of Decker. At the 1750 meter point they collided. The stadium froze. Suddenly Decker was flat on the infield, unable to get up or continue. A chorus of boos broke out, unsettling the inexperienced Budd who faded to finish a disappointing seventh. Puica, the Romanian Decker feared most, won the gold medal in 8:35.96.

What happened to Decker? Examination of the video tape showed that she appeared to catch Budd's heel with her foot about six strides before she fell, causing Budd to almost stumble and Decker to fall over Budd's splayed left leg. After the race, Budd was disqualified. She was reinstated following a British appeal, when the Jury examined tapes from six different angles and declared that Budd had not intentionally impeded Decker. The incident was a tragedy for both women and for the Games, which was robbed of what would have been a classic finale to the race.

The *New York Times* called it an "incredible disaster."

If the host nation had a stranglehold in any area, it was the sprints, as American athletes took the gold and silver medals in the 100 meter, 200 meter and 400 meter as well as both relays. Evelyn Ashford was an outstanding 100 meter champion in 10.97 seconds, an Olympic record, which wiped out the memory of the 1980 Olympic boycott and her own misfortune in the final of the 100 meter race at the 1983 World Championships. In that race, Ashford was overshadowed by her own teammate Valerie Brisco-Hooks, who earned three gold medals.

Brisco-Hooks served as an inspiration to those who feel that motherhood means an end to a track career. After her son was born, in 1982, Valerie had an urge to get back into shape through a return to sprinting. "I know for a fact that motherhood meant I had extra strength, and my recovery from training seemed to be much quicker," she said. Her coach, Bobby Kersee, persuaded her to look towards the 400 meters as her future, although she resisted — even disliked — the event. In June 1984 she became the first American woman to run under 50 seconds in the 400 meters.

...The situation was similar in the 200 meter, where Brisco-Hooks completed a difficult double in another Olympic record of 21.81. She overtook fast-starting teammate Florence Griffith at halfway and opened up a two meter lead by the finish. Along with a third gold medal in the 4 × 400 meter (relay) her 49.23 leg contributed to another Olympic record of 3:18:29.

...In the heptathlon, expanded from the five-event pentathlon of previous Games, it was one of the new events — the 800 meters — that provided the pulsating finish. Jackie Joyner was the pre-event favorite. Even after overcoming a disastrous long jump she still led marginally before the 800. In the long jump, Joyner had fouled her first two efforts and needed to take off way behind the board, losing a lot of distance, in order to ensure some points. Her 6.11 meter (20' ½") effort was well below her best, but kept her in the contest. All of this was despite the effects of a hamstring injury which was heavily bandaged.

In the 800 meters, which traditionally finishes off the competition, Joyner needed to stay within two seconds of the Australian Glynis Nunn and seven seconds of the West German Sabine Everts to secure the gold. Everts won the event in 2:09.05, but the Australian managed to drag herself 2.5 seconds clear of Joyner to earn the 36 points necessary to turn a 31-point deficit into a narrow five point win, 6390 to 6385.

George Vecsey wrote an article entitled "The Women's Olympics," for the *New York Times* on August 4. He writes:

Given free choice and an open ticket to the Olympics, a spectator or journalist could plot an entire two weeks without ever watching men compete. By doing this, the spectator would miss Carl Lewis and the male gymnasts and the decathlon and dozens of other male events, but perhaps for the first time in Olympic history, there are compelling female events every hour of every day.... But tomorrow morning, the Summer Games will belong to one event: the marathon, the female marathon, the first female marathon.

Nobody knows what heroics Grete Waitz of Norway or Joan Benoit of the United States or other runners may perform, but this race is already a crown jewel of these Games because it symbolizes the ultimate acceptance of female athletes as rugged, courageous, independent competitors, just like men.

...The runners will be seasoned competitors, who know each other and the wells of strength within their own bodies. But as Monique Berlioux, executive director of the International Olympic Committee has said of the inclusion of this race, "This is a major victory for the women, but it was not an easy one."

Sports Illustrated, July 18, published an issue entitled "Special Preview — The 1984 Olympics," which featured, in part, top track and field athletes. Kenny Moore's story named Kim Gallagher as a challenger for the 800 meter gold medal. Moore writes:

She's 20 and doesn't look even that because of her huge doe eyes and sparkling braces. She holds American junior records in the 800, 1,500 and 5,000 (2:00.07, 4:16.6 and 16:34.7, respectively). She set the 5,000 mark when she was only 15. For the five years ending last September, she was coached by her brother Bart. She quit running for three months last summer, then moved to Santa Monica and began again with Chuck DeBus of the Puma and Energizer club. This was with Bart's blessing. "And I love him even more since he's not my coach," says Kim.

"If you ran their physiological characteristics through a computer, she and Mary Decker would come out virtually identical," says DeBus. "Same speed. Same aerobic potential. Mary's just six years older." Decker and Gallagher also share a girlish directness that sometimes shades into faintly loony non sequitur. "Training has to be everything," Gallagher said at the U.S. Olympic trials in late June, "...but not too much."

...When Gallagher started running, her idol was Decker. She was eight; Decker, then 14, had just gained notice by beating 1972 Olympic silver medalist Niole Sabaite of the U.S.S.R. in a dual meet at 800 meters.

...Gallagher believes that Decker's U.S. record of 1:57.61 is within reach. "It seems like the only thing I think about all the time is the Olympics," she says. "I think it will take 1:56 to win the gold, and I think I'm capable of that."

More than capable. She possesses the rarest of attributes in a female middle-distance runner, the ability to accelerate late in the race. Traditionally, especially in Western countries, it has been the 800 woman who slowed down the least who won. But Gallagher has a real kick, and it gives her exciting tactical freedom.

Moore's article also discussed the performances of Ruth Wysocki and Mary Decker.

What Wysocki has is momentum. Her victory over Decker in the trials 1,500 was the revelation of the meet. No matter that Decker was running tired — she'd won the 3,000 less than 24 hours before — Wysocki's 4:00.18 was faster than Decker's winning time against the Soviets in the 1983 world championships in Helsinki. So she proved in one race that she can run the 1,500 with anyone in the world.

"She did two years of steady background mileage," says her husband, 10,000-meter runner Tom Wysocki.

"When she added the speed work, she was able to do it without cutting down on distance."

Wysocki became the first American runner to defeat her (Decker) at any distance since Manning in 1980.

As for Decker's race, Moore said, "But once together, the impatient natures of Budd and Decker may create a spectacular race, one that isn't tactical and jostling and infuriating and won with a late sprint by the way the men's races will certainly be. Decker loves to lead. Budd has never done anything else but lead. If each is uncomfortable in the way of the other, each will pass, and be passed and repassed."

"It will be a world-record pace, probably," says Dick Brown, Decker's coach.

The Olympic Results

100 meters. All three Americans were in the final with Evelyn Ashford and Alice Brown taking the 1–2 spots and Jeanette Bolden getting edged by Merlene Ottey for fourth. Evelyn set a new Olympic record with her 10.97 time.

"Alice Brown reacted first to the starter's pistol in the final and held everyone at bay until Ashford caught up with her at 20 meters," reported Hugman and Arnold.

The *New York Times* stated:

Miss Ashford is 27 years old, slim at 5 feet 3 inches and 115 pounds. Had the East Germans not stayed away from these Olympics she surely would have had a battle from Marlies Gohr and Marita Koch.

Without them, she was the favorite, her main threat being hamstring and buttock muscles that have suffered strains and tears. Here her body held up and she broke the Olympic of 11.01 seconds by Annegret Richter of East Germany in a 1976 semifinal.

On the victory stand, Miss Ashford cried from the start of the medal presentation to the end of the national anthem. She also cried last August in Helsinki, Finland during the first world championships of track and field, when a buttock muscle tore during the final and left her writhing in pain on the track.

Here, the tears turned to smiles after the medal ceremony.

"I was so happy it was over, I won and I ran under 11 seconds," she said. "I was stunned at first, I didn't realize what happened. Then he said 'new Olympic record' and it hit me."

Evelyn Ashford at her induction into the National Track and Field Hall of Fame, 1997.

Valerie Brisco at the 1984 Olympic Games. (AAF/LPI 1984.)

Evelyn Ashford is the only woman to break 11 seconds in an Olympic 100 meter final.

1. Evelyn Ashford	10.97	OR
2. Alice Brown	11.13	
4. Jeanette Bolden	11.25	

200 meters. "Florence Griffith certainly can't be accused of loafing in her heat and semi," reported *Women's Track and Field World*. "The long nailed-one sped to wins of 22.56 in her heat, nearly a second in front, then returned with a 22.33 semi ... again close to a second in front. She ripped off 22.04 in the final, her best ever, to chase Valerie Brisco across the line for the silver." Valerie Brisco set a new Olympic record of 21.81. Randy Givens was sixth in 22.36.

The *New York Times* said, "...Two years ago, Mrs. Brisco-Hooks had given birth to a son and was 40 pounds overweight. At her husband's urging, she started running again. Here, the 24-year-old Mrs. Brisco-Hooks won the 200-meter final by 2½ meters from Florence Griffith of Los Angeles."

1. Valerie Brisco-Hooks	21.81	OR
2. Florence Griffith	22.04	
6. Randy Givens	22.36	

400 meters. "Brisco, running with intensity, held off Cheeseborough," setting a new American and Olympic record of 48.83. Cheeseborough was under 50. with 49.05 and Lillie Leatherwood finished fifth in 50.25.

The *New York Times* reported: "The women's 400 meters, as expected, was a battle between the two women who had broken the American record three times between them this year. Both turned to the 400 this season after they had won national titles at 100 and 200 meters. Here, Mrs. Brisco-Hooks ran down Kathy Cook of Britain at the top of the stretch, and Miss Cheeseborough started to close in. But Mrs. Brisco-Hooks did not yield, and she won and set off an emotional binge."

1. Valerie Brisco-Hooks	48.83	OR
2. Chandra Cheeseborough	49.05	
5. Lillie Leatherwood	50.25	

800 meters. "USA lost Robin Campbell in the semis, but Wysocki and Gallagher moved into the final. Gallagher whipped through two fine prelim races, winning her heat in 2:00.48 over Romania's Melinte. Gallagher improved in the final to 1:58.63, but couldn't match the power of Melinte...." Ruth Wysocki finished sixth in 2:00.34.

2. Kim Gallagher	1:58.63
6. Ruth Wysocki	2:00.34

1500 meters. "Americans Missy Kane and Diana Richburg were eliminated in the first round heats, Kane just missing with 4:11.86 and Richburg fading to 4:13.35, far off her Trials time of 4:04.07."

Ruth Wysocki, the lone American in the final, finished eighth in 4:08.92.

8. Ruth Wysocki	4:08.92

3000 meters. Mary Decker fell and did not finish. Both Cindy Bremser and Joan Hansen made the final. Bremser finished fourth and Hansen eighth.

4. Cindy Bremser	8:42.78
8. Joan Hansen	8:51.53

Marathon. Joan Benoit won a stunning victory in this inaugural event in 2:24:52. The *New York Times* on August 6 ran a front page map of the marathon course which listed the times for Joan Benoit and Grete Waitz at nine points during the race.

3.1 miles	(Benoit 18:15; Waitz 18:21)
6.2 miles	(Benoit 35:24; Waitz 35:50)
9.3 miles	(Benoit 51:46; Waitz 52:37)
12.4 miles	(Benoit 1:08:32; Waitz 1:09:57)
15.5 miles	(Benoit 1:25:24; Waitz 1:27:15)
18.6 miles	(Benoit 1:42:23; Waitz 1:44:13)
21.7 miles	(Benoit 1:59:41; Waitz 2:01:12)
24.8 miles	(Benoit 2:17:23; Waitz 2:18:41
Finish	(Benoit 2:24:52; Waitz 2:26:18)

This was the first meeting between Miss Benoit, who set the world record in the 1983 Boston Marathon, and Mrs. Waitz, the five-time New York City

Valerie Brisco, 1999.

Mary Decker Slaney at the 1984 Olympic Games. (AAF/LPI 1984.)

marathon champion and the winner at the world championships last year at Helsinki. When Miss Benoit made her early surge, Mrs. Waitz chose to stay with a large pack rather than match it.

"Nobody came," Miss Benoit said. "And I didn't complain."

"I was afraid of the heat at the end," Mrs. Waitz said. "I was afraid of dying."

Miss Benoit's time was the third fastest by a woman in any marathon, and a record for a woman-only marathon.... Miss Benoit had said that the event would be a thinking person's race, and she certainly gave the field a lot to think about. "At first I hesitated," Miss Benoit said, "because I thought, this is the Olympic marathon, I'll look like a showboat, taking the lead and falling off the pace at the halfway mark and watching all the other people pass me."

She said she had decided two months ago to run her own race. "I was under control, I was very comfortable with the pace. I wasn't forcing the pace. I felt very natural with it."

She ran near the Pacific Ocean, along the Marina Freeway, and eventually uphill towards the Coliseum. Miss Benoit entered alone for a final lap and a victory lap all at once, and waved her white cap to the crowd. As Miss Benoit approached the stadium, she said she tried to avoid look-ing at her image on a mural on a wall adjoining the Coliseum. The mural, showing her breaking the tape at Boston, had been her inspiration earlier this year, when the pain in her knee reduced her from a world-record holding runner to just another walker.

"That was my first thought when my knee started to bother me," she remembered. "What about the wall mural? They put it up for no reason at all. I'm not going to be there."

But she was there, after a remarkable recovery from her arthrospic [sic] knee surgery on April 25. Only 17 days later, she easily finished first in the Olympic marathon trials.

Joan Benoit Samuelson at the 1984 Olympic Games. (AAF/LPI 1984.)

Julie Brown, more than fifteen minutes slower than her trial's qualifying time, was thirty-sixth in 2:47:33 and Julie Isphord-ing, the third American, did not finish.

1. Joan Benoit	2:24:52	EOR
36. Julie Brown	2:47:33	

100 meter hurdles. The 100 meter hurdle race ended in a close finish between the winner, Benita Fitzgerald, running a season best time, and the second place finisher.

Kim Turner, 13.06, was originally awarded fourth and then moved to the third spot. Pam Page finished eighth in 13.40.

1. Benita Fitzgerald	12.84
3. Kim Turner	13.06
8. Pam Page	13.40

400 meter hurdles. Judi Brown fin-ished second in 55.20. Sharrieffa Barksdale made it to the semifinal round with a 56.19 for fifth place in heat 1, while Angela Wright was sixth in the first round clocking 59.77.

2. Judi Brown	55.20

400 meter relay. The United States team of Alice Brown, Jeanette Bolden, Chan-dra Cheeseborough and Evelyn Ashford won by eleven meters with a time of 41.65.

Benita Fitzgerald *(left)* **and Evelyn Ashford** *(right)* **at the 1984 Olympic Games. (AAF/LPI 1984.)**

1600 meter relay. In the heats, Diane Dixon and Denean Howard ran legs, substituting for Valerie Brisco and Chandra Cheeseborough.

The United States won the final by almost three seconds. The team was comprised of Lillie Leatherwood, Sherri Howard, Valerie Brisco and Chandra Cheeseborough. The winning time was 3:18.29.

High jump. According to the *New York Times*: "With a PR going back for many years of 6' 2¾", Joni Huntley surprised everyone as she cleared 6' 3¼" and then hopped over 6' 4¼" along with five others.

"The bar was raised to 6' 5½" and out went Debbie Brill and Australia's Vanessa Brown and Maryse Epee of France.... But the surprise — again — was Huntley who cleared 6' 5½" along with Simeoni and Meyfarth. Simeoni and Meyfarth cleared 6' 6¾" and Joni Huntley won the bronze. Louise Ritter was eighth clearing 6' 3¼" and Pam Spencer tied for eleventh with 6' ¾"."

3. Joni Huntley	6' 5½"
8. Louise Ritter	6' 3¼"
11. Pam Spencer	6' ¾"

Long jump. Again, from the *New York Times*, "America's numero uno, the cheerful Carol Lewis, didn't make it to the final with a 21' 1¼" hop placing her 9th and missing out on the final three attempts. And it was Angela Thacker who eliminated Lewis on the last jump of the prelims. Thacker did it again to Jackie Joyner with her last jump in the final, pushing Joyner down to 5th just a half inch lower and just missing the bronze medal by three-quarters of an inch."

4. Angela Thacker	22' 3"	
5. Jackie Joyner	22' 2½"	

Shot put. Carol Cady finished in seventh place with a put of 56' 6½". Lorna Griffin was right behind in ninth with 55' 9¼" and Ramona Pagel was eleventh with a toss of 52' 8¼".

7. Carol Cady	56' 6½"	
9. Lorna Griffin	55' 9¼"	
11. Ramona Pagel	52' 8¼"	

Discus. Leslie Deniz moved into the first spot with her fifth throw of 212' 9" but ended up in second place after Ria Stalman's (Holland) final throw. Laura DeSnoo was tenth with 179' 11" and Lorna Griffin twelfth with 164' 7". The *New York Times* added, "Miss Stalman is an Arizona State graduate, Miss Deniz an Arizona State junior, and they had trained together."

2. Leslie Deniz	212' 9"	
10. Laura DeSnoo	179' 11"	
12. Lorna Griffin	164' 7"	

Javelin. Karin Smith placed eighth with a toss of 203' 7" and Cathy Sulinski tenth with 191' 6". Lynda Sutfin did not qualify for the final round. Her toss in the preliminary throws in group 1 was 183' 5".

8. Karin Smith	203' 7"	
10. Cathy Sulinski	191' 6"	

Karin Smith at the 1984 Olympic Games. (AAF/LPI 1984.)

Heptathlon. Jackie Joyner lost the event by five points. She was second with 6385 points. The long jump was her downfall. Normally a very strong event for her, she could only manage a 20' ½", taking off way behind the board and on the wrong foot, after fouling twice. Cindy Greiner compiled a personal best of 6281 points and finished fourth. Jodi Anderson dropped out after the third event, the shot put.

2. Jackie Joyner	6385
4. Cindy Greiner	6281

The Olympic Trials

The United States Olympic Track and Field Trials were held in the Los Angeles Coliseum, Los Angeles, California from June 16 through June 24. Twenty-one events were held for men and fourteen for women.

The first women's results reported by the *New York Times* were of the three Olympians from the women's shot put, Lorna Griffin, Carol Cady and Ramona Pagel and an announcement that, "Jane Fred-erick, the American record-holder

Jackie Joyner at the 1984 Olympic Games. (AAF/LPI 1984.)

in the heptathlon, who has high-jumped 6 feet 2¼ inches, started the heptathlon high jump at 5–7¼ and missed her three attempts. The 1972 and 1976 Olympian then dropped out of the competition."

Sunday's crowd of 20,552, reported the *New York Times*, witnessed 22-year-old Jackie Joyner win the heptathlon with 6,520 points, which broke Jane Frederick's 1982 American record of 6,458.

Wrote the *Times*: "Jodi Anderson (6,413) and Cindy Greiner (6,204) finished second and third in the heptathlon, also with personal records, to make the Olympic team. The heptathlon consists of seven events over two days. In today's last three events, Miss Joyner set an American heptathlon long-jump record of 22 feet 4¼ inches and a personal record of 148–11 for the javelin throw. Then she ran the 800 meters in 2 minutes 13.41 seconds."

In other events that day, "Kim Gallagher led the eight qualifiers for the women's 800-meter final in 1:59.28, her fastest ever.... Among the women who advance to the semifinals were Eve-lyn Ashford in the 100 meters (11.24 seconds) and Diane Dixon in the 400 meters (51.52 sec-onds, a career record)."

Reports in the *New York Times* about the other finals on the third day of competition stated, "Evelyn Ashford won the women's 100-meter dash.... Miss Ashford, a strong candidate for three gold medals in the Olympics, caught Alice Brown at the tape and beat her by inches, 11.18 seconds to 11.20. Jeanette Bolden finished third in 11.24 and also made the Olympic team.

Two and a half hours earlier, just before her semifinal, Miss Ashford suffered a cramp in her right hamstring. Before and after the semifinal, in which she finished fourth, the hamstring was iced and treated by a physiotherapist and then covered by elastic tape."

Jon Hendershott, in his book, *Track's Greatest Women*, describes the 100 meter final: "...Ashford's right leg was swathed in elastic bandages and tape from buttock to knee. And over all the wraps, she wore a pair of skin-tight leggings. But the muscle held firm and Ashford overhauled early leader Alice Brown at 70 meters to edge ahead for the victory in 11.18 to Brown's 11.20. 'I was going to run no matter what. I couldn't get to the Olympics any other way,' said Ashford, who threw her hands to her face beyond the finish to hide her tears of relief."

A crowd of 21,081 on Tuesday watched Chandra Cheeseborough win the 400 meters in an American record and twenty-year-old Kim Gallagher win the 800 meters in 1:58.50, the third fastest time by an American.

Litsky reported in the *New York Times*, "The women's 400 has undergone a revolution in this country this year. On May 13, Miss Cheeseborough lowered the American record to 50.52 seconds. On June 9, Valerie Brisco-Hooks reduced the record to 49.83.

Here, Mrs. Brisco-Hooks took a quick lead. Miss Cheeseborough caught her with 60 meters left and beat her by two meters. Mrs. Brisco-Hooks (49.79) and Lillie Leatherwood (50.19) finished second and third and also made the Olympic team."

On June 21, Peter Alfano wrote an excellent feature article in the *New York Times*, entitled "At 31, Francie Larrieu Still Pushes On."

For most of the leisurely run 3,000-meter heat, she stayed on the heals of Mary Decker, which is as close to the top as Francie Larrieu-Smith has been in recent years. Several years ago, before female track athletes were popular enough to be known as American sweethearts — featured in television commercials and seen smiling from larger-than-life billboards — it was Miss Larrieu who was the leader, chasing only her own ambition.

That was in the early and mid–1970's, when many people still did not consider it proper for a woman to sweat. Miss Larrieu was the dominant American in the 1,500 meters, helping to popularize what was then considered the ultimate distance event for women.

She is 31 years old now, and has overcome an athletic midlife crisis and a career-threatening foot injury to contend again for a place on the United States Olympic team. This is her fourth trip to the Olympic trials, which is a long run by anyone's standards.

"For about four years, I was the best by about five seconds," Miss Larrieu said after finishing second to Miss Decker in Tuesday's 3,000-meter heat, thus qualifying for the semifinal on Thursday, when competition resumes after a day off. "Even when Jan Merrill challenged me starting in 1976, I still felt in control. I always had to win the race.

"Then, in 1980, Mary came along and made me feel like a failure. I remember in 1972, when I was young, cocky and the one to beat and now I was a basket case. I didn't know what to do with myself. I decided that I just had to feel comfortable and be happy with doing my best. I guess it was a rationalization."

The fall from No. 1 is never an easy adjustment for an athlete who is accustomed to being held up as a standard of excellence, although Miss Larrieu did not achieve the success in international competition that she enjoyed at home. In the 1972 and 1976 Olympics, she failed to win a medal.

Even if she had won one, it is doubtful whether she could have cashed in financially on her success. Compared to the endorsement contracts and corporate subsidies that have enabled Miss Decker and other stars to open well-endowed trust funds, the under-the-table money available several years ago amounted to pennies, Miss Larrieu said.

"When I think about Mary," she said pausing for the right words, "what I feel most is envy for her talent. When I started and came up, things were different. But she deserves everything that she's gotten. And there's no reason why I still can't be there. Some of the best runners in the world are my age.

"Jan and I had a good go at the Pepsi," Miss Larrieu said, "and now, it seems like we have more of a camaraderie than a rivalry. We're all so far behind Mary that we're encouraging one another. And we're seeing our performances improve." The 3,000 meters will be a first-time Olympic event for women, and the Americans' chances have improved dramatically because of the Soviet Union's withdrawal.

...Miss Larrieu's 4:05.09 clocking in the 1,500 meters is still the third fastest by an American.

A *New York Times* article on June 22 described Evelyn Ashford's lost chance for winning more than two gold medals. "Miss Ashford had been favored to win Olympic gold medals in the 100-meter and 200-meter dashes and the 400-meter relay.... But when the injury (strained hamstring behind the right thigh) acted up this morning in her 200-meter heat, she stopped running after 50 meters. Pat Connolly, her coach, said she thought Miss Ashford would soon be sound and would be ready for Olympic relay workouts.

"Her body can't handle her speed," said Mrs. Connolly. "She runs so fast that she puts too much tension on the hamstring."

Mary Decker captured the first headlines for a woman when she won the 3,000 meters. The headline in the *New York Times* read, "Miss Decker Triumphs at 3,000 Meters." Frank Litsky described her as "the world's most successful distance runner."

> After the first 400-meter lap, she led by 9 meters. After 800 meters, she led by 25 meters. The lead got up to 50 meters as the other 11 finalists concerned themselves with their group and not the obvious winner.
>
> At the finish, Miss Decker had 40 meters over second-place Cindy Bremser (8:41.19). Joan Hansen (8:41.43) gained the third Olympic berth. Miss Bremser and Miss Hansen became the fastest Americans at this distance ever, except for Miss Decker.
>
> "I decided it would be senseless to try for a faster time tonight," said Miss Decker. "Tomorrow is going to be the deciding factor as to whether I'll double or not in the Olympics—how I feel during the race and how I react to running again tomorrow after tonight's race."
>
> The women's 100-meter hurdles had the crowd buzzing when it ended and buzzing even more when replay after replay on the giant scoreboard made it appear to be a four-way dead heat. It almost was.
>
> Pam Page led approaching the finish line. When Miss Hightower apparently stumbled clearing the last hurdle, Kim Turner and Benita Fitzgerald Brown caught her.
>
> The finish photograph showed that Miss Turner had won in 13.12 seconds. Mrs. Brown was second in 13.13, Miss Page third in 13.13, Miss Hightower fourth in 13.13 and Candy Young of Fairleigh Dickinson fifth in 13.26.
>
> Daniel LaMere of Swiss Timing, the chief of the photo-finish panel, said he had judged more than 10,000 races since 1960. This, he said, was the closest.
>
> Mamie Rallins, who coaches Miss Hightower, inspected the official photograph and filed a written protest. Officials reinspected the photograph and stood by their order of finish.

In the women's high jump, "Louise Ritter (6 feet 3½ inches), Pam Spencer (6–2¼) and Joni Huntley (6–2¼) were the only ones to clear 6–2¼ in the final. Miss Ritter, third in last year's world championships, has been hampered all season by injuries. This will be the third Olympic team for Miss Spencer, the second for Miss Ritter and Miss Huntley."

A second headline captured by Mary Decker was at the top of Monday's *New York Times*: "Miss Decker Upset in 1,500." The story proclaimed

> The impossible happened tonight as the nine-day United States Olympic track and field trials ended at the Los Angeles Coliseum. Mary Decker lost.
>
> Unheralded Ruth Wysocki of El Toro, Calif., who made the Olympic team Tuesday in the

800-meter run beat America's most celebrated distance runner by a meter in the woman's 1,500-meter final. By finishing second, Miss Decker also qualified for the United States Olympic team in that event. She previously qualified by winning the 3,000-meter final Saturday night.

The 25-year-old Miss Decker, from Eugene, Oregon, is the world champion and Olympic favorite at 1,500 and 3,000 meters. She last lost on the track in 1980 and on the road in 1981.

For years, Miss Decker had simply run away from other Americans at any distance. But in the 1,500 final, the opposition stayed close.

With a lap to go, Miss Decker led by 2 meters, and her victory seemed assured. But at the top of the final backstretch, Mrs. Wysocki edged by on the outside. Miss Decker quickly drew even, and they ran side by side around the last turn and into the final stretch.

The crowd of 31,482, the largest ever at a United States Olympic trials, was on its feet as the battle went on. Miss Decker again drew clear with 90 meters to go, and again most people assumed the race was over. But Mrs. Wysocki with her long stride, caught up with 60 meters to go, and with every stride she inched away from Miss Decker. With 3 meters left in the race, Mrs. Wysocki threw her arms high in celebration.

...Mrs. Wysocki is 27 years old, 5 feet 9 inches and 130 pounds. She ran previously under her maiden name of Ruth Kleinsasser and then her first married name of Caldwell. After 1978, when she became the national 800-meter champion, she quit running for four years because of knee and marriage problems. She is now married to Tom Wysocki, a nationally ranked distance runner. She had mixed feelings about a comeback, she said, because, "I was afraid to get that fit again so that I would get injured again."

"I thought Mary would blast off with 600 meters to go," she said. "I had no idea I could do this. I thought maybe I could sneak into third. I'm sure Mary won't let it happen again. I think Mary has run alone because too many people have let that happen. The gun goes off and they let her go."

Miss Decker said the loss would force her to rethink her Olympic plans.

"I think I'll have to pick one event or the other," she said, "in order to be my best at the Games. Right now, I don't have any idea which event I will run.

"The loss to Wysocki isn't that bad. In fact, it's good. I'm glad Ruth won. It gives me a chance to see how I react to a loss."

Miss Decker may have been glad Mrs. Wysocki won. But when Mrs. Wysocki attempted to join arms at the awards presentation, Miss Decker declined.

A second story devoted to a woman athlete was in Monday's *New York Times*. Peter Alfano's article was entitled "Kim Gallagher Runs With Goal."

...For others such as Kim Gallagher, a swift little runner from Fort Washington, Pa., the Olympic trials were an opportunity to be discovered in a sport that still suffers from a lack of fan recognition, even in an Olympic year.

She will represent the United States at the Olympics in the 800-meter run, her strongest event. Her attempt to make the Olympic team in the 1,500 failed tonight when she forced the pace against Mary Decker, the favorite, and tired badly in the latter part of the race. Miss Decker, the Greta Garbo of women's track, whom the other women had found as hard to catch as a puff of smoke, proved to be vulnerable tonight as she was overtaken in the last straight by Ruth Wysocki.

"I'd like to be as good as Mary," Miss Gallagher said. "I'd like to replace her as the best American woman runner. Maybe I shouldn't say that, but why not? I enjoy attention," she added. "I've worked hard for it. I'm just starting out, and someone like Mary is already established, so I can use all the publicity I can get. Beating her would open doors for me."

It isn't as if the 20-year-old Miss Gallagher laced on her first pair of running shoes a year or two ago. Actually, she was something of a child star back home in Pennsylvania. When she was 8 years old, she ran the mile in 5 minutes 32 seconds, then a world record for her age group, she said.

"I did it somewhere in Maryland," she said. "My brother, Bart, was there rooting me on, telling me I could do it. I was just running."

She had started running the year before when she followed Bart, who is two years older, to his track club one day. He treated her like most boys would their little sister.

"He told me I couldn't join the club and not to hang around him," Miss Gallagher said. "I remember I was wearing clogs, and all I knew was that I was ready to do track, whatever that was. I had to take off my clogs to run around. I remember I had long hair and looked like a pony," she added. "My idol was Mary Decker. When I won my first trophy and it was as big as me, I knew I wanted someday to make the Olympic team."

Bart Gallagher became his sister's coach and Miss Gallagher became the envy of her classmates. "I was in the second grade, saying, Tomorrow I am going to California," she said. "The kids said, wow."

When she was a student at Upper Dublin High School, she traveled to Europe to show off her running ability. Four years ago, at age 16, she qualified for the final of the 800 at the Olympic trials and encountered her first disappointment in track.

In that race, she started slowly, finished last and broke down in tears. "At the time," she said, "it was the biggest thing in the world to me and I was hurt a lot. I felt that I should not have bombed out by that much. Now it seems like nothing."

When the trials were over, the *New York Times* headline read "U.S. Track Team May Be Best Ever." The women mentioned as possible Olympic medalists in this final article were Evelyn Ashford, Mary Decker, Valerie Brisco-Hooks, Chandra Cheeseborough, Judi Brown, Jackie Joyner, and any one of the three 100 meter hurdlers. It was pointed out that this was the third Olympic team for Pam Spencer, Karin Smith, and Chandra Cheeseborough. The fourteen women's events produced three American records, the 400 meters, 400 meter hurdles and the heptathlon.

100 meters
1. Evelyn Ashford, Puma & Energizer Track Club	11.18	
2. Alice Brown, Tiger World Class Athletic Club	11.20	
3. Jeanette Bolden, Tiger World Class Athletic Club	11.24	
4. Diane Williams, Puma & Energizer Track Club	11.34	
5. Randy Givens, Bud Light Track America	11.35	
6. Jackie Washington, Team adidas	11.56	
7. Angela Thacker, Puma & Energizer Track Club	11.64	
8. Wendy Vereen, unattached	11.87	

200 meters
1. Valerie Brisco-Hooks, Tiger World Class Athletic Club	22.16	MR
(betters trials record of 22.47 by Brisco-Hooks in quarterfinals)		
2. Florence Griffith, Tiger World Class Athletic Club	22.40	
3. Randy Givens, Bud Light Track America	22.59	
4. Brenda Cliette, Bud Light Track America	22.81	
5. Mary Bolden, University of Tennessee	23.15	
6. Diane Dixon, Atoms Track Club	23.32	
7. Dannette Young, Alabama A&M	23.49	
8. Donna Dennis, Puma & Energizer Track Club	23.55	

400 meters
1. Chandra Cheeseborough, Athletics West	49.28	AR
(betters American record of 49.83 by Valerie Brisco-Hooks, 1984; betters trials record by Cheeseborough in semifinals)		
2. Valerie Brisco-Hooks, Tiger World Class Athletic Club	49.79	
3. Lillie Leatherwood, New Balance Track Club	50.19	
4. Sherri Howard, Puma & Energizer Track Club	50.40	
5. Denean Howard, Puma & Energizer Track Club	51.05	
6. Florence Griffith, Tiger World Class Athletic Club	51.11	

7. Diane Dixon, Atoms Track Club	51.26
8. Roberta Belle, Puma & Energizer Track Club	51.26

800 meters

1. Kim Gallagher, Puma & Energizer Track Club	1:58.50
2. Ruth Wysocki, Brooks Running Team	1:59.34
3. Robin Campbell, Puma & Energizer Track Club	1:59.77
4. Diana Richburg, Gazelle International	2:01.18
5. Cynthia Warner, Los Angeles Mercurettes	2:02.16
6. Claudette Groenendaal, University of Oregon	2:02.20
7. Delisa Walton, Team adidas	2:08.27

1500 meters

1. Ruth Wysocki, Brooks Running Team	4:00.18 MR
(betters trials record of 4:04.91 by Mary Decker, 1980)	
2. Mary Decker, Athletics West	4:00.40
3. Diana Richburg, Gazelle International	4:04.07
4. Missy Kane, Team adidas	4:06.47
5. Sue Addison, Athletics West	4:06.47
6. Darlene Beckford, Liberty Athletic Club	4:07.42
7. Louise Romo, University of California, Berkeley	4:09.29
8. Chris Gregorek, Athletics West	4:09.43

3000 meters

1. Mary Decker, Athletics West	8:34.91
2. Cindy Bremser, Wisconsin United Track Club	8:41.19
3. Joan Hansen, Athletics West	8:41.43
4. Cathy Branta, Wisconsin United Track Club	8:49.94
5. Francie Larrieu-Smith, New Balance Track Club	8:50.85
6. PattiSue Plumer, Puma & Energizer Track Club	8:57.02
7. Mary Knisley, Team Kangaroo	8:58.90
8. Cathie Twomey, Athletics West	9:06.71

5000 meters (exhibition)

1. Julie Brown, Team adidas	15:39.50
2. Betty Springs, Athletics West	15:39.72
3. Shelly Steely, University of Florida	15:40.97
4. Monica Joyce, Converse West/Ireland	15:42.03
5. Lisa Martin, Club Nike/Australia	15:43.21
6. Katie Ishmael, Wisconsin United Track Club	15:45.08
7. Carol Urish-McLatchie, Brooks Racing Team	15:45.28
8. Nan Doak, Hawkeye Track Club	15:47.64

10,000 meters (exhibition)

1. Joan Benoit, Athletics West	32:07.41
2. Katie Ishmael, Wisconsin United Track Club	32:37.37
3. Regina Joyce, Brooks Racing Team/Ireland	32:41.78
4. Marty Cooksey, Team Kangaroo	32:52.91
5. Lisa Martin, Club Nike/Australia	32:53.53
6. Margaret Groos, Athletics West	32:55.15
7. Carol Urish-McLatchie, Brooks Racing Team	33:03.16
8. Glenys Quick, New Zealand	33:04.96

10 kilometer walk (exhibition)

1. Esther Lopez, Southern California Road Runners	50:41.18
2. Teresa Vaill, Island Track Club	51:16.67
3. Susan Liers-Westerfield, Island Track Club	53:00.40
4. Susan Anderson, unattached	53:17.03
5. Carol Brown, Island Track Club	54:16.35
6. Debbi Lawrence, Team Kangaroo	54:52.10
7. Lizzie Kemp, unattached	55:22.22
8. Jeanne Bocci, Motor City Striders	56:16.78

100 meter hurdles

1. Kim Turner, Bud Light Track America	13.12
2. Benita Fitzgerald-Brown, Team adidas	13.13
3. Pam Page, Puma & Energizer Track Club	13.13
4. Stephanie Hightower, Bud Light Track America	13.13
5. Candy Young, Puma & Energizer Track Club	13.26
6. Patricia Davis, St. Augustine's College	13.40
7. Linda Weekly, Atoms Track Club	13.54
8. Arnita Epps, Texas Southern University	13.80

400 meter hurdles

1. Judi Brown, Team Nike	54.93	AR
(betters American record of 54.99 by Judi Brown, 1984)		
2. Angela Wright, Bud Light Track America	55.33	
3. Sharrieffa Barksdale, Team adidas	55.58	
4. Lori McCauley, Team adidas	55.60	
5. Leslie Maxie, Millbrae Lions Track Club	55.66	
6. Edna Brown, Atoms Track Club	56.78	
7. Robin Marks, Lay Witnesses for Christ	56.86	
8. Piper Bressant, University of Florida	56.93	

High jump

1. Louise Ritter, Pacific Coast Club	6' 3½"	MR
(betters trials record of 6' 1¾" by Paula Girvin, 1976)		
2. Pam Spencer, Puma & Energizer Track Club	6' 2¼"	
3. Joni Huntley, Pacific Coast Club	6' 2¼"	
4. Katrena Johnson, Puma & Energizer Track Club	6' 1¼"	
5. Mary Moore, Team adidas	6' 1¼"	
6. Phyllis Blunston, Team adidas	6' 1¼"	
7. Lisa Bernhagen, unattached	6'	
8. Shelly Fehrman, Team adidas and	5' 10¾"	
Debra Larsen, Team Nike		

Long jump

1. Carol Lewis, Santa Monica Track Club	22' 7¼"
2. Jackie Joyner, Tiger World Class Athletic Club	21' 10"
3. Angela Thacker, Puma & Energizer Track Club	21' 6¼"
4. Jodi Anderson, Puma & Energizer Track Club	21' 2½"
5. Donna Thomas, unattached	20' 10¾"
6. Kathy McMillan, Coast Athletics	20' 9¼"
7. Wendy Brown, Puma & Energizer Track Club	20' 5¼"
8. Janet Yarbrough, unattached	20' 3¾"

Shot put
1. Lorna Griffin, Athletics West   56' 1¼"
2. Carol Cady, Puma & Energizer Track Club   55' 7¾"
3. Ramona Pagel, San Diego State University   55' 7½"
4. Regina Cavanaugh, Puma & Energizer Track Club   55' 3¾"
5. Natalie Kaaiawahia, Arizona State University   55' 1"
6. Elaine Sobansky, Pennsylvania State University   53' 3½"
7. Sandy Burke, unattached   52' 10¾"
8. Bonnie Dasse, Coast Athletics   51' 6½"

Discus
1. Leslie Deniz, Arizona State University   202' 7" MR
   (betters trials record of 197' 6" by Lorna Griffin, 1980)
2. Laura DeSnoo, San Diego State University   190' 7"
3. Lorna Griffin, Athletics West   188' 2"
4. Carol Cady, Puma & Energizer Track Club   187' 2"
5. Pia Iacovo, University of Alabama   178' 9"
6. Lynn Anderson, University of Chicago Track Club   177' 11"
7. Gale Zaphiropoulos, Weight City Track Club   177' 3"
8. Julie Hansen, Puma & Energizer Track Club   176' 2"

Javelin
1. Karin Smith, Athletics West   200' 9"
2. Linda Sutfin, unattached   190' 7"
3. Cathy Sulinski, Millbrae Lions Track Club   182' 6"
4. Kate Schmidt, Puma & Energizer Track Club   179' 1"
5. Kathy Calo, unattached   178' 9"
6. Patty Kearney, Oregon International Track Club   177' 11"
7. Debbie Williams, Coast Athletics   175' 8"
8. Lori Mercer, University of Florida   167' 9"

Heptathlon
1. Jackie Joyner, Tiger World Class Athletic Club   6520
   (betters American record of 6458 by Jane Frederick, 1982)
2. Jodi Anderson, Puma & Energizer Track Club   6413
3. Cindy Greiner, Team Nike   6204
4. Patsy Walker, Team adidas   6153
5. Joan Russell, Coast Athletics   5841
6. Marlene Harmon, Puma & Energizer Track Club   5818
7. Debbie Larsen, Team Nike   5796
8. Kerry Bell, Coast Athletics   5698

In her book, *Running Tide*, Joan Benoit writes

Everything came tumbling down on April 10. I took a long run in the morning and, always hopeful, recorded in my diary, "No knee pain." At seven that evening I had a track workout at Harvard, where I ran three sub-five minute miles and felt terrific. I stopped to talk to John Babington before doing my cool-down laps, and when I began running again, there was the lock. It got tighter with each lap. The next morning I went out for a ten-mile run with a friend. I got to the subway station on Commonwealth Avenue near Boston College and had to stop; I wanted to gut it out, but something in the knee just wasn't right. I apologized to my friend and told him to go ahead because I'd have to walk from there. Later I called Dr. Leach and said I hated to be a pain in the neck, but I thought he'd better take another look at the pain in my knee. He gave me an appointment for the next day.

Always wanting to test myself, I ran twelve miles Thursday morning before seeing Dr. Leach. My diary entry says it all: "Last 3 + miles were completely miserable. Would have walked if I had had the time but was probably going through the motions of running slower than I would have walked. A real effort to lift my right leg over a twig." And that was no exaggeration — I remember stopping at every curb to step off with my left foot and drag the right down behind it.

Dr. Leach gave me another shot of cortisone. We both knew time was running out: the trials were slated for May 12 and it was now April 12.

After additional medical consultation, Joan decided on arthroscopic surgery. "The procedure had turned up a fibrous mass, called a plica, which had become inflamed and interfered with the joint."

The knee healed but while trying to make up for lost time running, she pulled the left leg hamstring muscle. After intensive daily therapy, she writes, "On May 9, three days before the trials, I gave myself a short speech: 'This is it. You have to go out and run at least fifteen miles. If you can't, there's no way you're going to run in the trials.' I ran two repeat loops that day for a total of sixteen miles. I was so unsure of my footing that I had to concentrate to put one foot in front of the other — it was like working a marionette. My stride was way off; there was nothing fluid in my motion. Running was a huge effort, and I knew if I overdid it I could rip the hamstring. The one consolation — besides making my goal — was my strong cardiovascular condition."

After the third or forth mile of the marathon, Joan and Betty Jo Springs broke away from the pack. At mile fourteen, Joan took the lead.

"In the last six miles I ran slower and slower, showing the disjointedness of my training. There were lots of turns in the course and I had to be especially careful about the way I planted my feet on them to avoid excess torque on the knee and hamstring. Miraculously, my legs held up and I finished first...."

Marathon Trials: Olympia, Washington, May 12

1.	Joan Benoit	2:31:04
2.	Julie Brown	2:31:41
3.	Julie Isphording	2:32:26
4.	Lisa Larsen	2:33:10
5.	Margaret Groos	2:33:38
6.	Janice Ettle	2:33:41

267 women qualified for the trials and 196 finished.

The Outdoor Nationals

San Jose City College in San Jose, CA hosted the championships from June 7 through the 9. The *New York Times* commented about the women's performances in the championships:

The 23-year-old Mrs. Hooks, from Los Angeles, became the first American woman to run 400 meters in less than 50 seconds. She won by 12 meters in 49.83 seconds, breaking Chandra Cheeseborough's four-week-old American record of 50.52 seconds. She also became the ninth fastest woman ever at this distance.

"It took Cheese, a sprinter, to show me 50 seconds could be broken," said Mrs. Hooks.

The 22-year-old Miss Brown, from East Lansing, MI, set an American record of 54.99 seconds for the 400-meter hurdles. She won by 5 feet from Miss Maxie, a high school senior from nearby Millbrae, CA.

Both bettered the year-old American record of 55.69 by Lori McCauley, a 1983 Rutgers graduate.

Miss Gallagher, from Fort Washington, PA, broke no records, but she did put in a full day. Within 52 minutes, she won the 800-meter final in 1 minute 59.87 and the 1,500 meters in 4:08.08. She won each race by 10 meters, in each case her fastest time ever.

---

100 meters
1. Merlene Ottey, unattached/Jamaica   11.12
2. Alice Brown, Tiger World Class Athletic Club   11.14
3. Diane Williams, Puma & Energizer Track Club   11.42
4. Wendy Vereen, unattached   11.54
5. Monica Taylor, unattached   11.77
6. Jennifer Inniss, Pasadena International Sports Club/Guyana   11.79

200 meters
1. Merlene Ottey, unattached/Jamaica   22.20
2. Grace Jackson, Atoms Track Club/Jamaica   22.33
3. Pam Marshall, Coast Athletics   22.67
4. Diane Williams, Puma & Energizer Track Club   23.08
5. Lori Smith, Team adidas   23.14
6. Merry Johnson, Metroplex Striders   23.34

400 meters
1. Valerie Brisco-Hooks, Tiger World Class Athletic Club   49.83   MR, AR
    (betters American record of 50.52 by Chandra Cheeseborough,
    1984, and meet record of 50.87 by Denean Howard, 1982)
2. Lillie Leatherwood, New Balance Track Club   51.45
3. Florence Griffith, Tiger World Class Athletic Club   51.56
4. Diane Dixon, Atoms Track Club   51.95
5. Charmaine Crooks, unattached/Canada   52.51
6. Denean Howard, Puma & Energizer Track Club   52.73

800 meters
1. Kim Gallagher, Puma & Energizer Track Club   1:59.87
2. Ruth Wysocki, Brooks Racing Team   2:01.54
3. Doriane Lambelet, Athletics West   2:05.68
4. Radious Guess, Colorado Flyers   2:05.74
5. Florence Walker, Greater Austin Track Club   2:06.62
6. Revah Knight, Police Athletic League/Jamaica   2:09.89

1500 meters
1. Kim Gallagher, Puma & Energizer Track Club   4:08.08
2. Francie Larrieu-Smith, New Balance Track Club   4:09.74
3. Cindy Bremser, Wisconsin United Track Club   4:09.94
4. Cathy Branta, Wisconsin United Track Club   4:11.72
5. Mary Knisley, Team Kangaroo   4:12.00
6. Deborah Pihl, unattached   4:12.94

3000 meters
1. Jan Merrill, Age Group Athletic Association   9:01.31
2. Shelly Steely, University of Florida   9:07.56
3. Suzanne Girard, Georgetown University   9:17.22
4. Paula Renzi, Pennsylvania State University   9:17.90
5. Margaret Wynne, Yale University   9:23.97
6. Avril McClung, Brigham Young University   9:25.03

5000 meters

1. Katie Ishmael, Wisconsin United Track Club	16:07.5
2. Nan Doak, Hawkeye Track Club	16:08.4
3. Glenys Quick, Metroplex Striders/New Zealand	16:11.5
4. Marty Cooksey, Team Kangaroo	16:14.8
5. Carol Gleason, California Polytechnic, San Luis Obispo	16:43.4
6. Peggy Grundham, University of Minnesota	16:43.8

The 10,000 meter run was held on the first day of the national championships. The *New York Times* reported:

> Bonnie Sons won the women's 10,000-meter run. No one else was close. No one else ran.
>
> The 10,000 is not an Olympic event, though an exhibition 10,000 will be run in the United States Olympic Trials, which start next Friday in Los Angeles. Many of the best 10,000-meter runners are resting for that race. Seventeen women were entered here, and on Wednesday 4 of the 17 were declared starters. Three of the four were scratched before the race.
>
> So the 18-year-old Miss Sons, a sophomore-to-be at Iowa State, ran by herself. Her time of 35 minutes 3.36 seconds was her slowest ever and far off her career best of 32:50.

10,000 meters

1. Bonnie Sons, Iowa State University	35:03.36

10 kilometer walk

1. Debbi Lawrence, Team Kangaroo	51:00.3
2. Esther Lopez, Southern California Road Runners	51:16.1
3. Susan Liers-Westerfield, Island Track Club	53:19.8
4. Chris Anderson, Liberty Athletic Club	53:50.4
5. Elizabeth Kemp, unattached	55:03.7
6. Karen Stoyanowski, West Valley Track Club	55:55.1

100 meter hurdles

1. Stephanie Hightower, Bud Light Track America	12.99
2. Benita Fitzgerald-Brown, Team adidas	13.12
3. Candy Young, Puma & Energizer Track Club	13.14
4. Kim Turner, unattached	13.17
5. Pam Page, Puma & Energizer Track Club	13.33
6. Deby Smith, Coast Athletics	13.56

400 meter hurdles

1. Judi Brown, Nike Track Club	54.99	AR
(betters American record of 55.69 by Lori McCauley, 1983; and meet record of 56.07 by Sharrieffa Barksdale, 1983)		
2. Leslie Maxie, Millbrae Lions TC	55.20	WJR
(betters world junior record of 55.61 by Radostina Shtereva, Bulgaria, 1984; and American junior record of 56.08 by Maxie in semifinals)		
3. Angela Wright Scott, Bud Light Track America	56.24	
4. Colleen Cozzetto, Moscow USA Track Club	57.41	
5. Sandy Farmer, Puma & Energizer Track Club	57.54	
6. Sybil Perry, Team Kangaroo	57.57	

4 × 110 yard relay

1. Hawkeye Track Club	45.04
(Vivien McKenzie, Elaine Jones, Jackie Moore, Davera Taylor)	

2. Atoms Track Club	45.07
3. Puma & Energizer Track Club	46.23

4 × 440 yard relay
1. Puma & Energizer Track Club	3:30.83
(Sherri Howard, Denean Howard, June Griffith, Robin Campbell)	
2. Police Athletic League	3:32.36
3. Puma & Energizer Track Club "B"	3:37.81

4 × 880 yard relay
1. Los Angeles Mercurettes	8:50.15
(Andrea Ward, Laurel Hacche, Trescia Palmer, Cynthia Warner)	
2. Metroplex Striders	8:50.23
3. San Jose Cindergals	9:20.39

880 yard sprint medley relay
1. Atoms Track Club	1:40.69
(Diane Dixon, Helena Nelson, Grace Jackson, Edna Brown)	
2. Musik International	1:46.57

High jump
1. Pam Spencer, Puma & Energizer Track Club	6' 4"
2. Louise Ritter, Pacific Coast Club	6' 2¾"
3. Katrena Johnson, Nike Track Club	6' 1½"
4. Frances Calcutt, Ohio Track Club and Joni Huntley, Pacific Coast Club	6' ½"
6. Lisa Bernhagen, Puma & Energizer Track Club	6' ½"

Long jump
1. Shonel Ferguson, unattached/Bahamas	22' ¼"
2. Jodi Anderson, Puma & EnergizerTrack Club	21' 6¼"
3. Jackie Joyner, Tiger World Class Athletic Club	21' 4¾"
4. Sabrina Douglas, St. Augustine's College	21' 1¼"
5. Meledy Smith, Puma & Energizer Track Club	21'
6. Sabrina Williams, Coast Athletics	20' 9¼"

Shot put
1. Ria Stalman, Team adidas/Holland	59' 1½"
2. Lorna Griffin, Athletics West	58' 3¼"
3. Regina Cavanaugh, Puma & Energizer Track Club	55' 1"
4. Elaine Sobansky, Pennsylvania State University	53' 1¾"
5. Peggy Pollock, Coast Athletics	52' 6"
6. Sandy Burke, unattached	52' ½"

Discus
1. Ria Stalman, Team adidas/Holland	221' 9" MR
(betters meet record of 206' 3" by Leslie Deniz, 1983)	
2. Carol Cady, unattached	206' 3"
3. Kathy Picknell, Bud Light Track America	194' 3"
4. Julie Hansen, Puma & Energizer Track Club	182' 6"
5. Lynne Anderson, University of Chicago Track Club	177' 5"
6. Francine Kaylor, Maccabi Track Club	176'

Javelin

1. Karin Smith, Athletics West	198' 11"
2. Lynda Sutfin, unattached	191' 11"
3. Kate Schmidt, Puma & Energizer Track Club	186' 6"
4. Susie Ray, Tiger World Class Athletic Club	184' 4"
5. Debbie Williams, Coast Athletics	177' 3"
6. Kathy Calo, unattached	177' 2"

Team scores:

1. Puma & Energizer Track Club	100
2. Tiger World Class Athletic Club	34
3. Team adidas	30

U.S. Heptathlon Championships: UCLA Drake Stadium, Los Angeles, California, May 19–20

1. Cindy Greiner, Athletics West	6154
2. Jodi Anderson, Puma and Energizer Track Club	5992
3. Debra Larsen, unattached	5856
4. Jill Ross, Canada	5728
5. Connie Polman-Tuin, Canada	5728

The Indoor Nationals

The indoor nationals were held in Madison Square Garden on February 27. The day of the indoor nationals a lengthy article entitled, "Carol Lewis, Herself," appeared in the *New York Times*.

When Carol Lewis was younger, she papered every inch of her bedroom with photographs of her favorite performers, always reserving the place of honor for Mikhail Baryshnikov.

The dancer is still on her wall, on her bookshelves, in her videotape collection, and in her heart, but there are no other celebrity photographs on the wall of America's best female long jumper. She recently woke up in the middle of the night and ripped all the other photos down.

It was a turning point in the thriving life of Carol Lewis. Instead of being surrounded by pictures of her favorite performers, she has decorated her room with banners culled and cajoled from the major sports networks. The lady didn't switch her major from computer sciences to broadcast journalism for nothing. Miss Lewis is in town for today's USA/Mobil Indoor track and field meet at Madison Square Garden. Because of a crowded meet program, her event will be held at 11:30 A.M. in the Garden, nearly eight hours before the evening session begins.

After trying to advance her American indoor long-jump record of 22 feet 2¼ inches, set on Feb. 4 in Dallas, Miss Lewis no doubt will be on hand this evening in case her older brother, Carl, needs a bit of ballast in his long jump. At the Wanamaker Millrose Games last month, Miss Lewis anchored down the wobbly far end of the runway, enabling Carl to set a world indoor record of 28 feet 10¼ inches.

Carol Lewis does not lack confidence. Since setting a goal of being a sports commentator in the very near future, she has arranged a University of Houston workshop semester in New York next fall, working for a network.

She knows she must prepare for a career beyond sports. Her parents, Bill Lewis and Evelyn Lawler Lewis, both fine athletes who are now track coaches in Willingboro, N.J., have instilled their work ethic in their youngest child.

With all her accomplishments and an apparently secure ego, Miss Lewis has only slight reservations about being occasionally described as Carl Lewis's younger sister.

...She sees Carl Lewis not as a celebrity but as an older brother who is "sometimes a little bit late when he says he'll be somewhere" and who dares her to run three 200-yard sprints in a row with him. She is not in awe of Carl Lewis as she is for Baryshnikov.

The day after the meet, the *New York Times* reported, "In the afternoon, Carl was one of only a few hundred spectators when Carol, his 20-year-old sister, defended her title successfully by extending her meet record to 21–8 on her sixth and last jump. Carol had already clinched the victory on a 21–6½ third jump, breaking the meet record of 21–5¼ she set last year."

In the hurdles, "Stephanie Hightower, who for the second straight year won the women's overall Grand Prix, captured the 60-yard hurdles in 7.43 seconds, only seven hundredths of a second off her world indoor record."

---

60 yard dash
1. Alice Brown, World Class Athletic Club   6.62
2. Chandra Cheeseborough, Athletics West   6.71
3. Sandra Howard, Puma & Energizer Track Club   6.76

220 yard dash
1. Valerie Brisco-Hooks, World Class Athletic Club   23.97
2. Alice Jackson, unattached   24.03
3. Wendy Vereen, New Jersey High School   24.14

440 yard dash
1. Diane Dixon, Atoms Track Club   53.82
2. Gwen Gardner, Los Angeles Mercurettes   54.15
3. Edna Brown, Atoms Track Club   54.18

880 yard run
1. Luybov Gurina, USSR   2:05.34
2. Robin Campbell, Puma & Energizer Track Club   2:05.61
3. Diana Richburg, Gazelle International Track Club   2:06.51

Mile run
1. Brit McRoberts, Canada   4:33.91
2. Jan Merrill, Age Group Athletic Association   4:35.16
3. Cindy Bremser, Wisconsin United Track Club   4:37.70

Two mile run
1. Kathy Branta, University of Wisconsin, Madison   9:49.39
2. Brenda Webb, Athletics West   10:03.39
3. Katie Ishmael, University of Wisconsin, Madison   10:09.18

60 yard hurdles
1. Stephanie Hightower, Bud Light Track Club   7.43
2. Deby LaPlante-Smith, Coast Athletics   7.52
3. Candy Young, Fairleigh Dickenson University   7:58

Mile walk
1. Teresa Vaill, Island Track Club   7:12.85
2. Maryanne Torrellas, Abraxas Track Club   7:26.37
3. Susan Liers-Westerfield, Island Track Club   7:29.32

4 × 160 yard relay
1. Tennessee State University   1:09.87
    (Angela Williams, Wanda Fort, Jackie Van Zant, Barbara Frazier)

2. Morgan State	1:10.97
3. Dynamite Track Club	1:11.74

4 × 440 yard relay

1. Atoms Track Club	3:38.15
(Tanya McIntosh, Edna Brown, Grace Jackson, Diane Dixon)	
2. Police Athletic League	3:41.78
3. Michigan State	3:48.64

Sprint medley relay (220, 110, 110, 440)

1. Tennessee State University	1:44.12
(Maxine McMillan, Wanda Fort, Barbara Frazier, Angela Williams)	
2. Ms. International	1:47.66
3. Police Athletic League	1:48.98

High jump

1. Tamara Bykova, USSR	6' 6¾"
2. Joni Huntley, Pacific Coast Club	6' 2¼"
3. Debbie Brill, Canada	6' 1¼"

Long jump

1. Carol Lewis, University of Houston	21' 8"
2. Jennifer Inniss, California State University, Los Angeles/Guyana	21' 5¼"
3. Irina Proskuryakova, USSR	21' 4"

Shot put

1. Meg Ritchie, Team adidas/Great Britain	58' 6¾"
2. Regina Cavanaugh, Rice University	55' 2¾"
3. Denise Wood, Team adidas	54' 7¼"

Team scores:

1. Atoms Track Club	12
2. World Class Athletic Club	10½
3. Tennessee State University	10

Sunkist Invitational (6 women's events): Los Angeles, January 20

60 yard dash	
Alice Brown	6.81
500 yard run	
Gwen Gardner	1:04.33
800 meter run	
Jarmila Kratochvilova, Czechoslovakia	2:02.85
Mile run	
Monica Joyce, Ireland	4:42.57
60 yard hurdles	
Deby Smith	7.54
Long jump	
Kathy McMillan	21' 2¾"

Vitalis/U.S. Olympic Invitational: Meadowlands Arena, Rutherford, New Jersey, February 11

55 meter hurdles
1. Stephanie Hightower, Nutri-Onix Track Club   7.46
2. Candy Young, Fairleigh Dickinson University   7.56
3. Benita Fitzgerald, Team adidas   7.72

Wilma Rudolph 55 meter dash
1. Chandra Cheeseborough, Athletics West   6.69
2. Alice Brown, World Class Athletic Club   6.72
3. Michele Glover, University of Houston   6.88

Betty Robinson 400 meters
1. Diane Dixon, Atoms Track Club   54.34
2. June Griffith, Puma and Energizer Track Club   54.46
3. Grace Jackson, Atoms Track Club   55.11

Madeline Manning 800 meters
1. Robin Campbell, Puma and Energizer Track Club   2:03.36
2. Diana Richburg, Gazelle International Track Club   2:03.64
3. Cynthia Warner, Los Angeles Mercurettes   2:06.53

Bufferin 3000 meters
1. Suzanne Girard, Georgetown University   9:06.86
2. Joan Benoit, Athletics West   9:06.99
3. PattiSue Plumer, Stanford University   9:07.20

Ford — Meadowlands 1500 meters
1. Brit McRoberts, Canada   4:39.27
2. Cindy Bremser, Wisconsin United Track Club   4:39.35
3. Sue Addison, Athletics West   4:39.72

Long jump
1. Carol Lewis, University of Houston   20' 10¾"
2. Jackie Joyner, World Class Athletic Club   20' 8"
3. Clair Conner, unattached   19' 11¾"

4 × 400 meter relay
1. Atoms Track Club   3:39.6
(Tanya McIntosh, Edna Brown, Grace Jackson, Diane Dixon)
2. Police Athletic League   3:40.89
3. Ms. International   3:42.75

The Vitalis Award of Excellence was presented to Stephanie Hightower, the outstanding meet performer.

Women's Track & Field World reported: "'The European Circuit' was not a happy place for Olympic champions. Only the USA's 100m champ Evelyn Ashford really was successful. Ashford ran four races, won four races and set a world record when she defeated East Germany's Marlies Gohr."

West Berlin, Germany: August 17

100 meters

Again, from *Women's Track & Field World*, "Evelyn Ashford led a 1-2-3-4 U.S. sweep of the 100 meters with a swift 10.94 after winning her heat in 10.92. Ashford was followed across the line by Griffith, Williams and Cheeseborough with Merlene Ottey 5th and Grace Jackson 6th."

1. Evelyn Ashford	10.94
2. Florence Griffith	10.99
3. Diane Williams	11.10
4. Chandra Cheeseborough	11.13

400 meters
2. Diane Dixon	52.23

1500 meters
2. Sue Addison	4:13.18
3. Joan Hansen	4:13.32
4. Cathie Twomey	4:17.60

100 meter hurdles
1. Benita Fitzgerald	13.11
3. Kim Turner	13.33
4. Candy Young	13.33

400 meter hurdles
2. Sharrieffa Barksdale	56.69
5. Angela Wright	57.94

Shot put
4. Carol Cady	55' ¼"

London, England: August 18

300 meters
2. Chandra Cheeseborough	35.49

100 meter hurdles
2. Kim Turner	13.31

Long jump
1. Carol Lewis	22' 1"

Zurich, Switzerland: August 22

"This is the 'biggie' of the European circuit and nearly everyone was on hand. In the feature event of the meet, Ashford whipped Marlies Gohr in world record time of 10.76 with Gohr clocking a not-so-bad time of 10.84 in her losing effort."

The *New York Times* continued, "Miss Ashford, who evened the record with her archrival at six victories each, cut 3-hundredths of a second off her mark set at Colorado Springs on July 3, 1983.

"Mrs. Gohr was faster out of the starting blocks but was passed by Miss Ashford after 40 meters."

100 meters		
1. Evelyn Ashford	10.76	WR
3. Diane Williams	11.04	

200 meters
4. Valerie Brisco-Hooks	22.26
5. Chandra Cheeseborough	22.47
6. Florence Griffith	22.68

200 meters (B race)
3. Randy Givens	22.90

800 meters
5. Kim Gallagher	2:00.23

3000 meters
4. Joan Hansen	8:49.43

100 meter hurdles
3. Stephanie Hightower	12.91
5. Benita Fitzgerald	12.98
8. Kim Turner	13.48

100 meter hurdles (B race)
2. Candy Young	13.35

High jump
5. Pam Spencer	6' 2"
6. Joni Huntley	6'

Cologne, West Germany: August 26

100 meters
1. Florence Griffith	11.26
2. Diane Williams	11.27

200 meters
1. Evelyn Ashford	22.76
3. Randy Givens	23.35

400 meters
2. Valerie Brisco	49.83
5. Diane Dixon	51.37

1500 meters
1. Ruth Wysocki	4:03.74

100 meter hurdles
2. Benita Fitzgerald	13.02
4. Kim Turner	13.20

400 meter hurdles
1. Sharrieffa Barksdale	56.31
3. Angela Wright	56.57

High jump
4. Pam Spencer   6'   ¾"

Long jump
2. Carol Lewis   20' 11¾"

Koblenz, West Germany: August 29

Women's Track & Field World reported: "Valerie Brisco ran her best-ever 100, winning in 11.08 over Williams, Kathy Cook, Alice Brown, Florence Griffith and Randy Givens."

100 meters
1. Valerie Brisco   11.08
2. Diane Williams   11.18
4. Alice Brown   11.25
5. Florence Griffith   11.31
6. Randy Givens   11.85

800 meters
3. Kim Gallagher   2:01.78
6. Sue Addison   2:02.46

3000 meters
3. Joan Hansen   8:56.93

Long jump
3. Carol Lewis   21' 5½"

Rome, Italy: August 31

100 meters
1. Evelyn Ashford   10.93
3. Valerie Brisco   11.14
4. Diane Williams   11.22

200 meters
1. Valerie Brisco   22.82
3. Randy Givens   23.18
4. Diane Dixon   23.67

800 meters
9. Kim Gallagher   2:02.04

100 meter hurdles
5. Kim Turner   13.12
7. Candy Young   13.23
8. Pam Page   13.45

400 meter hurdles
6. Angela Wright   58.97

High jump
8. Pam Spencer   6' ¾"

Paris, France: September 4

400 meters	
5. Diane Dixon	52.19
800 meters	
2. Ruth Wysocki	1:58.65
3. Kim Gallagher	2:01.70
4. Sue Addison	2:02.33
5000 meter run	
3. Joan Hansen	15:39.08
100 meter hurdles	
6. Pam Page	13.53
High jump	
8. Pam Spencer and Cindy Greiner	5' 10¾"
Shot put	
3. Carol Cady	52' 4¼"

London, England: September 8

"The big news of the meet," reported *Women's Track & Field World,* "was the win by Ruth Wysocki in the mile with a time of 4:21.78, second-best-ever by an American."

100 meters	
1. Valerie Brisco	11.25
2. Jeanette Bolden	11.33
200 meters	
2. Valerie Brisco	22.97
3. Randy Givens	23.17
Mile run	
1. Ruth Wysocki	4:21.78
100 meter hurdles	
3. Pam Page	13.73
100 meter hurdles "B" race	
3. Patsy Walker	13.73

8 Nation Meet: Tokyo, Japan, September 14

100 meters	
3. Jeanette Bolden	11.35
200 meters	
5. Zelda Johnson	24.52
800 meters	
6. Rose Monday	2:04.62

100 meter hurdles	
4. Kim Turner	13.30

4 × 100 meter relay	
4. USA	45.44

Long jump	
5. Gwen Loud	19' 11¾"

Javelin throw	
2. Karin Smith	212' 2"

Talence, France: September 15, 16

Vince Reel reports in *Women's Track & Field World*: "After failing to make the Olympic team due to a no-height in the high jump, Jane Frederick traveled to the climes of Europe and shortly after the Games promptly proceeded to set a new American record in the heptathlon at 6611—91 points better than Jackie Joyner's record.

Now she has done it again adding another 103 points as she won at Talence with 6714, a mark which puts her Number 5 on the All Time World List."

Final Grand Prix Standings

Overall Point Standings and Money Winnings

1. Stephanie Hightower, 90	$10,000.
2. Alice Brown, 57	$ 8,000.
3. Deby Smith, 55	$ 6,000.
4. Robin Campbell, 50	$ 4,000.
5. Gwen Gardner, 47	$ 2,000.

Other News and Honors

Track & Field News: Athlete of the Year

Evelyn Ashford

USA Rankings — *Track & Field News*

1. Evelyn Ashford
2. Joan Benoit
3. Valerie Brisco-Hooks
4. Chandra Cheeseborough
5. Jane Frederick

World Rankings — *Track & Field News*

1. Evelyn Ashford
5. Joan Benoit

A summary of the record accomplishments in women's track and field in 1984 can be found in the February 9, *Vitalis/U.S. Olympic Invitational Program.*

As expected, the Olympic year of 1984 turned out to be a banner one as far as new achievement in track and field was concerned.

...The renowned Carl Lewis has everyone holding his breath these days every time he jumps, but it was his sister, Carol, who kept setting new standards. Carol raised the American long jump record on three occasions, finally reaching the 22-foot mark in Dallas, Feb.4.

...Olympic sensation Valerie Brisco-Hooks, who won three Olympic gold medals, set American records in the 200 and 400 meters and contributed to an American record in the 1,600-meter relay.

Evelyn Ashford's Olympic gold medal was a climactic and gratifying experience after injury had threatened her from achieving the dream of a lifetime. But it was her world-record victory over Marlies Gohr in Zurich near the end of the season that was her crowning glory. Her 100-meter time of 10.76 seconds earned her accolades as Woman Athlete of the Year.

On August 3, in Eugene, Oregon, Mary Decker set a new world record for 2000 meters, reported *Women's Track & Field World.* Her time of 5:32.7 broke the time of 5:33.15 set by Zola Budd earlier in the year.

Alice Brown set an American record of 7.18 in the 60 meters on March 10 in Tokyo.

Cathy Branta won the national cross country title.

Prior to the start of the Olympic Games in July, the *New York Times* reported that the International Olympic Committee acted "to add the women's 10,000-meter run for the 1988 Olympics in Seoul, South Korea. This year for the first time, a women's 3,000-meter run and a women's marathon will be contested in the Olympics. A group of female distance runners sued to add the 5,000-meter and 10,000-meter runs as well for this Olympics, but the group lost in court. The men's program includes a 5,000, 10,000 and marathon, but not a 3,000."

Kim Gallagher died on November 18, 2002 at the age of 38.

Madeline Manning-Mims was inducted into the National Track and Field Hall of Fame. The following is from the National Track and Field Hall of Fame website.

Born January 11, 1948, Cleveland, Ohio

The first female middle distance star of world-class caliber, Madeline Manning-Mims was the 1968 Olympic 800-meter champion at Mexico City while attending Tennessee State University.

From 1967 to 1980, she won 10 national indoor and outdoor titles and set numerous American records as well. She also was a member of the 1972 and 1976 Olympic teams and in 1980, at the age of 32, won the U.S. Olympic Trials. Only the boycott of the Olympic Games that year kept her out of her fourth Olympiad. Coming out of retirement three times during her career, she also won a silver medal at the 1972 Olympic Games as a member

Doris Brown Heritage (left) and Madeline Manning, 1999.

of the 4 × 400-meter relay team. She was the 1975 Pan-American champion and in 1966 won the 400 at the World University Games.

Jackie Joyner (center) and Cindy Greiner (right) at the 1984 Olympic Games. (AAF/LPI 1984.)

American Records (as of January 1985)
(World records in bold)

100	**10.76**	**Evelyn Ashford**	**8/22/84**
200	21.81	Valerie Brisco-Hooks	8/9/84
400	48.83	Valerie Brisco-Hooks	8/6/84
800	1:57.9	Madeline Manning	8/78/76
	1:57.60p	Mary Decker	7/31/83
1500	3:57.12	Mary Decker	7/26/83
Mile	4:18.08	Mary Decker	7/9/82
2000	5:32.7	Mary Decker	8/3/84
3000	8:29.71	Mary Decker	7/7/82
5000	15:08.26	Mary Decker	6/5/82
10000	31:35.3	Mary Decker	7/16/82
100h	12.79	Stephanie Hightower	7/10/82
400h	54.93	Judi Brown	6/21/84
4 × 100mr	41.61	National Team	7/3/83
4 × 200mr	1:32.6	National Team	6/24/79
4 × 400mr	3:18.29	Olympic Team	8/11/84
4 × 800mr	8:19.9	National Team	6/24/79
	8:17.09p	Athletics West	4/24/83
Sprint medley r	1:36.79	Wilt's Athletic Club	6/20/82
Distance medley r	10:53.27	Villanova University	4/26/84
HJ	6' 6"	Coleen Sommer	6/26/82
	6' 7"p	Louise Ritter	9/1/83

LJ	22' 11¾"	Jodi Anderson	6/28/80
SP	62' 7¾"	Maren Seidler	6/16/79
DT	213' 11"	Leslie Deniz	4/7/84
JT	227' 5"	Kate Schmidt	9/10/77
Hepthalon	6714	Jane Frederick	9/15,16/84
Marathon/lp	**2:26:11**	**Joan Benoit**	9/12/82
Marathon/ptp	**2:22:43**	**Joan Benoit**	4/18/83

INTERVIEW: SHARRIEFFA BARKSDALE

(December 5, 2002) I started track as a freshman in high school. I started to run track because my brother ran track and I wanted to follow him and go to all the track meets but not knowing the talent that I had.

As a Hammond High School athlete we didn't have a track. I ran on grass. I mainly coached myself. Then I met a man named Ralph Boston who began to be my mentor. I enrolled in Hammond High School and I made it to States. I continued to make it to States each year. My last year at States I won all by myself—a one woman team. I won the 100, the 200, the long jump, the high jump and the 110 hurdles.

After high school I got a scholarship to the University of Tennessee. Terry Crawford coached me. When I got to the University of Tennessee, I knew I had a long road ahead of me because there was Benita Fitzgerald, there was Joetta Clark, and Delisa Walton Floyd — that type of caliber athlete. I knew my work was cut out for me.

When Terry brought me in, she brought me in on a partial scholarship. As time went on, Terry would tell me I was doing well and I could get a full scholarship. I eventually earned a full scholarship. Then Terry saw that I wasn't real good in the 100 meter hurdles and said, "Sharrieffa since you've been running some quarters, let's see you try the 400 meter hurdles." So, she put me in the 400 meter hurdles. My first 400 meter hurdle race was at Stanford University and I won. A man came over to me and he said, "How long have you been running these hurdles?" I said that this was my first time. It was Brooks Johnson. Brooks Johnson said, "If you stay with this one day you'll be on the Olympic team."

As time went on I became a four time All-American at the University of Tennessee. I was a 1984 Olympian. I was the first woman to go under 57 in the 400 meter hurdles. Then I became the American record holder. I made every team: the Pan American games, World University Games, World Championships, Sports Festivals and the list goes on and on.

I moved to Texas with Terry in 1984 — I followed her down to Texas. In 1985 I became the women's track coach at Florida A&M. I stayed there for about a year. I gave it up because the kids' mentality wasn't there. They didn't want it. They thought they could come to practice when they wanted. So I decided that this wasn't for me. I gave that up.

In 1986, I made a lot of teams. When we were at Eugene I was running to qualify for the Goodwill Games. I was fifteen meters ahead of the field and the only thing I could remember was that I heard the crowd say she's going on a world record pace. I hit the fifth hurdle and went down. I could not believe that I was on that pace and fell down and ended up getting up and coming in fifth place. I caught some of the girls at the line.

The biggest highlight of my career was when I made the 1984 Olympics. When I was training, a lot of the men athletes at the University of Tennessee were laughing because I would be out there at night training. They'd say, you're training but you're not going to make the team. I like people to tell me that I can't do something because I like to prove them wrong. I remember six months before the Olympic trials I had sprained my hamstring. Terry Crawford got me the best sports doctor who got me everything I needed to heal my hamstring so I could get out there and compete. I'll never forget coming down the chute, and all of a sudden I got sick and just threw up and I broke out into hives. I said, "Lord, you just did not bring me this far to leave me now." So, I got on the line and I ran. The only thing that I know is when we came across the finish line, it was Judi Brown-King, Angela Wright, Lori McCauley and me. It was almost a photo finish between Lori McCauley and me. I kept looking up there at the screen and kept looking at it and they kept replaying it but you couldn't tell who won. And I'm like, "Dear Lord, you gotta know —

please let me make it." Then all of a sudden they put the three names up there — Judi Brown-King, Angela Wright and Sharrieffa Barksdale. Oh, I can feel the tears and the emotion and excitement now because it was like, "Oh my God, I made it, I made it." I'll never forget when I got back to my hotel room. I had so many messages from my mom, from Tennessee and everything.

After I made the team and the Olympics were over, another big highlight of my career was going back to my home town. They honored me. They gave me the key to the city. They built a track and named it after me — Sharrieffa Barksdale Track. I got a street named after me.

Those were the big highlights of my life during track and field. But the most important — it makes me cry — are my children because I can instill the values in my children that I

Sharrieffa Barksdale, 2005.

had from my mom because my father died when I was nine years old. She is such a great woman because she has given me morals, determination, perseverance, a heart and persistent attitude. If you don't have the attitude, you can't make it.

I ended up quitting track. I tried to come back in '88 but I just didn't have it in my heart to run and if you are going to compete on a national level as an elite athlete you have to have it in your heart to give it all you can give. I didn't have it. So, I just hung up track.

I'm the assistant coach at Kentucky State University. I'm the head cross country coach at Kentucky State University for both men and women. I have a daughter who is eight years old and I have a son who is four years old.

INTERVIEW: ALICE BROWN HARRIS

(December 1, 2005) I got started probably when I was about eight years old. I used to just play in the street with the kids and realized that I had a little more speed than some of the little boys did. Fortunately the elementary school that I was going to had some after school activities for us; baseball, basketball and track. Actually my first love, I think, was baseball. As I got older I realized that baseball was not an Olympic sport. I thought, OK, then I want to do track or maybe gymnastics. One day during the '72 Olympics, that was my first Olympics that I actually saw on TV, I remember lying on the floor in front of the TV set. My sister came in and turned it. We just got into a really, really big fight. I told my mother that this event comes on only once every four years and that I should be able to watch it. She said, "Okay, I agree with you." They sat there and they let me watch it. And it was like, "Okay, I'm going to go there. I don't know what I'm going to do, but I'm going to go." And I think that was it. That just kind of stuck in my mind and track came alive, I think, when I went to junior high school. I realized that track was a spring sport and baseball was too. You couldn't do both at the same time. I had people that kind of influenced me at that time, especially my counselor. She also coached on her own in the afternoons. Her name was Miss Newman — Dr. Eddie Newman now. She helped me and she encouraged me to go ahead and continue to run. She would take us to little AAU meets on the weekend. That's how it started.

I went on to high school and ran with the Mercurettes. That was the first club team that I ran for. Because I wanted to go to the Olympics, I knew I needed just a little more than what the high school coaches could offer me. The bad side of that was that it was the Los Angeles

Mercurettes. I didn't live in L.A. at the time. What my parents had to do, actually my father, he would work and he would take me into Los Angeles because I couldn't drive at the time. I think I was only fifteen, and he would stay there and watch my practice and then drive me back home and then he would go back to work. He did that so often. It got to the point where it was affecting his job. So, it was like, okay, we trust you enough to drive yourself (laughter). I was close to sixteen. But I thought I knew how to drive. What ended up happening was I had to drive myself. My first experience on a freeway and the 110 freeway — I don't know if you've been on the 110 freeway going through Pasadena or not, it has the worst curves. It's the worst freeway I've been on to this day and I'm forty-something. I got on there and I said, "If I'm going to do this, I just have to do it — I have to go to practice everyday." I was scared — to — death. That's what I had to do until I was able to get my driver's license.

Once I started going there on a regular basis, I made a junior team. I was able to get a scholarship to Cal State, Northridge. Then I made the 1980 team which didn't go. At that point, it was kind of unusual because there were not a lot of females at that time getting full scholarships. The bottom line was that I wanted to go to the Olympics. The first university that I had enrolled in didn't have a track program and I was told that they did, that's why myself and several other athletes enrolled. I ended up going to Cal State, Northridge. Barbara Sworkes persuaded me to go there. Bob Kersee was the assistant coach there at the time. She told me certain things and brought to light some other things which made me think, OK, she really wants me to come here. I probably need to go there because she is looking out for me. So that's what I ended up doing. Then I made the '80 team which was a disappointment because I was thinking at the time not too many women got scholarships. At that time, outside of college, women did not have the opportunity to continue to run because there were not a whole lot of track clubs, and you couldn't afford to continue to train, once you got married and had kids. I thought that was pretty much the end of my career. So I thought, "Oh my gosh, this is it. I'm not going to have another opportunity to do this." Around the same time women athletes really started to evolve. The European track circuit started to offer more opportunities for American women. We would go over there and compete and as a result were able to maintain a lifestyle and receive money. USA Track & Field allowed us living expenses — that's what they called it at that time. We were allotted so much money a month to live on which allowed us to be able to train at the same time. It happened at the perfect time. I think it also happened because they realized it took away a lot of the athletes' dreams because some people were not able to come back in the next four years; some of us were and some of us weren't. I was fortunate to be able to come back and still be able to run well. I was able to continue to strive towards my dream for another four years, which is hard to do, a lot of people were not able to do it.

Alice Brown, 2005.

I think that just being stubborn, I don't know — made me go on. I think that was part of the reason why and I felt I was much better than that, so I continued to push myself. But, that old Evelyn Ashford had the nerve to come back too (laughter). I always wanted to do more and I always tried to push myself. I don't think it was so much Evelyn, I think it was more me pushing myself. She gave me the determination to continue to do it. If she can do it, I can do it. I think that's what it was more than anything else. I've always thought Evelyn was just a pretty runner, her and Edwin Moses; their technique was just so fluid. So, I don't want to take anything away from her but I always thought that I could do much better, so I pushed myself.

Two things I actually remember about the '84 games: the opening ceremony and "Reach Out and Touch." Even to this day when I hear Diana Ross sing that song it makes me teary-eyed. You can imagine 100,000 people in the stands — everybody embracing and holding hands, everybody rocking and singing that song. It was just electric. It was amazing. It was breathtaking. It was everything.

One thing that stands out in my mind when I was at the 1984 Olympics, I was at the starting line for the 100 meters, I heard my mother's voice. I have my game face on — I was concentrating, and I heard her voice holler at me and it just totally broke my concentration. It's like, okay Alice, gather yourself, get your mind back in focus because you have a job to do, and it took everything I had not to laugh. Because, how could I hear my mother's voice with all these people. So I had to gather myself and then after I did that and the race was over I didn't realize how much pressure it actually was until it was over. I felt like a ton had been lifted off my shoulders. When I heard the national anthem and I realized that ton was off my back I just couldn't help but cry. It was like all of that for eleven seconds of my life (laughter). After the 100m was over everything else was just icing on the cake for me.

I always push myself and that's why I went on to '88 hoping that I could do the same thing. I had a lot of ups and downs but I was trying to stay focused. At one point I was training myself. I recall one day that I was looking for a coach. I knew that I had to train but I also had to work. One morning when the time changed I was out on the track and it was still dark because of the time change. I didn't know there was someone else out on the track with me. The man ran up on me, he was just doing his morning jog. It scared me to death. I said, "Alice, something has got to change. Either you're going to have to start working part time, or you're going to have to make a decision. You know you want to do this, so you're going to have to sacrifice in another area." That's pretty much what I did. I had to cut back on my hours so that I would be able to train. Not only that but it was too much on me to do that and work full time. I ended up changing my schedule; I ended up finding another coach. It worked.

The Olympics in '88 was a totally different experience for me than '84. We were so close to home in '84 that we actually drove ourselves to the track. My coach, at that time, took us away from the atmosphere because it was our first participating Olympics and he wanted to make sure we stayed focused. We stayed outside of Los Angeles, maybe ten or fifteen miles. The '84 Olympics was my first one and it was my first gold and silver medals but in '88, the atmosphere of being around athletes from other nations, being in the Olympic village and just partaking in everything. That was another totally different experience. It was just amazing — the way they had it organized, the people, everything.

I can't be disappointed in the things I did over the years. I know I have been blessed. It has opened a whole lot of doors for me. I always thought I could do better so I always pushed myself. I really can't complain too much for not accomplishing what I wanted to accomplish. Everything I did I think I did to accomplish my goal. As a result, I have two golds and a silver and I had one American and world record, for 60 yards indoors. One year we had like three or four American records in the 4 × 100m relay. There's not a whole bunch more I could ask for even though I still want more (laughter). That's about the totality of it.

INTERVIEW: TASHA DOWNING

(June 26, 2004) I got started in track a long time ago, actually in 1976. I was about to turn seven. My brother would have me run against boys in the neighborhood for Kraft caramel candies. He would give me one and keep the rest. He would keep the change that he made from the races and no boy could beat me from age seven to about ten. So he made a lot of money off me. He put me in the Kendall Women's Classic. It was a meet for girls of all age groups. I got second in the 50 and it was on the 5 o'clock news and I have not stopped running since (laughter).

I ran for different club teams and then my father took over and started his own team, the Boston Bullets. Under my dad, I made the first world junior championship team that went to Athens, Greece in 1986. I was fifteen. I got fifth in the quarter. I was the fifth junior in the world. That was amazing to me. Even now I look back and go, "How'd I do that?" The best highlight was winning the 4 × 4. I think we ran 3:30, maybe 16. That record just got broken last year. The record was eighteen years old. So, I'm proud of that.

Tasha Downing, 2003.

After that, I ended up choosing the University of Florida under Coach Beverly Kearney. We were her first recruiting class and we were the first and still the only class to win NCAAs for the University of Florida. We won nationals. What I get so disappointed about is that I didn't actually win an individual championship. But, often times I won the SEC conference championship which is the toughest conference in track and field in the 400. I qualified for the Olympic trials in 1992 with a PR of 52.22 and right before the Olympic trials in the 60 meters I tore my hamstring from the back of my knee up to my gluteus. I was told I would never run again. They wanted to operate and I said no. If I run again, it would be God. That was in 1992 and in 2001, at almost 31 years of age, I ran my fastest ever in the quarter — 53.19 — and made the world championship team and anchored the team to a fourth place finish in Lisbon. So God is amazing and never say never (laughter).

I'm here today at the Master's Open Championships in Clermont, Florida and this is my last meet as a professional. I will take next year off. Hopefully God will bless me with a child and then I will come back and I will run masters until I can't walk [laughter]. Amen!

INTERVIEW: BENITA FITZGERALD MOSLEY

(December 5, 2002) I was about twelve years old and my middle school teacher, Gwen Washington, was also my gymnastics teacher. I had seen Olga Corbett compete in the '72 Olympics and I thought I wanted to be a gymnast. I was on a gymnastics team in my middle school. I took gymnastic lessons and I was tall, lanky and inflexible. I didn't make the best gymnast at all. My coach recognized that and although she put me on the team she still tried to steer me in a better direction. She had seen me run in a PE class and remarked how fast I was and how I could beat anybody in the school male or female and that I should come out for the track team. She encouraged me to do so when I was twelve in the seventh grade. So I did do that and started running hurdles and the 100 and the 50 yard dash and the 4 × 100 meter relay and the high jump, all in middle school. I won my events every year. That's how I got started. I guess a really bad gymnast turned great track star [laughter].

I went into Garfield High School. I grew up in northern Virginia a half an hour outside of D.C. When I went to high school, thankfully, I had a great school and a great community. That high school had won two straight state championships when I got in there my freshman year. My freshman year, Paula Girvin was a senior. She ended up making the Olympic team in '76 in the high jump. She didn't medal but she was definitely a hero in our community. I was a neighbor also. Her parents were good friends with my parents. Her sister and I are still best of friends. She was a great inspiration to me and a great role model for me as a freshman to see her set all those state records and national records and then go on to be an Olympian. In my freshman year we also won our third straight state meet title in track. I was running the hurdles, relays — even the mile relay and high jump — all in high school — and started at the national level at sixteen in my junior year. I won the junior national championships in the 100 meter hurdles. And the rest is history.

The first team was the most memorable in my younger career — just making that junior national team in 1978 going to Russia to compete against the Russian junior national team. We had two dual meets. Then we went to Great Britain and had a dual meet and to West Germany and had a dual meet. The one against the Russians, the first one the U.S. team won and the sec-

Benita Fitzgerald Mosley and son, 2002.

ond time they brought out a whole different team. Many of them had beards and moustaches and wrinkles. They didn't quite look eighteen or younger on the men's side and for sure on the women's side we saw some women who were quite a bit older and different from the ones we competed against the week before. But, it was during the cold war and they were definitely embarrassed on their home turf to have lost to the Americans so they pulled out all the stops a week later. It was definitely, definitely a memorable experience.

I then went to college at the University of Tennessee on a full scholarship. Terri Crawford was the head coach. John Miller coached me for a while. Loren Seagrave coached me for a while. Andy Roberts coached me for a while. I made my first Olympic team my freshman year 1980. Unfortunately because of the Carter boycott we didn't go to Moscow. I still regret that I didn't have that Olympic experience. Being eighteen years old and having that experience would have just so enriched my career and just catapulted me, I think, much quicker and farther. Thankfully, I was the only hurdler four years later to come back and make the Olympic team again. Candy Young and Stephanie Hightower unfortunately didn't make it in '84. I won the gold medal in the 100 meter hurdles just beating Shirley Strong from Great Britain by four hundredths of a second. It was a great race — highly competitive and definitely still the highlight of my track career. The next four years were up and down — probably more ups than downs — going through the post Olympic blahs a little bit the first year in '85. Then in '86, '87 and '88 coming back from battling some injuries and surgeries on my ankle. I retired in '88, just missing my third Olympic team by a hundredth of a second.

One real memorable experience was the '84 Olympic trials where four of us crossed the finish line within one hundredth of a second of one another and waiting twenty or thirty minutes for them to blow that photograph up and determine the winners. Unfortunately Stephanie did not make the team. It was so heartbreaking for her and for all of us, I think, because she was the American record holder at the time. You want your best competitors in the race with you. It was exciting, it was nerve-wracking, it was stressful. I'm glad my race, at least, was only twelve seconds because the jury was out for much longer than that.

Those are some of the highlights and the most memorable moments. I have a degree in industrial engineering. While I was competing I was an engineer for a while. When I retired in '88, I did it full time for a couple of years. Then I went into sports administration. Hal Connolly hired me. I was with the Special Olympics International in Washington, D.C. and I had gotten back to my home town area. He hired me as a regional director and got me into sports administration. I stayed in that field for about ten years in various capacities. I worked with the Special Olympics for a couple of years, then with the Atlanta Committee for the Olympic Games for a couple of years and for the U.S. Olympic Committee for five years, running their Olympic training center in San Diego and then all of the training centers. It was such an enriching and exciting time just to be able to give back in such a way that I was able to help and facilitate other athletes fulfilling their Olympic dreams. It was just a highlight and a blessing day to day to do that. I got a great job opportunity to leave Colorado and the USOC and become the President and CEO of an association that I feel very passionately about. It's called Women and Cable and Telecommunications. It's a twenty-five year old women's advocacy and professional association which really promotes and supports women leaders in the cable television industry. Our membership includes executives from cable programmers at HBO and ESPN, including the CEOs of Bravo, Lifetime and Oxygen, as well as cable operators like Comcast, Cox, and Time Warner Cable.

We promote women and offer them more opportunities to advance their careers. It's helping women achieve their dreams in a different arena.

INTERVIEW: STEPHANIE HIGHTOWER

(December 5, 2002) I'm a military brat. My father was stationed in Germany at the time. In your physical education classes they did the President's Physical Fitness Tests. People said, "Oh, you can run and jump." I was twelve years old. In the military, especially when your parents are stationed overseas, there are really strong athletic programs for youth and so I did everything. That is the way we stayed busy. The program was called Associations for Youth Athletics, AYA. You went every day. I did basketball, softball and they were just starting to develop track. So, I got involved in track. I beat all the boys — beat all the girls. So, it started there.

We moved back to the States, my freshman year in high school, to Kentucky. The school that I went to had been state champions for two years on the military installation and I decided that since they won two state championships in track, I wanted to be associated with a winning sport at that school. So, I went out for the track team as a freshman. Coach didn't really know where she wanted to put me, but since they didn't have a hurdler at the time — ours had graduated — she said, "So, you're running the hurdles." That's how it happened. It wasn't a matter of, I mean she had me run over the hurdles, I had okay form and she looked at me and said, "You're doing hurdles." That was it. It just sort of exploded from there. My freshman year I made it to the state finals. I wasn't successful but made it there. Then after that, my sophomore, junior and senior years in high school, I won the state championship in the hurdles, the 100 and the 200 and ran on some relays and ended up getting some scholarship offers. In 1976, when I graduated from high school, girls' sports was really starting to take off— so, I'm one of those beneficiaries from Title IX.

My lifetime dream at that time, knowing who Wilma Rudolph was and all those kind of things, that was when I graduated from high school in 1976, that was also the year of the Olympics — and after watching the Olympics — I knew that I wanted to be on an Olympic team. So, I tried to figure out where would be the best place for me to go to college. My dream was to go to Tennessee State, but at that time, Mr. Temple thought I was too slow coming out of high school — and I still tease him about that to this day. I had offers to the University of Kentucky but I really did not want to stay home in the state of Kentucky. Then, I had a partial scholarship offer to the University of Tennessee and that really wasn't enough financial aid for us.

My uncle was a professional football player and had been a star football player at Ohio State. His name is Paul Warfield. He then started recruiting me saying, "You need to come home to Ohio State, come back to Ohio. That's where your roots pretty much are." My family is from Warren, Ohio. So, I began looking at that school. But, at the time, they didn't have a track coach.

I was one of those then who couldn't go to Tennessee State and as a leap of faith went to Ohio

State. I was the first woman awarded a scholarship under Title IX for track and field at Ohio State and about a month and a half later they selected their coach, who happened to be Mamie Rallins — who happened to be a hurdler — who happened to be an Olympian. It was one of those sort of matches made in heaven. It was really a leap of faith and it was the best thing that could have happened to me.

I started at Ohio State with her and it was disastrous! I had been one of those athletes through high school who really didn't have to train very hard. I started at Ft. Knox, Kentucky — I have to back up a little — freshman and sophomore years. Then my father retired and we moved to Louisville and I graduated from Stewart High School. I had a different coach there who basically let me do whatever I wanted to do. She made me train a couple of days a week, but that was about it and I was still able to be very successful in track. So, by the time I got to college, I was a prima-donna and Mamie was this Olympic athlete and we immediately clashed.

I didn't know anything about cross country. She made me run cross country. Lost in the city, I don't know where I'm at, we're running on these streets — I don't know where I'm at. So, I basically said, "This isn't going to work." I called my father and said, "I'm coming home, come pick me up." He listened to me on the phone and then just slammed the phone down. He didn't listen to me anymore.

I figured out I couldn't go home so I had to make this work. Mamie and I had one of these love/hate relationships where she was always telling me what I couldn't do, I was too lazy to do this and do that. And so my whole purpose in life was to just basically show her that she was wrong — that I could do it. By the time that I was a senior at Ohio State, I had won Big 10 as a freshman, Big 10 indoors and outdoors from my freshman through my senior years. At that time, it was the AIAW. It turned into the NCAAs. I was AIAW champion for two years my junior and senior years at Ohio State. I made the Olympic team in 1980, the boycott year.

I stayed in Ohio to continue to train for another four years. I had that terrible, terrible accident in 1984 where I had been picked to win the gold medal and was undefeated going into the Olympic trials and had one of those unfortunate races and was awarded that alternate spot on the 1984 team. After that I wasn't sure I wanted to put all my eggs in one basket and make another Olympic team.

From 1984 through 1988, I still maintained and did very well in track. By 1988, I had married and priorities began to change in 1986. I ended up going to the Olympic trials in 1988. I think I ended up fourth again. I ended up finishing out that summer and then knew it was time to retire and look at other professional kinds of opportunities utilizing my degree. I did graduate from Ohio State in 1981.

It was time for me to start making a change and do some other things. What I've continued to try to do is stay actively involved in the sport sitting on the board of directors and now being Women's Track and Field chair. A lot of stuff that I've learned in this organization (USATF) and being actively involved in this organization, has been instrumental and I can apply it to a lot of what I do professionally as an administrator, as well as in my civic responsibilities in the community that I live in. I am President of the School Board in Columbus, Ohio. A lot of the focus and the drive and passion that I had as an athlete, I now use and apply not only in my work but also in my community and civic activities. I think you have to have that in this day and age because I don't think people are as engaged as they used to be, especially in the civic and political areas. I'm having a lot of fun taking what I learned as an athlete and now applying that in other things in life.

I can keep going on and on about memories in track. Making that Olympic team, even though it was boycotted, that was an incredible experience. Setting the American record over in East Germany in 1981 — that was very exhilarating and one of those sorts of life time memories. The series of world records that happened indoor season, which I will always have because we no longer run yards, that competition between me and Candy Young that went on and on in that series of indoor meets. Those are some of the memorable experiences.

One that's memorable, that I don't like to remember, that's been a life long lesson, is the 1984 trials. We play that over and over again. It was interesting, in Greece, last month, you know I'm the 2004 head manager for the Olympic staff. We went to do a site visit. We were in the airport and I turned the corner and there was a Swatch Watch and sitting on the side of their display case is a big — huge — probably a six foot photograph of that photo finish from the 1984 trials because it was determined to be the closest finish ever. You can still, as I sat there and looked at that damn thing for twenty minutes, you cannot tell who got second place. You cannot tell who got second place — and that was me being, I think, after how many years, being objective — you cannot see it. I don't care what anyone says, the race should have been run over. There's no way — and this is blown up — it's six feet — and you cannot tell — and me being women's chair, if that situation would have happened today, I would make them run the damn thing over. I don't care if they'd have to stay another day or come back in three hours, they would run that race again.

We had a situation a couple of years ago where an athlete didn't make another round. Part of it was because she ran in a semi round. Someone false started. The second gun didn't go off until she was down on the eighth hurdle. She walked back and rushed back into the blocks again. They didn't give her time to rest and then she got fourth place. I said, "Nope, she's going to run in lane nine," they're saying, "No, we can't run lane nine," and I'm saying, "That's a bunch of crap, you can't penalize that athlete because we didn't do our job as officials to call them back until she got to the eighth hurdle. Nor did we give her the amount of rest she needed. We can't penalize her for that."

As women's chair, I have the opportunity of really making sure that women are included in all facets of this organization and are really validated in a way. The reality is that women are beginning to carry the sport and have been for some time.

We have issues such as women coaches being displaced. Now that people see the value of women in sports, you have men who wouldn't even think about coaching women now wanting to.

If anything, I hope I will have the ability to begin to change things so that women do not have to be fighting these kinds of battles. We become validated as professionals in this field. We bring a lot to the sport and people respect what it is that we are out here trying to do and what we have accomplished.

INTERVIEW: JONI HUNTLEY

(December 2, 2004) I came from a small town in Oregon by the name of Sheridan. We didn't have a track other than a path around a field at the high school. My first memory of competition was at eight years old trying to qualify for a Junior State Olympic meet. I ran the 50-yard dash in the street to qualify and when I got to the meet I was disqualified for running outside my lane. I had no idea that I was supposed to run between two lines. My older brother Jerry, younger sister Sandy, and I would scissor-style jump into grass shavings using homemade standards and a bamboo pole. I could scissor over 4' 10" in 8th grade so I was content.

In 1971 I was a freshman in high school. I had a student teacher in my PE class, Marcia Miller, who had seen a Fosbury Flop movie in college. She drove me to a nearby university where I watched a movie with Dick Fosbury explaining the Fosbury Flop. I took the information and slowly changed my scissor style to more of a scissor layout style. I later progressed to the Flop by studying the style and getting the coaching I needed.

As sophomore, I went to my first girl's and woman's nationals and qualified for the 1972 Olympic trials. I was disappointed not to clear a height. I made my first international team in 1973. It was a junior team and the jumpers performed better than the senior team that year. The experience of travel and large competitions was wonderful.

My senior year in 1974 was filled with excitement. During the daytime all-comer meet in Portland, Oregon, the carpenters were preparing the track for the big evening meet. I jumped 5' 10¾" for my first American record bettering, Eleanor Montgomery's 5' 10½". The next weekend I became the first American to jump over 6 feet by clearing 6' ½" in San Diego. At the Oregon State High School Meet, I set national records in the high jump and 100 yard hurdles and won the 100 yard run and was second in long jump. Our team won the high point trophy but I was the only person who scored.

In 1974 I enrolled at Oregon State University to work with Berny Wagner, Dick Fosbury's coach. I won the 1975 Pan Am Games and was training for the 1976 Olympics when Coach Wagner decided to take a position in Saudi Arabia. I quit school in January and moved to Long Beach, California to train with Dave Rodda who had been a coach on the 1972 International Junior team. Rodda coached for the love of the sport. He would work all day at his job and then volunteer time each day of the week to coach the members of the Lakewood International team and others like me. There was never any money involved. I appreciate all he did for me and his athletes. He made it fun and we always knew it was "okay to play."

During the 1976 Olympic Games final, a Polish jumper moved my check mark and the officials stopped the competition while I re-measured. I watched as the cheater moved it again. The competition came to a halt while I yelled at the Polish jumper. It was a very emotional competition! I ultimately finished in a disappointing 5th place.

I moved down to Long Beach to finish my undergraduate degree at Long Beach and train with Rodda. In 1980 the U.S. boycotted the Olympics. There was no reason for me to be in California. I wanted to move back to Oregon. I remember exactly when I moved back to Oregon. I drove my truck with my Hobie Cat behind and my bed on top. Mount St. Helens had just erupted the day before so everything I took back to Oregon was covered with ash. Once I crossed the border I felt like I was home again.

Since the U.S. wasn't going to have the opportunity to compete in the 1980 Olympics, I had a busy indoor season and was injured before the trials. I always loved jumping on the indoor circuit. The closeness of the crowd always got my adrenalin flowing.

Joni Huntley, 2004.

I took a coaching job at Oregon State University for a couple of years because I felt I owed something to the sport that had given me so much. I really enjoyed it but it wasn't something I wanted to do for a career.

At the same time, I kept going to school and taking classes. I have always loved going to school. I didn't compete for two years but I missed it. I jumped in a couple of indoor meets in 1982. I started training but I was only training a couple of times a week and started jumping very well. I think the difference was being happy and having a well-rounded life. Many people thought I was "over-the-hill" or a "has-been." Louise Ritter was on the scene and she was doing so well there wasn't any pressure on me. I was training and jumping for fun.

In the 1984 Olympic Trials, I placed third and barely made the team. In one ranking for the Olympics, I was ranked 28th out of 30 jumpers. It was nice to be an underdog because I knew I would do well. To be able to go in and get a bronze medal was wonderful. I had three personal records in the Olympic games. I had not jumped higher outdoors since 1975. I was able to share the experience with my husband, John Rueter, who had been my training partner for a year.

I continued jumping after 1984 because I still loved it. It became a long goodbye to a big part of my life. When I was pregnant I was jumping. I competed in the 1986 nationals while pregnant and advanced to the finals by jumping over 6'.

At the 1987 nationals, I had my baby daughter, Sheridan, with me. I could hear Sheridan crying, so I brought her down to the field. I was rocking her in her stroller. I knew it was time to stop competing. I made the finals but withdrew and flew home to make the life I have now.

Last year, Howard Schmertz called and surprised me by telling me that I was being inducted into the Millrose Hall of Fame. Some of my favorite competitions were at Madison Square Garden and the Millrose Games. I took my family to New York. They were given a glimpse into my past and had a chance to meet my friends. The officials are the most wonderful people because they don't change. Athletes change, but the same officials volunteer year after year for twenty or thirty years. The trip was a wonderful experience for my family.

My daughter Sheridan is getting ready for college next year. She was named after the city that was so supportive to me as I was growing up. My other daughter, Courtney, is a sophomore in high school. My husband is an Environmental Sciences professor and my best friend. We live on a farm with horses, donkeys, dogs and cats. I've taught school for sixteen years and love my kindergarten classes each year. We work hard to keep our life simple and full of love. I will never forget the people I met and the memories made. They will always be a part of me.

INTERVIEW: PAM SPENCER

(March 2, 2003) I got started in track and field on a dare when I was in the sixth grade. They put a high jump pit in the gym because I lived in Montana and it was freezing outside. My two sixth grade coaches, my home room teachers actually, put the high jump pit out. I wasn't going to do it because I was very shy. My girlfriend said, "I dare you to." This is back when they had the burlap bags with the foam rubber and everybody is scissor-kicking. She dared me so I tried it. I was good at it, much to my amazement; I was very good at it. I kept jumping. I did it in the sixth grade and the seventh. That year I got something like third in the city which was a real big deal for me. I just loved it. So, I continued during high school. I did very well in high school. I think I was the second girl in the nation. Joni Huntley and I were within a week of each other in jumping six feet for the first time ever for an American woman. I'm still, to this day, not sure who got it first. I'd like to think it was me but I think it was her. It gave me the bug then.

I made my first Olympic team when I was seventeen. We went to Montreal in '76. I was so petrified. I thought, I made this Olympic team and I don't deserve to be here. I never trained a day in my life. I just had natural conversion ability from horizontal to vertical. I never trained. So consequently when I get to the Olympic games I'm doing everybody's workout little knowing that I should be tapering instead of doing all of these heavy workouts (laughter). I don't think it would have mattered. When I walked out into Olympic Stadium I, to this day, do not remember a thing. I remember walking out and seeing all the people. I remember trying not to cry so I wouldn't upset all my other competitors when I didn't qualify, then having to wait to leave until they were done and then walking out and getting drug tested. I'm thinking, I didn't even qualify and you want to drug test me. It was like adding insult to injury.

It was my first Olympic experience but it really motivated me from that point on to be worthy of the Olympic title so I started training very hard. I made my second Olympic team in 1980 when we didn't get to go. We boycotted. The very next year I set the American record. I think that was probably my prime time right there. In 1982, I had knee surgery. I did come back well enough for the '84 Olympic team but never got the same strength that I had prior to that. I finished my career in 1985.

I went to Seattle Pacific for three years and then went down to Cal State Northridge. I used to say I crammed four years into five and a half. I got my degree in philosophy and art history from Cal State Northridge.

I made one Olympic team when I was a freshman at Seattle Pacific. Then I moved to Cal State Northridge. Bobby Kersee and Chuck DeBus were the coaches there. There were eight Olympians on my team: Alice Brown, FloJo, Jackie, Julie Brown. We had a powerhouse. My PR was 6' 5½".

I am still very active coaching United States teams and I'm on the Athletes Advisory Board of Directors Executive Committee. I'm trying to give back to the sport that has blessed me for so many years. The first international team that they sent me on was to Tokyo, Japan with Mamie Rallins and a chaperone. I was fifteen. Mamie was thirty something and my chaperone was thirty something. I thought then that if they are going to let me go all over the world just for jumping over this silly little stick, I'm going to do it. I just enjoyed my career so much. To this day, I find it hard to believe the things that I got to do: meet the President, travel all over the world, just because I know how to jump over a stick well. You know, it seems kind of ironic and it sounds silly.

I'm here at the indoors because I'm the head coach of the indoor world championship team that is going to England. I was originally the assistant but Dr. Lyle came down with pneumonia so now I'm the head coach. I've been doing juniors for the past few years so this will be an experience to be back with the senior team.

I'm married and I have two children. I've been married for twenty years and I have a seventeen year old daughter and a thirteen year old son and we live in southern California. I teach high school and middle school art and physical education.

Interview: Ruth Wysocki

(January 12, 2006) Well, where do I start? It's been a long time. This is not a short story. Actually, I come from a family of three brothers and an athletic dad. So, we had a houseful of athletic people. My dad had run track in high school and college. He was fourth in the California State Meet in the 880 in 1946. As I was a youngster, my dad was in his mid to late thirties. He was playing a lot of pick-up basketball. The story from mom is that she was getting worried because my dad was gaining a little weight and his blood pressure was going up, yet he was playing guts out basketball. Apparently, she threatened him, "If you don't get yourself in shape, I'm not going to let you play basketball anymore because I don't want to be a non-working widowed mother with four kids!" [laughter]. My dad started jogging. This is just before the jogging craze in the '70s, this would be in the mid to late '60s. Just as he kind of got started running, he heard that there was a group starting that they were going to call master's running and actually have competitions for men that were over forty. He was approaching that. He thought, you know if I got in shape, maybe I could run. That's kind of the background.

In the midst of this, when I was a youngster, the recreation department in the summer would open up the junior college stadium and teach people how to use the starting blocks, long jump, etc. Every Friday they would have an all-comers track meet. I did those just for fun. I didn't train but we would go run these races and get ribbons. At the end of the summer, my dad realized that there was a local track club that was bringing kids to these meets. It was the next city over and he asked me if I wanted to join the track club. That's kind of how it all got started. My two older brothers were running high school track at the time and cross country. I joined this local club. I was about ten.

I started running and at that time, my first cross country season, eleven and under girls ran all of three quarters of a mile. That was very good for a half miler little girl. I would run these races and do pretty well. I'd win the local races. It got to where I won our district. We found out that the state meet was in Sacramento, the northern end of the state; we're at the southern end. My dad went out and raised money through service groups to fly us up to Sacramento so I could run these state championships. It would be the highlight of the year. We actually flew up in the morning, ran and flew home. We didn't even stay overnight [laughter]. But he managed to fundraise and do that. We went up there and I won the state meet. There was a local team, the Rialto Road Runners, I think they call it Southern California Road Runners now, and they won the team division and I won the individual. Their coach invited me to come to the national championships. I was so green at the time I didn't even know that such a thing existed. It was going to be in Frederick, Maryland. So, out we went, raising money again. Even though I was on a different team, this team invited me and included me in what they were doing. I ended up winning the national championship. They won the national team championship. That exposed me to a club that really went out and did things [laughter]; took it to another level. Rialto was an hour away from us. I joined their team but obviously could not get there on a daily basis. So, my dad became my coach for quite a while. On the weekends they would take me out to Rialto and I'd spend the weekend at somebody's house and we'd run together. Throughout my whole career, my dad was a very, very significant person. He was always the one who made the next step happen. To me, it just happened. Now, as an adult, I realize what he did to make it happen (laughter). That was the start.

My first track season as an eleven year old, I went to my very first AAU track meet and finished third. To me, that meant two people beat me. My first race I ran 2:44.1. My second race, the girl who won the week before wasn't there but the girl who got second was. I ran the race and won. Of course, I was thrilled; third one week and first the next. The announcer was Calvin Brown and I heard him say, "I think we have a new national record." National record, what's that? Somebody actually keeps track of what we're running out here, why would they want to do that? 2:33.1 was the record. Several of us took turns at breaking the record that season. I ended up with it: 2:30.2 at the end of the season.

The first year was successful. My dad sort of made sure I was where I needed to be without pushing or anything. I think the rest of my career was spent trying to do a little bit better than the last time. You don't go out trying to slay the dragon the first time. I talk to kids; I worked at a private school here for six years. I taught PE and coached. I started a middle school cross country team and then I had track and cross country for the high school kids. I would talk to kids and I'd say, "You've got to grow up playing soccer and baseball and this and this. But do you realize that this is a sport where you can win without crossing the finish line first?" That's really a big part of it.

"With early success, it kind of entices you to keep going. I don't know what would have happened if I wasn't any good at first. Would I have stuck with it or would I have kept on with my piano lessons? I don't know.

I look back on it. My parents had four kids. My mom was at home until the youngest went to school. Kind of a typical story maybe of that era. But, here was my dad, four kids, working full time. He would come home and train himself and train me. You just look at what they went through to make things happen. In addition to the running I had private piano lessons and violin lessons. I think the happiest day of my dad's life was the day I got a driver's license (laughter). Here's the key to the car — drive.

In '84 with the trials being in Los Angeles, I grew up in Southern California, so many of the officials, the timers, the starters, the people in the stands; these are all people who watched me grow up. There were a lot of significant people that were able to be there. It made it very significant when it happened; when it all took off. My high school coach video taped a lot of the meet and while the 1500 meters was shown on television, the 800 was not. He videotaped it, which was awesome. But he also had the tape going when I finally staggered around the track and caught my breath and I saw at the end of the coliseum my parents and my coach. So I ran up into the stands and on video he has me hugging my coach and hugging my dad. That's pretty cool [laughter]; pretty good memories.

The next significant thing for me was in high school, kinda with some connections, was the invitation later on to run with the Naturite team and Chuck DeBus. Again, I did not live where they were [laughter] and it turned out that there was sort of a little satellite group of track people training at Claremont College with Vince Reel, who was the editor of *Women's Track and Field World*. He was an excellent coach. His wife was Chi Cheng. He was coaching Marilyn Neufville who held the 440 record at the time. So I was able to connect with Vince Reel and train out at Claremont College and have that influence even though I was in high school. I had the opportunity to be a part of a group that was even bigger and better than what I had been a part of before. That made the whole high school thing memorable.

The other interesting thing throughout was kind of always being on the doorstep of the next big thing to happen for women. In some ways I feel that I had a part in things being better than they were [laughter]. For instance, when I was in high school, out here anyway, there were no high school sports for girls. It wasn't until toward the end of my high school career that they actually had girls running in CIF out here. My junior year, they didn't have a state meet, just a CIF meet. I won the 880 and the 440. They wouldn't let me run the 880 and the mile. Heaven forbid you should run that. But, they allowed me to run the 880 and the 440 with fifteen minutes rest. They were literally back to back events. I couldn't run the 880 and the mile which would have given me time to rest [laughter]. In my senior year, I wasn't allowed to run in the CIF because I trained with boys. My school did not have a girls' team. The coach was awesome in letting me be a part of the boys' team. He just treated me like one of the guys. It was probably the best thing to happen for my future. I had to stay with the boys, I couldn't run girls' track because I trained with boys — what a horrible thing to do [laughter]. We just put up with it then and got mad.

When I went to college I went to the University of Redlands just for a year because Vince Reel came out of retirement and was there. That was before the NCAA for women. They had the AIAW. We were eliminated from the AIAW because we filled out the forms wrong. These ridiculous things, but you realize now that we went through these things and now it's better for somebody else. I look later, all the way up to 1988 in making that trip to South Africa. When again, Ben Johnson had taken drugs and defrauded the whole Olympic movement but, Oh my gosh, these people had actually ran races in South Africa. We got four years suspension and he got two (laughter). We were worse than him. Now, Oh my goodness, there's South Africa in the forefront of sports. So I got to be a part of some pretty exciting things. I even look now at the money that people make and I think if I could only run now what I did then, I'd be making a fortune (laughter). But would I? The motivation would be different. Before it was because I really wanted to do it and the other is just chasing the dollars. But who knows? [laughter]

The other significant thing that happened is that I only went to the University of Redlands for a year. I realized that I had chosen the wrong school. Not that it isn't a wonderful place; it was just not the right place for me. I decided to drop out and come home to figure out what to do next. My dad, again unbeknownst to me, went to the local junior college coach who happened to be Vince O'Boyle. He is the now the long time head coach at UC Irvine. He had coached my brother. My dad said, "My daughter is dropping out of school, I think she is floundering, she doesn't seem really to know what she wants to do. I'd really like to see something stay consistent in her life. She seems to enjoy running; would you consider coaching her?" He said he would. Later he told me, when we got to know each other better, that he just put his head on his desk and said, "What have I just agreed to do? I've never coached a girl before. What do you do with a girl runner? I'll just put her in with my team and see what we can do." [laughter] So we modified some of the workouts that the guys were doing. But mostly I ran with them. We'd go for a run through town and I didn't want to be embarrassed by being last so I'd run my little tail off. I didn't want him to regret coaching me and I didn't want the boys embarrassed that they'd always have to wait for me. So I worked harder than ever.

That first year with him, I qualified for the Olympic trials in '76. I got the 800 all the way down to 2:03. I was fortunate throughout my running career to stay with Vince as a coach. I think probably this was one of the most significant things; through thick or thin, good or bad, the same person is there coaching you. If it doesn't go so well, you don't jump ship and go find somebody else. You ride it out, figure it out and move on. After '76, the feeling was — yeah, I made it to the finals of the 800 but I got dead last. I mean after running heats and stuff, I was whooped. But I realized going home from the meet that I was just eighth in the Olympic trials. I went from thinking, "How embarrassing, I just got dead last," to thinking "Oh my gosh, I just got eighth in the Olympic trials." Madeline Manning, at that point, was a little bit older. I'm thinking, "I'm only nineteen. Four years from now, that could really be my shot." That was the motivation to push through to '80. When the boycott was determined to happen, it really took the wind out of my sails and I kind of stopped for a while. I didn't even run those trials in '80 even though I qualified. I was having some foot problems and motivation problems mostly. I figured at the advanced age of twenty-three that that was my last chance [laughter].

About a year later I thought, "I don't want people thinking I'm washed up." I did win the national championship in the 800 in 1978. I didn't want people thinking that was just a fluke, that I had one good year and I just did that one thing. I decided to get serious about it again and made the unwise choice of deciding that what I needed was more mileage. I probably went from fifty miles a week, gradually building up, to eighty-five or ninety a week before my knee blew up [laughter]. I just can't hold up to that much. That kind of became the beginning of the end for me. In '81, the day after I found out what was wrong with my knee, my husband walked in and said, "I don't want to be married anymore." I just got blasted all the way.

When I met Tom, my husband now of twenty-three years, he was running and running well. I thought it was great. By then I was doing some running again. I was running every day but not racing. After two or three years of just running, I bet I was probably doing forty or fifty miles a week, just because it's what I did. He talked me into attempting to qualify for the Olympic trials in '84. He ended up getting hurt. In trying to heal his injury, the things that he was doing even diet-wise and stuff, of course, I was doing. All of a sudden I just started improving by leaps and bounds. Amazing things started to happen. I'm sure that because of having several years of a background without the stress and strain of racing and I was twenty-seven, which at the time was pretty much beyond over the hill [laughter] back then, everything just fell into place. Obviously 1984 was the highlight year as far as PRs, the Olympics. Even though the Olympics didn't go really great for me, when I got to Europe after the Olympics, I beat everybody that beat me in the Olympics including the Olympic champion. It was some kind of vindication that told me I belonged [laughter]. The years after that maybe were not as significant in that major way but kind of solidified that I belonged at that level.

My next retirement came in '88 after we went to South Africa and got suspended. After fighting to get reinstated, to kind of clear my name I guess, I thought, you know, I went to all this trouble to clear my name, I might as well race. I raced again in '92 and realized that I had given it about ninety-five percent and it wasn't fair. By then I had a child and it wasn't fair to my husband and child to just play with this. So I retired again.

Then in '95, I had people asking me about my past and telling me, "We see you running every day out in the street, why don't you try to go to the Olympics again?" I'm like, it's not that simple, guys (laughter). I looked that year and saw the top ten lists and realized that the top times really hadn't improved from ten years before. The girls weren't running any faster than we were in '84. I thought, gosh, I must be nuts to think this, I'm thirty-eight. But if I don't try I'll never know, right? [laughter] I started training again. Things just came together. I had an awesome year in '95. I ended up running in the world championships and breaking two minutes in the 800 again, which was cool. Heading into the Olympic year, I think I had an excellent chance of going again but I had an untimely hip injury about a month before the trials. I just couldn't quite make it back to where I was even several weeks before. I didn't make the team. But that's the way it goes. I decided that's not the way I wanted to go out, even though I told my husband I'm just going to run in '95 and '96. I'm not going to do this anymore. Then it became, I can't go out like this. So I raced one more year on the track in '97 when I turned forty. I decided to have some fun with it and do some racing on the roads just to enjoy it. I started going to some of the road races that I could never go to because they were in track season like Freihofers, Azalea Trail and Carlsbad. I just had a blast with the road racing and was fortunate to come up with some master's records out of it. It is kind of a nice way to come out of the racing scene, switching over to the road racing. It is definitely less stressful than the track. That's kind of that in as small a nutshell as I can put it [laughter].

5

1985

The Outdoor Nationals

The 110th Annual USA/Mobil Track and Field Championships were held June 14–16 at Indiana University Stadium, Indianapolis, Indiana. The meet qualified athletes for seven international meets.

Frank Litsky's article in the *New York Times* on June 15 noted that many of the top athletes including, Joan Benoit, Mary Decker-Slaney, Valerie Brisco-Hooks, Alice Brown, Jeanette Bolden, Jackie Joyner and Florence Griffith were missing from the meet. Athletes competing for the World Class Athletic Club of Los Angeles (Hooks, Brown, Bolden, Joyner and Griffith), were coached by Bob Kersee. Litsky writes:

> Kersee said all the women had lost their contracts with shoe companies, part of a wide cutback by most manufacturers. He said new contracts would depend on how well the athletes ran in Europe this summer, and that he did not want to expose them to serious injury now.
>
> The liberalized rules of amateur track allow athletes to be paid for many activities, including wearing certain running shoes. The money goes into individual trust funds. The athletes draw on their trust funds for living and training expenses, and get the balance when they retire.
>
> The money can be considerable. Lewis, Moses and Mrs. Slaney are said to earn more than $100,000 a year each from shoe companies. This is a post–Olympic year, when the companies usually cut back. But the cutbacks are unusually severe because rising production costs have left many manufacturers struggling.

Litsky also reported that Francie Larrieu-Smith won the women's 10,000-meter run in meet record time of 32 minutes 18.29 seconds. It was also the fastest in the world this year.

100 meters
1. Merlene Ottey-Page, Los Angeles Track Club/Jamaica — 10.98
2. Pam Marshall, Los Angeles Track Club — 11.21
3. Diane Williams, Puma Track Club — 11.23
4. Jennifer Inniss, Atoms Track Club/Guyana — 11.34
5. Michelle Finn, Bud Light Track America — 11.37
6. Kathrene Wallace, Texas Southern Track Club — 11.38

200 meters
1. Merlene Ottey-Page, Los Angeles Track Club/Jamaica   21.93
2. Pam Marshall, Los Angeles Track Club   22.39
3. Grace Jackson, Atoms Track Club   22.57
4. Brenda Cliette, Bud Light Track Club   23.05
5. Gwen Torrence, Bud Light Track Club   23.21
6. Ella Smith, Converse Track Club   23.23

400 meters
1. Lillie Leatherwood, New Balance Track Club   50.64
2. Diane Dixon, Atoms Track Club   50.79
3. Ilrey Oliver, Knoxville Track Club/Jamaica   51.96
      (Ilrey Oliver-Sparks died as a result of a car accident
      in December 2002)
4. Sharon Dabney, Puma Track Club   52.19
5. Tonya McIntosh, Atoms Track Club   52.47
6. Roberta Belle, Puma Track Club   52.75

800 meters
1. Claudette Groenendaal, Athletics West   1:59.48
2. Louise Romo, Los Angeles Track Club   1:59.63
3. Delisa Walton-Floyd, Pollitabs Sports Club   2:00.17
4. Joetta Clark, Athletics West   2:00.24
5. Veronica McIntosh, Villanova University   2:01.52
6. Julie Jenkins, Adams State College   2:03.14

1500 meters
1. Diana Richburg, Gazelle International   4:04.73
2. Darlene Beckford, Brooks Racing Team   4:06.46
3. Ruth Wysocki, Brooks Racing Team   4:07.42
4. Leann Warren, Team adidas   4:07.50
5. Suzanne Foster, Team Nike   4:08.76
6. Renee Odom, Houston Harriers   4:09.42

3000 meters
1. Cathy Branta, Athletics West   8:49.64
2. Cindy Bremser, Wisconsin United Track Club   8:49.66
3. Mary Knisley, New Balance Track Club   8:52.54
4. Kathy Hayes, Athletics West   9:02.14
5. Lesley Welch, unattached   9:02.92
6. Cathie Twomey, Athletics West   9:05.06

5000 meters
1. Suzanne Girard, unattached   15:47.50
2. Jan Merrill, Age Group Athletic Association   15:57.83
3. Anne Switzer, University of Texas, Austin   15:58.39
4. Chris McMiken, Los Angeles Track Club/New Zealand   15:59.89
5. Joan Hansen, Los Angeles Track Club   16:01.88
6. Jill Holiday, Brigham Young University   16:02.00

10,000 meters
1. Francie Larrieu-Smith, New Balance Track Club   32:18.29   MR
2. Kirsten O'Hara, University of California, Berkeley   32:40.76
3. Lynn Jennings, Athletics West   32:48.88

Left to right: Carol Lewis, Evelyn Lawler Lewis, the author and Judi Brown King, 1991.

4. Anne Audain, unattached/New Zealand	32:57.40	
5. Linda McLennan, Puma Track Club	33:03.82	
6. Robyn Root, California Polytechnic, San Luis Obispo	33:12.86	

100 meter hurdles

1. Rhonda Blanford, Los Angeles Track Club	12.85	MR
2. Stephanie Hightower, Bud Light Track America	12.92	
3. Benita Fitzgerald-Brown, Pollitabs Sports Club	13.04	
4. Pam Page, Los Angeles Track Club	13.06	
5. LaVonna Martin, Knoxville Track Club	13.11	
6. Rosalind Pendergraft, Auburn University	13.24	

400 meter hurdles

1. Judi Brown-King, Athletics West	55.10
2. LaTanya Sheffield, Los Angeles Track Club	55.53
3. Tonja Brown, World Class Athletic Club	56.34
4. Schowonda Williams, Louisiana State University	56.34
5. Sandra Farmer, Puma Track Club	56.61
6. Leisa Davis, Oklahoma State University	56.74

10 kilometer walk
1. Maryanne Torrellas, Abraxas Track Club   48:38.16 AR, MR
2. Teresa Vaill, Island Track Club   49:25.43
3. Debbie Lawrence, Danner Shoe   50:25.61
4. Esther Lopez, Southern California Road Runners   50:54.87
5. Susan Liers, Island Track Club   51:23.97
6. Gwen Robertson, Club Northwest   51:50.79

High jump
1. Louise Ritter, Pacific Coast Club   6' 3¼"
2. Coleen Sommer, Team adidas   6' 3¼"
3. Phyllis Blunston, Puma Track Club   6' 2"
4. Mary Moore, Washington State University   6' 2"
5. Joni Huntley, Pacific Coast Club   6' 2"
6. Pam Spencer, Los Angeles Track Club   6' 2"

Long jump
1. Carol Lewis, Santa Monica Track Club   22' 8½" w
2. Sabrina Williams, Coast Athletics   21' 2½" w
3. Esmeralda Garcia, Puma Track Club/Brazil   20' 11¾" w
4. Wendy Brown, Puma Track Club   20' 10½"
5. Pat Johnson, Pollitabs Sports Club   20' 10" w
6. Gwen Loud, Coast Athletics   20' 9" w

Shot put
1. Ramona Pagel, unattached   60' 4½"
2. Peggy Pollock, Coast Athletics   57' 7½"
3. Regina Cavanaugh, Puma Track Club   55' 7"
4. Carla Garrett, University of Arizona   54' 6½"
5. Carol Cady, Los Angeles Track Club   54' 4¾"
6. Dot Jones, University of California, Fresno   52' 8¾"

Discus
1. Carol Cady, Los Angeles Track Club   200' 9"
2. Penny Neer, Western Michigan Track Club   185' 2"
3. Lorna Griffin, Team Nike   179' 4"
4. Quennah Beasley, University of Oregon   179' 1"
5. Becky Levi, University of Arizona   178' 5"
6. Ramona Pagel, unattached   177' 2"

Javelin
1. Cathy Sulinski, Millbrae Lions Track Club   197' 8"
2. Lori Mercer, Florida State University   188' 8"
3. Lynda Sutfin, Los Angeles Track Club   187' 5"
4. Erica Wheeler, Puma Track Club   181' 1"
5. Susie Ray, World Class Athletic Club   177' 10"
6. Carla Battaglia, University of Indiana   175' 1"

Triple jump
1. Wendy Brown, Puma Track Club   43' 2½"
                                                                 (establishes MR)
2. Donna Thomas, Converse Track Club   43' 1"
3. Terri Turner, Team Nike   43'¼"
4. Esmeralda Garcia, Puma Track Club/Brazil   42' 9¾"

5. Yvonne Netterville, Purdue University	41' 3¾"
6. Easter Gabriel, Atoms Track Club	41'½"

4 × 100 meter relay

1. Puma Track Club "A"	43.95
(Randy Givens, Susan Shurr, Juliet Cuthbert, Wendy Vereen)	
2. Puma Track Club "B"	45.19
3. Michigan State University	45.74

4 × 400 meter relay

1. Police Athletic League	3:33.91
(Maxine McMillan, Angela Williams, Cynthia Green, Gail Emmanual)	
2. Puma Track Club "A"	3:36.35
3. Puma Track Club "B"	3:46.41

4 × 800 meter relay

1. Puma Track Club	8:36.88
(Francesca Castro, Michele Hopper, Tara Arnold, Karol Davidson)	
2. Metroplex Striders	8:42.28
3. Club Sota	8:48.59

800 meter sprint medley relay

1. Los Angeles Track Club	1:36.80
(Pam Page, Rhonda Blanford, Merlene Ottey-Page, LaTanya Sheffield)	
2. Puma Track Club	1:37.64
3. Atoms Track Club	1:41.17

Team scores:

1. Puma Track Club	105 points
2. Los Angeles Track Club	100
3. Athletics West	45

U.S. Heptathlon Championships: Indiana University Track Stadium, Indianapolis, Indiana, June 17–18

1. Jane Frederick, Athletics West	6587 w
2. Jolanda Jones, Houston Track Club	5765 w
3. Lana Zimmerman, Louisiana State University	5606 w
4. Lairi Young, Puma Track Club	5589 w
5. Janet Nicolls, unattached	5501 w
6. Susan Brownell, University of California, Santa Barbara Outreach	5404 w

The Indoor Nationals

The indoor nationals were held in Madison Square Garden on Friday, February 22.

A headline in the *New York Times* on Saturday, February 23 read "Dixon Betters 440-Yard Mark Twice." A finish-line photograph of Diane Dixon accompanied the story.

Miss Dixon's time of 52.20 seconds broke a record she had set only hours earlier, when she ran 52.77 in a heat. That time had broken a 20-day-old record of 52.99 seconds, set in Dallas by Valerie Brisco-Hooks, the winner of three gold medals at the Los Angeles Olympics, who also ran consecutive world indoor bests yesterday.

Miss Dixon's record runs became one of the highlights of the meet because of the uncertainty as to whether she would compete at all. Her coach, Fred Thompson, had discussed such a possibility with her Wednesday, in the aftermath of an episode that began Feb. 9 in the Vitalis/U.S. Olympic Invitational in the Meadowlands. There, Mrs. Brisco-Hooks was timed one-hundredth of a second faster than Miss Dixon in a 400-meter race. The finish was so close that upon studying a photograph the next day, Thompson appealed to meet officials to rule the race at least a dead heat, which they eventually did.

But Thursday, after reviewing the finish again, officials reversed the decision, reinstating Mrs. Brisco-Hooks as the winner. As a result, Thompson advised Miss Dixon not to run yesterday, in symbolic protest.

"But that didn't make any sense," Miss Dixon said. "I knew he was going to let me run. He was just upset at the time. He said he never wanted to take anything away from me. I wanted to set the record in the trials. After I did, he said he still wasn't satisfied. So I decided to try again in the final. After that race, I think he was satisfied. I think he had tears in his eyes."

The events entangling Miss Dixon, a 20-year-old sophomore at Baruch College who lives in Brooklyn, and Mrs. Brisco-Hooks have created something of a rivalry. One of the reasons Miss Dixon wanted the first record so much is that she had held it for nearly a year, at 53.17, until Mrs. Brisco-Hooks broke it in Dallas.

This was an electric night for Miss Dixon: She was presented with an Olympic gold medal for being a member of the United States 1,600-meter relay team. As an alternate, she had run the third leg of a first-round race.

Carol Lewis, the American indoor record holder, won her third consecutive meet long-jump championship with a distance of 21 feet 7½ inches, a half-inch off her meet record set last year.

...Alice Brown, the Olympic silver medalist at 100 meters, won the women's 60-yard dash in 6.56 seconds, just missing Evelyn Ashford's world indoor beat of 6.54, set three years ago.

---

60 yard dash
1. Alice Brown, World Class Athletic Club   6.56
2. Brenda Cliette, Bud Light Track America   6.80
3. Jennifer Inniss, Atoms Track Club   6.90

220 yard dash
1. Valerie Brisco-Hooks, World Class Athletic Club   22.95   WR, AR
2. Florence Griffith, World Class Athletic Club   23.38
3. Grace Jackson, Atoms Track Club   24.00

440 yard run
1. Diane Dixon, Atoms Track Club   52.20   AR, WR
2. Andrea Thomas, Dolfin Bronx International   53.45
3. Charmaine Crooks, Bud Light Track America   53.56

880 yard run
1. Cristina Cojocaru, Romania   2:04.15
2. Irina Podyalovskaya, USSR   2:04.73
3. Rose Monday, Puma Track Club   2:05.12

Mobil Mile
1. Doina Melinte, Romania   4:37.00
2. Fita Lovin, Romania   4:38.12
3. Ravilya Agletdinova, USSR   4:39.56

Two mile run
1. Cathy Branta, University of Wisconsin, Madison   9:40.54
2. Maricica Puica, Romania   9:41.60
3. Lynn Jennings, Nike/Boston   9:48.53

60 yard hurdles
1. Candy Young, Puma Track Club   7.57
2. Sharon Danville, New Balance Track Club   7.63
3. Patricia Davis, St. Augustine's College   7.65

One mile walk
1. Teresa Vaill, Island Track Club   6:58.70
2. Maryanne Torrellas, Abraxas Track Club   7:03.43
3. Esther Lopez, Southern California Road Runners   7:04.25

640 yard relay
1. Atoms Track Club   1:09.92
   (Jennifer Inniss, Helena Nelson, Robin DeSeignora,
   Easter Gabriel)
2. Tennessee State University   1:11.05
3. Dynamite Track Club   1:11.91

Sprint medley relay (440-110-110-220)
1. Tennessee State University   1:43.39
   (Maxine McMillan, Barbara Frazier, Jackie Van Zant,
   Angela Williams)
2. Atoms Track Club   1:46.46
3. Police Athletic League   1:46.64

Mile relay
1. Atoms Track Club   3:42.37
   (Grace Jackson, Stephanie Saleem, Robin DeSeignora,
   Diane Dixon)
2. Bud Light Track America   3:43.45
3. Rice University   3:46.50

High jump
1. Coleen Sommer, Atherton Track Club   6' 4¾"
2. Debbie Brill, Pacific Coast Club/Canada   6' 3½"
3. Joni Huntley, Pacific Coast Club   6' 1¼"

Long jump
1. Carol Lewis, University of Houston   21' 7¼"
2. Vali Ionescu, Romania   21' 4"
3. Dorothy Scott, Atoms Track Club   20' 10½"

Shot put
1. Bonnie Dasse, Coast Athletics   60' 6"
2. Regina Cavanaugh, Rice University   54' 11½"
3. Sandra Burke, unattached   54' 10"

Team Champion
Atoms Track Club

Sunkist Invitational: Los Angeles, January 18

The *New York Times* reported: "Mary Decker, competing tonight for the first time since her controversial collision with Zola Budd in the Olympics last August, ran a world-indoor best in the 2,000-meter run with a time of 5 minutes 34.52 seconds in the Sunkist Invitational indoor track meet at the Los Angeles Memorial Sports Arena. Miss Decker, who broke immediately to the lead and never trailed, finished more than 11 seconds ahead of Ruth Wysocki, who defeated her at 1,500 meters in last July's Olympic trials."

60 yards	
1. Alice Brown, World Class Athletic Club	6.72
440 yards	
1. Valerie Brisco-Hooks, World Class Athletic Club	53.41
800 meters	
1. Lee Arbogast, Athletics West	2:08.3
2000 meters	
1. Mary Decker, Athletics West	5:34.52 WR
High jump	
1. Debbie Brill, Canada	6' 5"

Vince Reel, editor of Women's *Track & Field World* commented, "That was it. Four women's events."

4th IAAF World Cup: Bruce Stadium, Canberra, Australia, October 4–6

100 meters	
7. Kathrene Wallace	11.86
200 meters	
5. Pam Marshall	23.15
400 meters	
3. Lillie Leatherwood	50.43
800 meters	
5. Joetta Clark	2:03.81
3000 meters	
3. Cindy Bremser	9:21.15
10,000 meters	
2. Mary Knisley	32:19.93
100 meter hurdles	
7. Pam Page	13.49
400 meter hurdles	
2. Judi Brown-King	55.10
4 × 100 meter relay	
5. USA	44.03
(Pam Page, Ella Smith, Susan Shurr, Pam Marshall)	

4 × 400 meter relay
5. USA   3:30.99
    (Susan Shurr, Roberta Belle, Judi Brown-King, Lillie Leatherwood)

High jump
7. Coleen Sommer   5' 10¾"

Long jump
3. Carol Lewis   22' 7"

Shot put
6. Ramona Pagel   56' 9½"

Discus
6. Carol Cady   185' 5"

Javelin
8. Cathy Sulinski   176' 5"

Team score:
5. USA 61

1st World Indoor Games: Palais Omnisports de Paris-Bercy, Paris, France, January 18–19

The inaugural World Indoor Games attracted 379 athletes from 144 countries. Almost 10,000 spectators watched the competition on the final day.

200 meters
5. Mary Bolden   23.89

400 meters
1. Diane Dixon   53.35

3000 meters
3. PattiSue Plumer   9:12.12

60 meter hurdles
4. Stephanie Hightower   8.12

3000 meter walk
6. Teresa Vaill   13:59.56   AR
    (betters American indoor record of 14:32.4 by
    Susan Liers-Westerfield, 1981)

Shot put
5. Ramona Pagel   56' 9¼"
8. Carol Cady   50' 8"

USA–USSR–Japan Triangular Meet: Olympic Stadium, Tokyo, Japan, September 21–22

100 meters
3. Pam Marshall   11.45
5. Kathrene Wallace   11.72

200 meters
4. Pam Marshall   22.96
5. Ella Smith   23.64

400 meters
3. Lillie Leatherwood   53.07
4. Roberta Belle   54.72

800 meters
3. Joetta Clark   2:04.59
5. Suzanne Girard   2:10.01

1500 meters
3. Leanne Warren   4:12.89
4. Suzanne Girard   4:22.79

3000 meters
1. Mary Knisley   8:49.97
4. Kathy Hayes   9:06.97

10,000 meters
3. Kellie Cathey   33:39.58
5. Robyn Root   35:18.43

100 meter hurdles
3. Pam Page   13.60

400 meter hurdles
3. Judi Brown-King   57.07
4. Schowonda Williams   59.95

4 × 100 meter relay
2. USA   43.59
   (Kathrene Wallace, Susan Shurr, Ella Smith,
   Pam Marshall)

4 × 400 meter relay
2. USA   3:34.69
   (Roberta Belle, Susan Shurr, Judi Brown-King,
   Lillie Leatherwood)

High jump
5. Jan Chesbro and Jan Clough   6' ¾"

Long jump
3. Carol Lewis   22' 9¾"
4. Sabrina Williams   19' 10¼"

Shot put
3. Ramona Pagel   55' 7½"
4. Peggy Pollock   54' 6"

Discus
3. Carol Cady   197' 8"
4. Penny Neer   179' 5"

Javelin
4. Lori Mercer   168' 9"
5. Cathy Sulinski   166' 3"

Team scores:

USSR	117	USA	50
USSR	120	Japan	48
USA	107	Japan	60

U.S. Women's Marathon Championships: Sacramento, California, December 1

1. Nancy Ditz	2:31:36
2. Janis Klecker	2:31:53
3. Maureen Custy	2:34:17
4. Margaret Cooke	2:35:39
5. Sue Schneider	2:35:59
6. Deborah Raunig	2:36:24

1st IAAF World Cup Marathon Championships: Hiroshima, Japan, April 13–14

29. Nancy Ditz	2:45:53
31. Debbie Raunig	2:46:13

U.S. Women's 10 Kilometer Road Race: Albany, New York, May 18 (Freihofer's Run for Women)

1. Betty Springs and Francie Larrieu Smith	32:14
3. Lynn Jennings	32:26
4. Lesley Welch	32:40
5. Suzanne Girard	33:00
6. Jan Merrill	33:06
403 finishers	

World Cross Country Championships: Lisbon, Portugal, March 24

5000 meters	
2. Cathy Branta	15:24
9. Betty Springs	15:44
15. Shelly Steely	15:51
16. Kate Keyes	15:54

The United States won with 42 points.

Other meet results:

The inaugural IAAF/Mobil Grand Prix meet hosted athletes from 21 countries at Bruce Jenner's Bud Light Classic on May 25th in San Jose, California.

There were six women's events: 100 meters, 200 meters, 800 meters, 400 meter hurdles, 3000 meters, and the high jump. There were twelve events on the men's program.

100 meters	
1. Valerie Brisco-Hooks	11.01 w
3. Alice Brown	11.15

200 meters	
2. Diane Dixon	22.92
3. Brenda Cliette	22.95

800 meters	
2. Joetta Clark	2:01.83
3. Robin Campbell	2:02.20

3000 meters	
1. Francie Larrieu	8:50.54
3. Lynn Jennings	9:05.65

400 meter hurdles	
1. Judi Brown-King	55.41
2. Tonja Brown	55.89
3. Sharrieffa Barksdale	58.03

High jump	
2. Louise Ritter	6' 3½"

Other News and Honors

Track & Field News: Athlete of the Year

Mary Slaney

USA Rankings — Track & Field News

1. Mary Slaney
2. Jackie Joyner
3. Valerie Brisco-Hooks
4. Joan Benoit
5. Judi Brown-King

World Rankings — Track & Field News

3. Mary Slaney
8. Jackie Joyner
9. Valerie Brisco-Hooks
10. Joan Benoit

At the Weltklasse Meet in Zurich, Switzerland on August 21, Valerie Brisco-Hooks won the 100 meters in 11.01 and later completed a splendid double by winning the 200 meters in 21.98, beating both the world leaders in the 100 and 200 meters: Marlies Gohr and Marita Koch.

Mary Decker-Slaney ran a close race against Zola Budd and Maricica Puica. All three runners passed the 1500 meter mark in four minutes flat. Mary held off a challenging Puica and won in a new world record time of 4:16.71.

Jackie Joyner, in finishing second in the long jump, set a new American record of 23' 9".

The IAAF World 15km Road Race Championship for Women was held in Gateshead, England on November 2. Judi St. Hilaire finished 50 meters behind the winner to take second in 49:25. Nancy Ditz was 16th in 51:57, Carol Urish-McLatchie 19th, and Sue Schneider 30th. The United States team placed third overall.

The outdoor Grand Prix became a reality in 1985.

Lynn Jennings won the national cross country championships. This was her first win.

Joan Benoit won the Sullivan Award.

Vince Reel, the editor of *Women's Track & Field World*, wrote in the May 1985 issue, "There will be just one more issue of *WTFW*."

Interview: Claudette Groenendaal

(December 5, 2005) I started running track in seventh grade. My first race was the 1320, which is three laps and I was third out of three people [laughter]. Then I went on to win the city meet from there. I was just stuck in that event, three laps. Of course, as I got older, they did not have that event. So, I did the 800 or the 1500 and found that I really enjoyed it. I worked hard at it and really did well.

I competed in junior high. As I competed, I would only just look at the next step ahead. In junior high I would only look to high school. Once I got to high school I thought about colleges. It never really occurred to me that one day I would be making a living doing what I was doing. It was something I never thought of. I just didn't know that people did that.

My sophomore year in high school, I defeated the big champion in Oregon and surprised everyone. I guess that was my high school claim to fame. I ran the 1500 in 4:24.

I selected the University of Oregon. It was a really fabulous place for a runner to be. The decision to go there was tough because there was another school that I was looking at, Stanford. I ultimately chose Oregon. There's just such a magic about the stadium and the arena. I remember as a high schooler going down for meets and just being so excited at seeing Rudy Chappa in the stands and getting to see him run, and Alberto (Salazar) and just so many fabulous meets. I have to say that excitement and that magic never left throughout all my years of running there. It's just really fabulous, as a Duck, to go to the meets even for regular dual meets and start to hear the announcers and you just get so excited. I know it wouldn't have been the same if I had gone to any other school in the country. I just can't imagine that same atmosphere. Eugene loves their runners and treats them very well. So, there were always articles in the paper, it was just a fabulous place to run, really wonderful.

My first two years at Oregon I ran cross country and I ran track and I improved. I wasn't anything to write home about. I went to nationals both years in the 1500 and made it to the final. I don't even remember, maybe I got eleventh one year, maybe I got twelfth the other year. I know I made it to the final and I know that I wasn't last but I was probably close to it. My times improved. I went from 4:24 probably to 4:19 and then 4:18.

My junior year was a big, big year for me. I ran indoors, 800 meters, and I think I got fourth in indoor nationals. I ran 2:07, which was a big PR, and then our first outdoor meet I ran 2:04, which was a huge PR for me. So, I went from the prior year, my best time being, I think, 2:11 in the 800. I concentrated on the 800 and then ultimately, that summer I went to Europe with Nike and I ran 1:59 in my very last race of the season. It was like a ten second difference. 2:04 was a huge milestone. It was at the Berkeley meet during spring break and then I went to nationals and I doubled in the 800 and 1500. I won the 1500. I shocked everyone. I remember thinking to myself with a lap to go, "If I'm there, no one is going to beat me." When you get in a bit of a zone, you just react. You don't think, you react and that's how my best races always are. You can hear the crowd from a distance but know nothing in particular. It's almost like they are far away and I just reacted. I would feel my races, not think them. I won, which was great. The next day I ran the 800 and got second. I used to suffer from blisters really badly. I remember not even being able to warm down after my 1500. My feet were throbbing all night long. It was almost like having severe burns. The blood would seep through my spikes. I wouldn't be able to take my spikes or my socks off without pulling off the skin. I would never feel it during the race. If I felt it during the race, I knew I was having a disastrous race. That was the case. I came back and ran the 800 and got second to Joetta Clark. That was '84. Then I went to the trials and ran a PR to make it to the finals and ran a PR in my first lap of the 800 [laughter] but still got sixth and ran a 2:02, so it was a second off the PR I set the day before. For me, it was the first time with the big guys and my first trials and I doubled with the 1500. I had all these intense, intense races in a week. It was very exciting.

Then I went to Europe. My first race was in Oslo and Doina Melinte, who became the Olympic champ that summer, was in the race. She won the race but there were a few British girls and people who had much faster times than I had. But I had the benefit of not knowing who they were. A few of them were a little bit prissy-looking and I remember thinking to myself, "There's no way in hell I'm going to let that girl beat me." One of them was one of my favorite athletes from another country. We became really good friends. Doina Melinte took the lead and with about a 300, 200 to go, I was getting really jostled around by all these girls who were a lot more aggressive. It was my first European race. The Bislett stadium again, in Europe, for me is like Eugene is. Two of the prissy-looking English girls passed me. So, of course, I had to beat them. I ended up knocking a second off and running 2 flat and getting second. I had six or seven more races that summer and my last race was in Oslo again. The whole summer, I really wanted to go under two minutes. When you're not in a race, the night before you think of exactly what the splits should be. The first 200 will be this, the next one and the 600 will be — it all seems so easy and doable when you are mapping it out the night before. But it doesn't work that way in a race. But I did it. It was my last race and I ran 1:59.98. That was really a turning point for me. I tell this to other runners who are striving for the sub 2 mark. You strive and strive for it and it's much more difficult because you're tense. It's something you're trying so hard for and you are trying to force it. Once you do it, it's that much easier to repeat it because you don't think about it. For me, I'm much better when I don't think about my race. I have to feel it and I have to react. It's not something I can tell myself to do. Your body just takes over. It doesn't always happen. My best races have always been feeling and reacting to the situation and racing — being competitive. Seeing an athlete and wanting to beat them and not thinking about what's going on. So, that was a turning point for me in 1984 because going into 1984 my best was 2:09 and I'd run 2:07 indoors; 2:04 the first race and then 1:59. So it was a huge breakthrough for me.

The next year at NCAAs I flipped what I did before. I won the 800 and set an NCAA record, which has been broken. I got second in the 1500 to Kathy Branta who then went on to double. She won the 3,000 as well. She's a really lovely girl. A week after that were outdoor nationals. It was my first test with the outdoor athletes where I was viable. I had gotten sixth in the trials in 1984. When I went to Europe I had beaten most of the Americans. But domestically I hadn't gone to a nationals and been one of the big players. I remember being very nervous going into the race [laughter]. I certainly wasn't expecting that I would go in and win. It's funny, because when I see tapes of that race, even knowing the final outcome, I still get nervous. That's exactly how I feel. At one point it looks like I'm not going to win. But then I do and it's great. I remember a great feeling of elation. It was similar to what I felt in '84 when I won the NCAAs in the 1500. It was like I was floating on a cloud. It was just the most amazing, incredible experience. There is just nothing quite like it. It was fabulous.

After that I went to Europe. In the interim, I actually started training with Luiz de Oliveira, the Brazilian coach. I trained with my college coach up through nationals and I started training with Luiz right after that. What we started to do immediately was to work on my speed, which was helpful in the 800. Other athletes that I competed with had 50 or 51 second quarter speed. My best was 56, I think. So when at the trials, my first lap was a 57, which was a second off my PR, I thought about it, which you should never do. "Wow, that's a second off my PR."

I had a summer of just amazing races and workouts where I was setting PRs, running a 54 on the way to a 500. We spent, between the first and second break, two or three weeks in Berne. At the end of that time, training like crazy, there was a race in Berne, which is where Mary set the American record 1:56.98. I was second in 1:58.33. It never occurred to me that that would be my fastest 800. Unfortunately, it was. Just on a side note, Mary and I warmed down together. I was always famous for my slow jogs warming down and warming up. She was notorious for running quickly. What she did on her warm downs was like four miles or something like that. I was so happy about what I did. I was elated. We were running and it was quite a bit faster than I wanted it to be, but I was too embarrassed to say anything. Then I started concentrating on noticing my breathing. I didn't want to show that I was feeling the exertion from the warm down. That just exacerbated it. It was quite a difficult run because I spent too much time trying not to breathe hard and it was a very uncomfortable run. That's just a funny side story.

1986 was another good year. I won nationals in the 800. Grand Prix was the 1500 in Europe that summer. I didn't get the opportunity to run as many 800s. I did run 1:58.55 but it wasn't a

PR. I ran a PR 1500 in Cologne, West Germany, 4:04.63. With 300 to go, there were about sixteen or seventeen women in the race — another one where I looked at it, you get nervous and you hope you do well — 300 to go and I was probably towards the back. I just said, "This is enough. There are so many people." I just got outside and raced it in and ran my PR. I think I was fourth; it might have been third.

Then in '87 I remember going into the year thinking if I only ran a 1:57 I would be disappointed. My training was going great. I was just getting stronger and stronger. The problem was, I think, I just did too much. I always had to monitor my anemia levels. I still trained and competed and went to Europe. I ran 1:59 but I got seventh at nationals and ran 2:01, which was exactly what I ran my first race of the season at Mt. Sac. I ran 2:01, 60.-60. We trained really well. It was a better training year than the year before. My body started crumbling, which it continued to do.

In '88, I moved to southern California and started training with Joe (Douglas) and the Santa Monica Track Club. I had periods where my training was incredible. Joe thought I would run — we thought I'd break all my old times with no problem. I'd have serious periods where I'd do 1200s in 3:12, just great, great training. Unfortunately, I had the anemia problems and I had undiagnosed thyroid problems. I think what happened was with all the training, it just caused different aspects to break down. I wasn't ever able to pin point it.

So, '85 and '86 were my best years and I had snippets. I continued to train and compete in Europe through '92–'93. I continued to go to the trials but I wasn't able to get back to where I was before. I never felt like I reached my potential. I learned a lot. If I were to go back, I would do things differently but I feel that I didn't come close to running my best times.

I was twenty-one and twenty-two when I ran my best times. I'm a very hard worker. I think I have a good attitude also. I get nervous but not unduly so. I run well under pressure. I had times where it looked like things would come together. I'd go to nationals and my iron levels would be really low. I'd start the season and my ferriten level would be, say, 120, and every six weeks I'd have it checked. It would go down twenty points and by the time I'd go to nationals, it would be really low.

In '96, actually the fall of '95, I was having problems where I couldn't even keep up with my teammates on jogs. That's when I was diagnosed with a thyroid problem. Around Thanksgiving of '95, I started taking thyroid medication and I felt an improvement almost immediately. I took each day as it came and worked as hard as I could on each day without worrying about the Olympic trials or getting ahead of myself. I made it to the trials. Unfortunately I was not fast enough to make the team. I ran 4:10 that summer, but it wasn't fast enough.

I had probably ten years of competing in Europe. I had the luxury of getting paid to do what I would have done anyway — what I loved to do, competing in Oslo, Zurich and all over. Oslo will always be one of my most special places to race because, until my last year, I'd always had great races there. I think I ran three PRs there. I will always have a fond place in my heart for Oslo. It's an amazing stadium. The stands are so close to the track. The spectators pound against the stands. There was electricity in the air. The races were always at night. It was magical as were all the races.

If you had told me as a seventh grader or even a tenth grader that I would then go on to do that, I didn't even know that existed. It was just really — I got to live a fantasy that all my running friends couldn't even have dreamed of. It was just an amazing experience that I will always cherish.

6

1986

The Outdoor Nationals

The 111th Annual USA/Mobil United States Outdoor Track and Field Championships were held in Eugene, Oregon at Hayward Field, University of Oregon from June 18 through June 21.

The *New York Times* on June 22 reported that a crowd of 8,488 watched the 23 finals on a sunny, breezy day, and described Diane Dixon's win in the 400 meters.

Miss Dixon is a 21-year-old Baruch College junior from Brooklyn. She has won the national 440-yard indoor title five times in six years.

Though she was favored here, her task was not easy. Hay fever made it difficult for her to breathe in this unofficial hay-fever capital of America. But she led from the start and won by 5 meters in 50.41 seconds. She had hoped to break 50 seconds for the first time, but she said that was unimportant.

"I'm small," she said, "and all that wind on the backstretch made it difficult. But there was no pain and no tension.

"Can you believe it? I'm a national champion, the champion of my country. We have 200 million people, and a little girl from Brooklyn won her first national championship. I'm still young and growing and learning. I'm not near my peak."

In the women's 1,500, Linda Detlefsen of Lake Ronkonkoma, L.I., held off Chris Mullen Gregorek by inches in 4 minutes 8.00 seconds, the fastest by an American this year.

"I never saw Chris," said a relieved Miss Detlefsen. "I have never been so nervous in my life."

The women's 400-meter hurdles were heartbreaking for Sharrieffa Barksdale. She was leading the favored Judi Brown-King by 3 meters when she ticked the 10th and final hurdle and fell. Mrs. Brown-King went on to win in 55.46 for her third straight national title. Miss Barksdale picked herself up and trotted in last in 58.65.

"I don't know if I could have caught her," said Mrs. Brown-King. "I feel bad for her."

---

100 meters
1. Pam Marshall, Mazda Track Club   10.80 w
2. Alice Brown, World Class Athletic Club   10.84
3. Evelyn Ashford, Mazda Track Club   10.85
4. Diane Williams, Puma Track Club   10.92
5. Gail Devers, World Class Athletic Club   11.00
6. Michelle Finn, Atoms Track Club   11.17

200 meters
1. Pam Marshall, Mazda Track Club   22.24 w

2. Randy Givens, Puma Track Club ... 22.70
3. Gwen Torrence, Georgia Track Club ... 23.01
4. Dannette Young, Alabama Agricultural & Mechanical University ... 23.06
5. Michelle Finn, Atoms Track Club ... 23.14
6. Odessa Smalls, unattached ... 23.47

400 meters
1. Diane Dixon, Atoms Track Club ... 50.41
2. Lillie Leatherwood, New Balance Track Club ... 51.29
3. Brenda Cliette, unattached ... 51.82
4. Chandra Cheeseborough, Athletics West ... 51.86
5. Alice Jackson, Mazda Track Club ... 52.37
6. Denean Howard, Puma Track Club ... 52.79

800 meters
1. Claudette Groenendaal, Athletics West ... 1:59.79
2. Delisa Walton-Floyd, Puma Track Club ... 2:00.00
3. Joetta Clark, Athletics West ... 2:00.32
4. Julie Jenkins, Brigham Young Track Club ... 2:01.55
5. Tina Parrott, Indiana Track Club ... 2:02.25
6. Essie Kelley, unattached ... 2:02.47

1500 meters
1. Linda Detlefsen, Athletics West ... 4:08.00
2. Chris Gregorek, Team Nike ... 4:08.02
3. Sue Addison, Reebok Racing Club ... 4:08.75
4. Alisa Harvey, Knoxville Track Club ... 4:08.95
5. Evelyn Adiru, Westchester Puma Track Club/Uganda ... 4:09.61
6. Lynn Jennings, Athletics West ... 4:10.87

3000 meters
1. Mary Knisley, New Balance Track Club ... 8:46.18
2. Cindy Bremser, Wisconsin United Track Club ... 8:46.56
3. PattiSue Plumer, Puma Track Club ... 8:52.57
4. Lesley Welch, Puma Track Club ... 8:52.60
5. Leslie Seymour, Club Sota ... 8:53.10
6. Brenda Webb, Puma Track Club ... 8:56.08

5000 meters
1. Betty Springs, Athletics West ... 15:30.99 MR
   (previous record 15:57.50 by Suzanne Girard, 1985)
2. Lorraine Moller, New Zealand ... 15:32.90
3. PattiSue Plumer, Puma Track Club ... 15:35.00
4. Suzanne Girard, Puma Track Club ... 15:41.77
5. Margaret Thomas, Athletics West ... 16:03.80

10,000 meter run
1. Nan Doak-Davis, Athletics West ... 32:29.68
2. Lynn Nelson, Reebok Racing Club ... 32:30.24
3. Marty Cooksey, Team Kangaroo ... 32:34.73
4. Ellen Reynolds, Etonic Track Club ... 32:49.05
5. Midde Hamrin, Sweden ... 32:50.00
6. Kathy Pfiefer, Reebok Racing Club ... 33:20.30

10,000 meter walk

1. Debbi Lawrence, unattached	50:28.86
2. Teresa Vaill, Team Rockport	50:55.81
3. Susan Liers, Team Rockport	51:29.90
4. Gwen Robertson, Team Rockport	53:12.77
5. Lisa Vaill, Team Rockport	53:32.17
6. Karen Rezach, Shore Athletic Club	54:01.5 ht

100 meter hurdles

1. Benita Fitzgerald-Brown, Mazda Track Club	12.83 w
2. Stephanie Hightower, unattached	12.90
3. Pam Page, Los Angeles Track Club	12.91
and Rosalind Council, Team Etonic	
5. LaVonna Martin, Team Nike	13.03
6. Sophia Hunter, Atoms Track Club	13.06

400 meter hurdles

1. Judi Brown-King, Athletics West	55.46
2. Sandra Farmer, Jamaica	56.25
3. Schowonda Williams, Louisiana State Track Club	56.48
4. LaTanya Sheffield, Mazda Track Club	56.62
5. Leisa Davis-Knowles, Oklahoma State Track Club	56.76
6. Gayle Kellon, World Class Athletic Club	57.96

800 meter sprint medley relay (100-100-200-400)

1. Southern California Cheetahs	1:40.1
(Lydia DeVega, Gayle Watkins, Gervaise McCraw, Janeen Vickers)	

No other entries

4 × 880 yard relay

1. Club Northwest	8:45.9 ht
(Sarah Bolender, Cynthia Henry-Balles, Susan Gregg, Sandra Gregg)	
2. Coast Athletics	8:45.9
3. Metroplex Striders	8:47.5

Triple jump

1. Wendy Brown, Puma Track Club	45' 2½" w
2. Sheila Hudson, South Bay Track Club	44' w
3. Yvette Bates, Southern California Cheetahs	42' 11"
4. Terri Turner, Team Nike	42' 9"
5. Janet Diggs, unattached	42' 4"
6. Renita Robinson, South Bay Track Club	42'

Sheila Hudson set a meet record of 43' 8¾" with her only non-windy jump; previous record 43' 2½" by Wendy Brown, 1985.

High jump

1. Louise Ritter, Pacific Coast Club	6' 4"
2. Jan Chesbro, Puma Track Club	6' 4"
3. Camille Harding, unattached	6' 2¾"
4. Katrena Johnson, University of Arizona	6' 1½"
5. Rita Graves, Kansas State University and	6' ½"
Latrese Johnson, University of California, Fresno	

Long jump
1. Carol Lewis, Santa Monica Track Club   22' 9" w
2. Sheila Echols, Louisiana State Track Club   22' 7¼" w
3. Jodi Anderson, Los Angeles Track Club   21' 10¾" w
4. Jennifer Inniss, Atoms Track Club   21' 10¼" w
5. Sabrina Williams, Coast Athletics   21' 9½" w
6. Dorothea Brown, Wisconsin United Track Club   20' 10¾" w

Discus
1. Carol Cady, Stanford Track Club   205' 9"
2. Ramona Pagel, Mazda Track Club   192' 1"
3. Pia Iacovo, Taunton Athletic Club   187' 4"
4. Becky Levi, unattached   186'
5. Lorna Griffin, unattached   182' 1"
6. Bonnie Dasse, Coast Athletics   179' 4"

Shot put
1. Ramona Pagel, Mazda Track Club   61' 1½"
2. Bonnie Dasse, Coast Athletics   59' 6¾"
3. Carol Cady, Stanford Track Club   55' 4¾"
4. Peggy Pollock, Coast Athletics   55'
5. Pam Dukes, Puma Track Club   54' 11½"
6. Connie Price, University of Chicago Track Club   53' 9"

Javelin
1. Helena Uusitalo, Finland   191' 9"
2. Donna Mayhew, unattached   183' 9"
3. Karen Szarkowski, University of Nebraska   182' 10"
4. Karin Smith, Athletics West   182' 8"
5. Cathy Sulinski, Puma Track Club   176' 11"
6. Lynda Hughes-Sutfin, Mazda Track Club   175' 5"

Heptathlon
1. Jane Frederick, Athletics West   6230
2. Cindy Greiner, Athletics West   6208
3. Jolanda Jones, University of Houston   5692
4. Lana Zimmerman, Louisiana State University Track Club   5613
5. Cathey Tyree, Purdue University   5563
6. Trish King, unattached   5442

Team scores:
1. Athletics West   85
2. Puma Track Club   72
3. Mazda Track Club   61

The Indoor Nationals

The indoor nationals were held in Madison Square Garden on Friday, February 28. An article appeared in the *New York Times* on the day of the meet predicting that Diane Dixon would run the fastest 400 of her life. "Diane Dixon of the Atoms Track Club is ready, according to her coach, Fred Thompson, 'to run the fastest quarter-mile of her life.' She is entered in the 440 after having set a world indoor best in the 500 last Friday at Los Angeles. In fact, in each of her seven major meets this season, she has established an American, meet or world best."

Jane Frederick (left) and Patty Van Wolvelaere, 1996.

However, a new record was not to be.

"Miss Dixon, unbeaten this indoor season, had a terrific struggle at the start," reported the *New York Times*.

"My coach said, whatever you do, don't let her get in front of you," she explained, referring to Sabine Busch of East Germany. Miss Dixon was in lane 2, next to Miss Busch. When they came off the first turn, the German got the lead briefly, but suddenly Miss Dixon sprinted for the next 15 yards, regained the lead, and never lost it.

"That was a tough one," she said. "I ran scared. I didn't run against the clock as I usually do. I just ran to win."

---

60 yard dash
1. Jeanette Bolden, World Class Athletic Club   6.57
2. Marlies Gohr, German Democratic Republic   6.62
3. Alice Brown, World Class Athletic Club   6.63

200 meters
1. Marita Koch, German Democratic Republic   22.89
2. Grace Jackson, Atoms Track Club   23.11
3. Florence Griffith, World Class Athletic Club   23.57

440 yard run
1. Diane Dixon, Atoms Track Club   52.52
2. Sabine Busch, German Democratic Republic   52.70
3. Charmaine Crooks, Mazda Track Club   53.77

800 meters
1. Sigrun Ludwigs, German Democratic Republic   2:05.93

2. Christina Cojocaru, Romania	2:06.65
3. Delisa Walton-Floyd, Puma Track Club	2:06.72

Mobil mile

1. Maricica Puica, Romania	4:35.00
2. Doina Melinte, Romania	4:35.30
3. Jo White, unattached	4:36.04

Two mile run

1. Lynn Jennings, Athletics West	9:28.15
2. Cindy Bremser, Wisconsin United Track Club	9:28.29
3. Ines Bibernell, German Democratic Republic	9:34.27

60 yard hurdles

1. Stephanie Hightower, unattached	7.44
2. Kerstin Knabe, German Democratic Republic	7.46
3. Yolanda Johnson, Colorado Flyers	7.52

3000 meter walk

1. Teresa Vaill, unattached	6:53.58
2. Lynn Weik, State University of New York/Stony Brook	6:56.27
3. Debbi Lawrence, Kansas City Walkers	7:09.83

One mile relay

1. Atoms Track Club	3:44.23
(Helene Nelson, Diane Dixon, Easter Gabriel, Grace Jackson)	
2. Delaware State College	3:46.06
3. Police Athletic League	3:48.19

High jump

1. Debbie Brill, Pacific Coast Club/Canada	6' 5½"
2. Andrea Bienias, German Democratic Republic	6' 4"
3. Joni Huntley, Pacific Coast Club	6' 2¼"

Long jump

1. Heike Drechsler, German Democratic Republic	23' ¾"
2. Jackie Joyner-Kersee, World Class Athletic Club	22' 10½"
3. Helga Radtke, German Democratic Republic	22' 4¼"

Shot put

1. Ramona Pagel, Mazda Track Club	60' 1¾"
2. Peggy Pollock, Coast Athletics	57' 7½"
3. Regina Cavanaugh, Rice University	55' 1"

Team Champion
Atoms Track Club

Sunkist Invitational (3 women's events): Los Angeles, January 17

60 yards

1. Nellie Cooman, Holland	6.71

800 meters

1. Jarmila Kratochvilova, Czechoslovakia	2:06.08

Mile
1. Lynn Williams, Canada   4:27.77

U.S. Marathon Championships (Twin Cities Marathon): Minneapolis, Minnesota, October 12

1. Kim Rosenquist	2:32:31	
2. Nancy Ditz	2:34:50	
3. Connie Prince	2:35:26	
4. Cathie Twomey	2:35:42	
5. Janice Ettle	2:37:23	

1st Goodwill Games: Lenin Stadium, Moscow, July 5–9

In the inaugural Goodwill Games, Jackie Joyner broke the world heptathlon record by over 200 points and became the first athlete over the 7000 point barrier. Her total of 7148 points included an American record in the 100 meter hurdles (12.85).

Ken Bastian described the final minutes in *Moscow '86 Goodwill Games*:

As Jackie Joyner stretched her weary legs just before her final event in the heptathlon — the 800 meters — the P.A. announcer boomed, in an unmistakably Russian accent, "We all hope Jackie Joyner will make it."

Joyner dug in her spikes for the start. She needed a time of 2:24.64. In the stands, her husband and coach Bob Kersee buried his head in his hands, unable to watch. Two minutes and 10.02 seconds later, Kersee peeked through his fingers to see his wife burst across the finish line to become the world's best all-around female athlete. The crowd roared its approval as the new world record holder, waving a red rose high in the air, made her victory lap while Kersee celebrated his wife's triumph with a victory dance of his own. "To do what Jackie has done is almost unheard of," he raved. "This is one of those magical moments in an athlete's life."

The *New York Times* reported, "Miss Ashford edged Heike Drechsler of East Germany in the 100-meter dash, with both clocking in at a sparkling 10.91 seconds."

100 meters		
1. Evelyn Ashford	10.91	
4. Alice Brown	11.14	
200 meters		
1. Pam Marshall	22.12	
4. Gwen Torrence	22.53	
5. Randy Givens	22.61	
(Race run in two sections)		
400 meters		
3. Lillie Leatherwood	50.47	
4. Diane Dixon	50.77	
12. Alice Jackson	52.91	
(Race run in two sections)		
800 meters		
7. Claudette Groenendaal	1:59.31	
8. Delisa Walton-Floyd	2:01.98	

1500 meters
7. Chris Gregorek   4:10.79
8. Linda Detlefsen   4:10.92

3000 meters
5. PattiSue Plumer   8:46.24
6. Mary Knisley   8:49.00
8. Cindy Bremser   8:53.74

5000 meters
3. Cindy Bremser   15:11.78
5. PattiSue Plumer   15:20.88
9. Betty Springs   15:41.39
14. Sue King   16:04.68
15. Joan Nesbit   16:08.50

400 meter hurdles
6. Judi Brown-King   56.06
8. Schowonda Williams   56.83
      (Race run in two sections)

Marathon
6. Katy Schilly-Laetsch   2:36:22
7. Maureen Custy   2:36:44
10. Julie Isphording   2:39:42

4 × 100 meter relay
1. USA   42.12
      (Michelle Finn, Diane Williams, Randy Givens, Evelyn Ashford)

10 kilometer walk
17. Teresa Vaill   51:19:50
19. Susan Liers   52:00:61
20. Debbi Lawrence-Spino   52:15:87

High jump
7. Louise Ritter (tie)   6' 2¼"
10. Jan Chesbro   5' 10¾"

Long jump
5. Carol Lewis   22' 7¾"
9. Sheila Echols   22' 1½"

Shot put
8. Bonnie Dasse   60' 1¾"
9. Ramona Pagel   57' 3¾"

Discus
9. Carol Cady   195' 9"
12. Ramona Pagel   176' 3"

Javelin
6. Donna Mayhew   184' 4"
7. Karen Szarkowski   165' 6"

Heptathlon
1. Jackie Joyner   7148   WR
11. Cindy Greiner   6095
17. Lana Zimmerman   4718

1st World Junior Championships

The 1st World Junior Championships were held in Athens, Greece from July 16 through July 20. 1,188 athletes representing 143 countries took part.

100 meters	
2. Caryl Smith	11.46
3. Maicel Malone	11.49
100 meter hurdles	
3. Tanya Davis	13.46
400 meter hurdles	
2. Kellie Roberts	56.80
4 × 100 meter relay	
1. United States	43.78
(Carlette Guidry, Caryl Smith, Denise Liles, Maicel Malone)	
4 × 400 meter relay	
1. United States	3:30.45
(Gisele Harris, Kandice Pritchett, Tasha Downing, Janeene Vickers)	

Pan American Junior Track and Field Championships: Winter Park, Florida July 4–6

100 meters	
1. Caryl Smith	11.56 w
200 meters	
1. Carlette Guidry	23.73
Long jump	
1. Carlette Guidry	21' ¾"
1500 meters	
1. Suzy Favor	4:26.84
100 meter hurdles	
1. Yolanda Johnson	13.38
Shot put	
1. Brandi Gail	46' 3¼"
4 × 100 meter relay	
1. USA	44.62
4 × 400 meter relay	
1. USA	3:35.81

The American women listed below were in the top 50 IAAF/Mobil Grand Prix.

5. Evelyn Ashford	16. PattiSue Plumer	33. Sue Addison
7. Valerie Brisco-Hooks	21. Benita Fitzgerald-Brown	43. Jackie Joyner-Kersee
8. Diane Dixon	22. Mary Knisley	45. Stephanie Hightower
12. Lillie Leatherwood	29. Pam Marshall	

Other News and Honors

Track & Field News: Athlete of the Year

Jackie Joyner-Kersee

Jackie Joyner-Kersee broke the world heptathlon record two times in twenty-six days. She became the first athlete to score more than 7,000 points and first American woman to dominate a multi-event.

USA Rankings — Track & Field News

1. Jackie Joyner-Kersee
2. Evelyn Ashford
3. Valerie Brisco-Hooks

4. Pam Marshall
5. Carol Cady

World Rankings — Track & Field News

1. Jackie Joyner-Kersee

8. Evelyn Ashford

Debbie Raunig was ranked in the top twenty performers in the world in the marathon with a time of 2:31:33.

Lesley Welch won the USA cross country championships.

Lynn Jennings placed second in the world cross country championships.

Diane Dixon bettered her indoor American record in the 400 meters in the 17th Annual Vitalis/U.S. Olympic Invitational indoor track meet on February 8. Her American record time was 52.13.

At the Los Angeles Times-GTE meet on February 22, Diane Dixon ran the fastest 500 yards indoors, setting a new world record of 1:02.29.

Jackie Joyner-Kersee broke the world record that she set in the Goodwill Games in Moscow in July during the United States Olympic Sports Festival in Houston, Texas in August. Her point total for the new heptathlon world record was 7,161.

No women athletes, coaches or contributors were enshrined in the National Track and Field Hall of Fame this year.

Jackie Joyner-Kersee won the Sullivan Award.

7

1987

The Outdoor Nationals

The USA TAC/Mobil National Outdoor Track and Field Championships were held in San Jose, California from June 23–27.

"The sun is blazing. The air is warm and dry. The Santa Cruz mountains loom in the background, providing a majestic view from the stadium at San Jose City College," wrote Michael Janofsky for the *New York Times*. He continues:

> But the talk is not so much of the USA/Mobil Track and Field Championships, which began today with competition in the women's heptathlon and the men's decathlon. No, for all the beauty and pristine weather of northern California and Jackie Joyner-Kersee's attempt to set another world record in the heptathlon, thoughts are centered many thousands of miles away — on Rome, where the world track and field championships will be held in August. Only the top three finishers in events here will qualify for Rome.
>
> ...The appeal of Rome, aside from the city itself, is the magnitude of the event. Not since the last world championships of 1983 in Helsinki will so many elite athletes have competed against each other. When Eastern bloc nations boycotted the 1984 Los Angeles Olympics, the Americans were left to fight it out with one another, for the most part.

Beneath a photograph of Valerie Brisco congratulating Jackie Joyner-Kersee, the headline read, "Joyner-Kersee First, But Misses Record." Janofsky reported in the *New York Times* on June 25:

> A record long jump helped America's foremost female track star, Jackie Joyner-Kersee, to win the heptathlon today in the USA/Mobil Track and Field Championships. But unexpected trouble in the javelin throw, the next-to-last event, kept her from setting the world heptathlon record a third consecutive time.
>
> Joyner-Kersee finished the seven events with 6,979 points — fewer only than her previous world-record totals of 7,158, set last August in Houston, and 7,148 of 27 days earlier in the Goodwill Games in Moscow.
>
> "Disappointed? No. I'm not disappointed," she said later. "I have my down moments. I'm a bit disappointed how I threw the javelin, but over all, I'm happy."
>
> Her long jump of 23' 9½" was a world heptathlon record.

Saturday and Sunday's stories in the *New York Times* featured Carl Lewis and Edwin Moses respectively. At the end of both articles, performances by women were reported.

In the women's triple jump, Sheila Hudson had a world-best mark of 45 feet 5¼ inches.

...Three women broke the American record in the 10,000 meter walk, with Maryanne Torrellas, a native of Queens, winning the event in 47:27.9 to break her record of 49:16.4. The others were Lynn Weik of Sayville, L.I., (47:36.5) and Debbi Lawrence of Overland Park, KA (48:30.3).

...Jackie Joyner-Kersee, who won the heptathlon Wednesday, won the long jump at 23' 4½", the best outdoor jump in the United States by a woman.

Evelyn Ashford, the world-record holder and Olympic champion in the 100 meters, was bothered by a hamstring injury for the second straight day. She failed to qualify for the final by finishing sixth. Diane Williams won the event with a wind-aided time of 10.90 seconds. In the 200-meter final Friday, Ashford finished fifth.

Valerie Brisco, the American record holder in the 400 meters, finished fourth, at 51.28 seconds, behind Lillie Leatherwood-King, Diane Dixon and Denean Howard. Leatherwood-King of Alabama, had the fastest time ever — 49.95 seconds — by an American collegian.

Regina Jacobs's winning time of 4:03.70 in the 1,500 meters was the fourth-fastest by an American.

100 meters

"The final, missing Evelyn Ashford after the WR holder suffered a slight hamstring tear in finishing 6th in her semi, was evenly divided between lightning starters and top-end speed merchants," reported *Track & Field News*.

Among the former, Alice Brown had the best getaway, beating Jeanette Bolden and Gwen Torrence in the first few steps. After running a PR 11.01 in the heats and semis, it was clear Alice was sharp and she led big until just past the halfway point. That's when she got company from burners Diane Williams and Pam Marshall, the latter looking to repeat her double of '86. Brown held on well and Marshall moved well, but it was Williams who finished best.

Running her finest race since gaining the World Championships bronze medal in 1983, the 25-year-old Puma TC runner flashed across the line in a windy (2.3) 10.90.

1. Diane Williams, Puma Track Club	10.90 w
2. Alice Brown, Stars and Stripes Track Club	10.93
3. Pam Marshall, Mazda Track Club	10.95
4. Gail Devers, World Class Athletic Club	10.99
5. Gwen Torrence, Athletics West	11.08
6. Michelle Finn, Atoms Track Club	11.11
7. Sheila Echols, Team Elite	11.12
8. Jeanette Bolden, World Class Athletic Club	11.17

200 meters

According to *Track & Field News*, "Pam Marshall was not entirely pleased with her lane assignment saying, 'I was so mad, I hate lane 1. I'm too tall.' But once she entered the straight, she displayed a burst of speed that propelled her past the field to a successful title defense. Florence Griffith, who had surprised many observers with her sharpness in the earlier rounds, led through the curve and hung on for 2nd." The automatic timing system malfunctioned.

1. Pam Marshall, Mazda Track Club	21.6 w
2. Florence Griffith, World Class Athletic Club	21.7
3. Grace Jackson, Atoms Track Club/Jamaica	21.8
4. Juliet Cuthbert, Los Angeles Track Club/Jamaica	21.8
5. Evelyn Ashford, Mazda Track Club	21.9
6. Pauline Davis, Coast Athletics/Bahamas	22.1
7. Gwen Torrence, Athletics West	22.2
8. Randy Givens, Puma Track Club	22.2

400 meters

Track & Field News reported:

At a press conference in early June, Valerie Brisco spoke quite casually about her superiority over the nation's other 400-meter runners. Her goals, she said, were her own AR of 48.83, which she would shoot for at TAC, and the gold medal at the World Championships this summer. She felt both were within her grasp.

It was, perhaps, this overconfidence that led Brisco to run a reckless race in San Jose that proved to be one of the meet's stunning upsets. Running in lane 3, Brisco made up the stagger on defender Diane Dixon (who drew lane 4) on the first turn, then continued to accelerate down the backstretch. She hit the 200 in a blistering 22.2.

"When I heard that split," she said later, "I knew I had made a mistake. I'm not used to going out that fast."

The Olympic champion held the lead around the second turn, but coming off the turn, it was apparent that she would soon be overtaken by Lillie Leatherwood-King, who always closes well, and by Dixon. They had gone out in a more conservative 23.8 and 23.5 and finished with 49.95 and 50.62.

Then Denean Howard provided the real shock by coming up on the inside to pass Brisco in the final 20m, thus dashing her hopes for Rome, 51.02 to 51.28.

Leatherwood-King's winning time is an American Collegiate record and she became only the fourth American in history to break 50 seconds.

1.	Lillie Leatherwood-King, Reebok	49.95
2.	Diane Dixon, Atoms Track Club	50.62
3.	Denean Howard, Stars and Stripes Track Club	51.02
4.	Valerie Brisco, World Class Athletic Club	51.28
5.	Sonja Friday, Mazda Track Club	51.69
6.	Denise Mitchell, University of Florida	51.72
7.	Rochelle Stevens, Morgan State University	51.81
8.	Tanya McIntosh, Atoms Track Club	52.08

800 meters

Said *Track & Field News*:

With Kim Gallagher out with a strep throat, and two-time defender Claudette Groenendaal strangely off form, the race was set up for SMTC teammates Essie Washington and Delisa Walton-Floyd. They took full advantage.

Washington towed the field through splits of 28.0 and 58.7, followed closely by Walton-Floyd, NCAA 3rd-placer Debbie Grant, Joetta Clark, NCAA winner Julie Jenkins and Groenendaal.

Past 400, Delisa moved strongly for the lead as she and Essie drew away from the rest, hitting 600 in 1:28.8. Behind them Groenendaal challenged gamely for 3rd while Grant fell back. They battled even down the homestretch with Washington prevailing only in the last 20m. Clark was an easy 3rd in the absence of the normal late strength of Groenendaal.

1.	Essie Washington, Santa Monica Track Club	1:59.07
2.	Delisa Walton-Floyd, Santa Monica Track Club	1:59.20
3.	Joetta Clark, Athletics West	1:59.45
4.	Julie Jenkins, Reebok Racing Club	2:00.50
5.	Debbie Grant, Villanova University	2:00.82
6.	Rose Monday, Track West	2:01.02
7.	Claudette Groenendaal, Team adidas	2:01.11
8.	Gail Conway, Santa Monica Track Club	2:04.12

1500 meters

Track & Field News reported: "There was no rush for the lead at the gun, 5000 3rd-placer

Left: **Diane Dixon and Denean Howard at the 1987 Pan American Games.** *Right:* **Delisa Walton, Joanne Terry Grissom and Essie Washington at the 1987 Pan American Games.**

Sylvia Mosqueda towing the pack through a leisurely 67.4 first lap. The pace remained through a Diana Richburg-led 2:14.9, with Angela Chalmers, defending champ Linda Sheskey and NCAA winner Suzy Favor in pursuit.

"Meanwhile, usual frontrunner Regina Jacobs had changed strategies. The Stanford grad hung back most of the race in 6th, but Richburg was making the third circuit interesting. Moving to 2nd at the bell, Jacobs followed Richburg's 63.8 and soon moved to her shoulder. With 250m remaining, Jacobs exploded and showed incredible drive in winning over Sheskey (4:05.80) by two seconds. Her final lap took only 60.6 and her last two just 2:04.9."

1. Regina Jacobs, Los Angeles Track Club   4:03.70
2. Linda Sheskey, Athletics West   4:05.80
3. Angela Chalmers, Team adidas/ Canada   4:06.43
4. Christine Pfitzinger, New Balance Track Club/New Zealand   4:06.47
5. Diana Richburg, Puma Track Club   4:07.32
6. Suzy Favor, University of Wisconsin, Madison   4:09.10
7. Teena Colebrook, Coast Athletics/Great Britain   4:10.85
8. Alisa Harvey, Nike Boston   4:11.65

3000 meters

"Pre-meet predictions ran true to form as Mary Knisley, who won this meet last year, and Cindy Bremser, who has never won a TAC outdoor title at any distance, battled it out. They let

Annette Hand, who likes to set the pace, do just that. The two veterans remained close, as did Brenda Webb and Leslie Seymour.

"That situation had to end eventually and Knisley, 28, moved up front with less than two laps remaining. She quickly strung out the pack, only Bremser managing to stick close by gun time. Seymour was about 20m back but was in good shape for the team, holding a 15m margin on Webb. Knisley gradually pulled away in a no-strain mode and was timed in 8:57.60. Working harder, but in full control, Bremser (8:58.80) was never threatened for 2nd by Seymour (9:02.64), who had nothing to worry about for 3rd," reported *Track & Field News*.

1. Mary Knisley, New Balance Track Club   8:57.60
2. Cindy Bremser, University of Wisconsin, Madison   8:58.80
3. Leslie Seymour, Club Sota   9:02.64
4. Brenda Webb, Puma Track Club   9:04.51
5. Anne Schweitzer, Puma Track Club   9:05.26
6. Annette Hand, University of Oregon   9:10.90
7. Sabrina Dornhoefer, Athletics West   9:12.85
8. Suzanne Girard-Eberle, Lady Foot Locker   9:14.10

5000 meters

"Six entered, 5 started and 4 finished the 5000 which, unlike all the other TAC championship events except the women's triple jump, did not lead to Rome, where the event will not be contested.

"Nan Davis, who as Nan Doak won the TAC 10 kilo last year, was the class of the field. But she took it easy on the competition. Not until there were only 800 meters remaining did she create much of a lead.... The diminutive Davis, 5 feet, 88 pounds, eschewed a title defense in the 10 in order to keep this year low-key in preparation for a major Olympic campaign," said *Track & Field News*.

1. Nan Davis, Athletics West   15:57.46
2. Maureen Cogan, Bob Schul Track Club   16:08.81
3. Sylvia Mosqueda, Team adidas   16:34.50
4. Tricia Clifford, University of Florida   17:08.05

10,000 meters

"'I didn't come here to run 33 minutes,' said Lynn Jennings. She wanted to run faster, perhaps approach her PR of 32:03.37, but after four laps in 5:20.0 it was clear that no one wanted to push the pace. So Jennings simply took off on her own. She passed 3200m in 10:14.2 for a blistering 4:54.2 second 1600, putting her more than 50m up on the field, as she cruised to her first-ever outdoor TAC title. Jennings, 6 days shy of 27, improved her seasonal best from 32:19.9 to 32:19.15, as she now owns three of the seven fastest times in U.S. history," *Track & Field News* reported.

1. Lynn Jennings, Athletics West   32:19.15
2. Francie Larrieu-Smith, New Balance Track Club   32:45.43
3. Lynn Nelson, Reebok Racing Club   32:52.55
4. Patty Murray, Team adidas   32:58.50
5. Marty Cooksey, Team Kangaroo   33:05.09
6. Judy Chamberlin, unattached   33:07.22
7. Cathie Twomey, Mike Manley Fitness   33:12.72
8. Ellen Lyons, Santa Monica Track Club   33:26.65

100 meter hurdles

"LaVonna Martin came to the meet looking to end the '80s dominance of the event by Stephanie Hightower (4 titles) and Benita Fitzgerald-Brown (2 titles). The new NCAA titlist did just that, and more, as she led the entire race and missed the AR by the narrowest of margins with her 12.80. Hightower's 12.79 of 1982 had escaped by a mere 0.01.... For Martin, a Tennessee junior, her almost–AR was a full-fledged Collegiate Record, taking down the 12.84 set by Fitzgerald-Brown (also for Tennessee) in 1983. She's also the third-fastest ever outside the Eastern bloc."

1. LaVonna Martin, Coast Athletics — 12.80 MR
2. Stephanie Hightower, Mazda Track Club — 12.99
3. Sophia Hunter, Atoms Track Club — 13.05
4. Rosalind Council, Mazda Track Club — 13.07
5. Benita Fitzgerald-Brown, Mazda Track Club — 13.13
6. Donna Waller, unattached — 13.26
7. Jackie Humphrey, Eastern Kentucky University — 13.28
8. Candy Young, Atoms Track Club — 13.50

400 meter hurdles

According to *Track & Field News*:

Judi Brown King's toughest hurdle came in advancing out of her semifinal. The three-time defending TAC champion stumbled, hit the eighth hurdle, and almost came to a dead stop. "I just kind of went into shock," she said, "but somebody yelled, 'Judi, run!'" As if on cue, JBK, who had fallen back to 6th, broke out of her trance, picked up the pace, and easily qualified by finishing 3rd.

The American record holder awoke with a "very sore" knee on Saturday but it didn't visibly affect her performance in the final. Down the backstretch, Brown King and Jamaican Sandra Farmer separated themselves from the rest of the field. Farmer had the edge as they entered the stretch, but with 80m to go JBK generated her characteristic stretch drive.

Earning a second consecutive trip to the World Championships, Brown King clocked 54.45, only 0.07 off her AR.

1. Judi Brown-King, Athletics West — 54.45 MR
2. Sandra Farmer, Stars and Stripes Track Club/Jamaica — 54.69
3. LaTanya Sheffield, San Diego Track Club — 55.05
4. Schowonda Williams, Mazda Track Club — 55.30
5. Sophia Hunter, Atoms Track Club — 55.40
6. Kathy Freeman, unattached — 56.10
7. Mimi King, University of Texas — 56.20
8. Rosalyn Bryant, Los Angeles Track Club — 57.97

10 kilometer walk

"After a couple of easy laps, 1985 champ Maryanne Torrellas, Debbi Lawrence ('84 and '86 winner), Teresa Vaill and Lynn Weik broke from the field. Torrellas captured the title with a new American record."

1. Maryanne Torrellas, Reebok Racing Club — 47:23.8 AR
2. Lynn Weik, unattached — 47:36.5
3. Debbi Lawrence, unattached — 48:30.3
4. Teresa Vaill, unattached — 48:57.2
5. Sara Standley, Southern California Road Runners — 50:53.3

6. Mary Howell, unattached   51:39.8
7. Karen Rezach, Shore Athletic Club   52:34.3
8. Viisha Sedlak, unattached   52:47.9

High jump
1. Coleen Sommer, Mazda Track Club   6' 5"
2. Louise Ritter, unattached   6' 4"
3. Phyllis Bluntson, Puma Track Club   6' 4"
4. Jane Clough, Puma Track Club   6' 4"
5. Yolanda Henry, Abilene Christian University   6' 2¾"
6. Rita Graves, Mazda Track Club   6' 1½"
7. Candy Cashell, unattached   6'
8. Camille Jampolsky, University of Oregon   6'

Long jump
1. Jackie Joyner-Kersee, World Class Athletic Club   23' 4½" MR
2. Jennifer Inniss, Atoms Track Club   22' 1¾"
3. Sheila Echols, Team Elite   21' 6"
4. Carol Lewis, Santa Monica Track Club   21' 4"
5. Sheila Hudson, Team adidas   21'
6. Cindy Greiner, Athletics West   20' 11¾"
7. Carlette Guidry, unattached   20' 5¾"
8. Veronica Bell, Southern California Cheetahs   20' 3¾"

Triple jump
1. Sheila Hudson, Team adidas   45' 5¼" WR
2. Wendy Brown, Puma Track Club   44' 4"
3. Terri Turner, Nike/Boston   42' 7"
4. Renita Robinson, South Bay Track Club   42' 5½"
5. Felicia Carpenter, Mazda Track Club   42' 2¼"
6. Yvette Bates, Southern California Cheetahs   41' 11½"
7. Tamara Compton, Fresno State University   41' 11¼" w
8. Nena Gage, George Mason University   41' 5¾"

Shot put
1. Ramona Pagel, Mazda Track Club   62' 3"
2. Pam Dukes, Puma Track Club   59' 5"
3. Bonnie Dasse, Coast Athletics   58' 11¼"
4. Connie Price, Coast Athletics   57' 3¾"
5. Peggy Pollock, Coast Athletics   57' 3½"
6. Regina Cavanaugh, Puma Track Club   55' 9¾"
7. Pinkie Suggs, Mazda Track Club   54' 9½"
8. Annette Bohach, Western Michigan Track Club   54' 8"

Discus
1. Connie Price, Coast Athletics   212' 5"
2. Carol Cady, Mazda Track Club   206' 1"
3. Ramona Pagel, Mazda Track Club   203' 2"
4. Kelly Landry, Mazda Track Club   193' 11"
5. Laura DeSnoo, San Diego Track Club   191' 5"
6. Lacy Barnes, Fresno State University   191' 2"
7. Becki Levi, unattached   182' 10"
8. Carla Garrett, University of Arizona   181' 5"

Left: Linda Detlefsen (left) and Pam Dukes at the 1987 Pan American Games. *Right:* Valerie Brisco (left) and Jackie Joyner with unidentified male at the 1987 Pan American Games.

Javelin
1. Karin Smith, Coast Athletics   203' 8"
2. Lynda Sutfin, Los Angeles Track Club   197'
3. Cathie Wilson, Coast Athletics   194' 3"
4. Donna Mayhew, South Bay Track Club   186'
5. Liz Mueller, Coast Athletics   181' 5"
6. Jeanne Villegas, unattached   180' 8"
7. Cathy Sulinski, Puma Track Club   174' 5"
8. Meg Warren, Mazda Track Club   174'

Heptathlon
1. Jackie Joyner-Kersee, World Class Athletic Club   6979   MR
2. Jane Frederick, Athletics West   6389
3. Cindy Greiner, Athletics West   6275
4. Jolanda Jones, University of Houston   5981
5. Wendy Brown, Puma Track Club   5896
6. Cathey Tyree, unattached   5806
7. Sheila Tarr, Track West   5755
8. Anita Sartin, Falcon Track Club   5607

Team scores:
1. Mazda Track Club   79

2. Athletics West	61
3. Coast Athletics	51

The Indoor Nationals

The indoor nationals were held in Madison Square Garden on Friday, February 27. The day before the meet, the *New York Times* featured a story on Jackie Joyner-Kersee after she won the Sullivan Award on Monday evening of that week. "...I was 9 years old when I had my first track competition," Jackie said. "I finished last, but the next week in practice I could feel improvement. My coach built a jumping pit in the back yard and the first time I tried it, he couldn't believe how far I jumped. When I was 12, I jumped 17–1."

After the Friday night meet, which had a record crowd of 15,859 in attendance, the *New York Times* headline read, "World Records Set in Long Jump and Triple Jump." The *Times* reported that "It was too bad that few people saw two of the most dramatic performances in the history of the national championships yesterday. But then, it was too bad that by the time a record crowd showed up in the evening at Madison Square Garden what didn't happen became almost as fascinating."

Besides Sergei Bubka failing to clear a height in the pole vault, Jackie Joyner-Kersee finished third in the hurdles and Valerie Brisco was second in the 200 meters. However, an American record was set by Diane Dixon in the first round of the 400 meters (52.)

55 meters
1. Anelia Nuneva, Bulgaria	6.64
2. Jeanette Bolden, World Class Athletic Club	6.79
3. Michelle Finn, Florida State University	6.83

200 meters
1. Grace Jackson, Atoms Track Club	23.51
2. Valerie Brisco, World Class Athletic Club	23.58
3. Alice Jackson, unattached	23.79

400 meters
1. Diane Dixon, Atoms Track Club	52.20
2. Lillie Leatherwood, unattached	53.00
3. Alice Jackson, unattached	53.53

800 meters
1. Christine Wachtel, German Democratic Republic	2:03.51
2. Svetlana Kitova, Union of Soviet Socialist Republic	2:03.97
3. Joetta Clark, Athletics West	2:04.05

Mobil mile
1. Doina Melinte, Romania	4:30.29
2. Darlene Beckford, Liberty Athletic Club	4:33.53
3. Julie Jenkins, Brigham Young University	4:39.56

3000 meters
1. Maricica Puica, Romania	8:43.49
2. Lesley Welch, Puma Track Club	8:44.68
3. Leslie Seymour, Club Sota	8:55.22

55 meter hurdles
1. Cornelia Oschkenat, German Democratic Republic   7.37
2. Yordanka Donkova, Bulgaria   7.49
3. Jackie Joyner-Kersee, World Class Athletic Club   7.64

3000 meter walk
1. Maryanne Torrellas, Abraxas Track Club   13:05.41
2. Teresa Vaill, unattached   13:15.97
3. Lynn Weik, unattached   13:43.47

One mile relay
1. Atoms Track Club   3:41.54
    (Robin DeSeignora, Diane Dixon, Easter Gabriel, Grace Jackson)
2. Rice University   3:43.41
3. Delaware State University   3:44.99

High jump
1. Tamara Bykova, Union of Soviet Socialist Republic   6' 3½"
2. Susanne Beyer-Helm, German Democratic Republic   6' 3½"
3. Debbie Brill, Pacific Coast Club/Canada   6' 1½"

Shot put
1. Ilona Briesenick, German Democratic Republic   66' 4½"
2. Ramona Pagel, Mazda Track Club   64'½"
3. Mihaela Loghin, Romania   63'¼"

Long jump
1. Heike Drechsler, German Democratic Republic   24'¼"
2. Galina Chistyakova, Union of Soviet Socialist Republic   22' 3¾"
3. Carol Lewis, Santa Monica Track Club   21' 11½"

Team Champion
Atoms Track Club (9th title — 4th consecutive title)

Sunkist Invitational (6 women's events): Los Angeles, January 16

60 meters
1. Juliet Cuthbert, Los Angeles Track Club   7.31

440 yards
1. Valerie Brisco-Hooks, World Class Athletic Club   55.02

800 meters
1. Joetta Clark, Athletics West   2:04.92

Mile
1. Brit McRoberts, Canada   4:39.18

Long jump (first year held)
1. Jackie Joyner-Kersee, World Class Athletic Club   21' 11¾"

Shot put (first year held)
1. Ramona Pagel, Mazda Track Club   65' ¾"

Maicel Malone (left) and the author at the 1987 Pan American Games.

10th Pan American Games: Indianapolis, Indiana, August 9–16

Indianapolis is the first American city in twenty-eight years to host the Pan American Games.

Maicel Malone carried the torch. Her picture was in the *New York Times* on August 8. When the huge torch was lighted at the Indianapolis motor speedway, after Vice President Bush declared the 10th Pan American Games open, Wilma Rudolph was deservedly selected to do the honors. With the headline on August 9 reading, "Pan Am Games Begin," the large photograph next to the story was that of Wilma Rudolph, hands held high above her head and smiling, holding the Pan American Games torch.

While Cindy Greiner became the first United States gold medalist of the Games with a record setting score of 6,184 in the heptathlon, the big news was Jackie Joyner-Kersee's long jump, which tied the world record. The *New York Times* said,

> Jackie Joyner-Kersee, who had to convince her husband/coach that she should compete in the long jump at the Pan American Games, proved her point tonight by matching Heike Drechsler's world record jump of 24 feet 5½ inches. She became the first American woman to hold or share the record.
>
> ...Joyner-Kersee's series of six jumps started slowly, with a jump of 23' 4¾" to lead a six-woman field.
>
> "I felt a little sluggish after that jump," she said, "I didn't feel that good. I knew I was either going to do something or mess it up."
>
> On her second attempt, she fouled, but said later she felt that had been her best jump in the series. "I had speed," she said. "My knees were up. I had my stride."
>
> On her next jump, she set an American record, at 23' 9½", and her next two jumps were 23' 8"

and 23' 5½". At that point in her career, she had the first, third and a tie for the fourth best jumps by an American.

Then came her sixth, and a lifetime of drama over the next 20 minutes. The electronic measuring device showed her distance to be close enough to the record that a hand-measure was called for. That's the rule in track and field.

Long moments ensued. Joyner-Kersee watched from a distance, not sure what to think.

"I didn't think it was a world record," she said. "But then, I started to think it might be something."

Finally, finally, the distance was flashed — the first world-record performance in track and field at the Pan American Games since 1975.

	Event	Place	Performance
Blunston, Phyllis	HJ	5	6' ½"
Brisco, Valerie	4 × 400mr	1	3:23.35 MR
Cooksey, Marty	10,000m	1	33:00.00
Devers, Gail	100m	1	11.14
	4 × 100mr	1	42.91
Dixon, Diane	400m	4	50.79
	4 × 400mr	1	3:23.35
Dukes, Pam	SP	5	54'
Echols, Sheila	4 × 100mr	1	42.91
Finn, Michelle	4 × 100mr	1	42.91
Floyd, Delisa Walton	800m	2	2:00.54
Friday, Sonya	4 × 400mr	DNC	alternate
Givens, Randy	200m	2	22.71 w
Greiner, Cindy	Heptathlon	1	6184 MR
Hightower-Leftwich, Stephanie	100mh	2	12.82
Howard, Denean	400m	3	50.72
	4 × 400mr	1	3:23.35
Jennifer Inniss	LJ	2	22' 5¾"
Jones, Jolanda	Heptathlon	3	5823
Joyner-Kersee, Jackie	LJ	1	24' 5½"
			(ties WR)
King, Judy Brown	400mh	1	54.23 AR
Knisley, Mary	3000m	1	9:06.75
Landry, Kelly	DT	5	176' 1"
Martin, LaVonna	100mh	1	12.81 MR
Mitchell, Denise	4 × 400mr	DNC	alternate
Molitar, Kathy	Marathon	4	2:59:58
Murray, Patty	10,000m	3	33:38.12
Pagel, Ramona	SP	1	60' 10¾"
Price, Connie	DT	3	195' 3"
Richburg, Diana	1500m	5	4:15.04
Seymour, Leslie	3000m	3	9:19.26
Sheffield, LaTanya	400mh	3	56.15
Sheskey, Linda	1500m	1	4:07.84
Sommer, Coleen	HJ	1	6' 5"
Stevens, Rochelle	4 × 400mr	1	3:23.35
Sutfin, Linda Hughes	JT	6	179' 3"
Torrellas, Maryanne	10,000m walk	3	47:35.12
Torrence, Gwen	200m	1	22.52
	4 × 100mr	1	42.91

	Event	Place	Performance
Warner, Debbie	Marathon	2	2:54:49
Washington, Essie	800m	4	2:04.66
Washington, Jackie	4 × 100mr	DNC	alternate
Weik, Lynn	10,000m walk	4	48:11.74
Williams, Diane	100m	2	11.25
Wilson, Cathie	JT	7	173'

Head Coach	Sue Humphrey
Assistant Coaches	Bob Kersee, Ed Parker
Head Manager	Nell Jackson
Assistant Manager	Louise Mead Tricard

U.S. Marathon Championships (Grandma's Marathon): Duluth, Minnesota, June 20

1. Janis Klecker	2:36:12
2. Janice Ettle	2:36:21
3. Martha White	2:38:02
4. Angella Hearn	2:39:55
5. Sarah Westover	2:41:31

Randy Givens at the 1987 Pan American Games.

2nd IAAF World Outdoor Track and Field Championships: Stadio Olympico Rome, Italy, August 29–September 8

After one day and four events in the heptathlon the *New York Times* reported that Jackie Joyner's "...point total for the first four events of the heptathlon — 4,256 — was the highest ever and 111 points more than the score she had after the first day of competition last summer in Houston when she set the current world record of 7,158 points. She is also 105 points ahead of the first-day total she had a month before that, at the Goodwill Games in Moscow, where she set her first world record.

"Joyner-Kersee led the field of 22 women with the best performances in three of the four events. First, she ran the 100-meter hurdles in 12.91 seconds. Then she high-jumped 6 feet 2¾ inches for an American heptathlon record. Then came a personal best in the shot-put with a throw of 52' 6" (only Jane Frederick, another American, threw farther today, 53' 5¾").

"Joyner-Kersee ended the day by running the fastest 200 meters at 22.95," continued the *New York*

Times. "[She] ... picked up her second gold — just three days after she won the heptathlon, making her the first man or woman since Harold Osborn of the University of Illinois in 1924 to win gold medals in multisport and individual events in the same major competition." She jumped 24' 1¾" in the long jump for the win.

---

100 meters
4. Diane Williams   11.07
8. Pam Marshall   11.19

200 meters
2. Florence Griffith-Joyner   21.96
4. Pam Marshall   22.18
5. Gwen Torrence   22.40

400 meters
5. Lillie Leatherwood-King   50.82
7. Diane Dixon   51.13

There was no American in the 800 meter final.

1500 meters
7. Diana Richburg   4:01.79
10. Linda Sheskey   4:08.33

3000 meters
10. Mary Knisley   8:50.99

10,000 meters
6. Lynn Jennings   31:45.43
13. Lynn Nelson   32:22.88
15. Francie Larrieu-Smith   32:30.00

Marathon
7. Nancy Ditz   2:34:54

100 meter hurdles
8. LaVonna Martin-Floreal   13.06

400 meter hurdles
7. Schowonda Williams   55.86
8. Judi Brown-King   56.10

High jump
8. Louise Ritter (tie)   6' 4"
11. Coleen Sommer   6' 4"

Long jump
1. Jackie Joyner-Kersee   24' 1¾" MR
7. Jennifer Inniss   22' 3¾"
11. Sheila Echols   20' 11¾"

No American women placed in the finals of the shot put, discus or javelin.

10 kilometer walk (road)
15. Lynn Weik   46:51
20. Debbi Lawrence   47:31
24. Maryanne Torrellas   48:27

4 × 100 meter relay
1. USA   41.58   MR
     (Alice Brown, Diane Williams, Florence Griffith-Joyner, Pam Marshall)

4 × 400 meter relay
3. USA   3:21.04
     (Diane Dixon, Denean Howard, Valerie Brisco-Hooks, Lillie Leatherwood-King)

Heptathlon
   1. Jackie Joyner-Kersee   7128   MR
   3. Jane Frederick   6502
  12. Cindy Greiner   6042

1st IAAF World Indoor Track and Field Championships: Hoosier Dome, Indianapolis, Indiana, March 6–8

A *New York Times* story prior to the start of the meet, written by Frank Litsky stated, "...The 17 American women will be fortunate to win one or two medals in their 11 events, and they have little chance for even one gold."

60 meters
6. Michelle Finn   7.19

200 meters
4. Alice Jackson   23.55

400 meters
2. Lillie Leatherwood-King   52.54

800 meters
6. Joetta Clark   2:03.92
8. Diana Richburg   2:05.86

1500 meters
7. Darlene Beckford   4:13.64

60 meter hurdles
8. Stephanie Hightower-Leftwich   8.26

3 kilometer walk
  8. Maryanne Torrellas   13:10.30
 13. Teresa Vaill   13:32.82

High jump
7. Katrena Johnson   6' 3¼"
9. (tie) Rita Graves   6' 2"

Long jump
9. Carol Lewis   20' 5¼"

Shot put
  6. Ramona Pagel   63' 2"
 11. Peggy Pollock   57' 4¾"

Other News and Honors

Track & Field News: U.S. Athlete of the Year

Jackie Joyner-Kersee

USA Top Five Rankings — *Track & Field News*

1. Jackie Joyner-Kersee
2. Florence Griffith
3. Jane Frederick
4. Pam Marshall
5. Louise Ritter

World Rankings — *Track & Field News*

1. Jackie Joyner-Kersee

Top American Road Women — *Track & Field News*

1. Lynn Jennings
2. Lisa Weidenbach
3. Lesley Welch
4. Marty Cooksey
5. Teresa Ornduff

Only three American women held world records: 100 meters, Evelyn Ashford, set in 1984 (10.76); Mary Slaney, mile run, set in 1985 (4:16.71) and, Jackie Joyner-Kersee, heptathlon, set in 1986 (7158).

Lynn Jennings won the United States cross country championships in November at Van Cortlandt Park in the Bronx, her second win in three years. She finished fourth in the world cross country championships.

Martha Watson was inducted into the National Track and Field Hall of Fame. The biography below is from the USA Track and Field website.

Martha Watson

Inducted: 1987, athlete

Born: August 19, 1946 — Long Beach, California

Another of the distinguished line of Tennessee State University athletes that included Hall of Famers Wilma Rudolph and Wyomia Tyus, Martha Watson dominated the American women's long jumping scene during much of her career. In 1964, just barely out of high school, she placed second in the long jump at the U.S. Olympic trials to qualify for the American team. She made three more Olympic teams (1968-72-76) as a long jumper, also running a leg on the U.S. 4 × 100m relay teams in 1972 and 1976. Watson won a total of eight U.S. long jump titles (five indoor, three outdoor) between 1964 and 1976. That included three straight at both the indoor nationals (1974–76) and outdoor nationals (1973–75). Twice, she bettered the American indoor record (20' 11½" in 1970 and 21' 4¾" in 1973). At the 1975 Pan American Games, Watson took a silver medal in the long jump and a gold medal in the 4 × 100m relay.

Championships

1972 Olympics: 400 m relay (4th)
1976 Olympics: 400 m relay (7th)
1973 USA Outdoors: Long Jump (1st)
1974 USA Indoors: Long Jump (1st)

1974 USA Outdoors: Long Jump (1st)
1975 USA Indoors: Long Jump (1st)
1975 USA Outdoors: Long Jump (1st)
1976 USA Indoors: Long Jump (1st)
1975 Pan-Am Games: Long Jump (2nd)
1975 Pan-Am Games: 400 m relay (1st)

Education

high school: Long Beach Poly (Long Beach, California)
undergraduate: Tennessee State (Nashville, Tennessee)

INTERVIEW: ROSE MONDAY

(November 30, 2001) I always knew I could run ever since I was a little kid. We would have relay races on the block and I would race kids. It was like the video we saw tonight — constantly racing. I grew up in southern California in the San Fernando Valley — Northridge.

It wasn't until I was thirteen and I beat all the high school boys in the neighborhood that my brothers and sisters, I'm the second of six kids, ran in and told my dad, "Dad, dad, sister beat the Snyders, she beat the Jones' and she beat the Johnsons" and my dad said, "She did?" That was eighth grade. He said, "We need to sign you up for a track team." I was painfully shy, even through college. I would not ever have been able to speak in front of people. To raise my hand in class, I would go into a deep sweat and my heart would race to like 180. I said, "Dad, I don't want to sign up for the track team. I just want to run on my block." I loved PE in my school. I would be the first one and beat all the boys and girls around the entire playground. It was just so much fun for me. He said, "We're just going to check it out." My dad was sort of an outgoing, very forceful person. I said, "Okay, just don't make me run in front of anyone." I knew he would say, "Run in front of everyone." He was like that. He said, "Okay, I promise I won't." Well, we got there and the first thing the coach said, it was an age group track team, let's see her run.

Well, I had hand-me-down clothes from the girl across the street that were too big and shoes that had holes in them and I was really embarrassed and did not want to run in front of those people. My dad said, "Get out there." You didn't argue with my dad. So, I got out there, ran 100 meters against these other kids with spikes on and track clothes on and I beat them. I think had that not happened I probably would never have run because I would have been so humiliated and embarrassed and never went back.

At that point I remember seeing the '72 Olympics on T.V. and just being in awe and thought, I want to do that. I knew that a vehicle to doing that would be to get a college scholarship to get good coaching. At the same time, I was in a public school. I went to Catholic school all my life, a small Catholic school. My parents had taken us out of Catholic school and put us all in public schools. I went to public school for eighth grade and a month of seventh grade. I really missed the Catholic school structure. I loved wearing a uniform. I loved all my friends that I grew up with from third grade — we were in the same school. Although I knew that they didn't have a track program I wanted to go there anyway. I went and started a track team there. I still have the records.

Art Venegas is one that I really credit for starting my career. He recognized my talents. He was my high school Spanish teacher. He was responsible for telling different coaches about me because I didn't have any coaching. My coach was a PE major who was volunteering as coach and knew nothing about track. I just went out and ran practice and didn't know what I was doing. I never made it to the state meet. I wasn't one of those kids that would be noticed by the big schools. But Art made sure I was noticed and got into the Arcadia Invitational and other meets like that.

I ended up going to Cal State Northridge on a scholarship. I did not develop until much later in my career. In fact, as a master's athlete, I'm running faster than I ran in college. It cracks me up. It doesn't make sense that you can be 42 and run faster than you did as this young college kid. In college I ran my freshman and sophomore years. I remember our coach handing us the national qualifying standards and saying nothing about a conference — maybe we weren't in a conference — because now I'm coaching at the University of Texas at San Antonio and the conference is the big thing and I'm thinking, how come I didn't know anything about that? We were given the national qualifying standards. This is it, I remember thinking. I did everything possible I could do to run well. The standard was 2:11 for the 800. I did not run that. But I was fast enough to run on the 4 × 8 and the 4 × 4. Those were the two events I ran. We won the national championships. The relay teams placed third but the team as a whole won the national championships. But I was in such good company that I was inspired by almost all of my competitors. Flo Jo was on my team, Kim Turner, a long jumper, Pam Spencer, Jodi Anderson, Kathy Weston and Kathy Costello. It goes on. Eighty per cent of our team made the Olympic team in 1980. It was just awesome. It was really an awesome experience.

Rose Monday, 2001.

I was injured in my junior year. My senior year I came back and was in an automobile accident in the very beginning of the year and I was in the hospital for two weeks and it smashed my knee. I ended up having surgery on my knee and have had back problems ever since then. My back always hurts. The doctors basically said you're not going to run again. Whenever someone tells me that, that's the first thing I remember. My high school's advisor for college was Brother Mark. He told me, you can't go to college. You don't have the grades to go to college. I'm thinking, I'm going to college. I'll show you. So that's the spirit of my personality.

My senior year I did not run either. In fact, Leroy Burrell sometimes jokes with me, "Do you have any eligibility left?" [laughter] Because I go to the University of Houston now and do these indoor meets and I beat all the college kids. It's so much fun. I do have eligibility. I could go to a Division 2 or a Division 3 school and still compete.

I started running again in 1983 and wanted to make the Olympic team in 1984. Skip Stolley, an awesome coach, coached me for thirteen years. I never really appreciated what a great coach he was until I coached for three years at the high school level and I realized how much work he puts into it and how much love he puts into it. He taught me why I was doing things, what I was doing and made me come to my first convention in San Diego because he thought that it would be a very good experience for me to be well-rounded and be involved in the politics. So I think even from that perspective how I got involved in the political aspect of the sport. He was a great coach and asked me what my goals were in 1983. I said I wanted to make the Olympic team. He said, "That's nice: all well and good, but I think maybe qualifying for the Olympic trials should be the goal." I remember thinking, "Hmm...." But, realistically, I look back on it and I had never competed in a national championship even as an open athlete. Here I want to go the Olympic trials and I want to be on the Olympic team.

I'm glad I had those high goals because I not only qualified for the Olympic trials but I finished ninth. I missed making the final by one. At the time I was devastated and was just sobbing. I remember being in the Coliseum in Los Angeles and just sobbing and feeling like I let my family down. It was just a terrible feeling. But then, I went away from that thinking, okay, the next one.

I then had a series of ups and downs and injuries and it wasn't until 1987 that I really started to run well. From 1983 to 1992, I competed on the European circuit, competed internationally for the United States, and was indoor champion in 1985. Finished fifth, sixth, seventh in nationals, that kind of thing—had awesome competitors that I raced with—but never made that Olympic team. When someone asked me about it a few years back, I still remember being upset. When they asked me to do this speech tonight — they wrote this speech and mentioned that I was proud to win my first world championship title as a master's athlete. I'm very proud of that but I was embarrassed to say that. My husband said, "Why are you embarrassed, Rose? You have accomplished so much in your career. Why can't you be proud of that?" It wasn't until Sandra and everybody else was saying, three time Olympian, and they were proud of what they did. I thought, I am proud of what I have done.

No, it's not been an Olympic team but I have been able to travel all over the world for free and get paid to do it. I met so many incredible friends. You may not see them for a year but you just pick up where you left off. You could call them on the phone and say, "So anyway." And they are just close friends — Julie Jenkins, I was her maid of honor. We were in Malmo, Sweden and all of us 800 runners were friends and we were all going shopping. We were coming down this beautiful spiral staircase and Charlie Jones was there and Craig Masback was commentating at the time. We all had these cute little short skirts on, we were all in our 20s and Charlie said, "Who are they?" Craig said, "That is the 800 field." And it was. We were the entire field going shopping, hanging out. They are awesome friends. I told Larry tonight. He inspired me. In this one particular situation, we were racing on the indoor circuit. I was running well. I competed in Ghent and won. I won in Barcelona. I got second in England. We were on our way to Greece. I'm still thinking it's sort of a fluke that I'm running well after I've been in Europe for three or four years now [laughter]. I couldn't believe that I'm doing this.

I competed in the 1988 Olympic trials in the 800 and the 1500. I got sick at the trials. That was the year I was picked by several publications to make the team.

In 1992 I competed in the Olympic trials. I had Mary Rose right after that and my father, in 1992, found out that he had cancer. They thought it was prostate cancer. I went and saw him every day because you never know with cancer. It turned out he passed away six weeks later. Looking back at that, I'm so glad I didn't make the Olympic team; I spent every day with my dad. My dad was my biggest fan besides my husband. He was just so proud of me. Even my mom, she's proud of me, but to this day she couldn't tell you what event I do. Oh, she probably knows. That's probably an exaggeration. But, my dad would just fly everywhere. He just loved it.

My sophomore year in college, Chuck told me that I was not fast enough for the 400. I had run a 54. I was a sprinter. I moved up. The 800 had a negative stereotype in my mind. The kids in high school who were slow ran the 800. The sprinters were the popular ones. It was like, if you were not good enough to sprint, you got thrown into the 800 or the mile. It wasn't like anyone wanted to do that event [laughter]. Even my dad said, "You're not doing that event, you're a sprinter." I always maintained that natural speed is what I have. Probably if I did a muscle biopsy I'd have 50% fast twitch and 50% slow twitch, which is ideal for a middle distance runner. But once I started to really train for the 800 with Skip, I actually loved that race. I still love the 400. The 800 is so tactical and I love the maneuvering and the mind games and that you have to think. It's not like going as fast as you can around the track, although that's mindless and I love to do that too. That's how I started doing the 800.

I did not like the 1500. I would complain and I never wanted to do the 1500 until the Grand Prix circuit had the 1500 every other year or the 800. All of a sudden it was a financial thing. I can't go to Europe. I said to Skip, "I want to learn how to run the 1500." He made me do the 1500 to help me do the 800 but it was with protest. I didn't want to do it and I didn't like it and I had an attitude about it. Now, this time I'm saying I want you to train me for this. I want to run better than a 4:28. So then I ran 4:28 and that year I ran 4:17. Granted, I was running two flats everywhere so I was really fit and because I did not run that many 1500's I had a big progression in the 1500.

I went to Europe and I raced in Nice and everyone was going on to Paris and I'm not running until the following week. They usually will bring you in a couple of days before but they are not going to pay for your hotel for a week so everybody said to me, just go ask the meet director if you can run in Paris. I said, "I just can't go ask him." So, I went over and introduced myself and he said, "I know who you are." I said, "Do you think there may be any room in your race?" and he said, "Of course, you can get into the race. I don't have any money left but I'll pay for your air fare, your hotel, and your food." And I'm excited and elated but very calm. I said, "That will be fine." Now I don't have to pay for a hotel for three or four days, which is what I was going to have to do. I'm excited to get into a hot 1500 and see what I could run because I had been running so well in the 800. Had he asked me my times, I'm embarrassed to say, I was prepared to lie because I wasn't going to tell him that 4:17 was my best. You can't even get into a hot 1500 in the United States with a 4:17. Thank God he never asked me because I would have been going to confession over that one. I would have said 4:14 because I was sure, I was sure I could do a 4:14. I just knew I could. So, I get in this race. It's the who's who of 1500's. Puica was in there, Paula Ivan was in there, Mary Slaney was in there, Ruth Wysocki was in there. It went on and on. World champion, she was ranked #5 in the world, and I'm in lane 13 with one leg on the grass. There's just not enough room for me on the track. Claudette Groenendaal was standing next to me and Claudette had blue panties on under her white briefs and it was pouring rain. It had poured and our hair was all straight and flat in our face and she said, "Rose, can you see my blue underwear?" And I looked and said, "Yes" [laughter]. She goes, "Do you think it looks bad?" And I said, "No one will even notice." Anyway, I ended up getting fifth and ran a 4:08.65. It was just, just the coolest moment of my life and broke that huge barrier for the 1500.

I never ran faster than the 4:08 but I ran several 4:09s, a bunch of 4:11s, a couple of 4:10s and so it was really fun at that point. Some coaches said, that's your race. You can't make it your race if somebody else says it's that. It still was hard for me. There were very few 1500s that after two laps I wasn't miserable. Even the one in Brisbane, oh my goodness, you can't believe how that race hurt. I'm standing on the grass and the first round of the 1500 is going for the semifinal. I'm timing it because they only take the first two qualifiers. I'm thinking, I'm going to get in on time because my legs are tired from the 800s and the 400 and I wanted to run as slowly as possible to qualify so that I could try and win a medal in all these events. All of a sudden I hear these women off to the side say, "Which is the one that won the 800?" and so I turned and looked and all of a sudden five women are pointing at me [laughter]. If they know, then they know how I ran it. They know that I can kick and they're going to push the pace, which I hate because I just wasn't in shape for that. So, sure enough, they pushed the pace in the semifinal. I won my heat. I just kind of surged at the end but it hurt. It was uncomfortable and my husband said "What's the matter?" I said, "John that really hurt." He said, "well, it's supposed to hurt." I go, "It's not supposed to hurt like that." If that one hurt, tomorrow is really going to hurt and I was thinking about the pain of the final of the 1500. The 400 final was an hour and ten minutes later and I'm thinking, tomorrow is going to be a fun day.

So, I get into the final and this other woman just pushed the pace. They pushed the pace from the beginning and I remember being miserable at the first lap. I thought, okay, just tuck in. I thought of every positive affirmation I have ever written or said; when the negative came in, the positive just kind of countered it. Okay, just tuck in, stay where you are, just one lap at a time, no, you're not dropping out, nobody cares if you get fifth place, you just won the 800, no, you're not getting fifth place, stay right here. Well, at the 800, this English woman just takes this huge lead, like a one hundred meter lead and I thought, well, you can try for one of the other color medals because you're not going to get that color [laughter] I could not go with her. Then the next lap, again just miserable, not sure when I'm going to make my move, thinking I'll wait until one hundred meters to go, just hanging on for dear life and with one lap to go—and this just goes to show you the power of affirmation and mental preparation—every single workout I did for the last two years since Gateshead, I knew I wanted to win that race. I wanted to win the 800 and I wanted to win the 1500. So every workout I would pretend like it's the last lap. I would say, this is the last lap, last lap. You think you can't go any faster and you end up running a faster rep or if it's the last 200—whatever the workout was—this is the last lap of the world championships, I would say that. It's funny because I got to the last lap, and, of course, the bell had rung because she's a hundred meters ahead. All of a sudden a loud voice just resonated in my head, "This is the last lap of the world championship," and I changed gears. It didn't matter how bad I felt—it was amazing—and I caught her at 150 meters to go. I thought, Oh my gosh, I'm going to catch her. I caught her and as I'm coming down the final stretch, I hear the crowd going crazy and all of a sudden I felt her, the girl that I beat in the 800, and I looked and I kind of moved out and the two of us were stride for stride for the last ten meters. When she leaned she lurched forward and leaned like you're supposed to—lean 101—not a dorky lean like I did. I did this sprawling ensemble, arching my back. I was so miserable the entire race that it was all I could do to finish, and so I lost by whatever—a hundredth of a second or something like that. But I was still really proud of that race too because of the mental barriers I overcame. It would have been easier for me to do just the 400 and the 800.

An hour later I ran a 59 in the 400. The winning time was 58.5. I'd already run 57. I could have won the 400 if I had just done the 400 and the 800 and not had the two 1500s, but I did drug testing for an hour and then went to warm up for the 400 final. My legs were just dead. I ended up fourth. I just couldn't muster anything out of them.

My best time in the half was 2:00.17. I ran 2 flat ten times and never broke that 1:59 barrier. My best time was run in 1987 in Olympic Stadium in Berlin.

I would tell anyone starting in track and field to have patience. Women do not develop until much later. It's been proven now. You can be a novice and a beginner and turn into a great star if you just have patience go out and train and do everything right and dream big. I just think dreaming big is huge. If I hadn't dreamed what I had dreamt and wished to be on an Olympic team or to break the records that I've broken I never would have done what I've done. I'm proud of those. They are hard work and it was fun and I've enjoyed it. But if I had listened to all the people who told me I couldn't do it or wasn't talented enough or I needed to take drugs or whatever — who knows. Thank God that I didn't listen to those people. It's really unfortunate that you have those people around. I've really tried to limit my association with people like that. Those kinds of people are unhealthy for your mind. So I would recommend to a young girl that she stay positive, that she write her dreams out and then go after them. You can do anything.

8

1988: The Seoul Olympic Year

Track and field events were held in Olympic Stadium from September 23 to October 2 in Seoul, South Korea.

	Olympic Event	Olympic Place	Olympic Performance
Ashford, Evelyn	100	2	10.83 w
	4 × 100mr	1	41.98
Brisco, Valerie	400m	4	50.16
	4 × 400mr	2	3:15.51 AR
Brown, Alice	4 × 100mr	1	41.98
Brown, Wendy	Heptathlon	18	5972
Cady, Carol	DT	11	208' 1"
Clark, Joetta	800m	DNQ	2:03.32 s
Dasse, Bonnie	SP	12	57' 9"
Dendy, Terri	4 × 400mr alternate		
Devers-Roberts, Gail	100mh	DNQ	13.22 qf
Ditz, Nancy	Marathon	17	2:33:42
Dixon, Diane	400m	5	50.72
	4 × 400mr	2	3:15.51 AR
Echols, Sheila	4 × 100mr	1	41.98
	LJ	DNQ	20' 10¾"
Gallagher, Kim	800m	3	1:56.91
	1500m	11	4:16.25
Greiner, Cindy	Heptathlon	8	6297
Griffith-Joyner, Florence	100	1	10.54 w OR
	200	1	21.34 WR
	4 × 100mr	1	41.98
	4 × 400mr	2	3:15.51 AR
Groos, Margaret	Marathon	39	2:40:59
Howard, Denean	400m	6	51.12
	4 × 400mr	2	3:15.51 AR

	Olympic Event	*Olympic Place*	*Olympic Performance*
Howard, Sherri	4 × 400mr	2	3:15.51 AR
Huber, Vicki	3000m	6	8:37.25
Humphrey, Jackie	100mh	DNQ	13.25 qf
Inniss, Jennifer	4 × 100mr alternate		
Jacobs, Regina	1500m	DNQ	4:18.09
Jennings, Lynn	10,000m	6	31:39.93
Joyner-Kersee, Jackie	LJ	1	24' 3½" OR
	Heptathlon	1	7291 WR
King, Trish	HJ	DNQ	5' 10¾"
Leatherwood, Lillie	4 × 400mr	2	3:15.51 AR
Lewis, Carol	LJ	DNQ	21' 2¾"
Malone, Maicel	4 × 400mr alternate		
Marshall, Pam	200m	injured	
Martin, LaVonna	100mh	DNQ	13.20 qf
Maxie, Leslie	400mh	DNQ	57.60 h
Mayhew, Donna	JT	7	202' 8"
Miles, Jearl	4 × 400mr alternate		
Nelson, Lynn	10,000m	11	32:32.24
O'Brien, Cathy	Marathon	40	2:41:04
Pagel, Ramona	DT	DNQ	188' 8"
	SP	DNQ	60' 10½"
Plumer, PattiSue	3000m	13	8:59.17
Price, Connie	DT	DNQ	187' 2"
	SP	DNQ	56' 1"
Ritter, Louise	HJ	1	6' 8" OR, AR
Sheffield, LaTanya	400mh	8	55.32
Slaney, Mary	1500m	8	4:02.49
	3000m	10	8:47.13
Smith, Francie Larrieu	10,000m	5	31:35.52
Smith, Karin	JT	DNQ	190' 1"
Sommer, Coleen	HJ	DNQ	6'½"
Sutfin, Lynda	JT	DNQ	184' 1"
Torrence, Gwen	100m	5	10.97 w
	200m	6	22.17
Walton-Floyd, Delisa	800m	5	1:57.80
Williams, Schowonda	400mh	DNQ	56.71 s
Young, Dannette	4 × 100mr	1	41.98

Terry Crawford, Head Coach
Fred Thompson, Assistant Coach
Dave Rodda, Assistant Coach
Dr. Ken Foreman, Assistant Coach
Bob Seaman, Head Manager
Martha Watson, Assistant Manager
Pearlie McDaniel, Assistant Manager

The Olympic Results

Elliott Denman in *Anthology of the Olympic Games* reported: "The American flag bearer, earning the cherished assignment by vote of the Olympic team captains, was three-time Olympic sprinter Evelyn Ashford, the defending 100-meter queen, of Walnut, CA.

According to *Track & Field News*, "For sheer athletic and visual impact, no figure in Seoul could match Florence Griffith Joyner. While her triumphs were not strictly unexpected, she had risen with such velocity to become the 'World's Fastest Woman' at the Trials that even those who had watched her in Indy longed for a conformational encore against the best in the rest of the world." The article continues:

Florence Griffith Joyner at her induction into the National Track and Field Hall of Fame, 1995.

> Flojo delivered staggering proof with two World Records, in her 200 semi and the final; another Indyesque series of mind-blowing 100 marks; and the third leg of the victorious U.S. 4 × 100.
>
> This made three golds, and she finished by anchoring the silver-minted 4 × 4 that pushed the Soviets under the old WR.
>
> ...The performance of the ever-fabulous Jackie Joyner-Kersee, with two golds and a heptathlon WR, was only marginally surpassed by Flojo's.
>
> ...Louise Ritter's victory ... produced tears-of-joy type tingles for many, as did Kim Gallagher's unexpected bronze race.

100 meters. In the first round, Florence Griffith-Joyner lowered the Olympic record from 10.97 to 10.88.

Track & Field News reported:

> For the final Flojo was spruced up with a white belt adorning her red and white uniform and her two-inch nails painted red, white and blue (one nail real gold). She blazed out of the blocks with a better reaction time (0.131) than any of the men had produced, and by 70m she was smiling.
>
> ...By 90m, the smile was a glorious grin. Five meters later, her arms were up in celebration as the gold was assured.
>
> ...Defending champ Ashford drove hard to the finish to edge Drechsler for the silver by 0.02 in 10.83.

Gwen Torrence finished fifth, in the same time as the fourth finisher.

1. Florence Griffith-Joyner	10.54 w	OR
2. Evelyn Ashford	10.83 w	
5. Gwen Torrence	10.97 w	

200 meters. FloJo had already broken the Olympic record in the second round with 21.76. In the semifinal she broke the world record with 21.56.

Although Grace Jackson of Jamaica was out of the blocks first, Griffith-Joyner took the lead off the first turn, continued pulling away from the field and was never challenged. *Track & Field News* reported,

"After the final Flojo said, 'This is the one I wanted more than any, the 200 gold and the record.' She continued, 'The time was fantastic. I knew it would be faster than the semi because I ran harder.'

"...Gwen Torrence ran a fine 22.17 but wound up just 6th. In all it was history's fastest race and produced the quickest times ever for places 1–8.... The major item of note in the heats was Pam Marshall's right hamstring injury. She had to be carried from the track."

1. Florence Griffith-Joyner	21.34	WR
6. Gwen Torrence	22.17	

400 meters. "...After a false start, Brisco, stuck in 1, bolted to the front (11.71/22.94). Halfway, she was leading by 0.47.... At 300, Bryzgina and Brisco were even (35.47).... Brisco (50.16) struggled home with a 27.22 second 200, but led a 4-5-6 American finish, Dixon and Howard running 50.72 and 51.12.... Of her front-running race Brisco said, 'I wanted to go out hard to get out front. I was in front, but once I got there, instead of me relaxing, I tried to find one more gear. And, honey, let me tell you, at 320 yards you can't find no more gears.'"

4. Valerie Brisco	50.16
5. Diane Dixon	50.72
6. Denean Howard	51.12

800 meters. Again, from *Track & Field News*:

...In the final ... Gallagher moved smartly from the gun.... The field closed up around the second turn and halfway down the straight, until Wodars took over the lead and began to stretch it out.... Gallagher (56.8) found herself 4th in a box. Wachtel (1:25.7) took the lead again with 200 to go, as Gallagher, out of the box and running hard to challenge Yevseyeva and Colovic, moved inside to save ground on the turn.

As they came off the final turn, Wodars moved alongside Wachtel and began to pull away, while Gallagher went past the tiring Yevseyeva on the inside and then made a nifty lateral move to spurt past Colovic into 3rd.

For a moment it looked as if the American might split the East German pair, or even win. But down the final straight Wodars forged a convincing 5m margin to win in 1:56.10 and Wachtel found enough strength to hold off Gallagher by 2m or so, 1:56.64 to 1:56.91.... Floyd finished strongly to end up just 3m behind Colovic (1:57.50) in a PR 1:57.80.

Joetta Clark was eliminated in the semis (2:03.32).

3. Kim Gallagher	1:56.91
5. Delisa Walton-Floyd	1:57.80

1500 meters. "...The chief question mark at the start of the race was if Slaney would be able to rally from her subpar showing in the 3000. Whether to lead or not was solved by the 25-year-old Ivan, who seized the front at the gun and, with Slaney on her shoulder and the '84 silver medalist Doina Melinte behind, punched her way through a 62.5 first 400."

At the finish, no one was close. Slaney had dropped back before the bell lap. She crossed the line in eighth place. Kim Gallagher was eleventh. The third American, Regina Jacobs finished eleventh in her heat.

8. Mary Slaney	4:02.49
11. Kim Gallagher	4:16.25

3000 meters. Vicki Huber was the top American finisher in sixth place with a time of 8:37.25. Mary Slaney finished tenth in 8:47.13 and PattiSue Plumer thirteenth in 8:59.17.

6.	Vicki Huber	8:37.25
10.	Mary Slaney	8:47.13
13.	PattiSue Plumer	8:59.17

10,000 meters. This was a new event on the Olympic program for women. Francie Larrieu-Smith was fifth in 31:35.52, a PR and just off Mary Slaney's AR of 31:35.3. Lynn Jennings was sixth in 31:39.93, also a PR. Their times ranked them numbers two and three on the all-time United States list. Nelson finished eleventh in 32:32.24.

5.	Francie Larrieu-Smith	31:35.52
6.	Lynn Jennings	31:39.93
11.	Lynn Nelson	32:32.24

Marathon. "...Nancy Ditz (2:33:42) led the American trio, as did she in Rome, finishing 17th. Margaret Groos (2:40:59) and Cathy O'Brien (2:41:04) were 39th and 40th."

100 meter hurdles. "...Americans Gail Devers (13.18), LaVonna Martin (13.20), and Jackie Humphrey (13.24) all qualified easily," said *Track & Field News*. In round two, Gail Devers advanced with a fourth place. Martin and Humphrey advanced on a time basis.

In the first semifinal, Martin was seventh and Devers eighth. In the second semifinal, Humphrey was seventh. No American women qualified for the final.

400 meter hurdles. Both LaTanya Sheffield and Schowonda Williams qualified for the semifinal round. In the first semi, Sheffield finished third in 54.36, the second fastest U.S. time ever. Williams was seventh in the second semi in 56.71 and did not qualify for the final.

"...Sheffield had hoped to run the race of her life — as she had in the semis — but ran out of steam after the fourth barrier and faded quickly, falling from 4th to 8th in the next 70m."

Leslie Maxie (57.60) was fifth in her heat and did not qualify for the semis.

8.	LaTanya Sheffield	55.32

4 × 100 meter relay. "...The Americans," wrote Walt Murphy for *Track & Field News*, "with Flojo and Ashford — the two fastest women in history — knew that they had the fastest team, but they were concerned about the Soviets ... Alice Brown, who also ran leadoff at L.A. in 1984, and last year in Rome (both gold medalists), ran her usual great turn and, combined with an excellent pass to Sheila Echols, gave the U.S. a meter's lead." Murphy continues:

> ...Echols ran well down the back stretch, but surrendered the lead to Kerstin Behrendt and Galina Maichugina on the pass to Griffith Joyner.
> Flojo passed Ingrid Lange and Marina Zhirova with a great curve, but Evelyn "froze" on the handoff, and found herself in 3rd as they straightened out for the stretch drive.
> Natalya Pomoshchnikova caught Gohr in the first 20m, only to suffer a cramp with 40 to go. Ashford, with a precarious grip on the baton, caught and passed Gohr with just 20m left and pulled away for the win, 41.98–42.09. She also wiped her brow after crossing the finish line.

The *New York Times* added, "Evelyn Ashford, in what could have been her farewell appearance, took the baton with 100 meters left and said goodbye to her competition. Ashford, after an awkward handoff from Florence Griffith Joyner, brought home the gold for the U.S. with an inspired anchor leg in the women's 400 meter relay."

4 × 400 meter relay. Again, from *Track & Field News*: "...The U.S. lament was that superstar Florence Griffith Joyner, recruited to run anchor, could not bring home a fourth gold, 'I gave it my all and everybody ran excellent times,' she said. 'Plus we got the American record.'

Alice Brown (left) and Dr. Ernie Gregoire.

"...Denean Howard opened with a solid 49.7 to give the U.S. a slight edge.... Diane Dixon and open bronze medalist Nazarova cruised easily together around the first turn until Dixon quickly made the cut to the pole. Just as suddenly, Nazarova assumed the lead at the top of the second curve, an edge the Soviets would never surrender." Dixon ran 49.2

"...Valerie Brisco snatched the baton for the Americans and persistently whittled down the Soviet lead, gaining ground strongly in the stretch. Brisco ran a blazing 48.5 leg.

"...The multi-medaled Flojo seemed content to settle in behind the open gold winner Bryzgina around the penultimate turn and down the final backstretch.... Midway in the final bend, Griffith Joyner got as close as she ever would, pulling to within a couple of strides of the Soviet's shoulder. But the Flojo lift never happened; she maintained a strong cadence throughout the lap but appeared never to vary it. Maybe she gained an inch or two.

"...Even though she was never able to find a higher gear, Griffith Joyner still produced the quickest U.S. leg of 48.1."

The Americans ran 3:15.51, a new American record.

The *New York Times* added,

> The capacity crowd of 70,000 at Olympic Stadium watched Griffith Joyner run three races in 135 minutes. First came a semifinal of the 400-meter relay, which the United States won despite ragged baton passing. Next was the final of that relay, in which the Americans put themselves in trouble with the last baton pass, from Griffith Joyner to Evelyn Ashford.
>
> Now Griffith Joyner had only 40 minutes before the 1,600-meter relay final. She started the anchor leg of that race a meter behind the Russians, fell 5 meters back, then closed the gap, but not all of it. The Americans' time of 3:15.51 was the second fastest in history. Griffith Joyner ran her anchor leg of 400 meters in 48.1 seconds, the fastest split for the Americans.

High jump. Again, from the *New York Times*:

Louise Ritter at the 1984 Olympic Games. (AAF/LPI 1984.)

...It was at 6' 4" that the major actors began to be identified, 6 jumpers continuing perfect, 1 missing once and 5 going out.

...6' 5" took care of Astafei and Andonova (and Chris Stanton). Bykova needed two tries, leaving Kostadinova, Ritter and Turchak tied for the lead. At 6' 6¼", Ritter's calf touched the bar, but it remained on.... They all followed the proper script at 6' 7", Kosta clearing cleanly, Ritter hitting with her back — but clearing — and Bykova going out (with bronze).

It would obviously be all over at 6' 8", equal to Ritter's AR, but a height which Kosta had cleared in 29 meets (and gone even higher in 25 of those) in her life.

But suddenly no one could clear, and six misses put them into a jump-off situation, the first since 1936. When Kostadinova missed, it was suddenly the bottom of the 9th with two out. Call it a hit and run, as Ritter's thigh brushed the bar, but it held. Ritter, it can well be imagined, went bonkers. After the initial rush was over, she ran to the stands, and one could see her face on the big screen mouthing, "Where's my mom?"

With a new American record, Louise became the first American to win the high jump in thirty-two years. Coleen Sommer and Trish King did not make the final.

1. Louise Ritter	6' 8"	OR, AR

Long jump. "...Nothing had changed when Jackie stood at the top of the runway for her fifth jump," reported Jim Dunaway for *Track & Field News*. The pressure was on, and one of the greatest come-through athletes in history responded with a superb 24 3½, the second-best non-windy jump of her life.

...Husband Bob leaped onto the track and after the mandatory hugging and kissing started her on a victory lap.

Of her winning effort, Jackie said, "All I wanted to do was concentrate on my consistency and get a good jump. I was fouling because I was trying to go faster. This was only my third long jump competition of the year."

...Carol Lewis, No. 2 all-time U.S. jumper, missed qualifying by a centimeter and third American Sheila Echols was another 10cm back.

1. Jackie Joyner-Kersee	24' 3½" OR

Shot put. The only American woman to qualify for the final was Bonnie Dasse. She missed her PR by 1'¾" and qualified 11th at 63' 9¾". In the final, she placed 12th with a put of 57' 9". Americans Ramona Pagel (60' 10½") and Connie Price (56' 1") did not qualify.

12. Bonnie Dasse	57' 9"

Discus. *Track & Field News* reported: "...The lone American in the final, Carol Cady, had a respectable 208' 1"." Ramona Pagel and Connie Price did not qualify for the final. Carol Cady finished in eleventh place.

11. Carol Cady	208' 1"

Javelin. "...Donna Mayhew was the loan U.S. entrant among the final dozen after her 202–0 took the last qualifying spot." Karin Smith (190' 1") and Lynda Sutfin (184' 1") did not qualify for the final. Mayhew placed 7th with her third throw in the final round of 202' 8".

7. Donna Mayhew	202' 8"

Heptathlon. The *New York Times* said, "Her lead was so substantial that Joyner-Kersee could have just about walked around the track twice and won the women's test of stamina and overall ability. But still on her mind was 1984, in Los Angeles, when she lost the Olympic gold by one-third of a second. Joyner-Kersee finished with 7,291 points, 76 more than her previous best."

"The trouble with being Jackie Joyner-Kersee is that you ultimately wind up competing against yourself, such was the case in these Olympics," continued *Track & Field News*.

100 hurdles: "A solid start. Aided by a modest 0.5 wind Jackie ran 12.69 for a heptathlon AR, missing the HWR by only 0.05."

High jump: "...Joyner-Kersee, straining a knee, topped out at 6' 1¼", an inch or so below expectations."

Shot: "...Jackie threw 51–10, her second best ever in a multi."

200m: *Track & Field News* continues: "Setter of the HWR of 22.30 at the OT, Joyner-Kersee couldn't expect to do as well here. But she did fine, sprinting all the way for a 22.56, second best ever. That burst of speed broke the actual competition wide open.

"Off to a great start for the first day, Jackie now needed some of the help made available by modern technology. Her knee was treated with ice, ultrasound and cross-fiber massage and she slept with mild electric current on the joint. Coach/husband Bob Kersee observed, 'After the first day people wrote off the World Record. They were people who don't know Jackie.'

Long jump: "Indeed, Joyner-Kersee came out flying, sore knee and all. She said she didn't keep her legs up as long as she hoped. But the result was a sensational 23–10¼. It broke both the HWR and open OR."

Javelin: "Her worst event, and the most erratic, the spear produced a less-than-average 149–10...."

800m: Again, from *Track & Field News*:

Finally it was WR time, Jackie needing 2:13.67 to surpass herself. She had had a better time in two of the last four big meets. It was no cinch then, but Jackie reminded, "I had always said that when the time came I would be able to do it."

And do it she did, pacing nicely and doing everything to put the record as far out as possible. Her 2:08.51, bettering a PR set six years ago, gave her more than enough....

Cindy Greiner, a veteran at 31, came up with a PR 6297, good for 8th, a better-than-expected finish. America's third entrant, newcomer Wendy Brown, was 18th at 5972.

1. Jackie Joyner-Kersee	7291	WR
8. Cindy Greiner	6297	
18. Wendy Brown	5972	

The Olympic Trials

The United States Olympic trials were held at the Indiana University Track Stadium in Indianapolis, Indiana from July 15 through the 23rd.

Headlines in the *New York Times* after the first day's events were of Carl Lewis's fast 100 meter time, but the photograph under the headline was of Valerie Brisco relaxing while having her foot massaged by her coach, Bobby Kersee.

The article by Frank Litsky said that while the heat and humidity were oppressive, Jackie Joyner-Kersee was "magnificent." Litsky writes:

After the day's four events, Joyner-Kersee totaled 4,367 points, the highest first day score ever. She was 222 points ahead of her world record pace and 593 points ahead of second-place Cindy Greiner.

She ran the 100-meter hurdles in 12.71 seconds and high-jumped 6 feet 4 inches, both American heptathlon records. Then she put the shot 51 feet 4¼ inches, a meet record, and won the 200-meter dash in 22.30 seconds, a world heptathlon record.

"Over all, I am pleased," she said, "but I can do better."

Headlines in Sunday's *New York Times* read, "Griffith Joyner Breaks World Mark in 100" and "Joyner-Kersee Snaps Record in Heptathlon."

On a windy, 98 degree day, "Jackie Joyner-Kersee shattered her world record for the women's heptathlon, totaling 7,215 points for the seven events over two days. Her sister-in-law, Florence Griffith Joyner, decimated the world record for the women's 100-meter dash, though her time of 10.49 seconds was beclouded by a controversy over whether there was too much aiding wind."

The 11,567 spectators were treated to a "day of incredible speed." Twenty-eight year old, Florence Griffith Joyner,

wearing a body suit with one of its legs cut off, ... won her heat by 4 meters in 10.60 seconds, the fastest 100 ever run to that point. It was far faster than Evelyn Ashford's 1984 world record of 10.76, but the following wind of 3.2 meters a second, or 7.15 miles an hour, ruled it out as a record. International rules say that for record purposes, a following wind cannot exceed 2 meters a second, or 4.47 miles an hour.

Two and a half hours after her heat, Griffith Joyner won her quarterfinal by almost 4 meters. Her time of 10.49 bettered Ashford's record by 27 hundredths of a second, an astounding margin. In the 20 years that only automatic times have been recognized, the record for the women's 100 had never been broken by more than 13-hundredths of a second.

Still no one seemed to quibble about Griffith Joyner's time. Lewis seemed to speak for everyone when he talked of her "unbelievable time." But wind, or lack of wind, was another matter.... The wind reading for Griffith Joyner's race was reported as 0.0, which meant there was no following or hindering wind. The wind reading for the next 100-meter quarterfinal was also 0.0. For the next one, it was 5 meters a second, or 11.18 miles an hour.

To many, the 0.0 readings seemed illogical. During the race, flags near the scoreboard were almost stiff from the wind. A wind-speed meter along the triple-jump runway, 15 feet from the sprint straightaway, read 2.9 meters a second. Officials on the field said the wind was swirling there all day. They said Omega officials told them there was a 92-degree crosswind during the race. Griffith Joyner said, "I didn't feel the wind like I did in the first race." But she also said, "I can't believe the time. I didn't think it was possible today."

Officials debated this issue and checked the wind gauge. Mike Gibbons, an Omega official said, "But as far as we're concerned," he said, "we're staying with it. We tested it after the next race and couldn't find anything wrong."

Monday's *New York Times* carried a photograph on the first page of Florence being lifted in the air by her coach, Bobby Kersee, along a side headline reading, "Griffith Joyner Keeps Going." Litsky wrote,

> Florence Griffith Joyner is for real. While the debate continued over her controversial and totally unexpected 100 world record of 10.49 seconds Saturday, she ran two more sensational 100s today at the United States Olympic trials.
>
> First, with an acceptable aiding wind of 2.68 miles per hour, she won her semifinal in 10.70 seconds. Two hours later, with an acceptable following wind of 3.58 miles per hour she won the final in 10.61 seconds. She beat Evelyn Ashford, the 1984 Olympic champion, by 2 meters, a wide margin at this level of competition.
>
> Thus, in two days, Griffith Joyner ran the fastest legal 100-meters ever —10.49, 10.70 and 10.61— plus a 10.60 with excessive wind in the first round. The next fastest legal time in the meet was Ashford's 10.81 in the final. Until Saturday, the world record was 10.76, set by Ashford in 1984.
>
> ...Griffith Joyner had never been a force at 100 meters, but she had won silver medals at 200 meters in the 1984 Olympics and at the 1987 world championships. So no one seemed surprised that she ran fast here, only at how fast she ran.
>
> "I'm a little bit surprised," said Griffith Joyner after the final. "My goal coming here was to go under 11 flat four times. I've been nervous. I was packed two weeks ago ready to go to the Olympic trials."

The *New York Times* reported on Tuesday that a nasty fall at the finish of the 800 meters almost cost Joetta Clark a berth on the team.

"'I could feel someone behind me,' said Clark. 'My legs got tight. I leaned, and my spikes caught the track and I fell. I hit my head and shoulder on the track. Look at this scrape on my shoulder. I didn't know I made the team until someone handed me a little flag.'"

Diane Dixon, who led from the start, held off Denean Howard by two hundredths of a second in the 400 meters.

Donna Mayhew's winning javelin throw of 208' 10" made her the third ranked American in history.

"Griffith Joyner Breaks U.S. Record in 200," was the headline of Michael Janofsky's article in Saturday's *New York Times*. "For the first time in the Olympic track and field trials, Florence Griffith Joyner wore a 'two-legger,' and the ever-changing decorations on her hand-painted fingernails showed palm trees, birds and moons on her left hand, random designs with rhinestones on her right." The story continues:

> Not that the new look made much difference in the way she ran tonight. She covered her 200-meter quarterfinal in 21.77 seconds to break the four-year-old American record of 21.81, held by the woman who was running two lanes to her right, Valerie Brisco.
>
> ...Through eight days of competition, she has been the meet's most stunning performer, setting a world record in the 100 meters, 10.49 seconds, and now a national record in the 200.
>
> To say nothing of her dazzling outfits, she designed, shiny spandex running suits. But until tonight, all of the one-legged variety in purple, black, lime, pink and blue. She described the two-legger as being "florescent golden yellow." "I like variety," she said. "I came here with 14 different outfits."
>
> ...The women's 200-meter competition began early in the day with 27 starters. Because six other athletes had entered but chose not to run, none in the group was eliminated from the second round tonight.

In the first race, Griffith Joyner won her heat in 21.96 seconds, which was only a meet record. "I pushed too much this morning," she said, comparing her two races. "I wasn't as balanced. I struggled with the curve. Tonight, the wind felt good, and I was a lot more relaxed. I took the curve a lot easier, and didn't try to push it at all."

Griffith Joyner, who finished second to Brisco in the 1984 Olympic Games, had run in the first of five heats in the morning race; Brisco had finished fourth in the fourth heat, wearing one shoe. It loosened on her with about 60 meters to go and she finally kicked it off with about 15 to go to finish in 23.69.

"I felt the shoe coming off around the curve and fought it," she said. "Then I decided to just let it go. It was a new pair of shoes."

In the second round, they were assigned lanes five and seven, and that was invitation enough for Griffith Joyner to go for a record.

"I wanted to take it from here while she's in the race," Griffith Joyner said. "I just liked it better that way."

Brisco finished behind Griffith Joyner in 22.36 seconds. Gwen Torrence, the 1987 N.C.A.A. champion, was the fastest of the other heat winners. Her time of 22.26 made her the sixth-best American performer ever. Alice Brown (22.53) and Dannette Young (22.70) won the other heats.

The crowd of 12,017 also saw Lynn Nelson win the 10,000 meters in meet record time of 31:51.27; thirty five year old Francie Larrieu Smith run 32:03.63 in the 10,000 meters to make her fourth Olympic team; and Jackie Humphrey win a close 100 meter hurdles.

In the 100-meter hurdles final of the 1984 Olympic trials, the first four women finished within a hundredth of a second. The race here was almost as close, with the first four separated by six-hundredths of a second, no more than two feet. Of those four, the one who was shut out was Benita Fitzgerald-Brown, the '84 Olympic champion.

Of the final nine events on the last day of the trials before a near capacity crowd of 13,796, Florence Griffith Joyner produced another outstanding performance in the 200 meters. Sunday's *New York Times* exclaimed, "Griffith Joyner Takes The 200." Michael Janofsky wrote

As she has often in previous days of the trials, Griffith Joyner overshadowed almost everyone else. Today, she won the 200-meter dash in 21.85 seconds, not a record but her fourth consecutive race under 22 seconds.

Pam Marshall, a two-time national champion, finished second in 21.93 seconds, and Gwen Torrence, a former N.C.A.A. champion, was third in 22.02. Both times were personal bests.

"The race was okay," said Griffith Joyner, who had run a wind-aided 21.90 in the semifinals two hours before. "I came to qualify for the Olympic Games and to stay healthy, and I accomplished that. I wanted to run the best curve of my life, and I feel when I run it strongly and relaxed, like I did today, I complete my purpose. Now I'm ready for my final goal, some Olympic gold."

Griffith Joyner's sister-in-law, Jackie Joyner-Kersee, also made the team in a second event. She won the long jump with an effort of 24 feet 5½ inches, but not without a scare. On her third attempt, she skinned her knee on the concrete pit and had to be assisted out of the landing pit.

...Sheila Echols and Carol Lewis, Carl Lewis's sister, also made the team in the long jump, Lewis with an effort of 22–7 on her final attempt.

...Mary Slaney ran the third-fastest time ever by an American in the women's 1,500, 3:58.92, a meet record....

Regina Jacobs was second behind Slaney in 4:00.26, and Kim Gallagher, who had won the 800 final last Monday, was third in 4:05.41.

Louise Ritter, the American record-holder, set a meet record winning the high-jump competition, clearing the bar at 6–6¼. Trish King and Coleen Sommer qualified by clearing 6–5.

Ramona Pagel and Connie Price placed first and second to qualify for the team in a second event. Both made it in the women's discus.

---

100 meters

"During the three early rounds and the final," commented *Runner's World*, "six women clocked legal sub–11-second marks ... because Devers-Roberts pulled out of the finals to save herself for her stronger event, the 100-meter hurdles, Torrence had a better chance to make the team. After she squeaked by Sheila Echols, Torrence lifted her legs in the air in a series of jubilant scissor kicks. 'I knew that Evelyn would run well, and we all knew how Florence was running, but the third spot was wide open,' said Torrence after her victory lap. 'I felt that if I performed here as I had in practice, that spot would be mine.'"

1. Florence Griffith-Joyner, World Class Athletic Club	10.61
2. Evelyn Ashford, Mazda Track Club	10.81
3. Gwen Torrence, Athletics West	10.91
4. Sheila Echols, Athletics West	11.00
5. Alice Brown, unattached	11.04
6. Dannette Young, Reebok Racing Club	11.19
7. Jennifer Inniss, Atoms Track Club	11.21
Gail Devers-Roberts DNS	

200 meters

Runner's World, commenting on Griffith Joyner said,

The other competitors in the 200 only got to see the eye-catching costume from the rear — which is just what third-finishing Gwen Torrence had expected. "If you're going to wear outfits like that," said Torrence, already Griffith Joyner's 100-meter Olympic teammate, "then you better do something in them."

Griffith Joyner eased around the curve as relaxed as ever, taking the lead from a fading Alice Brown. She powered through the straight, finishing in 21.85, the fourth-best U.S. performance ever.

1. Florence Griffith Joyner, World Class Athletic Club	21.85
2. Pam Marshall, World Class Athletic Club	21.93
3. Gwen Torrence, Athletics West	22.02
4. Valerie Brisco, World Class Athletic Club	22.11
5. Alice Brown, unattached	22.39
6. Dannette Young, Reebok Racing Team	22.52
7. Wendy Vereen, Morgan State University	22.93
8. Diane Williams, unattached	22.98

400 meters

"After the gun sounded," reported *Runner's World*, "Dixon and the youthful Indianapolis favorite Maicel Malone zipped through the first 200 meters with Denean Howard a step back. Nearly dead even after dropping Malone at the end of the second turn, Dixon and Howard hurtled down the straight. At the tape, Dixon outleaned Howard, edging her by 2 one-hundredths of a second."

1. Diane Dixon, unattached	50.38
2. Denean Howard, Tyson International	50.40
3. Valerie Brisco, World Class Athletic Club	50.53
4. Lillie Leatherwood, Reebok Racing Team	50.68
5. Sherri Howard, Tyson International	51.63
6. Maicel Malone, Nike Coast Track Club	51.98
7. Jearl Miles, Young Achievers Sprint Club	52.14
8. Terri Dendy, Reebok Racing Team	52.82

800 meters

"Gallagher took the lead at 600 meters after Essie Washington, the 1979 Pan American

Florence Griffith Joyner (right) at the 1988 Olympic Trials — 200 meters. (©www.photorun.net)

Games champ, stumbled for the second time in the Trials competition," reported *Runner's World*. The article continues:

> Washington had been a late entry in the final after officials ruled that a foul caused her first fall in the semis. She eased home in last place.
>
> By contrast, Gallagher won jubilantly in a PR and meet record 1:58.01.... Delisa Walton-Floyd (1:59.20) followed Gallagher's lead and had second place to herself with 60 meters left. But third-finishing Joetta Clark wasn't sure of her place or possible Olympic status as she pumped toward the finish. With Debbie Marshall matching her every step, Clark lunged at the line. "It was a combination of tripping and diving," she said. "I had to do something."

1. Kim Gallagher, Los Angeles Track Club   1:58.01   MR
2. Delisa Walton-Floyd, unattached   1:59.20
3. Joetta Clark, Athletics West   1:59.93
4. Debbie Marshall, Team Elite   1:59.97
5. Julie Jenkins, Reebok Racing Club   2:01.62
6. Kathleen Harris-Rounds, unattached   2:01.86
7. Karol Davidson, University of Texas   2:04.35
8. Patricia Melton, Liberty Athletic Club   2:04.88
9. Essie Washington, Houston Track Club   2:18.2 ht

1500 meters

According to *Runner's World*:

Coming in as the clear front-runner in the '88 Trials, Mary Slaney had a plan. On the comeback trail, she plotted to win the 3000, then win the 1500 as in her Helsinki World Championships double and maybe run close to her American record PR. "If the conditions aren't atrocious, I can go for the American record," said Slaney, after a classy win in the 3000. "In the finals (the others) will go with me, well, at least until the third lap."

But she didn't count on Regina Jacobs, who, with a game plan of her own, caught Slaney on — guess where? — the bell lap and threatened to make lightening strike twice. Slaney powered home in 3:58.92, a meet and stadium record and the third-fastest American time ever. Jacobs finished solidly in second place clocking a PR 4:00.46.

1. Mary Slaney, Athletics West	3:58.92	MR
2. Regina Jacobs, unattached	4:00.46	
3. Kim Gallagher, Los Angeles Track Club	4:05.41	
4. Ruth Wysocki, unattached	4:06.58	
5. Julie Jenkins, Reebok Racing Club	4:06.66	
6. Diana Richburg, Puma Track Club	4:09.68	
7. Alisa Harvey, Athletics West	4:09.73	
8. Sabrina Dornhoefer, Athletics West	4:12.07	

3000 meters

"Slaney displayed her distinctive style as she took off with typical 'catch-me-if-you-can' strategy," stated *Runner's World*. The article goes on:

Everyone fell in behind her, a concession to her years-old role as the country's pacesetter. She slowed after the first 1000 meters only when it seemed that the 98-degree heat and 55 percent humidity might offer a bigger challenge than her opponents. Her time, 8:42.53, marked her fastest of the season.

Only Vicki Huber dared to run with Slaney. She caught up at midrace and shared the lead until the last lap, but never tried to pass. Still, the move made her an Olympian at 21, and her second-place 8:46.48 broke her collegiate record.

Third-finisher PattiSue Plumer, sixth in this event in the '84 Olympic Trials and once an NCAA 5000-meter champion for Stanford, ran the race of her life. She shadowed Slaney early on, but fell back into fifth place later. A bell-lap rally, including a last-stretch duel with Sabrina Dornhoefer, saved her Olympic dreams. As Dornhoefer stumbled and fell from exhaustion 10 meters short of the finish, Plumer ran on to an 8:49.21.

1. Mary Slaney, Athletics West	8:42.53
2. Vicki Huber, Villanova University	8:46.48
3. PattiSue Plumer, unattached	8:49.21
4. Sabrina Dornhoefer, Athletics West	8:57.63
5. Mary Knisley, New Balance Track Club	9:02.05
6. Ruth Wysocki, unattached	9:03.01
7. Leslie Seymour, Club Sota	9:10.26
8. Annette Hand, University of Oregon	9:14.73

100 meter hurdles

"Humphrey, 22 and with no international experience, beat a stellar field," reported *Runner's World*. By the eighth hurdle, she had raced away from runner-up Gail Devers-Roberts (12.90), who had set the 12.61 American record two months ago, and third-place LaVonna Martin (12.93), the '87 Pan American Games champion on the same track. That trio edged out Benita Fitzgerald-Brown and Kim McKenzie (formerly Turner), the Olympic gold and bronze medalists in Los Angeles."

1. Jackie Humphrey, Eastern Kentucky University   12.88
2. Gail Devers-Roberts, World Class Athletic Club   12.90
3. LaVonna Martin, unattached   12.93
4. Benita Fitzgerald-Brown, Mazda Track Club   12.94
5. Kim McKenzie, Mazda Track Club   13.01
6. Patricia Davis, Mazda Track Club   13.04
7. Stephanie Hightower-Leftwich, Mazda Track Club   14.02
8. Rhonda Blanford, Denver Track Club   15.00

400 meter hurdles

Runner's World reported that Sheffield took off quickly at the gun "with Leslie Maxie right with her through the first five hurdles. On the curve, Schowonda Williams caught up to the leaders, and the three ran dead even through the final three hurdles. At the finish, Williams crossed the line first, tying Judi Brown King's 54.93 meet record, just ahead of runner-up Maxie. Sheffield edged fourth-place Linetta Wilson by four one-hundredths of a second and a lean."

1. Schowonda Williams, Tyson International Track Club   54.93   equals MR
2. Leslie Maxie, Millbrae Lions Track Club   55.29
3. LaTanya Sheffield, San Diego Track Club   55.70
4. Linetta Wilson, University of Nebraska   55.74
5. Judi Brown-King, Athletics West   56.56
6. Kathy Freeman, Tyson International   56.89
7. Gayle Kellon, World Class Athletic Club   57.18
8. Leisa Knowles, San Diego Track Club   57.73

5000 meters (exhibition)
1. Andrea Ward, Santa Monica Track Club   16:25.50
2. Carmen Ayala-Troncoso, Nike Coast Track Club   16:28.51
3. Desiree Scott, unattached   16:29.97
4. Judy Bogenschutz, Indiana Track Club   16:40.28
5. Marty Geissler, Nike Boston Track Club   16:42.70
6. Carey Hill, unattached   16:50.54
7. Mary Shea, Michigan State University   16:51.46
8. Celsa Boman, unattached   16:52.96

10,000 meters

This event was run for the first time for women as an Olympic event in Seoul.

Runner's World reported "Fifty-three women came together early in the week to race for the 18 spots in the final." The story continues:

...After jockeying for position through the middle miles, Nelson made her big break with six laps to go. Francie Larrieu Smith, running strong in second, gave chase, but never caught up. Margaret Groos, winner of the Marathon Trials, dropped out, apparently a victim of stomach cramps.

That left Athletics West teammates Lynn Jennings and Nan Doak-Davis fighting for the last spot on the team. Jennings had ruled 10,000 meter racing in the United States the last three years.

...And then came a surprise. Over the last mile, even as Jennings and Doak-Davis swapped places several times, a tall figure loomed in their shadows. It was Lisa Weidenbach, the unlucky soul who had placed fourth in both the 1984 and 1988 Marathon Trials.

Of course, with Jennings and her aided last-lap sprint, a fairy-tale ending for Weidenbach seemed highly unlikely. She did manage to catch Jennings and Doak-Davis with 500 meters to go. Doak-Davis kicked at the bell, briefly circling her teammate. But then Jennings shifted gears and roared down the backstretch. "I figured I'd better run safe than sorry," she said moments later, explaining her wait-'til-the-bitter-end approach. "I never thought it would be a runaway by any-one, because the stakes are too high."

1. Lynn Nelson, Reebok Racing Club	31:51.27
2. Francie Larrieu-Smith, New Balance Track Club	32:03.63
3. Lynn Jennings, Athletics West	32:07.74
4. Nan Doak-Davis, Athletics West	32:14.05
5. Lisa Weidenbach, Team adidas	32:15.88
6. Betty Geiger, Athletics West	32:33.04
7. Cathie Twomey, Nike Portland Track Club	32:38.11
8. Marty Cooksey, Team Kangaroo	32:40.35

10 kilometer walk

1. Debbi Lawrence, Team Os-Cal	47:52.15
2. Teresa Vaill, unattached	48:56.44
3. Sara Standley, Southern California Road Runners	50:04.98
4. Wendy Sharp, unattached	50:16.02
5. Maryanne Torrellas, Reebok Racing Club	50:38.01
6. Victoria Herazo, Valley Track Club	50:38.27
7. Viisha Sedlak, unattached	51:27.17
8. Deirdre Collier, University of Wisconsin, Parkside	51:32.96

High jump

1. Louise Ritter, Mazda Track Club	6' 6¼"	MR
2. Trish King, Reebok Racing Team	6' 5"	
3. Coleen Sommer, Athletics West	6' 5"	
4. Rita Graves, Mazda Track Club	6' 2¾"	
5. Latrese Johnson, unattached and Amber Welty, Idaho	6' 2¾"	
7. Felicia Hodges, Temple University	6' 1½"	
8. Jan Wohlschlag, Nike Coast and Shelly Fehrman, Nike Coast	6' 1½"	

Long jump

1. Jackie Joyner Kersee, World Class Athletic Club	24' 5¼" w
2. Sheila Echols, Athletics West	22' 7"
3. Carol Lewis, Santa Monica Track Club	22' 7" w
4. Yvette Bates, Southern California Cheetahs	22' 7" w
5. Jennifer Inniss, Atoms Track Club	21' 7½"
6. Claire Connor, Louisiana State University	21' 7½" w
7. Cindy Greiner, Athletics West	21' 7¼" w
8. Julie Goodrich, University of Oregon	21' 1¼" w

Triple Jump (exhibition)

1. Renita Robinson, South Bay Track Club	44' 4¾" w
2. Angela Goodman, unattached	42' 2¾" w
3. Julie Lewis-Harris, Louisiana State University	41' 11½"
4. Robyne Johnson, unattached	41' 4½" w
5. Starlite Williams, unattached	41' 2¼"
6. Brenda McDonald, Auburn University	41' 2¼" w

| 7. Kim Batten, Florida State University | 40' 5" w |
| 8. Laketa Ziegler, Auburn University | 40' 1½" |

Shot put

1. Ramona Pagel, Mazda Track Club	63' 5" MR
2. Bonnie Dasse, Nike Coast Track Club	61' 9½"
3. Connie Price, Athletics West	59' 6¼"
4. Pam Dukes, Nike Coast Track Club	57' 9¾"
5. Regina Cavanaugh, unattached	57' 3¾"
6. Carol Cady, unattached	55' 10¼"
7. Carla Garrett, University of Arizona	54' 11½"
8. Jennifer Ponath, Reebok Racing Club	54' 6¾"

Javelin

1. Donna Mayhew, South Bay Striders	208' 10"
2. Karin Smith, Nike Coast Track Club	185' 3"
3. Lynda Sutfin, Los Angeles Track Club	184'
4. Niki Nye, University of Texas	181'
5. Durelle Schimek, California Polytechnic, Pomona	176' 11"
6. Teri Okelberry, Weber State University	174' 10"
7. Lori Mercer, Nike Coast Track Club	166' 2"
8. Meg Foster, Mazda Track Club	165' 10"

Discus

1. Connie Price, Athletics West	201'
2. Ramona Pagel, Mazda Track Club	201'
3. Carol Cady, unattached	199'
4. Becky Levi, unattached	191' 8"
5. Carla Garrett, University of Arizona	183' 5"
6. Kathy Picknell, Nike Coast Track Club	178' 6"
7. Laura Lavine, Reebok Racing Club	176' 6"
8. Penny Neer, Nike Coast Track Club	175' 1"

Heptathlon, July 15–16

According to *Runner's World*,

At the end of four events [Joyner-Kersee] had racked up 4367 points, smashing her own first-day world best by 111 points. She posted a heptathlon PR in the 100-meter hurdles (12.71), a heptathlon American record high jump (6' 4") and a heptathlon world record 200 meters (22.30). In the shot put she was a mere 14" shy of her heptathlon best with a 51' 4¼" mark. Despite a second day with three-digit temperatures, Joyner-Kersee nonetheless long jumped 22' 11" and came within an inch of her javelin best with a 164' 4" heave. With six events down, Joyner-Kersee needed only 757 points to erase the world record, which translated to a 2:25.02 in the dreaded 800 meters.

Although she boasts a 2:09.69 PR, the 800 has sometimes been a stumbling block in the past. At the World Championships last year, a tired, dehydrated Joyner-Kersee missed the mark by 2.2 seconds when a 2:16.29 800 left her 30 points away. "My biggest problem with that race is my own mentality," said Joyner-Kersee, who admits she's scared of the event. "But I've been working with Brooks Johnson [Stanford University coach] to get over that fear."

She wasn't running scared in Indianapolis as she finished a half-step behind Greiner in 2:20.70 to reach a new world-record total of 7,215, a 57-point increase on her previous mark. The real race, however, heated up behind the leaders as Jane Frederick, 36, battled hamstring problems and newcomer Wendy Brown for the third spot on the team. In the end, Brown, 22, who was a wee kindergartner when Frederick made her first of two Olympic teams in 1972 as a pentathlete, ended Frederick's hopes. "I didn't expect to be on the team," said a wide-eyed Brown, a recent graduate of the University of Southern California. "I felt a tremendous amount of pressure going into the 800. I just tried to stick with Jane until the last 100 and then kick."

The *New York Times* added:

> Jackie Joyner-Kersee completed her remarkable assault on another world record today in the heptathlon, finishing with 7,215 points at the United States track and field Olympic trials to become the first athlete to break 7,200 points, for her third world record in two years.
>
> By going over 7,000 points for the fourth time — no other athlete has done it even once — she passed her previous mark of 7,158, set in 1986, and extended her consecutive victory streak in the heptathlon to nine.

1. Jackie Joyner-Kersee, World Class Athletic Club	7215	WR
2. Cindy Greiner, Athletics West	6226	
3. Wendy Brown, Mazda Track Club	6079	
4. Jane Frederick, Athletics West	6048	
5. Anita Behrbaum, Champions in Action	5839	
6. Crystal Young, Boise State University	5621	
7. Trish King, Reebok Racing Club	5611	
8. Terri Turner, Tyson Track Club	5604	

Marathon Trials: Pittsburgh, Pennsylvania, May 1

Track & Field News wrote,

> ...Groos became just the fourth American to break 2:30 and the first new member of the club since 1983. Ditz and O'Brien also claimed PRs.
>
> Groos took the lead for good in the 22nd mile, while Ditz, 33, fought off O'Brien challenges at 23 and 25M.
>
> Groos finished comfortably as the 20-year-old O'Brien, youngest runner in the field (just as in 1984, when she finished 9th), maintained a comfortable margin over Weidenbach, the 4th place finisher, just as in '84.

1. Margaret Groos	2:29:50	MR
2. Nancy Ditz	2:30:14	
3. Cathy Schiro-O'Brien	2:30:18	
4. Lisa Larsen-Weidenbach	2:31:06	
5. Kim Rosenquist-Jones	2:32:16	
6. Deborah Raunig	2:32:36	
7. Maureen Custy-Roben	2:33:19	
8. Lynn Nelson	2:33:31	

224 women qualified — 159 finished

The Outdoor Nationals

The USA/Mobil Outdoor Track and Field Championships were held in Tampa, Florida at the University of Tampa, from June 16 through the 18.

The first report on June 16 in the *New York Times* stated:

Despite a painful knee injury, Jane Frederick of Santa Barbara, CA. took an impressive lead in the heptathlon today as the USA/Mobil Outdoor Track and Field Championships began.

The 36-year-old Frederick totaled 3,863 points for the four first-day events. Cathey Tyree of Gibson County, TN. was second with 3,508 points, and Sheila Tarr of Bakersfield, CA. was third with 3,495.

...Frederick has won nine national heptathlon and pentathlon titles, starting in 1972. Last year she won the bronze medal in the world championships. Jackie Joyner-Kersee of Long Beach, CA., who won the gold medal, is not competing here. Frederick has the best performances in each event here: 13.74 seconds in the 100-meter hurdles, 6 feet 1¼ inches in the high jump, 47' 7" in the shot-put and 24.14 (wind aided) in the 200-meter dash.

Frederick jammed her left knee in the high jump. She said that if the pain continued in the long jump, the first heptathlon event Thursday, she would quit the competition.

Final results in two events were reported on Friday. Carol Urish McLatchie of Topeka, Kansas, won the 10,000 meter run in 34:25.33 and the heptathlon was won by Sheila Tarr of Las Vegas, Nevada, in a personal best. "Jane Frederick of Santa Barbara, Calif., the heptathlon leader after the first day, dropped out of the competition with injuries," reported the *New York Times*. Stephanie Hightower fell on the first hurdle and was eliminated from the 100 meter hurdles.

Saturday's *New York Times* carried a feature article on Brian Cooper entitled, "Cooper Emerging As a Threat in 100." At the end of the story, Litsky reported that, "Women's meet records were set by Kim Turner McKenzie in the 100-meter hurdles (12.84 seconds), Brenda Webb in the 5,000 meters (15:18.71) and Jan Chesbro Wohlschlag in the high jump (6 feet 5½ inches)." Webb's time was the fastest in the world this year.

On Saturday, Vickie Huber won her first national title. Frank Litsky wrote a small article about her entitled "Huber Has Eyes On Olympic Games":

...The scene was the final night of the USA/Mobil Outdoor Track and Field Championships at Pepin/Rood Stadium. The 21-year-old Villanova junior from Wilmington, DE. won the women's 1,500 meters in 4 minutes 7.40 seconds, her fastest ever.

Huber has won the national collegiate 3,000 meter title the last two years. She will run the 3,000 in the United States Olympic trials July 15–23 in Indianapolis. The race here was designed to sharpen her speed, and it did.

Before the race, Marty Stern, the Villanova women's coach, told her: "When you finish, I want your fuel tank empty. But I don't want you to run out of gas."

As it turned out, Huber had a little fuel left, but she did not need it. Until the last 100 meters, it seemed she might because Sabrina Dornhoefer and Alisa Harvey were a step behind.

"I knew people were there, because my heels were being clipped and I heard breathing behind me," Huber said.

In the final straightaway, the fast pace and the 90-degree heat told on the others, and they faded badly. Huber beat Dornhoefer by 12 meters and Harvey by 20.

The only double winner of the four-day championships was Sheila Echols. She won the women's 100 meters Friday night and the long jump at 21 feet 1½ inches tonight.

100 meters

1.	Sheila Echols, Athletics West	11.04
2.	Esther Jones, Louisiana State University	11.24
3.	Michelle Finn, Atoms Track Club	11.32
4.	Dawn Sowell, unattached	11.34
5.	Andrea Thompson, Florida State University	11.54
6.	Tina Iheagwam, Nigeria	11.60
7.	Zelda Johnson, Southern California Cheetahs	11.63
8.	Pam Reynolds, Mazda Track Club	11.81

200 meters
1. Gwen Torrence, Athletics West   22.71
2. Diane Dixon, unattached   22.84
3. Rochelle Stephens, Nike Track Club   23.13
4. Dawn Sowell, unattached   23.21
5. Esther Jones, Louisiana State University   23.29
6. Michelle Finn, Atoms Track Club   23.82
7. Cathy Roberts, Nike Coast Track Club   24.04

400 meters
1. Lillie Leatherwood, Reebok Racing Club   50.70
2. Maicel Malone, Nike Coast Track Club   51.01
3. Jearl Miles, Young Achievers Sprint Club   51.35
4. Celena Mondie, University of Illinois   51.45
5. Tanya McIntosh, Atoms Track Club   51.76
6. Terri Dendy, Reebok Racing Club   52.19
7. Denise Mitchell, Nike Coast Track Club   52.24
8. Alice Jackson, Coca Cola Track Club   54.49

800 meters
1. Joetta Clark, Athletics West   1:59.79
2. Julie Jenkins, Reebok Racing Club   2:00.68
3. Debbie Marshall, Team Elite   2:00.83
4. Karol Davidson, University of Texas   2:01.03
5. Kathy Harris, unattached   2:01.46
6. Linda Sheskey, Athletics West   2:02.99
7. Jane Brooker, unattached   2:03.52
8. Celeste Halliday, Villanova University   2:05.09

1500 meters
1. Vicki Huber, Athletics West   4:07.40
2. Sabrina Dornhoefer, Athletics West   4:09.15
3. Alisa Harvey, Athletics West   4:10.49
4. Evelyn Adiru, Westchester Puma Track Club/Uganda   4:12.29
5. Rosalind Taylor, University of Maryland   4:13.42
6. Leslie Seymour, Club Sota   4:13.54
7. Pam Raglin, Louisiana State University   4:14.10
8. Sue Foster, Dominos Racing Team   4:14.87

3000 meters
1. Lynn Jennings, Athletics West   8:55.42
2. Joan Nesbit, New Balance Track Club   9:05.68
3. Trina Leopold, University of Texas   9:08.95
4. Lori Bearson, U.S. Army   9:10.98
5. Eleanor Simonsick, Moving Comfort   9:13.39
6. Darlene Beckford, Liberty Athletic Club   9:14.40
7. Shelly Steely, Team adidas   9:17.79
8. Sam Resh, unattached   9:18.28

5000 meters
1. Brenda Webb, Tiger Track Club   15:18.71   MR
2. Betty Geiger, Athletics West   15:46.50
3. Anne Schweitzer, Nike Texas   15:57.90

4. Colette Goudreau-Murphy, Athletics West   16:11.46
5. Carmen Ayala-Troncoso, Nike Texas   16:27.19
6. Marty Geissler, Nike Boston   16:40.61
7. Janet Smith, North Carolina State University   16:46.75
8. Maria Pazarentzos, Reebok Racing Club   16:50.70

10,000 meters
1. Carol Urish-McLatchie, Etonic   34:25.33
2. Judy Bogenschutz, Indiana Track Club   34:44.33
3. Wiley Fulham, Liberty Athletic Club   35:40.82
4. Susan Lupica, Boston Athletic Association   36:10.12
5. Anne Kuiken, DePaul University   36:29.30

10 kilometer walk
1. Maryanne Torrellas, Reebok Racing Club   48:25.3
2. Teresa Vaill, unattached   48:32.5
3. Wendy Sharp, unattached   50:50.3
4. Victoria Herazo, Valley Race Walkers   52:22.3
5. Mary Howell, Oregon International Track Club   52:43.2
6. Karen Reach, Shore Athletic Club   52:55.9
7. Sara Standley, Southern California Road Runners   54:30.8
8. Martha Iverson, Front Range Walkers   56:24.1

100 meter hurdles
1. Kim McKenzie, Mazda Track Club   12.84   MR
   (previous record, Rhonda Blanford, 12.85, 1985)
2. Benita Fitzgerald-Brown, Mazda Track Club   12.85
3. Lynda Tolbert, Arizona State University   13.12
4. Donna Waller, Goldwin Track Club   13.13
5. Rhonda Blanford, Denver Track Club   13.15
6. Patricia Davis, Mazda Track Club   13.16
7. Tananjalyn Stanley, Louisiana State University   13.24
8. Candy Young, Atoms Track Club   13.44

400 meter hurdles
1. Schowonda Williams, Louisiana State University   55.24
2. Leslie Maxie, Millbrae Lions Track Club   55.33
3. Victoria Fulcher, University of Illinois   55.88
4. Kathy Freeman, Louisiana State University   56.57
5. Arnita Epps, Southern California Cheetahs   56.80
6. Lori McCauley, Atoms Track Club   57.78
7. Rosie Edeh, unattached/Canada   57.88
8. Jennifer Harlan, Mountain West Track Club   58.23

Triple jump
1. Wendy Brown, Mazda Track Club   45' 4¼"
2. Nena Gage, Reebok Racing Club   42' 7"
3. Angela Goodman, Purdue University   42' 5½"
4. Renita Robinson, South Bay Track Club   42' 3¼"
5. Starlite Williams, unattached   41' 10¾"
6. Julie Lewis, Louisiana State University   40' 1¼"

High jump
1. Jan Wohlschlag, Nike Coast   6' 5½"   MR
2. Coleen Sommer, Athletics West   6' 3½"
3. Amber Welty, Idaho State University   6' 2¼"
4. Rita Graves, Stars and Stripes Track Club   6' 2¼"
5. Vicki Borsheim, University of Washington and   5' 11½"
     Jane Clough, Ather Track Club
7. Melinda Stott, Texas A&M University   5' 11½"
8. Mary Moore, unattached, Jolanda Jones, Houston Track Club 5' 11½"
     and Tonya Mendonca, Fresno State University

Long jump
1. Sheila Echols, Athletics West   21' 1½"
2. Claire Connor, Louisiana State University   21' ½"
3. Wendy Brown, Mazda Track Club   21'
4. Yvette Bates, Southern California Cheetahs   20' 11¾"
5. Julie Lewis-Harris, Louisiana State University   20' 9¼"
6. Nena Gage, Reebok Racing Club   20' 8½"
7. Shirley Scipio, St. Augustine's College   20' 4¼"
8. Sabrina Williams, Nike Coast   20' 1¾"

Shot put
1. Connie Price, Athletics West   62' 10" MR
2. Pam Dukes, Nike Coast   58' 1"
3. Peggy Pollock, Nike Coast   56' 9"
4. Jennifer Ponath, Reebok Racing Club   55' 5"
5. Carol Cady, unattached   54' 11"
6. Annette Bohach, Western Michigan Track Club   54' 4¾"
7. Regina Cavanaugh, unattached   54' 4½"
8. Dot Jones, unattached   53' 8¼"

Discus
1. Lacy Barnes, Fresno State University   203' 9"
2. Carol Cady, unattached   203' 4"
3. Penny Neer, Nike Coast   199' 2"
4. Becky Fettig, Club Sota   186' 10"
5. Kelly Landry, Mazda Track Club   185' 7"
6. Connie Price, Athletics West   178' 3"
7. Laura Lavine, Washington State University   177' 3"
8. Pam Dukes, Nike Coast   173' 1"

Javelin
1. Donna Mayhew, South Bay Track Club   194' 10"
2. Linda Sutfin, unattached   181' 5"
3. Marilyn Senz, US Army   180' 2"
4. Niki Nye, University of Texas   171' 5"
5. Sherrie MacKinney, University of North Carolina   162' 4"
6. Meg Foster, Mazda Track Club   159'
7. Erica Wheeler, Stanford University   158' 9"
8. Karen McGovern, Gateway Track Club   121' 9"

Heptathlon
1. Sheila Tarr, Track West   5881 w
2. Teri LeBlanc, University of Missouri   5518 w

3. Jill Lancaster, unattached		5513 w
4. Kerry Bell, Nike Coast		5490 w
5. Angela Taylor, unattached		5468 w
6. Laura Kirkham, Indiana Track Club		5267 w
7. Clara Lock, Marquette University		5159 w

Team scores:

1. Athletics West	96
2. Reebok Racing Club and Nike Coast Club	42
4. Mazda Track Club	38

The final article in the *New York Times* was entitled "Questions Abound Before Trials Start." The article questioned the talents of Vicki Huber and Brenda Webb in the Olympic trials. "Huber, a Villanova junior, has won the last two national collegiate titles in the women's 3,000 meters and will run that distance in the Olympic trials. But she was not sure she could run with the best postgraduates until her convincing victory in the 1,500 meters here in 4:07.40, her career best. 'This meet really didn't feel that different,' she said, 'until they introduced people as American champions. I still think the Olympic trials will blow me away.'"

About Brenda Webb, Frank Litsky wrote, "At age 34, the 5-foot-2-inch, 90-pound Webb is running faster than ever. She won the women's 5,000 meters in 15:18.71 and became the fifth-fastest American ever. But the 5,000 is not an Olympic distance, so Webb must decide whether to run 3,000 or 10,000 meters in the Olympic trials. In the Olympic trials, Webb would face Mary Decker Slaney in the 3,000 and Margaret Groos, Francie Larrieu Smith and probably Lynn Jennings in the 10,000."

The Indoor Nationals

The indoor nationals 100th anniversary meet was held in Madison Square Garden on Friday, February 26.

The *New York Times* headline on February 27 read "Torrence Keeps Streak Alive."

...Gwen Torrence at first believed she had extended her winning streak in sprint races with a photo-finish victory over Evelyn Ashford in the women's 55-meter dash. But after nearly all of the spectators had left, an announcement was made that the race had been ruled a dead heat, leaving Torrence with a 40-race unbeaten streak.

...Torrence and Ashford, the world record holder, were timed in 6.66 seconds. "She thought I had won," Torrence said, "I thought she had won."

Eventually, they were both right. But at first, after Torrence had been declared the winner, Ashford smiled and looked for the difference. "You outleaned me," Ashford said. "You won by your ponytail, or something."

Diane Dixon came from behind to win her sixth consecutive national 400-meter championship and her seventh in eight years, after breaking her national record of 51.95 seconds in a preliminary heat.

Dixon, who was voted the outstanding female performer, was shocked by her American record. She had been bothered by a sore hamstring muscle and a headache.

When she was told of the record, she said, "Stop playing." But there it was—51.95, surpassing the mark of 52 seconds she established in a preliminary heat at the national championships last year.

"I really had tears in my eyes," Dixon said. "I could not believe I ran that fast."

After Brisco took the early lead last night and the announced crowd of 14,643 became involved in the race, the thought occurred to Dixon that her record had come hours too soon.

Dixon made her move on the final backstretch, but Brisco, the gold medal winner at the Los Angeles Olympics and the only runner to defeat Dixon indoors this year, held on.

"I still couldn't get by her," Dixon remembered. "I said, My God, the race is almost over."

Her last burst — the decisive one — came after the last turn, when Dixon moved past Brisco in the final 25 meters.

Joyner-Kersee had problems from the start of the 55-meter hurdles. She slipped coming out of the starting blocks. She hit the fourth hurdle with her trailing knee, and hit the fifth hurdle with her trailing foot.

She still had a chance to challenge Julie Rocheleau of Montreal, who had also struck the fourth hurdle. "I felt like I was gaining on her," Joyner-Kersee said.

But as Joyner-Kersee strained to make up the difference, she stumbled and slid, face-down, across the finish line.

Maryanne Torrellas won the 3,000 meter walk in an American record time of 12:45.38.

---

55 meters
1. Gwen Torrence, Athletics West and   6.66
   Evelyn Ashford, Mazda Track Club
3. Sheila Echols, Athletics West   6.74

200 meters
1. Grace Jackson, unattached/Jamaica   23.07
2. Natalya Pomoshchnikova, USSR   23.38
3. Terri Dendy, George Mason University   23.93

400 meters
1. Diane Dixon, unattached   52.51
2. Valerie Brisco, World Class Athletic Club   52.90
3. Terri Dendy, George Mason University   52.98

800 meters
1. Mitica Junghiatu, Romania   2:03.27
2. Joetta Clark, Athletics West   2:03.41
3. Debbie Marshall, Team Elite   2:05.83

Mile
1. Doina Melinte, Romania   4:36.68
2. Alisa Harvey, Athletics West   4:39.61
3. Sheila Ralston, Track West   4:42.24

3000 meters
1. Sabrina Dornhoefer, Athletics West   9:03.59
2. Christine McMiken, Reebok Racing Club/New Zealand   9:05.81
3. Nan Davis, Athletics West   9:13.44

3000 meter walk
1. Maryanne Torrellas, Reebok Racing Club   12:45.38   AR
2. Teresa Vaill, unattached   12:47.32
3. Lynn Weik, unattached   13:24.88

55 meter hurdles
1. Julie Rocheleau, Canada   7.40
2. Lynda Tolbert, Arizona State University   7.50
3. Kim McKenzie, Mazda Track Club   7.54

4 × 400 meter relay
1. Rice University   3:46.17
   (Robin Bryant, Michele Lynch, Maureen Stewart/Costa Rica, Tanya McIntosh)

2. Seton Hall University	3:52.31
3. Concorde Track Club	3:52.62

High jump
1. Louise Ritter, Mazda Track Club	6' 4"
2. Debbie Brill, Pacific Coast Club/Canada	6' 2¾"
3. Jan Wohlschlag, Nike Coast Track Club	6' 1¼"

Shot put
1. Ramona Pagel, Mazda Track Club	61' 3"
2. Pam Dukes, Nike Coast Track Club	59' 3½"
3. Bonnie Dasse, Nike Coast Track Club	59' 1¼"

Long jump
1. Sheila Echols, Athletics West	21'
2. Jennifer Inniss, Atoms Track Club	20' 11"
3. Terri Turner, Nike Track Club	20' 9¾"

Team Champion
Athletics West

Sunkist Invitational (Three women's events): Los Angeles, January 22

440 yards
1. Diane Dixon, unattached	53.41

800 meters
1. Kim Gallagher, Los Angeles Track Club	2:07.99

Mile
1. Lynn Williams, Canada	4:36.18

Other News and Honors

Track & Field News: U.S. Athlete of the Year

Florence Griffith-Joyner

United States Top Five Rankings — Track & Field News

1. Florence Griffith-Joyner
2. Jackie Joyner-Kersee
3. Louise Ritter
4. Evelyn Ashford
5. Kim Gallagher

World Top Ten Women — Track & Field News

1. Florence Griffith-Joyner
2. Jackie Joyner-Kersee

Top American Road Women — *Track & Field News*

1. Lynn Jennings
2. Margaret Groos
3. Lisa Weidenbach
4. Nancy Ditz
5. Betty Geiger

Associated Press World Women's Athlete — Jackie Joyner-Kersee

Pat Rico was the women's track and field chair. She stepped down from that position at the end of 1988.

Jackie Joyner-Kersee set an American indoor record in the long jump of 23' ½" at the Vitalis/U.S. Olympic Invitational Track and Field Meet at the Meadowlands Arena in New Jersey.

Lynn Jennings won her third cross country title, the second consecutive title.

Florence Griffith-Joyner won the Sullivan Award.

The National Track and Field Hall of Fame inducted two women. The biographies below are from the USA Track and Field website.

Barbara Ferrell

Born July 28, 1947, in Hattiesburg, Mississippi. During a five-year span, Ferrell appeared in the 1968 and 1972 Olympic Games, the 1967 Pan American Games and the 1967 and 1970 World University Games. In 1967 and 1968, she had a hand in six world records, two at 100 meters, two at 200 meters and two in the 4 × 100 meter relay. At the 1968 Olympics in Mexico City, Ferrell won a gold medal in the 4 × 100 meter relay, was second in the 100 meters and fourth in the 200 meters. She won the Olympic Trials 100 meters in 1972, but was injured later and finished seventh in both the 100 and 200 at the Munich Olympics.

Evelyne Hall (Adams)

Born September 10, 1909 in Minneapolis, Minnesota. In one of the closest finishes in Olympic history, Evelyne Hall was second to Babe Didrikson in the 80 meter hurdles in the 1932 Olympic Games in Los Angeles. Hall led going over the last hurdle, but Didrikson beat her to the tape by a scant two inches. Both were timed in 11.7, a new world record.

Evelyne won three American indoor titles (1931, 1933 and 1935). She was the outdoor 80 meter hurdle champion in 1930.

American Outdoor Records (World Records in bold print)

100	**10.49**	**Florence Griffith Joyner**	**7/16/88**
200	**21.34**	**Florence Griffith Joyner**	**9/29/88**
400	48.83	Valerie Brisco	8/6/84
800	1:56.90	Mary Slaney	8/16/85
1000	2:34.8	Mary Slaney	7/4/85
1500	3:57.12	Mary Slaney	7/26/83
Mile	**4:16.71**	**Mary Slaney**	**8/21/85**
2000	5:32.7	Mary Slaney	8/3/84
3000	8:25.83	Mary Slaney	9/7/85
5000	15:08.26	Mary Slaney	6/5/82

Florence Griffith Joyner (left center) and Louise Ritter at their induction into the National Track and Field Hall of Fame, 1995.

	15:06.53p	Mary Slaney	6/1/85
10,000	31:35.3	Mary Slaney	7/16/82
Marathon (loop)	2:26:11	Joan Benoit-Samuelson	9/12/82
Marathon (point to point)	2:21:21	Joan Benoit-Samuelson	10/20/85
100h	12.61	Gail Devers	5/22/88
	12.61p	Jackie Joyner-Kersee	5/28/88
400h	54.23	Judi Brown-King	8/12/87
5kW	22:40.3	Teresa Vaill	4/23/87
10kW	47:23.8	Maryanne Torrellas	6/27/87
(road)	46:28	Maryanne Torrellas	5/3/87
	46:17p	Maryanne Torrellas	8/28/88
4 × 100	41.55	National Team	8/21/87
4 × 200	1:32.6	National Team	6/24/79
4 × 400	3:15.51	National Team	10/1/88
4 × 800	8:19.9	National Team	6/24/79
	8:17.09p	Athletics West	4/24/83
SpMed r	1:36.79	Wilt's Athletic Club	6/20/82
DistMed r	10:48.38	Villanova University	4/28/88
HJ	6' 8"	Louise Ritter	7/8/88
		Louise Ritter	9/30/88

LJ	24' 5½"	Jackie Joyner-Kersee	8/13/87
TJ	45' 5¼"	Sheila Hudson	6/27/87
SO	66' 2½"	Ramona Pagel	6/25/88
DT	216' 10"	Carol Cady	5/31/86
JT	227' 5"	Kate Schmidt	9/10/77
Heptathlon	**7291**	**Jackie Joyner-Kersee**	**9/23, 24/88**

American Indoor Records

50	6.13p	Jeanette Bolden	2/21/81
60	7.18	Alice Brown	3/10/81
		Gwen Torrence	2/14/88
200	22.95y	Valerie Brisco	2/22/85
400	51.95	Diane Dixon	2/26/88
800	1:58.9	Mary Slaney	2/22/80
1000	2:37.9	Joetta Clark	3/9/86
1500	**4:00.8**	**Mary Slaney**	**2/8/80**
Mile	4:20.5	Mary Slaney	2/19/82
3000	8:44.68	Leslie Lehane	2/27/87
5000	15:25.02	Brenda Webb	1/30/88
50h	6.85	Candy Young	1/15/83
60h	7.88	Jackie Joyner-Kersee	2/14/88
3000w	12:45.38	Maryanne Torrellas	2/26/88
4 × 200	1:36.8yp	Morgan State University	3/7/81
4 × 400	3:37.88	University of Texas	3/14/81
	3:35.49p	Louisiana State University	3/14/87
4 × 800	8:25.5	Villanova University	2/7/87
	8:24.72	**Villanova University**	**3/14/87**
HJ	6' 6¾"	Coleen Sommer	2/24/82
LJ	23'½"	Jackie Joyner-Kersee	2/13/88
SP	65'¾"	Ramona Pagel	2/20/87

INTERVIEW: TERRY CRAWFORD (THE 1988 OLYMPIC COACH)

(February 6, 2006) It was almost by chance that I got in track and field. Something that got me sort of thinking about my ability in track and field is that I just happened to be the fastest kid in the phys ed class back in the late 60's when I was in high school. I had a physical education teacher that really sort of encouraged me about my athletic ability. At that point that was pre Title IX and there were really no school opportunities for women to be on sports teams. I just sort of played every sport I could in phys ed class and did the annual field day at my small school. I grew up in a small country town in East Tennessee called Greenville. Interestingly enough, my senior year I had done well at the annual field day, and there was a local guy in my town who had gone on to college and had done some running at the University of Tennessee. He came home in the summer, after I graduated, and called me and encouraged me to start running. He said he would take me to some all comer meets down in Knoxville, Tennessee. So really, without him encouraging me and getting me to some official track meets in the summer after my senior year, I don't know if I'd be in the sport of track and field today. His name was Kent Buwley. He is still a businessman today in my hometown. He really was sort of my inspiration and mentor in terms of starting to do a little coaching with me. He bought me my first pair of track spikes. That was really something I cherished. It was sort of like getting a gold watch just to have a real pair of track shoes.

I went down to start to run some of the summer AAU meets in Knoxville, where a group of people hosted them to give young people a chance to go on to the regional meet and to national meets. I ran in those and a couple of people who were in track and field in Knoxville encouraged me. I'd already decided that I was going to the University of Tennessee for college. They really encouraged me to contact them when I got there and they would help me continue to run and get me involved in their small club — the Knoxville Track Club. So I did that as a freshman, not really knowing what it was all about or what training entailed or anything.

I joined the Knoxville Track Club when I got to the University of Tennessee as a freshman. After that, I was very fortunate to have a couple of guys who took me under their wings and started coaching me and saw some potential in me. They gave me an opportunity to become a track runner and I was sort of a club all by myself. There were two or three other girls who were in high school who came out to practice occasionally but it was really just me. The other thing that was really a big boost to me was that when they felt that I was good enough to start going to some bigger meets and the club did not have a lot of funding, they called Ed Temple, who of course was in Nash-ville with his famous Tigerbelles. They asked if I could tag along with them to some meets. If they got me to the meets, then Coach Temple would take me under

Terry Crawford, 2006.

his wing and let me hang out with the Tigerbelles at the hotel, and would get me to the meet and make sure I had all the information. Thanks to Ed Temple — that was a huge boost to me in terms of getting started, especially when I started going to the national meets with the AAU. I would always hook up and I made some great friends on the Tigerbelle team like Martha Watson, Madeline Manning and Mattline Render. I would always travel with them. We'd go to all the indoor meets in Chicago, New York and Canada. They were great. They just took me in and showed me the ropes. That's how my career got started.

Fortunately, they moved me up and I went from being a sprinter to being a 400 meter runner to being an 800 meter runner. That's where I had my best success, in the 800. I started making U.S.A. teams. I went to school in 1966 and really got started. I was really fortunate that I improved enough to make the 1968 Olympic trials in the 400. I went out to California and made the finals in my first Olympic trials. I finished seventh. I think that was a big piece that made me think about what I wanted to accomplish in running. It set my path for the next four years. I really realized that maybe I had a shot at being a national caliber, world class athlete. I think after those 1968 Olympic trials I went home and was really committed to train and try to really have a shot at making the 1972 Olympic team. During the next four years I made several international teams. I went to Russia and ran. I made the Pan Am Games team. I made the USA-Russian team. I sort of climbed the ladder to become one of the better quarter milers and 800 meter runners in the United States. I think my best ranking was second one year behind Cheryl Toussaint or behind Madeline Manning, I can't remember.

I went on to qualify for the 1972 Olympic trials in the 800. I was one of three people who had made the Olympic standard. I ended up getting hurt six weeks before the trials. I strained a hamstring, which so often happens when people are at their best. They have misfortunes. I went to the trials and did poorly. I didn't really have a chance to make the team even though I had my standard. Unfortunately, that was a long, debilitating injury, a hamstring strain which turned into a back problem. I spent a year trying to get over it and that was really discouraging to me. I had just graduated from college and I had a chance to start a teaching career and start coaching. I was really teetering whether I could compete at the level that I had and go on.

After 1973 I had a chance to come back to the University of Tennessee and start a master's program and actually help them start a women's track team because Title IX had just passed. Tennessee was one of the first schools in America to start to support women's athletics. The three sports that they wanted to support initially were their basketball team: Pat Summit was the first basketball coach; they started a volleyball team and then asked me to help with the track team as a graduate student. So Pat and I started out as coaches there as graduate students. I tried the first year to coach and train, to keep my own training going. That was just too hard, impossible. So I stepped aside from my own running and started to put my full energy into my coaching at Tennessee. I went on to develop a really successful program at Tennessee. I coached there for eleven years. I had some great athletes that put Tennessee on the map; people like Benita Fitzgerald, Delisa Walton, Sharrieffa Barksdale and Joetta Clark — athletes who went on and were great U.S. Olympians. I really had great success attracting some of the top talent in women's track in the mid and late 70s to Tennessee. That was a program that leaped ahead and became the model for women's college track programs since we were one of the first to really get going in college other than the Tigerbelles and what Bert Lyle did at Texas Woman's University. They were well ahead of Title IX. After winning a national championship at Tennessee in 1980, an AIAW championship, finishing well indoors a couple of times, and having many national champions and internationalists and Olympians, in 1984 I moved to the University of Texas, Austin. I took over the track program there as head coach. I went on during the nine years that I was there to win five national championships. I don't keep up with All-Americans and all that. I couldn't begin to tell you how many All-Americans I've had. I had several Olympians there. I am most proud of the five national championships. In one year — we are still the only women's team to ever do this — we won what is called the "triple crown." In 1986, we won the cross country championships, the indoor championships and the outdoor championships. We are the only women's team to have ever won all three in the calendar year. That was sort of special. I have a lot of great memories of the teams and the successes we had at Texas.

In 1992, I had an opportunity to look at making a move to Cal Poly. They were changing their program from Division 2 to Division 1 and they were combining the program and looking for head coaches to coach men and women. I just felt it was time for a change in my career. I was very intrigued with the opportunity to coach both men and women because I had always been a women's coach. I applied for the job and got it. Coincidentally, they also hired one of my old mentors, Brooks Johnson. We came to Cal Poly together as head coaches with the idea that we would try to turn Cal Poly into a national power. I've been here now fourteen years. The only thing probably that has held us back as an emerging D1 program that did not have the financial resources like a Texas or a Tennessee is that we have been slow-going getting fully funded scholarship-wise. It has kept us from leaping ahead to be the program that I really envisioned. We have had quite a bit of success since I have been here. We have had three national champions. We had a national champion last year in the high jump in Sharon Day. We had an Olympian here on our women's team: Stephanie Brown, who made the 2004 Olympic team. We've taken smaller steps than I did at Tennessee or Texas and again I think it's based on the funding that we've had. It's been a great change for me in terms of working with both men and women. That's really been exciting for me. I like the blend of the two teams: the dual gender and the dual coaching opportunities for me and my staff. I've been very happy here. Hopefully, I will finish my career in terms of retiring here sometime at Cal Poly. That's pretty much it.

In the meantime I've done a number of things within the coaching community. I'm active in USATF. I started at Tennessee getting involved in USATF from a coaching level after I had been an athlete. I've been a coach of many international teams culminating in 1988 when I was the head Olympic coach. We had a great, successful Olympic team, winning more gold medals than any Olympic team up to that point in time. I had an opportunity to be with some great athletes on that team: FloJo, Evelyn Ashford, Jackie Joyner-Kersee, and Louise Ritter, who won a gold medal. It was really a great team, great experience. I've done a little international coaching since then on cross country teams and so forth. But it's really sort of a step back from that. Very typically, after an Olympic experience you feel like you've done it all. I also got very involved working administratively within USATF, where I'm a certified official. I was also President of Division 1 Association of the United States Track Coaches Association and then went on to be president for two years over all the divisions. I enjoyed that work in terms of trying to give back to the sport and be a leader and a mentor for other coaches. Currently I'm chairperson of the Coaches' Advisory Committee and I sit on the Board of Directors of USATF.

That sort of brings you up to date. I try to focus my work right now with what I'm doing at Cal Poly. I'm also excited about Coaches' Advisory taking on a more invested role with USATF to make sure the voice of the coaches are heard and the opportunities are there to recognize what coaches do for our sport on a national and international level.

As far as great moments in my career go, I was pleased with my career but I feel that I didn't accomplish as much as I would have liked because it got cut short due to an injury. I was really fulfilled as a coach. I had great moments. Every national championship that you win is just a fantastic feeling of accomplishment. You are so happy for your athletes when you can bring a group of young people together in a team effort like that. It's just a huge satisfaction. I watched one of my athletes win a gold medal at the 1984 Olympics when Benita Fitzgerald crossed the finish line. To have an athlete make an international team or win a national championship is just a great feeling of reward for what you contributed.

If there's one feeling that I'll always cherish, it's the sense of pride that I got when I walked in with the United States delegation into the opening ceremonies at the 1988 Olympics. That is the icing on the cake in terms of being in the sport of track and field; to wear a USA uniform whether it's as an athlete or a coach. Those opening ceremonies will always be very touching to me in terms of what that meant to me.

INTERVIEW: DR. EVIE DENNIS

(December 1995) I actually got started in track and field following my daughter around. You know, you will spend your time with the children doing what they're doing. She came home one day from elementary school and said, "Mom, I want to run with this track club." I brushed her off. But being one who is persistent, she just kept at it. Then I found out that the person she was talking about would go to their field days and pick out the kids who were winning the blue ribbons and would recruit them for his track club. She persisted and just kept after me and I finally said, "Okay, tell the man to call me." He did and he came to visit me. He told me what was going on in the whole AAU movement. So I allowed her to run with him.

The first meet they competed in, indoors, I looked at them and they were running in cut off blue jeans and t-shirts and the other teams had nice uniforms. So one of the other mothers and I decided that we were not going to let our kids look like this. The other mother was Pam Greene's mother. Pam competed in the Olympics in Munich. So we took out our sewing machines and made uniforms for them. We even got sophisticated enough to be able to silk screen the team name on them which, at that time, was the Denver All-Stars.

I became the president of the club and one thing led to another. This was in the late 60s, 68 and 69. I started attending the Rocky Mountain Association meetings. I got appointed as women's track and field chair, then region chair. Then I became an officer in the association. They used to go to conventions all the time and then come back and tell me what the new rules were. I said, "I don't need you to do this and tell me, I need to go." So that was the beginning of them taking people who were chairs of committees of the Rocky Mountain Association to conventions.

At the convention, there were a lot of things going on. But I looked at the sport being controlled by men. I thought that either they were rich and retired or just retired. I decided one day to run for vice president of the AAU. I did. I ran against two men. They felt we would have to go to two votes. We only had one ballot and I won. When I was inducted, Bob Helmrich was the president and said, "Well, we've never really had a situation like we have now. The officers have always been able to share rooms and the men always wore tuxedos." I said, "I think I can take care of the tuxedo but you must get ready to buy another room" [laughter].

Dr. Evie Dennis at her induction into the National Track and Field Hall of Fame, 2004.

From then on I got involved with the Olympic committee around 75–76. I found the same thing at the management level, the officers' level. I thought this group needed some help also. So I ran. Bob Helmrich ran at the same time. That group had first, second and third designations. So I ran for second vice president and I beat him out. He was third vice president. He had said to me, "Maybe you'd make a good secretary. I said, "No, I can't be a secretary. I already have two secretaries." I ran unopposed. I won and I was there for two terms; eight years. I was about to be elected for a third term but I was going to have more job responsibilities and I think Helmrich wanted George Steinbrenner on his team.

I still am part of the board of directors. I have the Chef de Mission assignment for Seoul for the U.S. team. It's the first time that a woman has held that position. Sometimes people think that being first is nice. But any woman doing these things has to prove herself. I worked very hard and I was pretty successful.

I was pro-tem president of TAC when Dr. LeRoy Walker left the position. That was about a year in 1978. In 1984, I was vice president of the U.S.O.C. and I lived and worked in the Olympic village. Some of my other team assignments were: Chef de Mission–Pan American Games, Caracas; Pan American Games, Havana; Olympic Games, Seoul; World Championships, Stuttgart; World Championships, Gothenburg; Assistant Chef de Mission, Pan American Games, Winnipeg; Special Assistant, Olympic Games, Sydney; U.S.O.C. President's Stand-In, Paralympic Games, Sydney.

Dr. Dennis was a deputy superintendent and superintendent of Denver Public Schools. In 2004, she was inducted into the National Track and Field Hall of Fame.

INTERVIEW: DR. ERNIE GREGOIRE
(COACH, SOUTHERN CALIFORNIA CHEETAHS)

(December 3, 2004) My experiences in track and field have been all my pleasures because I've gotten more than I've given, I'm sure.

I started in track and field back in 1968 with the Southern California Cheetahs, which is an all girls track club. I got involved really because of my oldest daughter, who wanted to high jump. We started working and the next thing you know she became involved and started running cross country. One thing led to another and I became a full time coach for the Southern California Cheetahs. I'm still involved and loving every moment of it.

I think my career has been very, very exciting. I started with an age group team coaching high school track, coaching community college track — then on eventually into international track. I've had a chance to be on a whole score of international teams starting in 1980. I was in the Sports Festival and then in 1981, it was my first one with you, Barquisimeto, Venezuela, with the junior Pan American team. I've been head coach of several teams and I've been on the Olympic staff. In 2006, I'll be on the indoor World Championship team. It's been a great, great run and I've enjoyed it.

Dr. Ernie Gregoire, 2004.

More importantly, I've met so many great people. The kids that I've been involved with have all done extremely well. I'm not just talking track and field, but as human beings, as people. I'm so proud of them. They are just a joy to be with.

Getting involved on the international scene came through a long process of development work. I started with a group of kids in '70, '71, '72. They got better and better and those kids stayed with me for at least ten years. So by 1980 the kids were really, really doing well. We had one young lady, Dolly Fleetwood, who made our first international team. She was on the World Cup in Montreal in 1979.

In 1980, I became the coach of the Olympic Festival and my junior kids began to blossom. By 1984, my junior kids had done really, really well and in addition to that, Larry Myricks came into our program. So now we had an international star in addition to emerging juniors. We had about five people at the 1984 Olympic trials. One, of course, was Larry Myricks, who made the team; Gail Watkins, who was a finalist; Zelda Boldon, who didn't make the finals but was in there, and Tanya Byrne, the high jumper. We had four or five kids at the trials and we had one kid make the team. So that was very good.

By 1988, that junior group had become very, very prolific. Michelle Taylor had gone to college at USC and was NCAA runner-up two years in a row. Gervaise McCraw was a great college runner, so was Tanya Byrne, as I mentioned before, a great college high jumper. Zelda Boldon was at Arizona State. We had a lot of our kids move on to college. Some you never heard of but they did extremely well. Gayle Kellon, as a junior, was one of the best. We have several kids who have become doctors, we have kids who became lawyers. Although they didn't do extremely well in college athletics, the college athletic experience for them through track and field took them a long, long ways — took them a long ways.

Coming forward to 1988, I had my first medalist — Larry Myricks. He won a bronze medal in the '88 Games.

Moving on into the 90s, our group was expanded by about five or six people who were really professional athletes. LaVonna Martin and her husband Edrick Floreal were in our group. Larry Myricks, of course, Arnita Epps, his then wife, who was a junior champion, was with us in Barquisimeto when I first met her. She said to me there, "I really want to work with you. I'll be there to train with you some day." Sure enough, four years later she came out to train with us. Of course, Natasha Kaiser-Brown and her husband Bryan was in our group. We had a great travel group.

Coming forward to 2000, I guess between 1996 and 2000, our brightest star was Angela Williams. She won four NCAA championships in a row. That's a record that can never be broken. It can be tied, but it can never be broken. We're real proud of that. In 2004, we had two people make the team. Angela Daigle made the team as an alternate for the relay and Tony Allmond made the team. He was second in the long jump. So it's been rewarding and there have been so many kids in the program. I can't name them all right now.

I am a retired educator. I retired in 1996 as Dean of Special Programs at Mt. San Antonio College. Although I'm retired, I continue to work with the Mt. Sac Relays, which I've been doing for over thirty-five years now as the marketing director for them. As of December 31 this year, I will no longer be the marketing director. But I'm still coaching the horizontal jumps and the sprints at Mt. San Antonio College and I have a very good group of Southern California Cheetahs — a very, very good group that I am working with.

My family — that's my Olympic gold medal; that's my Heisman Trophy; that's my Superbowl. My wife Eugenia, three kids — Monique, Ernest and Angelique; seven grandkids; one great-grandchild and one on the way — just Superbowl people.

Then, of course, I've got my two dogs [laughter]. It's a wonderful family. It's what keeps me grounded.

Let me digress for just a moment. I think there are certain sources of personal power; things that make us strong; things that make us tick. One source of personal power is God and family. I think if you have God in your life and you have a great family, you have a great chance of making it. I'm just very, very blessed that I have a great family. I am what they help me to be — no question about that. I would not be the person I am without my family.

INTERVIEW: LaTanya Sheffield

(December 5, 2003) Well, I played around with [track] a little in high school in Downey, California in 1979. That was my first experience with track and field on an organized level. I had a wonderful time. I believe that it was an extension of my brother and me running around in our apartment and all of that. The love for just being physical probably came from all of that.

LaTanya Sheffield, 2003.

In high school I was not a sensation to say the least. I was a sprinter. The big deal was the Howard sisters, Denean and Sherri Howard. My fastest 400 was 60 flat on a relay. So no one was knocking on my door — no one was asking for any assistance on any other relay squad in college.

My brother, Rahn Sheffield, who is the head coach at San Diego State, said, "LaTanya, I think you may have some talent, but we'll have to see." He took me out on the track during the summertime and he had me run a quarter. He asked me about four times to stop — slow down while I was running the 400 meters. I'm running the quarter and I'm thinking, you want me to run fast but you asked me to slow down — whatever — and he was so excited as he saw the results on the stopwatch.

I wasn't concerned about running in college. I just knew that I was going to college but I didn't have any idea that there was competition before me. So Rahn encouraged me to try out for the track team at San Diego State. Of course, as soon as I got on the track and looked at all of the girls and all these bodies — and I'm just kind of hitting 5' 3" and holding, maybe 115, you know — I just thought that these girls are too massive for me. But I started training with them and then we eventually had to go through a tryout period in college at San Diego State. The coach said, if you do not run a specific time, then you will not be on the team. And that's all I needed to hear. I was so afraid that there was a possibility that I would not be able to be on the team. It's one of those things where if someone tells you that you can't do something then you really would be hurt.

I ran a 300 meter race in a squad track meet. And I ran a really fast time, a really fast time. I want to say like 38 or 37 seconds for a 300 as a freshman. I broke their record and everyone was kind of excited. I really didn't know what was going on. But for about 18 or 20 years, that record stood. So in hindsight, I can say now, "Wow, you were a great kid." And now I can celebrate what they were celebrating at the time because I really didn't have any clue.

I think that was the springboard of my success and wanting to succeed and know that I was a viable entity on the team; being able to contribute no matter what the size or height or weight of any athlete. So I just went on from there.

A year later, at San Diego State, my coach was Fred LaPlante, the husband of Deby LaPlante as well as Monica Joyce Jewell — at the time he was married to Monica Joyce Jewell — he recommended that I run the 400 hurdles. Rahn, my coach, my brother, recommended that I run the 400 hurdles. Of course, I thought the two were out of their mind. I'm thinking 100, 200 — 400 would be really a big, huge push because that 300 hurt, at the time.

Then I went out and tried it and I won. The very first race that I ran, I won. I ran a NCAA qualifying time. At the time, I had no idea what NCAA was, so I wasn't as excited because I didn't know what was before me. Now, in hindsight, as an NCAA champion, I can celebrate.

I eventually went on to break the American record at the NCAAs and again, as I say, it was exciting at the time, but it was even more exciting because that record held for eleven years. That girl was good! [laughter] I think about those things now. The people that were in my race, again at the time, I knew that they were very good. I just had no idea what type of history we were establishing. In the race were Jackie Joyner and Sandra Farmer. There were many greats, Schowonda Williams. Many, many greats were there and just really were wonderful in helping me perform as an elite athlete. And I say they helped me because they allowed me to understand the sport through analyzing them and being friends as well as being competitors. They allowed me to learn the difference between competition mentality and disposition on the track and then be a friend off the track. They allowed me to grow as an athlete and as a person by never giving up a race. I always had to run hard for everything I got. And, so, that person that was being built and created is the person now. I am really happy about that. After all that has been said and done, after all the accomplishments and all the work, I can't count on one hand how many races I lost. There are just too many to be true [laughter]. But when it's all said and done, I like me and I like my character and the life's lessons that I learned and it's okay to lose and it's okay to win.

At this point, I am pursuing a mentorship amongst the other hurdlers that are developing now. I am available to them for questions, for answers and being a role model — whatever it takes to help them get to the level of an elite athlete. Not just to define an elite athlete as an Olympian, because certainly the Olympics were a great, great moment for me — the Goodwill Games, a great, great moment for me — all of that — but being the person is even better — being the complete person. All those life lessons, they really come back full circle with what you have to be and do in your own personal life. Those are the monumental things that have happened along my way. The emotions, all of that can really never be captured by words. They are all emotional instances.

In 1985, I was a kid competing at the NCAA level. I was familiar with competition, but I didn't realize to become an NCAA champion would require an American record performance. In that winning performance I became many things: a champion, an American record holder and the fastest 400 hurdler in the world — whew! That was huge! There are a lot of athletes that go through their lives not even able to experience that. It's unbelievable — because you sleep in your bed, at least one night, knowing that you're the best in the world. That's huge. Nothing else can be better than that. In fact, my coach at the time, my brother (he moved to San Diego State and ended up becoming my coach), told me the night before, "You're going to break the American record tomorrow and I just want you to get prepared for it." I mean, what do you say to something like that? Whew, that was something. So, I wrote my mom on a postcard that Rahn said that I was going to break the American record tomorrow and we'll see. I went and mailed that to her and sure enough, the next day, that's exactly what happened. Even more importantly, I beat the postcard home [laughter]. We still have that in print and something to frame. And, again, I didn't know what else could be because that was a major moment in my career.

In 1988, to make the Olympic team — to place third at the trials and the media not even think of you as a contender and to be the only finalist in the Games — those are moments that are not like each other — they are not like each other. I was more mature three years later. I look back at those moments and think how incredible: to not only make the team but to go on to the finals. I think, you know what, it can't get any better than this; it absolutely can't get any better than this.

Then to marry and have my coach on my shoulder, on my arm, walking down the aisle together, and he's like, "I don't know, are you sure?" — "Yes, I'm sure." Just being supported the whole way: my coach taking me to an American Record, my coach taking me to the Olympic Games, and now my coach is walking me down the aisle. "Then my coach is my brother. It can't get any better.

And then to go on and have babies — have a child and come back to track and field. And then to have another child. People thought I was out of my mind.

Those who knew me, knew my will to continue to compete, especially my husband, Keith. To do it again — and make a Goodwill team — get a gold medal in the Olympic Sports Festival. That was huge. That was extraordinary. That was when Craig Masback was the commentator. You know, in hindsight I had no idea how every level would be so emotional — so emotional. Every moment was so different, so pivotal. I've been able to see it really clearly: that with each experience, I was evolving from a mom holding on to the bed rails in labor to competing in the international Goodwill Games.

Every moment is certainly a blessing and being able to give back to the community of track and field has just been wonderful. My daughters, who are now twelve and nine years old, have allowed me an opportunity to see what youth athletics have to offer. I never even competed in youth track and field. They are allowing me to do that. I explain to the both of them, "You don't have to be asleep to have a dream!"

It's just really wonderful to be able to go through this journey. God has just blessed me tremendously, with being able to see it and I hope He continues to allow me to see it, but not through the eyes of a competitor: through the eyes of a mother. I'm really happy — no complaints.

INTERVIEW: MARYANNE TORRELLAS DANIEL

(December 5, 2002) I was in high school in New York City, Richmond Hill, Queens, and I started running because I didn't quite fit in with the gymnastics team. I found that I really liked the discipline of running; you put yourself on the line and it's only you out there, you either make or break your own performance.

In my sophomore year I tried out for the boy's cross country team as there was no girl's team at the time. I remember fondly how I was initially met with resistance, but then quickly became one of the boys as its third "man." My team was often taunted by other teams for having a girl with a long blonde ponytail. We would just smile and respond by beating them. It was an exciting time for women's athletics, Title IX stormed the country and girls' teams sprang up.

I loved the 880 and back in the mid 70s it was actually considered a distance event. My coaches, Larry Parrish and Don Dauch, were innovative with speed and strength training, as well as mental preparation. They enabled me to unleash a 2:11, one of the top high school times. I won city champs, Glenn Loucks Games and several invitationals. I had dreams like every runner who starts to do better as they go along, the ultimate: of making an Olympic team, especially watching people like Madeline Manning, Mary Decker, Doris Brown and many others who did so well.

I earned a scholarship to St. John's University in New York, upped my distance to 3000 meters and unfortunately had many injuries.

While I was at St. John's, my cousin and teammate, Peter Timmons, who was a national class racewalker, introduced me to the technique as a way to stay fit while I recovered from several stress fractures. I could push without the pounding. I would watch Peter's smooth, powerful, fluid stride and try to mimic it. I instantly liked the feeling of using the upper body and abdominal muscles when pressing the pace.

I dabbled in race walking, sort of on-and-off between running comebacks. It wasn't until after I got married and had my first child that I decided this is really what I'd like to do: let's see how good I can get at it. Qualifying by the skin of my teeth for my first nationals in '83, I started out sensibly in the back of the pack, but my competitive instincts led me past one athlete after another. Way beyond my wildest dreams, I finished 4th and that put me on a USA team that went over to Norway and competed in a world championship. I remember being so thrilled to wear a USA uniform and compete in a country that lined the streets with people and cheered for everyone. I was so thrilled that I performed way beyond my expectation and set an American record.

That was the beginning of a long racewalking career that had many ups and downs. I won six national championships, held half a dozen American records, won an '87 Pan American Bronze, Mobile Grand Prix and made over 20 national teams.

The most memorable race was a 1500 meters at the Olympic Invitational '88. From the gun,

Maryanne Torrellas Daniel, 2002.

Anne Peel, a Canadian national champion, and I battled for the lead. She was a feisty competitor, pushing her way through from the inside lane, and she gained a few steps on me. At 1000m, the announcer had the full stadium cheering for her attempt at the world record. She was flying, but there was no way I was going to let her go. Back and forth we exchanged the lead on the last lap. The crowd was deafening as we pushed shoulder to shoulder. Then, in one of those magical slow motion-in-your-mind steps, I beat her to the tape, earning a world best that stood for a few years.

I happen to be very good at having tragedies happen right before the Olympic Trials. In 1988, I blew out my left knee and needed surgery. Then in 1992, I blew out my right knee and needed cartilage surgery. The worst was having a sudden onset of heart valve damage just prior to the '96 Olympic Trials. Not fully understanding how an athlete who never had any heart trouble before could possibly have a problem, I raced and had to be carried off the track. I had held the American records in between, but what counts, of course, is the trials finish. While I had to let go of the dream of ever competing in the Olympics, there was something that came along to take its place.

I had become a sports massage therapist some years before and, being a young therapist, I didn't think my chances were so good when I applied to be part of the Olympic Games medical staff. As if one door opens as another closes, when I returned home from the trials there was a letter waiting assigning me as the track and field massage therapist. I was ecstatic. Working on all the Olympians was quite an experience. It was a special feeling at the closing ceremony in Atlanta, being on the field with all the athletes in wild celebration. It wasn't the path I had dreamt of, but here I was, I had made the Olympics. I learned that it was very satisfying to give back to the sport I loved so much. I began to coach a team and volunteer my time as an official. I have been fortunate to be selected as assistant manager for the Pan Am Team, head manager for a world championship team, as well as being a part of the medical staff for several international teams.

When you are an athlete competing, you often don't stop to think of all the hard work it takes to put on a meet — all the officials that make the events happen. I began to realize that there weren't all that many female officials, so I joined their ranks.

If I were to give advice to a runner converting to walking, I would tell them that you need a lot of patience because in the beginning, you have the cardio component, but all the intrinsic muscles are going to need time to adjust to new biomechanics. Just like any other technique event, you want to make sure you are being as efficient as possible. Typically the shins are sore from plantar flexion, gluts and hamstrings from the straight leg motion. By progressively adding more racewalking to a running program, you'll get to the point where you'll be able to go fast enough to go into oxygen debt and all those wonderful other things that happen — the endorphins that get set off — it will just take a little bit of patience by slowly making the transition.

My coaching philosophy includes running training for a racewalker as long as the emphasis is on the racewalking. I have always done some running while I was race walking; in fact, I had my best 10k run when I was in the best racewalking shape in 1987.

I try to balance family, (I have four boys) massage and officiating. Sometimes it's a crazy household, but I wouldn't change a thing. I also haven't given up competing. I found the Masters level to be very exciting. The camaraderie and fun with other competitors is what engages me. To go to a meet and watch a grey-haired man hurdle gracefully, a 50-year-old sprinter whiz by like she's 25, or a 72-year-old pole vaulter — now that's the endurance of the competitive spirit. I'm looking forward to my own master's American record and possibly a world master's. This is my second year of competing with one kidney and I want to see how far I can go.

I have only one kidney because I gave the other one away. Interestingly enough, my cousin Peter, the one who taught me how to racewalk, needed a kidney transplant. It was a shock to our family that something could be wrong with his kidneys; after all, he was such a great athlete. We learned being fit was no guarantee. Peter was like a brother to me and I had no hesitation when I found out I was a match. Like any major surgery, it took a while to recover, but one can do very well on one kidney, although there didn't seem to be any statistics on racing at a high level, so I'm sort of an experiment. I'm happy to say, Peter is doing well. We fool around and e-mail each other kidneys to tell of the day we had. My left kidney seems far too happy with its new owner, getting adequate water, rest, attending plays and symphonies — it's making my right kidney jealous.

I'm looking forward to an upcoming marriage that will take place on a mountaintop and to sharing my life with a man who has been involved in track and field for most of his life. It is our vision that we will be able to work with young racewalkers and bring them to their potential, giving them the tools to be the best they can be. We both feel so blessed to have had so many people help in our athletic careers; it's just a natural thing to want to give back.

9

1989

The Outdoor Nationals

The USA/Mobil Outdoor Track and Field Championships were held in Robertson Stadium, Houston, Texas from June 13 to June 17.

The *New York Times* featured Dawn Sowell in a story about the meet on June 17. Thomas George wrote

> ...Sowell racing for Flo-Jo International, ran the second-fastest time this year in the women's 100 meters at 10.91 seconds, topping Sheila Echols of Athletic [sic] West (11.12) and Esther Jones of LS United (11.13). Two weeks ago, representing Louisiana State, she ran the fastest time this year, 10.78, in the National Collegiate Athletic Association outdoor championships.
>
> ...Sowell and Burrell both set stadium and meet records.
>
> "Dawn! Dawn!" yelled Al Joyner, the 1984 Olympic triple jump gold medalist, who with his wife, Florence Griffith Joyner, is Sowell's new mentor. "Dawn! Dawn! You ran sooo-oo well!"
>
> "Flo-Jo and Al are different kinds of people," said Sowell, who trailed Echols in the first 30 meters. "With them, in just a short time, I'm learning to put myself out there and just hang. Sheila Echols always starts fast, but I wasn't looking over my shoulder, just at the finish line. I'm learning that I have a talent and not to waste it."

After the finals of the men's and women's 400 meter hurdles, Thomas George's feature story in the *New York Times* entitled "Husband and Wife Take Hurdles Titles" read,

> Their devastating defeat in the Olympic Trials last year seemed a bit farther away today for David Patrick and Sandra Farmer-Patrick. They became the first husband-wife pair to win a national event in the same year in 29 years—both winning the 400-meter hurdles....
>
> The pair's hopes to make the Olympic team were dashed last year when both narrowly missed making the squad. Here, however, both set stadium records with Farmer-Patrick also setting an American record and this year's world-leading mark of 53.75. Patrick won in 48.83, as the duo matched the 1960 feat of Hal and Olga Connolly, who won the hammer throw and discus throw, respectively.
>
> "I'm not jealous," Patrick said, smiling, of his wife's new American record. "We're on the same team."
>
> That's doubly true, since the pair runs for Flo-Jo International. They reside in Austin, TX., have been married for a year and a half and never train together.
>
> "Never!" Farmer-Patrick said. "He thinks he's the expert, and it causes too much friction when we train, but now maybe I can teach him a thing or two. I don't know if anything will ever help

us get over last year and the Olympic trials. That was like a dream shattered. But this helps distance that. Maybe we're on to a couple of world records. Yeah, that would help us forget it even more."

George also noted that, "Ramona Pagel of the Mazda Track Club tossed the shot put 62 feet ½ inch to win the women's title.

"I'm excited about going to Europe to meet up with the Eastern Europeans, because they have started to respect me more as a competitor," she said. "We really need to work on promoting shot put in the United States. And that has to start at the junior high level."

---

100 meters

"Many of the biggest American stars — indeed, most of the box-office names — chose to bypass the Houston activities, for one reason or another," said Scott Davis in *Track & Field News*.... That unfortunately deprived the meet of both high-level competition and much-needed positive publicity.

"An hour after a 10.95 semi victory, Sowell found herself behind defending champion Sheila Echol's storming start in the final. But she cruised by Echols at 30m and left her and the field behind en route to a 10.91 meet-record win," reported Howard Willman in *Track & Field News*.

1. Dawn Sowell, Flojo International	10.91	MR
2. Sheila Echols, Athletics West	11.12	
3. Esther Jones, Louisiana State University	11.13	
4. Anita Howard, University of Florida	11.14	
5. Pauline Davis, Bahamas	11.16	
6. Dannette Young, Reebok Racing Club	11.25	
7. LaMonda Miller, unattached	11.26	
8. Michelle Finn, Atoms Track Club	11.29	

200 meters

Scott Davis reported Dannette Young's win in *Track & Field News*, "Running in lane 6 in the final, the 25-year-old Florida native bolted out of the blocks prior to the gun and was charged with a false start.

"She was out well on the restart and ran a strong turn with Esther Jones in pursuit. Off the turn, Young was the clear leader and she moved smartly to the win in 22.29, just off her PR of 22.23."

1. Dannette Young, Reebok Racing Club	22.29
2. Esther Jones, Louisiana State University	22.53
3. Diane Dixon, Athletics West	22.72
4. Michelle Finn, Atoms Track Club	22.88
5. Carlette Guidry, University of Texas	22.90
6. Wendy Vereen, Atoms Track Club	23.41
7. Rosie Williams, University of Oregon	23.70

400 meters

"With the entire Olympic squad absent, the 1-lapper featured many of the nation's up-and-coming young runners," reported John Parks for *Track & Field News*.

Rochelle Stevens "cruised away from the field early. She maintained her lead the rest of the way to win in 50.75. That dropped her PR from 51.23 and moved her all the way from No. 19 to No. 9 on the all-time U.S. list."

1. Rochelle Stevens, Atlantic Coast Club	50.75
2. Jearl Miles, Reebok Racing Club	51.52
3. Celena Mondie, University of Illinois	51.55
4. Terri Dendy, Reebok Racing Club	51.64
5. Lillie Leatherwood, Reebok Racing Club	51.75
6. Natasha Kaiser, Nike South	51.89
7. Sandie Richards, Jamaica	52.09
8. Michelle Taylor, Southern California Cheetahs	52.17
9. Maicel Malone, Nike Coast	52.20

800 meters

"Joetta Clark had little trouble defending her title, even though her father, controversial high school principal Joe Clark, was in the hospital recuperating from open-heart surgery," said Walt Murphy in *Track & Field News*. "Clark patiently worked her way up from 7th, took the lead for good on the backstretch, and pulled away to a 2:01.42 win. It was the first 2:00-plus winning time since 1982 and the slowest winner since 1979."

1. Joetta Clark, Athletics West	2:01.42
2. Debbie Marshall, unattached	2:01.99
3. Meredith Rainey, Atoms Track Club	2:02.90
4. Sylvia Brydson, Louisiana State University	2:03.43
5. Celeste Halliday, Nike-Boston	2:03.47
6. Rose Monday, Track West	2:04.91
7. Julie Jenkins, Reebok Racing Club	2:05.81
8. Tara Arnold, Stars & Stripes Track Club	2:08.05

1500 meters

Bob Hersh wrote in *Track & Field News*:

Olympian Regina Jacobs settled into the middle of the pack and stayed there for nearly 700m, where she moved up to 2nd. She held that position around the turn, and then took over the lead just past the 800 (2:20.5), a mark reached first by Wisconsin's Suzy Favor in a pedestrian 2:20.1.

Thereafter, the 25-year-old Californian was in complete command of the race, a 64.3 third circuit opening up a margin of 15m and stringing out what had been a closely bunched field.

1. Regina Jacobs, Team New Balance	4:11.80
2. Suzy Favor, Nike North	4:12.29
3. Diana Richburg, Gazelle International	4:12.32
4. Gina Procaccio, Sallie Mae Track Club	4:13.95
5. Teena Colebrook, Nike Coast Track Club/Great Britain	4:14.50
6. Alisa Harvey, Athletics West	4:14.59
7. Darcy Arreola, California State University, Northridge	4:18.35
8. Kathy Franey, Villanova University	4:19.25

3000 meters

According to Troy James of *Track & Field News*,

PattiSue Plumer and Sabrina Dornhoefer talked beforehand and agreed not to let a slow pace rob either in a kicker's race. A pair of kilometers just over 3:00 quickly shed the pack and it was just the two of them left.

Coming off the final turn, Dornhoefer was the first to strike, and a homestretch battle reminiscent of their Trials struggle — where Plumer grabbed the final Olympic spot and both grabbed IVs — began in earnest.

The Missouri grad held a step and a half lead with 80m to go, but Plumer began to come back. ...She pulled even, then moved on with 20m to go to win by 0.18 in 9:00.05.

1. PattiSue Plumer, Athletics West	9:00.05
2. Sabrina Dornhoefer, Athletics West	9:00.23
3. Gwyn Hardesty, Nike Boston	9:12.17
4. Sammie Resh, Reebok Racing Club	9:16.58
5. Annette Hand, Nike Portland	9:19.15
6. Shelly Steely, Florida Athletic Club	9:20.61
7. Elizabeth Johnson, Nike Texas	9:23.49
8. Trina Leopold, Nike Texas	9:25.75

5000 meters

"With no World Cup berth at stake, the 5000 became an orphan, with only four contestants toeing the line," said Roy Conrad in *Track & Field News*.

"Rowland, 5th in the NCAA, was unpressed to the wire, winning by more than 8 seconds at 16:12.36."

1. Mindy Rowland, Dominos Racing Team	16:12.36
2. Lisa Stone, Athletes In Action	16:20.94
3. Ann Henderson, unattached	16:34.06
4. Andrea Ward, Santa Monica Track Club	17:18.35

10,000 meters

"The 26-year-old Davis led at the halfway mark in 16:28.9, already pulling away.

...She cranked out a series of 77-second laps to cruise home 20 seconds in front," said Jon Hendershot of *Track & Field News*.

1. Nan Doak-Davis, Athletics West	32:34.59
2. Colette Murphy, Athletics West	32:54.86
3. Judy Chamberlin, unattached	32:56.06
4. Martha Geissler, Nike Boston	33:40.22
5. Suzanne Jones, Harvard University	33:47.08
6. Lisa Vaill, unattached	34:15.46
7. Roxanne Polo, Metroplex Striders	34:23.47
8. Judy Bogenschutz, Indiana Track Club	34:31.50

100 meter hurdles

Stanley, McKenzie and Tolbert "started superbly, but coming off the first hurdle, Stanley landed off balance and injured her knee. She crashed the next barrier badly and was finished.

"Arizona State junior Tolbert began to build a lead over McKenzie at the fourth barrier. She streaked across the finish with an 0.16 margin and a 12.75 that makes her the No. 4 American of all time," stated Jeff Hollobaugh in *Track & Field News*.

1. Lynda Tolbert, Nike Coast Track Club	12.75	MR
2. Kim McKenzie, Mazda Track Club	12.91	
3. Candy Young, Atoms Track Club	13.15	
4. LaVonna Martin, Reebok Racing Club	13.16	
5. Cinnamon Sheffield, Louisiana State University	13.20	
6. Jackie Humphrey, Athletics West	13.21	
7. Donna Waller, Southern California Cheetahs	13.34	

400 meter hurdles

"Finding herself behind early, Farmer-Patrick turned it up a notch: nearest pursuers Schowonda Williams, Victoria Fulcher and Kathy Freeman were more than 2m down at the halfway point," said Howard Willman in *Track & Field News*. "As the field entered the home-stretch, Farmer-Patrick's lead was more than 5m. She added nearly 10m more as she flashed across the finish in 53.75 to smash Judi Brown King's American Record of 54.23. It also made her history's No. 9 performer."

1. Sandra Farmer-Patrick, Flo-Jo International	53.75	AR
2. Victoria Fulcher, Nike North	55.87	
3. Janeene Vickers, unattached	56.01	
4. Schowonda Williams, Athletics West	56.21	
5. Kathy Freeman, Louisiana State University	57.17	
6. Sametra (Mimi) King, Boston University	57.37	
7. Countess Comadore, Southern University	58.09	
8. Arnita Epps, Southern California Cheetahs	60.00	

10 kilometer walk

"After missing most of '88 with an injury, Lynn Weik is back stronger than ever," reported Bob Bowman in *Track & Field News*. "Three days short of her 22nd birthday, she knocked almost 40 seconds off Maryanne Torrellas's AR, set in this meet two years ago, to win going away in 46:44.1."

At the mid point, only Teresa Vaill was with Lynn Weik. Both were under the old American record.

1. Lynn Weik, Walk USA	46:44.1	AR
2. Teresa Vaill, Walk USA	47:21.9	
3. Maryanne Torrellas, Reebok Racing Club	48:25.7	
4. Debbi Lawrence, Nike Track Club	48:41.5	
5. Wendy Sharp, unattached	49:07.1	
6. Sara Standley, Southern California Road Runners	49:24.4	
7. Victoria Herazo, California Walkers	49:57.3	
8. Susan Liers, Walk USA	50:00.1	

High jump

"The battle for 1st went back-and-forth between the Texas natives: Wohlschlag took the lead at 6' ½"; Ritter regained it with a first-try make at 6' 2¾"; at 6' 4", Lou missed her first and Wohlschlag soared over. Most expected the battle to climb higher, but the defending champ's was the last clearance of the day," reported Jeff Hollobaugh in *Track & Field News*.

1. Jan Wohlschlag, Nike Coast Track Club	6' 4"
2. Louise Ritter, Mazda Track Club	6' 4"
3. Shelley Fehrman, Nike Coast and	
Yolanda Henry, 4 Winds Track Club	6' 2¾"
5. Latrese Johnson, Azusa Pacific University and	
Tonya Mendonca, Stars and Stripes Track Club	5' 11¼"
7. Candy Cashell, unattached and	
Sissy Costner, Auburn University	5' 11¼"

Long jump

Defending champion Sheila Echols led the competition from the start with a 21' 5½" jump. "...Connor's fourth-try of 21-6 then edged her ahead," reported *Track & Field News*.

1. Claire Connor, Louisiana State University	21' 6"
2. Sheila Echols, Athletics West	21' 5½"
3. Gwen Loud, Stars and Stripes Track Club	21' 3½"

4. Terri Turner, Nike Track Club   20' 11¾"
5. DeDee Nathan, Indiana Track Club   20' 10¾"
6. Wendy Brown, Bee-Fit Track Club   20' 9¾"
7. Jennifer Inniss, Athletics West   20' 9¾"
8. Janet Harvey, Nike Coast Track Club   20' 9"

Triple jump

"...Sheila Hudson had little trouble. She showed that more than any other American in the TJ's brief history she's able to put together the three phases which give the event its name," reported *Track & Field News*.

"All three phases came together in round 5, as she stretched out to a windy 45–6½, almost 2 feet up on Diana Wills (43–9¾ w). Hudson closed with 45–1, the No. 7 mark in U.S. history."

1. Sheila Hudson, Nike Coast Track Club   45' 6½" w
2. Diana Wills, U.S. Army   43' 9¾" w
3. Renita Robinson, Reebok Racing Club   43' 1¾" w
4. Cynthia Rhodes, Austin Striders   42' 3½"
5. Diane Sommerville, Jamaica   42'
6. Juliana Yendork, Southern California Cheetahs/Ghana   41' 7¾" w
7. Jocelin Wilson, George Mason University   41' 4½" w
8. Yolanda Taylor, Texas A&M University   41' 3¼"

Shot put

"Ramona Pagel took up where she finished her three previous TACs — on top. Her first round throw of 61-9 would have won by almost a yard but she improved to 62–½ in the second round.... The 27-year-old Pagel wasn't all that thrilled with the situation, despite her win. "The lack of a big field was a negative factor," she explained, noting that only 13 showed up for the event. "I'm glad for myself that they cancelled the qualifying rounds, but it can only hurt our event," reported *Track & Field News*.

1. Ramona Pagel, Mazda Track Club   62' ½"
2. Connie Price, Athletics West   59' ¾"
3. Bonnie Dasse, Nike Coast Track Club   57' 1½"
4. Peggy Pollock, Nike Coast Track Club   54' 8"
5. Pam Dukes, Nike Coast Track Club   54' 8"
6. Kathy Picknell, Nike Coast Track Club   53' 7½"
7. Carla Garrett, University of Arizona   51' 8¼"
8. Dot Jones, unattached   50' 10¼"

Discus

"Connie Price made the competition for the national title a moot point on the second throw of the whole event, reaching her winning distance of 201–11. It was the second title for the 6' 3"/205 Missouri native, who also won in 1987 and took the Olympic Trials in '88," said *Track & Field News*.

1. Connie Price, Athletics West   201' 11"
2. Lacy Barnes, unattached   196' 2"
3. Ramona Pagel, Mazda Track Club   190' 2"
4. Carla Garrett, University of Arizona   187' 9"
5. Kelly Landry, Nike Coast Track Club   184' 8"
6. Laura Lavine, unattached   179' 9"

| 7. Penny Neer, Nike Coast Track Club | 177' 11" |
| 8. Colleen Rosensteel, University of Florida | 175' 4" |

Javelin

"...Veteran Karin Smith, at 33 the oldest thrower in the competition, led the finals with her opening-round 187–2 until Mayhew reached 199–6 in the 2nd frame.... Just four throwers after Mayhew, Bahamian Laverne Eve produced the throw of her life, the jav flying in a high arc and biting the turf at 212–6," reported *Track & Field News*. As the first American, Mayhew retained her national title.

1. Laverne Eve, Louisiana State University/Bahamas	212' 6"
2. Donna Mayhew, Nike Coast Track Club	199' 6"
3. Karin Smith, Nike Coast Track Club	188'
4. Marilyn Senz, Mazda Track Club	181' 3"
5. Niki Nye, Nike Coast Track Club	177' 3"
6. Julia Solo, University of Virginia	169' 2"
7. Lorri LaRowe, Austin Striders/Canada	167' 5"
8. Durelle Schimek, Nike Coast Track Club	164' 1"

Heptathlon

Track & Field News reported:

Shooting for TAC title No. 10, 37-year-old Jane Frederick held a 162-point lead after the first day but couldn't start day two as her left Achilles flared up.

That left NCAA champ Jolanda Jones, 23, with the lead and Gea Johnson just 30 back.

Since Jones is a very good 800 runner, it seemed unlikely that she would lose to either Johnson (by about 1½ seconds) or Sharon Hanson (by about 3½).

But Johnson and Hanson were up to the challenge. In an exciting finish, Hanson took the race in 2:15.13, while Johnson fell across the line 4th in 2:16.60. Jones stayed as close as she needed (2:16.86) to take the win with 6006w."

1. Jolanda Jones, Houston Track Club	6006 w
2. Gea Johnson, Nike Coast Track Club	5990 w
3. Sharon Hanson, Nike Coast Track Club	5983 w
4. Cathy Tyree, Stars and Stripes Track Club	5873 w
5. Teri LeBlanc, University of Missouri	5805
6. Anita Behrbaum, Nike Coast Track Club	5802
7. Jamie McNeair, Purdue University	5775
8. Terri Turner, Nike Track Club	5755 w

The Indoor Nationals

The indoor nationals were held on Friday, February 24 in Madison Square Garden.

"McKenzie Ends Joyner-Kersee's Streak," read the headline in the *New York Times* on February 25. Jackie Joyner-Kersee's winning streak ended. Diane Dixon kept hers intact. Gwen Torrence took the first step toward a new one.

...The meet was especially important for American competitors. The top two finishers qualified for the world indoor championships next month in Budapest, provided their performances met the predetermined standards.

Dixon's winning time in the 400, 53.28, provided a comfortable margin over Jearl Miles (54.36) and gave her a seventh-consecutive national indoor title and eighth overall.

Sandra Farmer Patrick.

Torrence's victory in the women's 55-meter dash in 6.61 followed a loss in her last meet a week ago in Los Angeles. By finishing second to Dawn Sowell, she ended a 49-meet victory streak that spanned four indoor seasons.

"This was my best start this indoor season," Torrence said. "I wanted it real bad. I was determined to win. I knew if I got a good start, I would beat them."

A second headline proclaimed, "Griffith Joyner Retiring; Other Interests' Cited."

...Florence Griffith Joyner, the 29-year-old three-time gold medalist at the Seoul Olympics last summer and the world-record holder at 100 and 200 meters, said she would announce her retirement at a news conference today.

...Speculation that she might retire began earlier this winter, when it became apparent she would not compete in any indoor meets. At the same time, her Olympic success was beginning to generate interest from a variety of sources, including book publishers, motion-picture and television producers, even a toy company that wants to manufacture a "Flojo" doll.

---

55 meters
1. Gwen Torrence, Athletics West   6.61
2. Carlette Guidry, University of Texas, Austin   6.77
3. Tina Inheagwan, Southern California Cheetahs/Nigeria   6.78

200 meters
1. Alice Jackson, Coke Track Club   23.64
2. Terri Dendy, Reebok Racing Club   23.74
3. Laurel Johnson, Bronx Express/Jamaica   24.08

400 meters
1. Diane Dixon, Athletics West   53.28
2. Jearl Miles, Young Achievers Sprint Club   54.36
3. Tanya McIntosh, Rice University   54.42

800 meters
1. Joetta Clark, Athletics West   2:02.60
2. Essie Washington, Houston Track Club   2:03.34
3. Diana Richburg, Gazelle International Track Club   2:04.27

Mile
1. Linda Sheskey, Athletics West   4:43.09
2. Rosalind Taylor, University of Maryland   4:43.39
3. MaryEllen McGowan, unattached   4:45.00

3000 meters
1. Elaine Van Blunk, Nike Track Club   9:16.46

2. Judy Bogenschutz, Indiana Track Club   9:18.43
3. Rita Cecil, Liberty Athletic Club/Canada   9:28.24

55 meter hurdles
1. Kim McKenzie, Mazda Track Club   7.39
2. Jackie Joyner-Kersee, Mazda Track Club   7.43
3. Candy Young, Atoms Track Club   7.57

3000 meter walk
1. Teresa Vaill, Walk USA   13:12.74
2. Lynn Weik, Walk USA   13:24.21
3. Susan Liers, Walk USA   13:52.80

4 × 400 meter relay
1. Rice University   3:44.66
    (Robyn Bryant, Michelle Lynch, Tanya McIntosh, Rosie Edeh)

High jump
1. Louise Ritter, Mazda Track Club   6' 5"
2. Jan Wohlschlag, Nike Track Club   6' 4"
3. Yolanda Henry, 4 Winds Christian Track Club   6' 2¼"

Long jump
1. Jennifer Inniss, Athletics West   21' ½"
2. Nena Gage, George Mason University   20' 4¼"
3. Sonya Henry, Rice University   20' ¼"

Shot put
1. Ramona Pagel, Mazda Track Club   62' 6½"
2. Connie Price, Athletics West   60' 10½"
3. Beth Bunge, unattached   49' 9¼"

20 lb. weight (exhibition)
1. Virginia Young, St. John's University   60' 2"   AR
2. Bonnie Edmondson, unattached   54' 6½"
3. Shirl Dorsey, George Mason University   54' 4"

Team scores:
1. Athletics West   29
2. Mazda Track Club   19
3. Walk USA   10

Sunkist Invitational (4 women's events): Los Angeles, January 20

60 yards
1. Jackie Joyner-Kersee, Mazda Track Club   6.68

440 yards
1. Diane Dixon, unattached   53.64

800 meters
1. Essie Washington, Houston Track Club   2:07.98

Mile
1. Linda Sheskey, Athletics West   4:38.24

5th IAAF World Cup: Barcelona, Spain, September 8–10

The *New York Times* reported: "David and Sandra Farmer-Patrick each won gold medals yesterday in the 400-meter hurdles at the World Cup meet in Barcelona, Spain, becoming the first married couple to win the same track event at a major international meet."

100 meters
1. Sheila Echols   11.18

200 meters
4. Dannette Young   23.08

400 meters
4. Rochelle Stevens   52.16

800 meters
9. Joetta Clark   2:01.94

1500 meters
9. Regina Jacobs   4:30.78

3000 meters
3. PattiSue Plumer   8:54.33

10,000 meters
4. Nan Doak-Davis   32:23.09

100 meter hurdles
3. Lynda Tolbert   12.86

400 meter hurdles
1. Sandra Farmer-Patrick   53.84 MR

High jump
5. Jan Wohlschlag (tie)   6' 3¼"

Long jump
6. Claire Connor   20' 8"

Shot put
6. Ramona Pagel   61' 7"

Discus
7. Connie Price   173' 6"

Javelin
6. Donna Mayhew   181' 8"

4 × 100 meter relay
3. United States   42.83
    (Sheila Echols, Esther Jones, Dawn Sowell, LaMonda Miller)

4 × 400 meter relay
4. United States   3:27.29
    (Celena Mondie, Rochelle Stevens, Terri Dendy, Jearl Miles)

The United States finished fifth with a point score of 84½.

2nd IAAF World Indoor Track and Field Championships:
Budapest, Hungary, March 3–5

60 meters
  2. Gwen Torrence   7.07 AR

400 meters
  2. Diane Dixon   51.77

60 meter hurdles
  4. Kim McKenzie   7.92

High jump
  5. Jan Wohlschlag   6' 3¼"
  9. Yolanda Henry   6' 3¼"

Long jump
  8. Jennifer Inniss   19' 9"

Shot put
  9. Ramona Pagel   58' 1¼"
 10. Connie Price   57' 3¾"

USA–USSR–Great Britain–West Germany Quadrangular Meet:
Alexander Stadium, Birmingham, England, June 23–24

100 meters
1. Esther Jones   11.20 w
2. LaMonda Miller   11.35

200 meters
2. Diane Dixon   23.21
4. Michelle Finn   23.40

400 meters
2. Rochelle Stevens   52.08
4. Jearl Miles   52.69

800 meters
1. Joetta Clark   2:02.08
6. Sylvia Brydson   2:04.21

1500 meters
3. Suzy Favor   4:14.20
4. Diana Richburg   4:15.78

3000 meters
1. PattiSue Plumer   8:53.20
5. Sabrina Dornhoefer   8:57.93

100 meter hurdles
5. Candy Young   13.26
8. LaVonna Martin   13.81

400 meter hurdles
3. Janeene Vickers   56.66
5. Victoria Fulcher   57.41

5000 meter walk
4. Teresa Vaill   22.47.05

4 × 100 meter relay
2. USA   43.72
    (LaMonda Miller, Michelle Finn, Carlette Guidry, Esther Jones)

4 × 400 meter relay
1. USA   3:26.40
    (Jearl Miles, Celena Mondie, Terri Dendy, Natasha Kaiser)

High jump
1. Jan Wohlschlag   6' 4¾"
3. Yolanda Henry   6' 4"

Long jump
4. Terri Turner   21' ¾" w
5. Claire Connor   21' ¾" w

Shot put
2. Ramona Pagel   63' 7"
7. Connie Price   56' 9¼"

Discus
2. Lacy Barnes   190' 5"
6. Connie Price   175' 5"

Javelin
2. Donna Mayhew   204' 2"
7. Karin Smith   182' 10"

Team scores:
1. Soviet Union   169
2. United States   160
3. Great Britain   119
4. West Germany   99

World Cross Country Championships: Stavanger, Norway, March 19

(6000 meters)
 6. Lynn Jennings   22:59
16. Margaret Groos   23:20
21. Carla Borovicka   23:28
25. Annette Hand   23:32
29. Sabrina Dornhoefer   23:45

The United States placed third in the scoring with 68 points.

U.S. Marathon Championships (California International Marathon): Sacramento, California, December 3

1.	Nan Doak	2:33:11
2.	Linda Somers	2:33:37
3.	Lissa Kindelan	2:35:31
4.	Rose Gutierrez	2:35:55
5.	Mary Alico	2:36:26

World Marathon Cup: Milan, Italy, April 15–16

1.	Sue Marchiano	2:30:48
8.	Gordon Bloch	2:37:17
38.	Charlotte Thomas	2:48:12
45.	Pat Wassak-Hinson	2:54:33

The United States placed second in the scoring with a total time of 7:56.17.

World Race Walking Cup: L'Hospitalet, Spain, May 27–28

10 kilometer walk

21.	Lynn Weik	46:38
23.	Teresa Vaill	46:45
41.	Deborah Lawrence	48:10
44.	Wendy Sharp	48:18
79.	Maryanne Torrellas	53:07

The United States placed ninth in the scoring with a total of 162 points.

World Games: Helsinki, Finland, June 29

200 meters

2.	Esther Jones	22.74
3.	Dannette Young	22.82
5.	Sheila Echols	23.12

800 meters

4.	Joetta Clark	2:03.48

3000 meters

4.	Sabrina Dornhoefer	8:57.46

400 meter hurdles

1.	Sandra Farmer-Patrick	54.05
4.	LaTanya Sheffield	57.14

High jump

1.	Jan Wohlschlag	6' 4"

Long jump
5. Sheila Echols	21'	4"
6. Jennifer Inniss	20'	10"
8. Claire Connor	20'	4½"

Final Standings of the Mobil Grand Prix Final: Monte Carlo, Monaco, May 27–September 1

American women in the top ten

100 meters
  2. Sheila Echols
  4. Esther Jones
 10. Dawn Sowell

800 meters
  4. Joetta Clark
  7. Claudette Groenendaal

Mile
  4. Diana Richberg
 10. Julie Jenkins

3000 meters
  1. PattiSue Plumer

400 meter hurdles
  1. Sandra Farmer-Patrick
  3. Schowonda Williams
  5. Kathy Freeman
  8. LaTanya Sheffield

High jump
  1. Jan Wohlschlag

Long jump
  9. Jennifer Inniss
 10. Carol Lewis

Shot put
  5. Ramona Pagel

Other News and Honors

Track & Field News: U.S. Athlete of the Year

Sandra Farmer-Patrick

Women's World and American Rankings — *Track & Field News*
(American rankings in bold)

100 meters
2. Dawn Sowell
3. Sheila Echols
5. Evelyn Ashford
6. Esther Jones

1. Dawn Sowell
2. Sheila Echols
3. Evelyn Ashford

200 meters
2. Dawn Sowell
8. Dannette Young
9. Esther Jones

1. Dawn Sowell
2. Dannette Young
3. Esther Jones

400 meters
4. Rochelle Stevens
5. Diane Dixon
10. Natasha Kaiser

1. Rochelle Stevens
2. Diane Dixon
3. Natasha Kaiser

800 meters
10. Joetta Clark

1. Joetta Clark
2. Julie Jenkins
3. Diana Richburg

1500 meters
No American women were in the top ten.

1. Suzy Favor
2. Diana Richburg
3. PattiSue Plumer

3000 meters
4. PattiSue Plumer

1. PattiSue Plumer
2. Sabrina Dornhoefer
3. Vicki Huber

5000 meters
2. PattiSue Plumer

1. PattiSue Plumer
2. Carla Borovicka
3. Lisa Brady

10,000 meters
No American women were in the top ten.

1. Nan Davis
2. Colette Murphy
3. Judy Chamberlin

Marathon
3. Kim Jones
4. Lisa Weidenbach

1. Kim Jones
2. Lisa Weidenbach
3. Sue Marchiano

100 meter hurdles
5. Lynda Tolbert

1. Lynda Tolbert
2. Kim McKenzie
3. Tananjalyn Stanley

400 meter hurdles
1. Sandra Farmer-Patrick
9. Schowonda Williams

1. Sandra Farmer-Patrick
2. Schowonda Williams
3. Jackie Joyner-Kersee

10 kilometer walk
No American women were in the top ten.

1. Lynn Weik
2. Teresa Vaill
3. Debbi Lawrence

High jump
4. Jan Wohlschlag
7. Louise Ritter

1. Jan Wohlschlag
2. Louise Ritter
3. Yolanda Henry

Long jump
No American women were in the top ten.

1. Sheila Echols
2. Jennifer Inniss
3. Carol Lewis

Triple jump (American women)
1. Sheila Hudson
2. Renita Robinson
3. Diana Wills

Shot put
No American women were in the top ten.

1. Ramona Pagel
2. Connie Price
3. Bonnie Dasse

Discus
No American women were in the top ten.

1. Lacy Barnes
2. Connie Price
3. Ramona Pagel

Javelin
No American women were in the top ten.

1. Donna Mayhew
2. Karin Smith
3. Marilyn Senz

Heptathlon
No American women were in the top ten.

1. Jolanda Jones
2. Gea Johnson
3. Sharon Hainer

Lynn Jennings won the cross country championships for the fourth time, her third consecutive.

The *New York Times* reported on February 22 that Florence Griffith Joyner "received the Jesse Owens Award last night for athletic excellence and international understanding."

Ed Temple.

The following two coach/contributors were inducted into the National Track and Field Hall of Fame. The biographies are from the USATF website.

ED TEMPLE   COACH

Born September 20, 1927, Harrisburg, Penn.

Although still relatively young in chronological terms, Ed Temple has compiled a coaching record that would be the envy of someone twice his age. After graduating from Tennessee State University, Temple became the Tigerbelles head track coach and his record may never be equaled.

Already a member of four other Halls of Fame, Temple has watched his women athletes win 23 Olympic medals, 13 of them gold. Olympic champions who have come under his tutelage include Wilma Rudolph, Mae Faggs, Wyomia Tyus, Edith McGuire and Madeline Manning Mims, all Hall of Famers. His Tigerbelle teams were perennial national champions, capturing a total of 34 team titles, 16 indoors, 13 outdoors and five in the junior meet. Twice he has been honored as the head coach of the U.S. Olympic women's team and twice more he has been the Pan American Games women's head coach. Civically active in Nashville in several areas, Temple is also the author of a book published in 1980, *Only the Pure in Heart Survive*.

NELL JACKSON   ATHLETE   COACH

Born July 1, 1929, Athens, Georgia. Died April 1, 1988.

One of the pioneers in women's track and field, Nell Jackson served the sport as an athlete, coach and administrator. At the time of her death, she was serving as TAC's secretary and had previously been a TAC vice president.

While a student at Tuskegee Institute (where she was coached by Hall of Famer Cleve Abbott), she was a member of the 1948 Olympic team and also competed in the first Pan American Games in 1951, taking second in the 200 meters and running on the winning sprint relay team. A former

American record holder in the 200, Jackson later became a coach at Tuskegee, Illinois State, Illinois and Michigan State. She was the U.S. Olympic women's head coach in 1956 and 1972 and was the first African American to be named head coach of a U.S. Olympic team. Administratively, she served many organizations, including the U.S. Olympic Committee and the International Amateur Athletic Federation, as well as being an officer of The Athletics Congress (forerunner of USA Track & Field) since 1979. A renowned scholar, she conducted more than 50 workshops and clinics in track and field and was director of physical education at the State University of New York in Binghamton.

Geigengack Award

This award was presented posthumously to Nell Jackson who died in April 1988, while serving as The Athletic Congress's secretary. She had been one of TAC's officers since the Congress's inception in 1979.

INTERVIEW: SANDRA FARMER PATRICK

(January 30, 2006) I started competing, I hate to mention dates, probably back in the late 70s [laughter] through the Colgate Women's Games in Brooklyn, New York. It's a program that's run by Fred Thompson of the Atoms Track Club. I went out to the Colgate Games on a whim, just to get a free t-shirt. I was very successful that day. I placed fifth overall. Not knowing that there were a series of five meets to qualify to compete at Madison Square Garden, I never went back to any of the other meets. However, that one event that I went to qualified me to go to Madison Square Garden to compete in the finals. I had no idea, no concept of what track and field was about. Surprisingly, we received mail that said, "You've qualified to be in the semifinals of the Colgate Women's Games." Still not knowing what was involved, another free t-shirt [laughter] was enough motivation. So, of course, I went back. Again, without any training, I did well at the semifinals, which qualified me to compete at Madison Square Garden. Wow, it was an incredible experience; I recall getting a huge bag with Colgate products, t-shirt, sweatshirts, and meeting so many sports heroes. As a child, life couldn't have been any better — to just run down the straightaway. And you were given this great opportunity.

While I was competing at the Colgate Games, I was recruited by a young man named Don Johnson out of New York, the coach of the Flashettes Track Club. I still was clueless as to what I was getting into. I went to one or two practices. It wasn't part of my regular routine in terms of my family tradition and how I was raised. Church took priority over everything. I didn't go to many practices but I do remember showing up with a suitcase to go to a national championship because all my friends were talking about it. I was so clueless, I showed up, suitcase packed, but the coaches told me that I couldn't travel with the team, because I hadn't been to practice [laughter]. So I had to go back home. It was that day that I realized it was a little more serious. After that, I explained everything to my mom and told her that I had to go to practice to be a part of the track team. It was always a conflict competing on Sundays, because that day was dedicated to the Lord. As time evolved and I began to have more and more success in the sport, my mom, who was raised with a very traditional Pentecostal faith, started loosening up a little and every once in a while she'd let me go to an event on a Sunday. That's when they had most of the qualifying events. That's basically how it got started, out of Brooklyn, New York.

I won several academic scholarships at the Colgate Women's games, which paid for my private school education. I was recruited very heavily out of high school. I had a choice of just about any college that I wanted to go to. I did my collegiate years at the University of Arizona. Again, I think when I was in college I really didn't understand the importance of sports and the value and benefits that were involved. I kind of went to school and went through the motions.

It was maybe my junior year in college. Accidentally, if you would, I made the Olympic team for Jamaica [laughter]. Here it was the Olympic Games, Los Angeles, California. I ended up in the finals of the Olympic Games. Everyone is talking about medals and money. And I am wondering how did I get here to be a part of this?

I was a finalist in the 1984 Olympic Games and I had one more year of college and that's when

I decided to look at it a little bit more seriously. In doing that, I had to make a very hard decision. I knew at that time that I could make the Jamaican team. It was a lot easier to make than the U.S. team. Again, I made the finals. Obviously I beat out a lot of the Americans to make the Olympic final. However, I did not want to go to the Olympics just to say, 'I'm an Olympian." So I raised the bar some and I said, "You know what, I'm going to compete for the U.S." I knew that would help my development because I would get more financial support; I would get more competition.

In 1988, I switched and decided to run for the United States instead of Jamaica. That was my defining year. In 1988, when I had a guaranteed spot on the Olympic team for Jamaica, I gave that up to run for the United States and consequently I was disqualified at that Olympic trials and unable to go to the 1988 Olympic Games. I was very heartbroken and very disappointed but as I said before, it was my defining year. I developed a lot of strength and character after that. I really took another look and got really serious and got very, very motivated. I really needed to be on top of my game. Following that was the 1989 season where I went undefeated; broke the American record and just had a very, very successful year. Of course, I went around on a campaign and said, "This is my Olympic year." It was 1989. It was a really great year in terms of competition for me and being Sports Woman of the Year for the USOC. A lot of great things happened that year because of the determination and character that I developed from the 1988 season.

After that, I went on with my career but I have to say that the highlight of my career would probably be in 1993, Stuttgart. I won the silver medal in the 1992 Olympic Games. That was a great accomplishment: Stuttgart in 1993 was the epitome of performance excellence for me. When I speak to kids, I truly enjoy sharing that story. I took second place and went under the old world record, but yet I still did not win the race. However, that second place race was the best race of my life. If I had to run that race over again, the outcome would have been similar. The best executed race, I did everything that I was supposed to do on that particular day. To me, that was very victorious. Most people would probably think winning a major event would be a career highlight, but the highlight of my career was when I crossed the line and passed out, with nothing left — my personal best. There were some disappointing and mixed emotions after the competition. I continued to question myself: you take second place, you didn't win. Again, like I said, that was my personal accomplishment. There's not a title or a medal that could be attached to that.

Sandra Farmer Patrick.

I tell young children that sports in general are a great confidence-builder. It's good for wellness and fitness. It helps you to stay focused and determined and to really build good character for all areas in life. Sports are a good foundation. Whatever it may be when you're young, just get active, and get into sports whatever it might be, whether it's basketball, volleyball, golf. As you get into middle school and high school, that's a good time to really start looking at track and field a little more seriously, especially in high school if you want to pursue it on an international level. As kids, try all the sports that you are interested in and get ready for high school; that's really when you zone in and need to really get focused on a specific sport. Especially if you are considering a technical event like the jumps or the hurdles or the throws. I'm not necessarily a proponent of starting very, very young in a specific sport — some sports you need to start young and develop — but it's best that you start early in sports. You can always transition later on. Several athletes have done that. Jackie Joyner-Kersee did it. She did basketball and then she transferred over into track and field. Others have done it as well. The main thing is to stay active and get involved in athletics. Track and field has afforded me a unique opportunity to demonstrate academic and athletic excellence.

Currently I am the USOC representative for track and field; I'm also the Athlete's Advisory Chair. When I retired it was a nice transition. It was a sport that I've done for so long and it's given me so much that I wanted to give back. Now I work behind the scenes, just using some of my experiences to try to help better the quality of life for athletes competing. Our sport has become more professionalized — the things that we would have loved to have when we were competing. It's really gratifying just seeing the changes and the evolution that the sport has gone through. Being involved allows me to utilize my experience, trying to bridge that gap for our athletes. Being involved at this level helps to create better competition and performance excellence for our elite athletes. I'm really enjoying proven results, which keeps me busy. Any athlete issue that comes up I'm there to provide input, guidance and advocate on the athletes' behalf.

10

1990

The Outdoor Nationals

The USA/Mobil National Outdoor Track and Field Championships were held at Cerritos College in Norwalk, California from June 12 to June 16. Athletes who qualified were eligible to compete in the Goodwill Games held in July and August in Seattle, Washington.

"In Thursday night's only final," reported Frank Litsky in the *New York Times*, "Colette Murphy won the women's 10,000 meters in 32 minutes 20.92 seconds."

On June 15, in his article "Lewis Blasts to a Victory Over Witherspoon in 100," Litsky said,

Among the women's winners were Michelle Finn in the 100 meters (10.20 seconds, with Evelyn Ashford third), LaVonna Martin in the 100-meter hurdles (12.90 seconds), Sheila Hudson in the triple jump (46 feet 2 inches, wind-aided) and Debbi Lawrence in the 10-kilometer walk (46 minutes 14.4 seconds, an American record).

Mary Slaney, recovering from her latest leg injuries, was the 12th and final qualifier for Saturday night's 1,500-meter final, although she decided not to run it. She ran eighth in her semifinal in 4:18.40.

The *New York Times* on Sunday ran this headline, "Slaney, 'Not Fit to Race,' Bows Out."

It was uncharacteristic. It was almost embarrassing. But it could have been predicted.

To be brutal, Mary Decker Slaney, the best middle-distance runner in American track history, looked awful Friday night in the USA/Mobil Outdoor Track and Field Championships. She barely qualified for tonight's 1,500 meter final, and she decided not to run it. "I'm healthy," she said. "I'm fit. But I'm not fit to race."

She is almost 32 years old. She has been a world class runner since she was 14. She has broken five world records. Until last year, she held all eight United States records from 800 to 10,000 meters. She won two world championships in 1983. She achieved all that despite frequent injuries, the latest batch of which kept her out of competition from the winter of 1989 until last week. She has had three operations in the last year. Two were on her left Achilles' tendon. One was on her left calf, two and a half months ago.

...Friday night's race was only her fourth time on a track this year. The first and third times were in workouts. Between them was a race last week in which she achieved a qualifying time for this meet.

---

100 meters

Track & Field News reported that after a false start Michelle Finn led from the start to the finish in the 100 meters.

1. Michelle Finn, Atoms Track Club	11.20
2. Carlette Guidry, Longhorn Track Club	11.25
3. Evelyn Ashford, Mazda Track Club	11.30
4. Sheila Echols, Nike International	11.33
5. Dannette Young, Reebok Racing Club	11.42
6. Pauline Davis, Nike International/Bahamas	11.45
7. Grace Jackson, Jamaica	11.46
8. Esther Jones, Louisiana State University	11.54

200 meters

"...After a Young false start, Finn took the lead and held it through the curve. Two lanes to her left, Young headed her entering the stretch. But the long legs of the 6 ft, 136 lb. Jackson closed fastest, the Jamaican besting Young 22.48–22.55," reported *Track & Field News*.

1. Grace Jackson, Jamaica	22.48
2. Dannette Young, Reebok Racing Club	22.55
3. Pauline Davis, Nike International/Bahamas	22.75
4. Michelle Finn, Atoms Track Club	22.76
5. Mary Onyali, Nike International/Nigeria	22.78
6. Celena Mondie-Milner, University of Illinois	22.97
7. Gwen Torrence, Nike South Track Club	23.37
8. Wendy Vereen, Atoms Track Club	23.45

400 meters

"...On the second turn, Stevens made her move and led entering the final straight, but Malone's finish was overwhelming. She gained steadily on Stevens and Leatherwood and overtook them with about 40m to go to win by 0.28 in 51.23, the slowest winning time since '81," stated *Track & Field News*.

1. Maicel Malone, Nike Coast Track Club	51.23
2. Rochelle Stevens, Nike International	51.51
3. Lillie Leatherwood, Reebok Racing Club	51.60
4. Natasha Kaiser, Southern California Cheetahs	51.69
5. Jearl Miles, Reebok Racing Club	51.90
6. Delisa Floyd, FloJo International	52.26
7. Wendy Watson, University of Oklahoma	52.53
8. Tasha Downing, University of Florida	57.72

800 meters

Track & Field News reported:

Meredith Rainey was the last qualifier from the first round, having spent the week before the meet graduating from Harvard instead of training.

In the final, two-time defending champ Joetta Clark and Essie Washington moved down the backstretch and were three abreast with Julie Jenkins at 600 (1:30.0), with Rainey just a stride back. Around the last turn Clark fell back slightly and Rainey went wide to challenge for the lead.

Jenkins, Clark and Rainey hit the straight even, but Rainey's 51.56 speed could not be denied. She moved to the lead with 80m to go and finished a full stride up on Jenkins (2:00.91), whose strength prevailed to outlast a disappointed Clark (2:01.14).

1. Meredith Rainey, Atoms Track Club	2:00.70
2. Julie Jenkins, Reebok Racing Club	2:00.91
3. Joetta Clark, Nike International	2:01.14

4. Celeste Halliday, Nike Indiana Track Club   2:02.16
5. Adina Valdez, Westchester Track Club/Trinidad & Tobago   2:04.79
6. Cynthia Bayles, unattached   2:04.99
7. Essie Washington, Nike Houston   2:05.23
8. Michelle Taylor, Southern California Cheetahs   2:06.39

1500 meters

"...Favor followed Claudette Groenendaal's dawdling pace for 2 laps (2:23.6), then took the lead. Plumer ran midpack and had reached the collegiate star's shoulder with 300 remaining.

"The pair upped the ante 200m from home, and though Plumer narrowed the 2m margin Favor had built by mid–home-stretch, she came up 0.21 short of the winner's 4:13.47," reported *Track & Field News.*

1. Suzy Favor, University of Wisconsin, Madison   4:13.47
2. PattiSue Plumer, Nike International   4:13.68
3. Alisa Hill, unattached   4:15.44
4. Gina Procaccio, Sallie Mae Track Club   4:16.51
5. Linda Sheskey, Nike South Track Club   4:16.84
6. Kathy Franey, Villanova University   4:17.56
7. Darcy Arreola, Nike Coast Track Club   4:18.16
8. Sheila Carrozza, Run-Tex Track Club   4:18.63

3000 meters

Track & Field News reported:

...The finish was as anticlimactic as it was exciting. Peters, despite 4:14.4 speed, simply doesn't have the tools to outkick a happy and healthy Jennings. Looking like a sacrificial lamb, Peters modestly upped the pace.

On the final circuit, the 5 ft. 5, 108 lb. Jennings waited until it was more than safe to begin her patented destruction of the pacemaker.

A 64.8 closer—with a 30.1 last 200—brought her home in 8:51.97 for her second title at this distance.

1. Lynn Jennings, Nike International   8:51.97
2. Annette Peters, Nike West Track Club   8:54.64
3. Valerie McGovern, University of Kentucky/Ireland   8:57.73
4. Trina Painter, Nike Texas   9:07.04
5. Kathy Kanes, Pilo Track Club   9:09.97
6. Libbie Johnson, Nike Coast Track Club   9:11.16
7. Gwyn Hardesty, Nike Boston   9:12.78
8. Carmen Ayala-Troncoso, Nike Texas   9:15.75

5000 meters

According to *Track & Field News,*

...On the last circuit, the two vets hammered around the final turn, Dornhoefer a couple of strides behind. On the straight, the Missouri grad accelerated remarkably and attempted to pass on the inside.

"She left it open for me, then closed it off," said Dornhoefer, who chopped her stride and gave Plumer a sound push. "I expected something like that; that's how it goes."

Plumer crossed in 15:45.67, Dornhoefer in 15:46.20. "Tough!" said the 28-year-old victor of her nasty double effort. "It wasn't easy."

1. PattiSue Plumer, Nike International   15:45.67
2. Sabrina Dornhoefer, New Balance Track Club   15:46.20

3. Sammie Gdowski, Reebok Racing Club	15:51.54
4. Brenda Webb, Asics Track Club	16:01.33
5. Chris McNamara, unattached	16:01.44
6. Laurie Gomez, North Carolina State University	16:07.11
7. Shelly Steely, unattached	16:08.16
8. Kate Fonshell, Villanova University	16:12.45

10,000 meters

"Colette Murphy followed the pace of Cathy O'Brien for the first 3000 (9:43.3), but 100m later the Indiana grad surged ahead decisively. O'Brien and Sylvia Mosqueda dogged Murphy's heels, but could never get really close," wrote *Track & Field News*.

1. Colette Murphy, Nike Indiana Track Club	32:20.92
2. Cathy O'Brien, New Balance Track Club	32:25.93
3. Sylvia Mosqueda, Mazda Track Club	32:41.02
4. Laura LaMena, unattached	33:01.84
5. Margaret Groos, Nike South	33:10.01
6. Anne Letko, Nike Running Room	33:21.87
7. Lisa Vaill, Warren Street Track Club	33:32.36
8. Shelly Steely, unattached	33:37.83

100 meter hurdles

"LaVonna Martin lined up with her main competition—Kim McKenzie and Lynda Tolbert—on either side. But after the gun was fired, it was clear there was no match for Martin this time," said *Track & Field News*. The 23-year-old Tennessee grad raced away cleanly from the field. Her 2m victory in 12.90 produced her first TAC win since 1987.

1. LaVonna Martin, Reebok Racing Club	12.90
2. Candy Young, Atoms Track Club	13.16
3. Lynda Tolbert, Nike International	13.18
4. Jackie Humphrey, Nike South Track Club	13.32
5. Rosalind Council, unattached	13.35
6. Kim McKenzie, Mazda Track Club	13.38
7. Michelle Freeman, Jamaica	13.39
8. Kathy Freeman, LS United	13.51

400 meter hurdles

According to *Track & Field News*,

...Farmer-Patrick was playing catch-up throughout the race. By the eighth hurdle the UCLA junior was still leading; then came the charge. SFP caught her at the last barrier and appeared poised for a win. Vickers even stumbled on the 10th, but the UCLA junior planned to play her trump. "Nobody can run the last 50m with Janeene," says coach Bobby Kersee. Vickers regained herself for a last-minute charge, besting the favorite with a PR of 54.80 and moving to No. 4 on the all-time U.S. list.

1. Janeene Vickers, World Class Athletes	54.80
2. Sandra Farmer-Patrick, FloJo International	55.18
3. Schowonda Williams, Nike International	55.61
4. Victoria Fulcher, Nike South Track Club	56.06
5. LaTanya Sheffield, San Diego Track Club	56.36
6. Countess Comadore, Southern University	56.39
7. Kim Batten, Florida State University	58.34
8. Tracy Mattes, University of Wisconsin, Madison	58.86

10 kilometer walk

"...Lawrence, Teresa Vaill and Sara Standley walked a tightly contested race until Lawrence broke away just after the halfway mark to add to the titles she won in '84 and '86," said *Track & Field News.*

1. Debbi Lawrence, Parkside Athletic Club	46:14.4 AR
(American record; previous record 46:44.1, Lynn Weik, 1989)	
2. Teresa Vaill, Natural Sport	46:54.2
3. Sara Standley, Natural Sport	47:08.5
4. Wendy Sharp, Natural Sport	47:39.6
5. Debora Van Orden, unattached	48:28.8
6. Victoria Herazo, California Walkers	48:47.8
7. Viisha Sedlak, Easy Spirit	49:14.9
8. Zofia Wolan, Wolverine Pacers Athletic Club/Poland	50:06.6

High jump

After a shaky start at the lower heights, Yolanda Henry scaled the next three heights with ease.

"...With the bar at 6–8¼, Henry had a good first shot at Ritter's AR; her last two tries weren't as impressive. 'I was so tired by then,'" she explained to *Track & Field News* reporter Jeff Hollobaugh.

1. Yolanda Henry, Mazda Track Club	6' 5"
2. Phyllis Blunston, Southern California Cheetahs	6' 4"
3. Vicki Borsheim, Westwood Track Club	6' 4"
4. Jan Wohlschlag, Nike International	6' 2¾"
5. Angie Bradburn, University of Texas	6' 2¾"
6. Latrese Johnson, Azusa Pacific University	6' 1½"
7. Julieann Broughton, Nike Coast Track Club	6' 1½"
8. Mary Moore, Club Northwest	6' ½"

Long jump

"Very few people expected to see Jackie Joyner-Kersee lose. None of them did, as she indicated once again just what a chasm there is between her and the rest of the nation's long jumpers. The Olympic champ leaped 23' 2¾" on her fifth attempt to win by more than a foot," said *Track & Field News.*

1. Jackie Joyner-Kersee, McDonald's Track Club	23' 2¾"
2. Sheila Echols, Nike International	22' 2¼" w
3. Cindy Greiner, Nike Coast Track Club	21' 11¾" w
4. Christy Opara, Nigeria	21' 6¾"
5. Jennifer Inniss, unattached	21' 6"
6. Sheila Hudson, Mizuno Track Club	21' 4¾"
7. Gwen Loud, Stars & Stripes Track Club	21' ½" w
8. Wendy Brown, unattached	20' 9¾"

Triple jump

"By the time she finished, AR holder Sheila Hudson had produced the longest jump ever by an American, a just-windy (2.1mph) 46–2 in the fifth round."

1. Sheila Hudson, unattached	46' 2" w
2. Wendy Brown, unattached	45' ¼" w
3. Diana Wills, U.S. Army	44' 4"

4. Robyne Johnson, unattached	43' 7"
5. Donna Crumety, St. Joseph's University	42' 3½"
6. Juliana Yendork, Southern California Cheetahs	41' 11¼" w
7. Camille Jackson, Louisiana State University	41' 5¾"
8. Kathy Harrison, Nike South Track Club	41' 4½"

Discus

"Connie Price, 28, won her third platter title but was somewhat non-plussed by her performance. 'It was okay,' she said. 'It wasn't great. But I'll take it — a win is a win.'"

1. Connie Price-Smith, Nike North Track Club	191' 6"
2. Lacy Barnes, Nike Track Club	187' 5"
3. Penny Neer, Nike Coast Club	186' 2"
4. Ramona Pagel, Mazda Track Club	180' 2"
5. Carla Garrett, Nike Coast Club	178'
6. Kelly Landry, Florida Athletic Club	176'
7. Laura Lavine, unattached	175' 1"
8. Tracie Millett, World Class Athletes	171' 1"

Shot put

"Connie Price dominated the shot, all five of her fair throws — topped by a winning 60' 10¾" — surpassing defending champ Ramona Pagel's best of 58' 5¼".... Price's win capped a notable weight double. She is the first to accomplish the feat since Hollander Ria Stalman in 1984, and the first American in a quarter century, the most recent being Lynn Graham in '65," reported Dave Johnson for *Track & Field News*.

1. Connie Price-Smith, Nike North Track Club	60' 10¼"
2. Ramona Pagel, Mazda Track Club	58' 5¼"
3. Bonnie Dasse, Nike Coast Club	58' 2"
4. Grace Apiafi, Southern California Cheetahs/Nigeria	53' ¼"
5. Pam Dukes, Nike Coast Club	52' 10¼"
6. Deb Corley, unattached	51' 7"
7. Christy Barrett, Indiana State University	51' 3¾"
8. Katrin Koch, Indiana University/West Germany	50' 2½"

Javelin

"Karin Smith had been red hot over the previous month, taking the U.S. lead with a near–PR performance at *Pre* [the Prefontaine Meet held yearly in Eugene, Oregon]. The 34-year-old vet left little room for a challenge as she quickly established the lead with an opening 206' 3".

"'It's really unusual for me to get a good throw to start a competition,' she said. 'It usually takes me a few throws to warm up before I get a good one. I was relieved to get it over with early,'" said *Track & Field News*.

1. Karin Smith, Nike Coast Club	206' 3"
2. Laverne Eve, Nike South/Bahamas	193' 11"
3. Donna Mayhew, Nike Coast Club	193'
4. Marilyn Senz, Mazda Track Club	185' 9"
5. Erica Wheeler, unattached	173' 10"
6. Paula Berry, University of Oregon	171' 10"
7. Durelle Schimek, Nike Coast Club	167' 11"
8. Kim Hyatt, University of Oregon	165' 3"

Heptathlon

Track & Field News reported:

"Retired" a year ago, Cindy Greiner is basically back where she was in 1988. Her winning score of 6262w was just 35 points off her 6297 PR from Seoul and the third best of her career.

The 33-year-old Oregon State alum was unsure of where her conditioning was in the hurdles and high jump, but led from the shot on to the finish.

1. Cindy Greiner, Nike Coast Club	6262	w
2. Gea Johnson, Nike Coast Club	6135	w
3. Sharon Hainer, Nike Coast Club	6030	
4. Jamie McNeair, Purdue University	6016	
5. Kym Carter, Oregon International Track Club	6003	w
6. Cheryl Wilson, Stars & Stripes Track Club	5916	w
7. Cathy Tyree, Nike Coast Club	5847	
8. Debra Larsen, Nike Coast Club	5731	w

Hammer throw (exhibition)

1. Bonnie Edmondson, unattached	174'	9"	MR
2. Virginia Young, St. John's University	165'	5"	
3. Mary Teeman, Rhode Island College	164'		
4. Angela Vaughn, Rutgers University	157'	3"	
5. Shirl Dorsey, George Mason University	155'	6"	
6. Sonja Fitts, St. John's University	153'	7"	
7. Christine Spinosa, Syracuse University	144'	10"	
8. Donna McDonough, Athletes in Action	142'	5"	

Team scores:

Nike International	79
Nike Coast Club	72
Reebok Racing Club	42

The Indoor Nationals

The USA/Mobil Indoor Track and Field Championships were held on Friday, February 23, in Madison Square Garden, New York.

"The North American indoor track and field season, which lumbered along at an innocuous pace for two months, ended tonight with a flurry of outstanding performances in the final event of the Grand Prix circuit, the USA/Mobil championships," wrote Michael Janofsky in the *New York Times*.

Lynn Jennings set an American record in the 3,000 meters and Diane Dixon, in winning the 400 meters, became the top winning woman in the eighty-four year history of the meet. Janofsky goes on:

...In a scintillating women's 3,000-meter race, Jennings passed Vicki Huber with two laps to go to finish in 8 minutes 40.45 seconds, lowering Lesley Lehane's four-year-old record by 4.23 seconds.

PattiSue Plumer, who passed Huber just before the last turn and Huber also ran faster than Lehane, Plumer in 8:41.45 and Huber in 8:42.13.

"With the personnel in that race, it was inevitable that the pace would be that fast," said Jennings, who last month ran the world's fastest 5,000 meter indoors.

55 meters
1. Michelle Finn, Atoms Track Club   6.61
2. Dawn Sowell, Flo-Jo International   6.65
3. Sheila Echols, Nike International   6.75

200 meters
1. Grace Jackson, unattached/Jamaica   23.53
2. Angela Williams, unattached/Trinidad and Tobago   23.57
3. Lamonda Miller, Nike South Track Club   23.94

400 meters
1. Diane Dixon, Nike International   53.50
2. Maicel Malone, Arizona State University   53.87
3. Toinette Holmes, Arizona State University   55.12

800 meters
1. Joetta Clark, Nike South Track Club   2:04.32
2. Svetlana Kitova, Union of Soviet Socialist Republic   2:04.67
3. Diana Richburg, Gazelle International   2:05.69

Mobil mile
1. Doina Melinte, Romania   4:27.62   MR
2. PattiSue Plumer, Nike International   4:31.29
3. Alisa Harvey, unattached   4:31.78

3000 meters
1. Lynn Jennings, Nike International   8:40.45   AR
2. PattiSue Plumer, Nike International   8:41.45
3. Vicki Huber, Nike International   8:42.13

55 meter hurdles
1. LaVonna Martin, Reebok Racing Club   7.44
2. Lynda Tolbert, Arizona State University   7.45
3. Kim McKenzie, Mazda Track Club   7.49

Shot put
1. Ramona Pagel, Mazda Track Club   60' 4½"
2. Connie Price-Smith, Nike North Track Club   59' 2"
3. Bonnie Dasse, Nike Coast Track Club   53' 3¾"

20 lb. weight throw (non–championship event)
1. Virginia Young, St. John's University   59' 11¾"
2. Shirl Dorsey, George Mason Track Club   59' 2"
3. Christine Spinosa, Syracuse University   54' 7¼"

Long jump
1. Jacinta Bartholomew, Atoms Track Club/Grenada   21' 2½"
2. LaShawn Simmons, Southern California Cheetahs   20' 8½"
3. Claire Connor, Louisiana State Track Club   20' 5¾"

High jump
1. Jan Wohlschlag, Nike International   6' 4"
2. Vicki Borsheim, unattached   6' 2¼"
3. Angela Bradburn, University of Texas,   5' 10¾"
       Felicia Hodges, unattached, Connie Long, unattached

3000 meter walk
1. Teresa Vaill, Natural Sport — 12:53.17
2. Anne Peel, Top Form Lions Athletics/Canada — 13:10.69
3. Victoria Herazo, California Walkers — 13:37.10

4 × 400 meter relay
1. Atoms Track Club — 3:48.96
   (Ashaley Williams, Alicia Moss, Dawn Salazar, Maxine Wynter)
2. Fairleigh Dickinson University — 3:49.4

Team champion:
Nike International

Sunkist Invitational (5 women's events): Los Angeles, January 19

50 meters
1. Angela Bailey, Canada — 6.34

440 yards
1. Diane Dixon, unattached — 53.18 — MR

800 meters
1. Teena Colebrook, California Polytechnic, San Luis Obispo — 2:06.19

Mile
1. PattiSue Plumer, Nike International — 4:33.01

50 meter hurdles
1. Linda Tolbert, Arizona State University — 6.89 — MR

Goodwill Games: Seattle, Washington, July 22–26

100 meters
1. Carlette Guidry — 11.03
2. Sheila Echols — 11.05
3. Michelle Finn — 11.05
5. Evelyn Ashford — 11.24

200 meters
1. Dannette Young — 22.64
4. Michelle Finn — 23.00

400 meters
3. Rochelle Stevens — 51.54
4. Maicel Malone — 51.73
8. Lillie Leatherwood — 52.77

800 meters
6. Julie Jenkins — 1:59.81
7. Meredith Rainey — 2:00.45
8. Celeste Halliday — 2:01.08
9. Joetta Clark — 2:01.94

1500 meters
3. PattiSue Plumer   4:10.72
4. Suzy Favor   4:11.45

3000 meters
1. PattiSue Plumer   8:51.59
3. Lynn Jennings   8:52.34
6. Annette Peters   8:56.89

5000 meters
3. Sabrina Dornhoefer   15:38.87
4. Shelly Steely   15:41.23
5. Sammie Gdowski   15:59.72
6. Brenda Webb   16:00.85

10,000 meters
2. Cathy O'Brien   32:05.40
5. Sylvia Mosqueda   32:13.37
6. Colette Murphy   32:33.96

100 meter hurdles
3. LaVonna Martin   12.89
6. Candy Young   13.11
7. Linda Tolbert   13.14

400 meter hurdles
1. Sandra Farmer-Patrick   55.16
2. Schowonda Williams   55.65
4. Michelle Freeman   57.71

4 × 100 meter relay
1. USA   42.46
    (Carlette Guidry, Sheila Echols, Michelle Finn, Evelyn Ashford)

4 × 400 meter relay
2. USA   3:24.53
    (Natasha Kaiser, Rochelle Stevens, Lillie Leatherwood, Maicel Malone)

High jump
2. Yolanda Henry (tie)   6' 3½"
5. Vicki Borsheim   6' 2¼"
6. Jan Wohlschlag   6' 2¼"
8. Phyllis Blunston   6' 1¼"

Long jump
3. Sheila Echols   21' 4¼"
4. Cindy Greiner   21' 3½"
5. Jennifer Inniss   20' 6½"
6. Sheila Hudson   20' 1¾"
7. Gwen Loud   19' 11¾"

Shot put
6. Ramona Pagel   60' 3¼"
7. Connie Price   59' 10¼"

Discus
| 7. Lacy Barnes | 189' 9" |
| 8. Connie Price | 187' 9" |

Javelin
| 3. Karin Smith | 193' 4" |
| 4. Donna Mayhew | 192' 4" |

Heptathlon
| 1. Jackie Joyner-Kersee | 6783 |
| 4. Gea Johnson | 5963 |

IAAF World Cross Country Championships: Aix-les-Bains, France, March 24

(6000 meters)
1. Lynn Jennings	19:21
33. Sabrina Dornhoefer	20:07
34. Elaine Van Blunk	20:07
44. Shelly Steely	20:20
103. Leanne Martin	21:11
117. Janet Smith	21:24

The United States team placed fifth.
This was Lynn Jennings's fifth cross country title and her fourth consecutive win.

Junior women (4400 meters)
12. Melody Fairchild	14:37
23. Jamie Park	14:57
72. Deena Drossin	15:49
90. Rebecca Spies	16:09
96. Shelley Smathers	16:16
105. Amy Giblin	16:27

The United States junior team finished third.

IAAF/Mobil Grand Prix Series

Mobil Banespa International: Sao Paulo, Brazil, May 20

100 meters
| 1. Dannette Young | 11.54 |

200 meters
1. Dannette Young	23.02
2. Rochelle Stevens	23.18
7. Lillie Leatherwood	24.29

400 meters
1. Rochelle Stevens	51.01
6. Lillie Leatherwood	51.87
7. Jearl Miles	53.55

100 meter hurdles
1. LaVonna Martin   13.16
3. Jackie Humphrey   13.52
5. Kim McKenzie   13.55

Javelin
4. Karin Smith   192' 10"
5. Donna Mayhew   191' 10"

Bruce Jenner's Bud Light Classic: San Jose, California, May 26

200 meters
1. Dannette Young   22.89
3. Michelle Finn   23.20
4. Celena Mondie-Milner   23.29

400 meters
2. Rochelle Stevens   51.42
4. Natasha Kaiser   51.55
7. Pam Irby   53.91

Other News and Honors

Track & Field News: U.S. Athlete of the Year

PattiSue Plumer

Track & Field News— American Women in Top Ten World Rankings

7. PattiSue Plumer   10. Jackie Joyner-Kersee

U.S. Top Five Rankings — Track & Field News

1. PattiSue Plumer   4. Yolanda Henry
2. Jackie Joyner-Kersee   5. Carlette Guidry
3. Lynn Jennings

World and United States Rankings by Event — Track & Field News
(U.S. rankings in bold)

100 meters   1. **Dannette Young**
3. Carlette Guidry   2. **Michelle Finn**
4. Michelle Finn   3. **Esther Jones**
5. Evelyn Ashford
7. Sheila Echols   **400 meters**
                                     8. Rochelle Stevens
1. **Carlette Guidry**
2. **Michelle Finn**   1. **Rochelle Stevens**
3. **Evelyn Ashford**   2. **Maicel Malone**
                                     3. **Lillie Leatherwood**
200 meters
3. Dannette Young   **800 meters**
                                     7. Julie Jenkins

1990

1. Julie Jenkins
2. Meredith Rainey
3. Delisa Floyd

1500 meters
No American women ranked in the top ten in the world.

1. Suzy Favor
2. Lynn Jennings
3. PattiSue Plumer

3000 meters
1. PattiSue Plumer
4. Lynn Jennings

1. PattiSue Plumer
2. Lynn Jennings
3. Vicki Huber

5000 meters
1. PattiSue Plumer
2. Lynn Jennings
9. Annette Peters

1. PattiSue Plumer
2. Lynn Jennings
3. Annette Peters

10,000 meters
No American women ranked in the top ten in the world.

1. Colette Murphy
2. Cathy O'Brien
3. Sylvia Mosqueda

Marathon
5. Francie Larrieu-Smith
6. Lisa Weidenbach

1. Francie Larrieu-Smith
2. Lisa Weidenbach
3. Kim Jones

100 meter hurdles
6. LaVonna Martin

1. LaVonna Martin
2. Candy Young
3. Lynda Tolbert

400 meter hurdles
3. Sandra Farmer-Patrick
5. Janeene Vickers
6. Schowonda Williams
9. Kathy Freeman

1. Sandra Farmer-Patrick

2. Janeene Vickers
3. Schowonda Williams

10 kilometer walk
No American women ranked in the top ten in the world.

1. Debbi Lawrence
2. Lynn Weik
3. Teresa Vaill

High jump
4. Yolanda Henry
7. Jan Wohlschlag

1. Yolanda Henry
2. Jan Wohlschlag
3. Vicki Borsheim

Long jump
7. Jackie Joyner-Kersee

1. Jackie Joyner-Kersee
2. Sheila Echols
3. Cindy Greiner

Triple jump (No world rankings — event too new)
1. Sheila Echols
2. Wendy Brown
3. Diana Wills

Shot put
No American women ranked in the top ten in the world.

1. Connie Price
2. Ramona Pagel
3. Bonnie Dasse

Discus
No American women ranked in the top ten in the world.

1. Lacy Barnes
2. Connie Price
3. Penny Neer

Javelin
No American women ranked in the top ten in the world.

1. Karin Smith
2. Donna Mayhew
3. Marilyn Senz

Heptathlon
1. Jackie Joyner-Kersee

1. Jackie Joyner-Kersee
2. Gea Johnson
3. Cindy Greiner

Doris Brown Heritage (left), Roger Kingdom and the author, 2004.

Doris Brown-Heritage was inducted into the National Track and Field Hall of Fame. The following biography is from the National Track and Field Hall of Fame website.

DORIS BROWN-HERITAGE

Born September 17, 1942, Tacoma, WA.

In whatever area Doris Heritage has embraced in track and field, she has met with exceptional success. A five-time world cross country champion as an athlete, she also is an outstanding distance coach at Seattle Pacific University. She is the first woman member of the Cross Country and Road Running Committee of the International Amateur Athletic Federation (IAAF), the world's governing body for the sport. Despite her busy schedule, she still runs and in 1988 won the master's national cross country title in Raleigh, North Carolina. Heritage first came into international prominence in 1967 when she won the world cross country championship. She won the next four as well, and overall, represented the U.S. on nine world cross country teams. She was also on two Olympic teams, placing fifth in the 800 meters in 1968. An injury just before the competition forced her to drop out of the 1972 Olympic 1,500. She was second in the 1971 Pan American 800. In all, she won 14 national titles and set a world record for the 3,000 meters in 1971. As a coach, she was an assistant at both the 1984 Olympics and the 1987 Outdoor World Championships.

INTERVIEW: PattiSue Plumer

(December 5, 2002) I had been interested in running track since I was very young. My father went on a mystery trip to Mexico when I was about six years old and during that time, I knew he was attending the Mexico City Olympics. So, in my sort of very young child's mind, I figured if I watched T.V. I might see him at the Olympics. Just sort of the excitement of the events coupled with the fact that I thought my dad was there watching it; I wanted to be in the Olympics ever since then. To me, the Olympics was track and field. There really wasn't anything else. I knew nothing. I was six years old. I had no perspective on what it meant at that point. But it was a seed that was planted very early and I just couldn't believe it twenty years later when I actually made the team.

My parents were divorced and my mother worked as most mothers do when they're in that situation. I was really fortunate to live at that time in southern California during a time that running was actually available and it wasn't very crowded. It was a golden age in California, I think. There were lots and lots of after school programs for the kids. I did a lot of different sports, lots of different programs, but one of them that the city offered was an eight week track program. I did my first one when I was in second grade and it was terrific. It was a short exposure to track. Even then, I don't remember exactly how well I did but I was pretty good in sprints and I actually remember throwing the shot put, but I really did well in the distance events.

They had a cross country program. I entered that at one point. I took off running — I was ahead of everybody — the last 100 yards I got passed by everybody, like I was dead — and then I threw up!

After California, I moved to Colorado with my dad.

Before that, I had a really wonderful PE teacher, Debbie LaHecka. She was the coach of the track team in my elementary school, which had a sixth grade. You were eligible to compete in the middle school if you wanted to. So I did. I competed on the track team as a sixth grader. She really was the first, probably one of the first people who said, "You're really good and you could really do something with this."

I just sort of showed up and beat a lot of people and I remember the only person who beat me, and this was Orange County which had a pretty competitive program, was the girl who qualified for the Olympic Trials in swimming as a twelve year old. I wish I knew her name. She was the one person who was a better distance runner than me. But I didn't train. I just showed up and ran. That's how I got started and it showed that I was better than most. I really pretty much beat everybody in the longer distances and I just kept running in high school sports.

I didn't train year round. I really didn't think about training year round until I was somewhere in the middle of high school. I really had a good track coach. One year the track coach was the football coach. One year the track coach was a driver education teacher. One year I had very good coaches — the Randalls — a husband and wife. He coached football and she coached other sports and they coached track together — they didn't really know what they were doing. I remember when I met them; they came to me when I was speaking out in Colorado after I made an Olympic team. Or maybe they wrote me a letter — I can't remember — but they said, "We're so glad we didn't ruin you" [laughter].

They were wonderful people though. They really cared and even though they didn't know a whole lot about track and they certainly didn't know a lot about coaching someone with talent and potential, they admitted it. They didn't try to pretend that they knew what they were doing and we really worked together. That was my best year in high school, my sophomore year, and that was the year they coached. My next years were okay, but that was my best year.

I won everything I ran in Colorado but when I got to the state meet, my best finish was third in my sophomore year in the mile. In my junior year I was fourth. That's all they had. In my senior year, they added the two mile (1980) and I was fourth in both the mile and two mile. I was always good, always very good but I don't think I was a prodigy. I wasn't setting state records. I trained hard during the season. I did everything I was supposed to do but I never really thought about it; it just didn't occur to me until I was probably in my late teens that you would do this all year round.

I think that's why I had a long career. My career was ended by a fluke as opposed to overuse injuries. I had an injury that was not attributed to overuse; it was just a freak accident and so bad that had it not occurred, I probably could have really successfully run for another three years. I think part of that is because I did a lot of sports growing up. My body wasn't over-taxed. It was allowed to grow normally and naturally. It's an advantage of running, in a sense; it's not as tiring as the longer distances. When I was in high school, I thought, I don't have any help doing this, I have no track coach, no track club, no nothing. But I think when I look back, had I stayed in California, I think I would have been scooped up by one of these track clubs at eleven or twelve years old and would've run year round — I'm sure I never would have kept going. I think I would have been burned out by the time I got to college.

I didn't get a scholarship to college. Stanford had just hired a new coach the year before, Brooks Johnson. It was the first time they were offering scholarships. I was in Colorado, for gosh sakes. My first choice was Georgetown and I sent a letter saying I wanted to run and I didn't get anything back. It was a running joke with Coach Gag for a long time. He wasn't the coach actually at the time but we just joked about Georgetown in general. Honestly, there was no way I would have gone to Georgetown. Stanford's a better school but it wasn't because I knew that. I went there because I knew it was a good school and they said I could run track and I had a really good financial aid package. That was probably because the track program wanted me and helped with that, but I was not eligible. I never had a track scholarship — not ever. I had an academic scholarship. I was also eligible for financial aid; my father didn't have any money.

PattiSue Plumer, 2002.

I didn't really need it. I kind of thought it was a good thing not to take a scholarship away from an athlete who couldn't come any other way. It didn't really bother me. It was a little hard when the tuition came due. I really wasn't ready and I wasn't eligible for it in my last two years.

One of my favorite moments as an athlete and there are many — but I'd have to put it right up there — certainly in the top five — was the moment that I put on my Stanford jersey for the first time. I remember that I was in a hotel in Fresno, California and I just put on this uniform and I looked in the mirror and said, "I am a Class C collegiate athlete. I am a varsity collegiate athlete." I didn't care how I did. This was my goal: just to make the traveling team.

An important coach in my life was Lance Harger. I was invited by Lance to go to this training camp in Colorado Springs and he was the coach there. He sat down with me on the last day and said, "Where are you going to school?" I said, "I'm going to Stanford." He knew me all through Colorado. He was watching me run. But I wasn't even the best athlete there. He said, "Who else is on the team?" I knew the names of people but I didn't know who they were. He said, "You know, you can make it. You can make an impact, you can be a scoring person on the team immediately." And I was just stunned. It never even occurred to me that this could be something I could do. It was really great because he opened my mind to the fact that I could do this, but I didn't know if he was right. I didn't know what he knew. I was still questioning that premise but in my mind, at least, I thought I might be a scorer on the team and so I went there with the least amount of credentials of anybody that was recruited to the program.

My first year really wasn't very good. We didn't qualify for nationals but we had some very good athletes. I was the second top scorer at our regional meet. The first year Brooks wasn't really my coach but I made a huge improvement. But that meant nothing because I was still nothing on the collegiate level.

In my very first track meet at Stanford I was dead last, but I could not have been happier because I broke five minutes for the mile for the first time. That was quite an accomplishment and I was so happy; dead last but I ran under five minutes. By the end of the season, in my freshman year, I qualified for the nationals in the 3000 meters in my last meet of the season. I qualified: I ran 9:39.9, which was 11:41 in my senior year in high school. So that was over a minute's improvement. I had run 11:21 as a sophomore, but not in an official high school meet. So in one year I went from 11:41 down to 9:40 — over a minute's improvement. I just couldn't believe that I qualified for nationals. It was not in my thought processes at the beginning of the year.

Just about a week before, I found out that [Brooks] would take me to the nationals. I didn't qualify for finals. I was the first non-qualifier. But, actually, I was sick. I didn't know it at the time. I had a mono-like virus. I didn't know that until I got home. I was anemic that year. But I've never been anemic and hadn't had it diagnosed. I just thought I was tired because it was the end of the season—finals and everything else. So I didn't qualify for finals. I was so upset and all I remember about that meet is that Brooks was yelling at me. Yelling and yelling and yelling at me. He was talking to me. I must be good. It was the first time that he ever paid attention to me. And so I knew at that point, because the man doesn't waste that kind of energy on athletes that have no potential. He just would have said, good job, good effort.

I was thinking that next year I could qualify for three events at the nationals. That was my goal, I thought maybe. I was so afraid to even mention it. It would have been about a twenty second jump in the 3000 for All-American. So I was very nervous about it. I said three events. And he goes, anything else. And I go, maybe All American in the 3000. And he sat there and he goes, "If that's the only thing you want to accomplish you just might as well quit the team now." I had done a lot of acting in high school and I was in a freshman play, so it was kind of hard for me to choose between running and theatre. And he said, "Go to your theatre arts, go to your plays. We don't need you on the team. I have a whole boat load of people coming in who want to win nationals; if you're not one of them, then I don't want you on the team." I was so shocked that he put me in that category to win national championships. I said, "Think I could win national championships?" He said, "Think I'd be having this conversation with you?" So now I got the concept of national championships in my brain. When I was seven years old and didn't have a clue, I thought about it but not when I was running and training and saw what it took. I left there and decided I would give it a year. I would give running one more year. I would just do running and I would see at the end of a year if I was doing well. If not, I would go back to theatre. I knew I could pick it up in a year, it didn't matter.

That was another turning point at the moment when I made a commitment. I made an emotional commitment and I really started to believe it. I had a good year and we were a great team. It was the best in the nation. I was number three on the team.

He sent me to this meet in Canada. I didn't go with him. He sent me with another coach and I remember he gave me instructions: go to the front and run, it wouldn't matter who was in it; just go to the front. I didn't like it too much but I said, "okay." And I went there. I had no clue. I remember walking out on the track and it was unbelievable, it was like a who's who in women's track and field at that point. About the only one missing was Mary Slaney. Francie Larrieu was in it, the Canadian champion, and our national American champion. It was the first time I competed against people who were out of college who were national champions and internationally ranked. My first international meet, my first indoor meet, I didn't even know how to run on an indoor track. It was like a 160 meter track and I was thinking, what am I going to do? I don't know what to do. There were hundreds of people packed into this tiny fieldhouse, screaming like crazy. Well, I figured, if [Brooks] was here he wouldn't tell me to do this. There's no way he'd tell me to go out with the leaders. So I don't. Of course, I don't go out with the leaders. And I go out, I was really in never-never land. I was running around the track going round and round in circles. I was getting dizzy practically. And I remember thinking, you know, I didn't go with the leaders but I was supposed to. With a couple of laps to go, I started running fast and I passed two people and I ended up fourth in this race. And I was four seconds off the lead. I think I ended up being 9:32 something and the person who won ran 9:29. I sat there, and I got it. It was like the light bulb went on in my head. When he heard, he was really pissed because I didn't go out on the lead. If I had listened to him and gone out on the lead, I might not have won but boy, would I have had a race because I did nothing right. I still managed to get fourth, I still managed to get an eight second PR and I still managed to do all these things but I was not in the race ever, mentally or physically, and I thought, he's right. I got it. I got it. Like the light bulb went on in my head and I knew. I knew that I had just been using excuses like I wasn't good enough, I didn't have good coaching, I never ran as a youth. I was putting up all these reasons why I couldn't be successful in order to have an excuse for when I failed. I realized that my biggest enemy was myself. I had to just go out there and give myself a chance and let the chips fall where they may. But I was good enough to be with the leaders at any rate.

When I got home, my coach was sick. I went and I begged him, I begged him—I said, "Please let me go to any other meet. I'll show you. I got it. I got it. I really got it." And he said no. The L.A. Times meet was coming up and I really wanted to go to this meet and he said no. There was this little tiny meet in Pocatello, Idaho and I ran my PRs in the 400. I think I ran like the 4 × 4, I got a PR in that event, I got a PR in the indoor mile. Every race I ran, I got it. I beat everybody on our team. Obviously, they're national champions — I beat them all. He still wouldn't send me. So two days before the meet he relented. I went out with Mary Slaney in that race. I held her off. I was the only person she didn't lap. But I ended up getting third. I ended up getting passed by Joni Hansen. But I ran 9:11, which was a leading collegiate time. I ran 9:39 three or five months before and I ran 9:11 indoors and I got it. That was the change. The rest you can look up. I mean, the rest is when I was fit and not injured. I broke records, I had good meets, I had bad meets. But that was really the defining moment in my career, in terms of men- tally allowing myself to be amongst the best. I got it that we could all make the Olympic team if we had the right frame of mind and the right training and the right confidence. He was actually talking to me too, not just everybody else. So that was really the message that changed me.

After that my career was a very good career on many levels. What really defined me as an ath- lete happened. That was just a matter of training and timing. That's the problem with distance running in our country. We really focus on getting in shape and not focus on racing. It may be great for a long road racing season but it doesn't do a lot for trying to get on an Olympic team and winning a medal.

One of the highlights of my career, I already shared with you. Certainly winning the 5,000 meters and setting the collegiate record when I was at Penn Relays. That was in 1983 when I was a junior. My career has a lot of high points in college. I don't think any moment can match that moment when I put on my jersey. I love the fact that I went out and I left my collegiate season with a national championship. The last race of my college career was a national championship. I had three or four races in college that I look back on with pride: when I got the collegiate record at Penn, when I beat Joan Benoit in the 3000 meters at the Meadowlands and set the collegiate indoor record. I think it still stands — I'm sure it still stands today — it may be the oldest record on the books.

As for post college — making my first Olympic team — I mean, gosh, that was fabulous, unbe- lievable — and what I went through to get there was really, really challenging. The previous year and a half had been physically and emotionally challenging. At that point, when I made the Olympic team I was going to school full time as a law student. I was working, actually I was working two jobs. I was an RA, a resident assistant in a dorm, living in a dorm and training. I made an Olympic team and I graduated from law school in three years — from Stanford. I feel like they make this way too hard. It's not rocket science, running, you know, but you do the things you need to do — it doesn't take twelve hours a day. Making that team was really fabulous, and how I made it, and everything about it was really fabulous. It was in 1988 in Indianapolis. It was 116 degrees on the track. I wasn't in very good shape at that point. I had had plantar fasciitis back in 1987 and just as I had gotten better, I got a really bad case of pneumonia. I didn't start training until February, actually March 1st. I started to really jog — really jog more than thirty minutes. My first time on the track was April 15. It was really, really, hard. Every race was hard. Everything was hard.

Winning the Olympic trials was fabulous. 1990 was a great year. I was healthy and strong. No injuries. I felt great and I just felt that I could do anything I wanted to on the track. My regrets that year were that I did not run a 10,000 because I felt really confident that I could have run very fast in that race. That's one of those regrets. I wish I had done more things in that year when I was really in good shape. That whole year was good. It is a little hard to pick one thing, but winning the Goodwill Games in Seattle was probably the highlight of that year for me. It was great competition, great crowd, running 4:16.68 in the Mercedes Mile against the best field ever compiled. Anybody who was ever anybody was in that race. I was the only American in the race. I had wanted to drop out, I was tired, I had traveled around the world, literally around the world to get there. I think that was my greatest physical accomplishment ever.

I won so easily in 1990. I ran so many races in 1990 that I wish I had done more. They weren't providing rabbits in women's races then; that's why Ingrid Christiansen had to ask me as a friend, she paid me well, but she asked me as a friend if I would pace her because nobody else would do it. She paid me out of her own money to do this for her because I was the only one who was running fast enough to pace her through the time that she wanted to run.

I never got an opportunity to run a really good time. I could have had the world record at sub 8:45 race pace [laughter]. I just won everything. People would just go for second. They just let me go.

The one thing that still causes me occasional sleepless nights is the fact that I did not win a medal in the '92 Olympics. That was really hard. What made it harder was the fact that in 1991 I chose — I didn't choose, my coach chose — to drop the 3,000 meters for the year to focus on speed and I didn't run the 3,000 at the world championships. It was won in a time that I certainly would have medaled. I beat everybody in that field regularly and it was really hard to watch that race go by and not to have a good race in the 1500. The Olympics is a tricky thing. There are very few people that walk away happy.

Now I am finishing my final term as chair of the Athletes Advisory Committee of USA Track & Field. I was chair for four years and I was vice-chair for two years before that. I was an event leader for four years before that.

This past year I have focused primarily on this job as AAC chair because it's been pretty demanding and I have children. I work part-time doing parenting education, but before that I ran a family resource center.

I'm going to take some time. In the last five months I've been to Madrid, Lausanne, here, Indianapolis, Chicago — all for track and field and not making a dime for it, spending a lot of time away from my family, and I'm tired. I really want some time where I don't have a trip coming up, where I don't have to get things done immediately. I teach two days a week — that's enough and I have two very active kids — two girls — and I'm involved in school. I'm also very involved with Stanford. I'm one of the four founders of the track foundation, a local organizing post for both the U.S. Open meet and the national championships. Particularly in June, that keeps me really busy. I did not exist last year in my house in June. Between those two meets and the AAC, it was pretty crazy.

But I'm taking a break from this organization for a while. I'm not looking for a job right now anywhere unless someone has a part-time position that's emotionally engaging and only requires me to work half days and pays a lot. If you know one of those, I'll take that!

11

1991

The Outdoor Nationals

The 1991 USA/Mobil National Outdoor Track and Field Championships were held in Downing Stadium, Randalls Island, New York from June 13 to June 15.

The *New York Times* reported, "The national outdoor track and field championships returned to Randalls Island yesterday for the first time in 25 years...."

Early stories in the *New York Times* mainly dealt with Butch Reynolds's suspension and Dan O'Brien's record-setting marks in the decathlon. Mention was made of Jackie Joyner-Kersee capturing the heptathlon and Lynn Jennings winning the 10,000 meters.

The *New York Times* went on:

There were examples yesterday of grit, and grace. Rosalind Taylor of Philadelphia fell and was trampled by several runners during a 3,000 meter semifinal. She rose, rejoined the pack, and qualified for the final with a fourth place finish.

Tananjalyn Stanley, who came into the 100-meter hurdles with the fastest time for an American this year, tripped on a hurdle during a preliminary heat and failed to qualify. It was the second time in three years this had happened to her at the national championships.

Marion Jones, the 15-year-old Oxnard, CA. sprinter who enjoys shopping malls and Laker games, ran two competitive 100-meter dashes to qualify for the final.

There was an American record in the women's 10,000-meter race walk, by Debbi Lawrence of Kenosha, WI. in 46:06.13.

Six athletes repeated victories: Suzy Hamilton in the 1500, PattiSue Plumer in the 5000, Debbi Lawrence in the 10 kilometer walk, Yolanda Henry in the high jump, Jackie Joyner-Kersee in the long jump and Karin Smith in the javelin.

---

100 meters

Sieg Lindstrom wrote for *Track & Field News*: "...Finn blew out of the blocks best but saw the 5 ft. 7, 146 lb. Guidry rush by and away early to a 2½-foot win. 'I felt strong from start to finish,' the 22-year-old Texan said after finishing in a PR 10.94, a time only seven Americans have bettered. As Finn began to fade (eventually to 6th) Torrence pulled ahead of the rest of Guidry's chasers at halfway and ran 11.02, her best since '88. Ashford (11.12) reached 3rd at 75m and finished a full 10th up on Esther Jones."

1. Carlette Guidry, University of Texas	10.94
2. Gwen Torrence, Nike South Track Club	11.02

3. Evelyn Ashford, Mazda Track Club	11.12
4. Esther Jones, Louisiana State University	11.22
5. Dannette Young, Reebok Racing Club	11.23
6. Michelle Finn, Mazda Track Club	11.27
7. Sheila Echols, Nike International	11.30
8. Marion Jones, unattached	11.46

200 meters

Ed Fox reported for *Track & Field News*: "...Young was out quickly and held a short lead around the curve, with Torrence and prep phenom Marion Jones about even behind her. As the running sorted itself out down the straight, it was Torrence who was fastest of all, catching Young with 40m to go and maintaining a 4–5m lead to the finish, 22.38–22.44."

1. Gwen Torrence, Nike South Track Club	22.38
2. Dannette Young, Reebok Racing Club	22.44
3. Esther Jones, Louisiana State University	22.72
4. Marion Jones, unattached	22.76
5. Michelle Finn, Mazda Track Club	23.29
6. Tamela Saldana, University of Texas	23.57
7. Michele Collins, Nike Houston	23.74
8. Shantel Ransom, unattached	23.75

400 meters

"...Rochelle Stevens went out quickly, but at halfway it was world indoor champ Diane Dixon who controlled the race. This wasn't indoors, though, and coming out of the turn, the long-striding defending champion, Maicel Malone, led.

"The 5 ft. 6, 125 lb. Leatherwood, in the meantime, had run down Dixon on the turn, and with 30m left nabbed Malone.

"Reebok teammate Jearl Miles (50.19 PR) ran a similar race and caught Malone soon after. The Arizona State junior tied up just before the line as Dixon edged past for 3rd, 50.30 to a PR 50.39," reported Jeff Hollobaugh.

1. Lillie Leatherwood, Reebok Racing Club	49.66
2. Jearl Miles, Reebok Racing Club	50.19
3. Diane Dixon, Atoms Track Club	50.30
4. Maicel Malone, Nike Coast Track Club	50.39
5. Rochelle Stevens, Nike International	51.03
6. Natasha Kaiser, Southern California Cheetahs	51.82
7. Celina Mondie-Milner, unattached	51.91
8. Tasha Downing, Mazda Track Club	52.65

800 meters

Celeste Halliday took the lead at the start. According to reporter Jed Brickner, "...But 80m out Halliday seemed to soften. Rainey — with the slightest possible lead — and Floyd drew away. Never separated by more than a body-width, they clawed towards the finish. Floyd, a 29-year-old mother of two, dove for the tape and emerged with not only bad bruises to her right cheek and both shoulders and a big bandage on her forehead, but also a narrow victory over her 22-year-old rival, 1:59.82 to 1:59.87."

1. Delisa Floyd, Sports Track Club	1:59.82
2. Meredith Rainey, Atoms Track Club	1:59.87
3. Joetta Clark, Joe Clark International	2:00.48

4. Celeste Halliday, Nike Indiana Track Club	2:00.69
5. Diana Richburg, Gazelle International Track Club	2:02.01
6. Michelle Bennett, Villanova University	2:02.80
7. Debbie Marshall, unattached	2:03.77
8. Julie Jenkins, Reebok Racing Club	2:06.32

1500 meters

Jed Brickner wrote: "PattiSue Plumer and newly married Suzy Hamilton (nee Favor) reached the bell in 3:04.4 and drew away from the pack. Plumer still led through 1200 (3:20.3) but, running on the outside of the innermost lane, was leaving too tempting a target for the defending champion. With 250 to go Hamilton charged through the hole to the lead, sharing at least three exchanges of elbows with the surprised Stanford lawyer."

The *New York Times* added:

...Favor had made like Dennis Rodman once more and elbowed her way along the inside past PattiSue Plumer into first place in the 1,500-meter final at the Mobil national track and field championships on Randalls Island. She picked her spot along the east end at Downing Stadium, then held on in a stadium record 4 minutes 6.13 seconds. The wonderfully arrogant move, with 250 meters to go, had caught Plumer unaware, and left her annoyed at herself and Favor.

"She'd have a hard time doing that in an international field," said Plumer, who finished second in 4:06.59 and won a 5,000-meter final less than an hour later. "There was a lot of contact. It's a bad habit to get into. I was drifting, but she took a chance on a hole that wasn't wide enough for her to go through."

1. Suzy Hamilton, Reebok Racing Club	4:06.13
2. PattiSue Plumer, Nike International	4:06.59
3. Darcy Arreola, Nike CoastTrack Club	4:09.32
4. Alisa Hill, Southern California Cheetahs	4:09.70
5. Ceci St. Geme, Asics International Track Club	4:11.97
6. Stephanie Best, Cornell University	4:13.11
7. Claudette Groenendaal, Santa Monica Track Club	4:13.25
8. Nnenna Lynch, Villanova University	4:14.87

3000 meters

Shelly Steely "...took the lead from the get-go, heading off Judi St. Hilaire, Annette Peters and Sammie Gdowski. At halfway (4:27.5), Peters — who had beaten Steely in a last lap kick at Mt. SAC — stuck closest, a step behind. Fine. But Steely had planned surges with 1000 and 600m left. The strategy worked as her closing 2:52.2 kilo (with a 67.6 last lap) brought her home in, yes, a PR 8:49.00, more than 15m ahead of Peters (8:52.07 PR)," reported Sieg Lindstrom for *Track & Field News*.

1. Shelly Steely, Mizuno Track Club	8:49.00
2. Annette Peters, Nike West	8:52.07
3. Judi St. Hilaire, Nike International	8:52.66
4. Sabrina Dornhoefer, New Balance Track Club	8:54.49
5. Sammie Gdowski, Reebok Racing Club	9:02.10
6. Rosalind Taylor, Nike South Track Club	9:06.48
7. Nicole Birk, Brigham Young University	9:09.07
8. Gwyn Coogan, Nike Boston	9:11.87

10,000 meters

Lindstrom continued: "...Jennings's strong finish left Larrieu Smith (32:50.00) more than 20m behind. Letko won a tight backstretch battle with Van Blunk (32:54.42) and nearly got up to 2nd with her 32:50.37."

1. Lynn Jennings, Nike International   32:45.88
2. Francie Larrieu-Smith, New Balance Track Club   32:50.00
3. Anne Letko, Nike Running Room   32:50.37
4. Elaine Van Blunk, Nike Running Room   32:54.42
5. Colette Murphy, Nike Indiana Track Club   33:10.76
6. Trina Painter, Nike Texas Track Club   33:15.54
7. Mindy Schmidt, Nike North Track Club   33:19.37
8. Inge Schuurmans, Mountain West Track Club   33:20.13

100 meter hurdles
1. Gail Devers-Roberts, World Class Athletic Club   12.83
2. Dawn Bowles, Louisiana State University   12.89
3. Arnita Myricks, Southern California Cheetahs   12.99
4. Cheryl Dickey, unattached   13.13
5. Mary Cobb, Louisiana State University   13.22
6. Yolanda Johnson, unattached   13.23
7. Kim McKenzie, Mazda Track Club   13.23
8. Jackie Humphrey, Nike South Track Club   13.26

400 meter hurdles
Ed Fox wrote for *Track & Field News*:

Favorite Sandra Farmer-Patrick made up the stagger on NCAA 3rd-placer Kim Batten by the second hurdle, and by No. 8, beginning the run for home, the AR holder had a 5m lead on defender Janeene Vickers. But Batten, despite her slow start ("A lot of people thought I was out of it early"), was running the race of her life. Down by 8m at the top of the homestretch, she confidently began an irresistible drive to the finish line, while Farmer-Patrick and Vickers tied up.

It became one of those familiar final-hurdle scenes where the leader is struggling and the strong pursuer flashes past and goes on to win handily. Batten's world-leading 54.18 was a shocker, cutting almost a second off the PR 55.11 she had set in the semis and also capturing the Collegiate Record."

The *New York Times* referred to Kim Batten, 22, of Rochester, New York as, "an unfamiliar name."

1. Kim Batten, Florida State University   54.18   MR
2. Sandra Farmer-Patrick, Flo Jo International   54.72
3. Janeene Vickers, unattached   54.89
4. Schowonda Williams, Nike International   55.43
5. Kathy Freeman, Nike International   55.93
6. Tonja Buford, University of Illinois   56.45
7. Ann Graham, Nike Atlantic Coast   56.52
8. Tonya Lee, Knoxville Track Club   57.62

10,000 meter walk
"...She'll be 30 in October and, after a first-rate 15th in the World Cup, is at the top of her game. Challenged by Lynn Weik at 23 laps, Lawrence responded with a surge that carried her to a track AR of 46:06.36, breaking the 46:10.26 she set last year," wrote Elliott Denman for *Track & Field News*.

1. Debbi Lawrence, Propet Walkers   46:06.36   AR
2. Lynn Weik, Natural Sport   46:12.83
3. Victoria Herazo, California Walkers   46:26.49
4. Michelle Rohl, Parkside Athletic Club   48:21.09

5. Lynda Brubaker, unattached	48:37.28
6. Debora Van Orden, unattached	48:40.58
7. Maryanne Torrellas, unattached	48:42.39
8. Teresa Vaill, Natural Sport	48:46.31

High jump

"Yolanda Henry defended her title decisively. She cleared every height on first attempt until the bar was raised to 6' 4¾". Her one miss at that height did not matter since Sue Rembao, the only other jumper alive by then, couldn't clear it at all," reported Bob Hersh of *Track & Field News*.

1. Yolanda Henry, Mazda Track Club	6' 4¾"
2. Sue Rembao, unattached	6' 3½"
3. Tisha Waller, University of North Carolina	6' 2¼"
4. Tanya Hughes, Nike Coast Club	6' ¾"
and Jan Wohlschlag, Nike International	
6. Angie Bradburn, unattached	6' ¾"
7. Vicki Borsheim, Mizuno Track Club	6' ¾"
8. Felicia Hodges, New York Pioneer Club,	5' 11¼"

Latrese Johnson, Azusa Pacific University, Louise Ritter, Mazda Track Club

Long jump
1. Jackie Joyner-Kersee, McDonald's Track Club	22' 8"
2. Sheila Echols, Nike International	21' 11½" w
3. Cindy Greiner, Nike Coast Track Club	21' 9"
4. Gwen Loud, Keiser Track Club	21' ¾" w
5. Julie Bright, Mizuno Track Club	20' 11½"
6. Juliana Yendork, Mazda Track Club	20' 9¾"
7. Lisa Payne, University of Wisconsin	20' 9"
8. Sharon Couch, University of North Carolina	20' 7"

Triple jump
1. Carla Shannon, unattached	44' 4¼"
2. Sheila Hudson, Mizuno Track Club	44' 1½" w
3. Donna Crumety, St. Joseph's University	44' ¾"
4. Robyne Johnson, unattached	44'
5. Diana Wills, U.S. Army	43' 9¼"
6. Cynthea Rhodes, University of Texas	43' ¼"
7. Kim Austin, University of North Carolina	42' 4¾"
8. Wendy Brown, Stars and Stripes Track Club	41' 5¾"

Shot put

"...Pagel, 29, handily regained the title Price-Smith took from her in 1990 by racking up five marks superior to her rival's best. Price-Smith had done exactly the same thing last year," wrote Garry Hill for *Track & Field News*.

1. Ramona Pagel, Mazda Track Club	60' 2½"
2. Connie Price-Smith, Nike North Track Club	58' 6¾"
3. Pam Dukes, Nike Coast Track Club	56' 5¼"
4. Bonnie Dasse, Nike Coast Track Club	55' 5¾"
5. Eileen Vanisi, University of Texas	55' 4¼"
6. Christy Barrett, Indiana State University	52' 10¼"
7. Tracie Millett, unattached	51' 9¾"
8. Sharron Simmons, unattached	51' ¼"

Discus

Dave Johnson wrote for *Track & Field News*:

The biggest news of the early rounds was 200-footer Connie Price-Smith, who fouled her first two attempts. Price-Smith, who has won the most important domestic meet in each of the last four years — TAC titles in '87, '89 and '90 and the Olympic trials in '88 — then reached a paltry 157–10 on her third attempt. It left her 12th and out of a chance for an additional three throws.

Lacy Barnes, the '88 champ, effectively won the event with her first throw, as her 194–1 was to stand up as better than any other thrower, even though she later improved to 199–10.

1. Lacy Barnes, Nike Coast Track Club	199'	10"
2. Pam Dukes, Nike Coast Track Club	191'	1"
3. Penny Neer, Nike Coast Track Club	190'	10"
4. Carla Garrett, Nike Coast Track Club	188'	8"
5. Kelly Landry, Nike Coast Track Club	185'	1"
6. Carol Finsrud, unattached	181'	7"
7. Edie Boyer, Minnesota Track Club	181'	2"
8. Ramona Pagel, Mazda Track Club	180'	4"

Javelin

"...The veteran Smith, 35, handled things best, her first round 197–6 standing up for her seventh national title (with her second-shortest distance). Her two other fair throws would have sufficed for the win," reported Richard D. Smith.

1. Karin Smith, Nike Coast Track Club	197'	6"
2. Paula Berry, University of Oregon	191'	7"
3. Donna Mayhew, Nike Coast Track Club	188'	1"
4. Marilyn Senz, unattached	180'	8"
5. Julia Solo, unattached	174'	6"
6. Ashley Selman, Nike Coast Track Club	172'	11"
7. Durelle Schimek, unattached	172'	4"
8. Kim Hyatt, University of Oregon	171'	5"

Heptathlon

Jon Hendershott reported for *Track & Field News*: "Like Dan O'Brien, Jackie Joyner-Kersee got off to a fast start and never let up. She hurdled 12.77, a U.S. leader (even if lacking a wind reading), then cleared 6' 2¼", put 51–3 and sped 23.42, all event leaders, to total 4191 for the first day.... She long jumped 22' 10½", another U.S. pacer. Her final two events (142–0/2:22.12) were modest by her standards but she still totaled 6878 points. That's the No. 8 U.S. (and JJK) performance ever and her highest since her WR 7291 in Seoul.

"Cindy Greiner claimed 2nd (6186) to join Jackie on their fourth major team (after LA, Rome and Seoul)."

1. Jackie Joyner-Kersee, McDonald's Track Club	6878
2. Cindy Greiner, Nike Coast Track Club	6186
3. Kym Carter, Nike Oregon	6183
4. Sharon Hainer, Nike Coast Track Club	6123
5. DeDee Nathan, Nike Indiana Track Club	5955
6. Jamie McNeair, Purdue Area Track Club	5919
7. Trevaia Williams, University of Nevada, Las Vegas	5861
8. Terri Hairston, Nike Houston	5679

2000 meter steeplechase (exhibition)

1. Teressa DiPerna, unattached	7:12.76

2. Marissa Sutera, Westchester Track Club	7:20.10
3. Martha Obindinski, Pennsylvania State University	7:47.43
4. Kaci Holt, unattached	8:39.68
5. Laurie Black, New York Pioneer Club	8:57.18

Hammer throw (exhibition)

"In the only final yesterday," the *New York Times* reported, "Bonnie Edmondson won the hammer throw with a toss of 169.'"

1. Bonnie Edmondson, unattached	169'
2. Pam Dukes, Nike Coast Track Club	163' 6"
3. Sonja Fitts, St. John's University	162' 5"
4. Michele Curcio, unattached	147' 5"
5. Heather Ewing, Fitchburg State University	147' 2"
6. Maureen Magnan, U.S. Naval Academy	145' 4"
7. Laura Carlson, New Haven Age Group Track Club	142' 7"
8. Sarah Washburn, Lafayette College	140' 10"

Team scores:

1. Nike Coast Track Club	78
2. Nike International	53
3. Reebok Racing Club	40

Kim Batten was voted the outstanding female athlete of the meet.

The Indoor Nationals

The USA/Mobil National Indoor Track & Field Championships were held in Madison Square Garden, New York on February 22.

"It has become rather commonplace for Diane Dixon to win another national title in the women's 400-meter race," wrote Michael Janofsky in the *New York Times*. He goes on:

...But what Suzy Favor did to Doina Melinte of Romania — now, that was a little surprising, as the North American indoor track and field season ended last night in Madison Square Garden with 11,483 watching the USA/Mobil national championships.

For Dixon, it was the ninth consecutive year she had won here and 10th over all. But unlike some of her previous victories, this one not only anointed her national champion and qualified her for the United States team that will compete in the world indoor championships next month in Seville, Spain. It also made her the women's overall North American Grand Prix champion for the second time since 1986. And it gave her a prominent place in history, with more national titles than all but two athletes in the 85 years the meet has been held."

"I wanted to break the record tonight," said Dixon, whose first title came in 1981 when she was 16 years old. "But the boards don't agree with my knees."

60 meters

1. Michelle Finn, Mazda Track Club	7.16	MR
2. Gwen Torrence, Nike South Track Club	7.17	
3. Teresa Neighbors, Houston Track Club	7.22	

200 meters

1. Rochelle Stevens, Nike International	23.65
2. Celena Mondie-Milner, unattached	23.80
3. Dannette Young, Reebok Racing Club	23.87

400 meters
1. Diane Dixon, Atoms Track Club   52.38
2. Jearl Miles, Reebok Racing Club   52.39
3. Rochelle Stevens, Nike International   53.61

800 meters
1. Meredith Rainey, Atoms Track Club   2:03.07
2. Lyuobov Tsjoma, Union of Soviet Socialist Republic   2:03.84
3. Joetta Clark, Joe Clark International   2:04.42

Mile
1. Suzy Favor, Reebok Racing Club   4:37.55
2. Doina Melinte, Romania   4:37.59
3. Alisa Harvey-Hill, Southern California Cheetahs   4:38.49

3000 meters
1. Margareta Keszeg, Romania   8:49.61
2. PattiSue Plumer, Nike International   8:55.37
3. Shelly Steely, Mizuno Track Club   8:56.82

60 meter hurdles
1. Kim McKenzie, Mazda Track Club   8.12
2. Aliuska Lopez, Cuba   8.21
3. Cheryl Wilson, unattached   8.21

3000 meter walk
1. Teresa Vaill, Natural Sport   12:49.95
2. Sara Standley, Natural Sport   13:09.72
3. Victoria Herazo, California Walkers   13:11.34

Triple jump
1. Juliana Yendork, unattached   43' ½"   MR
2. Diane Sommerville, Anderson Track Club/Jamaica   42' 9¼"
3. Robyne Johnson, unattached   42' 8¼"

Long jump
1. Carol Lewis, Santa Monica Track Club   21' 6¼"
2. Cindy Greiner, Nike Coast Track Club   20' 7½"
3. Shunta Rose, University of Nevada, Las Vegas   20' 3¼"

Shot put
1. Connie Price-Smith, Nike North Track Club   61' 10½"
2. Ramona Pagel, Mazda Track Club   60' 6½"
3. Peggy Pollock, Nike Coast Track Club   53' 3½"

20 pound weight throw
1. Sonja Fitts, St. John's University   59' 7¼"
2. Angela Vaughn, Rutgers University   51' 5"
3. Sondra Hinson, Rutgers University   51' 4½"

High jump
1. Yolanda Henry, Mazda Track Club   6' 5"
2. Angela Bradburn, unattached   6' ¾"
3. Jan Wohlschlag, Nike International   6' ¾"

4 × 400 meter relay
1. Seton Hall University	3:49.03
(Veronica Harris, Marie Bynoe, Shana Williams, Flirtisha Harris)	
2. University of Maryland	3:50.20
3. Bronx Express	3:58.62

Winning team:
Mazda Track Club

Sunkist Invitational (Four women's events): Los Angeles, January 18

50 meters
1. Michelle Finn, Mazda Track Club	6.25	MR

440 yards
1. Diane Dixon, Atoms Track Club	53.25

800 meters
1. Charmaine Crooks, Canada	2:06.30

Mile
1. Suzy Favor, Reebok Racing Club	4:39.39

11th Pan American Games: Havana, Cuba, August 3–11

Name	Event	Place	Performance
Barnes, Lacy	DT	3	197' 11"
Bowles, Dawn	100mh	4	13.24
Bright, Julie	LJ	3	21' 5¼" w
Buford, Tonja	400mh	3	57.81
DeNinno, Lynn	Marathon	5	2:49:34
Dornhoefer, Sabrina	3000m	1	9:16.15
Downing, Tasha	4 × 400mr	1	3:24.21
Dukes, Pam	DT	4	183' 7"
Ettle, Jan	Marathon	4	2:49:22
Gaines, Chryste	100m	2	11.46
	4 × 100mr	3	44.62
Gdowski, Sammie	3000m	8	9:31.64
Hainer, Sharon	Heptathlon	2	5770
Halliday, Celeste	800m	3	2:01.41
Hill, Alisa	800m	2	1:59.99
	1500m	1	4:13.12
Howard, Anita	100m	5	11.70
	4 × 100mr	3	44.62
Hughes, Tanya	HJ	4	5' 10¾"
Kaiser, Natasha	400m	4	51.20
	4 × 400mr	1	3:24.21
Lawrence, Debbi	10k walk	2	46:51.53
Loud, Gwen	LJ	8	20' 5¼"
Malone, Maicel	4 × 400mr	1	3:24.21

Name	Event	Place	Performance
Mayhew, Donna	JT	2	191' 9"
Miles, Jearl	400m	3	50.82
	4 × 400mr	1	3:24.21
Miller, Lamonda	4 × 100mr	3	44.62
Murphy Colette	10000m	8	36:22.24
Myricks, Arnita	100mh	3	13.23
	4 × 100mr	3	44.62
Nathan, DeDee	Heptathlon	1	5778
Pagel, Ramona	SP	3	58' 3¼"
Ransom, Shantel	200m	7	23.97
Saldana, Tamela	200m	DNQ	24.19 h
Senz, Marilyn	JT	5	174' 8"
Sheskey, Linda	1500m	8	4:31.59
Smith, Connie Price	SP	2	60'½"
Van Blunk, Elaine	10000m	7	36:10.91
Weik, Lynn	10k walk	4	47:54.05
Williams, Schowonda	400mh	5	57.95
Wohlschlag, Jan	HJ	3	5' 10¾"

3rd IAAF World Indoor Track and Field Championships: Seville, Spain, March 8–10

The *New York Times* featured a story on the victory of Diane Dixon in the 400 meters: "The tears trickling down Fred Thompson's cheeks into creases of a smile told the entire story. For all the joys Diane Dixon has brought him, none matched this one. Now she was a world champion; he was a world champion coach. Never before had an American woman won a gold medal in an indoor world championship. The 26-year-old Dixon became the first by winning the women's 400 meters in 50.64 seconds, an American record and the sixth-fastest time ever run indoors.

"...This was her first international title — she has 10 national titles, the last nine in a row."

60 meters
4. Gwen Torrence	7.13	
7. Michelle Finn	7.23	

400 meters
1. Diane Dixon	50.64	AR
5. Jearl Miles	52.00	

800 meters
6. Meredith Rainey	2:04.82

1500 meters
7. Alisa Hill	4:08.54
8. Gina Procaccio	4:19.51

3000 meters
8. Elaine Van Blunk	8:58.23

60 meter hurdles
7. Kim McKenzie   8.05

3 kilometer walk
9. Victoria Herazo   13:09.90

4 × 400 meter relay
3. United States   3:29.00   AR
    (Teri Dendy, Lillie Leatherwood, Jearl Miles, Diane Dixon)

High jump
 4. Yolanda Henry   6' 3¼"
11. Angie Bradburn   6' 2"

Long jump
 8. Carol Lewis   21' 6"
11. Cindy Greiner   20' 11¼"

Triple jump
9. Robyne Johnson   42' 1¼"

Shot put
7. Connie Price-Smith   61'
9. Ramona Pagel   59' 4¼"

3rd IAAF World Outdoor Track and Field Championships: Tokyo, Japan, August 23–September 1

100 meters
2. Gwen Torrence   11.03
5. Evelyn Ashford   11.30
8. Carlette Guidry-White   11.52

200 meters
2. Gwen Torrence   22.16
6. Dannette Young-Stone   22.87

400 meters
5. Jearl Miles-Clark   50.50
7. Lillie Leatherwood   51.53
8. Diane Dixon   51.73

No American women qualified for the 800 meter final.

1500 meters
12. PattiSue Plumer   4:06.80

3000 meters
 7. Judi St. Hilaire   8:44.02
 8. Annette Peters   8:44.02
14. Shelley Steely   8:53.70

10,000 meters
5. Lynn Jennings   31:54.44

Marathon
13. Joy Smith   2:39:16
14. Maria Trujillo   2:39:28

100 meter hurdles
2. Gail Devers   12.63

400 meter hurdles
3. Janeene Vickers   53.47
4. Sandra Farmer-Patrick   53.95
5. Kim Batten   53.98

No American women qualified for the high jump final.

Long jump
1. Jackie Joyner-Kersee   24' ¼"

Shot put
11. Connie Price-Smith   59' 5 ½"

No American women qualified for the discus or javelin final.

10 kilometer walk (road)
19. Debbi Lawrence   45:58
25. Lynn Weik   46:49
27. Victoria Herazo   47:10

The American team dropped the baton in the heats and did not qualify for the 4 × 100 meter relay final.

4 × 400 meter relay
2. USA   3:20.15
    (Rochelle Stevens, Diane Dixon, Jearl Miles-Clark, Lillie Leatherwood)

The *New York Times* reported: "...Joyner-Kersee's demise in the heptathlon came at the top of the curve in the last of the four events contested within 10 hours, the 200-meter sprint. Leading the 27 other women after the first three events and the seven in her heat of the 200, she pulled up, hopped for several meters, her face contorted, before crumbling to the track in agony.

"Although it later became clear that the injury, a strained hamstring muscle in her right leg, was not as severe as it first appeared, she was forced to retire from the competition and sentenced to a month or more of rest and recovery."

Heptathlon
10. Cindy Greiner   6216
20. Kym Carter   5909

IAAF World Cross Country Championships: Antwerp, Belgium, March 24

This was Lynn Jennings's second world cross country title. She won the United States cross country championships for the sixth time, her fifth consecutive.

1. Lynn Jennings   20:24
19. Annette Peters   21:10

| 28. Elaine Van Blunk | 21:18 |
| 29. Gwyn Coogan | 21:19 |

The United States placed fourth with 77 points.

Other News and Honors

Track & Field News: U.S. Athlete of the Year

Jackie Joyner-Kersee

World Rankings — Track & Field News
(U.S. rankings in bold)

7. Jackie Joyner-Kersee

1. Jackie Joyner-Kersee
2. Gwen Torrence
3. Gail Devers-Roberts
4. Sandra Farmer-Patrick
5. Janeene Vickers

100 meters
3. Gwen Torrence
5. Carlette Guidry
6. Evelyn Ashford
10. Esther Jones

1. Gwen Torrence
2. Carlette Guidry
3. Evelyn Ashford

200 meters
3. Gwen Torrence
5. Dannette Young

1. Gwen Torrence
2. Dannette Young
3. Carlette Guidry

400 meters
6. Lillie Leatherwood
7. Jearl Miles
9. Maicel Malone

1. Lillie Leatherwood
2. Jearl Miles
3. Maicel Malone

800 meters
No American women were ranked in the top ten.

1. Meredith Rainey
2. Delisa Floyd
3. Joetta Clark

1500 meters
6. Mary Slaney
10. PattiSue Plumer

1. Mary Slaney
2. PattiSue Plumer
3. Suzy Hamilton

3000 meters
8. PattiSue Plumer

1. PattiSue Plumer
2. Annette Peters
3. Shelly Steely

5000 meters
No American women were ranked in the top five.

1. Shelly Steely
2. Annette Peters
3. PattiSue Plumer

10,000 meters
5. Lynn Jennings

1. Lynn Jennings
2. Francie Larrieu-Smith
3. Anne Marie Letko

Marathon
5. Kim Jones
6. Francie Larrieu-Smith

1. Kim Jones
2. Francie Larrieu-Smith
3. Joan Samuelson

100 meter hurdles
2. Gail Devers

1. Gail Devers
2. Dawn Bowles
3. Tananjalyn Stanley

400 meter hurdles
1. Sandra Farmer-Patrick
3. Janeene Vickers
4. Kim Batten

1. **Sandra Farmer-Patrick**
2. **Janeene Vickers**
3. **Kim Batten**

10 kilometer walk
No American women were ranked in the top ten.

1. **Debbi Lawrence**
2. **Lynn Weik**
3. **Victoria Herazo**

High jump
8. Yolanda Henry

1. **Yolanda Henry**
2. **Sue Rembao**
3. **Tisha Waller**

Long jump
2. Jackie Joyner-Kersee

1. **Jackie Joyner-Kersee**
2. **Carol Lewis**
3. **Sheila Echols**

Triple jump
No American women were ranked in the top five.

1. **Sheila Hudson**
2. **Diana Wills**
3. **Juliana Yendork**

Shot put
No American women were ranked in the top ten.

1. **Connie Price-Smith**
2. **Ramona Pagel**
3. **Pam Dukes**

Discus
No American women were ranked in the top ten.

1. **Lacy Barnes**
2. **Penny Neer**
3. **Carla Garrett**

Javelin
No American women were ranked in the top ten.

1. **Karin Smith**
2. **Paula Berry**
3. **Donna Mayhew**

Heptathlon
2. Jackie Joyner-Kersee

1. **Jackie Joyner-Kersee**
2. **Cindy Greiner**
3. **Kym Carter**

Francie Larrieu-Smith, 38, ran 31:28.92 for an American record in the 10,000 meters at the Texas relays in April.

Roxanne Andersen was inducted this year into the National Track and Field Hall of Fame. The biography below is from the National Track and Field Hall of Fame website.

ROXANNE ANDERSEN   COACH

Born June 26, 1912, Montreal, Quebec. Died September 6, 2002.

As Roxy Atkins, she was a top sprinter-hurdler for Canada in the thirties, placing fourth at the 1934 British Empire Games, forerunner of the present Commonwealth Games. She won the 1934 U.S. indoor hurdles title, defeating future Hall of Famer Evelyne Hall Adams. In 1936, she ran for Canada at the Berlin Olympics. After marrying and moving to California following World War II, she became a U.S. citizen. Anderson pioneered women's and age group track and field programs and her activities were later used as a model for national programs.

By the fifties, she was active in the governance of American track and field. She has served on the women's track and field national committee—first for the AAU, later TAC—continuously since 1953. In 1958, Andersen co-chaired the women's track and field committee. She's been a staff member for many national teams, including both the U.S. Olympic team (1956) and Pan American Games teams (1971, 1983). Andersen has authored several articles on the sport. Still an active official, Roxy Andersen received the President's Award for years of meritorious service to athletics in 1982.

Arnita Epps Myricks Champion, 2001.

Interview: Arnita Epps Myricks Champion

(November 30, 2001) I'm from Virginia Beach, Virginia. I started running in the third grade. It was a fluke. My oldest sister used to be very active, very athletic. I remember her telling me that I used to run flat-footed because she could hear me. That's how she heard me coming up on her — clunk, clunk, clunk. She was the one that really taught me and inspired me to run on my toes. From then, running was a hobby. It was just something I enjoyed. It continued from elementary school, through junior high, and high school. I was an All-American, which earned me a scholarship to Texas Southern University in Houston, Texas.

I started running the sprints, the 100 meters. When I first started hurdling it was a fluke. It was in high school and we were losing the meet. My coach said, "If you can just hurdle, if you can just jump over them, we will win this meet because I know you can do it." It was the worst thing because I hit every hurdle. But I won it [laughter] and we won the meet. Then she said, "I'm going to make you a hurdler." I thought to myself, "No, you're not because that hurt. That really hurt" [laughter]. From then on she taught me how to bring my trail leg around and not just jump the hurdles. She gave me that vision of running the hurdles. It's just an extension of your high knee lift going over the hurdle and that's how she made me see it. It's not jumping them, it's running them. All you have to do is extend or bring your knees up higher, just a little bit more to go over. I said, "I can do that" [laughter]. And that's when I started. That was in 1979. I was a freshman in high school and did the hurdles, high jump and long jump all the way through high school. I was undefeated in the high jump through high school. I figured that if I could do the hurdles, I could jump over the bar and land in a soft pit [laughter]. It was a lack of fear and in the long jump, the speed carried me through. I had awful form — awful technique. It was just the speed; I just hydroplaned right up in the air because I was just flying. I also anchored the relays. The funny thing was, just give it to Arnita and she'll win it. I hate that: you guys are just going to loaf around and then I have to go to work. But they would always put me last and I would always bring it home.

My college coach did not want anything to interfere with my hurdling. He saw that I had talent. He just perfected it. But he did let me run the relays. He was the one that threw me into the

Arnita Epps Myricks Champion (left), the author and Jean Gregoire, 2001.

400 hurdles. He said if you can hurdle and you can run the 400, you can do the 400 hurdles. The first time, I thought, you're crazy because it hurt [laughter]. It hurt like mad. But in college I basically stuck with the hurdles. I got my degree in psychology.

I went to my first Olympic trials in 1984. I really think that the immaturity of being young just flawed me because I was so into the Games in L.A. I can remember the gun and everything in L.A. other than my race. From then on I continued training with my coach, Ernie Gregoire, that's what brought me to California. In 1982, I met him for the first time in Caracas, Venezuela. I was a member of the junior Pan American team. That is where I got my first gold national medal. From then, I knew that I wanted him to train me because of the inspiration and dedication that he showed during that time. Coming to California, I knew that I had my work cut out for me because everyone was running well. However, Coach Gregoire told me his motto was, "If it is to be, it's up to me." That motto stays with me today, not only through athletics, but also in my professional career and in whatever I endeavor to do.

So after graduating from college and moving to California, I went on to pursue the '88 games. It seems as though each final in the Olympic trials something happened. The '88 games, when I was supposed to go to Seoul, Korea in the 400 meter hurdles, I bombed. In '92, Barcelona, I bombed. In '96 I was not able to make the Olympic trials because of surgery on my Achilles. I looked at it and said, "You know, I might as well just hang it up." However, I was able to take that mentality, that commitment from athletics, into the academic arena. I pursued my masters and achieved my masters and now I'm pursuing my doctorate. I look at each hurdle, each circumstance, as a hurdle and I take it full charge, the same way that I did in athletics. If I can't seem to go over it, I'll go around it. Nothing can stop me — nothing.

The first highlight of my career was in Venezuela — the first gold medal that I won. The pinnacle of my career was in 1991 when I made the world championship team. 1991 was like a magical year, it was like a fantasy. I got married in 1991 and made the world championship team with my husband — traveling and just running as though nothing else mattered. That was the highlight and that took me into 1992 just knowing there was nothing impossible for me. Making that world championship team in '91 was it. I PRed in 1991. It was at the world championships in Tokyo, Japan. I made it to the semis. The top two went to the final and I was third.

Coach Gregoire took us all over Europe: France, Germany, Italy, Spain. Each competition taught me that if I put my mind to it, I was unbeatable and unstoppable. Overseas, it was like the Superbowl. They really support athletes. Even if you got eighth place it was like you were a winner. They would ask you for your autograph. It didn't matter that you got eighth place. That actually taught me a lot — it's not how you finish, but how you finish mentally and how you come back with it. In the competition I would say that I was ranked in the top five in each event. The Soviets really dominated the 400 hurdles. Now the USA is dominating.

My first advice to young athletes is, "If it is to be, it's up to me." My second advice is really let them know that there's nothing impossible for them — nothing impossible. If they put their minds to it, they can do the impossible. I look at it, if you have impossibility, then you have a possibility. Nothing's impossible.

Have fun; enjoy it every second because you never get that second chance. You can't look back and say, "Oh, I wish I would have done that." Do it. Just for the sake of doing it, do it. Reach for the stars.

Dr. Ernie Gregoire and Arnita Epps Myricks Champion, 2001.

INTERVIEW: ALISA HARVEY

(February 25, 2005) I started running as a grade schooler. I was about ten or eleven years old and the Hershey Hall of Fame track series is how I started getting into running. They would do it during the summer time. My parents would drive me to the track meets. I wouldn't train or anything, I just did it for fun. I would do the 400 and 800. I wanted to be a sprinter. I had just seen the Wilma Rudolph movie back in the 70s and I wanted to be a sprinter. So I started out doing those summer youth group track meets.

Then I ventured out from there as I got into high school. I joined the track team but I also wanted to be a gymnast and a cheerleader. For the first two years I was a gymnast and a cheerleader [laughter]. Finally, after my sophomore year the track coach said, "Let's focus on track and field." He thought that's what it would be for me for my future and gymnastics was just too dangerous. I had fallen off the uneven bars the year before. I almost killed myself [laughter] and I didn't want to do that. It took me a while. It was a tough transition.

I started out again as a sprinter. I wanted to be a 100 and 200 meter runner — and I was. I would come in third and fourth in the 200 or they'd put me in the 100 and I'd do the whole blocks thing and all that. But what eventually happened was there was a girl on our team at the time who smoked cigarettes and she was an 800 meter runner back in '81. She had to go on vacation and I took her spot in the 800 meters. I won that race and that's where I stayed. I guess something natural happened there.

I had a big body. Puberty really hit me hard somewhere early in high school. During all that time, I was 14, 15, 16; I was heavy and very full-chested. I ran decent times but it wasn't very, very fast. I wasn't looking at a college career or anything beyond what I was doing there. My miles were like six minutes and my 800 — 2:40. During the summer I joined another track club-type thing. I kept the running up and stopped the cheerleading and stopped the gymnastics and focused on the sport. I did cross country my junior year and was developing into a better runner. I did the mile and the two mile sometimes and, of course, cross country. I got pretty good. I made regionals. By the time I was a senior I was being sought after by colleges. By the time I graduated I had one of the top times in the country in the mile and 800. That's my beginning. That's how I started.

After high school I had a really big jump that summer after I graduated. I won the state meet in Virginia in the 800 and the 1600. It was 2:13 in the 800 and 4:55 in the mile. But that summer I dropped to 2:06 and 4:45. I just had phenomenal summer training like a track athlete finally. I dropped the weight and the body was changing a little—getting stronger and all that. I had already gotten my scholarship to Tennessee—Lady Volunteers—and I started my college career.

College was pretty successful. I started out with Terry Crawford at the time and then changed to Gary Schwartz after my freshman year. By the time I graduated I had nine All-Americans. I did cross country, indoor and outdoor track. I ran 800 meters and 1500 meters; mostly 1500 meters because when I first got there, Joetta Clark was at Tennessee and, of course, she was the 800 meter runner for Tennessee. But I was on that relay my freshman year. The biggest thing in my college career, I think, was that I was on the relay with Joetta Clark, Karol Davidson, who went to Texas, and Cathy Rattray, a Jamaican runner. We still have the Penn Relays 4 × 800 record. It's a twenty year record now going on the twenty-first year. I set that record with Joetta then and that was my big thing—the 800 meters—even though I didn't get to do it as much because she was doing it and Karol was doing it and they had other girls doing it. But, after that year, my sophomore year, I would do the 8 and the 15 pretty regularly. I was the SEC champion many times and then the NCAA champion in 1986. I was the NCAA champion in the 1500 meters. But my senior year in 1987 I was second in both events. Suzy Favor-Hamilton beat me out in the 1500 meters and Julie Jenkins beat me in the 800 meters. So I had good company but they got me in both those events. I started to cry and someone in the stands said, "Would you stop that crying?" I had run well but I was exhausted from not getting any one win. I had two darn good performances, though. I ran a 2:01 in the 800 after running a 4:08 in the 1500. So it was a very good meet but I just didn't get a win out of it [laughter].

From there, right out of college, I did get a contract with Athletics West. That was such a great thing to happen when you're coming out of school. You don't know what you're going to do—should you run? I got the contract, moved to train with Robert Vaughn, now Dr. Robert Vaughn, coach of Francie Larrieu. So I got to know Francie Larrieu very well. She was like a mentor. I got to talk to her for hours about anything. She just knew it all. Also Mary Knisley was down there and a few others. I was living and training with them for a few months before the '88 trials, which were a disaster for me. I made it to the '88 trials in the 1500 meters. I was doing great. I made it to the finals. On the final day hormones hit and I had a horrible stomach and I finished seventh.

The next year I went and got married [laughter]. Well, I hadn't gotten married yet. I moved to California—left Texas and moved to California with my fiancé and started training with Dr. Ernie Gregoire out at Mt. San Antonio College. At that point, somewhere in there, I joined the Southern California Cheetahs and got married. I was also working for J.C. Penny's for the Olympic Job Opportunities Program. That was helping me out as far as finances. I had a very successful time with them. That was the early 90s: '88, '89, '90. For three or four years there I trained with the Southern California Cheetahs. I trained with some good runners: Alice Brown, Michelle Taylor, a half-miler, Larry Myricks, a jumper, Arnita Epps Myricks, she was out there. I ran 2:01 every time I stepped on the track. I was 2:01 in indoors; 2:01 in outdoors before I had any babies, no babies yet. The 1500 was still my main focus. But what kept eluding me was a national championship. I could not win a national championship. At that time Suzy had come on strong and she was just hard to beat at that mile distance. I look back now and I think maybe it was because even though I had the OJOP program, I still had to work. My schedule could have been a little bit easier. It would have been a little easier for me. I could have trained a little bit harder. But you never know. It may not have worked that way.

In 1991, which I think was my best year, I had a bad nationals performance. I missed the world championships team. It was a hot day at Randall's Island. I finished fourth in the 1500 meters. I just knew I should have been in the top two to make that world championship team. I was in the lead and everything. I think the mistake I made was to have a little glass of wine the night before the finals. I think that cost me; it was very hot that day and I had heat stress. So I finished fourth, but fortunately, the Pan American Games were that summer and these girls did not want to go. So I was next in line.

I went to the Pan American Games in the 1500 meters. What happened was, Coach Gregoire was one of the coaches of the team. When we got there, Diana Richburg decided not to run the 800. She didn't show up for the plane when we got to Florida. So they didn't have an 800 meter runner. They only had one. So [Coach Gregoire] asked me, "Do you want to do it Alisa?" [laughter]. "Of course!" So I did the 800 and the 1500 in the Pan American Games in Havana. Those, I think, were my best performances ever. I went up against Anna Quirot. I just surprised myself there. Maybe it was because I was half starved [laughter]. We didn't eat too much there. They were shipping in water and food for us because the food was kind of suspect, that's it [laughter]. We were drinking lots and lots of water.

Alisa Harvey, 2005.

Jearl Miles was on the team. Natasha Kaiser was on the team. Great team. We had a lot of fun. Beautiful island, but it was a weird experience. It's hard to say — no luxuries there — we didn't have the luxury. It was a hand made stadium and we appreciated it there. It was beautiful weather every day. You took your showers and you had a good time.

But I managed to win the 1500 meters in 4:13 — an easy win — it was just 4:13. I didn't have a lot of competition. It was so darn hot that you weren't going to run that much faster. I forget what the temperature was, but it was hot down there. The 800 meters was a hot race. Their national star, the Cuban star Anna Quirot, was there and Fidel Castro was there for the final of the 800 meters. The gun went off. We take off, and coming around the first lap, I was dead last. Anna was in the lead. I was dead last. It was amazing. So as I come through the curve, I started picking people off one by one. By the backstretch with 200 meters to go I was behind Anna. I had worked my way up right behind Anna. The crowd stood up and started screaming at that point. They thought I was going to go by her. I came up on her and then she put it in another gear. We kicked it in. I think she was 59 low and I was 59 high (1:59.99). That was my best. I left that competition with a gold medal in the 1500 and a silver in the 800 and a great time — my fastest time at that point, my PR.

I made a few indoor world championships: Budapest in '89, Seville in '91— I ran 7th in 4:08. So '91 was a good year for me. I think that was my best year.

Let's see — '92, the trials. I qualified in both the 8 and the 15. Again, 2:01 every day of the week but I got at the trials and I was 6th place in both the 800 meters and the 1500 meters. Coach Gregoire was heartbroken. I was heartbroken. I was working hard. It was hot. My last race — it was three rounds for each race — I was worn out. I tried but I just couldn't make the team.

In '93 I had a race and beat Regina Jacobs at the nationals and made the world championships team. Regina was coming out of the back stretch in the 1500 meters and I passed her and she dropped out. I finished behind Annette Peters. I came in second in the 1500 meters and made the Stuttgart world championships team. I got there and didn't do very well. But that year I decided to have my child. So in '94 my little girl, now ten years old, was born [laughter]. She's almost eleven. I had my daughter, Virginia. I came right back into it pretty strong. In '93 I was ranked number one miler in the U.S. So '94 — baby year.

About '95 I came back into it pretty strong. I still, at that point, came back into 2:01 indoor and 4:31 indoor mile. I still didn't get an indoor championship because of Suzy and Joetta and Meredith [laughter]. I'm like always a bridesmaid. I had a lot of competition with some very good athletes in my day. But who doesn't, I guess. I think if I had to do it again I may have waited on the baby thing. But who can second guess life? That's just the way it is. My baby girl is my pride and joy.

Let's see. 1996, the trials. Another stressor. Atlanta, 1996. I had a pretty good season leading up to the trials. I chose to do both: the 800 meters and the 1500 meters. I didn't know which would be better. The 800 was the first race. The only thing that happened was in the finals. I went out in 56.7; I think that was my time exactly [laughter]. I came through ahead of Meredith in 56.7 and, coming around the back stretch at the 200 meter mark, Meredith passed me and then at the 100 meters to go, everyone else did. I finished sixth. I just went out too hard. I just lost it for myself there. I don't know what happened to me. I just lost focus probably. I wasn't thinking. It felt really easy and I just got awed by where I was. So that one was really devastating for me because I knew I really should have been on that team. I did come back in the 1500 meters but my head wasn't in it. My heart wasn't in it. I still made it to the finals. But it was just going through the motions because of the 8; I could taste that one. I vowed to quit at the end of that year. I remember meeting somebody on the bus going back to the hotel who said, "Alisa, you feel really bad now but you'll be back at it." I said, "No, I'm stopping now."

I picked myself up from that destruction. The low point, I think, in my career was '96 and I managed to go on. That was my divorce. That was a bad year. I moved out of New York and went back home to Virginia. I did stop running. I stopped track and field pretty much to take care of the baby. I was living with mom and had two jobs. What happened was I got back into it because I was doing road races for money. The next thing you know, I was running fast in road races for money. I jumped into a track meet at home in Fairfax and ran 2:04. So I'm like, here I go again [laughter]. It's amazing what you can do when you put your mind and your body to it. I tried to do office jobs; I tried to even do waitressing. But it just didn't make any sense if I could make that kind of money doing something I enjoy. I got involved in personal training at a local gym and I managed to meet some people who owned a running store. I'm still working there now. The woman who owned the store is a runner herself, former runner, and that job allowed me to get back to track. I could work there and she'd let me go to competitions and come on back. So it was really good to get that kind of employment—someone who was understanding.

In '97, '98 I started doing more road races, like the local 10 miler and stuff and getting my name out there. It wasn't track and field but it was fun. Oh, the Goodwill Games: I was working two jobs. I was training myself and I thought, well, let me give it a try. I had done the 10 miler like two months beforehand. So I decided to go to the nationals. It was in New Orleans in '98. I ran the 1500 meters. It was the only race I put myself in and I was third in that race. I remember I just couldn't believe how well I was doing during the race. When I came across the line I collapsed because it was so hot. I asked how I placed; they told me I was third.

I went to the Goodwill Games that year and ran my PR in the mile—4:28, I think it was. The next year I got a coach. It was a big mistake and it didn't work for me at all. I should not have done that; I was doing fine coaching myself. I did a fun commercial with New Balance in Japan. Then the next year I went with the Avon Corporation through Kathy Switzer. She met me at one road race in Baltimore. The next thing you know I was doing speaking engagements for Avon across the country. It was quite lucrative. It was a nice job to have to keep myself going and the baby and all that. That was in '98, '99, and 2000. I did Milan with them. I went to the world global race in Milan in '99. I kind of made a name, a 10k kind of niche. With Avon, I was speaking to high school kids or grade school kids, women's groups, women's track clubs. We traveled all over the country. It was a nice kind of side step from what I had been doing and I tried to transition that into another kind of career.

In 2000, I met my second husband. The Olympic trials in 2000 were a nightmare. I had qualified the year before running 2:01 in the 800 and I qualified for the 1500 meters somewhere—probably the mile time. But I had gotten myself so worn out that I decided that the way I was going to do these trials was to lose a lot of weight and be thin fast. So I proceeded to starve myself for a few months before the trials and got down to about 102 pounds. It was horrible. They were in Sacramento and I did not make it out of the first round in the 1500 meters and I didn't make it out of the second round in the 800 meters. I don't know how I made it to the second round of the 800 meters. It was just a low point in my life. I had worked myself into an eating disorder, and I knew better because I've seen athletes like this before. Bad way to go. I drove out to the trials to begin with and I drove myself home from Sacramento to Virginia. I had a long time to think about that. I ended that mess and stopped running for a while.

I met my husband and I got pregnant a year later with my now three year old. That was kind of a nice change. I got into coaching in 2002 after the baby was born — a little girl, Kyah, she was born on February 22 in 2002. I started coaching at George Mason University, women's distance, and I'd bring Kyah along with me. I've been there ever since. I'm still coaching at Mason and running and training with the women I coach. I do that because there's a small group of us and it gives them someone to train with and something to look at doing. That's why I'm here: I compete in the college meets and still at age 39 I find that I'm way ahead and don't have people to race with. So, for me, for fun, I'm here to compete against the national best because I can actually be in a race with people around me. My time is still now at 2:06 in a race I ran recently by myself, no one near me. It's fun but I'm still at the point where I can't do masters because they are not going to be competitive yet. So that's where we are now. That's my career [laughter].

Alisa's 800 PR is 1:59.7

12

1992: The Barcelona Olympic Year

The Olympic Games were held in Barcelona, Spain from July 25 to August 9.

Name	Event	Place	Performance
Ashford, Evelyn	100m	DNQ	11.29
	4 × 100mr	1	42.11
Berry, Paula	Javelin	DNQ	160' 9"
Buford, Tonya	400mh	DNQ	55.04
Carter, Kym	Heptathlon	11	6256
Clark, Joetta	800m	7	1:58.06
Coogan, Gwyn	10,000	DNQ	33:13.13
Couch, Sharon	LJ	6	21' 10¼"
Dasse, Bonnie	SP	DNQ	54' 8¾"
Devers, Gail	100m	1	10.82
	100mh	5	12.75(fell)
Dukes, Pam	SP	DNQ	54'
Echols, Sheila	LJ	7	21' 8¾"
Finn, Michelle	200m	7	22.61
	4 × 100mr	1	42.11
Garrett, Carla	Discus	DNQ	190' 6"
Greiner, Cindy	Heptathlon	9	6300
Guidry, Carlette	200m	5	22.30
	4 × 100mr	1	42.11
Hamilton, Suzy	1500m	DNQ	4:22.36
Herazo, Vicki	10,000m walk	27	48:26
Hill, Denean	4 × 400mr	2	3:20.92
Hughes, Tanya	HJ	11 (tie)	6' 2"
Jacobs, Regina	1500m	DNQ	4:21.55
Jenkins, Julie	800m	DNQ	2:06.53
Jennings, Lynn	10,000m	3	31:19.89
Jones, Esther	4 × 100mr	1	42.11
Kaiser, Natasha	400m	DNQ	50.60

Name	Event	Place	Performance
	4 × 400mr	2	3:20.92
Kersee, Jackie Joyner	LJ	3	23' 2½"
	Heptathlon	1	7044
Klecker, Janis	Marathon	21	2:47:17
Lawrence, Debbi	10,000m walk	26	48:23
Martin, LaVonna	100mh	2	12.69
Mayhew, Donna	Javelin	12	182' 8"
Miles, Jearl	400m	DNQ	50.57
	4 × 400mr	2	3:20.92
Neer, Penny	Discus	DNQ	181' 11"
O'Brien, Cathy	Marathon	10	2:39:42
Pagel, Ramona	SP	11	59' 10¼"
Patrick, Sandra Farmer	400mh	2	53.69
Peters, Annette	3000m	DNQ	8:52.77
Plumer, PattiSue	1500m	DNQ	4:04.23
	3000m	5	8:48.29
Rainey, Meredith	800m	DNQ	2:01.33
Rembao, Sue	HJ	DNQ	6' 2¾"
Rohl, Michelle	10,000m walk	20	46:45
Smith, Connie Price	Discus	DNQ	192' 5"
Smith, Francie Larrieu	Marathon	12	2:41:09
St. Hilaire, Judi	10,000m	8	31:38.04
Steely, Shelly	3000m	7	8:52.67
Stevens, Rochelle	400m	6	50.11
	4 × 400mr	2	3:20.92
Tolbert, Lynda	100mh	4	12.75
Torrence, Gwen	200m	1	21.81
	100m	4	10.86
	4 × 100mr	1	42.11
	4 × 400mr	2	3:20.92
Vickers, Janeene	400mh	3	54.31
Welty, Amber	HJ	DNQ	6' 2"
Young, Dannette	4 × 400mr	2	3:20.92

The Olympic Results

100 meters. "...Devers was not the favorite yesterday," wrote Elliott Denman of the *Asbury Park Press*. "She wasn't even slated to medal, in the experts' analyses. The top choice was U.S. teammate Gwen Torrence, who had won the U.S. Trials." Denman goes on:

"...Well, they had it all wrong. It was the closest 100-meter final, men or women, in Olympic history, with the first five finishers bunched within 5/100.... It was so close the finalists had no clear idea where they finished. For agonizing moments, they stayed on the track, awaiting a replay of the finish-line photo on the giant electronic scoreboard. At last, Devers got the good news — and started off on a 400-meter victory dance."

Track & Field News described the race:

...The final had Devers and Cuthbert in lanes 2 and 3, while the big three of Ottey, Torrence and Privalova owned the choice real estate of 4-5-6.

Privalova made the most of her first few strides, but Devers was right behind. The Russian held a narrow margin over much of the distance, but by 80m Ottey, Torrence and Cuthbert had pulled themselves into contention. If anyone had a lead at that point, it was lost on the naked eye.

With the exception of Onyali, Nuneva and Allen, this was anybody's race, and the five contenders drove to the line knowing it, clawing for every fraction of an inch. With 10m to go, it was even tighter. So tight that Ottey, perhaps 12 inches behind the leader, seemed to be out of it.

From any angle but dead on the finish line, the first four were inseparable.

1. Gail Devers	10.82
4. Gwen Torrence	10.86

200 meters. *Track & Field News* recounted the race: "...In 6, Torrence had made herself the clear favorite in her semi. Privalova readied herself in 3, Guidry in 7.

"For 100m it looked as if Ottey had finally capitalized on her experience. She ran a smooth, strong turn, and came into the straight even with Torrence, Cuthbert and Privalova. Torrence, however, started *really* running once she hit the straight. Pulling steadily away from the Jamaicans, she was not challenged as she streaked to victory in 21.81 into the 0.6 wind."

1. Gwen Torrence	21.81
5. Carlette Guidry	22.30
7. Michelle Finn	22.61

400 meters. "...Jearl Miles and Natasha Kaiser, were unfortunate enough to have drawn the same semi as the three eventual medalists," reported *Track & Field News*. Miles was just out-toughed by Britain's Smith (who PRed) and Kaiser's characteristic late rush was good only for 6th. Said Miles, 'Close doesn't count right now.'

...For Stevens, running within 0.05 of her PR was apparently satisfactory: 'Now I'm gonna go on a cruise, kick back and say, 'I was in the Olympic finals.'"

6. Rochelle Stevens	50.11

800 meters. Meredith Rainey placed third in heat five and did not qualify for the semis. Julie Jenkins was third in heat three but qualified for the semis on her time of 1:59.96. She was eliminated in the semis, finishing eighth in the second semi.

Joetta Clark PRed in semi one, placing forth in 1:58.22 and making the final. She ended up seventh in the final but ran another PR 1:58.06.

7. Joetta Clark	1:58.06

1500 meters. Suzy Hamilton finished eleventh in heat one in 4:22.36 and did not qualify for the semis. Regina Jacobs placed seventh in heat two (4:13.87) and then finished twelfth in semi one (4:21.55) and did not move on to the final. Only PattiSue Plumer made it to the final round. She finished tenth with a PR of 4:03.42.

10. PattiSue Plumer	4:03.42

3000 meters. Annette Peters running in heat three did not qualify for the final (4/8:52.77). Both Shelly Steely and PattiSue Plumer did qualify; Plumer on place (3/8:47.58) and Steely on time (6/8:44.22). In the final Steely was seventh and Plumer finished fifth.

5. PattiSue Plumer	8:48.29
7. Shelly Steely	8:52.67

10,000 meters. *Track & Field News* reported: "...Gwyn Coogan never felt good in her heat and did not qualify, but finished in a respectable 33:13.13. Judi St. Hilaire found another gear, however, and finished 7th to advance to the final with a PR 32:13.99. 'When Elana made the break, I tried to go with her, but I couldn't,' Jennings said. 'So I decided to sit back and go for the bronze.'

"...In the race for the bronze, Jennings began a long kick with 350 to go and crossed the finish in American record time (31:19.89), less than two seconds ahead of Zhong."

| 3. Lynn Jennings | 31:19.88 | AR |
| 8. Judi St. Hilaire | 31:38.04 | |

Marathon. "With Cathy O'Brien in 10th, Francie Larrieu 12th and Janis Klecker 21st, the U.S. put three women across the line before any other nation," said *Track & Field News*.

10. Cathy O'Brien	2:39:42
12. Francie Larrieu-Smith	2:41:09
21. Janis Klecker	2:47:17

100 meter hurdles. "...Devers drew lane 2 for the big race, with Tolbert, Martin, Patouli-dou and Donkova in adjacent corridors. Martin got a fine start, but Devers sped to the lead by the fourth obstacle," said *Track & Field News*. The article continues:

"Devers steamed toward the line, as the Martin-Tolbert-Patoulidou-Donkova foursome scrapped tightly behind her. Video replays later showed Devers taking one furtive glance to her right for an instant before she rose to the final barrier. That was all it took — the sole of her lead foot slammed into the bar and she stumbled forward. Momentarily prone, she sprawled/crawled across the line almost parallel to the track. Amazingly, she still clocked 12.75."

The *New York Times* said, "...It might have been an even more glorious day for the United States were it not for a stumble by Gail Devers, the 100-meter gold medalist, in the women's 100-meter hurdles. Her right leg hit the top of the final hurdle, and she stumbled the remaining 10.5 meters before belly-flopping across the finish line. She was leading by an uncatchable margin to the point of her error and still managed to finish fifth, just missing third by five one-hundredths of a second."

2. LaVonna Martin	12.69
4. Lynda Tolbert	12.75
5. Gail Devers	12.75

400 meter hurdles. Tonja Buford finished sixth in the second semi in 55.04 and did not advance to the final.

"...The American record holder made a strong run on the turn in spite of a bad hurdle at No. 7, and coming into the stretch she still had a narrow edge over Gunnell.

"...Farmer-Patrick — a strong finisher, but a leaper who laughingly allows herself to be called 'the fastest ugly hurdler ever' — lost the lead at hurdle 9 and stuttered at the final jump. She was unable to gather enough momentum to catch the fleeing Gunnell," said *Track & Field News*.

| 2. Sandra Farmer-Patrick | 53.69 |
| 3. Janeene Vickers | 54.31 |

10 kilometer walk. Michelle Rohl was the first American finishing twentieth with a PR of three seconds. Debbi Lawrence was twenty-sixth and Victoria Herazo twenty-seventh.

20. Michelle Rohl	46:45
26. Debbi Lawrence	48:23
27. Victoria Herazo	48:26

4 × 100 meter relay. The Russian team had a lead of almost 2m at the last exchange. "...Torrence drew even with her rival — this looked more like the 200 — and forged on to cross half a meter ahead," said *Track & Field News*.

1. United States	42.11	
(Evelyn Ashford, Esther Jones, Carlette Guidry, Gwen Torrence)		

4 × 400 meter relay. Natasha Kaiser led off in lane 6. Torrence then took the baton and moved the team into first place. Jearl Miles held the lead and passed to Rochelle Stevens. Stevens held the lead until the final 60 meters.

2. United States	3:20.92	
(Natasha Kaiser, Gwen Torrence, Jearl Miles, Rochelle Stevens)		

High jump. Sue Rembao (6' 2¾") and Amber Welty (6' 2") did not make the final. Tanya Hughes finished in a tie for eleventh place.

11. Tanya Hughes	6' 2"

Long jump. This is the fist time since 1984 that the United States had three women in the final.

3. Jackie Joyner-Kersee	23' 2½"
6. Sharon Couch	21' 10¼"
7. Sheila Echols	21' 8¾"

Shot put. Neither Pam Dukes (54') nor Bonnie Dasse (54' 8¾") made the final. Ramona Pagel qualified with a toss of 59' 1½" and finished in eleventh place in the final.

11. Ramona Pagel	59' 10¼"

Discus. None of the three Americans qualified for the final round. In the preliminaries Connie Price-Smith threw 192' 5", Carla Garrett 190' 6", and Penny Neer 181' 11".

Javelin. Of the two Americans entered in the javelin only Donna Mayhew made the final. Paula Berry tossed the spear 160' 9" in the qualifying round. Mayhew threw the javelin 200' 11" in that round.

12. Donna Mayhew	182' 8"

Heptathlon. Jackie Joyner-Kersee led the entire way to win the gold medal.

1. Jackie Joyner-Kersee	7044
9. Cindy Greiner	6300
11. Kym Carter	6256

The Olympic Trials: New Orleans, Louisiana, June 19–28

"Three defending champions (in four events) held their ground in New Orleans: Jackie Joyner-Kersee (LJ, Hept), Connie Price-Smith (DT), and Donna Mayhew (JT)," stated *Track & Field News*. "If Karin Smith ends up being named to the team in the javelin, it will be her fifth Olympic squad. Ashford is on her fourth. Pagel and Greiner have been on three."

100 meters

Jeff Hollobaugh reported for *Track & Field News*: "...When the gun sounded for the final,

Torrence and Devers got away best and Guidry doomed herself with a bad start. Running side-by-side, Torrence and Devers matched strides for 50m, and Torrence — no longer holding back — used her longer stride to pull away. At the line, a mere 0.05 separated the two, Torrence the victor in 10.97."

1. Gwen Torrence, Mazda Track Club   10.97
2. Gail Devers, Foot Locker   11.02
3. Evelyn Ashford, Mazda Track Club   11.17
4. Carlette Guidry, Nike International   11.18
5. Marion Jones, Thousand Oaks
   High School, California   11.29
6. Esther Jones, Nike International   11.33
7. Sheila Echols, Nike Track Club   11.40
8. Michelle Finn, Mazda Track Club   11.44

200 meters

Jeff Hollobaugh continues: "...In the final-delayed by two false starts — Torrence did not explode with the gun. Instead, Michelle Finn rocketed away best, with Carlette Guidry in tow. Torrence struggled to catch up.... [She] dug deep and passed the Texan, cruising to the finish in 22.03, just 0.01 off her PR. Guidry, who had PRed at 22.41 in the semis, maintained for another lifetime best, 22.24."

Evelyn Ashford at the 1992 Olympic Trials. Photograph by Victah Sailer, ©www.photo run.net

1. Gwen Torrence, Mazda Track Club	22.03	
2. Carlette Guidry, Nike International	22.24	
3. Michelle Finn, Mazda Track Club	22.51	
4. Marion Jones, Thousand Oaks High School, California	22.58	AJR
5. Dannette Young, Reebok Racing Club	22.68	
6. Esther Jones, Nike International	22.90	
7. Dyan Webber, unattached	23.01	
8. Chryste Gaines, Stanford University	23.04	

400 meters

Track & Field News goes on: "...In the final Stevens got out fastest, making up the stagger on the slow-starting Natasha Kaiser by 100m. She continued to fly down the backstretch, with Dannette Young and Mackey also running well at that point. On the last turn, veteran Jearl Miles came on strong, and was nearly even with Stevens and Mackey when they entered the straight. Gradually, Stevens moved back into the lead, with Miles assuming 2nd and finishing 0.08 behind Stevens' 50.22."

1. Rochelle Stevens, Nike Track Club   50.22
2. Jearl Miles, Reebok Racing Club   50.30
3. Natasha Kaiser, Southern California Cheetahs   50.42
4. Dannette Young, Reebok Racing Club   50.46
5. Denean Hill, unattached   50.89

6. Anita Howard, University of Florida	51.30
7. Lillie Leatherwood, Reebok Racing Club	51.31
8. Kendra Mackey, unattached	51.72

800 meters

"The tough twosome of four-time Trials veteran Joetta Clark, 29, and Meredith Rainey, still just 23, was favored as the finalists emerged," wrote Jed Brickner for *Track & Field News*.

He continues:

...Halliday led from the start, towing the field through splits of 27.7 and 58.7 with Jenkins and Hill at the head of the tight bunch behind her. Clark (59.1) languished in 7th.

...Around the last turn the trailing three stalked Halliday and a team berth. Then at the top of the stretch Celeste moved out slightly from the rail and it was all over. Jenkins came through on the inside, Clark and Rainey flew by on the outside and for the second straight year, Halliday was left short, even though she scored a PR 1:59.87 in the now-familiar 4th spot.

Clark pulled away to win in a PR 1:58.47 and pronounced that she was ready to contend for a medal.

1. Joetta Clark, Foot Locker	1:58.47
2. Julie Jenkins, Reebok Racing Club	1:59.15
3. Meredith Rainey, Nike Boston	1:59.18
4. Celeste Halliday, Nike Indiana Track Club	1:59.87
5. Debbie Marshall, unattached	2:01.07
6. Alisa Hill, Foot Locker	2:01.38
7. Jasmin Jones, Nike South Track Club	2:02.22
8. Nekita Beasley, Foot Locker	2:02.31

1500 meters

Rodney Staggs reported for *Track & Field News*: "...Making a strong move down the backstretch with 250m remaining, Jacobs blew by Slaney, who had settled into 2nd behind PattiSue Plumer on the second lap. Jacobs then overtook former Stanford teammate Plumer coming out of the final curve.

"...An ailing Plumer (head cold) held off onrushing Suzy Hamilton for the runner-up spot. Plumer, who had earlier in the week PRed in winning the 3000, turned in her second-best time ever, 4:04.04. Hamilton passed Slaney entering the final straight on her way to a PR 4:04.53."

1. Regina Jacobs, unattached	4:03.72
2. PattiSue Plumer, Nike International	4:04.04
3. Suzy Hamilton, Reebok Racing Club	4:04.53
4. Mary Slaney, Foot Locker	4:05.43
5. Gina Procaccio, Sallie Mae Track Club	4:07.68
6. Alisa Hill, Foot Locker	4:08.32
7. Fran ten Bensel, unattached	4:08.91
8. Jasmin Jones, Nike South Track Club	4:09.34

3000 meters

A headline in the *New York Times* read, "Slaney, Slowed by Injury, Fails to Gain 3,000 Berth." Frank Litsky reported:

For 20 years, Mary Decker Slaney has been a dynamic middle-distance runner and orthopedic patient. For every world or American record, and there have been dozens, she seems to have been done in by an injured ankle or calf or leg or something else.

Tonight, in the United States Olympic track and field trials, it was something else. She finished sixth in the women's 3,000-meter final, largely because a foot injury in December had wiped out

Left to right: Regina Jacobs, PattiSue Plumer and Suzy Favor at the 1992 Olympic Trials. Photograph by Jack McManus, ©www.photorun.net

three months of heavy training and left her short of conditioning. Only the first three finishers made the Olympic team. Slaney, almost 34 years old, will have another chance later in the week in the 1,500 meters.

A crowd of 13,902 watched PattiSue Plumer win the race in 8 minutes 40.98 seconds, the second-fastest time in the world this year.

Sieg Lindstrom reported for *Track & Field News*, "...At the start of the final Slaney led and Plumer got into 2nd by the end of the first homestretch. Gina Procaccio and Annette Peters followed.... At 5½ laps Plumer moved to the lead, but not without a fight from Peters. Steely always lurking just behind, drew even with Plumer on the outside with just under a lap left and the pair pulled away. Plumer's glance over her shoulder on the final backstretch, though, said it all. Its message: 'I can handle Shelly; who else is there?' 'Nobody close' was the answer, and off the final turn Plumer let it out to finish 2m up at the end of her 64.2 closer."

1. PattiSue Plumer, Nike International   8:40.98
2. Shelly Steely, Mizuno Track Club   8:41.28
3. Annette Peters, Nike West Track Club   8:42.31
4. Joan Nesbit, New Balance Track Club   8:51.92
5. Sabrina Dornhoefer, New Balance Track Club   8:55.57
6. Mary Slaney, Foot Locker   9:02.60
7. Fran ten Bensel, unattached   9:03.69
8. Laurie Gomez-Henes, North Carolina State University   9:08.12

Mary Decker Slaney (left) and PattiSue Plumer at the 1992 Olympic Trials. Photograph by Errol Anderson, ©www. photorun.net

10,000 meters

Mike Fanelli wrote for *Track & Field News*: "...With exactly 8 laps remaining, Jennings displayed her dominance for the first time, surging into familiar 1st place territory. Her gearshifting soon pared the field to five, but she didn't keep the hammer down, forcing Mosqueda and Painter to seesaw back into the lead.... Laps of 70 and 69 brought the elated Jennings (32:55.96) home 1st with Coogan (33:04.64) overtaken in the final 20m by the furiously finishing St. Hilaire (33:03.39) for a New England sweep."

1. Lynn Jennings, Nike International   32:55.96
2. Judi St. Hilaire, Nike International   33:03.39
3. Gwyn Coogan, adidas Track Club   33:04.64
4. Sylvia Mosqueda, Nike West Track Club   33:17.11
5. Trina Painter, Nike Texas Track Club   33:33.41
6. Anne Marie Letko, Nike Running Room   33:47.20
7. Elaine Van Blunk, Nike Running Room   33:54.89

100 meter hurdles

"...The 5 ft. 3, 115 lb. Devers led the final from the gun. Despite running up on some hurdles, she turned in another solid technical race and let her 10.95 speed carry her to another meet record," wrote John Parks for *Track & Field News*.

The *New York Times* added, "Jackie Joyner-Kersee, the leading qualifier in the heptathlon, failed to gain the final of the 100-meter hurdles when she finished fifth in her semifinal behind Gail Devers, the American record holder...."

1. Gail Devers, Foot Locker   12.55   MR
2. LaVonna Martin, Reebok Racing Club   12.71
3. Lynda Tolbert, Nike International   12.74
4. Monifa Taylor, University of Florida   12.80
5. Donna Waller, unattached   13.02
6. Arnita Myricks, Southern California Cheetahs   13.63
      dnf— Dawn Bowles, Foot Locker, Cheryl Dickey, Nike South

400 meter hurdles

David Woods reported for *Track & Field News*:

...Attired in a sheer uniform with tutu designed by Lauren Sheehan, the 29-year-old SFP opened a wide lead by the sixth hurdle and broke the meet record by more than a second with her 53.62, only 0.25 off her own AR.

...Going in, it appeared unlikely that anyone would break into the Janeene Vickers-SFP-Kim Batten trio that finished 3-4-5 in the World Championships last year. That feeling was confirmed when they had the three fastest times in the semis.

In the final Batten led Vickers off the eighth hurdle and they were even off the ninth, but suddenly NCAA champ Tonja Buford stormed up on the inside. She passed both on the run-in as she PRed at 54.75. Vickers edged Batten for the last spot on the team, 54.80–54.89.

The *New York Times* reported that Sandra Farmer Patrick was "...overjoyed because her husband, David Patrick, made the team in the men's 400-meter hurdles. They are the first husband-wife combination on a United States Olympic track team since Harold Connolly (hammer throw) and Olga Fikotova Connolly (women's discus throw) in 1960."

1. Sandra Farmer-Patrick, Flo Jo International	53.62
2. Tonja Buford, University of Illinois	54.75
3. Janeene Vickers, World Class Athletic Club	54.80
4. Kim Batten, Reebok Racing Club	54.89
5. Schowonda Williams, unattached	56.30
6. Connie Ellerbe, West Virginia University	56.55
7. Sandra Cummings, Mizuno Houston	58.12
8. Countess Comadore, Reebok Racing Club	58.15

10,000 meter walk

"Not much of a surprise for 1st, as the U.S.'s premier woman, Debbi Lawrence, quickly separated herself from all challengers around 3km," reported Bob Bowman for *Track & Field News*. "The 30-year-old Wisconsin native then settled into a comfortable pace all the way to the finish. Her time of 45:46, good under the conditions, was a little over a minute off her AR of 44:42 set last month."

1. Debbi Lawrence, unattached	45:46
2. Victoria Herazo, California Walkers	46:21
3. Michelle Rohl, Parkside Athletic Club	46:50
4. Debby Van Orden, unattached	47:32
5. Cindy March, Golden Gate Race Walkers	47:52
6. Lynn Weik, Natural Sport	48:01
7. Lynda Brubaker, unattached	48:33
8. Kim Wilkinson, Monterey Peninsular	49:37

High jump

"NCAA champ Tanya Hughes added the Trials crown to her growing list of titles with a first-attempt clearance of 6' 3½".

"It was a height none of the others could master, which was unfortunate for runner-up Amber Welty, because if she had it would have been the requisite Olympic qualifier," wrote Kevin Saylors for *Track & Field News*.

1. Tanya Hughes, Nike Coast Club	6' 3½"
2. Amber Welty, unattached	6' 2¼"
3. Sue Rembao, Reebok Racing Club	6' 2¼"
4. Vicki Borsheim, Mizuno Track Club	6' 2¼"
5. Angie Bradburn, unattached	6' 2¼"
6. Yolanda Henry, Mazda Track Club	6' 2¼"
7. Karol Damon, Goldwin Gym	6' 1¼"
Denise Gaztambide, unattached (tied)	
Shelley Nixon, Nike Coast Club (tied)	

Long jump

Tom Jordan reported for *Track & Field News*: "Defending Olympic champ Jackie Joyner-Kersee overcame cramping calves to make her third Olympic team on her first attempt. Jumping into the north pit, with a runway still damp from a rainstorm an hour before the start of the event, JJK launched a put-paid leap of 23' 2¾", farther than the PR of anyone else in the competition. Indeed, it's farther than any other American has ever jumped, though JJ herself has done it in 17 other meets."

1. Jackie Joyner-Kersee, McDonald's Track Club	23'	2¾"
2. Sheila Echols, Nike International	22'	8"
3. Sharon Couch, unattached	21'	10¾"
4. Julie Bright, Mizuno Track Club	21'	6¼"
5. Tonya Sedwick, World Class Athletic Club	21'	3¼"
6. Sheila Hudson, Mizuno Track Club	21'	½"
7. Gwen Loud, Keiser Track Club	20'	10¾"
8. Shunta Rose, University of Nevada, Las Vegas	20'	9"

Triple jump (exhibition)

1. Sheila Hudson, Mizuno Track Club	46'	8¼" AR, MR
2. Robyne Johnson, unattached	44'	5¼" w
3. Diana Orrange, unattached	43'	5¼"
4. Claudia Haywood, Rice University	43'	2½"
5. Cynthea Rhodes, unattached	42'	10¾"
6. Dana Boone, unattached	42'	2¾"
7. Karen Pittman, George Mason University	41'	11"
8. Leah Kirklin, University of Florida	41'	10½"

Shot put

According to Roy Conrad of *Track & Field News*:

Not since Earlene Brown in '60 had the shot and discus gone to the same winner at the Trials.

With that goal in mind, discus winner Connie Price-Smith rose above her big-meet problems of the past and dominated the shot field. Price-Smith's first heave of 59' 11¼" put her in the lead for good.

"...Winning the double was a season goal of mine and I wanted it real bad," said Price-Smith. "It was important to me because a double win hasn't been done in a while."

While a double win was important to Price-Smith, trying both at the Games is not, and she announced that she would not contest the shot, giving the spot instead to 4th-placer Dukes. "I was in the drug-testing room when I found out," said the ecstatic Dukes, who just minutes before had thought she was doomed to spend '92 as she had in '88, as an alternate. "I just started crying."

1. Connie Price-Smith, Nike Coast Track Club	62'	6½"
2. Ramona Pagel, Mazda Track Club	59'	6¾"
3. Bonnie Dasse, Nike Coast Track Club	58'	5¼"
4. Pam Dukes, Nike Coast Track Club	57'	4¼"
5. Dawn Dumble, World Class Athletic Club	54'	3¾"
6. Christy Barrett, Terre Haute Track Club	53'	11"
7. Melisa Weis, unattached	52'	4"
8. Beth Bunge, unattached	51'	6¼"

Discus

"...Favorite Connie Price-Smith had little difficulty winning the event on her second throw (193–8). She then hit a big 202–6 in round 5, becoming the only competitor to reach the darker green pseudo-turf, missing Leslie Deniz's meet record by an inch," reported Ed Fox for *Track & Field News*.

1. Connie Price-Smith, Nike Coast Track Club	202' 6"
2. Carla Garrett, Nike Coast Track Club	198' 7"

3. Penny Neer, Nike Coast Track Club   193' 6"
4. Kelly Landry, Boston Athletic
   Association   191' 6"
5. Becky Levi, unattached   191' 1"
6. Lacy Barnes, Nike Track Club   190' 3"
7. Edie Boyer, Minnesota Track Club   179'
8. Kristin Kuehl, Concordia College   177' 11"

Javelin

Janet Vitu wrote for *Track & Field News*: "...After fouling on her first attempt, the 32-year-old Mayhew opened the second round with 181–7 to take the lead. Meg Foster countered with 183–7, moving briefly into 1st. Mayhew responded quickly in the next stanza with a toss of 187–6 to reclaim her position, and after three rounds the standings for the first three places were Mayhew 187–6, Foster 183–7 and Erica Wheeler 176–1. The order remained the same until the penultimate frame, when Marilyn Senz launched a PR of 186–7 which catapulted her from 6th to 2nd.... Mayhew extended her best to 189–1 in the final round."

Left to right: **Erica Wheeler, Lynn Cannon and Bonnie Edmondson.**

1. Donna Mayhew, Nike Coast Track Club   189' 1"
2. Marilyn Senz, Tennessee Air National Guard   186' 7"
3. Meg Foster, Team Florida   183' 7"
4. Erica Wheeler, unattached   177' 11"
5. Cathie Harris, Rebel West   175' 3"
6. Paula Berry, Nike Oregon International   173' 8"
7. Jill Smith, Nike Oregon International   171' 7"
8. Lynda Sutfin, unattached   171' 7"

Heptathlon

The *New York Times* reported: "...Jackie Joyner-Kersee is perhaps the most gifted athlete in track and field. She has been by far the best in the heptathlon since the event was introduced in 1981. Since the 1984 Olympics, where she finished second, she has now competed in 16 heptathlons, winning 14 and dropping out of 2 because of injuries.... After opening day 2 with a heart-stopping first jump on which she twisted her right ankle, JJK spanned 22' 10¾" w on her final attempt to virtually assure herself a third Olympic trip."

"Her 6695 was her worst score since '85, but was still more than 400 points ahead of Cindy Greiner's 6223," reported Glen McMicken for *Track & Field News*.

1. Jackie Joyner-Kersee, McDonalds Track Club   6695
2. Cindy Greiner, Nike Coast Track Club   6223
3. Kym Carter, unattached   6200
4. DeDee Nathan, Nike Indiana Track Club   6162
5. Sharon Hanson-Hainer, Nike Coast Track Club   6078
6. Jamie McNeair, Reebok Racing Club   5853
7. Crystal Young, Southern California Cheetahs   5700
8. Angie Taylor, Nike North Track Club   5690

2000 meter steeplechase (exhibition)

1. Gina Willbanks, unattached	6:57.61
2. Barbara Bolden, unattached	7:00.98
3. Christine Morgan, unattached	7:04.73
4. Teresa DiPerna, unattached	7:04.81
5. Coleen Kenney, unattached	7:14.13
6. Marisa Sutera, unattached	7:18.45
7. Maria Fonseca, unattached	7:20.91
8. Tami Micham, unattached	7:22.44

Hammer (exhibition)

1. Sonja Fitts, St. John's University	185' 4"	MR
2. Alexandra Earl-Givan, Southern Connecticut University	181' 4"	
3. Bonnie Edmondson, unattached	177'	
4. Michelle Thompson, Pennsylvania State University	170' 11"	
5. Maureen Magnan, Navy	166' 5"	
6. Liz Legault, University of Rhode Island	162' 1"	
7. Lisa Acosta, Syracuse University	156' 1"	
8. Crystal Corbeil, Northeastern University	155' 1"	

Marathon: Houston, Texas, January 26

1. Janis Klecker	2:30:12
2. Cathy O'Brien	2:30:66
3. Francie Larrieu-Smith	2:30:39
4. Lisa Weidenbach	2:33:32
5. Christine McNamara	2:34:35
6. Joy Smith	2:35:09

118 women qualified for the trials and 64 finished.

The Indoor Nationals

The indoor national championships were held in Madison Square Garden, New York on Friday, February 28.

William N. Wallace wrote for the *New York Times*:

...Joyner Kersee's two championships were the first for her indoors, and were achieved with expected ease. Indoor competition has not appealed to one of track and field's most notable performers. She jumped 22' 5¼", in the afternoon before a sparse gathering, then won the hurdles in 8.07 seconds at night.

"...The two 60-meter dashes for men and women, events that push the physical limits of the Garden's track configuration, were of record quality.... Finn, the defending champion, and Gwen Torrence were side by side right down the track, Finn ahead by inches at the end in 7.07, an American and meet record.

...Diane Dixon, who has hard times outdoors, continued to thrive indoors. She won the women's 400-meter run in 53.16 seconds for the 10th straight time and 11th over all. Her first title came when she was a 16-year-old prodigy running for the Atoms Track Club of Brooklyn. This time Dixon fled from the field and won by 12 feet while easing up.

...Lynn Jennings, the two-time women's world cross country champion, took charge early in a field of 13 runners in the women's mile on the tight track and no one could challenge her. Jennings' winning time of 4:37.4 was not so special but the performance was.

"I really ran a strategic race," said Jennings. "I took the lead on the third lap and it really gave me a chance to have a competitive, aggressive race, a tune-up for the world cross country championship next month."

---

60 meters
1. Michelle Finn, Mazda Track Club   7.07   MR, AR
2. Gwen Torrence, Mazda Track Club   7.08
3. Teresa Neighbors, Mizuno Houston Track Club   7.15

200 meters
1. Dyan Webber, unattached   23.69
2. Dannette Young, Reebok Racing Club   23.79
3. Rochelle Stevens, Goldwin Track Club   23.98

400 meters
1. Diane Dixon, Nike Track Club   53.16
2. Jearl Miles, Reebok Racing Club   53.66
3. Natasha Kaiser, Southern California Cheetahs   54.00

800 meters
1. Maria Mutola, Mozambique   2:01.49
2. Meredith Rainey, Nike Boston Track Club   2:01.86
3. Joetta Clark, Joe Clark International Track Club   2:02.03

Mobil mile
1. Lynn Jennings, Nike International Track Club   4:37.39
2. Alisa Hill, Southern California Cheetahs   4:38.37
3. Jennifer Lanctot, Boston Athletic Association   4:39.12

3000 meters
1. Shelly Steely, Mizuno Track Club   8:51.29
2. Gina Procaccio, Sallie Mae Track Club   8:57.31
3. Rosalind Taylor, Nike South Track Club   9:08.97

60 meter hurdles
1. Jackie Joyner-Kersee, McDonald's Track Club   8.07
2. Jackie Humphrey, Nike South Track Club and   8.09
    Kim McKenzie, Mazda Track Club

Shot put
1. Connie Price-Smith, Nike Coast Track Club   60' 6¾"
2. Ramona Pagel, Mazda Track Club   58' 11½"
3. Pam Dukes, Nike Coast Track Club   56' 10"

Triple jump
1. Claudia Haywood, Rice University   42' 5½"
2. Dana Boone, Middle Tennessee State Track Club   42' 3½"
3. Diana Wills-Orrange, U.S. Army   42' 2¼"

20 lb. weight throw
1. Sonja Fitts, St. John's University   62' 10"
2. Pam Dukes, Nike Coast Track Club   61' 5½"
3. Lacy Barnes, Nike Track Club   59' 8½"

Long jump
1. Jackie Joyner-Kersee, McDonald's Track Club   22' 5¼"
2. Dana Boone, Middle Tennessee State Track Club   20' 7¾"
3. Shana Williams, Seton Hall University   19' 9½"

3000 meter walk
1. Debbi Lawrence, Prevention Magazine Walker's Club   12:47.51
2. Victoria Herazo, California Walkers   12:54.52
3. Teresa Vaill, Natural Sport Track Club   12:57.52

High jump
1. Angie Bradburn, unattached   6' 5"
2. Yolanda Henry, Mazda Track Club   6' 2¼"
3. Jan Wohlschlag, Nike Track Club   6' ¾"

4 × 400 meter relay
1. Seton Hall University   3:43.53
    (Keisha Caine, Shana Williams, Julia Sandiford, Flirtisha Harris)
2. Jeuness Track Club   3:44.11
3. University of Houston   3:45.21

Team champion:
Mazda Track Club

Sunkist Invitational (5 women's events): Los Angeles, February 15

50 meters
1. Michelle Finn, Mazda Track Club   6.13   MR, AR

440 yards
1. Janeene Vickers, World Class Athletic Club   55.16

800 meters
1. Maria Mutola, Mozambique   2:03.92

Mile
1. Suzy Favor-Hamilton, Reebok Racing Club   4:32.39

Long jump
1. Jackie Joyner-Kersee, World Class Athletic Club   22' 10"

6th IAAF World Cup: Havana, Cuba, September 25–27

100 meters
6. Sheila Echols   11.72

200 meters
5. Dyan Webber   23.60

400 meters
1. Jearl Miles   50.64

800 meters
2. Joetta Clark   2:01.60

1500 meters
3. Alisa Hill   4:18.41

3000 meters
4. Joan Nesbit   9:12.09

10,000 meters
5. Anne Marie Letko   34:14.18

100 meter hurdles
5. Kim McKenzie   13.36

400 meter hurdles
1. Sandra Farmer-Patrick   55.38

High jump
6. Amber Welty (tie)   5' 8¾"

Long jump
4. Sharon Couch   21' 4¾"

Triple jump
4. Sheila Hudson   43' 10¾"

Shot put
4. Connie Price-Smith   58' 5¾"

Discus
7. Connie Price-Smith   174' 3"

Javelin
5. Donna Mayhew   188'

4 × 100 meter relay
7. USA   45.03
   (Kim McKenzie, Kendra Mackey, Wendy Vereen, Dyan Webber)

4 × 400 meter relay
4. USA   3:33.43
   (Terri Dendy, Kendra Mackey, Ann Graham, Jearl Miles)

Team score:
4. USA   79

20th IAAF World Cross Country Championships: Boston, March 21

Track & Field News wrote of Lynn Jennings, after her third consecutive win: "At 32 years of age, the Princeton-born athlete had reached peak form in the discipline, having just taken her fifth American title, also on the Franklin Park course a few kilometers from her home.

"...Apart from her victories in 1990 and 1991, she finished second at Neuchatel in 1986, fourth in 1987 and 1988 and sixth in 1989.

"For her part, Lynn Jennings took on the task of leading the race herself." She was challenged at different points in the race and the lead group eventually was narrowed to three with Jennings winning after a sprint finish.

The *New York Times* added:

...Jennings grew up in nearby Harvard, MA., and first raced in Franklin Park as a high school sophomore as a member of the boys' team at Bromfield School. Two of the three state high school titles she won came there, as well as other victories later on, including several when Princeton engaged Harvard in dual meets (Jennings graduated from Princeton in 1983). She won her sixth national cross country title four months ago.

"This one surely stands alone," she said after her third consecutive world cross country victory. "...The crowd support was unbelievable. I've never experienced anything like it. It felt like a local race, with everyone yelling my name. I'll never forget it."

1.	Lynn Jennings	21:16
4.	Vicki Huber	21:34
30.	Annette Peters	22:13
42.	Sylvia Mosqueda	22:22
47.	Melinda Schmidt	22:28

The United States placed second in the team scoring.

IAAF/Mobil Grand Prix Final: Turin, Italy, September 4

200 meters

3.	Gwen Torrence	22.10
8.	Dyan Webber	23.58

400 meters

4.	Jearl Miles	50.70
7.	Rochelle Stevens	52.37

5000 meters

8.	Shelly Steely	15:33.22

100 meter hurdles

1.	Gail Devers	12.73
3.	Lynda Tolbert	12.89
4.	LaVonna Martin	12.96
8.	Kim McKenzie	13.29

Long jump

2.	Jackie Joyner-Kersee	22' 10¾" w

IAAF/Mobil Grand Prix Standings

6.	Gwen Torrence
9.	Gail Devers
11.	Jackie Joyner-Kersee
20.	LaVonna Martin
26.	Jearl Miles

Other News and Honors

Track & Field News: U.S. Athlete of the Year

Jackie Joyner-Kersee

Track & Field News — World Rankings

4. Jackie Joyner-Kersee
5. Gail Devers
7. Gwen Torrence

World and U.S. Top Ten Rankings — *Track & Field News*
(U.S. rankings in bold)

1. Jackie Joyner-Kersee
2. Gail Devers
3. Gwen Torrence
4. Sandra Farmer-Patrick
5. Lynn Jennings
6. La Vonna Martin
7. Janeene Vickers
8. PattiSue Plumer
9. Lynda Tolbert
10. Carlette Guidry

100 meters
2. Gwen Torrence
3. Gail Devers
6. Evelyn Ashford
8. Carlette Guidry

1. Gwen Torrence
2. Gail Devers
3. Evelyn Ashford

200 meters
1. Gwen Torrence
6. Carlette Guidry
9. Michelle Finn

1. Gwen Torrence
2. Carlette Guidry
3. Michelle Finn

400 meters
4. Gwen Torrence
8. Rochelle Stevens
9. Jearl Miles

1. Gwen Torrence
2. Rochelle Stevens
3. Jearl Miles

800 meters
8. Joetta Clark

1. Joetta Clark
2. Meredith Rainey
3. Julie Jenkins

1500 meters
9. PattiSue Plumer

1. PattiSue Plumer
2. Regina Jacobs
3. Suzy Hamilton

3000 meters
6. PattiSue Plumer
7. Shelly Steely

1. PattiSue Plumer
2. Shelly Steely
3. Annette Peters

5000 meters
No American women were in the top five.

1. Shelly Steely
2. Annette Peters
3. PattiSue Plumer

10,000 meters
3. Lynn Jennings
10. Judi St. Hilaire

1. Lynn Jennings
2. Judi St. Hilaire
3. Gwyn Coogan

Marathon
No American women were in the top ten.

1. Janis Klecker
2. Cathy O'Brien
3. Francie Larrieu-Smith

100 meter hurdles
1. Gail Devers
3. LaVonna Martin-Floreal
4. Lynda Tolbert

1. Gail Devers
2. LaVonna Martin-Floreal
3. Lynda Tolbert

400 meter hurdles
1. Sandra Farmer-Patrick
4. Janeene Vickers
7. Tonja Buford
8. Kim Batten

1. Sandra Farmer-Patrick

2. Janeene Vickers
3. Kim Batten

10 kilometer walk
No American women were in the top ten.

1. Debbi Lawrence
2. Victoria Herazo
3. Michelle Rohl

High jump
No American women were in the top ten.

1. Tanya Hughes
2. Sue Rembao
3. Angie Bradburn

Long jump
3. Jackie Joyner-Kersee

1. Jackie Joyner-Kersee
2. Sheila Echols
3. Sharon Couch

Triple jump
5. Sheila Hudson

1. Sheila Hudson
2. Robyne Johnson
3. Leah Kirklin

Shot put
No American women were in the top ten.

1. Connie Price-Smith
2. Ramona Pagel
3. Pam Dukes

Discus
No American women were in the top ten.

1. Connie Price-Smith
2. Carla Garrett
3. Penny Neer

Javelin
No American women were in the top ten.

1. Donna Mayhew
2. Marilyn Senz
3. Meg Foster

Heptathlon
1. Jackie Joyner-Kersee

1. Jackie Joyner-Kersee
2. Cindy Greiner
3. Kym Carter

Sports Illustrated, in its July 22 Olympic Preview edition, featured Jackie Joyner-Kersee on the cover throwing the javelin. In the same edition, Kenny Moore wrote a short piece about the long friendship between the two long jumpers, Heike Drechsler and Jackie Joyner-Kersee and a feature entitled, "A Long Run Gets Longer," about Francie Larrieu-Smith.

> ...No runner alive can bring greater steadfastness of dream to the race than Larrieu Smith. This is not simply because she is now 39 and still running 23 seasons after setting her first American record on the track or because she has made the U.S. Olympic team for the fifth time. No, it is because the force that drives her red blood drives it more powerfully than ever.
> In April 1991 she ran 10,000 meters at the Texas Relays in 31:28.92, breaking Mary Decker Slaney's American record of 31:35.3, which had stood for nine years. Then Larrieu Smith placed second to Portugal's Rosa Mota in the 1991 London Marathon with 2:27:35, a good time considering that she and Mota were fighting a head wind for the last 13 miles. "She can do two and a half minutes faster," says Larrieu Smith's coach, Robert Vaughan. That puts her under Joan Benoit Samuelson's Olympic record of 2:24:52.
> There is no precedent for what Larrieu Smith has done. In January she earned a spot on the Olympic team when she finished third (2:30:39) in the U.S. Olympic Marathon Trials in Houston. "I'm really the first woman I know of who's going to hit the over-40 masters' circuit who came up as an age-grouper and never quit," she says.
> ..."Well, first, I never at the beginning thought I'd go this long, but I got into that fairy-tale world of running, and just when the bubble was about to burst, sponsorship became legal and money races came in, and that let me stay in the sport without changing focus. I was blessed that what I loved could become my job. Then, emotionally, I was made to see that if I loved running, surely there would be a race for me to win, and there was. And when that race turned into the marathon, I looked at runners like Carlos Lopes, winning the L.A. men's Olympic marathon at 37, and Joyce Smith placing 11th in the women's race at 46, and then Pricilla Welch running 2:26 at 42, and they all gave me hope. You know what it really was? It was never really feeling like quitting."

The newsletter of the Women's Track and Field Committee reported: "The Women's Sports Foundation recognized Jackie Joyner-Kersee by honoring her as Amateur Sportswoman of the Year. With her victory in Barcelona, Joyner-Kersee has now won back-to-back Olympic gold medals in the heptathlon. Joyner-Kersee has said her long-term goal is to finish her career on American soil at the 1996 Olympic Games in Atlanta."

World Records Held by American Women

100 meters	10.49	Florence Griffith-Joyner	7/16/88
200 meters	21.34	Florence Griffith-Joyner	9/29/88
Heptathlon	7291	Jackie Joyner-Kersee	9/23, 24/88

American Records

100m	10.49	Florence Griffith-Joyner	7/16/88
200m	21.34	Florence Griffith-Joyner	9/29/88
400m	48.83	Valerie Brisco-Hooks	8/6/84
800m	1:56.90	Mary Decker-Slaney	8/16/85
1000m	2:34.04	Julie Jenkins	8/17/90
1500m	3:57.12	Mary Decker-Slaney	7/26/83
Mile	4:16.71	Mary Decker-Slaney	8/21/85
2000m	5:32.7	Mary Decker-Slaney	8/3/84
3000m	8:25.83	Mary Decker-Slaney	9/7/85
5000m	15:00.00	PattiSue Plumer	7/3/89
10,000m	31:19.89	Lynn Jennings	8/7/92
Marathon	2:21:21	Joan Samuelson	10/20/85
100mh	12.61	Gail Devers	5/22/88
	12.61	Jackie Joyner-Kersee	5/28/88
	12.48	Gail Devers	9/10/91
400mh	53.37	Sandra Farmer-Patrick	7/22/89
5k walk	22:36.8	Theresa Vaill	4/28/90
10k walk	45:28.4	Debbi Lawrence	7/19/91
4 × 100mr	41.55	National Team	8/21/87
4 × 200mr	1:32.57	Louisiana State University	4/28/89
4 × 400mr	3:15.51	National Team	10/1/88
4 × 800mr	8:19.9	National Team	6/24/79
Sprint Medley r	1:36.79	Wilt's Athletic Club	6/20/82
Distance Medley r	10:48.38	Villanova University	4/28/88
HJ	6' 8"	Louise Ritter	7/8/88
			9/30/88
LJ	24' 5½"	Jackie Joyner-Kersee	8/13/87
TJ	46' 8¼"	Sheila Hudson	6/20/92
SP	66' 2½"	Ramona Pagel	6/25/88
DT	216' 10"	Carol Cady	5/31/86
JT	227' 5"	Kate Schmidt	9/11/77
Heptathlon	7291	Jackie Joyner-Kersee	9/23, 24/88

INTERVIEW: BONNIE EDMONDSON

(December 2, 2004) I'm really excited to share some of my experiences with you.

I think I got started in track and field because of the influence of my family. Both of my older brothers were athletes so they were a very positive influence for me. My parents were absolutely supportive and always made sure I had the same opportunities as my brothers did. So right from the start I was involved in sports. I was a three-time state champion in Connecticut in the shot put and state champion in the discus, one year, as well. I was also All-State in basketball and volleyball.

My initial focus in college was basketball and also track and field, but basketball was going to be my primary sport. I remember one day hearing about a friend of mine, who was a thrower, how she had qualified for the Olympic trials. At that moment, I thought, that's what I want to do. So I left basketball and I concentrated on track and field year round. I went to Eastern Connecticut State University, a small division three school, and they didn't have a throws coach per se. So I called Bob Kennedy who was the throws coach at the University of Connecticut. I drove 15 minutes up the road to UConn to train with him. It just so happened that Andy Bessette, who was an Olympian in the hammer throw, was training with Bob Kennedy (one of the best hammer coaches around). I saw Andy throwing and I said, "That looks like fun — I want to try that." And so, he took me under his wing and taught me how to throw the hammer.

That was back in '84 — this was long before the women's hammer was contested regionally or nationally. A few women were throwing in the northwest but that was about it. Then we started looking around for competitions and they were few and far between.

So, we started talking. What does it take to get the hammer as a recognized event? Some people said it will never happen and others were more optimistic. They said, well, you have to start with baby steps. So we set off with baby steps. I think I have been so fortunate; fortunate in some regards and frustrated in others, in that we were able to get together a group of people (pioneers if you will) that really pushed the movement and started going forth and saying how do we do this? What do we have to do to get this a recognized event? And so, little by little, it became a regional event. Washington State was doing some and so we had both coasts working on this and things began to happen.

It wasn't recognized as an Olympic event until the 2000 Olympic Games in Sydney. So you look at 1985 to 2000 — 15 years. I never, ever envisioned that it would take that long to get to where it is and so I have a true appreciation for the work that went into this — and the politicking — and the encouraging others to stick with it and making the movement. Pat Rico, former President of USATF and member of the IAAF Women's Committee was a great supporter of this, as was Lynn Cannon, chair of the USATF Women's Track and Field Committee. I kept calling them — hopefully, not bugging them — but keeping a voice in their ears and reminding them to make sure to advocate for us. I remember back in 1990 — that was the first year that it was an exhibition at the USATF nationals. I was warming up and there was Jackie Joyner-Kersee on my left side and Carl Lewis on my right side, and I'm thinking, "Wow, I made it" [laughter]. I was fortunate to win the nationals that year and then repeat in 1991 at Randall's Island, New York.

In 1992, at the trials in New Orleans, I think that was really a tell-tale sign for me. A person was escorting us out to the field and he turned to us — there were probably about 10 to 12 female throwers — and he said, "We're giving you a chance here, don't embarrass me." And so, with that I thought "Who does this guy think he is?" We were angry but we were also psyched and motivated and said we're going to put on a serious performance here. We had three of the top throws (distances) ever in the United States. I think we really answered the call and put on a great show. With any of the events, athletes that finished in the top three got a little American flag. I remember them giving us American flags and Sonja Fitts, Alexandra Givan and I took a victory lap around the track but I remember thinking when we finished that that was it. There wasn't a ticket to Barcelona waiting for us. It was an incredible high but then it was a complete low and at that point it really impassioned me to really make a difference with this and to do everything I could to rally the troops, so to speak, to get these opportunities for women.

That nice nucleus of throwers and coaches and other supporters really committed to making this happen. It was fascinating to be a part of such a movement. I often wonder if that small group of people really realize what they were a part of. The first international opportunity for us was the Pan Am Games and, of course, the world championships and Olympics in 2000 — that was the progression. So it's been a very awesome experience.

I retired from throwing in '97. Jeri Daniels Elder, who was the development coordinator, asked me if I'd be interested in focusing on junior development. Of course, I want to stay in this. This is my love; as you can tell, I'm very passionate. This is great stuff. So Jeri and I have worked side by side in trying to create opportunities with development. It's fascinating to see. I look back and I really hope the throwers now appreciate the opportunities that are there. I think most of them do but I think that until someone goes through something where they don't have something and then through hard work it becomes a reality, only then can you truly get that feeling of "Wow, we made it."

I think our group of throwers is just top, top quality people — athletes and outstanding individuals. Just to see what's happened with the evolution, as far as distances go, too. I think that given the opportunity people will rise to the occasion. This is what we have been trying to say all along — like, hey, give us a chance — put it in this meet, put it in that meet. I think, for the most part, most people were very supportive and so we were very lucky with that.

Bonnie Edmondson, 2004.

As far as professionally, gee, I'd like to say I was a professional hammer thrower [laughter]. I started off as a high school English teacher in Connecticut. I taught English for one year and health education for eight years and was also one of the track and field coaches at the high school while I was the development coordinator. I also was a throws coach at UConn as a graduate assistant.

I currently have been at the State Department of Education in Connecticut for seven years as a health education consultant and HIV prevention coordinator. I was also recently elected as president of my national association, the Society of State Directors of Health, Physical Education, and Recreation. That is very challenging and rewarding. I am also hoping to finish my doctoral dissertation in educational leadership this spring. While working, I've been able to stay active with USATF and participate in clinics around the country. We made an instructional video tape for beginning throwers. One of our junior athletes, her dad was very passionate about creating opportunities for young women and donated some money for us to make an instructional video, which was just great. We printed 500 videos and they are all gone now so we need to do a second printing of it. It's basic hammer throwing. People have really embraced it and young women watch it. I wish I had something like that when I was coming through the pipe line to see and say, "Wow, I can be like that."

I think my job at the State Education Department is not really conducive to having a coaching position as well, so I miss the coaching part significantly since I've been in this job. But I got a call out of the blue about seven months ago from a guy who used to go to college with my brother. He has a fifteen-year-old daughter and a twelve-year-old son who want to learn the hammer. So I said I would be happy to meet and go over some things. That was five months ago and we're meeting on a weekly basis now. She has just taken off. That really makes me smile. I feel very lucky to give back to someone now and the son is doing great as well.

I think I've been very fortunate and I can say without a doubt that my experience as an athlete, coach and coordinator continue to shape my life everyday.

INTERVIEW: CINDY GREINER

(December 4, 1992) I was born in 1957 and the first time I started to compete in track and field was in the fourth grade. Fortunately, for me, my aunt and uncle raised me. I lived in San Diego until I was nine years old, until I was in third grade. My mother had died when I was very young, like five months old. I lived with my grandmother and she had gotten old. My aunt and my uncle were going to raise me from the age of nine on. They lived in South Dakota except that he worked in California in the winter time six months out of the year and South Dakota the other six months. I was really lucky to actually have gotten into that family because I was in a Catholic school and then when I went in to live with them in the third grade, I was put into a public school. I went back to South Dakota. We were in South Dakota usually from about April to October. My uncle had a summer resort.

The following year, my fourth grade year, I came back and went to a public school in San Diego. The public school had an after school program. It was mainly, I think, to just give kids something to do. They had six weeks of team handball, six weeks of softball, six weeks of basketball, and six weeks of track and field. John Adams was the name of the school. They had arts and crafts on Saturday. It was a really great situation. I was from a low to middle class kind of family. It was a place where we could go and hang out and be with our friends. It was all kind of centered around athletics. They had a person, sort of like the coach. I started in fourth grade. We played basketball and I had a great time but I loved track. We played flag football and that was my true love. We were really good.

One thing that was interesting to recall was that I wasn't really fast. I remember running and high jumping. We did this program from fourth to eighth grade with this program after school. We'd come back to our same house we had in San Diego for the six months my uncle would work there and we'd do all these sports together. I don't know what years I did what but I can remember always sprinting, always being on the relays and high jumping — I loved to high jump. I remember jumping 4' 4". No one knew anything about track. We just kind of did this for fun and we tried to do well.

I never was really that fast. We ran on these tracks that were kind of gravel. They weren't cinder and they certainly weren't synthetic. They were kind of dirt gravel. I guess that's kind of maybe the way it is in San Diego. A lot of the kids used to run barefoot. I was really tenderfooted. I had these big old clunky shoes on. I don't even think they were tennis shoes. I think they were leather shoes that were just old school shoes that weren't any good any more for school. I was good athletically like in flag football or even in running; we had four people in our little group and we had maybe fifteen or twenty girls there and there were probably four of them that were faster than me. One day I took my shoes off because that's what they did. It was amazing: I just blew everyone away. Of course, I had bloody feet at the end. But it was worth it. I think I ran from then on without my shoes. It was amazing the difference when I took my shoes off but, you know, you're in fourth or fifth grade and you don't even think of those kinds of things.

So I did that and I competed in these after school programs and I really got to where I loved track. In South Dakota, when I went back there was nothing there, not even a PE program. In San Diego we had PE.

There were quite a bit of drugs going around and I have to say that we, my friends and I, were involved in that to some extent and this was something that got us away from all that. We smoked and did all these things and we were a little bit delinquent in a way. But we loved sports. I think that if it wasn't for the athletic part of it we would have gone just totally in the wrong direction. It was always there and it was something we loved to do. I think we were generally good kids but living in a big city like that and in a lower income family, there were just too many other tempting things to do.

I did not ever want to go back to South Dakota. I loved it in San Diego. But there were things I liked about South Dakota too: we water skied. My aunt and uncle had a summer resort and I got to water ski. It was always those kind of things that interested me.

By the end of my eighth grade year, I was in junior high rather than being in grade school because junior high was seventh, eighth and ninth grades in San Diego. There was a much different situation even though I still competed in the after school program. School itself wasn't as fun. I was in a big junior high. There were a lot of problems with just different cliques of kids and drugs became more prevalent. My aunt and uncle decided, well, we're going to keep our kids in South Dakota. San Diego is not a good place for them. I think that was a really good move because I think I was starting to hang out with the wrong kind of kids. Even these kids that I was hanging out with who were good athletes — athleticism became less important to them — boys and drugs and alcohol and smoking became much more important. I was kind of caught in between. I still wanted to be kind of cool but I still loved track and field. My aunt and uncle made a conscious decision to move to South Dakota and stay there year round. It was somewhat difficult for them because they had this summer resort so he had to make all his money in a five month period of time and then we had to try to live on that.

Well, we got back to South Dakota and I was getting more mature and I was liking South Dakota better and better. They didn't have any type of PE or after school program for girls at all: no track, no basketball no volleyball — nothing. It was a very small school. As a matter of fact, my graduating class was thirty-seven kids. So, anyway, what happened was that I asked the assistant boys' basketball coach if we could have a track team my freshman year. He said, "cool."

I was a freshman and a girlfriend of mine was a senior and she liked to run. So, we got about fifteen of the girls signed up and we had about two meets that year. I was so excited. Maybe track had only been around five years in South Dakota and we were a small school. We were a B school. The coach's name was Gary Miller and I will always thank him for doing that. We didn't have girls track. This was South Dakota. I think now it was probably chauvinistic. That's the way things were. I didn't know that. I don't think he got paid for it and it was a lot of work and he just did it out of the goodness of his heart.

What I did was I long-jumped and I high-jumped. I think I sprinted. I ran like a 75. What was funny was that we didn't have a track. We had a dirt circular area that was probably a little more than 400 meters. It was a practice field for football. They didn't play football out there. I think it was just where they jogged. It was kind of beaten down. We didn't really have workouts. I can remember once in a while we had to run this four mile loop. But all we did was walk it and talked and had a good time. I was serious about track but I didn't like to do stuff like that. We had a high jump area of foam bags that we had the whole four years that I was there. They got broken down more and more by the time I was a senior and we had a metal triangular bar. I scissored. I remember trying to learn to flop and landing on that bar several times and being in the foam pits. I can remember picking that bar up on more than one occasion, probably my first instance of being a javelin thrower, and just wailing on that thing because I hurt myself. I'd land on it on my back and he didn't know what I was doing. It was also kind of funny that the high jump area had a little piece of cement right before you took off so you couldn't wear spikes; the same with the long jump runway. It was this little cement path maybe forty feet long. But, you couldn't wear spikes on it because it was cement. Me and this girl who started the team had our own spikes. My aunt and uncle went out and bought me a pair of spikes from Sears. She had a pair of spikes and we thought they were really cool. I had them the whole four years I was there. We didn't have starting blocks. We didn't have hurdles. I was fast. I liked the 100 but I didn't run it because I had a really close friend who ran it and I would beat her and I didn't want to beat her. It was the only thing that she could win. But I did long jump and I did high jump and I almost always won. But I did the scissors.

My sophomore year we got to go to the conference meet and the state meet. In the state meet I got second in the long jump. My junior year I went to state meet and I won. I was totally shocked. "Wow, I can't believe I won." Also I remember during that time frame trying to find books and magazines on track and field and there was no such thing, especially in South Dakota. There was a girl from an A school and she was very fast. She got to go the junior nationals in Florida. I was thinking that since I won the state meet I was going to get to do that. But I didn't. I didn't have any of those opportunities. I did get to go to an AAU meet in Aberdeen, South Dakota my junior year. I think I won that or got second but I didn't get to go anywhere. I was really disappointed. They also had at South Dakota State University a track and field camp. I really wanted to go to it. It was like $150. So I couldn't go. I really wanted to do this stuff and I really wanted more information. There was no where to get it. So it was kind of a drag for me.

My senior year I went to the state meet in three events. I ran the 200, I high-jumped and I long-jumped. In the high jump I scissored and I jumped 5' 1". In the long jump I got second. Then I ran the 200. Another girl showed me how to use the starting blocks as we were warming up. I can remember thinking, "Sprint out, float the corner and sprint the straight-a-way. That's how I did it. I got sixth in the 200. I don't remember how I placed in the high jump. But I loved the high jump. That was my favorite event. I didn't do it well but I loved it. I think back now, I jumped 5' 1" scissoring, what could I have done with flopping? I wish I could have done that but we didn't have the facilities. It was kind of a big deal when I won the state meet. They put my picture in the paper. All four years of track I was the most valuable athlete on our team. And that was a big deal to me. The girls voted for me. I got a little plaque. I was the big superstar. It didn't go to my head or anything. It was just something I loved.

People were supportive of me. The town was supportive. It was a nice community I lived in. It was Wilmot, South Dakota. It was a small farming community. I graduated from there and said, "What am I going to do?" My sister lived in Oklahoma, I was going to go to college and I was trying to decide what school to go to. Track didn't enter into it although I wanted to run track. I didn't talk to any coaches or anything. I think that I knew that Oklahoma had a track program. I went to the University of Oklahoma because my sister lived in Oklahoma City. They had a track program but they didn't have any scholarships. I ran track there for two years. The first year we had a woman coach. She was also the women's basketball coach. But she wasn't very good.

We had a group of ten women on the team my freshman year in 1975-76. I kept trying to qualify for the AIAW meet in the long jump. I tried and tried but I couldn't do it. It was a big shock for me to go to Oklahoma because we had these regular workouts and that was great but we had to run like eight miles in the morning — every morning. They made me run cross country and I'm definitely not a cross country runner. Maybe today I could do it. At the time I didn't have the experience or background but I would always do terribly and I hated it. I would do it because it was part of track and field.

In my sophomore year I started working more on the pentathlon and I qualified for nationals. I got a stress fracture right before nationals in my ankle but I went anyway. It was at UCLA. I got last. I shouldn't have been there. I couldn't high jump. I couldn't run the curve. It was disappointing but I made the AIAW nationals and that was a big deal.

Starting in my junior year, the men took over the program because they combined it. The woman coach was gone which was actually good. She was a basketball coach and that's all she cared about. I started to train with the men's coaches and they were better. But, my boyfriend, who is now my husband, had joined the army during that time. He was stationed in Washington, D.C. It was a very traumatic period of time for me so I just bagged it. After being there for six months without him, I moved to Washington, D.C., where he was. I tried to go to school there. I wanted to go to the University of Maryland, but it was a very long haul even though it was only seven miles from our house. If you went through D.C., it was an hour drive and once again gas was expensive. If you took the beltway around it was thirty-five miles. I didn't want to go to college and not be able to run track. So I didn't go, I worked. We were pretty poor. I worked at a drug store and just waited. I moved there at Christmas time of 1977. I dropped out of track for almost a year and a half. We got married in May. He got out of the army the following February, so I missed two track seasons.

We moved to Oregon. We lived in a town that was about twenty miles from Oregon State. I just went there because that was the closest school. Oregon was about forty miles away, although Oregon had a better track program. Gary Winkler was there and he was a very good coach. But I still didn't do very well. They made me run the 800. Will Stephens was there. I didn't get a scholarship, although they did have scholarships. We had Kathy Weston on our team and Robin Campbell. I just admired Kathy Weston. I was just in awe of her. I couldn't talk to her. "I can't talk to you; you're an Olympian and I could never be an Olympian." My big goal was to try to qualify for the Olympic trials. In Washington, D.C., I kept running and lifting weights just to stay in shape because I knew I was going to run track.

Will Stephens had his favorites but he still took care of me and Gary took care of me. I was a walk-on and there were a lot of scholarship athletes and I always felt out-classed. It wasn't them that made me feel that way, it was me. So I trained and I competed and went to nationals. I high-jumped and long-jumped because I was doing the heptathlon in 1980-1981. They had already changed it to the heptathlon. I started to train for the heptathlon. I didn't qualify for nationals in the heptathlon. I qualified in the two mile relay because Kathy Weston was there. I ran 2:12 on the two mile relay team. I remember with Will being the coach there I did the 400 meter hurdles. I did all the events. I remember going up against the University of Oregon. It must have been my junior year because Will got really sick with cancer. I don't think he was there my senior year. I think Joni was running the show. They had Lexi Miller, one of the top intermediate hurdlers, and Lisa Nichols. Lexi was very good. There was a big crowd in the stands for this dual. I remember coming around the curve in the 400 and I didn't have any confidence in myself. These people were really good. I was just doing all of these events to add points and stuff. I remember coming around that curve and those two were in front of me. I can remember Will screaming, "You better split them" and I mean this huge crowd of people and I'm like, "Oh my gosh" and I just started sprinting and I did split them. Just things like that pop into my head. I kind of laugh and wonder what kind of things were motivating me. I remember running the Portland indoor and I ran the 800 and Will was there and I ran really terribly. I remember he was totally disgusted with me. I never did that again. That very same year I ran a 2:12 and I think I ran like three minutes or something. It went on and on. This track was like 180 meters. We did lap after lap and we were just dying, this other athlete and me. It was embarrassing. I was embarrassed. Will was embarrassed.

My senior year Joni Huntley came and Gary left. I have to say Joni really inspired me. We fought. She kicked me off the team twice because I was so negative. She'd say, "That looked really good." She was very positive. I'd say, "It looked terrible." She just couldn't handle that after a while. She'd say, "You're out of here." I did score a lot of points my junior year, so I got scholarship tuition for one quarter of my senior year. There were other people that got lots more but I was just happy to get that. It gave me some confidence that someone actually respected me and that I was worth some money. Joni comes and we had these fights. But I loved her. She demanded a lot. She expected a lot. I had to kind of walk on eggshells once in a while. She wanted you to be successful. She knew what it took to be successful. I really respected her. Here she was an Olympian and American record holder. I had jumped 5' 5" with Gary and Joni came in and we had a lot of high jumpers. We had three on scholarship and then there were another three of us that could high jump as well. With Joni, all of a sudden I jumped 5' 11". As soon as I started high jumping well, pretty soon everything else fell into place. Then I started hurdling well. Then I started throwing the shot well. Then I started long jumping well.

Then what happened is we had these good high jumpers, the ones that were on scholarship and they were good but some of them were kind of head cases. We had duals and you could have three athletes in each event. I was very consistent. So I always got to go on the team as a high jumper and a long jumper and the relays. The people who were on scholarship had to have jump offs to see who would take the second two or one spot. I'm on the team in every event I want to be on, practically. I was consistently doing well, especially in my senior year. At a conference meet I did the heptathlon, the 4 × 4, the 4 × 1, the 400 meter hurdles, the 100 meter hurdles, the high jump and the long jump. I did all of those events. I saw Jackie do the same thing. Jackie and I actually competed against each other, since I took those two years off with my husband. Jackie was actually a sophomore or freshman when I was a senior.

I went to the AIAW nationals that year. I finally qualified in the heptathlon, the first time ever it was in Texas. I got fourth. It rained, it was horrible weather. I opened at a reasonable height for me which was 5' 4". I missed my first two attempts. What happened was Joni Huntley was in the stands and she did this little clapping with her hands which meant that I wasn't doing my best. I heard that clapping and thought, "Oh, that's what I'm doing wrong." So I went back and made that attempt. Here it was, the first really big meet that I'm at and I did that. That year I went to the TAC meet and it was in Spokane. They were taking the top four to Russia. I had never been out of the country before in my life. Well, there's no way I'm going to go. Actually in the AIAW nationals Jackie had gotten third and I had gotten fourth. A girl from Nebraska had won and Patsy Walker had gotten second.

I think that about the time that I got out of college I was trying to figure out whether I could continue on. I always tell the story to my kids now that I had a throwing coach and I remember asking him if I should compete after college. He said "No, don't bother. Just go off and get a good job. It's really hard to go beyond college." Then I remember asking Joni Huntley, who was an Olympian, if I should keep training. I wanted to hear "Yes, keep training." We all want to hear that. We all want to give up our entire lives to be track stars. Joni said, "Oh, absolutely, you're going to make the Olympic team." She was the first person that ever said that to me and here she was, an Olympian. I use that with my kids. I said, in 1981 I had a coach that probably didn't know me as well and probably wasn't as competitive in that same kind of sphere. One coach was telling me give it up and three and a half years later I got fourth at the Olympic Games. I always use that with them: don't let people tell you that if you have something in your heart that you want to do, you can't do it.

So, anyway, after I got out of college I had to figure out how we were going to support ourselves. I was married and my husband was working. But you just can't go off and play track. You have to help out. I was fortunate that I was able to get on with Athletics West, which was run by Nike. They had brought some coaches in from Poland. They brought the male coach in, Andrzej

Krzesinska. He was going to coach some of the Athletics West pole vaulters and decathletes. His wife, who was a dentist in Poland — and she actually happened to be also the gold medalist in the long jump and world record holder back in the 50s — she came too. So they said, when I went to approach Nike to see if they could help me with some money, they said, "Boy, do we have an opportunity for you." They really didn't want any hepthathletes of my caliber, right? If you're the world record holder, yeah. They were mostly distance runners. They said, "Well, we'll give you some money and sponsor you but you'll have to train under this coach." I was like, "Oh! I wanted to train under the coach at the University of Oregon." Joni had moved on. They said, "Yeah, you can train down here in Eugene but you have to train under Ela Krzesinska." And I was like, "Oh no." But actually it turned out pretty well. The first year was a little rough because they were definitely Eastern European, Polish, and this is in 1985. Most of the U.S. athletes weren't being trained by any type of Eastern European methods. So some of the stuff we did for warm-ups and all that were not really very American. The stuff you see today, all those weird kind of drills, the Eastern Europeans did that but the Americans didn't at the time. So here I was doing all these drills. People were looking at me — weird. They would have us do these crazy things. For example, when we would warm up, we would play soccer. No Americans played soccer. We'd jog two laps and then they'd stretch and then you did your work out. They never did anything like that. Their workouts were not centered on doing laps on the track. You didn't run 400s. You ran your workout on the long jump runway. You'd take twenty jumps that day. You'd go over 200 hurdles but you would never spend hours and hours just running on the track. Put a hurdle in front of you for goodness sakes; you're a hepthathlete. I think over time, most of the American coaches have transitioned into that theory. You have a lot of work to do. So those were my coaches.

I made the Olympic team in 1984 with them. In my event at the time, Jane Frederick was probably one of the top three hepthathletes in the world and she didn't make the team. She no-heighted in the high jump. And so, there I was. I made the team and got third place. It was actually between me and my training partner, Patsy Walker. It came down to the 800. We'd been training together for a year or two in Eugene. She moved out there and trained under Ela. Actually Patsy was a great high school and a great college athlete. She had a lot of potential. So 1984 is really important. You have to make an Olympic team to continue in track and field, to get sponsorship, coaches and all that other stuff so you can keep training. The first day was pretty even. I was a much better long jumper than she was. She was a much better javelin thrower. We were about the same in the 800. And so, it was pretty even after the first day. Like, oh no. Jane had already no-heighted in the high jump. So, we knew Jackie was in the number one spot; Jodi Anderson was in the number two spot and the third was up for grabs. And we knew that and it was us and we were training partners. I remember we long-jumped and she beat me in the long jump. I'm a pretty good long jumper and she beat me in the long jump. So then, I was behind. And then we get ready to throw the javelin and I'm a terrible javelin thrower. I'm the worst javelin thrower there is. And I beat her in the javelin. So then we went into the 800 and I think there might have been eighteen points difference or something, some minuscule amount. All I had to do was just stay in front of her. I remember running the 800 and it was dark. The lights were on in the L.A. Coliseum. We were coming around that home stretch and I remember I was in a box. Jackie had me in a box. I remember yelling at her 'cause Patsy went flying around me. I remember yelling at Jackie to move. She moved out and so then I could go and chase Patsy. I ended up beating her in the 800 and making the team. But it was so close. I only beat her by 51 points. It was 6204 to 6153. So then I made the team. It was tough for both of us because we both wanted to be on the Olympic team together.

That was my first Olympic trials. And then, of course, I went to the Olympics and got fourth and that was great. I didn't even realize that I was in the money. I think there were only around 100 points between fourth and first. It was just so new to me. I couldn't even believe I was there in the first place. It's too bad that I wasn't a little more mature when that happened. We had the boycott from some of the Eastern Bloc countries so it was a little easier to medal that year. That was exciting and everything and it helped me establish myself as a credible hepthathlete and be able to continue to keep competing.

I kept competing with those same coaches through the '88 Olympics. I really felt like after '84 that I was on my way to becoming one of the top three hepthathletes in the world. But it just never happened. I trained really hard and everything. I do think that I had the tools but maybe mentally I wasn't as tough as I probably could have been. I don't know. Reflecting back — why could I never put a meet together? I remember the Polish coach, Ela, I'm very close to her, I remember her saying to me "You never have any luck. You have the worst luck of anybody I ever met." I don't know if it was luck or bad focus. I even think of Barcelona. I was high jumping so well in practice a couple of days before. If I jump well in practice, I jump really well in the meet. I get to the meet and my steps were off and I couldn't figure it out. It was just things like that. You look back and you think there are some things that I coulda, shoulda, woulda done, but wasn't 100 per cent focused as I should have been. It is hard in the heptathlon because there are seven events. I think of people like Jackie, not to take anything away from Jackie because she's great, but Bobby helped her a lot. He took a lot of pressure off her. I think when you're out there and you're stressed out and you're trying to make things happen sometimes you just need someone to take over for you. I think that's why they made such a great pair. He knew that if she was sagging he could get her back on track. She had a ton going for herself but that was probably just that ten percent over the top that helped her shatter the world record every time versus just breaking it.

In '88 I still had Ela for a coach. I got injured one year. I think it was '85. I came back in '86 and I was shocked at how much I didn't improve relative to some of the others. Still in the top three in the U.S. and the top ten in the world, but I was hoping to be up in the top three or four in the world.

After the '88 Olympic Games I finished my MBA. I had been going to graduate school for the last three years while I was training. Then I had gotten a job at Hewlett Packard and moved to Boise and retired. But I didn't really want to retire. I was 31 at the time. I really didn't want to retire because I started track late in South Dakota and didn't really get into the elite level until my senior year of college. I really didn't feel like I was finished. As it turned out, Ed Jacoby lived over here. So after taking a year off and working at H P, I talked him into coaching me. He was a men's jump coach for the Olympics and a really great jump coach. So I trained under Ed. It was great training under Ela. She helped me with my long jumping and hurdling. Then I came and trained under Ed and he really helped me a lot. He was great to train with. I was still working at H P. I would go and work out at 6 o'clock at night. He would show up there every night. It would just be him and me every night. If it was decent weather we'd be out in the stadium with the big football lights on — just me and him. If it was in the winter time, we'd be inside the basketball arena. There was a little track upstairs. It was just him and I doing the workouts together. My husband would come up and film once in a while.

But that is what made '92 probably good for me. I had this great relationship with Ed; I didn't have very much pressure anymore. I had a job and I knew that this was my last go-around. I was going to be 35 at the '92 Olympics. I went into it probably with a pretty good attitude. I still thought I could medal, but if I didn't it wouldn't be the end of the world. The first Olympics I got fourth, the second Olympics I got eighth, and the last Olympics I got ninth. But each Olympics I did better. I scored higher. It's pretty cool because right between fifth, sixth, seventh, eighth, ninth there are probably 50 or 100 points separating me. Whereas first, second, third there's probably 500, 600 points away.

Anyway, I felt like it was a really great ride. I met a lot of great people. It was fun at the end. In '92 a lot of people came up to me and said, "We're going to miss watching you." You don't realize that you have that impact on other people. You have such great friends. Even today, there are still people that I communicate with. Even as hectic and busy as our lives are and I'm living up here in Boise it really was a big part of my life and it made me who I am, I think. It really made you open your eyes to different cultures; how different people attack things; how people become successful; how to motivate yourself and how to organize; how to have compassion for others — all those things. To look at the glass as half full; it's not half empty. I think a lot of us learned in track that you come in as a prima donna, but you learn a lot along the way. The world does not revolve around you. It was a great experience for me.

INTERVIEW: ROBYNE JOHNSON

(December 1, 2005) My father was a track guy. Actually he did the same events that I did: the long jump, triple jump and the hurdles. He was the junior college national record holder at

Compton Junior College in California. He became a track coach after he finished his career. He kind of always wanted me to do some events. But I didn't want to run in front of people. It actually took one of his friend's daughters who was running in a track meet, an all comers meet in California, who said, "Oh, why don't you try it?" I wound up winning. I was nine or ten years old. Once I won I kind of caught the bug. I guess it's not so bad to run in front of people.

After that, I remember the little organizations at parks. Those rec centers were really popular then around '76, '77. One of the rec clubs was going to the Arco Jesse Owens Meet, and I was asked to go. I don't know. I was always the fastest in my junior high, grammar school and everything like that. Alright, I'll go. I ended up long-jumping there and winning. Actually Jesse Owens put the medal around my neck and everything. It was wonderful. I have pictures from that and I have his signature on my medal. I won a trip to the national Arco Jesse Owens Games where I competed against Jackie Joyner-Kersee. I met her for the first time. I wound up making a junior team with her in 1980 and we were roommates. So it's just kind of funny in track how you keep running into the same people.

It's really been in my family forever, it seems, for me. I remember seeing my father compete. I just got the bug. I just started competing and I wound up doing fairly well. We went to the age group nationals, the AAU nationals and the junior Olympics.

I went to a very good high school in Berkeley, California. The Berkeley High School track team, in 1981, won both the boys and girls high school state championships. It was the first time that it was ever done in California history and it still remains the most points ever scored at a high school meet. We broke five national records that night. So it was great.

I went on to the University of Texas. I was a five time All-American in the triple jump. I loved it there and competed in a national championship in my freshman year in 1982.

I competed in four Olympic trials. I competed a lot longer than I should have [laughter]. I competed until I was thirty-seven and I almost PRed at thirty-seven. I competed in the '88 trials. I was fourth. I decided I was quitting track and I retired. It lasted a year. I came back again in '90 and actually did fairly well. '90 was USA vs. Great Britain. I was on that indoor team. In '91, in the indoor world championships, I finished eighth. '92 was probably my best year. I was ranked number two U.S. and number seven in the world. I was ranked in the top ten for the women's triple jump for ten years in a row. I guess that's a good thing. Like I said, '92 was my best year. I finished second at the Olympic trials. Unfortunately, the triple jump was not an official Olympic event. It was an exhibition. But I kept going. I got to go over to Europe a couple of times. To me, it was just a blast.

In '96, I didn't have a great year. Unfortunately, my mother passed away two months before the Olympic trials and I just really couldn't get myself together. But I still kept going.

In 2000, I competed in my last Olympic trials. I retired right after that meet. I had almost PRed a couple of weeks before the trials.

It was a great career though. It took me all over the world. I met all my friends. It's just the best experience I've ever had in track and field. And now I continue: I'm the development coordinator for USATF in the women's triple jump. I'm the director of track and field and cross country and the head track coach at Boston University. It's gone on. I coached at Penn State for six years; Ryder University for two; Cal Berkeley for ten and now I'm at Boston University. So, nineteen years later, I'm still involved in track and field, coaching. I think I competed for twenty-three years. I've had great experiences in high school, college and after college. So I love track and field [laughter].

13

1993

The Outdoor Nationals

The USA/Mobil Outdoor Track and Field Championships were held in Hayward Field, University of Oregon, Eugene, Oregon from June 15 to 19.

Filip Bondy of the *New York Times*, wrote an article entitled, "Tolbert's Victory Prevents a Devers Sweep."

...At a hot and humid Hayward Field, Tolbert overcame favorite Gail Devers, plus medical problems that included a torn hamstring, stress fractures in both her feet and chronic anemia. She edged Devers in a photo finish, winning the women's 100 meter hurdles in 12.72 seconds to foil an historic attempt at a double by her more famous rival.

...For Devers, who captured the 100-meter dash on Thursday, it is always something. No American athlete, male or female, has ever pulled off a sprint-hurdle double at the national championships. She almost did it at the 1992 Olympics in Barcelona, but tripped over the final hurdle and failed. Something else in Spain went unnoticed: her tumble also caused Tolbert to slow and to finish fourth in that race.

Tonight, Devers started too slowly and didn't care to press the matter. Her hamstrings were sore from a total of six heats and finals in three days.

"I made the team," Devers said, about qualifying for the world championships in Stuttgart, Germany, with her second-place finish in 12.73 seconds. "It doesn't make sense to kill yourself to win a race when you just have to make the team. I could be lying on the ground."

While Devers was cooling down after the race, Tolbert was bawling with relief. She received comfort from an old friend, Pearlie McDaniel, from her hometown of Washington, D.C. Tolbert had missed the indoor season because of the torn hamstring and an assortment of other ailments. "I wasn't feeling good about myself," Tolbert said. Now, she did.

In other finals that produced the fastest times in the world this year, Sandra Farmer-Patrick won the women's 400-meter hurdles in 53.96.

As the national championships ended today before a near-capacity crowd of 10,653, two other races produced the best times in the world this year. One of these performances was the 50.43 that Jearl Miles ran to win the 400 meters.

In the women's 200 meter dash today, Gwen Torrence held off Dannette Young and Michelle Finn before her hamstring began to ache again. Torrence crossed the finish line in 22.57, then limped through a victory lap. She now will have to decide whether she is strong enough to compete in both the 100 and 200 at Stuttgart.

Not all the drama involved impressive times. The women's 1,500 meter race was ponderous, but created both an uplifting and heart-wrenching story. Annette Peters, the local schoolteacher from Eugene who won the 3,000 meters on Thursday, became a double-winner here before some boisterous hometown fans with a come-from-behind victory in 4:11.53.

Second place went to Alisa Hill who was fading. Several yards behind, Suzy Hamilton, the telegenic star of sneaker commercials, surged at Gina Procaccio for the third and last spot on the United States team. As Hamilton neared the finish line, she collapsed and tumbled onto the track. She stayed there for several minutes, a fourth-place finisher with no ticket to Germany.

"I had nothing left," Hamilton said, after being helped off the track. "I just completely tightened up."

The team selected here to represent the United States at the World Track and Field Championships in Stuttgart, Germany, Aug. 13–22, is a relatively strong one, but there are some weak spots. Ernie Gregoire, the women's coach stated, "We'll take our lumps this year, but we are building." "We'll be ready for the '96 Olympics."

---

100 meters

Shawn Price reported for *Track & Field News*: "...Devers came out even with NCAA winner Holli Hyche and previous national champions Gwen Torrence and Michelle Finn, then established a lead after 20m. She increased her margin all the way to the finish in recording a windy 10.82 and becoming the eighth different winner of the event in as many years."

1. Gail Devers, Nike International   10.82 w
2. Gwen Torrence, Mazda Track Club   11.03
3. Michelle Finn, Santa Monica Track Club   11.07
4. Wenda Vereen, Goldwin Track Club   11.13
5. Sheila Echols, unattached   11.14
6. Holli Hyche, Indiana State University   11.18
7. Cheryl Taplin, Louisiana State University   11.19
8. Teresa Neighbors, Mizuno Houston   11.24

200 meters

Gwen Torrence "...charged out, and was even with Dannette Young and Chryste Gaines through the curve, with Michelle Finn a meter back. Torrence pulled away for a clear lead but had to slow at the finish as she recorded a windy 22.57. Across the line she started to hobble, this time favoring her left leg," wrote Shawn Price.

1. Gwen Torrence, Mazda Track Club   22.57 w
2. Dannette Young, Reebok Racing Club   22.68
3. Michelle Finn, Santa Monica Track Club   22.81
4. Flirtisha Harris, Seton Hall University   22.99
5. Wenda Vereen, Goldwin Track Club   23.04
6. Kim Graham, Clemson University   23.09
7. Chryste Gaines, unattached   23.19
8. Carlette Guidry-White, Nike International   23.21

400 meters

According to *Track & Field News*: "...Keeping her prerace strategy allowed the 26-year-old Miles to claim her first national title. "I wanted to be in the lead with 300m to go and I think I was," she said. "With 40m to go I was very tired. What I try to do when I'm very tired is to keep my form."

"Running in lane 5, the 5 ft. 7, 130 lb. Miles followed Maicel Malone down the backstraight. Heading into the curve Miles gained control and ran away with a world-leading 50.43."

1. Jearl Miles, Reebok Racing Club   50.43
2. Natasha Kaiser-Brown, Southern California Cheetahs   50.93
3. Michele Collins, unattached   51.77
4. Youlanda Warren, Louisiana State University   52.13

5. Maicel Malone, Mazda Track Club	52.21
6. Terri Dendy, Anderson International	52.40
7. Rochelle Stevens, Maybelline Track Club	52.56
8. Kendra Mackey, Mazda Track Club	54.80

800 meters

"Debbie Marshall led the first lap in 59.6, followed closely by last year's Olympians, Julie Jenkins, Meredith Rainey and Joetta Clark. With 150m to go, Clark and Jenkins flew past the fading Marshall, with Rainey in close pursuit," reported Bob Hersh for *Track & Field News*. "Clark soon established a commanding lead and won the race decisively in 2:01.47 for her fourth national outdoor title."

1. Joetta Clark, Foot Locker Athletic Club	2:01.47
2. Amy Wickus, University of Wisconsin	2:02.22
3. Julie Jenkins-Donley, Reebok Racing Club	2:02.23
4. Meredith Rainey, Nike Boston	2:02.27
5. Sarah Renk, University of Wisconsin	2:03.49
6. Nekita Beasley, Atoms Track Club	2:03.72
7. Debbie Marshall, Tinley Track Club	2:04.17
8. Nicole Teter, Nike Coast Track Club	2:04.98

1500 meters

Ed Fox reported for *Track & Field News*: "Regina Jacobs towed the field through the first 1200, but around the penultimate curve her legs turned to lead and Alisa Hill bounced ahead. Suzy Hamilton and Gina Procaccio followed Hill, and that looked like the team for Stuttgart.

"But whoa! A white-and-blue blur flew around the last curve and simply ran past everyone. It was hometown heroine Annette Peters, showing the same newfound finishing speed that had won her the 3000. Her 31.4 last 200 made her the winner in 4:11.53, as Hill struggled home 0.90 back."

1. Annette Peters, Nike West	4:11.53
2. Alisa Hill, Foot Locker Athletic Club	4:12.43
3. Gina Procaccio, Sallie Mae Track Club	4:12.51
4. Suzy Hamilton, Reebok Racing Club	4:12.73
5. Kathy Franey, Reebok Racing Club	4:13.54
6. Darcy Arreola, Nike Coast	4:14.04
7. Kristen Seabury, Nike Boston	4:16.70
8. Claudette Groenendaal, Santa Monica Track Club	4:18.53

2000 meter steeplechase (exhibition)

1. Marisa Sutera, Westchester Track Club	7:27.30
2. Tami Micham-Grimes, Northeast Louisiana University	7:45.02
3. Kelly Conery, Club Northwest	8:16.58
4. Laurie Black, Crunch Track Club	8:45.31
(only competitors)	

3000 meters

Sean Hartnett wrote for *Track & Field News*:

The 3000 field was full of questions. Fortunately, local 1st-grade teacher Annette Peters had the answers—a pace few could sustain, and a kick that no one could match.

Laura Mykytok pulled the field through a quick 69.5 opener, then Peters took over and set the cruise at 71.5 pace for the next five laps. At 1600m (4:44.9), half the field was still in contention, with Shelly Steely on Peter's shoulder. But another 71-second lap shaped the race as Peters and Steely pulled 10m clear.

At the bell, Peters abandoned the 71-second pace. Lifting on the backstretch, she opened a 2m gap on the straining Steely, and hit high gear over the last furlong (31.8) to claim a 25m victory in a U. S.-leading 8:48.59.

1. Annette Peters, Nike West   8:48.59
2. Shelly Steely, Mizuno Track Club   8:52.99
3. Sheila Carrozza, Team Run-Tex   8:55.03
4. Gina Procaccio, Sallie Mae Track Club   8:56.80
5. Kathy Franey, Reebok Racing Club   9:02.17
6. Libbie Johnson, Mizuno Track Club   9:04.41
7. Clare Eichner, University of Wisconsin, Madison   9:05.93
8. Rosalind Taylor, Sallie Mae Track Club   9:06.41

5000 meters
1. Christine McNamara, unattached   16:11.85
2. Carmen Troncoso, Nike Texas   16:24.29
3. Kate Fonshell, Nike Boston   16:27.30
4. Heather Shutt-Warner, University of Alabama   16:32.26
5. Maria Pazarentzos, Reebok Racing Club   16:33.85
6. Amy Legacki, Nike Indiana   16:34.39
7. Stacia Prey, Nike Boston   16:36.72
8. Shelley Taylor, University of Arkansas   16:41.44

10,000 meters
"...Jennings forged to the lead and through the first kilo in 3:05.3, roughly a 30:30 pace that at halfway moderated to 31:50," wrote Sieg Lindstrom for *Track & Field News*.

"On her heels were Anne Marie Letko and Elaine Van Blunk. Here was the Stuttgart team, but Letko and Van Blunk lacked times better than the Stuttgart standard of 32:40.0. At 2km, when Letko went up front, the trio tacitly agreed to pursue qualifiers and began alternating the lead. With one lap left Jennings pulled out a 66.4 kick and charged away to win in 31:57.83. Letko's 32:00.37 and Van Blunk's 32:07.19 were PRs and the desired WC qualifiers."

1. Lynn Jennings, Nike International   31:57.83 MR
2. Anne Marie Letko, Nike Running Room   32:00.37
3. Elaine Van Blunk, Nike Running Room   32:07.19
4. Chris McNamara, unattached   32:50.84
5. Laurie Gomez-Henes, adidas Track Club   32:55.24
6. Trina Painter, New Balance Track Club   32:59.31
7. Inge Schuurmans, Mountain West Track Club   33:39.37
8. Caryn Landau, Georgetown University   33:48.89

100 meter hurdles
"...Tolbert was first out of the blocks, with Devers close behind. Nothing, not even the ten intervening hurdles, changed that, and Tolbert crossed the line first with a windy 12.72, a scant 0.01 ahead," reported Dave Johnson for *Track & Field News*.

1. Lynda Tolbert, Nike International   12.72 w
2. Gail Devers, Nike International   12.73
3. Dawn Bowles, Foot Locker Track Club   12.89
4. Marsha Guialdo, Nike Coast Track Club   12.97
5. Cheryl Dickey, Nike South   13.00

6. Monifa Taylor, University of Florida   13.07
7. Doris Williams, Goldwin Track Club   13.14
8. Tiffany Smith, unattached   13.21

400 meter hurdles

"Leading from the start, Sandra Farmer-Patrick had an uncommonly clean and efficient race for one who sometimes appears to be leaping hedges and fences instead of skimming hurdles on a synthetic track," reported Dave Johnson. "The Olympic silver medalist's time of 53.96 was the fastest in the world this year...."

1. Sandra Farmer-Patrick, Reebok
    Racing Club   53.96
2. Kim Batten, Reebok Racing Club   54.57
3. Tonja Buford, Mazda Track Club   54.63
4. Trevaia Williams, Atoms Track Club   55.94
5. Kellie Roberts, Anderson International   56.28
6. Sandra Cummings, unattached   58.13
7. Janeene Vickers, unattached   60.10

10,000 meter walk

Bob Bowman reported in *Track & Field News*: "Coming from behind is not an easy task in this event, but that's what veteran Debbi Lawrence did in winning her sixth title in the last decade.

"Teresa Vaill, winner of the World Cup Trials over an injured Lawrence, had taken control at the

Sandra Farmer Patrick at the 1993 National Championships. Photograph by Victah Sailer, ©www.photorun.net

gun and looked determined to win her first crown after many close misses. It was again not to be as Lawrence reeled her in over the last 3km for a 45:55–46:04 victory."

1. Debbi Lawrence, Natural Sport Track Club   45:55
2. Teresa Vaill, unattached   46:04
3. Sara Standley, unattached   48:16
4. Debby Van Orden, unattached   48:47
5. Lynda Brubaker, unattached   49:06
6. Dana Yarbrough, unattached   49:07
7. Susan Armenta, Parkside Athletic Club   49:22
8. Cindy March, Golden Gate Race Walkers   49:32

High jump

For *Track & Field News*, Kevin Saylors reported: "...Five cleared 6' 2¼" and any clearance at 6' 3½" would have won the competition — no one could. Both Hughes and Connie Teaberry shared clean records through 6' 2¼". In their jump-off, each missed a fourth time at 6' 3½" before the bar retreated to 6' 2¾". Hughes, jumping first, cleared to apply the pressure. A Teaberry miss later, she had again won in Eugene."

1. Tanya Hughes, Nike Coast Track Club   6' 2¾"
2. Connie Teaberry, Goldwin Track Club   6' 2¼"
3. Sue Rembao, Reebok Racing Club   6' 2¼"
4. Tisha Waller, Goldwin Track Club   6' 2¼"

5. Angela Bradburn, unattached	6' 2¼"
6. J. C. Broughton, Nike Coast Track Club	6' 1¼"
and Karol Damon, Goldwin Track Club	
8. Denise Gaztambide, unattached	6' 1¼"

Long jump

Jackie Joyner-Kersee "...soared in impeccable fashion before calling it a day, cranking out four marks better than anyone else could manage. Three times she produced the best U.S. distance of the year, topped by a 23' ½" in the fourth round," reported Garry Hill for *Track & Field News.*

1. Jackie Joyner-Kersee, unattached	23' ½" w
2. Sheila Echols, unattached	21' 10" w
3. Sharon Couch, Asics International	21' 6¾" w
4. Camille Jackson, Louisiana State University	21' 2" w
5. Trinette Johnson, Florida State University	20' 9¾" w
6. Julie Bright, Mizuno Track Club	20' 7¼" w
7. Shana Williams, Seton Hall University	20' 6¼"
8. Tamara Cuffee, George Mason University	20' ½" w

Triple jump

Garry Hill writes: "One of the best tactical moves in the sport is to get out ahead early, and that's just what Claudia Haywood did, having more than a foot's margin over favored Sheila Hudson at the end of the first round.... She applied even more pressure in the second round, becoming the second-farthest American ever with a windy 45' 5¾"."

1. Claudia Haywood, Athletes-in-Action	45' 5¾" w
2. Sheila Hudson, Mizuno Track Club	44' 9¾" w
3. Cynthea Rhodes, unattached	44' 2¾" w
4. Wendy Brown, unattached	44' 1½" w
5. Lisa Austin, University of Texas, Arlington	42' 10¼" w
6. Robyne Johnson, unattached	42' 7½" w
7. Leah Kirklin, Mazda Track Club	42' 7" w
8. Tiombé Hurd, James Madison University	42' 4¾" w

Shot put

Connie Price-Smith became "...the fourth woman ever to win a nationals shot/discus double three times.

"The issue was never in doubt as Price-Smith opened with the longest throw of the day, and on each of her four (there's that number again) subsequent legal throws was better than runner-up Ramona Pagel could manage.

"It was the fifth year in a row that the two had finished in some permutation of 1–2," reported Garry Hill.

1. Connie Price-Smith, Nike Coast Track Club	62' 5"
2. Ramona Pagel, unattached	58' 1¼"
3. Stevanie Wadsworth, Texas Christian University	56' 3"
4. Melisa Weis, University of Colorado	54' 6"
5. Dawn Dumble, University of California, Los Angeles	54' 3¾"
6. Peggy Pollock, unattached	54' 3¼"
7. Eileen Vanisi, University of Texas	51' 11¼"
8. Beth Bunge, unattached	51' 9"

Discus

"Except for a second round foul, Connie Price-Smith improved with each throw, having three good enough to win. She finally iced the cake with the biggest American toss of the year, 208' 5", leading her to animated hand-slapping with Carla Garrett, whose 193' 4" gave her the third Stuttgart spot," reported Ed Fox.

1. Connie Price-Smith, Nike Coast Track Club	208'	5"
2. Kris Kuehl, unattached	197'	4"
3. Carla Garrett, Nike Coast Track Club	193'	4"
4. Janet Hill, Goldwin Track Club	184'	10"
5. Danyel Mitchell, Louisiana State University	184'	8"
6. Pam Dukes, Nike Coast Track Club	184'	1"
7. Lacy Barnes, Nike International Track Club	183'	2"
8. Lynda Lipson, University of North Carolina	181'	

Javelin

Kevin Saylors reported, "Two-time Olympian Donna Mayhew wasted no time in establishing herself as the best javelin thrower in town. The 5 ft. 4, 150 lb. Nike Coaster, entering the meet as the only U.S. 200-footer of the year, effectively ended the competition by reaching just 183' 10" on her first throw. No one else came within a foot; Mayhew herself had three longer throws. Even her sole qualifying round effort (191–1) would have won."

1. Donna Mayhew, Nike Coast Track Club	206'	7"
2. Heather Berlin, unattached	182'	8"
3. Erica Wheeler, Mizuno Track Club	181'	1"
4. Nicole Carroll, unattached	176'	11"
5. Lynda Lipson, University of North Carolina	172'	11"
6. Meg Foster, unattached	172'	8"
7. Ashley Selman, Oregon Track Club	171'	
8. Cindy Herceg, University of Florida	170'	5"

Hammer throw (exhibition)

1. Sonja Fitts, unattached	180'	2"
2. Elizabeth Legault, unattached	175'	5"
3. Bonnie Edmondson, Nike Coast Track Club	173'	7"
4. Christel Kittredge, University of Rhode Island	163'	6"
5. Jana Tucker, Idaho State University	157'	1"
6. Claudine Rice, Westfield State University	156'	11"
7. Lisa Peterson, St. John's University	156'	10"
8. Kim Johnson, Syracuse University	152'	11"

Heptathlon

"In her first heptathlon since retaining her Olympic title, Jackie Joyner-Kersee prevailed over Eugene's renowned pollen and her breathing problems while compiling a year — pacing total of 6770 points.... [She] never was even remotely threatened by her foes and her windy long jump of 23' 2½" served to lock up her third consecutive nationals win," reported Jon Hendershott.

1. Jackie Joyner-Kersee, unattached	6770
2. Kym Carter, unattached	6038
3. DeDee Nathan, Nike Indiana Track Club	6038
4. Kelly Blair, Oregon Track Club	5828

5. Shana Williams, Seton Hall University	5641
6. Clare Look-Jaeger, Nike Coast Track Club	5557
7. Denise Brungardt, Wichita State University	5513
8. Terry Roy, University of Connecticut	5513

Team scores:

1. Reebok Racing Club	58
2. Nike Coast Track Club	53½
3. Nike Track Club	30

The Indoor Nationals

The USA Mobil National Indoor Track and Field Championships were held in Madison Square Garden on Friday, February 26.

The *New York Times* on Saturday featured a photograph of the finish of the 60-meter dash with Gail Devers winning and Carlette Guidry-White to her right. Filip Bondy wrote,

> ...Devers set an American indoor record of 6.99 seconds, starting fast and then rocketing faster halfway down the track to put away Teresa Neighbors, a distant second in 7.21. Devers was only seven hundredths of a second off the world indoor record, set this year by Irina Privalova of Russia. Devers's stride, oft maligned and tinkered with, approached perfection.
>
> ...Lynn Jennings continued her remarkable season, uninterrupted by an emergency appendectomy on Dec. 31 in Britain. "The incision was tiny," she insisted. The week after surgery, Jennings ran 65 miles. Last night, Jennings kicked passed Margareta Keszeg of Romania for a graceful victory in the women's 3,000 meters, at 9:00.52.
>
> .... Debbi Lawrence won the Grand Prix award as the women's indoor champion with her triumph in the 3,000-meter race walk.

60 meters
1. Gail Devers, Nike International Track Club	6.99	AR
2. Teresa Neighbors, Mizuno/Houston Track Club	7.21	
3. Michelle Finn, Santa Monica Track Club	7.24	

200 meters
1. Rochelle Stevens, Maybelline Track Club	23.51
2. Dyan Webber, unattached	24.02
3. Flirtisha Harris, Seton Hall University	24.59

400 meters (2 section final)
1. Jillian Richardson, Canada	53.24
2. Jearl Miles, Reebok Racing Club	53.26
3. Kim Batten, Reebok Racing Club	53.95

800 meters
1. Maria Mutola, Nike International/Mozambique	1:59.63	MR
2. Joetta Clark, Foot Locker Track Club	2:01.60	
3. Meredith Rainey, unattached	2:03.67	

Mobil mile
1. Shelly Steely, Mizuno Track Club	4:30.23
2. Alisa Hill, Foot Locker Track Club	4:31.02
3. Jasmin Jones, adidas USA	4:39.21

3000 meters
1. Lynn Jennings, Nike International Track Club
9:00.52
2. Margareta Keszeg, Romania
9:02.23
3. Kathy Franey, Reebok Racing Club
9:04.75

3000 meter walk
1. Debbi Lawrence, Natural Sport
12:35.79 MR
2. Victoria Herazo, California Walkers
13:08.73
3. Sara Standley, unattached
13:48.24

60 meter hurdles
1. Michelle Freeman, Nike Track Club/Jamaica
7.90   MR
2. LaVonna Martin, Reebok Racing Club
7.93
3. Dawn Bowles, Foot Locker Track Club
8.11

4 × 400 meter relay
1. Seton Hall University
3:45.12
   (Julia Sandiford/Barbados, Shana Williams, Keisha Caine, Flirtisha Harris)
2. Seton Hall University "B"
3:50.59
3. New York Pioneer Club
3:57.83

High jump
1. Yolanda Henry, unattached
6' 3½"
2. Angela Bradburn, Nike Track Club
6' 2¼"
3. J.C. Broughton, University of Arizona
6' ¾"

Long jump
1. Christy Opara, Southern California Cheetahs/Nigeria
20' 7¾"
2. Sharon Couch, Asics Track Club
20' 6½"
3. Shana Williams, Seton Hall University
20' 6½"

Triple jump
1. Sheila Hudson, Mizuno Track Club
44' 3¼" MR
2. Cynthea Rhodes, unattached
43' ½"
3. Tiombé Hurd, James Madison University
42' ¾"

Shot put
1. Connie Price-Smith, Nike Coast Track Club
59' 9½"
2. Ramona Pagel, unattached
59' 4¼"
3. Pam Dukes, Nike Coast Track Club
54' 3¼"

20 pound weight throw
1. Sonja Fitts, unattached
61' 1¼"
2. Pam Dukes, Nike Coast Track Club
61' 1¼"
3. Bonnie Edmundson, Commonwealth Track Club
57' 9"

Team scores:
1. Seton Hall University   12
2. Reebok Racing Club   11
3. Nike International Track Club,   10
     Nike Coast Track Club, Mizuno Track Club

Sunkist Invitational (5 women's events): Los Angeles, February 20

50 meters
1. Gail Devers, Nike International Track Club
6.10   MR, AR

440 yards
1. Sandie Richards, Jamaica   52.9   MR

800 meters
1. Maria Mutola, Mozambique   2:01.00   MR

Mile
1. Shelly Steely, Mizuno Track Club   4:32.40

50 meter hurdles
1. Jackie Joyner-Kersee, World Class Athletic Club   6.84   MR, AR

4th IAAF World Indoor Track and Field Championships: Toronto and Ontario, Canada, March 12–14

"Lynn Jennings had a great dream," reported the *New York Times*. The article continues:

In one year, she would win world track and field championships indoors and outdoors plus the world cross country title outdoors.

It may happen, but not this year. Tonight, in the world indoor championships, Yvonne Murray, a 28-year-old Briton, won the women's 3,000-meter title. The 32-year-old Jennings, from Newmarket, N.H., took the bronze medal, as she did in the Olympic 10,000 meters last year.... Jennings has won the last three world cross country championships, and on March 28 in Spain she will go for four straight. In tonight's race, she said, she and the other 3,000 meter finalists had themselves to blame when they let Murray get away.

60 meters
1. Gail Devers   6.95
5. Teresa Neighbors   7.26

200 meters
5. Wenda Vereen   23.34
6. Dyan Webber   23.34

400 meters
3. Jearl Miles   51.37
6. Kim Batten   52.70

800 meters
3. Joetta Clark   1:59.86

1500 meters
9. Alisa Hill   4:29.67

3000 meters
3. Lynn Jennings   9:03.78
8. Kathleen Franey   9:13.16

60 meter hurdles
2. LaVonna Martin-Floreal   7.99

4 × 400 meter relay
3. United States   3:32.50
   (Trevaia Williams, Terri Dendy, Dyan Webber, Natasha Kaiser-Brown)

Medley relay
1. United States   3:45.90
   (Joetta Clark, Wenda Vereen, Kim Batten, Jearl Miles-Clark)

High jump
7. Angela Bradburn (tie)   6' 4¼"

Shot put
9. Connie Price-Smith   59' 4¾"

Pentathlon
6. Kym Carter   4566
9. DeDee Nathan   4128

4th IAAF World Outdoor Track and Field Championships: Stuttgart, Germany, August 14–23

The *New York Times* reported:

Gail Devers beat Merlene Ottey of Jamaica by an eyelash tonight to win the women's 100-meter title in the world outdoor track and field championships. The time was 1 hour 40 minutes — the first 10.81 (sic.10.82) seconds of that for Devers to run the race and the rest for a jury of appeals to decide on a protest by the Jamaicans who insisted Ottey had won or at least tied for first.

Tonight, Ottey was foiled again. With 15 meters left in the race, she trailed Devers by a foot. As Ottey closed in, Devers stumbled. They lunged for the finish line, Devers thrusting her head forward, Ottey with a lesser lean.

Within three minutes, the judges had studied the photo-finish picture and declared Devers the winner. Ottey was second, a hundredth of a second slower. The Jamaican federation protested, and the jury studied the original photograph and one from a reverse angle. It finally announced that by a majority vote, Devers had indeed won.

100 meters
1. Gail Devers   10.82   MR
3. Gwen Torrence   10.89

200 meters
2. Gwen Torrence   22.00
8. Dannette Young-Stone   23.04

400 meters

"Miles barreled to the front with 50 meters left, Kaiser-Brown closed fast and Miles held her off by 2 meters. Miles ran 49.82 seconds and Kaiser-Brown 50.17, the fastest ever for each," reported the *New York Times.*

1. Jearl Miles-Clark   49.82
2. Natasha Kaiser-Brown   50.17

800 meters

"Meredith Rainey, a Harvard graduate who had never won a major title, was leading with 200 meters to go when others challenged her, knocked her off balance and left her to finish in fifth place," commented the *New York Times.*

5. Meredith Rainey-Valmon   1:59.57

There were no American women in the final of the 1500 meters.

3000 meters
10. Annette Peters   8:45.56

10,000 meters
 5. Lynn Jennings   31:30.53
 8. Anne Marie Letko-Lauck   31:37.26
21. Elaine Van Blunk   33:42.85

The *New York Times* reported, "In the women's marathon, 35-year-old Kim Jones led for the first 18 miles. Then she fell back and finished eighth. 'I felt really good,' Jones said. 'I just got very tired, and I couldn't go any longer. I was waiting for someone to help me out with the pace, but they were all pretty content where they were so I did pay the price.'"

Marathon
 8. Kim Rosenquist-Jones   2:36:33
19. Jane Welzel   2:46:08

100 meter hurdles
With the win in the hurdles, "Devers became only the second athlete, female or male, to win an Olympic or world sprint-hurdles double. The first was Fanny Blankers-Koen of the Netherlands in the 1948 Olympics," reported the *New York Times*.

1. Gail Devers   12.46   AR
3. Lynda Tolbert-Goode   12.67
6. Dawn Bowles   12.90

400 meter hurdles
"The women's 400-meter hurdles was a marvelous race. Farmer-Patrick set an almost suicidal pace and led by two feet coming off the last hurdle. But she stumbled from exhaustion, and the relentless Gunnell caught her five meters from the finish. Both lunged for the line, and Gunnell barely won," reported the *New York Times*.

Both women bettered the existing world record.

2. Sandra Farmer-Patrick   52.79   AR
4. Kim Batten   53.84
5. Tonja Buford-Bailey   54.55

High jump
7. Tanya Hughes   6' 3¼"

There were no American women in the long jump or triple jump final.

Shot put
12. Ramona Pagel   58' 3¾"

There were no American women in the discus or javelin final.

10 kilometer walk (road)
22. Teresa Vaill   46:58
37. Debbi Lawrence   48:53
43. Sara Standley   51:01

Heptathlon
"Bob Kersee had no doubt," reported the *New York Times*. "'It was her greatest victory ever,' he said. Jackie Joyner-Kersee who often disagrees with her husband and coach, agreed this time.

'I believe this was my greatest triumph,' she said, 'because of the competition and the situations I put myself in. I learned to test my strength, my character and my heart. This is one I'm going to enjoy.'"

1. Jackie Joyner-Kersee	6837
6. Kym Carter	6357
17. DeDee Nathan	5785

4 × 100 meter relay
2. USA	41.49 AR

(Michelle Finn, Gwen Torrence, Wenda Vereen, Gail Devers)

4 × 400 meter relay
1. USA	3:16.71 MR

(Gwen Torrence, Maicel Malone-Wallace, Natasha Kaiser-Brown, Jearl Miles-Clark)

21st IAAF World Cross Country Championships: Amorebieta, Spain, March 28

3. Lynn Jennings	20:09
21. Annette Peters	20:37
68. Kathleen Franey	21:25

The United States placed tenth in team scoring.

Other News and Honors

Track & Field News: Athlete of the Year

Gail Devers

Top Ten Women — World Rankings — Track & Field News

2. Gail Devers
8. Jackie Joyner-Kersee
9. Sandra Farmer-Patrick

U.S. and World Top Ten Rankings — Track & Field News
(U.S. rankings in bold)

1. Gail Devers	**100 meters**
2. Jackie Joyner-Kersee	1. Gail Devers
3. Sandra Farmer-Patrick	3. Gwen Torrence
4. Jearl Miles-Clark	8. Michelle Finn
5. Gwen Torrence	**1. Gail Devers**
6. Natasha Kaiser-Brown	**2. Gwen Torrence**
7. Lynda Tolbert	**3. Michelle Finn**
8. Kim Batten	**200 meters**
9. Lynn Jennings	2. Gwen Torrence
10. Annette Peters	9. Dannette Young

1. Gwen Torrence
2. Dannette Young
3. Holli Hyche

400 meters
1. Jearl Miles-Clark
2. Natasha Kaiser-Brown
4. Gwen Torrence
9. Maicel Malone

1. **Jearl Miles-Clark**
2. **Natasha Kaiser-Brown**
3. **Gwen Torrence**

800 meters
6. Joetta Clark
8. Meredith Rainey

1. **Joetta Clark**
2. **Meredith Rainey**
3. **Amy Wickus**

1500 meters
There were no American women ranked in the top ten.

1. **Alisa Hill**
2. **Annette Peters**
3. **Shelly Steely**

3000 meters
There were no American women ranked in the top ten.

1. **Annette Peters**
2. **Lynn Jennings**
3. **Gina Procaccio**

5000 meters
3. Annette Peters

1. **Annette Peters**
2. **Laura Mykytok**
3. **Kathy Franey**

10,000 meters
5. Lynn Jennings
8. Anne Marie Letko-Lauck

1. **Lynn Jennings**
2. **Anne Marie Letko-Lauck**
3. **Elaine Van Blunk**

Marathon
There were no American women ranked in the top ten.

1. **Kim Jones**

2. **Kristy Johnston**
3. **Linda Somers**

100 meter hurdles
1. Gail Devers
4. Lynda Tolbert
8. LaVonna Martin-Floreal
9. Dawn Bowles

1. **Gail Devers**
2. **Lynda Tolbert**
3. **LaVonna Martin-Floreal**

400 meter hurdles
2. Sandra Farmer-Patrick
3. Kim Batten
5. Tonja Buford-Bailey

1. **Sandra Farmer-Patrick**
2. **Kim Batten**
3. **Tonja Buford**

10 kilometer walk
There were no American women ranked in the top ten.

1. **Teresa Vaill**
2. **Debbi Lawrence**
3. **Sara Standley**

High jump
There were no American women ranked in the top ten.

1. **Tanya Hughes**
2. **Angie Bradburn**
3. **Yolanda Henry**

Long jump
2. Jackie Joyner-Kersee

1. **Jackie Joyner-Kersee**
2. **Sheila Echols**
3. **Sharon Couch**

Triple jump
There were no American women ranked in the top ten.

1. **Sheila Hudson**
2. **Claudia Haywood**
3. **Cynthea Rhodes**

Shot put
There were no American women ranked in the top ten.

1. **Connie Price-Smith**
2. **Ramona Pagel**
3. **Dawn Dumble**

Discus

There were no American women ranked in the top ten.

1. **Connie Price-Smith**
2. **Kris Kuehl**
3. **Carla Garrett**

Javelin

There were no American women ranked in the top ten.

1. **Donna Mayhew**
2. **Erica Wheeler**
3. **Heather Berlin**

Heptathlon

1. Jackie Joyner-Kersee
8. Kym Carter

1. **Jackie Joyner-Kersee**
2. **Kym Carter**
3. **DeDee Nathan**

The *New York Times* reported that Wilma Rudolph, along with Arnold Palmer, Ted Williams, Muhammad Ali and Kareem Abdul-Jabbar, received the first National Sports Awards at Constitution Hall in Washington, D.C., on Saturday night, June 19. The final paragraph quoted Wilma as saying, "'If I left the earth today my great moment would be knowing that I have tried to give something to young people.'"

President Bill Clinton added Florence Griffith-Joyner as a co-chair to the President's Council on Physical Fitness and Sports.

It was reported by *American Track & Field* that 345,700 girls participated in track and field during the 1993-1994 school year in the United States, making it second only to basketball.

Lynn Jennings won her eighth national cross country title, the seventh consecutive win.

Sandra Farmer-Patrick was the overall Grand Prix winner of $100,000.

Evelyne Hall Adams, 83, died on April 20. Evelyne won the silver medal in the 80 meter hurdles in the 1932 Olympic Games.

Jean Shiley Newhouse was inducted into the National Track and Field Hall of Fame. The biography below is from the National Track and Field Hall of Fame website.

JEAN SHILEY (Newhouse)   HIGH JUMP

Born November 20, 1911, Harrisburg, PA.

When women first competed in Olympic track and field at the 1928 Games in Amsterdam, one of the youngest competitors in the field was Jean Shiley, a 16-year-old student at Haverford Township High School in Pennsylvania.

She placed fourth in the high jump in 1928, then dominated U.S. women's high jumping for the next three years, winning national titles in 1929, 1930 and 1931. She tied Babe Didrikson for the title in 1932 and both competed in the Olympic Games in Los Angeles where they staged one of the greatest one-on-one duels in Olympic history. Didrikson was the women's star of the Games but in the high jump they matched each other jump for jump and each cleared 5' 5" to set a world record. In the jump-off for 1st place at 5' 5¾" each made the height but Didrikson's "diving roll" style was ruled inadmissible and Shiley was awarded the gold medal. That world record was to stand for seven years and it remained the American record until 1948. Shiley also set the American indoor record in 1929 and 1930 and the latter mark of 5' 3¼" remained the American indoor record for 38 years. A 1933 graduate of Temple University, she was the captain of the 1932 Olympic women's track and field team and remained active until 1936 when she was declared a "professional" for teaching swimming and serving as a lifeguard.

INTERVIEW: NATASHA KAISER BROWN

(December 3, 2004) I went to the University of Missouri and got injured; I tore a cartilage in my knee. I had just learned the drills. I got it [laughter]. I was so proud that I had it and then I just did it wrong. I was out for a while but then came back and ended up running great. I had the fastest time in the world in the 300 meters — 300 yards and did everything: NCAAs, made a

The author (left) and Jean Shiley Newhouse on her induction into the National Track and Field Hall of Fame, 1993.

couple of teams — it was just a wonderful spot. But then again in my sophomore year I got injured. I had a series of things — sprained my ankle, my hamstring, my foot fell — disastrous.

My junior year we had a new coach, Darroll Gatson. He coached, I think, Alabama and somewhere else before he came to me. He was a 400 meter runner out of Michigan, and a great athlete. He had a different mentality on how to do things. It was so different from what I had been taught. It was so different from what I had been taught with Coach McGuire because he used sport psychology, which taught you to feel your event and know it and understand how your body works and what's your best emphasis and put it out there. And then I've got this other guy saying, "Yeah, that could work but just run your butt off and this is how you're gonna do it. You're going to run this in such and such a time and this in such and such a time." It was really frustrating because I didn't like him [laughter] because of the way he was. He was so direct and just kind of, shut up and do it. Not necessarily that blunt. But it just came across that way. So I honestly never struggled. I left his office the day I met him and went right next door to Coach McGuire and I told him, "I don't like him." He said, "Just give him time, give him time." So, from the moment he said that, I thought, okay, let's do it. This is who I have for the next two years; make this thing work. I completely put everything into his hands. I just trusted completely whatever he said, that's what I was going to do. It was totally different to do that. Actually, I only had him for a year. He came at the end of my junior year for my senior year. It was interesting: we had a great connection since he ran the 400 but we had different personalities. I'm everybody's friend all the time. Whether I win the race or not and he is only your friend after the race [laughter]. Regardless of what happens, I'm your friend later. It's hard for me to warm-up alone and to do some stretching and stuff and see your friends go by and they start to wave and then they see him standing over me with the dark sunglasses [laughter]. And I'm saying "Why isn't anyone coming over to talk to me?" and then I look up. He says, "They are not your friends."

It's kind of hard to overcome that aspect of it. But anyway, we did some great races together and I remember them because they were so strategic. We would walk the track and he would point out what to do and where to do it. I would just execute that. It was tough.

Once I got away from him — we trained together from '90 to '92 — I ended up being an NCAA collegiate record holder indoors because we put together a great race. I was in a slower section. It was a two heat final. It was fine. I knew how to run the race. There wasn't any question. I could run by myself. It was so in my head.

Then we went outdoors and I ran into Pauline Davis, whom he had coached. So, you get on the line and you're doing exactly the same thing that somebody else is doing before you get in the blocks [laughter]. Wait a minute! It's like, who wants this more. Pauline obviously wanted it more. I ended up being second which is still okay. I wound up with 50.80 or something. So, that was good. Then we were off to the trials.

I'm going to skip to '92.' 91 was a great year but I also had a sciatic injury and I just kind of made a world championship team on the relay as an alternate. So, '92 comes along and now I have this perfect package of a sports psychologist and then I

Natasha Kaiser Brown, 2004.

have this other coach who is all about strategy and how we're going to get through it. Instead of saying, they're taking four to the next round at the Trials — you just win the heat. Don't even worry about it, just win it. I'm thinking, he's talking about winning and I'm coming in here with probably the eighth fastest time [laughter]. Yeah, okay, good luck. But, I trust him because we've been here before. I was engaged. So, no matter what happens out here, I still have this guy who's going to love me. It was a perfect grouping of people. Brian was going to jump later in the week so it was just about me for the next five days. Every day we had the same regimen. We did all the stuff, all the warm-ups, we walked to the track together. It went great. The first heat I won. The second round I won. The third round I was second. Then we had a day off before the finals. It's just stress. I can't eat and it's making me nervous. I'm wondering what my competition is doing. You're in the hotel where you see them all. We got to the final event. There was another young lady who was having a hey day. She was just doing phenomenally. A lot of people were running well but this girl came out of no where and was doing great and running wonderful times like 50.40s, 50.60s early. My coach said to run the same way that you've been running and you're going to be fine. Don't change anything. This is not the time now to think, "I'm going right back to here." Just run what you've been doing. So, the gun goes off. I get to the 300 meter mark, I'm in lane six, and I look up and I'm in last place. I know that they are only taking three. In my mind I'm doing the math and I'm counting 1, 2, 3, 4, 5, 6, 7, 8. So, I put my head down, and this is my trademark, the last hundred meters. I put my head down and I dig and I'm running and I look up again and I'm one, two, three, four, five. This is better. I'm going to focus on the line. I knew that there was a clear winner but then all of us — it was just a blanket. I had already seen where Kim Batten had done this in the hurdles, the same kind of thing. They gave her the flag and she took a victory lap and then she didn't make the team. I was not about to run around this joker and celebrate and not be on the team. So I bent over and they gave the first two people the flag and then they came to me. And, I'm no, no, no. I need to see the photo. I'm not taking my lap. I've got family here and they are going to think that I'm on the team and I'm not. So just go. They convinced me to take the lap. It's so weird because you're so tired. This is the fourth fastest race of my career. I've got this flag and I'm thinking I made the team. But I don't know this. Everybody is excited. The people are running down and they're hugging you. And you think you might not really be on the team, and, sure enough, I made it. My husband just missed making the team. I think he was fifth. He went into the first part fine. He automatically qualified. It was a bittersweet end. I was going overseas right after the trials. He was going to come over later.

I went overseas and I couldn't get it going. I was so flat. I was running like 51s [laughter]. I couldn't get it. He came over later to compete at a really small meet, I think in Germany. My manager and I took the train to go and watch him. I wasn't planning to compete in the meet. He said, "I got you in the meet if you want to do it." So, we go to the meet. It's like a six lane, beautiful little track, small, low key meet. For some reason, it comes back and I run a 50.60. It was easy and I thought that's going to be 52. It was amazing. I didn't speak the language and I was confused over what section I was going to be in. A lot of the pressure was off because I didn't expect much from it. I'll do what I can. It was wonderful. Then I was back on and I went to the Olympic camp which was in France.

I then went over to Barcelona and we were there for twelve days. It's a great experience. All the best athletes are there. That makes it exciting. You are in the village with everybody. There are boxers and gymnasts—being awakened at 4:00 A.M. by the boxing club!

The running was very exciting. I had been there in 1989 so I was familiar with the facilities. My whole goal was to get to run there. Because even though I made the Olympic team and I had the title, until I ran in the Olympics, I didn't consider myself an Olympian. There's so much pressure not to false start and not screw up so I could get at least one 400 in [laughter], so I could say, now, I'm an Olympian. It was horrible. We were waiting and waiting and waiting. For some reason there was a delay. Then, finally we get to start it. I'm trying to stay relaxed and they said "Ladies, ten minutes"—ten minutes is an eternity. Finally, we run the race and I make it through. I'm like, okay, let's go to the next round. So, we get to the third round. The women who know how to run this thing obviously know that you don't run fast early. I'm just running with the trial mentality. It's not that. It's know who you need to beat and then go to the next round. So, I get to the third round and I had already run my best races [laughter]. I get to the starting line and in my heat are the three medalists plus Jearl Miles, who was also my roommate. In the other heat is the other American. In our heat there were not only 49s but a lot of 50s. I'm getting fifth [laughter]. It was horrible. It was horrible. Jearl got fourth, I think, or was it was fifth and sixth [laughter]. Anyway, we don't make it in. Then you have this devastating feeling. What just happened here? I don't understand this.

We go to the 4 × 4 prelim round and I get put on the relay as anchor leg. The coach, at the time, said to me that I should be the fastest because I ran the slowest. I don't understand the logic. But I'm happy being there because I want to be in the finals. I get to anchor in the prelims. That's great. The next day, he moved me to lead off leg. Oh no, lead leg [laughter]. Anything but lead leg. I hate the open quarter and you put me in lead leg? [laughter]. It's a thrill because the way it's set up is you walk out from under the tunnel and you set your blocks. It's nine o'clock at night and it's beautiful out. The sky is clear. I look up on the screen and the screen has my face on it. Okay, be cool. I'm thinking this image is going back home. I'm trying to look relaxed. Well, we get in the blocks and the gun goes off. It's a false start. So, now you have to do this all over again. I run a nice leg but it was not stellar by any means. We hand off with the German team at exactly the same time. But the cool thing was that I got to beat Cathy Freeman [laughter]. We go on to get the silver. It's an exciting time because we're on a relay and everybody wants to win. They give it everything they have. It was exciting to me at that moment. You get a medal. I really didn't care which medal we earned, I just wanted a medal. I looked for my parents. I kind of knew where they were and I found them. I gave my mom the medal. She was just so proud. She put it on. I walked them to the trolly, which took a long time, and they get on and take off. Then I walked back to the stadium to get my ride back to the village and everybody's gone [laughter]. I had to get a ride back with Michael Johnson, who had his own personal van and driver. But it was pretty scary when you're not right around the corner from the village.

In '93, I'm roommates again with Jearl. We've been going 1–2 at every major meet. We get to the qualifying for the world championship and she's first and I'm second. Now, we're going into the world championships and we have a different attitude. Okay, we're going to be in the finals. We may not win the world championships but we are going to be in the finals. That was the deal. So, we went through it with the mentality of winning the heat but being smart with it. So, if winning it means 52, run 52. We got through the rounds and we had some of the fastest times going in. In the final, I was ready for that one. I felt great. There are only a handful of quarters that I can remember wanting to run and that was one. The gun goes off and I get to 250m coming off the turn and I'm with people. I'm actually in the race and not watching them go through the turn. I got to 300 meters and I'm thinking I just won a car because I don't really see any-one — if I'm ahead of people, it's my race. I'm envisioning this car and its color, then out of the corner of my eye I see someone. I'm trying to not look at them but think now, I'm forced to run it. I'm trying to close on this girl but I can't get her and it ends up — it's Jearl [laughter]. I look at the clock and it had 49 — I was 50.1— second in the world, not bad. Then it was a whole different atmosphere on the awards stand. I don't have three other people to help me get it. It's my medal. It was awesome. It was just unbelievable the emotions that came with that race, and then to be standing on the awards stand hearing the national anthem.

In '95 I had a stress fracture and was completely out.

Then in '96 for the trials, I worked my butt off. I only had three months. So I really was not in shape. But I made the team. I was sixth or seventh, but I made it. It was a whole different world in '96. An alternate is a whole different thing. You're down there. You don't get the same communications. People say they care about you and they try. But it was frustrating. Then when I got back from some races, I had a message on my phone, asking "Where are you? You're supposed to be in the village in Atlanta." I'm thinking, "How would I know this?" I call them and I make arrangements to fly there. I go to the Olympic practice. Where is everybody? They picked the pool. We warmed up and the coach told us there will be six people in the pool, and I'm not in the six. Why was I here again? What was the rush? So, I'm like, "Okay," we go and we do the handoffs and, you know, I can't say that I'm hurt by it, I kind of am but I understand why because I've been injured most of the year. To put me on is a risk. But, then I think, the one thing that I've done consistently well are the relay legs so, why would I not run; I have so much knowledge with this and so much history. So, we practice. We go back and I think I went home. There was no reason to be there. I'm not even in the pool. Once they declare the pool, that's it. So, some of the people said, "Oh, you're leaving." But, they kind of understood. To me it was kind of a waste of money to fly a person out there because it was short notice and the ticket prices are high. You know, you could have called me [laughter] and that would have been okay.

Anyway, it was frustrating. I ended up writing letters to everybody on the staff thanking them for letting me be part of it and for allowing me to be an Olympian. I wrote to the head coach and said, "While I don't agree with your decision, I respect it; you have to make the decisions you have to make." I didn't want it to sound like this disgruntled athlete. I wanted to make it like I understand it, no hard feelings. But, it was kind of tough because you've gone to this level and someone is telling a former Olympian that you're not good enough to be here — anyway.

So, then I came back in '97 and made a world championship team with my husband. I actually made the indoor and outdoor teams. In the indoor one we set an American record in the 4 × 4. It was another strange circumstance, the way that the rounds fell. You had two rounds of the 4 and then the 4 × 4 prelims, and then another round. Yeah, it was really kind of weird to come back and try to get all that in. It was real confusing. We didn't have enough bodies to run the prelim in the 4 × 4. So, I ended up sacrificing the 400 for the 4 × 4. But I thought maybe if I'm good enough I can make both of these. I didn't make it in the 400, just the relay. That's kind of always been my love. So, we got to the relay final. It was fun. I love indoor track. I'm tall and it's awkward but it's so fast and it's so strategic — it's just a war. You get in there and it's elbows and its spikes. You don't think about the 400, you just think about: gotta get through it, gotta get to the front, and it's wonderful and we got the American record.

Then I went outdoors. I ran the first round of the world championship 4 × 4 and didn't run the finals, which was totally fine by me. In the prelim round, I thought, yeah, this ain't working and I was running great but I could tell that my heart was changing. I finished out '97.

I ran a little in '98. I didn't make any teams in '98 although I did run well. I think I ran 50.80 in Japan in May. I had a lot of sciatic pain now. I had a lot of random pain in my legs. I really had to stop and wait for that to dissipate. I didn't like that and I was thinking, thirty something, kids would be good, you know. Life, I kinda just wanted to get on with it and not end when I was on the bottom. Yeah, it's that time. I just wanted to go out kind of in the middle, not at the top because, "Why you stopping here?" [laughter].

I got out in '98 and had my first born in '99 and tried to come back, just to see if it's still there, in 2000. And it wasn't. But it was still fun trying.

Coaching then became real important to me. I was still coaching as an assistant coach as I was learning a lot. Then it was coaching more and running less and finally I was coaching a lot, and I liked that better. It worked into a full time coaching position. I was at Missouri forever [laughter]. I thought if I were going to make a move in coaching, to be a head coach, it needed to be soon. If I were going to go somewhere, it needed to be now because I would get to the age where I was no longer a viable candidate. I don't want to get locked in. I really wanted to do my own thing. I could see how I could take the good stuff from every coach that I had and the philosophy of Coach McGuire and kind of build my own program doing things a little differently.

One of the other assistant coaches was leaving for Illinois State. He was coming to tell me that one of the coaches at Drake University had passed away, which was my hometown and I love it. But I was devastated because I don't know the guy but he was the same age as our coach. No, there's a job opening. You're not hearing what I'm saying. I said to him, "Why don't you look into it. It would be a good job for you."

My house was on the market to be sold. Not only that, my husband and I were talking and praying about our future and trying to decide to stay or leave Missouri.

Here I am also, an assistant coach, wanting to do my own thing. I'm thinking, we need to go somewhere else. He said, "Well, where?" At the time, I had not heard about the Drake job. I don't know. I hadn't gotten my resume together; hadn't looked at it; hadn't updated it. He said, okay. So, we got temporary housing. In the meantime we got an offer on the house, which we accepted. It was awesome how everything unfolded. Just about the time that the temporary housing expired, I got the job at Drake. So, it's really strange. The timing was perfect. I moved back home. I had finally recruited some really good athletes. My thoughts were that if I could ever get to the point that I had an athlete that could beat me, not necessarily in the 400, but the 100 and 200, I'd retire. I recruited this young lady, Avis Evans. I was running the 100 and 200 with her and she beat me in both events. She got me in the 100 by an edge. I said, "Okay, yeah, but we'll try the 200." I figured I could get her. I couldn't get this girl for anything. I think she finally read it somewhere a couple of years ago because someone interviewed me about it. She said, "I didn't know that."

It's been awesome. It's been exactly what I've been looking for, what I want out of a job. It's so family friendly. I can bring my kids to work and they can play in the field house and it's fine. If they stay in my office, it's fine.

Whatever I need, I have. Now, we're getting a new outdoor track. I can't complain. It's been really good for me.

14

1994

The Outdoor Nationals

The USA/Mobil National Outdoor Track and Field Championships were held in Knoxville, Tennessee from June 13 to 18.

A headline in Friday's *New York Times* read, "In 100, Devers and Mitchell Are First to the Finish Line."

James Dunaway wrote,

...Devers, the defending Olympic 100-meter champion, got off to a terrible start but edged ahead in the final strides to beat Carlette Guidry by a foot, clocking 11.12 seconds to Guidry's 11.15. Devers, who suffered a back injury in an auto accident three and a half weeks ago, was more relieved than exultant.

"The injury never healed," she said. "I've been cautious all week. I didn't run the first 50 meters at all. I prayed I wouldn't have to be carried off the track, and I made it through."

...Sheila Hudson-Strudwick won her fifth national title by equaling her American record of 46 feet 8¼ inches.

Teresa Vaill, of Kingston, N.Y. [sic.] set an American record in the women's 10,000-meter race walk, winning in 45 minutes 1.46 seconds to defeat Michelle Rohl of La Grange, GA. by 20 meters. Both broke the former record of 45:28.4 held by Debbi Lawrence, who finished fourth.

One other final was scheduled for today, but it didn't happen. The women's 10,000 meters was barely underway when thunderstorms and lightning forced Referee Lynn Cannon to abandon the race after 3 of the 25 laps. The race will be run tomorrow.

In a second *New York Times* article, it was reported that "Jackie Joyner-Kersee didn't compete in the heptathlon here, but she did come away with a double victory today. First, she dominated the women's long jump, winning for the sixth straight time by nearly two feet with 23' 5¼". Two hours later she treated the 100-meter hurdles field in a similar manner, beating LaVonna Floreal, the 1992 Olympic silver medalist, by more than two meters, in 12.88 seconds to Floreal's 13.06.

"...Joetta Clark, of Somerset, N.J., won the women's 800 in 2:00.41 in a hotly contested race with Amy Wickus of the University of Wisconsin (2:00.60) and the Brooklyn native Meredith Rainey (2:00.65)."

Track & Field News reported: "Sheila Echols, the '88 titlist, got the best start and led for the first half of the race. Devers, who had come out of the blocks quite slowly, began to move well at the 60m mark and moved to a slight lead over Echols and '91 winner Carlette Guidry,

307

who was also running very well. Guidry and Devers appeared to be even with 5m to go, but the Olympic champ had the best lean, and was able to garner the victory, 11.12–11.15."

100 meters
1. Gail Devers, Nike International	11.12
2. Carlette Guidry, adidas Track Club	11.15
3. Cheryl Taplin, unattached	11.26
4. Sheila Echols, Goldwin Track Club	11.27
5. Dannette Young, Reebok Racing Club	11.37
6. Chryste Gaines, Mizuno Track Club	11.45
7. D'Andre Hill, Louisiana State University	11.48
8. Wenda Vereen, Goldwin Track Club	11.58

200 meters

"Young got the best start and ran the turn strongly with Guidry and Chryste Gaines in hot pursuit. As they entered the straight, Guidry challenged for the lead. She and Young ran together for the next 70m, virtually even. Guidry edged ahead in the last 10m to capture the win in 22.71," reported *Track & Field News*.

1. Carlette Guidry, adidas Track Club	22.71
2. Dannette Young, Reebok Racing Club	22.81
3. Chryste Gaines, Mizuno Track Club	23.33
4. Flirtisha Harris, Seton Hall University	23.34
5. Wenda Vereen, Goldwin Track Club	23.46
6. Shantel Twiggs, University of Northern Iowa	23.65
7. Richelle Webb, University of Michigan	23.66
8. Omegia Keeys, Indiana State University	23.79

400 meters

Track & Field News reported: "In the final Malone came out early and made up the stagger on Miles after 100m. She continued to lead through 300, looking terrific, but then Miles and Kaiser-Brown began to make up some ground as Malone faltered. The trio headed down the final straight, battling each other, fatigue, heat and humidity. Malone was holding on for dear life over the last 20m as the other two closed down. Kaiser-Brown forged a lead with 5m to go to take the victory in 50.53. Miles lunged desperately at the tape but was unable to catch Malone. Only 0.05 separated the three."

1. Natasha Kaiser-Brown, Foot Locker Athletic Club	50.73
2. Maicel Malone, Asics International	50.77
3. Jearl Miles, Reebok Racing Club	50.78
4. Kim Graham, adidas Track Club	51.43
5. Michele Collins, Mizuno Track Club	51.63
6. Rochelle Stevens, Nike Atlantic Coast Track Club	52.42
7. Sheryl Covington, Florida State University	52.60
8. Crystal Irving, Atoms Track Club	52.80

800 meters

"Joetta Clark took the lead from the gun and never relinquished it. Running confidently all the way, she passed the 400 mark in 58.9 and withstood Meredith Rainey's challenge at the top of the homestretch. Then she held off Amy Wickus's late rush at the end, just like last year. Clark's win made her the first woman ever to win three 800 titles in a row," reported Bob Hersh for *Track & Field News*.

1. Joetta Clark, Foot Locker Athletic Club	2:00.41
2. Amy Wickus, University of Wisconsin	2:00.60
3. Meredith Rainey, Foot Locker Athletic Club	2:00.65
4. Jane Brooker, Athletes in Action	2:01.13
5. Nekita Beasley, Atoms Track Club	2:01.66
6. Tosha Woodward, Villanova University	2:01.69
7. Jennifer Buckley, Kent State University	2:05.82
8. Shola Lynch, Foot Locker Athletic Club	2:08.11

1500 meters

Track & Field News wrote: "Jacobs moved to the fore entering the gun lap and sprinted to a 63.2 final circuit that brought her home in 4:07.71, 0.44 up on Suzy Hamilton."

1. Regina Jacobs, Mizuno Track Club	4:07.71
2. Suzy Hamilton, Reebok Racing Club	4:08.15
3. Kathleen Franey, Reebok Racing Club	4:08.79
4. Sarah Thorsett, Nike North Track Club	4:10.24
5. Juli Speights, Reebok Enclave	4:10.56
6. Kristen Seabury, Nike Boston Track Club	4:10.97
7. Kari Anne Bertrand, Reebok Enclave	4:12.94
8. Kelly Rabush, Reebok Enclave	4:14.58

2000 meter steeplechase (exhibition)
1. Gina Wilbanks, Athletes in Action	6:58.85
2. Marisa Sutera, Westchester Track Club	7:00.45
3. Teressa DiPerna, unattached	7:07.40
4. Frances Childs, unattached	8:22.46
5. Phil Raschker, unattached	8:24.60
6. Laurie Black, New York Pioneer Club	9:14.86

3000 meters
1. Annette Peters, Nike International	9:01.69
2. Libbie Johnson, Mizuno Track Club	9:07.25
3. Joan Nesbit, New Balance Track Club	9:14.74
4. Polly Plumer, Asics International	9:15.99
5. Liz Wilson, Sporthill Track Club	9:17.23
6. Becky Spies, Villanova University	9:20.97
7. Cassie McWilliam, Nike North Track Club	9:22.25
8. Cheri Goddard, Reebok Enclave	9:24.10

5000 meters
1. Ceci St. Geme, Asics International Track Club	15:57.71
2. Jennifer Rhines, Villanova University	16:04.02
3. Misti Demko, Asics International Track Club	16:10.85
4. Sam Gdowski, Reebok Racing Club	16:12.05
5. Carmen Troncoso, Nike Texas Track Club	16:26.93
6. Lauren Gubicza, Asics International Track Club	16:30.99
7. Cathy Palacios, Asics International Track Club	16:39.20
8. Lucy Nusrala, Reebok Racing Club	16:51.37

10,000 meters

"In one of the more unusual developments of the meet, the race was stopped after three plus laps when lightning and a hard downpour caused officials — in perhaps an unprecedented decision?— to intervene," reported *Track & Field News*. "An athletes meeting resulted in a 9–8 vote not to try again the same night. When the race was restarted the next evening, the race was controlled immediately by a pack of four: newly naturalized Olga Appell, Gwyn Coogan, Anne Marie Letko and Jennings. Coogan went to the lead with 850m to go, trying to force a long drive. But when Appell went past with 300m left, the race was over."

Lynn Jennings dropped out when the heat got to her.

1. Olga Appell, Reebok Racing Club	32:23.76
2. Gwyn Coogan, adidas Track Club	32:24.81
3. Anne Marie Letko, Nike Running Room	32:41.67
4. Carole Zajac, Villanova University	33:09.18
5. Laura LaMena-Coll, Reebok Racing Club	33:43.89
6. Elaine Van Blunk, adidas Track Club	34:43.79
7. Laura Craven, unattached	34:16.09
8. Vicki Mitchell, Nike Boston	34:17.77

100 meter hurdles

According to *Track & Field News*, "An explosive start was the decider in the 100H as Jackie Joyner-Kersee claimed her second title of the championships. It was the first time she had entered this event at the nationals since 1984, and the first time she had ever made the final."

1. Jackie Joyner-Kersee, Honda Track Club	12.88
2. LaVonna Martin-Floreal, Reebok Racing Club	13.06
3. Cheryl Dickey, Nike South Track Club	13.25
4. Sherlese Taylor, St Augustine's College	13.43
5. Lynda Tolbert-Goode, Mizuno Track Club	13.50
6. Allison Williams, unattached	13.55
7. Anjanette Kirkland, Texas A&M University	13.59
8. Ayo Atterberry, University of North Carolina	13.95

400 meter hurdles

"Batten, who was fourth in the 400-meter hurdles in last year's world championships, won her second national title with a smooth, powerful race. She was clearly in the lead by the second hurdle. The former Rochester, N.Y., high school star drew away to a 10-meter margin...," reported Jim Dunaway in the *New York Times*.

1. Kim Batten, Reebok Racing Club	54.51
2. Tonja Buford, Nike International	55.87
3. Trevaia Williams, Atoms Track Club	56.55
4. Connie Ellerbe, Nike South Track Club	56.77
5. Tonya Williams, University of Illinois	56.77
6. Keisha Marvin, unattached	56.93
7. Sandra Cummings-Glover, Mizuno Track Club	57.62
8. Countess Comadore, Reebok Racing Club	1:00.98

10,000 meter walk

Elliott Denman wrote for *Track & Field News*: "A silver medalist five times in the last six years, Vaill left no doubt this time and had only a late rush by Michelle Rohl — America's Barcelona leader — to worry about.... 'I knew Michelle was closing on me, but I had a lot left,' said Vaill.'"

1. Teresa Vaill, unattached	45:01.46	AR
2. Michelle Rohl, Parkside Athletic Club	45:07.58	

3. Debora Van Orden, unattached   47:00.30
4. Debbi Lawrence, Natural Sport Track Club   47:16.00
5. Dana Yarbrough, unattached   47:20.28
6. Victoria Herazo, California Walkers   48:10.93
7. Lynda Brubaker, Phast   48:22.13
8. Sally Richards-Kerr, High Altitude Race Walkers   49:18.00

High jump
    "In a replay of the indoor nationals in Atlanta, Angela Bradburn went at it with Tisha Waller. As in Atlanta, Waller came in with the campaign's best mark, but Bradburn went one height higher to claim the win," said *Track & Field News*.

1. Angela Bradburn, unattached   6' 3½"
2. Tisha Waller, Goldwin Track Club   6' 2¼"
3. Karol Damon, Goldwin Track Club   6' 1¼"
4. Connie Teaberry, Goldwin Track Club   6' 1¼"
     and Tanya Hughes, unattached
6. Yolanda Henry, unattached   6' 1¼"
7. Gwen Wentland, unattached   6' 1¼"
8. Sue Rembao, Reebok Racing Club   6'

Pole vault (first exhibition)
1. Melissa Price, unattached   10' 8"
2. Phil Raschker, unattached   10' 8"
3. Jocelyn Chase, unattached   10' 4"
4. Shannon Walker, Air Time Athletics   10' 4"
5. Pam Reynolds, unattached   9' 8"
6. Melissa Feinstein, Air Time Athletics   9' 8"
7. Alissa White, Air Time Athletics   9' ¼"
8. Adrian Williams, Lincoln High School   8' 8¼"

Long jump
    Track & Field News continued: "A breezy tailwind blew as Jackie Joyner-Kersee sped down the sun-drenched runway for her first jump, and although getting little from the board, she landed 22' 11¼" away, enough to win by more than a foot."

1. Jackie Joyner-Kersee, Honda Track Club   23' 5¼" w
2. Sheila Echols, Goldwin Track Club   21' 7½"
3. Terri Turner-Hairston, Mizuno Track Club   21' 6¾" w
4. Cynthea Rhodes, unattached   21' 6" w
5. Sheila Hudson, Reebok Racing Club   21' 4¾"
6. Sharon Couch, Asics International   21' 3½" w
7. Dawn Burrell, University of Houston   21' ½"
8. Tamara Cuffee, Anderson International Track Club   20' 3¾"

Triple jump
1. Sheila Hudson, Reebok Racing Club   46' ¼" ties   AR
2. Diana Orrange, Prime Time Sports   46' ½"
3. Carla Shannon, unattached   44' 10¾"
4. Roshanda Glenn, unattached   44' 10¼"
5. Cynthea Rhodes, unattached   44' 8¾"
6. Telisa Young, University of Texas, Austin   43' 10"
7. Robyne Johnson, Anderson International Track Club   43' 6½"
8. Karyn Smith, unattached   43' 1¾"

Shot put

"Five-time champion Connie Price-Smith recorded one of the best series in U.S. history, including a 64' 3¾" winner that moved her ahead of Bonnie Dasse into the No. 2 slot on the all-time U.S. list. All six of her tosses were past the 61-foot mark, including four beyond 62, as she added almost a foot to her PR."

1. Connie Price-Smith, Nike Coast Track Club	64' 3¾"	MR
2. Ramona Pagel, Nike Coast Track Club	58' 9¼"	
3. Dawn Dumble, unattached	57' 3¾"	
4. Eileen Vanisi, University of Texas, Austin	55' 5¾"	
5. Peggy Pollock, unattached	54' 9¼"	
6. Stevanie Ferguson, Texas Christian University	54' 7½"	
7. Valeyta Althouse, University of California, Los Angeles	54' 1"	
8. Melisa Weis, Goldwin Track Club	52' 5¼"	

Discus

"Since 1987 only two women have claimed national discus titles, and they battled it out again this year, with favored Connie Price-Smith edging Lacy Barnes for a record-equaling title No. 6."

1. Connie Price-Smith, Nike Coast Track Club	195'	1"
2. Lacy Barnes, Nike Track Club	193'	7"
3. Kristin Kuehl, unattached	188'	2"
4. Dawn Dumble, unattached	187'	
5. Carla Garrett, Nike Coast Track Club	185'	6"
6. Edie Boyer, unattached	183'	6"
7. Alana Preston, University of Tennessee	176'	11"
8. Pamela Dukes, Nike Coast Track Club	176'	

Hammer throw (exhibition)

Fitts won her third straight title on her last try.

1. Sonja Fitts, unattached	190' 6"	MR
2. Alexandra Givan, New Haven Age Group	188' 5"	
3. Bonnie Edmondson, Nike Coast Track Club	182' 11"	
4. Liz Legault, Boston Athletic Association	181' 2"	
5. Leslie Coons, University of South Carolina	176' 1"	
6. Debbie Templeton, Stanford University	174' 6"	
7. Tina Rankin, Cornell University	160' 4"	
8. Ericka Dice, University of California	160'	

Javelin

1. Donna Mayhew, Nike Coast Track Club	193' 4"
2. Nicole Carroll, San Mateo Athletic Club	185' 4"
3. Lynda Lipson, Klub Keihas	182' 3"
4. Paula Berry, Nike Track Club	180' 5"
5. Erica Wheeler, Mizuno Track Club	173' 4"
6. Kim Hyatt, Nike Oregon International Track Club	172' 8"
7. Jenny McCormick, Stanford University	171' 4"
8. Cindy Herceg, unattached	170' 11"

Heptathlon

1. Kym Carter, Nike Club West	6371
2. Jamie McNeair, Purdue Area Track Club	6323

3. DeDee Nathan, Nike Indiana Track Club	6189
4. Kelly Blair, unattached	5907
5. Sharon Hanson, Nike Coast Track Club	5886
6. Clare Look-Jaeger, Nike Coast Track Club	5746
7. Theresa Roy, unattached	5645
8. Peggy Odita, Sacramento Track Club	5602

Team scores:

1. Reebok Racing Club	76
2. Nike Coast Track Club	43
3. Mizuno Track Club	37

The Indoor Nationals

The USA/Mobil National Indoor Track and Field Championships were held, for the first time, in the Georgia Dome, Atlanta, Georgia, March 4–5.

"USA Track and Field, the sport's national governing body, has said that leading athletes wanted the meet moved because they could run faster times on Atlanta's 200-meter banked track with a Mondo, plastic-like surface than they could on the Garden's 146-meter, tight banked-board oval," said the *New York Times*.

Frank Litsky writes:

Gwen Torrence and Jackie Joyner-Kersee shattered their American records today in the USA/Mobil national indoor track and field championships.

Torrence won two titles in 77 minutes, and her usually dour manner dissolved in smiles. But Joyner-Kersee, two and a half hours after she won the long jump, hit the last two hurdles in the 60-meter hurdles and crashed, hurting her left foot and her pride.

For 108 years, these national championships had been held in one Madison Square Garden or another in New York. Now, because of rising costs and falling attendance in New York, the meet has moved for at least 10 years to the Georgia Dome, the site five Sundays ago of Super Bowl XXVIII.

...Torrence won the women's 60-meter dash by a meter in 7.10 seconds. Then she won the 200 meters by 4 feet in 22.74 seconds, bettering the American record of 22.84 she set in Friday night's preliminaries.

...Joyner-Kersee ran more than her heart out. In the women's long jump, she sailed 23 feet 4¾ inches on her second round, breaking her 1992 American record of 23' 1¼". Then she was about to win the hurdles when she almost broke her left foot.

After three of the five hurdles, Joyner-Kersee was leading and the crowd, announced at 19,080, was whooping it up. Then Joyner-Kersee hit the fourth hurdle hard and the last one harder and fell.

Her foot was bruised but not broken, confirmed after x-rays were taken at a local hospital.

Twenty-eight-year-old Gwen Torrence of Decatur, Georgia was voted the outstanding female athlete of the meet.

60 meters

1. Gwen Torrence, Mazda Track Club	7.10
2. Esther Jones, Nike International	7.23
3. Sheila Echols, Goldwin Track Club	7.24

200 meters

1. Gwen Torrence, Mazda Track Club	22.74	AR
2. Carlette Guidry, unattached	22.92	
3. Dannette Young, Reebok Racing Club	22.95	

400 meters
1. Maicel Malone, unattached   51.72   MR
2. Jearl Miles, Reebok Racing Club   51.99
3. Natasha Kaiser-Brown, Mizuno/Southern California Cheetahs   52.15

800 meters
1. Maria Mutola, Nike International/Mozambique   2:00.52
2. Joetta Clark, Foot Locker Athletic Club   2:01.80
3. Jane Brooker, Athletes in Action   2:04.32

Mobil mile
1. Hassiba Boulmerka, Algeria   4:31.91
2. Gina Procaccio, Sallie Mae Track Club   4:35.48
3. Kristin Seabury, Nike Boston Track Club   4:37.01

3000 meters
1. Kathy Franey, Reebok Racing Club   9:14.64
2. Cassie McWilliam, Nike North Track Club   9:15.97
3. Lauren Gubicza, Asics International Track Club   9:19.21

3000 meter walk
1. Debbi Lawrence, Natural Sport   13:13.20
2. Victoria Herazo, California Walkers   13:15.85
3. Susan Armenta, Parkside West Track Club   13:49.86

60 meter hurdles
1. Michelle Freeman, Reebok Racing Club/Jamaica   7.98
2. LaVonna Martin-Floreal, Reebok Racing Club   8.08
3. Lynda Goode, Nike Track Club   8.10

4 × 400 meter relay
1. Rice University   3:39.29
   (Pam Brooks, Tanisha Mills, Vonda Newhouse, Melissa Straker)
2. University of Illinois   3:39.93
3. University of Nevada, Las Vegas   3:40.90

High jump
1. Angela Bradburn, unattached   6' 6"
2. Tisha Waller, Goldwin Track Club   6' 4¾"
3. Nicole Hudson, unattached   6' 2¼"
   and Gwen Wentland, unattached

Long jump
1. Jackie Joyner-Kersee, Honda Track Club   23' 4¾"AR
2. Cynthea Rhodes, unattached   21' ½"
3. Jackie Edwards, Mizuno Track Club/Bahamas   20' 10"

Triple jump
1. Sheila Hudson, Reebok Racing Club   45' 3½" MR
2. Cynthea Rhodes, unattached   45' 2¼"
3. Diana Wills-Orrange, unattached   44' 1½"

Shot put
1. Ramona Pagel, unattached   60' 8½"
2. Connie Price-Smith, Nike Coast Track Club   55' 9¾"
3. Pam Dukes, Nike Coast Track Club   52' 8¼"

20 pound weight throw
1. Sonja Fitts, unattached   57' 3¾"
2. Pam Dukes, Nike Coast Track Club   56' 2"
3. Sandy Sparrow, Idaho State University   52' 3¼"

Team scores:
1. Reebok Racing Club   24
2. Nike Coast Track Club   10.2
3. Mazda Track Club   10

Sunkist Invitational (5 women's events): February 19, Los Angeles

50 meters
1. Irina Privalova, Russia   6.08   MR

440 yards
1. Angela Reed, University of Arkansas   54.91

800 meters
1. Maria Mutola, Mozambique   2:00.21   MR

Mile
1. Suzy Hamilton, Reebok Racing Club   4:38.43

50 meter hurdles
1. Jackie Joyner-Kersee, Honda Track Club   6.87

New York Grand Prix: May 22

Jim Dunaway wrote in *Track & Field News*, "After a foul, and a 22' 11¾" (7.00) jump which found her several inches behind the board, Jackie Joyner-Kersee sped down the runway for her third long jump attempt and came down at 24' 7" (7.49), 4cm past the AR of 24' 5½" she set at the '87 Pan-Am Games in Indianapolis."

100 meters
1. Carlette Guidry, unattached   11.31
6. Wenda Vereen, Goldwin Track Club   11.66
8. Chryste Gaines, Mizuno Track Club   11.84

400 meters
2. Jearl Miles, Reebok Racing Club   50.68
3. Natasha Kaiser-Brown, Southern California Cheetahs 51.01

800 meters
2. Joetta Clark, Foot Locker Athletic Club   2:00.29
5. Nekita Beasley, Atoms Track Club   2:04.71
8. Debbi Marshall, New Balance Track Club   2:05.32

Mile
1. Kelly Rabush, Reebok Enclave   4:36.57
2. Kate Fonshell, Nike Boston   4:37.51
3. Kari Bertrand, Reebok Enclave   4:37.55

4. Cheri Goddard, Reebok Enclave 4:38.27
5. Lauren Gubicza, Asics Track Club 4:38.53
6. Cathy Stanmeyer, Reebok Enclave 4:51.60

100 meter hurdles
2. Jackie Joyner-Kersee, Honda Track Club 13.12
3. LaVonna Martin-Floreal, Reebok Racing Club 13.13
4. Lynda Tolbert-Goode, Mizuno Track Club 13.25
5. Dawn Bowles, Foot Locker Athletic Club 13.26
6. Monifa Taylor, Reebok Racing Club 13.26

Long jump
1. Jackie Joyner-Kersee, Honda Track Club 24' 7"   AR

San Jose Grand Prix: San Jose, California, May 28

100 meters
1. Gail Devers, Nike International Track Club 10.77 w
2. Carlette Guidry, unattached 10.97
4. Sheila Echols, Goldwin Track Club 11.13
6. Wenda Vereen, Goldwin Track Club 11.33
7. Chryste Gaines, Mizuno Track Club 11.34

400 meters
3. Natasha Kaiser-Brown, Foot Locker Athletic Club 50.89
5. Maicel Malone, Mazda Track Club 52.08
7. Kim Graham, unattached 52.33

1500 meters
1. Gina Procaccio, Sallie Mae Track Club 4:08.77
3. Suzy Hamilton, Reebok Racing Club 4:09.12
5. Juli Speights, Reebok Enclave 4:10.47
7. Kelly Rabush, Reebok Enclave 4:12.55
8. Ceci St. Geme, Asics Track Club 4:12.85
9. Darcy Arreola, Reebok Racing Club 4:14.44
10. Lauren Gubicza, Asics Track Club 4:15.65
11. Jennifer Bravard, unattached 4:20.07
12. PattiSue Plumer, Nike International Track Club 4:21.00
13. Shola Lynch, Foot Locker Athletic Club 4:30.08

3000 meters
1. Annette Peters, Nike West Track Club 8:58.3
2. Lynn Jennings, Nike International Track Club 8:59.2
3. Kathy Franey, Reebok Racing Club 9:00.0
4. Libbie Johnson, Mizuno Track Club 9:01.4
5. Fran ten Bensel, New Balance Track Club 9:10.7
6. Cathy Palacios, Asics Track Club 9:18.1
7. Melody O'Reilly, Nike Running Room 9:18.7
8. Elaine Van Blunk, Nike Running Room 9:22.6

100 meter hurdles
2. Jackie Joyner-Kersee, Honda Track Club 12.75
3. Lynda Tolbert-Goode, Mizuno Track Club 12.90

4. Cheryl Dickey, Nike South Track Club   13.03
5. LaVonna Martin-Floreal, Reebok Racing Club   13.08
6. Dawn Bowles, Foot Locker Athletic Club   13.17
7. Sharon Couch, unattached   13.27
8. Marieke Veltman, World Class Athletic Club   13.80

Long jump
1. Jackie Joyner-Kersee, Honda Track Club   23' 11½"
6. Sheila Echols, Goldwin Track Club   21' 3½"
7. Sharon Couch, unattached   20' 10"

Discus
2. Connie Price-Smith, Nike Coast Track Club   198' 3"
3. Kris Kuehl, unattached   192' 6"
4. Dawn Dumble, unattached   183' 2"
5. Edie Boyer, unattached   181' 2"
6. Lacy Barnes, Nike International Track Club   180' 10"

7th IAAF/Mobil World Cup: London, September 9–11

100 meters
8. Sheila Echols   11.81

200 meters
8. Chryste Gaines   24.21

400 meters
3. Jearl Miles   51.24

800 meters
5. Joetta Clark   2:03.76

1500 meters
6. Kathy Franey   4:21.48

3000 meters
7. Cassie McWilliam   9:26.50

10,000 meters
7. Laura La Mena-Coll   33:43.66

100 meter hurdles
7. Sherlese Taylor   14.10

400 meter hurdles
7. Tonya Lee   59.61

4 × 100 meter relay
5. United States   43.79

4 × 400 meter relay
5. United States   3:30.99

High jump
8. Karol Damon   5' 10¾"

Long jump
8. Sheila Echols   20' 5¼"

Triple jump
2. Sheila Hudson-Strudwick   45' 11"

Shot put
6. Dawn Dumble   51' 3¼"

Discus
6. Connie Price-Smith   187' 1½"

Javelin
7. Donna Mayhew   168' 11½"

U.S. Women's Marathon Championship (Grandma's Marathon): Duluth, Minnesota, June 18

1. Linda Somers, Asics Track Club	2:33:42
2. Kellie Archuletta, New Balance Track Club	2:38:08
3. Roxi Erickson, unattached	2:39:08
4. Regina Joyce, Mizuno Track Club	2:39:36
5. Lynn Nelson, Reebok Racing Club	2:40:04
6. Barbara Acosta, unattached	2:40:15

IAAF/Snickers World Cross Country Championships (6220m): Budapest, Hungary, March 26

27. Gwyn Coogan	21:33
39. Lucy Nusrala	21:40
44. Carmen Ayala-Troncoso	21:43

Other News and Honors

Track & Field News: Athlete of the Year

Jackie Joyner-Kersee

Top Ten Women — World Rankings — Track & Field News

1. Jackie Joyner-Kersee
5. Gwen Torrence

Top Ten Women — U.S. Rankings — Track & Field News

1. Jackie Joyner-Kersee
2. Gwen Torrence
3. Kim Batten

4. Maicel Malone
5. Jearl Miles
6. Annette Peters

7. Sheila Hudson-Strudwick
8. Carlette Guidry

9. Regina Jacobs
10. Connie Price-Smith

Wilma Rudolph, 54, died on Nov. 12 in Tennessee. The *New York Times* commented, "Rudolph was a handsome, regal woman, 6 feet tall, charming, graceful and gracious. Over seven days, she became the first woman to win three gold medals in track and field in one Olympics."

Jackie Joyner-Kersee long jumped 24' 7" in the Reebok New York Games in May to break her 1987 American record by 1½".

Jackie Joyner-Kersee was the overall grand prix winner.

Helen Stephens, 75, died on January 17 in St. Louis. Helen won the gold medal in the 100 meters in the 1936 Olympic Games in Berlin, Germany.

Olga Appell won the national cross country championships.

The National Track and Field Hall of Fame inductees included Lillian Copeland and Kate Schmidt. The biographies below are from the National Track and Field Hall of Fame website.

LILLIAN COPELAND

Born: November 25, 1904 — New York, New York. Deceased: February 7, 1964.

Events

Discus Throw — 40.60 m
Javelin Throw — 38.30 m

A world or American record holder in three throwing events, Lillian Copeland was only a part-time competitor in 1932, when the Olympics were held in Los Angeles. As a student at the University of Southern California, she took time away from her studies to prepare for the trials. There, she finished third in the discus, before winning the gold medal at the Games on her final throw. The first great American woman weight thrower, Copeland won nine national AAU titles in three events. She was the shot put champion from 1925 through 1928 and again in 1931, the discus champion in 1926 and 1927, and the javelin champion in 1926 and 1931. Copeland set world records in the javelin in 1926, 1927 and 1928, but neither that event nor the shot was on the Olympic program. However, she did win a silver medal in the 1928 Amsterdam Olympics. Four years later, she won gold in that event with an Olympic record of 133' 2". Amazingly quick for a weight thrower, she was a member of a 440-yard relay team that set a national record in 1928. Copeland worked for the Los Angeles County Sheriff's Department and was a juvenile officer for 24 years.

Records Held

World Record: Javelin Throw — 38.30 m (February 26, 1927–)
American Record: Discus Throw — 40.60 m (August 2, 1932–)

Championships

1925 AAU: Shot Put (1st)
1926 AAU: Shot Put (1st)
1926 AAU: Discus Throw (1st)
1926 AAU: Javelin Throw (1st)
1927 AAU: Discus Throw (1st)
1927 AAU: Shot Put (1st)
1928 AAU: Shot Put (1st)
1931 AAU: Shot Put (1st)
1931 AAU: Javelin Throw (1st)

Education

undergraduate: University of Southern California (Los Angeles, California)

Occupations

Juvenile officer, Los Angeles County Sheriff's Department

KATE (KATE THE GREAT) SCHMIDT

Born: December 29, 1953 — Long Beach, California

Events

Javelin Throw — 69.32 m

Kate Schmidt had the good luck to grow up in Long Beach, CA., a mecca of javelin throwing during the 1960s. A year after she took up the event, she almost made the Olympic team in 1968

at age 14 and won the woman's nationals the following year. Nicknamed "Kate the Great" with good reason, she totally dominated the American women's javelin throwing scene for a decade. She broke the American javelin record 10 times, culminating with a throw of 227' 5" that has held up as the record for more than a quarter century. At the time, that throw was a world record and established her place on the international scene. Schmidt was third at the 1972 and 1976 Olympic Games and was also a member of the 1980 Olympic team that didn't compete. She just missed making the 1984 team when she placed fourth. She won seven national titles and placed in the top three in 12 of 13 national championships from 1972 to 1984.

Records Held

World Record: Javelin Throw — 69.32 m (September 11, 1977)

Championships

1972 Olympics: Javelin Throw (3rd)
1976 Olympics: Javelin Throw (3rd)
1969 USA Outdoors: Javelin Throw (1st)

Education

undergraduate: UCLA (Los Angeles, California)
undergraduate: Long Beach State (Long Beach, California)

The author and Kate Schmidt (right).

INTERVIEW: CECI HOPP ST. GEME

(March 10, 2006) I grew up in Greenwich, Connecticut. I went out for the indoor track team in my sophomore year which would have been probably 1979. I went out for indoor track to get in shape for the spring tennis season. I was a ballet dancer and a tennis player. But I just discovered that I was a much better runner than a tennis player [laughter]. This is when I met Bill Mongovan, who was one of the track coaches and club coach in the area for the Gateway Track Club. Bill had the most influence on me as a high school runner with both his coaching and knowledge of the sport.

I quickly had a lot of success on the high school level. By my senior year in high school, I was the national cross country champion; back then it was called Kinney, now it's Foot Locker. I ran 17:12 for a 5k. I won the regionals in Van Cortlandt Park. By the end of my senior year I won the U.S. junior nationals at 3000 meters in 9:21. I think that meet record was just broken last year. I ran a 4:42 .6 mile in high school. My competition back then was a young lady named Kim Gallagher [laughter]. She was very fast and a two minute 800 meter runner up to the mile and I was coming down from cross country and the two mile.

I went on to get a scholarship to Stanford University in Palo Alto. At the time, I remember, I never really thought in high school that I would get an athletic scholarship. I definitely caught the first wave of female athletes benefiting from Title IX.

For me running had always been kind of an extracurricular activity to help me get into college. My dad went to Columbia and was pushing the Ivy Leagues but I was recruited by a pretty famous track coach named Brooks Johnson, who was also an Olympic track coach, and I went all the way out to California. There I won the NCAAs at 3000 meters in my freshman year; I was 10th in cross country at NCAAs in 3000 meters in 1982; I had the world junior record in 3000 meters in 8:57. That was broken by Zola Budd and then a bunch of Chinese women [laughter]. It's still the American junior record. From there on out, my sophomore year I was the PAC 10 cross country champion and third at NCAAs in cross country. That was pretty much my college career. I struggled with a lot of injuries thereafter.

I retired for a couple of years after college. I had two children. I came back in 1991 and I finished fifth in the country in the 1500 meters. My best mile time was 4:27 and my best 1500 meter time, 4:11. I tried to make the Olympic team in 1992 and dropped out of the trials with a foot injury. I had another baby in 1993 and I came back in 1994 and won the USATF national championships 5000 meters on the track in 15:50. I finished second in the 1993 cross country nationals to Lynn Jennings. 1994 was a big year for me on the track. I was trying to hold on for the 1996 Olympics but I had some injury problems and ended up retiring there. I had three more babies in '95, '97 and '98.

Probably what put me on the map on a national level would be winning the Kinney cross country nationals in Balboa Park in San Diego as a senior in high school. I really didn't get to the national level until my senior year. Bill Mongovan was very instrumental in taking me beyond the little Connecticut pond [laughter]; also finishing second at the cross country nationals to someone like Lynn Jennings, who was the world champion at the time. I did that only seven months after having my third child. It was one of those races that just stands out in my mind. It was probably the first time where I remember thinking, "Why am I doing this?" [laughter] "Why am I out here in Missoula, Montana, seven degrees? I don't have to be doing this anymore." And then my brain just clicked and went, you know what, you have nothing to lose, you have three babies at home waiting for you — happy whether you win or lose — and let's see what you can do. That's probably where my running career kind of changed over to just having fun with it — less pressure and see what I could do. To be a mother out there — that's where I feel that I kind of have been blazing a little bit of a trail as a female athlete after children. I would never have had the opportunities I had in high school and college if I were any older than I am. I am probably the first age group to truly benefit from Title IX.

I am now a master's runner [laughter]. My two oldest daughters are seventeen and eighteen and they run at Corona del Mar High School and I am assistant coach to their amazing coach Bill Sumner. I was the top master's finisher at the cross country nationals this past fall. I do a lot of road racing, 5ks. I've gotten my 5k down to 16:20.

Annie is the California state champion in 1600 meters. She was 13th at the cross country nationals. She is a strong runner and is going to Stanford also on a track scholarship. So that's a lot of fun for us. Our other daughter Christine is the number 5 or 6 girl on the high school cross country team and the team was ranked number 1 in the country this fall.

So that's my story. Definitely track and field and running has been a life long sport and activity for me. That's probably one of the things I'm proudest about: that I've been able to reach the top of the national level in high school, college and now as a master's runner. I'm having more fun with it now than ever.

INTERVIEW: PHILIPPA "PHIL" RASCHKER

(December 2, 2004) I got started in track and field when I was ten. Before that, I had done a few other sports. I did that through age twenty until I came to the United States in the late 60s.

I was really surprised coming from Europe. I had always thought that the United States was a dream country for doing track and field but there was just nothing available for women. So, I came to a screeching halt. I didn't do a thing for a couple of years. Then, when I started again, I was called the grandma of the team because the other girls were so much younger and I was 22 (actually 23). I was called grandma, what would they call me now? [laughter]

I did that for a number of years while I was living up north. Then we moved closer to the south, to Rocky Mount, North Carolina and again there was nothing available for women, absolutely nothing. So, what they did have at that point was some cross country running and some YMCA 5 ks. So, I tried that. But, I'm really a sprinter/jumper and it didn't go well with me. I tried it for two years and couldn't do it.

In 1979, I saw results from a masters meet in Raleigh, North Carolina, which was just about an hour away from where I lived. Hey, I can do that! So, I called the newspaper and asked where I could get more information and they gave me all of the information. I hooked up with that meet the following year (1980) which was the Southeastern Masters Championships. That was the first time I participated in the masters program. I did the 100, 200 and long jump. Even then, in the masters program in 1980, when I went to the meet they didn't have the long jump for women. I had to jump with the men. They didn't have the women's pentathlon. You had to do the men's version. That was 1980 — amazing! Anyway, a little while later I got together with Phil Mulkey. He was in the decathlon in the 1960 Olympics in Rome. So, of course, he was an all around athlete. He was pole vaulting in addition to many of the other events in the masters program. I found out that any event that was open for the men was also open for the women in the masters program. So, it didn't matter if we were 50, 60 or 70 years old as a woman; they were not concerned that we as women couldn't do an event. So, that was absolutely marvelous.

I was really intrigued by the pole vault and Phil did the pole vault. We took one of his long, heavy sticks — my gosh — the man weighed something like 180 pounds and was 6 feet tall and here I was barely 5' 4" weighing, at that point, barely 100 pounds. We cut it off and made it shorter. I couldn't jump that high anyway. So, we shortened it, which made it a little better but the circumference of the pole, you know, I couldn't get my hand around it. It didn't matter. So, we started from scratch jumping into the long jump pit. This was about 1983. That's how I learned, little by little. I really thought it was a great event. I also picked up other events. I picked up the triple jump, which we didn't have at that time in the open — what else? I guess the triple jump and the pole vault were two events that I did that were not available to the women in any other program than the masters.

We had the first exhibition jumping event in 1994 in the national championships. We had the steeplechase, as well as the first exhibition pole vault at the open nationals in Knoxville. At that time, we didn't have the right height and didn't know what the steeplechase was going to be. I think we had only four entrants and so the girls were asking, who would do the steeplechase with them. I said, "I will help you out." So, I did the steeplechase.

That was the first time we did the women's pole vault. The winner of the event was Melissa Price. This was 1994. I think she was seventeen years old. We both jumped 10' 8" but because she had fewer misses, she went to the inaugural Goodwill Games for the pole vault in St. Petersburg and I stayed home [laughter]. That would have been really great. You know, it didn't matter that we both jumped the same height; I barely missed it.

That was the first time we did the pole vault officially, as an exhibition. The following year in 1995 was the first year that it was officially done in Sacramento. I was again, very fortunate that time. I didn't have any misses all the way through and I had a lot of endurance. There were a lot of kids there. I was 48 years old, so, they were kids. We ended up — Melissa Price won the competition, Stacy Dragila got second and I got third. Shortly after that we had our world masters games in Buffalo. I think I won 8 or 9 gold medals and several world records. Then I said, "Okay, I'm going home now and rest until the end of the year." But, I wasn't home a couple of hours, it seemed, and I got this phone call from Indianapolis. They said, "You are being selected for our first women's international pole vault competition in a dual meet, USA vs. Great Britain." Hey! I'm tired but I'm going to go.

That was the first time that we had an international competition in the pole vault and, of course, the oldest other woman there was Ruth Wysocki (age 38) running — and me — and all those young athletes.

That was very, very exciting. I think I was even late getting over there. The team was already gone and I sort of hauled myself over there. So, that was really great and exciting. At that age, who would have ever thought, certainly not me — in that event. That was '95.

'96 was the first time we had it indoors. I went to that one. Then injuries got me, youth got me and even though I loved the pole vault, I was not willing to do just the pole vault. I like all the other events and I'm good at all the other events. I was not willing to give that up and just do the pole vault. So, I continued to do the sprints, hurdles and jumps and the heptathlon, but at the same time doing the pole vault. Probably, if I had not done all the other events, I could have done quite a bit better because I had the speed and I have the strength. Everything was there but, heck, you can't look back. I made my choices and I don't regret it. I had a great time with it. From there, all the kids came up in the rank and file.

In 1997, we still did not have it in the schools but I was recruited by Mike Spino for a

Philippa "Phil" Raschker, 2004.

scholarship at the NAIA for Life College for basically doing the heptathlon and the pole vault. It was 1996, and my good friend, Josh Culbreath, said we really need to get the pole vault in the college program and they were the first division that got the women's pole vault in. I got the scholarship, which was again, one of the highlights of my life; 50 years old and you get a scholarship. I hadn't gone to college in Germany so I still had my eligibility and the NAIA doesn't have an age limitation. So, you can be 100 years old; if you can get a point, they'll give you a scholarship, I guess [laughter]. I could have scored well with them.

My problem was that when I started with Life College, I was asked if I had ever received money and I said "No." Nothing occurred to me. I went home that night and said, "Wait a minute, I did get money." In our masters program we used to have 100 meter age graded races. We had these races where you win your division in the 100 and then have an age graded handicapped race at the end of the national championships. *National Masters News* was, at that time, putting up some money. The winner of the men's and women's race (women) would get a hundred dollars. That's what my prize money was. So, that's what came to me that night. The next day I went to the coach and told him I received some money when I was around 45 and 46 years old. At one point, I received one hundred dollars and another few times I got fifty dollars. Altogether it came to four hundred dollars over several years for four different events. So, he said we need to report that and see what they are going to do. And so the NAIA as a body, said, sorry, she can't run. She got prize money. Even though, of course, my entry fees alone have always run over one hundred dollars in the first place [laughter] besides the cost of traveling. So, it's not like I got rich on it! That was the beginning and the end of my college career.

That was my second highlight. Just even being asked for a scholarship to a college. I had great team members. It would have been a lot of fun. I was really looking forward to that.

And then, I guess my next highlight has been winning thirteen Outstanding Athlete of the Year awards from USATF with the masters program. Of course, that's a wonderful honor and I'm still trying to get a few more.

My last highlight was when I was nominated by the National Senior Games Association (NSGA) for the AAU Sullivan Award and made it through the rounds. The first round was being accepted by the committee. The next round was a vote of the top 10 and I made the top 10, and, wow, that was terrific. Then, of all things, the final vote for the top 5 who would be invited to New York for the final big splash; and I made the final 5. So, here I was with Michael Phelps (swimming), Apollo Ono (speed skating), Diana Turasi (basketball) and the other basketball players, LeBron James and Phil Raschker. We were there for the big celebration in April 2004 for the 2003 Sullivan Award. Michael Phelps won it. Their policy is not to announce place 2, 3, 4 or 5 — but just being there. Apollo Ono was 23, he was the oldest one. And, then there was me — 57 years old [laughter]. It was an incredible honor which I'm very proud of— having had that opportunity — the people that gave me that opportunity.

So, now, I just continue to train and I can't do as much as I used to. I think our bodies tell us not to do as much and I've been crazy about that because I love all my events.

My goal is still doing better in the pole vault. I know I can do so much better. So, maybe now is the time. I have to cut back on some of the other events because it's just too much for the body to do all the jumping and sprinting and hurdling and heptathlon and, of course, we do have the decathlon. Maybe I need to focus on just a few events. So, maybe the pole vault would really be the one. I know I have more speed than anyone else in the world in my age group, because I am the fastest in the sprints. I've got the speed and the strength and now I need the technique. That's a little more difficult since I am not with Phil Mulkey anymore. I don't have anyone I can go out with and doing the pole vault by yourself is not good.

You can do the drills on the track, but other than that, you develop bad habits and you don't know what you're doing. Besides, I don't have a pit even if I wanted to do at least some drills. I need to find a coach locally. Watch out! If I can really find a coach to train me and just concentrate on the pole vault, there's some good heights in me!

15

1995

The Outdoor Nationals

The USA/Mobil Outdoor Track and Field Championships were held in Hughes Stadium, Sacramento, California from June 14 to June 18.

Jeff Hollobaugh reported in *The Record*:

Gwen Torrence, the Olympic 200 champ, came to Sacramento hurting from a muscle tear behind her right knee. After one round of the 100, no one bet on her to make it. Even her husband (and coach) Manley Waller said the chances were only "slim" that she would continue. Said Torrence, "I thought, I'll never know if I don't try. I'm just going by chance right now. Hopefully chance is enough."

"It was for the semis, though the Atlanta sprinter cramped at the finish. But then, in the final, she came alive, running as if she warmed up at Lourdes. Her 11.04 topped the field and gave her the second U.S. 100 title of her career. In the 200, Torrence looked even better. She cruised the turn in a windy 22.03. It was title No. 5 for her, and the second time she had managed the double.

"In the 100,' she said, "I came to get 3rd, but this is my event, so I wanted to win."

Athletes such as Sheila Hudson-Strudwick helped to provide the thrills that make meets into treasured memories. America's best triple jumper rode a heady gust out to 48' 1¼". Not a record, but it was the best leap ever by an American, by a longshot. Hudson-Strudwick knew it, bounding down the track to the signboard, hopping up on a chair, and posting the numbers herself for all the fans to see.

Just as joyful was Kim Batten, who won the 400 hurdles in 54.74 just four weeks after an emergency appendectomy and a warning by doctors to rest for a few months. "I'm very, very happy," she said. "I felt the only thing that should stop Kim was Kim."

---

100 meters

"A three week-old hamstring pull in her right leg was the problem and Torrence was in obvious pain after each of the preliminary races," reported *Track & Field News*.

"In the final, she got off to a lightning start and was in control of the race by the 20m mark, looking like the normal Torrence."

To date, this is the third fastest time in the world.

1. Gwen Torrence, Mazda Track Club		11.04
2. Carlette Guidry, Team adidas		11.12
3. Celena Mondie-Milner, MidAtlantic Track Club		11.22

4. D'Andre Hill, Louisiana State University	11.34
5. Chryste Gaines, PowerAde Athletic Club	11.45
6. Sabrina Kelly, unattached	11.47
7. Cheryl Taplin, Nike International Track Club	11.48
8. Inger Miller, unattached	11.62

200 meters

"The reigning Olympic champ got a fine start and went through the first 100 in 11.2," said *Track & Field News*. "She was never challenged and won her fifth title easily in a windy 22.03."

1. Gwen Torrence, Mazda Track Club	22.03 w
2. Carlette Guidry, Team adidas	22.57
3. Celena Mondie-Milner, MidAtlantic Track Club	22.76
4. Aspen Burkett, University of Illinois	22.77
5. Chryste Gaines, PowerAde Athletic Club	23.07
6. Kenya Walton, University of Tennessee	23.28
7. Zundra Feagin, Louisiana State University	23.28
8. Dannette Young-Stone, Reebok Racing Club	23.31

400 meters

"Just before the home straight, Miles began to move. She sliced through the pack to go from last to first in 30m or so, and then pulled away to win in 50.90."

1. Jearl Miles, Reebok Racing Club	50.90
2. Kimberly Graham, Nike Track Club	51.48
3. Maicel Malone, Asics Track Club	51.56
4. Rochelle Stevens, Posner Track Club	51.97
5. Nicole Green, PowerAde Athletic Club	52.02
6. Camara Jones, University of Oregon	52.23
7. Youlanda Warren, Louisiana State University	52.25
8. Michele Collins, Mizuno Houston Track Club	52.56

800 meters

According to *Track & Field News*, "In the final turn, Rainey revived and although second surges are tough in an 800, pulled away to win in 2:00.07. Clark's strong final 200 took her by Wickus on the inside 80m from home."

1. Meredith Rainey, Foot Locker Athletic Club	2:00.07
2. Joetta Clark, Foot Locker Athletic Club	2:01.02
3. Amy Wickus, University of Wisconsin	2:01.26
4. Jill Stamison, Nike North Track Club	2:01.85
5. Alisa Hill, Foot Locker Athletic Club	2:02.59
6. Nicole Teter, Central Coast Track Club	2:03.71
7. Debbie Marshall, unattached	2:05.79
8. Nekita Beasley, Nike Track Club	2:08.40

1500 meters

USATF Report interviewed Regina Jacobs: "I'm very happy with my race. It's really good practice for the world championships. A lot of times it gets strategic like that in the rounds. I was very surprised by the time. While this is the trials, this is another opportunity to practice. I felt so easy the first three laps. That's my third 1500 in the last eight days and my second 4:05 (in that stretch). I definitely have a shot at going under 4 this year."

1. Regina Jacobs, Mizuno Track Club 4:05.18
2. Suzy Hamilton, Reebok Racing Club 4:07.07
3. Sarah Thorsett, PowerAde Athletic Club 4:07.49
4. Ruth Wysocki, Nike Coast Track Club 4:08.22
5. Kathy Franey, Reebok Racing Club 4:09.40
6. Amy Rudolph, Providence College 4:11.18
7. Kate Fonshell, Asics Track Club 4:13.02
8. Cheri Goddard, Reebok Enclave 4:14.20

3000 meter steeplechase (exhibition)
1. Chris Morgan, Track West 10:51.92
2. Melissa Teemant, Brigham Young University 10:56.90
3. Teressa DiPerna, unattached 11:07.02
4. Monica Townsend, Reebok Aggies Track Club 11:07.16
5. Gina Wilbanks, Athletes in Action 11:26.42
6. Pam Allie-Morrill, Frog's Racing Team 11:27.24
7. Kristin Diggs, Sacramento Track Club 11:29.42
8. Gretchen Lohr, Track West 11:48.70

5000 meters

"Laura Mykytok took the pace out from the start," said *Track & Field News*.

"At 4k, Joan Nesbit briefly took the lead, but Mykytok and Procaccio passed her back, taking Libbie Johnson along with them. In the closing laps, Mykytok, weakened by the wind, was unable to break away. With 150 left, Procaccio unleashed her miler's speed and shot past Mykytok for the victory in 15:26.34."

1. Gina Procaccio, New Balance Track Club 15:26.34
2. Laura Mykytok, Nike Track Club 15:27.52
3. Libbie Johnson, Mizuno Track Club 15:28.27
4. Joan Nesbit, New Balance Track Club 15:29.35
5. Cheri Goddard, Reebok Enclave 15:29.68
6. Annette Peters, Nike International Track Club 15:39.84
7. Katy McCandless, Asics Track Club 15:45.87
8. Shelly Steely, Mizuno Track Club 15:47.58

10,000 meters

Track & Field News reported: "Anne Marie Lauck was the principal early leader of a pack which dwindled to four at the midway point, reached in 16:04.22. With 500m, Lauck let go, and Henes was doing all she could to keep a pace going that might discourage Jennings. It wasn't enough, and Jennings blasted past with 300m to go."

1. Lynn Jennings, Nike International Track Club 31:57.19
2. Laurie Henes, Team adidas 32:05.32
3. Anne Marie Lauck, Nike Track Club 32:07.43
4. Olga Appell, Reebok Racing Club 32:19.60
5. Trina Painter, New Balance Track Club 32:41.35
6. Colette Murphy, Team adidas 32:45.37
7. Nan Doak-Davis, Team adidas 32:51.27
8. Laura LaMena-Coll, Reebok Racing Club 33:23.04

100 meter hurdles

Track & Field News continues: "Dawn Bowles and Doris Williams got out ahead of her, but Devers closed the gap by the second hurdle and eased to a 12.77 win."

1. Gail Devers, Nike International Track Club   12.77
2. Marsha Guialdo, unattached   12.98
3. Doris Williams, Goldwin Track Club   13.03
4. Dawn Bowles, Foot Locker Athletic Club   13.04
5. Cheryl Dickey, unattached   13.10
6. Donna Waller, unattached   13.25
7. Monifa Taylor, Reebok Racing Club   13.25
8. Lynda Goode, Goldwin Track Club   13.34

400 meter hurdles

"Six days after running a world-leading 53.88 in Sao Paulo on May 14, Kim Batten underwent an emergency appendectomy. So her 54.74 clocking, good enough to defend her title and turn back Tonja Buford, stands as testimony to her toughness."

1. Kim Batten, Reebok Racing Club   54.74
2. Tonja Buford, unattached   54.82
3. Trevaia Williams, Atoms Track Club   55.43
4. Sandra Farmer-Patrick, Nike International Track Club 55.63
5. Tonya Williams, University of Illinois   57.17
6. Rebecca Russell, unattached   57.36
7. Tonya Lee, MidAtlantic Track Club   57.61
8. Michelle Johnson, University of Arizona   58.92

10,000 meter walk

"Vaill, the 32-year-old defending champion, quickly showed her determination as she took the early lead and drove hard all the way for a wire-to-wire victory."

1. Teresa Vaill, unattached   45:01.00
2. Michelle Rohl, Brooks Athletic Club   45:16.14
3. Debbi Lawrence, NaturalSport Track Club   45:45.92
4. Victoria Herazo, California Walkers   45:52.63
5. Debby Van Orden, unattached   46:02.99
6. Lynda Brubaker, LaGrange Track Club   47:26.41
7. Dana Yarbrough, LaGrange Track Club   49:02.13
8. Susan Armenta, California Polytechnic, Pomona   49:15.18

High jump

"...Only Acuff, at 19 the youngest in the field, could scale 6' 4¾" and the title was hers."

1. Amy Acuff, University of California, Los Angeles   6' 4¾"
2. Tisha Waller, Goldwin Track Club   6' 3½"
3. Connie Teaberry, Goldwin Track Club   6' 3½"
4. Gwen Wentland, Nike Track Club   6' 3½"
5. Yolanda Henry, Nike International Track Club   6' 1¼"
   and Clare Look-Jaeger, Nike Coast Track Club
7. Angela Bradburn, PowerAde Track Club   6' 1¼"
8. Tanya Hughes, unattached   6' 1¼"

Pole vault (exhibition)
1. Melissa Price, Kingsburg High School   12' 9" AR
   (betters American record of 12' 6", by Price earlier in season)
2. Stacy Dragila, Idaho State University   11' 5¾"
3. Phil Raschker, World Elite Track Club   10' 10"

4. Melissa Feinstein, Air Time Athletics   10' 10"
5. Shannon Walker, Air Time Athletics   10' 10"
    and Tyra Holt, Stanford University
7. Nikki Hyles, unattached and Kristi Draher, Mira Mesa High School   10' 6"

Long jump
1. Jackie Joyner-Kersee, Honda Track Club   22' 7" w
2. Marieke Veltman, World Class International   22' 1½" w
3. Sharon Couch, Olsten Corporation   21' 11" w
4. Shana Williams, Reebok Racing Club   21' 9" w
5. Tonya Sedwick, Nike Track Club   21' 8¾"
6. Vonetta Jeffrey, University of Alabama, Birmingham   21' 4¾" w
7. Tameka Roberts, University of Texas, San Antonio   21' ½" w
8. Cynthea Rhodes, unattached   20' 10" w

Triple jump
1. Sheila Hudson-Strudwick, Reebok Racing Club   48' 1¼" w
2. Cynthea Rhodes, unattached   46' 4" w
3. Diana Orrange, Prime Time Track Club   45' 7" w
4. Amanda Banks, unattached   45' 2¼" w
5. Wendy Brown, Maccabi Track Club   44' 4¾" w
6. Carla Shannon, unattached   44' 1½" w
7. Robyne Johnson, Anderson International Track Club   43' 8"
8. Tiombé Hurd, James Madison University   43' 7¾"

Shot put
    This was Connie Price-Smith's fourth consecutive national title and sixth overall in the shot.

1. Connie Price-Smith, Reebok Racing Club   62' 6"
2. Ramona Pagel, Nike Coast Track Club   61' 2¼"
3. Eileen Vanisi, Reebok Racing Club   57' 8¼"
4. Valeyta Althouse, Bruin Track Club   57' 5"
5. Dawn Dumble, Reebok Racing Club   56' 5¼"
6. Amy Christiansen, Brigham Young University   51' 7¾"
7. Tressa Thompson, University of Nebraska   51' 5½"
8. Collinus Newsome, University of Illinois   50' 6¾"

Discus
1. Edie Boyer, unattached   205' 4"
2. Pamela Dukes, Nike Coast Track Club   195'
3. Danyel Mitchell, unattached   194' 9"
4. Melisa Weis, Goldwin Track Club   194' 4"
5. Connie Price-Smith, Reebok Racing Club   192' 8"
6. Dawn Dumble, Reebok Racing Club   189' 9"
7. Carla Garrett, Nike Coast Track Club   187' 4"
8. Erica Ahmann, California Polytechnic, San Luis Obispo   177' 7"

Hammer (exhibition)
1. Dawn Ellerbe, University of South Carolina   181' 8"
2. Sonja Fitts, New York Athletic Club   180' 7"
3. Alexandra Earl-Givan, New Haven Athletic Association   178' 10"
4. Leslie Coons, unattached   176'

5. Bonnie Edmondson, Nike Coast Track Club	175' 3"
6. Lisa Misipeka, unattached	168' 8"
7. Kiza Brunner, Boston Running Club	167' 11"
8. Kiyomi Parish, unattached	167' 1"

Javelin

1. Donna Mayhew, Nike Coast Track Club	194' 1"
2. Ashley Selman, Asics Track Club	191' 4"
3. Erica Wheeler, Mizuno Track Club	183' 9"
4. Chris Stancliff, U.S. Navy	178' 10"
5. Nicole Carroll, San Mateo Athletic Club	178' 2"
6. Lynda Lipson, Klub Keihas	172' 1"
7. Jenny McCormick, San Mateo Athletic Club	168' 8"
8. Heather Berlin, University of Minnesota	167' 2"

Heptathlon

Jere Longman wrote in the *New York Times*:

...Jackie Joyner-Kersee won her sixth national heptathlon championship with 6,375 points, her most pedestrian performance since she won a silver medal in the 1984 Summer Olympics.

A struggling Joyner-Kersee, suffering a hamstring injury, a tender Achilles' tendon and asthma, nearly collapsed from weakness after four events on Wednesday. Today, after the long jump and a mediocre javelin throw, she strained through the 800 meters, tugging irritatingly at an allergy mask covering her face.

Her 800 time of 2 minutes 26.39 seconds was her slowest in eight years. That followed a 200-meter time of 24.36 seconds on Wednesday that was her slowest ever.

"This was a very embarrassing performance," said the 33-year-old Joyner-Kersee, who was competing in her first heptathlon of the season. 'I'm not washed up. I just need to put it together.'"

1. Jackie Joyner-Kersee, Honda Track Club	6375 w
2. Kym Carter, Nike Track Club	6354
3. Kelly Blair, Reebok Racing Club	6354
4. DeDee Nathan, Nike Indiana Track Club	6283
5. Sharon Hanson, Nike Coast Track Club	6202
6. Tonya Sedwick, Nike Track Club	6074
7. Ali McKnight, Nike Coast Track Club	5787
8. Sheila Burrell, University of California, Los Angeles	5735

Team scores:

Reebok Racing Club	75
Nike Track Club	37
Nike Coast Track Club	35½
Nike International Track Club	26½
Team adidas	25

Gwen Torrence was named the Outstanding Female Athlete of the meet.

The Indoor Nationals

The USA Mobil Indoor Track and Field Championships were held in the Georgia Dome, Atlanta, Georgia on March 3–4.

The *New York Times* featured an article on Michael Johnson's world record 400 meters in the indoor nationals. The article said, "...Sheila Hudson-Strudwick set an American women's indoor record with a triple jump of 46' 8¼", and Carlette Guidry-White set another national record in winning the 200-meter dash in 22.73 seconds."

Track & Field News reported that in the 60 meters, "[Gwen] Torrence won by an eyelash over Guidry, with each clocking a PR 7.04. A mere 0.004 separated them in the photo finish, and several minutes elapsed before Torrence was credited with the victory."

60 meters

1. Gwen Torrence, Mazda Track Club	7.04	
2. Carlette Guidry-White, Team adidas	7.04	
3. Chryste Gaines, unattached	7.18	

200 meters

Torrence scratched. Carlette Guidry-White won breaking Torrence's American record set here last year.

1. Carlette Guidry-White, Team adidas	22.73	AR
2. Dannette Young-Stone, Reebok Racing Club	22.83	
3. Juliet Cuthbert, Mizuno Track Club/Jamaica	22.84	

400 meters

"Jearl Miles trailed Maicel Malone for the first 300. But the former Arizona State star was unable to hold on as Miles moved by her on the far turn with relative ease and cruised in with a 50.99, the second-fastest ever by an American," reported *Track & Field News*.

1. Jearl Miles, Reebok Racing Club	50.99	MR
2. Maicel Malone, Asics Track Club	51.92	
3. Sandie Richards, Reebok Racing Club/Jamaica	52.00	

800 meters

Track & Field News reported: "Maria Mutola led wire-to-wire to capture the title in 1:58.41, the No. 6 performance of all-time. Meredith Rainey ran valiantly in an effort to catch the African star but came up a bit short. Rainey's time of 1:59.61, however, is inferior only to Mary Slaney's 15-year-old 1:58.9 among U.S. marks."

1. Maria Mutola, unattached/Mozambique	1:58.41	MR
2. Meredith Rainey, Foot Locker Athletic Club	1:59.61	
3. Joetta Clark, Foot Locker Athletic Club	1:59.85	

Mobil mile

"Regina Jacobs ran away from Hassiba Boulmerka in the last half mile to win by more than 7 seconds in 4:26.54."

1. Regina Jacobs, Mizuno Track Club	4:26.54	MR
2. Hassiba Boulmerka, Algeria	4:33.78	
3. Kristen Seabury, New Balance Track Club	4:34.40	

3000 meters

"...After leading at both kilo marks, Jennings was pushed by Ireland's Sinead Delahunty for the last 800. They traded the lead over the last 3 laps, but on the final backstretch, Jennings sprinted to the front and Delahunty was unable to cover the move."

1. Lynn Jennings, Nike International Track Club	8:57.62	
2. Sinead Delahunty, New Balance/Ireland	8:58.33	
3. Joan Nesbit, New Balance Track Club	9:01.80	

Michelle Rohl at the 1999 National Indoor Championships.

60 meter hurdles

"...Goode was smooth while Jackie Joyner-Kersee stumbled out of the blocks and got into a bit of a hop mode over the sticks. JJK pulled even at hurdle 3, but Goode drew away at the last barrier," reported *Track & Field News*.

1. Lynda Tolbert-Goode, unattached	7.93
2. Jackie Joyner-Kersee, Honda Track Club	7.97
3. Michelle Freeman, Reebok Racing Club/Jamaica	7.98

3000 meter walk

1. Michele Rohl, Brooks Athletic Club	13:04.99
2. Victoria Herazo, California Walkers	13:11.76
3. Joanne Dow, unattached	13:28.22

20 lb. weight throw

Track & Field News reported: "Sonja Fitts won last year with a 57-footer. This time she had to loft the 20lb. ball out to 62' 7¼", the No. 3 toss ever, to stay ahead of Pam Dukes. Dukes' 61' 10¼" made her No. 2 on the all-time list."

1. Sonja Fitts, New York Athletic Club	62' 7¼"
2. Pam Dukes, Nike Coast Track Club	61' 10¼"
3. Dawn Ellerbe, unattached	60' 8"

High jump

"Gwen Wentland (PR) won a stirring competition over Tisha Waller (=PR), as both cleared 6' 5". With Wentland ahead on misses, the bar went to 6' 6¼" and both had two good attempts," said *Track & Field News*.

1. Gwen Wentland, Kansas State University	6' 5"
2. Tisha Waller, Goldwin Track Club	6' 5"
3. Yolanda Henry, unattached	6' 4"

Triple jump

According to *Track & Field News*, "Hudson-Strudwick looks to have improved the jump phase of her technique, and she put a strong finish on the competition itself as well, leaping 46' 8¼" on her final attempt to establish a new AR by 2¼ inches. The mark also equals her outdoor AR as the best U.S. jump ever."

1. Sheila Hudson-Strudwick, Reebok Racing Club	46' 8¼" AR
2. Cynthea Rhodes, unattached	44' 6"
3. Juliana Yendork, Southern California Cheetahs	44' 1¼"

Shot put

Track & Field News said, "Defender Ramona Pagel captured her sixth title, hitting 61' 3½" in round 2. Pagel was never challenged, as Connie Price-Smith finished 2nd at 58' 8½"."

1. Ramona Pagel, Nike Coast Track Club	61' 3½"
2. Connie Price-Smith, Reebok Racing Club	58' 8½"
3. Eileen Vanisi, Reebok Racing Club	57' 2¼"

Long jump

Jackie Joyner-Kersee won easily. She then passed her remaining jumps in order to get ready for the hurdles.

1. Jackie Joyner-Kersee, Honda Track Club	22' ¾"

2. Shana Williams, unattached   20' 10¾"
3. Jackie Edwards, unattached/Bahamas   20' 8½"

Pole vault
1. Melissa Price, unattached   11' 7¾"
2. Kate Staples, unattached/Great Britain   11' 5¾"
3. Tyra Holt, Stanford University   10' 10"

4 × 400m relay
1. University of Tennessee   3:38.64
   (Cheryl Finley, Kim Townes, Saidah Jones, Sue Walton)
2. Rice University   3:38.95
3. Eastern Michigan University   3:39.18

Distance medley relay
1. Auburn University   11:19.45
   (Eusheka Bartley, Nichole Bartley, Janet Trujillo, Rachel Sauder)
2. Stanford University   11:22.72
3. University of North Carolina   11:22.87

Point score:
Reebok Racing Club   23
Honda Track Club, Nike Coast Track Club and Team adidas   8

Sunkist Invitational (Five women's events): Los Angeles, February 11

500 yards
1. Sandie Richards, Jamaica   1:02.64 MR

800 meters
1. Maria Mutola, Mozambique   2:01.05

Mile
1. Sarah Thorsett, Nike North Track Club   4:38.64

50 meter hurdles
1. Jackie Joyner-Kersee, Honda Track Club   6.82 MR

High jump
1. Angela Bradburn, unattached   5' 11½"

12th Pan American Games: Mar del Plata, Argentina March 17–25

Name	Event	Place	Performance
Batten, Kim	400mh	1	54.74
Berry, Paula	Javelin	5	177' 5"
Bradburn, Angie	HJ	3	6' 3¼"
Buford, Tonja	400mh	2	55.05
Burrell, Dawn	LJ	5	20' 2¼"
Coogan, Gwyn	10,000m	7	33:32.49
Cuffee, Tamara	LJ	6	19' 11¾"
Damon, Karol	HJ	4	6' 2"

Name	Event	Place	Performance
Demko, Misti	5000m	5	16:04.56
Dendy, Terri	4 × 400mr	2	3:31.22
Fitts, Sonja	Hammer	3	183' 11"
Gaines, Chryste	100m	1	11.05 w (ties MR)
	4 × 100mr	1	43.55
Givan, Alexandra	Hammer	1	193' 4" MR (new event)
Harris. Flirtisha	400m	3	52.51
	4 × 100mr	1	43.55
	4 × 400mr	2	3:31.22
Irving, Crystal	400m	4	52.69
	4 × 400mr	2	3:31.22
Jenkins, Karol	HJ	4	6' 2"
Keeys, Omegia	200m	3	23.24
Kuehl, Kristin	Discus	3	186' 9"
LaMena, Laura	10,000	5	33:16.15
Lipson, Lynda	Javelin	7	166' 9"
Martin, Jennifer	Marathon	2	2:44:10
McNeair, Jamie	Heptathlon	1	6266 MR
Nathan, DeDee	Heptathlon	3	5879
Pagel, Ramona	SP	2	60' 8½"
Rabush, Kelly	1500m	5	4:25.04
Rainey, Meredith	800m	1	1:59.44
Rohl, Michelle	10k walk	2	46:36.52
St. Geme, Ceci	5000m	10	16:43.15
Shannon, Carla	TJ	5	43' 10" w
Smith, Connie Price	SP	1	62' 10¾"
Thorsett, Sarah	1500m	1	4:21.84
Trujillo, Maria	Marathon	1	2:43:56
Twiggs, Shantel	100m	7	11.57
	4 × 100mr	1	43.55
Vaill, Teresa	10k walk	DQ	
Webb, Richelle	200m	DNQ	23.59 s
	4 × 100mr	1	43.55
Williams, Allison	100mh	4	13.30
Williams, Trevaia	4 × 400mr	2	3:31.22

5th IAAF World Outdoor Track and Field Championships: Gothenburg, Sweden, August 5–13

100 meters
1. Gwen Torrence   10.85
4. Carlette Guidry-White 11.07

200 meters

"Her winning time of 21.77 seconds was disqualified today after a track judge ruled that Torrence had stepped out of her assigned lane, thus gaining an advantage over opponents by running a shorter distance around the curve," reported the *New York Times*.

Gwen Torrence (1st-DQ'd)

400 meters
3. Jearl Miles-Clark   50.00
7. Maicel Malone-Wallace   50.99

800 meters
5. Meredith Rainey-Valmon   1:58.20

1500 meters
7. Ruth Wysocki   4:07.08

5000 meters
Gina Procaccio   DNF

10,000 meters
12. Lynn Jennings   32:12.82
14. Anne Marie Letko-Lauck   32:22.54

Marathon
 7. Linda Somers   2:32:12
16. Kim Jones-Rosenquist   2:37:06

100 meter hurdles
1. Gail Devers   12.68

400 meter hurdles
1. Kim Batten   52.61   WR
2. Tonja Buford-Bailey   52.62

High jump
8. Amy Acuff (tie)   6' 4"

Long jump
6. Jackie Joyner-Kersee   22' 1½" w

Triple jump
There were no American women in the final.

Shot put
7. Ramona Pagel   61' 8½"
9. Connie Price-Smith   61' 5"

There were no American women in the final of the discus or javelin.

10 kilometer walk (road)
15. Michelle Rohl   44:17   AR
22. Teresa Vaill   45:02
24. Debbi Lawrence   45:03

Heptathlon
 5. Kym Carter   6329
 8. DeDee Nathan   6258
10. Kelly Blair-LaBounty   6229

4 × 100 meter relay
1. USA   42.12
    (Celena Mondie-Milner, Carlette Guidry, Chryste Gaines, Gwen Torrence)

D'Andre Hill ran in qualifying round.

4 × 400 meter relay
1. USA   3:22.39
      (Kim Graham, Rochelle Stevens, Camara Jones, Jearl Miles)

Nicole Green ran in qualifying round.

5th IAAF World Indoor Track and Field Championships: Barcelona, Spain, March 10–12

60 meters
3. Carlette Guidry   7.11
7. Chryste Gaines   7.22

200 meters
There were no American women in the final.

400 meters
5. Jearl Miles   52.01

800 meters
There were no American women in the final.

1500 meters
1. Regina Jacobs   4:12.61
4. Kristen Seabury   4:16.77

3000 meters
2. Lynn Jennings   8:55.23
3. Joan Nesbit   8:56.08

60 meter hurdles
6. Cheryl Dickey   8.19

4 × 400 meter relay
3. USA   3:31.43
      (Nelrae Pasha, Tanya Dooley, Kim Graham,
         Flirtisha Harris)

High jump
7. Tisha Waller   6' 4"

Long jump
There were no American women in the final.

Triple jump
 8. Sheila Hudson-Strudwick 45' 6½"
12. Cynthea Rhodes   42' 4¾"

Shot put
2. Connie Price-Smith   62' 8¾"

Pentathlon
2. Kym Carter   4632
9. Jamie McNeair   4365

Kim Batten at the 1995 World Champion-ships. Photograph by Ace Lyons, ©www.photo run.net

IAAF/Mobil Grand Prix Final: Monaco, September 9

200 meters	
1. Gwen Torrence	22.20
3. Carlette Guidry	22.71
800 meters	
6. Meredith Rainey	1:58.42
400 meter hurdles	
1. Kim Batten	53.49
2. Tonja Buford	53.69
4. Sandra Farmer-Patrick	54.61
High jump	
8. Tisha Waller	6' 2¾"
Shot put	
6. Connie Price-Smith	61' 2¾"
8. Ramona Pagel	60' 1"

U.S. Women's World Cross Country Team Trials: Birmingham, Alabama, February 18

1. Joan Nesbit, New Balance Track Club	21:01
2. Gwyn Coogan, Team adidas	21:24
3. Liz Wilson, New Balance Track Club	21:27

USATF Women's Cross Country Championships: Portland, December 4

According to the *New York Times*: "...Appell charged away from the 168-runner field at the start, leading Jennings by 10m after the first quarter-mile.... Passing through the mile in 5:00, Appell continued to extend her lead over a chasing pack of seven that included Jennings, '91 and '92 nationals runner-up Gwyn Coogan, marathon Olympian Cathy O'Brien, and '93 runner-up Ceci St. Geme. By 4km on the cold, frozen turf of the flat 5875m course, Appell had opened up 19 seconds on the pack, a margin that she extended to 22 by the finish line, which she crossed in 18:15."

1. Olga Appell, Reebok Racing Club	18:15
2. Gwyn Coogan, Team adidas	18:37
3. Lynn Jennings, Nike International Track Club	18:41
4. Sinead Delahunty, Ireland	18:44
5. Cathy O'Brien, New Balance Track Club	18:45
6. Ceci St. Geme, Asics Track Club	18:47
7. Lucy Nusrala, Reebok Racing Club	18:51
8. Kate Fonshell, Asics Track Club	18:59
9. Kristen Seabury, New Balance Track Club	18:59
10. Lisa Senatore, New Balance Track Club	19:02

IAAF/Snickers World Cross Country Championships: Durham, Great Britain, March 25

6. Joan Nesbit	20:50
14. Olga Appell	21:07
37. Gwyn Coogan	21:32
54. Katy McCandless	21:45

The United States team placed fifth, scoring 111 points.

IAAF/Reebok World Race Walking Cup: Beijing, China, April 29, 30

34. Michelle Rohl	45:57
42. Victoria Herazo	46:25
52. Debby Van Orden	47:08
53. Lynda Brubaker	47:55

IAAF Grand Prix Standings

3. Gwen Torrence
7. Kim Batten
8. Tonja Buford

Other News and Honors

Track & Field News: U.S. Athlete of the Year

Gwen Torrence

Top Ten Women — World Rankings — Track & Field News

2. Gwen Torrence
4. Kim Batten
7. Gail Devers

Top Ten Women — United States Rankings — Track & Field News
(World rankings in bold)

1. Gwen Torrence	**100 meters (world)**
2. Kim Batten	**1. Gwen Torrence**
3. Gail Devers	**4. Carlette Guidry**
4. Tonja Buford	**9. Celena Mondie-Milner**
5. Jearl Miles	**10. Chryste Gaines**
6. Meredith Rainey	
7. Carlette Guidry	1. Gwen Torrence
8. Connie Price-Smith	2. Carlette Guidry
9. Jackie Joyner-Kersee	3. Celena Mondie-Milner
10. Regina Jacobs	

200 meters
1. Gwen Torrence

Torrence's double makes her the first American woman to top both dashes two years in a row.

1. Gwen Torrence
2. Carlette Guidry
3. Celena Mondie-Milner

400 meters
3. Jearl Miles
7. Maicel Malone

1. Jearl Miles
2. Maicel Malone
3. Kim Graham

800 meters
6. Meredith Rainey
8. Joetta Clark

1. Meredith Rainey
2. Joetta Clark
3. Amy Wickus

1500 meters
10. Regina Jacobs

1. Regina Jacobs
2. Ruth Wysocki
3. Suzy Hamilton

3000 meters
No American women were ranked in the top ten in the world.

1. Gina Procaccio
2. Laura Mykytok
3. Lynn Jennings

5000 meters
No American women were ranked in the top ten in the world.

1. Lynn Jennings
2. Gina Procaccio
3. Laura Mykytok

10,000 meters
No American women were ranked in the top ten in the world.

1. Lynn Jennings
2. Anne Marie Lauck
3. Laurie Henes

100 meter hurdles
1. Gail Devers

1. Gail Devers

2. Marsha Guialdo
3. Doris Williams

400 meter hurdles
1. Kim Batten
2. Tonja Buford-Bailey
5. Sandra Farmer-Patrick

1. Kim Batten
2. Tonja Buford
3. Sandra Farmer-Patrick

10 kilometer walk
No American women were ranked in the top ten in the world.

1. Michelle Rohl
2. Teresa Vaill
3. Debbi Lawrence

High jump
10. Amy Acuff

1. Amy Acuff
2. Tisha Waller
3. Gwen Wentland

Pole vault
No American women were ranked in the top five in the world.

1. Melissa Price
2. Stacy Dragila
3. Shannon Walker

Long jump
8. Jackie Joyner-Kersee

1. Jackie Joyner-Kersee
2. Marieke Veltman
3. Sharon Couch

Triple jump
No American women were ranked in the top ten in the world.

1. Sheila Hudson-Strudwick
2. Cynthea Rhodes
3. Diana Orrange

Shot put
6. Connie Price-Smith
10. Ramona Pagel

(These are the first American women ranked in the world in the shot put since 1960.)

1. Connie Price-Smith
2. Ramona Pagel
3. Valeyta Althouse

Discus

No American women were ranked in the top ten in the world.

1. Edie Boyer
2. Pam Dukes
3. Danyel Mitchell

Hammer

No American women were ranked in the top five in the world.

1. Sonja Fitts
2. Dawn Ellerbe
3. Alexandra Givan

Javelin

No American women were ranked in the top ten in the world.

1. Donna Mayhew
2. Ashley Selman
3. Nicole Carroll

Heptathlon

9. Kym Carter

1. Kym Carter
2. Jackie Joyner-Kersee
3. Kelly Blair

Benita Fitzgerald, 34, was appointed director of the new United States Olympic Committee Training Center in Chula Vista, California.

Florence Griffith-Joyner, Valerie Brisco and Louise Ritter were inducted into the National Track and Field Hall of Fame. The biographies below are from the National Track and Field Hall of Fame website.

VALERIE BRISCO

Born: July 6, 1960—Greenwood, Mississippi

Events
200 m — 21.81
400 m — 48.83

More than a decade before Michael Johnson galvanized world attention with his 200m/400m doubles, Valerie Brisco became the first person to perform that feat in the Olympics. Her stage was ideal: the 1984 Los Angeles Olympics, just miles from her home at that time. She set American records in both individual events, running 21.81 in the 200m and 48.83 in the 400m. She won her third gold medal that year when she anchored the U.S. 4 × 400m relay team that set an American record with its time of 3:18.28. In 1988, Brisco won her fourth Olympic medal when she ran the third leg on the 4 × 400m relay team that broke the world record but finished second to the USSR team. Her previous running career barely hinted at her true abilities. She won the 1979 AIAW 200m championship while a student at California State-Northridge and was on the 4 × 100m relay team that won a gold medal at the Pan American Games. After marrying and giving birth to a child, she put her running career on hold. She finally underwent a rigorous training program in time to emerge as a superstar in 1984, winning the national indoor 200 and outdoor 400 titles that year. She became the first American woman to break 50 seconds in the 400 meters with her time of 49.83. In 1985, she set an indoor world record of 52.99 in the 400-yard run, and she was the national champion in the outdoor 400m in 1986. In 1987, she won a relay gold medal at the Pan American Games and a bronze medal as a member of the 4 × 400m relay at the World Outdoor Championships.

Records Held
World Record: 400 m — 52.99
World Record: 1,600 m relay
American Record: 200 m — 21.81 (August 9, 1984)
American Record: 400 m — 48.83 (August 6, 1984)
American Record: 1,600 m relay — 3:18.28

Championships
1984 Olympics: 200 m — 21.81 (1st)
1984 Olympics: 400 m — 48.83 (1st)

Valerie Brisco and Ed Levy, Coach, New York Pioneer Club, on Brisco's induction into the National Track and Field Hall of Fame, 1995.

1984 Olympics: 1,600 m relay — 3:18.28 (1st)
1988 Olympics: 1,600 m relay (2nd)
1987 World Outdoors: 1,600 m relay (3rd)
1979 Association of Intercollegiate Athletics for Women: 200 m (1st)
1984 U.S. Indoors: 200 m (1st)
1984 U.S. Outdoors: 400 m — 49.83 (1st)
1986 U.S. Outdoors: 400 m (1st)
1987 Pan Am Games: (1st)

Education
undergraduate: California State-Northridge (Northridge, California), 1979

Occupations
Athlete

FLORENCE GRIFFITH-JOYNER

Born: December 21, 1959 — Los Angeles, California. Deceased: September 21, 1998

Events
100 m — 10.49
200 m — 21.34

The nickname "Flo-Jo" has come to denote blazing speed, grace, flair and awesome talent. "Flo-Jo" is, of course, Florence Griffith Joyner, who was to the 1988 Olympic games what Wilma Rudolph was to the 1960 Rome Games. Even before the 1988 Olympics, Flo-Jo was a world record holder. Seoul merely confirmed her greatness. Her records set during those wild days of 1988 are standards that probably will prevail well into the 21st century. She still holds the women's world record of 10.49 for 100 meters and 21.34 for 200 meters and no one has come close to threatening them. Her 10.49 at the Olympic Trials in Indianapolis was one of the most eye-popping performances in track and field history. An outstanding sprinter before 1988, she showed her early promise at Jordan High School, where she anchored the relay team that posted the nation's fastest time of the year. After transferring from Cal State Northridge to UCLA, she won the NCAA 200m championship in 1982 and the 400m title in 1983. She was a silver medalist in the 200m at the 1984 Olympics and also medaled at the 1987 World Outdoor Championships, taking second in the 200 and running on the winning 4 × 100m relay team. At Seoul in 1988, she won three gold medals (100, 200, 4 × 100) and one silver (4 × 400), setting a world record in the 200. It was Flo-Jo's golden moment and it will be tough to repeat. She won the Sullivan Trophy in 1988. Flo-Jo married Al Joyner, 1984 Olympic triple jump champion, in 1987.

Records Held

World Record: 100 m — 10.49 (July 16, 1988)
World Record: 200 m — 21.34 (September 29, 1988)

Championships

1984 Olympics: 200 m (2nd)
1988 Olympics: 100 m (1st)
1988 Olympics: 200 m (1st)
1988 Olympics: 400 m relay (1st)
1988 Olympics: 1,600 m relay (2nd)
1987 World Outdoors: 200 m (2nd)
1987 World Outdoors: 400 m relay (1st)
1982 NCAA: 200 m (1st)
1983 NCAA: 400 m (1st)

Education

high school: Jordan (Los Angeles, California)
undergraduate: Cal State-Northridge (Northridge, California)
undergraduate: UCLA (Los Angeles, California), 1983

Occupations

Clothing designer

LOUISE RITTER

Born: February 18, 1958 — Dallas, Texas

Events

High Jump — 2.03 m

The premier women's high jumper in the United States for a decade from 1979 to 1989, Dorothy Louise Ritter surprised the world by winning the gold medal at the 1988 Olympics in Seoul. She won the event in a jump-off against Stefka Kostadinova of Bulgaria, the world record-holder and favorite. But Ritter's credentials were impressive in their own right. Starting in 1979, she raised the American record from 6' 4¼" to the present mark of 6' 8". She was on three Olympic teams, including 1988, and was third at the 1983 World Outdoor Championships. Ritter won 10 national championships, indoors and outdoors, and was world-ranked nine times, including her best placing of second in 1988. A graduate of Texas Woman's University, where she was the national collegiate champion, she also starred in basketball. She previously was one of the nation's best high school jumpers, clearing 5' 11½" at Red Oak (Texas) High School in 1976. She later became assistant track coach at Southern Methodist University and head track coach at Texas Tech.

Records Held

American Record: High Jump — 2.03 m (July 8, 1988)

Championships

1984 Olympics: High Jump (8th)

1988 Olympics: High Jump (1st)
1983 World Outdoors: High Jump (3rd)

Education
high school: Red Oak (Red Oak, Texas)
undergraduate: Texas Woman's (Denton, Texas), 1981

Occupations
Coach

INTERVIEW: PAM DUKES

(December 1993) I grew up in New Jersey. My parents moved there when I was four. Essentially, I got started in track and field almost by accident. I was always very athletic and I tried just about every sport. I was really into softball. I was a pitcher. I had a very good arm. Mr. Dennison, the track coach at my school, Freehold Township High School, kept harassing me, telling me that I'd be a great shot putter and I looked at him like he was from Mars because I couldn't imagine why anybody would throw the shot put at that point. He kept harassing me and I kept putting him off. One day he brought the shot put out to my softball practice. He told me that if I threw it once, he'd leave me alone. I said fine. So, he was prepared. He had a tape measure, he had the whole nine yards. And I said, I've seen people throw before so I had some clue as to what to do. So, I went down in the position and I let it go and he quickly measured it. As it turned out, the school record at the time was, I believe, 33 feet and I had just thrown it like 30 feet plus maybe 31 feet. He told me, "You know, you'd really be a great shot putter.

So, that evening I went home and talked to my parents. I've been really fortunate because I had a great support group with my family. Everything I tried they supported me. They bought me the drum set I wanted; they got me cheerleading shoes. You name it. And I said, "I'm thinking about this track thing, what do you think?" And they thought, you know, that's great, maybe there are more track scholarships than softball, you never know, you may excel at that. So, that very next year I went out for track as a sophomore and I won states that year. It was pretty much a Cinderella story.

My second year, I won states indoor and outdoors and I had the second best throw in the country at 46' 8". That qualified me for the junior nationals at UCLA. As it turned out, my coach couldn't accompany me to that meet so I took my mom as my coach. We went to that meet and we were sitting in the UCLA lobby one day and we were registering. I saw this guy sitting over on the couches with his feet up on the table and this big straw hat on and he really looked like a bum to me. And, I remember, I even remarked to my mom, "Gosh, they just let anybody in here, don't they?" It turns out that was Coach Brooks Johnson, the head coach at Stanford. I went upstairs for whatever reason and my mom sat down. He started talking to her and she found out who he was; he started getting interested in me. What are her grades like and so forth? It turned out that I had an excellent GPA in high school, I think I had close to 3.8. I was an Honor Society member and so forth but I didn't do that great on the SATs the first time. He was really interested in me taking them again.

So, at that point we left and I started getting all those recruiting letters. In 1982, I'll never forget my first recruitment letter. It was the University of Hawaii. I thought, "Wow, they're going to give me a scholarship," and I was going there. The next day I got something from Arizona and I said, "Okay, I'm going here." I must have switched 40 or 50 times. It was hysterical. As it came down, I decided to apply to LSU, University of Florida and Stanford, knowing full well that I wasn't going to get into Stanford [laughter]. At that point, I was pretty much leaning to going to LSU. I went to the school visits that they pay for and, at that point, I wanted to be a lawyer. When I got to the University of Florida, they took me straight to track and that's all we did was stay at the track. I thought they're obviously interested in my education — not. Then I visited LSU and they took me straight to the law school. They took me all around campus. I didn't even see the track till the very end. I thought, now these guys, I like what they're talking about. I actually didn't get a chance to visit Stanford, at that point. But I've seen pictures. I've seen they play college football on Saturdays. I knew it was a nice place.

Pam Dukes, 1993.

I'll never forget another girl from my school who was actually ranked higher than me in our class rankings applied to Stanford also. We were the only two. One day I got the mail and there was a letter from Stanford and I thought here's my rejection letter. I opened it up and it said "We are pleased to announce that you have been admitted." I just started screaming and I called my mom at work. I said, "Mom, are you sitting down?" She said, "Yes" and I said I just got word from one of the schools. She said, "And?" I said, "I got into Stanford." She said, "You're going." There wasn't even a pause. She just said "You're going." And at that point, I had so much trust in my family: they had really been a support basis and never steered me wrong and if they think I should go to Stanford, then I'm going, even though it's all the way across the country and I was really sort of a home body. I felt that this is going to set me up and would give me a good education because there's no way to go to Stanford and not get a good education. As it turned out, I think, one of the reasons my mom picked Stanford was not only because of its academic excellence, but also that she got along really well with Coach Johnson. In a way, they are a lot alike. They are very opinionated; they stand up for what they believe in; and I think they are very caring individuals. A lot of people may not see that necessarily in Coach Johnson, sometimes he can come off a little abrasive, but once you get to know him and you observe what he does, he really does care about his athletes and about the sport of track and field.

Ever since I went there, like every student, I had trouble in school the first year. I thought I could party all year and not study like I did in high school [laughter]. I got bad grades; I was on probation; they called my folks—oh my gosh! Sophomore year I did a little better, but not that much. Finally, I realized that doing the sport at this level was a sacrifice. It wasn't a sacrifice for me in high school, it was easy. Now, it was a sacrifice. In order to get to the next level I would have to give up something. I remember one speech Coach Johnson gave to everybody, "You can always have a social life. There's always going to be people around. When you're trying to compete at a Division 1 NCAA level, you are either going to be training or studying. It's that simple."

As it turned out, my sophomore year I made All-American. I was in the top eight in the United States. My junior year I went to the financial aide office to pick up my information and I got my stipend check to go pay to register. The check was for a lot more money than I was used to. I thought maybe they raised the fees. So, I went to go pay and I got money back. Everything was paid for. My parents didn't owe anything. I was surprised and I thought they screwed up. You know, how you hear about the IRS screwing up and you think you got all this money. So I called Coach Wollman, who was my direct coach at Stanford and he said, "Oh, didn't I tell you we put you on full scholarship?"

I thought, "Oh my gosh," and I called my mom and she screamed and yelled, and said, "We are so proud of you."

Based on how I did the year before, that even gave me more motivation to apply myself and between my junior and senior year, I improved 5 feet in the shot, 13 feet in the discus and I went from getting Cs and Ds to As and Bs. All I really did was to decide to try to apply myself. Stanford can be very intimidating because you are surrounded by every school's valedictorian. I don't know many students that have the confidence level to know that they belong and they're not worried about everybody else. You think, well, I'm not really going to try because I can't compete with these people. And I decided that they didn't let me in here because they thought I was cute or something [laughter]. They let me in because they knew that I could do the work and I applied myself and I ended up graduating with Honors.

My senior year, Brooks told me he wanted me to come back a year because I had eligibility. I thought, Well, I'm graduating on time, how are we going to work this? It turns out that Stanford has a co-term program where you can go to school and get your bachelors and masters degrees. I put an application in and thought they're not going to accept me, I'm way past the deadline. They let me in the program. I ended up getting my masters degree while I went on and won the indoor championships in the shot put in my graduate year.

A lot of this is all tied to Brooks. He kind of steered me in a direction and things have worked out. That's one of the reasons why this year I'm actually going to be moving down to where he is now, San Luis Obispo, and training under him. Some people have discouraged me because he's not a throws coach. But, at this level, I pretty much know how to throw the implement. I need someone to watch, guide me and give me some specifics and stuff. But, I don't need someone there every day telling me, get your left foot here, do this, do that.

One of the reasons I'm going with Brooks is because he is a person who builds self-esteem in athletes. It's simple. You can see it in all of his athletes. You can see it in PattiSue Plumer. You can see it even more so when he worked with Butch Reynolds through all of the controversy he went through. It's just there. It permeates. And that is what I need. If there is one thing that is lacking it's for me to believe that I can actually be the best in the country, not one of the best. I know that I can be one of the best but now I have to move to the next level and become the best. I know that by just being around him; whenever he's around I do better. So, why knock it at this point. I'm still going to work with Coach Wollman back in Texas in the shot put and the man who helped me throw 200 feet in the discus is still in the Stanford area. I'll drive up once a month and work with him. At this point, I'm going to do this because I believe I've gotten stale at Stanford. I need a change. I think every athlete reaches a point where they have done the best they can with the circumstances and they need to try something different. Now is the perfect time, three years out from the Olympics, that I go there and see what happens.

I made the Olympic Festival, I started college in 1982, so I guess it was in 1983 or '84, I made my first Olympic Festival and I haven't missed one since. They call me grandma and they make me captain and they tell everyone that if they have any questions, ask Pam. That was my first big team.

Then I started making teams like the World University Games. My first one was in 1987, I think. I went to Zagreb, Yugoslavia. That was a real experience for me and probably with all of the people I was with. I was with a lot of the people who are stars now. I was real good friends with Michael Powell. We all know who Michael Powell is now. I still tease him: "I remember when you were in Yugoslavia."

I made the Pan American Games in 1987 in Indianapolis. I went to Germany in 1989.

In 1991, I made my first world championship team and we went to Japan. That was really a thrill to me. That was the biggest meet I had ever gone to. I also went to the Pan Ams in Cuba in 1991. That was a real experience. It was really an eye-opening experience. One of the things I learned the most from going to these meets and leaving the U.S. is realizing how lucky you are. If you could see the poverty level in Cuba, people waiting on line for a loaf of bread, deterioration of the housing facilities, the old cars, I've never seen cars that old in my life. These things are running. I hear people complaining about what they have here. It's unbelievable. It refreshes you. It gives you a better perspective on what you have and makes you grateful. I got off the plane from Cuba, in Florida, and I kissed the ground and I had a hot dog. I was so happy to be home. I think that's one of the great things about competing in track and I met a lot of great people.

Of course, the big team I made was last year's Olympic team in Barcelona. That was a great experience for me. I was surrounded by people I watch on T.V. all the time. I turned around and Jim Courrier was standing next to me. Your brain is just swimming. It's nice because they see you as an equal. Oh, you're an athlete too, "No, you're Jim Courrier," and I just kind of fool around [laughter]. I actually befriended Jennifer Capriati. We hung around a little bit. I guess she's a lot younger than some of the tennis players so she still has more of an adolescent kind of feeling about life. She's out having fun, enjoying things. And, then to find out that she actually won was really special for me; she was my friend, I hung out with her and she's got the gold. That was nice.

Of course, the highlight of it were the opening ceremonies which were unbelievably awesome, spectacular. I can't compare it to anything. We met the dream team. A lot of them came to the village. I opened the door and Patrick Ewing was standing there and I know I was sweating, my hair, I'm losing the curl and I just thought, I cheered for you, you don't know how big a fan." I kept saying, "My family is gonna die," and he just kept laughing at me. And I said, "You don't seem to understand how big you are in my household." So I ran off and got my camera and got pictures with all these people. I gave them to my relatives and they just think I'm the greatest thing in the world. I got pictures with Cosby, I was with Ewing, I was with Barkley. I mean it's experiences like that that I'll cherish forever. Granted, these other special athletes tour and meet people but to actually be there almost as an equal with them, you really can't express in words. All this was happening because I competed in track and field. If I can get one point across to young athletes out there, they always want to be Carl Lewis, and I tell them when you see Carl in Europe at the world championship meet, I'm there too. I'm in the stands cheering for him. I just finished competing and now I'm cheering for him. Not everybody can run fast but you can possibly throw things or you can possibly jump. There are a lot of things you can do. I don't think you should sit there and try to attain something that you are not destined to do. If it turns out that you have a vertical of 40 inches, and you can jump, maybe you should high jump. Maybe you can be the next Hollis Conway. If you can jump far, maybe you can be the next Michael Conley or Mike Powell. You shouldn't just say I want the glamour of that and if I can't be Carl I'm not going to do track, because Carl's not there alone. We are all there with him. We all get most of the same experiences.

That's pretty much the highlight. I know a lot of the great athletes now. So we have a camaraderie going on. Granted, you always want to beat each other but afterwards we all get together and hang out and talk about training schedules. I met one girl who can bench 350 pounds. This is well over 100 pounds more than me. I'm taller than her. Just to get to know somebody like that. Some people say women shouldn't be that strong, they're intimidated. But, I am in awe of someone with that much strength as a female. That's the kind of thing I enjoy. Not only do I get to meet people like this but I can learn from them. Now, I can push myself. I'm sure there are women out there who would never think to go over 200 and now knowing that there's a female out there who can, well, now maybe you can do 210 or 215, you don't know. Just experiencing what other people have accomplished, I think, kind of infuses your own training.

One of the good things for me at this convention, especially the general meeting that they had yesterday, just seeing the medalists and the clips from T.V., it gets me excited. I'm a part of it. I want to go run, I want to go to the weight room. I can't wait to get back to run this hill I run. When I go back home, I think, "Michael Johnson is not sitting home watching Oprah, so get out there." I'm really grateful to track and field.

Now, it's my turn to turn around and say to other athletes, "Look, I did it and so can you. Don't give me excuses because there are too many excuses out there. At least try. If you only make the world championship team, that's too bad [laughter]. We're so sorry for you. You really have to test yourself."

Profile: Michelle Rohl

(Information provided by Michelle Rohl) I was born in Madison, Wisconsin in 1965. We lived just a few blocks from the UW campus, where my dad was going to grad school, but at the time, my family had no connection with anyone in athletics. My parents both grew up on farms and didn't have the opportunity to be in any sports. My mom was about as athletic as a girl was allowed to be back then, though. As a matter of fact, I always say that it was due to Jack LaLane that I was born. She watched his show to stay in shape, and even during the sixties when exercise during pregnancy was taboo, she went into labor with me while exercising with Jack LaLane.

I don't think my parents, or anyone else, could have guessed that I would grow up to be an athlete. I was a very small, timid child (I entered school in 1970 at a whopping 29 lbs.). I hated physical education because I wasn't the most coordinated child and I was always afraid of the ball. Even though I was consistently the last one picked for kickball, I was usually the first one in when we ran our 600 yd race every year. In third grade I won my first ribbon at an area elementary track meet. I was third in the 880. I guess that was the beginning of my athletic career. I sat on the bench for the whole basketball season, but I knew I could run. I floundered through middle school wondering what I was going to excel at, as most middle schoolers do I suppose. Since I went to parochial school we didn't have much opportunity for athletics as girls. Besides my not so inspiring basketball career, there was really nothing. But, in 8th grade, inspired by the challenge from a boy in my class, I began to seriously train for our annual 8th grade 1½ mile race in physical education. I ran three miles a week to prepare for it. Well, I thought this was big mileage! As it turned out, I did beat this boy, I always loved to beat boys.

We moved that summer, so I had to start high school in a new town. It was a difficult transition for me, and I think my parents were worried (probably justly) that I might start hanging with the wrong crowd. My older sister was telling us on the way home from school one day that a girl in her class was on the school's first ever girls cross country team. I thought that sounded really neat, but I was too shy to join the team; so my dad made me. He said, "Tomorrow you have to ask your gym teacher about joining cross country." This was so hard for me, because I was ridiculously shy. He gave my name and phone number to the coach (later I found out that he told him he didn't think I would be that good). The coach called and invited me to come out and run.

Our cross country race was two miles at the time. I informed my coach that I'd never actually run that far, but I'd give it a try. I remember crossing the finish line after my first race. I was so tired and disappointed, because it seemed like everyone beat me. I saw Coach Johnson running towards me at the finish line, probably to tell me I'm not good enough to be on the team, I thought. Instead he gave me what would become a very familiar smile and handshake. "Michelle," he said, "that was a great race, you were the first JV runner in. I'm so proud of the way you ran out there."

I have to say, this was definitely the turning point of my athletic career. In grade school I kind of got an idea that I might be good at running, but it wasn't until I received the much needed positive feedback from my coach that I knew running was what I was going to work hard to excel at. I hope all high school coaches know what an impact they can have on their young athletes. I was at a crossroads in my life at that time. I could have decided to waste high school with parties or fooling around, instead I gained a new sense of self-worth and pride in my abilities. I was putty in Coach Johnson's hands. Whatever he told me to do, from that day to graduation, I did, because I wanted only to get better. I soon became the best runner on our team, and eventually the best in the conference.

Though I wasn't a state stand-out in high school, I ran fast enough to obtain an athletic scholarship from UW-Parkside in 1984. Though it was hard for me to make the transition to a new coach, I soon came to trust and admire Coach Dewitt as much as I did my high school coach. After I was accepted at Parkside, Coach sent me a workout schedule to do over the summer to get ready for the season. It was really hard to start doing "real" workouts, and train seven days a week, but Coach had done the Olympic Trials that year for the 50K walk. He said the Olympics really inspired him to train and that I should watch the Olympics to help inspire me to do my training over the summer. Even as an 18 year old, I was told that achieving the status of

Olympian was within my grasp. It was more a matter of consistency and dedication than talent, Coach told us. (Coach knows consistency and dedication, he's never missed a day of training in over 25 years!) When I showed up for our first day of practice, and saw the Hall of Fame cabinet with Olympian Jim Heiring's picture in it, I was impressed, but also hungry to achieve the same status. Coming into college as a 5:24 miler, I really had no business even dreaming of such things, but Coach never suggested that it was impossible. He just consistently drew me back to the immediate goals and stepping stones that I needed to achieve along the way. "First let's concentrate on qualifying for nationals, you just need to worry about breaking five minutes this season." He helped me make goals that were realistic for me, and helped me stay focused on myself, not how others were doing in comparison. I can't control how others race.

Well, so far I haven't mentioned a word about racewalking. I was a runner all the way through college. I never really gave walking a serious thought, because I was enjoying more success than I would have ever thought possible as a runner. I had 100% confidence in Coach DeWitt, and if he told me I could be a national champion, I believed it and just went out and did the job. I graduated from Parkside with 15 All-Americans to my credit, and two individual national championships, along with a team national championship in cross country. I did do one walking workout my sophomore year. We were running Corbit Fartlek at the same time that the walkers were walking it (many national and international class walkers trained along with our cross country team). I told coach I was tired and asked if I could race walk this workout instead of run it. Coach knew I didn't know what I was getting into, but he let me go ahead and do it. It turned out to be a lot harder than I thought, but I was determined to keep up with the others. Actually, Jim Heiring said I was really tough. This was inspiring, since he was definitely my idol. I did manage to finish that workout, but I was never so sore in my life! I could hardly train the rest of the week. I decided to stick with running and leave the walking to the tough athletes. Coach did say that I had good technique for a beginner, and that if I ever decided to walk I could probably be pretty good at it. Just a seed planted in the back of my head.

Well, my senior year of track was going great, until I got Achilles tendonitis. I couldn't run a step without great pain, but walking didn't seem to bother it. Since I could keep up with the walkers on a workout, Coach had me do all walking workouts in the weeks prior to NAIA nationals. I didn't run a step. I ended up being second to Leah Pells at nationals, but finished off my college career with three more All-American races (1500, 3000, and relay). Not bad off only walking training. This was 1988, again an Olympic year. I wanted to qualify for the Olympic trials in the 1500, but I was a disappointing .02 seconds off the standard.

The next year, again I tried to make that jump to the elite level at 1500, but I had a hard time making the transition from college to post-collegiate running. Lack of funds made it difficult to get to races where the competition was, I couldn't get sponsorship unless I could go to those races, so it was a frustrating circle. Women's walking was just starting to come into its own at this time. Deb Lawrence had just won the exhibition 10K walk at the Olympic trials, and it was set to be an official Olympic event in 1992. As I came down to my last week to qualify for U.S. nationals in 1989, Coach told me that I had two choices. I could try to qualify in 1500 at Northwestern, but there would be no competition, and it would be really hard to run 4:20, or I could try and qualify in the walk. I thought this was a preposterous idea. I had never even raced over a mile, and that was a slower time than I would have to average for 10K to qualify for nationals in the walk. But Coach said that after seeing the way I walked prior to NAIA nationals last year, he was sure I could do it. As usual, I trusted him. On Thursday I started my walking training. On Saturday I did my first 10K race, and qualified for nationals. I was too sore to train for several days after that, but two weeks later I competed in U.S. nationals as a 10K racewalker. I was 10th, good enough to make it to Olympic Festival. The third race of my walking career, I was 6th there.

I guess you could call those three races of 1989 the beginning of my walking career, but it was short-lived. Having married a walker, Mike Rohl, in 1987, 1990 brought us a surprise little bundle of joy, Molly Elizabeth, born July 7th. Obviously, I was not too competitive that year. I did train every day right up until I went into labor. I was going to do eight hard quarters on July 4th like I'd read that Alberto Salazar's wife did to go into labor, but it didn't work. I only made it to four and gave up. Instead, I went into labor three days later while running 10 × 100M strides. I mostly ran during that pregnancy because race walking was less comfortable.

I really consider 1991 to be my first year of walking. That is when I really started to train for walking specifically. There was plenty of competition right in my area, and I decided that it would be easier to juggle training and caring for a baby if I didn't have to travel much. Also, the same financial restraints were keeping me from running. I finished 4th at nationals that year, just missing making Pan Am games. That was okay because I didn't really want to leave my baby anyway. So basically, as the Olympic trials approached in 1992, I was still a new face in the crowd. I'd never qualified for any U.S. team before (I was the only person I knew who didn't have a USA uniform). We went into serious credit card debt, getting me to races, since I didn't qualify for any USATF or USOC funding at the time. We were on the verge of bankruptcy so I really felt I had to do well at the trials.

As the new kid on the block, I was definitely the dark horse to make the team. The only people who believed in me were my husband and coach. But, of course, if Coach said I could make the team, he was right, so I just went out and did the job. As a result of making the team, and having to leave my husband and baby at home, we lucked out and had the opportunity to make an MCI commercial. This got us out of credit card debt. Phew, the gamble was worth it. To this point my whole race walking career had been a story of holding back. I couldn't go as fast as I wanted to, because I was still waiting for my technique to catch up with the cardiovascular ability that I had achieved as a runner. I raced very conservatively at the trials because it was important to just make the team and not get in trouble with the judges. At the Olympics I decided that I was tired of holding back. I wanted to see what the judges thought of my technique when I was going as hard as I could. No one expected anything of me, so I had nothing to lose. It was 95 degrees and 100% humidity in Barcelona that day. Everyone was 2–3 minutes off their PR in that race. I walked my fastest time of my life, to get 20th place, the first American, in fact, the first from the western hemisphere. Many people had said that my making the team was a fluke; I guess they were eating their words after that.

Coming home after a great Olympics, in the best shape of my life, I was looking forward to taking my walking to a new level. Then I found out I was pregnant with #2. Sebastian Miles arrived on May 13th of 1993. It was a harder pregnancy to train through, but I did a pretty good job. We moved to La Grange, GA, right after Seb was born, to start preparing for the Atlanta Olympics. LaGrange provided us with free housing, but again, we were living in abject poverty. Mike was going to graduate school 45 minutes away, so he was gone most of the day with the car. I would walk two miles to the track everyday pulling Molly and Seb in the wagon with their sand toys. Theoretically, they were supposed to play in the long jump pit with sand toys while I did my workouts. Mostly, Molly just chased me around the track crying, "Just one more K, Mommy, please, just one more K," and Seb would crawl into lane one and grab at my ankles as I walked by. It was really hard. Eventually, they learned that the steeplechase pit was way more fun than sand. Molly would chase me with the hose and spray me if she was ready to go home. I had to stop many workouts prematurely, just because my kids were wet, sandy, and cold so I had to take them home.

Still more eventually, we found a godsend of a woman, who babysat my children for free. In return, I would come after my workouts, and help her with the other kids that she took care of. In addition, I squeezed in as many hours as I could at my job in the nursery at First Baptist Church. It didn't pay much, but at least I could take the kids with me. After I set an American record at 10K in 1994, I was getting a little support from USATF (basic grant), but still, there were many times that we just didn't have enough money for groceries.

A lot of people have helped us along the way during these hard times. Our babysitter, who would even take the kids overnight when I had to race, was wonderful. My parents were always my biggest sponsor. In addition, many people in LaGrange, and the walking community opened their doors to us when we needed help.

In 1995, I continued to shatter American records at many distances. I got a silver medal at Pan Am games. I was 15th at world championships. I was walking better than any American woman had ever walked. Still, I lacked any real sponsorship.

Getting to races was still a significant financial strain. Molly started school and school responsibilities started stretching me even more thin. (I thought it would get easier as they got older, ha!) I started feeling a lot of pressure to perform well in Atlanta. People were calling me the U.S.'s only hope for a walking medal (15th to 3rd would be a pretty big jump). I couldn't commit any more time to training at that point, because I still needed to work and take care of my family.

In 1996, I took the kids and went to New Mexico to train at altitude. This was my first attempt at altitude training so it was a little hit and miss. I walked a huge American record at 5K at Penn Relays, but I didn't quite hit it right for the Olympics. I had hoped for a top 10 finish, but had to be satisfied with 14th. Still, this was the highest place a U.S. walker had finished in a couple of decades. Molly, Sebastian, and my whole family was there to cheer me on during the race. This was inspiring. Coach DeWitt, still my only coach, was also there, and I always race better when he is there.

1996 had been such a stressful year for me that I really had intended to retire after the Olympics. I got pregnant again and had #3 on August 25th, 1997. I was very casual about my training during that pregnancy, but I actually got back into shape very quickly after Ayla Frances was born. Again, the need for money swayed my decision to return to walking. There were some fall money races that year (though nothing compared to what the runners make). We needed the money, so seven weeks after Ayla was born I was 2nd to Deb Lawrence at the first of a series of prize money races that fall. It soon became apparent that I was going to continue walking. I walked an American record for 10K in the spring, after I took my family of five to the Jemez Mountains to do altitude training. I was now home schooling so I was free to travel with the family and not be held down by school restraints. Though home schooling requires a significant time commitment, it has been tremendously rewarding to our family.

In 1998, I had to come back to reality and get a real job again. I worked for Headstart every day from 7:30 to 12:00. I still home schooled the kids in the afternoon. To this day, I'm not sure how I squeezed in training. We had a treadmill, and I did a lot of workouts late at night. Living in the north woods of Wisconsin didn't lend itself well to winter training outside anyway. I was 2nd at nationals that year. Joanne Dow, the "new" kid on the block, won at our new distance of 20K. Actually, having Joanne on the scene has been a great relief to me. She is also a mom of two, and like me, she puts her family first.

It is nice to have someone I can relate to on the national team. She also got a bronze medal at Goodwill Games and I had to settle for 4th. This was the first time I had ever been beaten by an American in an international event. This inspired me to train harder in 1999. While I was genuinely happy for Joanne, it kind of bugged me that people were saying I wasn't going to be able to make the transition to 20K. I had to prove them wrong. I always train best when I'm in the process of proving people wrong. I came back in '99 and won nationals with a new American record. En route to this I made sure I held every record from 3K up to 20K. People were saying I could never train at a high level with three kids, so I just had to.

In 2000, we made a more permanent move to New Mexico. We live at 9000 ft. in a little mountain town called Cloudcroft. We train down in the desert in beautiful White Sands National Monument. We love it here. The kids are going to school this year in a very good little school. I miss home schooling, but it's probably good for them. My training is going very well, now that I have more time to actually do it. Making a third Olympic team is not really part of my goals this year, although I expect that if I achieve my other goals that will also happen. I want to continue to lower my records at every distance this year. There are still a couple of records I don't have (indoor mile and 3K, and road 5K), and I hope to achieve those times this year or next. I don't have many years left before my legs retire to winning my age group in the local "Pumpkin Chase" and I want to leave a legacy of records that will be challenging for our crop of new Olympic hopefuls.

Obviously, making money has not been a priority in my life or I wouldn't have spent it being a race walker. But, right now, I'm getting ready to go out the door to run barefoot through the sand dunes of White Sands National Monument (It's a recovery day). My life has been unique and challenging and I can't think of any other way I'd rather have wasted it.

16

1996: The Atlanta Olympic Year

The Games of the XXVI Olympiad were held from July 19 to August 4 in Atlanta, Georgia.

	Olympic Event	Olympic Place	Olympic Performance
Acuff, Amy	HJ	DNQ	6'¾"
Althouse, Valeyta	SP	DNQ	59' 7"
Appell, Olga	10,000m	DNQ	34:12.54
Bailey, Tonja Buford	400mh	3	53.22
Batten, Kim	400mh	2	53.08
Blair, Kelly	Heptathlon	8	6307
Carroll, Nicole	JT	DNQ	179' 7"
Clark, Joetta	800m	DNQ	2:00.38
Devers, Gail	100m	1	10.94
	100mh	4	12.66
	400mr	1	41.95
Dickey, Cheryl	100mh	DNQ	12.92
Fonshell, Kate	10,000m	DNQ	32:48.05
Gaines, Chryste	4 × 100mr	1	41.95
Goode, Linda Tolbert	100mh	7	13.11
Graham, Kim	400m	DNQ	51.13
	4 × 400mr	1	3:20.91
Guidry, Carlette	200m	8	22.61
	4 × 100mr	1	41.95
Hamilton, Suzy	800m	DNQ	2:00.47
Henner, Juli	1500m	DNQ	4:27.14
Herazo, Victoria	10k walk	DQ	
Hill, Aretha	DT	DNQ	183' 10"
Hill, D'Andre	100m	DNQ	11.20
Huber, Vicki	1500m	DNQ	4:14.82
Hudson, Sheila	TJ	10	46' 2¾"
Jacobs, Regina	1500m	10	4:07.21

	Olympic Event	Olympic Place	Olympic Performance
Jennings, Lynn	5000m	9	15:17.50
Kersee, Jackie Joyner	LJ	3	22' 11¾"
	Heptathlon	DNF	
Lauck, Anne Marie	Marathon	10	2:31:30
Lawrence, Debbi	10k walk	20	45:32
Lowery, Sharon Hanson	Heptathlon	9	6292
Malone, Maicel	400m	DNQ	51.16
	4 × 400mr	1	3:20.91
Mileham, Lacy Barnes	DT	DNQ	188' 7"
Miles, Jearl	400m	5	49.55
	4 × 400mr	1	3:20.91
Miller, Inger	200m	4	22.41
	4 × 100mr	1	41.95
Nesbit, Joan	10,000m	DNQ	32:33.48
Orrange, Diana	TJ		no mark
Pagel, Ramona	SP	9	60' 7¾"
Patrick, Sandra Farmer	400mh	DNQ	54.73
Powell, Suzy	DT	DNQ	184' 6"
Rainey, Meredith	800m	DNQ	1:59.36
Rhodes, Cynthea	TJ	DNQ	45' 9¼"
Rohl, Michelle	10k walk	14	44:29
Rudolph, Amy	5000m	10	15:19.77
Slaney, Mary	5000m	DNQ	15:41.30
Smith, Connie Price	SP	5	63'¾"
Somers, Linda	Marathon	31	2:36:58
Spangler, Jenny	Marathon	DNF	
Stevens, Rochelle	4 × 400mr	1	3:20.91
Stone, Dannette Young	200m	DNQ	22.49
Teaberry, Connie	HJ	DNQ	6' 2¾"
Torrence, Gwen	100m	3	10.96
	4 × 100mr	1	41.95
Veltman, Marieke	LJ	DNQ	21' 3½"
Waller, Tisha	HJ	9	6' 4"
Wheeler, Erica	JT	DNQ	175'
Williams, Shana	LJ		no mark
Wilson, Linetta	4 × 400mr	1	3:20.91

The Olympic Results

100 meters. "At the gun," reported *Track & Field News*, "Devers's shorter legs unfurled like springs and her advantage was immediate. Torrence broke slightly ahead of Ottey, whose start was unremarkable." The article continues:

"Between 60 and 70m, though, the Jamaican's velocity stood out in the group. She drew even with Devers at the line, as the American threw her shoulders forward and eyed her opponent. To a viewer right on the finish line and two stories up, Devers appeared an obvious winner.... A meter before the line, Devers was clearly ahead, and so it seemed, she would finish that way. Not so. It was a near dead-heat, with Torrence just two ticks behind."

The Atlanta Olympic Stadium, 1996.

Gail's winning time was 10.94. Torrence finished third in 10.96. D'Andre Hill placed 6th in the first semi in 11.20.

The *New York Times* pointed out that this was Gail Devers's second consecutive Olympic gold medal in the 100 meters.

1. Gail Devers	10.94
3. Gwen Torrence	10.96

200 meters. Two American women were in the final. Inger Miller finished fourth in 22.41 and Carlette Guidry placed eighth in 22.61. Dannette Young was fifth in the first semi in 22.49.

4. Inger Miller	22.41
8. Carlette Guidry	22.61

400 meters. Jearl Miles placed fifth in 49.55, the fastest time by an American since Valerie Brisco's American record in 1984. Maicel Malone and Kim Graham finished sixth and fifth respectively in the first semi.

5. Jearl Miles	49.55

800 meters. No American women were in the final. Joetta Clark finished third in heat four in 2:00.38 and Suzy Hamilton was fourth in 2:00.47 in heat five. Meredith Rainey advanced to the second semi, placing seventh in 1:59.36.

1500 meters. Regina Jacobs placed tenth in 4:07.21. She was the only American in the final. Juli Henner was tenth in the first heat in 4:27.14 and Vicki Huber placed ninth in the second heat in 4:14.82.

Gail Devers, 1999.

10. Regina Jacobs	4:07.21

5000 meters. Lynn Jennings finished strong, capturing the ninth spot in 15:17.50. Amy Rudolph was right behind in tenth in the time of 15:19.77. Mary Slaney placed seventh in the second heat in 15:41.30 and did not make the final.

9. Lynn Jennings	15:17.50
10. Amy Rudolph	15:19.77

10,000 meters. No American women were in the final. Kate Fonshell ran 32:48.05, finishing in ninth spot in the first heat. Olga Appell (34:12.54) and Joan Nesbit (32:33.48) were in the second heat, finishing 17th and 13th respectively.

100 meter hurdles. Gail Devers finished fourth in 12.66 and Linda Tolbert-Goode seventh in 13.11. Cheryl Dickey placed fifth in the third heat of the quarter round in 12.92 and did not make the semis.

4. Gail Devers	12.66
7. Linda Tolbert-Goode	13.11

400 meter hurdles. "In the final," wrote Jim Dunaway for *Track & Field News*, "Buford-Bailey was in lane 4 and Batten in lane 6, with Hemmings between them in lane 5. They were all off well, and Hemmings quickly took the lead, virtually making up the stagger on Batten down the backstretch. By halfway, the three protagonists had clearly begun to put away the rest, and Hemmings had a 2m lead on the two — Americans. Around the turn, Batten and Buford-Bailey slowly pulled themselves up to the Jamaican, and at the eighth barrier they were virtually even.

"But Hemmings not only fought off the challenge, she found another gear and opened up her lead a second time. By the final hurdle she was 2m up on Batten, and she made it nearly four by the time she crossed the line in 52.82, her second OR in two races. Batten took 2nd (53.08), with Buford-Bailey 3rd (53.22)...." Sandra Farmer-Patrick did not qualify for the final.

2. Kim Batten	53.08
3. Tonja Buford-Bailey	53.22

10 kilometer walk. "Top Americans Michelle Rohl (14th) and Debbi Lawrence (20th) improved 6 places on their Barcelona performances with solid efforts," reported *Track & Field News*. "Rohl's 44.29 is the No. 2 time in U.S. history, behind only her AR 44:06, but she said, 'I'm just disappointed with the time and the place.'" Victoria Herazo was disqualified.

14. Michelle Rohl	44:29
20. Debbi Lawrence	45:32

4 × 100 meter relay. "Inger Miller, 24, caused American hearts to flutter when she took off early as Gail Devers steamed down the backstretch on the second leg," reported *Track & Field News*. The story continues: "Devers made the pass no more than two steps before the end of the zone as they stretched the limit almost to the breaking point. Miller then churned the second curve to come from behind and give the U.S. an unbeatable lead.

"...Miller outran Sevatheda Fynes by almost a full 10th and sent Torrence away with a meter's lead after another safe pass. When Torrence (9.97) emulated her strong anchor of four years ago the U.S. was assured of a fourth consecutive gold."

The *New York Times* reported: "...Miller made history, too, as she and father Lennox ('68 silver/'72 bronze in the 100) became the first father-daughter pair to win Olympic medals." Their time was the fastest in the world this year.

1. USA	41.95
(Chryste Gaines, Gail Devers, Inger Miller, Gwen Torrence)	

4 × 400 meter relay. Dave Johnson wrote for *Track & Field News*: "The team of Rochelle Stevens, Maicel Malone, Kim Graham and Jearl Miles stood on the top of the victory podium after barely holding off the challenge of upstart Nigeria, which led for more than half of the race." It took sterling legs by Graham and Miles to secure the U.S. win.

Johnson continues:

...Opening the gap around the turn and down the backstretch, Miles looked like a winner. But haunting her was Nigerian anchor Fali Ogunkoya, the 400 bronze medalist who had run 49.10 in the open to beat Miles by two places and 0.45 seconds. Ogunkoya was running the same type of leg as Graham had, eating up the margin on the last turn.

Coming into the homestretch the lead was down to 3m and Miles tried to surge to the finish. Ogunkoya tried valiantly to close the last bit of the margin, stride by stride inching closer. Time became interminable as the mental calculations were made: Was the rate at which Ogunkoya was cutting the lead enough to let her get to the finish first? Was the distance to the finish now short enough for Miles to hold on? Some 40m out the Nigerian began to slow, but so did her American rival, fighting now to maintain most of what was a 2m-plus margin. The question changed: Would they both stay on their feet? Form broken in both runners, they struggled to the finish. Miles barely held on, her 49.47 giving the U.S. a 3:20.91 victory, barely a meter (0.13 seconds) ahead of Ogunkoya (48.90) and Nigeria (3:21.04 NR).

The *New York Times* said, "Miles defiantly maintained the lead to the finish."

1. USA	3:20.91
(Rochelle Stevens, Maicel Malone, Kim Graham, Jearl Miles)	

High jump. Of the U.S.'s three high jumpers only Tisha Waller made the final. Waller tied for ninth place at 6' 4". Connie Teaberry jumped 6' 2¾" and Amy Acuff injured her ankle and jumped 6' ¾."

9. Tisha Waller (tie)	6' 4"

Long jump. "...So Jackie Joyner-Kersee began the last approach of her Olympic career, hit about half the board and took off into sultry night air lit by a sea of flashbulbs," reported *Track & Field News.* "She cut into the sand as the partisan crowd erupted, a roar repeated moments later when the 22' 11¾" distance lit up the readerboard. Jackie had moved into 3rd and at least temporarily the bronze medal." When the competition was over, Jackie had her sixth Olympic medal, which put her on the top of the United States Olympic medal list. Marieke Veltman and Shana Williams did not qualify for the final.

Tim Layden reported in *Sports Illustrated*, "Jackie Joyner-Kersee became, at 34, the most decorated woman in U.S. Olympic track and field history with her sixth medal, a bronze in the long jump. She took the medal on her sixth jump, which was five more than she hoped to take on a right hamstring so badly injured that she doddered down the runway looking more like a grandmother than an Olympian. 'I said to myself, This is it Jackie, this is it,' she said later. 'This isn't the way you wanted it to be, but this is your last shot. If the leg is going to pull, it's going to pull.' She pounded hard off the takeoff board and hit the sand 22' 11¾" away, a bronze medalist by one inch."

The *New York Times* added, "It was a rewarding moment for Joyner-Kersee, who was seeking a fourth career gold medal and sixth over all after struggling with a hamstring injury and dropping out of the heptathlon earlier in the Games. 'Of all the medals I've won,' Joyner-Kersee said, 'this one is special because I really had to work for it.'"

3. Jackie Joyner-Kersee	22' 11¾"

Triple jump. Sheila Hudson placed tenth with a mark of 46'. Cynthea Rhodes and Diana Orrange did not qualify for the final.

10. Sheila Hudson	46'

Shot put. At one point in the competition, Connie Price-Smith was in third place with her 63' ¾" put. However, her final placing was fifth. "She became only the third American (joining Earlene Brown '56/'60 & Carol Cady '84) to take all six throws in an Olympic final, while recording the best U.S. finish since Brown's bronze in '60," reported *Track & Field News.* Ramona Pagel finished ninth with a put of 60' 7¾" while Valeyta Althouse did not qualify for the final.

5. Connie Price-Smith	63' ¾"
9. Ramona Pagel	60' 7¾"

Discus. None of the American women (Lacy Barnes-Mileham, Suzy Powell and Aretha Hill) qualified for the final.

Javelin. Neither of the two entries from the United States (Nicole Carroll and Erica Wheeler) qualified for the final.

Heptathlon. John Hendershott wrote for *Track & Field News*: "An Olympic era ended at the eighth barrier in the third heat of the heptathlon hurdles. Two-time champion Jackie Joyner-Kersee, her right upper leg heavily wrapped to protect a tender hamstring, sped through a furious downpour toward hurdle No. 8. As JJK trailed the leg over the barrier, the hamstring grabbed and the WR holder grimaced in pain. She flew over the last two hurdles in ungainly fashion, yet clocked 13.24."

The *New York Times* added, "An hour and a half after the hurdles, Joyner-Kersee returned to the field for the high jump portion of the heptathlon. She took a few practice jumps. Then she left the field."

Kelly Blair finished in eighth place and Sharon Hanson in ninth.

8. Kelly Blair	6307
9. Sharon Hanson	6292

Marathon. *Track & Field News* interviewed American Linda Somers, after she placed 31st in the marathon: "'I knew I was in trouble at the 5K mark. I felt lousy the whole way. It was just one of those days when I didn't have it. I had a really bad calf cramp from about 13M on. It made it hard to go up the hills. I really wanted to drop out. If it had been any other race, I would have. I can't believe I finished.'" The article goes on:

"The highest American marathon placer, Anne Marie Lauck, collapsed immediately after crossing the line in 10th. 'I don't know about this marathon thing,' said Lauck, who has still only run a handful of 26-milers. 'Every single one I've done, I've gotten to the 23M mark and said to myself, Why am I doing this? This is not fun. I figure it's got to get better. There's got to be one where it feels better, because I've yet to feel great in a marathon.'"

Lauck finished in 2:31:30, Somers, who had calf cramping problems, in 2:36:58 and Spangler, who had foot problems, dropped out at eleven miles.

10. Anne Marie Lauck	2:31:30
31. Linda Somers	2:36:58

The Olympic Trials

The Olympic Trials were held in Centennial Olympic Stadium in Atlanta, Georgia from June 14 to 23.

The *New York Times*, on Sunday June 16, reported:

In an upset that would have been unimaginable four years ago, Joyner-Kersee, 34, lost the heptathlon to Kelly Blair of Eugene, Ore. with a lifeless race in the 800 meters. It was the first completed heptathlon that she did not win since the 1984 Summer Olympics when Joyner-Kersee finished second to Glynnis Nunn of Australia. She has won two gold medals in the event, holds the world record and is considered by many to be the top track and field athlete of all time. "I don't like losing," a defiant Joyner-Kersee said. "I am not going out this way." In the women's 100 meters, Gwen Torrence demonstrated why she will be a candidate for four gold medals this summer as she matched her personal best with a victory in 10.82 seconds. It was the fastest time in the world this year and one of the fastest women's 100 meters ever as five runners finished below 11 seconds.

Gail Devers, the defending Olympic champion who has essentially not run the 100 meters for two years because of a painful injury to a muscle in her left buttock, finished second in 10.91. D'Andre Hill, the two-time national collegiate champion from Louisiana State, also made the Olympic team with a personal best of 10.92 seconds.

100 meters

After the first two rounds of the 100 meters, Jere Longman in the *New York Times* reported: "...Gail Devers, the Olympic champion at 100 meters, who has seldom run the event the past two years because of a balky hamstring, ran the fastest time of the first two rounds today, 10.96 seconds. Gwen Torrence, the world champion and Olympic favorite, ran 10.99."

"Devers was drawn in 3, Torrence in 4," reported *Track & Field News*. "Devers was marginally quicker out of the blocks and for the first half of the race they ran even. But when it came time to lift, Torrence's elevator went a floor higher. She steadily pulled away, crossing the line in a PR-matching 10.82. Devers (10.91) just held off the fast-closing Hill (10.92 PR)."

1. Gwen Torrence, Nike International Track Club   10.82
2. Gail Devers, Nike International Track Club   10.91
3. D'Andre Hill, Louisiana State University   10.92
4. Inger Miller, PowerAde Track Club   10.96
5. Chryste Gaines, PowerAde Track Club   10.96
6. Dannette Young-Stone, Reebok Racing Club   11.06
7. Carlette Guidry, Team adidas   11.07
8. Cheryl Taplin, Nike International Track Club   11.11

200 meters

"Guidry and Young-Stone, just 7th and 6th in the 100 final, ran the best first 100s here, out of lanes 3 and 5," stated *Track & Field News*. "Between them was Torrence, not seemingly sharp at all as she entered the straight a step behind. But she wasn't in 3rd, as out in lane 8 was the unheralded Miller, who had never before even made a nationals final. As they raced up the straight, it soon became apparent that Torrence's magic lift, which had served her so well in the 100, was out of order. Guidry slashed across the line in a PR 22.14, with Young-Stone's 22.18 also being a lifetime best.

"The winning mark gave Guidry the yearly world lead and moved her to No. 8 on the all-time U.S. list, with Young-Stone climbing to No. 9."

1. Carlette Guidry, Team adidas   22.14
2. DannetteYoung-Stone, Reebok Racing Club   22.18
3. Inger Miller, unattached   22.25
4. Gwen Torrence, Nike International Track Club   22.25
5. Zundra Feagin, Louisiana State University   22.33
6. Celena Mondie-Milner, PowerAde Track Club   22.55
7. Cheryl Taplin, Nike International Track Club   22.59
8. Kisha Jett, University of Florida   23.09

400 meters

Track & Field News reported: "The 25-year-old Malone, who missed the '92 Trials while pregnant, roared off the blocks like she was sprinting only half the distance. She covered the opening 200 in 23.78, with just New Orleans winner Rochelle Stevens (23.99) within hailing distance.... Now, into the last half of the title contest, Malone continued to stretch her lead. Her 36.22 at the 300m led Miles by nearly 0.4. But the lactic acid caught up with Malone midway in the homestraight. She still was able to stave off Miles' rush, which looked for a few strides like it might reel in the faltering leader.

"'...Adrenaline got to me,' Malone admitted. 'The last 100 hurt and it took a prayer to get through.' Miles added, 'Maicel always goes out fast. I just tried to run my own race, catch her and not break. But it was the hardest 50.6 of my life.'"

1. Maicel Malone, Asics Track Club   50.52
2. Jearl Miles, Reebok Racing Club   50.61
3. Kim Graham, Asics Track Club   50.87
4. Rochelle Stevens, Posner Track Club   51.16
5. Linetta Wilson, South Bay Track Club   51.49
6. Natasha Kaiser-Brown, Foot Locker Athletic Club   51.52

7. Nicole Green, PowerAde Track Club   51.95
8. Youlanda Warren, unattached   52.10

800 meters

Track & Field News wrote:

Alisa Hill made sure the final would be fast. She went out at 27.0 and hit the 400 in 56.8. Behind her were Rainey and the other favorite, Joetta Clark (both 56.7), then Amy Wickus and Suzy Hamilton, with a gap to Michelle DiMuro, Kathi Rounds and Tosha Sumner.

Down the backstretch, Hamilton went past Wickus into 4th. A second or two later, Rainey stormed past Hill in a full sprint which carried her past 600 in 1:26.1. Behind her, Clark and Hamilton also passed the struggling Hill.

Rainey came into the final straight with a 10m lead and didn't slow down until she crossed the line in 1:57.04, just 0.14 off Mary Slaney's '85 American Record.... Clark (1:58.22) had no trouble holding 2nd, but Hamilton (1:59.04) pitched to the track in her desperation to hold 3rd as she was almost caught by the unheralded Rounds (1:59.28), who sprinted up from far back to PR for the second race in a row.

1. Meredith Rainey, Foot Locker Athletic Club   1:57.04
2. Joetta Clark, Foot Locker Athletic Club   1:58.22
3. Suzy Hamilton, Reebok Racing Club   1:59.04
4. Kathi Rounds, unattached   1:59.28
5. Michelle DiMuro, Asics Track Club   1:59.85
6. Alisa Hill, unattached   2:00.06
7. Tosha Woodward-Sumner, Goldwin Track Club   2:00.82
8. Amy Wickus, Nike International Track Club   2:01.63

1500 meters
1. Regina Jacobs, Mizuno Track Club   4:08.67
2. Juli Henner, Reebok Racing Club   4:09.49
3. Vicki Huber, Asics Track Club   4:11.23
4. Amy Wickus, Nike International Track Club   4:12.06
5. Sarah Thorsett, PowerAde Track Club   4:12.34
6. Kathy Franey, Nike International Track Club   4:12.34
7. Sarah Schwald, Nike International Track Club   4:13.00
8. Cheri Goddard, Reebok Racing Club   4:13.10

5000 meters
1. Lynn Jennings, Nike International Track Club   15:28.18
2. Mary Slaney, Nike International Track Club   15:29.39
3. Amy Rudolph, Reebok Racing Club   15:29.91
4. Libbie Johnson, Mizuno Track Club   15:30.77
5. Annette Peters, Nike International Track Club   15:39.91
6. Cheri Goddard, Reebok Racing Club   15:41.80
7. Kim Jones, Nike International Track Club   15:53.58
8. Elva Dryer, unattached   15:55.82

100 meter hurdles

Track & Field News said, "In the final Goode was out of the blocks first, but Devers passed her by the second hurdle. Dickey and Morrison also got away well and ran even. By midway Devers and Goode were clear of the field and finished in that order, running 12.62 and 12.69. Dickey and Morrison continued to run even until hurdle 8, where Morrison whacked the barrier and faded to last."

1. Gail Devers, Nike International Track Club   12.62
2. Lynda Tolbert-Goode, Goldwin Track Club   12.69
3. Cheryl Dickey, unattached   12.76
4. Dawn Bowles, Southern California Cheetahs   12.93
5. Tonya Lawson, LaGrange Track Club   12.94
6. Tananjalyn Stanley-Boutte, unattached   12.97
7. Kim Carson, Louisiana State University   13.04
8. Melissa Morrison, unattached   13.45

400 meter hurdles

The *New York Times* reported, "Kim Batten, the world champion and world record-holder in the women's 400-meter hurdles, had this small problem in March. She couldn't train. In fact, she had trouble walking. She had aggravated an ankle injury during a photo shoot. If she made it to the Olympic trials, she feared it might be only as a spectator.

"...Batten recovered sufficiently to run the fastest time in the world this year and win the Olympic trials tonight in 53.81 seconds. '...I'm so happy I'm here, with the injuries I've had,' Batten said."

According to *Track & Field News*: "...It was two-time NCAA champ Tonya Williams — drawn in lane 1, unfortunately — who went flying to an immediate lead. Batten caught the Illini by the third hurdle, but by No. 5 had yielded to Buford-Bailey as Farmer-Patrick remained close while Williams receded.

"Around the second turn Batten crept back up, and at the top of the stretch she led Buford-Bailey by perhaps a foot and Farmer-Patrick by a yard. Though briefly threatened by Trevaia Williams, their margin and the order remained the same down the long homestretch. The trio crossed the line within 0.26, recording the year's three quickest times...."

1. Kim Batten, Reebok Racing Club   53.81
2. Tonja Buford-Bailey, Nike International Track Club   53.92
3. Sandra Farmer-Patrick, Nike International Track Club   54.07
4. Trevaia Williams, Atoms Track Club   54.87
5. Rebecca Buchanan, Anderson International Track Club   55.69
6. Tonya Williams, University of Illinois   55.94
7. Tonya Lee, unattached   56.59
8. Rosa Jolivet, Texas A&M University   57.53

10,000 meters

Track & Field News wrote, "Racing just the sixth 10K of her life, Kate Fonshell provided one of the biggest surprises of the meet. With the on-track temperatures still nearly at 90, early leaders Sylvia Mosqueda and Gwyn Coogan faded quickly."

1. Kate Fonshell, Asics Track Club   32:37.91
2. Olga Appell, Reebok Racing Club   32:43.79
3. Joan Nesbit, New Balance Track Club   32:46.77
4. Lynn Nelson, Mizuno Track Club   33:05.03
5. Laurie Henes, adidas USA   33:16.59
6. Trina Painter, New Balance Track Club   33:19.50
7. Laura LaMena-Coll, Moving Comfort Racing Team   33:30.93
8. Carole Zajac, Nike International Track Club   33:36.32

10 kilometer race walk (June 22 — Olympic road course)

"After a cautious start," said *Track & Field News*, "'92 Trials winner Debbi Lawrence, 34, took the lead at the 3km mark and was never challenged as she literally walked away from the field for a 46:05 clocking as temperatures approached triple digits."

1. Debbi Lawrence, Natural Sport Walking Club   46:05
2. Michelle Rohl, Parkside Athletic Club   46:37
3. Victoria Herazo, California Walkers   48:12
4. Debby Van Orden, unattached   49:13
5. Sara Standley, Asics Track Club   49:23
6. Teresa Vaill, unattached   49:36
7. Dana Yarbrough, LaGrange Track Club   50:12
8. Kim Wilkinson, Monterey Peninsula Walkers Club   50:47

High Jump

"Acuff and Waller led the field with no misses," reported *Track & Field News*. The article continues:

Teaberry, who had needed a pair at 6' 2¼", stood only 6th. Acuff was the only one to clear on first attempt. What a surprise that she would end up only 3rd.

A PR-equaling clearance by Karol Jenkins briefly put her in 2nd, but she was quickly dropped a spot by Teaberry. The big surprise was Waller, who missed for a second time and found her Olympic hopes in jeopardy. Digging down deep, she came up with a masterful clearance to keep her hopes alive, but would need to clear another height to make the team.

The bar went to 6' 4¾", and she did it straight-away while the others all missed twice. Jenkins missed her third, then Teaberry provided the last clearance of the competition to slip ahead of Acuff."

1. Tisha Waller, Goldwin Track Club   6' 4¾"
2. Connie Teaberry, Goldwin Track Club   6' 4¾"
3. Amy Acuff, University of California, Los Angeles   6' 3½"
4. Karol Jenkins, unattached   6' 3½"
5. Tanya Hughes-Jones, unattached   6' 2¼"
6. Angela Bradburn, PowerAde Track Club   6' 2¼"
7. Gwen Wentland, Nike International Track Club   6' 2¼"
8. Erin Aldrich, Lake Highlands High School, Texas   6' 2¼"

Shot Put

Track & Field News said, "Price-Smith could have won with her 61' 7" opener, just as Pagel could have secured 2nd with her initial 58' 11¼". However, both used round 5 to improve, Pagel to 61'¼" and then Price-Smith to 62' 7¾" as the very next thrower. Price-Smith thus won her fifth consecutive national title, and sixth in the last seven years. Pagel claimed her fifth straight 2nd-place finish behind Price-Smith since '92, but still earned a spot on her fourth Olympic squad. Price-Smith earned a third team berth, although she threw only the discus in '92."

1. Connie Price-Smith, Reebok Racing Club   62' 7¾"
2. Ramona Pagel, Nike Coast Track Club   61' ¼"
3. Dawn Dumble, Reebok Racing Club   58' 2"
4. Valeyta Althouse, Reebok Racing Club   57' 9½"
5. Amy Christiansen, Brigham Young University   57' 7½"
6. Teri Steer, Southern Methodist University   56' 8½"
7. Eileen Vanisi, Reebok Racing Club   56' 6½"
8. Tressa Thompson, New Balance Track Club   55' 3¾"

Discus

"Suzy Powell used a PR 198' 9" to win, while Washington's Aretha Hill reached 190' 5" for

3rd," reported *Track & Field News*. "At 19 (with Powell three weeks the younger), they'll be the youngest members of the U.S. team. Between them, vet Lacy Barnes-Mileham (195' 9") took 2nd to complete the threesome of first-time Olympians."

1. Suzy Powell, University of California, Los Angeles	198'	9"
2. Lacy Barnes-Mileham, Nike International Track Club	195'	9"
3. Aretha Hill, University of Washington	190'	5"
4. Carla Garrett, unattached	188'	10"
5. Melisa Weis, Goldwin Track Club	187'	10"
6. Dawn Dumble, Reebok Racing Club	187'	2"
7. Erica Ahmann, California Polytechnic, San Luis Obispo	185'	9"
8. Seilala Sue, Aquinas High School, Florida	181'	5"

Heptathlon

Jere Longman wrote in the *New York Times*:

Jackie Joyner-Kersee is likely to win the heptathlon at the United States track and field trials. Her chances for a third gold medal in the Olympics are far more uncertain. At 34, she can get through the seven events, but she can no longer get through them healthy.

In an ordinary performance today, Joyner-Kersee took the lead despite a sprained ankle, hamstring spasms and a cold as she delivered her worst high jump in a dozen years, at 5 feet 10 inches. She only remotely resembled the woman who is generally considered history's greatest female track and field athlete.

...On the encouraging side, Joyner-Kersee scored higher today, with 3,916 points, than she did on the first day at last year's national championships. Her shot put of 50' 6¾" was more than 4 feet farther than her best throw at the 1992 Summer Olympics and her longest throw in three years.

...This year, she has been training voraciously, up to eight hours a day, using cross-training methods such as pool running to relieve the stress on her body. She said, however, that the strenuous training sometimes made it difficult to retain muscle mass. She has lost as much as four pounds a week, she said.

"This is my last Olympic Games," Joyner-Kersee said on Thursday. "I don't want to make my last hurrah the biggest thing. I want the biggest thing to be what I do on the track."

"Jackie Joyner-Kersee has so dominated the U.S. heptathlon scene, it took some real digging to unearth her last loss to an American in a multi she finished," reported *Track & Field News*. "Try the '83 nationals, to Jane Frederick. Now Kelly Blair — who was 12 years old when JJK last lost — can claim the distinction of a win over The Great One. A PR 6406 for the Oregon grad edged JJK by just 3 points, as veteran Sharon Hanson grabbed 3rd with her career-best 6352."

"'...Sometimes it doesn't go your way,' Joyner-Kersee said," reported William C. Rhoden in the *New York Times*. "'That doesn't mean to me that I should quit or I should give up. It means that I should find a way to bounce back. I have five weeks to get that hunger back, because I can't come to these Olympic Games and perform at this level.' ... Joyner-Kersee has made her fourth Olympic team. Her concern is what shape she'll be in next month...."

1. Kelly Blair, Nike International Track Club	6406
2. Jackie Joyner-Kersee, Honda Track Club	6403
3. Sharon Hanson, unattached	6352
4. DeDee Nathan, Nike Indiana Track Club	6327
5. Jamie McNeair, Reebok Racing Club	6287
6. Kym Carter, Reebok Racing Club	6281
7. Wendi Simmons, Nike Coast Athletics	6078
8. Corissa Yansen, Purdue University	5912

Long jump

"A PR 23–0 by Williams to lead the qualifying 'inspired me,' JJK said, reported *Track & Field News*. 'I thought the final could be a great competition.' In perfect health, Joyner-Kersee hoped to jump 7.40 (24' 3½"). But fear about pulling the hamstring haunted her. She put all she had into her first effort to grab the lead. JJK then passed five times as the jumpers battled both swirling winds and the 113 degree infield heat. She took her final jump. It was 23' 1¼" w, enough to put her in first place."

1. Jackie Joyner-Kersee, Honda Track Club	23'	1¼" w
2. Shana Williams, Nike Track Club	22'	9"
3. Marieke Veltman, Reebok Racing Club	22'	7"
4. Sharon Couch, Goldwin Track Club	22'	1¾"
5. Sheila Hudson, Reebok Racing Club	21'	11¾" w
6. Gwen Loud, Nike Track Club	21'	11"
7. Tonya Sedwick, unattached	21'	10¼"
8. Sheila Echols, unattached	21'	8¼"

Triple jump

1. Cynthea Rhodes, unattached	46'	1½"
2. Sheila Hudson, Reebok Racing Club	46'	1¼"
3. Diana Orrange, Nike Track Club	45'	5"
4. Wendy Brown, unattached	45'	3½"
5. Telisa Young, unattached	44'	11"
6. Nicole Gamble, University of North Carolina	44'	2"
7. Amanda Banks, unattached	44'	1¼"
8. Lisa Austin, unattached	43'	3¾"

Javelin

According to *Track & Field News*: "Carroll had led after round two (180' 7"), but NCAA champ Dean responded with a third-round 187' 4", only 15 inches shy of the PR she had set in qualifying. Paula Berry's 182' 3" also passed Carroll." Carroll's 184' 5" passed Berry in frame four, but Lipson got her best of the day in five to move into 2nd. It was time for some heroics, and on her last throw Carroll got them, pulling out a 188' 11" before sweating out the final tosses by Dean and Berry."

1. Nicole Carroll, unattached	188'	11"
2. Windy Dean, Southern Methodist University	187'	4"
3. Lynda Lipson, Klub Keihas	184'	9"
4. Paula Berry, unattached	182'	3"
5. Erica Wheeler, Mizuno Track Club	181'	11"
6. Meg Foster, unattached	179'	9"
7. Kristin Dunn, unattached	176'	4"
8. Jen McCormick, San Mateo Athletic Club	170'	9"

Pole vault (exhibition)

"Stacy Dragila, 25, picked up her third outdoor AR of the year, scaling 13' 9¼" before failing three times in an attempt to become America's first 14-footer," reported *Track & Field News*.

1. Stacy Dragila, unattached	13' 9¼"	AR
2. Melissa Price, Fresno State University	12' 9½"	
3. Tiffany Smith, No Limit Sports	12' 5½"	
4. Jocelyn Chase, University of California, Los Angeles	12' 1½"	

5. Melissa Feinstein, Weston High School, Massachusetts   12' 1½"
6. Alexa Harz, unattached   11' 9¾"
    and Kellie Suttle, Bell Athletics
8. Glenda Smith, No Limit Sports   11' 9¾"

Hammer (exhibition)

Track & Field News wrote: "What do you do if you're the American Record holder, you have two fouls in the final of the USATF Championships, and you are in danger of not making the final eight? You take a 2-turn safety throw ... that puts you in the lead. Dawn Ellerbe's 186' 3" gave her the top spot and three more attempts, but Leslie Coons, a former AR holder, hit 188' 6" in the 5th to overtake Ellerbe. Ellerbe answered right back at 193' 9" for a nationals record and the eventual winning mark, as both fouled in the 6th round."

1. Dawn Ellerbe, University of South Carolina   193' 9"   MR
2. Leslie Coons, University of Southern California   188' 6"
3. Katie Panek, Wichita State University   184' 10"
4. Crystal Corbeil, Boston Athletic Association   184' 4"
5. Kiyomi Parish, Pomona Pitzer College   183' 5"
6. Molly Duggan, Nike International Track Club   182' 9"
7. Paulette Mitchell, New Balance Track Club   179' 1"
8. Dawn Tabla, Brigham Young University   177' 11"

3000 meter steeplechase (exhibition)

"BYU's Courtney Pugmire is one of the few runners with anything approaching national-class credentials to try this new discipline. Her debut-race 10:23.47 was nearly 30 seconds faster than last year's winner," said *Track & Field News*.

1. Courtney Pugmire, Brigham Young University   10:23.47
2. Sarah Heeb, University of Kansas   10:25.44
3. Rae Henderson, Reebok Racing Club   10:35.93
4. Lesley Lehane, unattached   10:39.79
5. Shane Wille, University of Colorado   10:54.18
6. Chris Morgan, Beach Track Club   10:54.49
7. Monica Townsend, Reebok Racing Club   11:05.86
8. Jennifer Latham, Los Feliz Flyers   11:08.88

Marathon Trials: Columbia, South Carolina, February 10

"Jenny Spangler became the first member of the '96 Olympic team when she broke the Women's Marathon Trial tape in 2:29:54," reported Sean Hartnett in *Track & Field News*. Her victory was thoroughly unexpected, yet convincing, as the 61st seed controlled the race from the first mile.

Hartnett continues:

> ...Undaunted by her company, the 32-year-old Spangler took control in the sixth mile, vigorously charging hills and dropping under 5:45 pace. By 10M (57:27), only Somers, Lauck, Coogan and Kristy Johnston opted to match Spangler's defiant assault on a Columbia course known for its challenging second half, with significant hills at 14, 22 and 24M.
>
> Spangler forced the pace again at 12M, and after two uphill miles only Lauck remained in contact. A 5:22 downhill 16th mile dropped Lauck, who admitted, "I didn't want to risk not making the team at that point. I just said, 'No way,' and let her go."

Jenny Spangler competed in two previous marathon trials: 1984 and 1988. Her trials' qualifying time was 2:43:02.

1. Jenny Spangler, Santa Monica Track Club	2:29:54	PR
	(course record)	
2. Linda Somers, adidas USA	2:30:06	PR
3. Anne Marie Lauck, Nike Running Room	2:31:18	
4. Gwyn Coogan, adidas USA	2:33:51	
5. Kristy Johnston, Reebok Racing Club	2:34:21	
6. Ann Schafers-Coles, Santa Monica Track Club	2:38:47	

The Indoor Nationals

The USA Track and Field Indoor Championships were held in Atlanta, Georgia on March 1 and 2.

"Joetta Clark was competing in her 18th national indoor meet, no less, and she made it clear from the start that none of the desire for victory was missing," wrote *Track & Field News.* "...She moved to an early lead and was never headed."

Gwen Torrence won her heat of the 200 in American record time. *The Atlanta Journal-Constitution* reported, "...With the Atlanta Games just 4½ months off, Torrence staged a wonderful performance Saturday afternoon at the USA/Mobil Indoor Track and Field Championships, dominating the 60- and 200-meter fields while reaffirming her status as the world's top women's sprinter. Attired in a bright, two-piece pink running outfit, Torrence dusted the 60-meter field and then brought the Georgia Dome crowd to its feet with an American indoor-record 22.33 seconds in the 200—eclipsing the mark she'd set only a night earlier."

The *New York Times* ran a four column story on Michael Johnson's victories in the 200m and 400m and simply stated, "Gwen Torrence dominates the women's sprints."

60 meters		
1. Gwen Torrence, Mizuno Track Club	7.05	
2. Celena Mondie-Milner, PowerAde Track Club	7.17	
3. Holli Hyche, adidas USA	7.24	
200 meters		
1. Gwen Torrence, Mizuno Track Club	22.33	AR
2. Dannette Young, Reebok Racing Club	22.71	
3. Carlette Guidry, adidas USA	22.97	
400 meters		
1. Maicel Malone, Asics Track Club	51.49	
2. Jearl Miles, Reebok Racing Club	51.57	
3. Shanelle Porter, U.S. West	52.06	
800 meters		
1. Joetta Clark, Foot Locker Athletic Club	2:00.90	
2. Julie Jenkins-Donley, unattached	2:01.16	
3. Alisa Hill, unattached	2:01.65	
Mile		
1. Stephanie Best, Mountain West Track and Field Club	4:34.67	
2. Sarah Thorsett, PowerAde Track Club	4:35.00	
3. Kathy Franey, Nike Track Club	4:35.73	

3000 meters
1. Joan Nesbit, New Balance Track Club   8:56.01
2. Amy Rudolph, Reebok Racing Club   9:00.58
3. Fran ten Bensel, New Balance Track Club   9:14.52

60 meter hurdles
1. Michelle Freeman, Reebok Racing Club/Jamaica   7.91
2. Tonya Lawson, Anderson International Track Club   7.98
3. Cheryl Dickey, Nike Track Club   8.08

3000 meter walk
1. Michelle Rohl, Parkside Athletic Club   12:55.90
2. Maryanne Torrellas, Abraxas Track Club   13:09.35
3. Victoria Herazo, California Walkers   13:12.29

4 × 400 meter relay (on time basis)
1. Louisiana State University   3:36.37
    (La Tarsha Stroman, Charlene Maulseed, Sheila Powell,
       Astia Walker)
2. University of North Carolina   3:37.65
3. Florida State University   3:37.82

Distance medley relay
1. Auburn University   11:19.69
    (Amanda Patrick, Eusheka Bartley, Janet Trujillo,
       Rachel Sauder)
2. University of Alabama   11:33.70
3. University of North Carolina   11:34.02

High jump
1. Tisha Waller, Goldwin Track Club   6' 6¼"
2. Angela Bradburn, PowerAde Track Club   6' 3½"
3. Clare Look-Jaeger, Nike Coast Track Club   6' 3½"

Pole vault (non-scoring event)
1. Stacy Dragila, unattached   13' 5¼" AR
2. Melissa Price, California State University, Fresno   13' 1½"
3. Kellie Suttle, Bell Athletics   12' 7½"

Long jump
1. Shana Williams, Nike Track Club   22' 3½"
2. Marieke Veltman, Reebok Racing Club   21' 2½"
3. DeDee Nathan, Nike Indiana Track Club   21'¾"

Triple jump
1. Sheila Hudson, Reebok Racing Club   46' 7½"
2. Cynthea Rhodes, unattached   45' 8½"
3. Carla Shannon, unattached   44' 3¼"

Shot put
1. Connie Price-Smith, Reebok Racing Club   61' 9"
2. Ramona Pagel, Nike Coast Athletics   58' 11½"
3. Valeyta Althouse, University of California, Los Angeles   58' 8½"

20 pound weight throw
1. Dawn Ellerbe, University of South Carolina		65' 1¼"
2. Lisa Misipeka, University of South Carolina		60' 7¼"
3. Gladys Nortey, Iowa State University/Canada		59' 1¼"

Point score:
Reebok Racing Club	22
Nike	18
Mizuno Track Club	11

Los Angeles Invitational (formerly the Sunkist Invitational— four women's events): Los Angeles, February 24

50 meters
1. Denice Juan Ball, Southern California Cheetahs	6.25

800 meters
1. Michelle DiMuro, Nike International Track Club	2:06.23

Mile
1. Stephanie Best, Mountain West Track and Field Club	4:40.63

Shot put
1. Valeyta Althouse, University of California, Los Angeles	59' 3¼"

USATF Cross Country Championships: Stanford, California, December 7

In winning this ninth national victory, 36-year-old Lynn Jennings now holds the record for the most U.S. titles won, man or woman.

The *New York Times* added, "Lynn Jennings became the winningest runner in United States cross country championships history by capturing her ninth women's title in Stanford, Calif."

1. Lynn Jennings, Nike International Track Club	21:06
2. Olga Appell, Reebok Racing Club	21:13
3. Amy Rudolph, Reebok Racing Club	21:21

24th IAAF World Cross Country Championships: Stellenbosch, South Africa, March 23

25. Joan Nesbit	21:19
48. Liz Wilson	21:49
52. Carole Zajac	21:53
84. Kristin Hall	22:45
116. Lucy Nusrala	24:31

The United States placed 13th in the team standings.

VII Pan American Race Walking Cup: Manaus, Brazil, September 21–22

10 kilometer walk	
2. Michelle Rohl	49:10
3. Debbie Van Orden	49:43
7. Sara Standley	51:27
11. Dana Yarbrough	53:18
Victoria Herazo	DQ

Other News and Honors

Track & Field News: Athlete of the Year

Gail Devers

Top Ten American Women — Track & Field News

1. Gail Devers	6. Jearl Miles
2. Kim Batten	7. Connie Price-Smith
3. Gwen Torrence	8. Inger Miller
4. Tonja Buford-Bailey	9. Regina Jacobs
5. Jackie Joyner-Kersee	10. Sheila Hudson

There were no American women on the world list.

Gwen Torrence was on the cover of *Newsweek* magazine, the June 10 edition.

Pat Rico, the first vice-president of USATF, was elected for a four year term as president of the governing body. With the departure of the executive director, one of her first tasks as president was to lead a search for a replacement. This led to the selection of the current CEO, Craig Masback, a lawyer, world-class miler and sportscaster.

After years of discussion, Pat also initiated a two year restructure of USATF with the goal of streamlining the governance of the sport of track and field.

Margaret Jenkins, 92, died this year. She was a member of the 1928 Olympic team and placed ninth in the discus in the 1932 Olympic Games.

Essence magazine, in its January edition, ran an article entitled "Olympic Legends." The track and field stars featured were Willye White, Mae Faggs and Alice Coachman.

Cleve Abbott was inducted into the National Track and Field Hall of Fame. The biography below is from the National Track and Field Hall of fame website.

CLEVE ABBOTT

Born: December 9, 1894 — Yankton, South Dakota. Deceased: April 16, 1955.

Career Highlights

• As coach of women's track and field at Tuskegee Institute, Abbott won 14 national outdoor championships

One of the pioneer coaches of women's track and field, Cleve Abbott was head coach of the women's team at Tuskegee Institute from 1936 to 1955. During that period, his Golden Tigers won 14 national outdoor titles, including eight in a row. Tuskegee athletes won 49 indoor and outdoor individual titles. Six of his athletes were on the Olympic team, including gold medalists Alice Coachman and Mildred McDaniel. Three of his athletes — Coachman, McDaniel and Nell

Jackson — have been inducted into the Hall of Fame. He was still coaching at Tuskegee when he died in 1955. An outstanding athlete while in high school and college, Abbott was hired to teach and coach at Tuskegee Institute in 1915 by the great educator, Booker T. Washington. He had exceptional success as Tuskegee's football coach, winning nine national titles over a 32-year period. In addition to being an outstanding coach, Abbott served on the women's committee of the former National AAU (a predecessor of USA Track & Field) and twice was on the U.S. Olympic Track and Field Committee. He is also a member of the Alabama Sports Hall of Fame.

Education

high school: Watertown (Watertown, South Dakota), 1912
undergraduate: South Dakota State (Brookings, South Dakota), 1916

Occupations

Coach / athletic director

World Records (held by American women as of January 1996)

100 meters	10.49	Florence Griffith-Joyner
200 meters	21.34	Florence Griffith-Joyner
400 meter hurdles	52.61	Kim Batten
Heptathlon	7291	Jackie Joyner-Kersee

(12.69, 6' 1¼", 51' 10", 22.56, 23' 10¼", 149' 10", 2:08.51)

American Records (as of January 1996)

100m	10.49	Florence Griffith-Joyner
200m	21.34	Florence Griffith-Joyner
400m	48.83	Valerie Brisco
800m	1:56.90	Mary Slaney
1000m	2:33.93	Suzy Hamilton
1500m	3:57.12	Mary Slaney
Mile	4:16.71	Mary Slaney
2000m	5:32.7	Mary Slaney
3000m	8:25.83	Mary Slaney
5000m	14:56.04	Amy Rudolph
10,000m	31:19.89	Lynn Jennings
Marathon	2:21:21	Joan Benoit-Samuelson
100mh	12.46	Gail Devers
400mh	52.61	Kim Batten

4 × 100mr   41.49   1993 World Championship Team
    (Michelle Finn, Gwen Torrence, Wendy Vereen, Gail Devers)

4 × 200mr   1:32.55   Louisiana State University
    (D'Andre Hill, Karen Boone, Eureka Hall, Cheryl Taplin)

4 × 400mr   3:15.51   1988 Olympic Team
    (Denean Howard, Diane Dixon, Valerie Brisco, Florence Griffith-Joyner)

4 × 800mr   8:17.09   Athletics West
    (Sue Addison, Lee Arbogast, Mary Decker, Chris Mullen)

Sprint medley relay   1:36.79   Wilt's Athletic Club
    (Brenda Morehead, Jeanette Bolden, Alice Brown, Arlise Emerson)

Distance medley relay   10:48.38
    (Kathy Franey, Michelle Bennett, Celeste Halliday, Vicki Huber)

5k walk	20:56.88	Michelle Rohl
10k walk	44:41.87	Michelle Rohl
HJ	6' 8"	Louise Ritter
PV	13' 9¼"	Stacy Dragila
LJ	24' 7"	Jackie Joyner-Kersee
TJ	47' 3½"	Sheila Hudson
SP	66' 2½"	Ramona Pagel
DT	216' 10"	Carol Cady
HT	209' 2"	Dawn Ellerbe
JT	227' 5"	Kate Schmidt
Heptathlon	7291	Jackie Joyner-Kersee

INTERVIEW: LACY BARNES MILEHAM

(December 4, 2006) I actually got started in the short sprints. But, at the end of my seventh grade year I had major surgery and had to have a kidney removed. Based on that, I came back and wasn't quite as quick as I used to be. I started pulling muscles and that sort of thing, because of the training. I had two coaches, in particular, who basically said, "Throw these." These were both the shot and the discus. Neither of the two coaches knew what they were doing. It was one of those things where they were looking in books and said, "Here, throw it this way." Later on we found out that they actually taught me how to throw the discus wrong, but [laughter] I guess I've managed okay. That was Linda Rolfs and Fred Parker. These are two redheads who basically knew that I needed to stay engaged and that was their way of helping me do that. So, that's pretty much how I got started throwing—the discus, in particular.

From there, I actually went on and did well with a high school coach, Alan Stephens. He basically brought me along, he and his wife Rita Stephens, who is now deceased. They helped me in such a way that I was able to get an athletic scholarship to Fresno State. I guess one highlight was doing well enough in high school. There was one particular meet that I can think about, where I threw twenty feet further than my best mark at the time [laughter]. So, it was one of those things that stood out. At that point, Alan started to really focus in on trying to talk to different coaches here and there to possibly help me gain access into a four year institution on an athletic scholarship.

I went to Fresno State right out of high school and managed to do quite well there. Tom Pagani was the coach at the time. He likes to remember a particular track meet at the University of Oregon where I actually went from my best of 157 at the time to 177 [laughter], so another twenty feet. That meet was quite a highlight as well. From there, I guess Matthew Mileham, my husband, actually started to talk about how well I could do if I wanted to. So, that's when I kind of hunkered down. I had some natural talent and I started to work a little harder at that time, and things went well [laughter].

I didn't have quite the successes that Connie had, but what's funny is I remember her clasping my arm walking into the stadium in 1996. She looked at me and said, "Finally, this will be my best opening ceremony because you are here, and I've been waiting for you" [laughter]. My first attempt to actually make an Olympic team was in 1988. I failed. 1992 was my second attempt, and I failed again. Then I finally made it in '96. It was rain that literally washed my dreams away in '88. '92 a couple of injuries here and there kind of slowed me down. But, then in '96, I pulled things together. It was a rough go at trials, but I managed to make the team on my fourth throw. It was one of those things that I think all of the pressures of the two attempts before—the psychological aspects of it all—I had to overcome quite a few demons [laughter], and I managed. That was '96.

Now, I haven't really thrown in a while. I never announced a retirement or anything like that, but when my car was stolen with all of my equipment in 2002, I just assumed [laughter] that, well—I was done [laughter]. So, I haven't really picked up a discus since then; I don't actually have any to pick up anyway. The thing is, I still have an opportunity to live a dream that I've had for a long time. My daughter is competing again. She had a full scholarship to the University of Washington when she graduated from high school, but dropped out after a year. She worked in

Lacy Barnes Mileham, 2005.

Seattle for several years before she found her way back to Cal State, Bakersfield, where she's been doing very well. I know that she'll be at trials in 2008. My promise to myself is that I'm going to finish my doctorate in the next year or so and between now and then think about buying a case of duct tape, dust off a little [laughter] bone dust [laughter] and see if I can go out and make a trials mark. I always wanted to compete in trials with her; I might have the opportunity to do so. I know that she will be there, so that's something to look forward to. So, I'm not done, done, done. I think. We'll see [laughter]. We'll just say, to be continued [laughter]. I think that's pretty much my story.

INTERVIEW: JOE DOUGLAS (COACH, SANTA MONICA TRACK CLUB)

(February 24, 2006) Well, I was raised in the 1940s, 50s and part of the 60s. It was a pretty macho society. Women could only run short distances. When I was teaching school, I noticed that the women were successful in everything from the brain power to the muscle power. They were very competitive. While I was coaching at Westchester High School in Los Angeles, California, I asked some of the girls to come out and train. They did, and they became very successful high school runners. When I started the Santa Monica Track Club in 1972, I had some young women join the club and train with the SMTC. We were successful in cross country and on the track. Some of the women ran under two minutes in the 800m. Running for the SMTC in the women's 800m at the 2006 Indoor National Championships today is Frances Santin, who I think is going to surprise everyone at this meet in Boston.

The attitudes of the women are what attract me to them. They want to achieve and they are disciplined. That is the attitude the men had until about 1996, and then their attitudes began to be less disciplined. I didn't see the sacrifice it takes for track athletes to be the best that they can be. I was actually going to quit coaching and then this young lady came to me and said, "Would you coach me?" I said, "What do you run?" She said, "The intermediate hurdles." I said, "No." She said, "I also can run the 800m." She said, "Please coach me. If you tell me to lick dirt off the floor, I will." I thought to myself, "Oh my gosh, I'm going to continue coaching for a few more years." As I said previously, you're going to see Frances have a very successful meet this weekend.

I worked with a lot of young women and one of the good distance runners I coached was a young lady named Ellen Lyons. The 5,000 and 10,000 meters were not official Olympic women's events in 1984, but they did have an exhibition 5,000 meters at the Olympic trials. Ellen won the Olympic trials 5,000m for women. Later on, I coached Dorianne Lambelet, Gail Conway and Claudette Groenendaal in the 800m. I had so many women runners it is hard to remember all of them as you get older. I was very fortunate to coach these female athletes. They are focused and they run the best they can. I don't care if they win, place, or show as long as they do their best. That is the characteristic that will make them successful in track and in life.

I remember I had one young lady who was a girlfriend of one of my ex-students. I don't believe she had run under 4 hours in the marathon. She trained well and ran 2:54:00 in the marathon. Her name was Terry Hom. She also ran a 36:59 in the 10k. That shows the success you can achieve with a good attitude. I think it's unfortunate that women didn't start competing in the distance events much earlier. We had some great women but they just didn't have the stage to show their abilities.

In 1995 an ex-athlete of mine, Willie Rios, sent a woman athlete named Jenny Spangler to me. I looked at her and I thought she was about in her early 20s. I asked her how old she was. She said, "I'm 32." "Oh my gosh," I said, "young lady, your HGH is high." She started training and had the perfect attitude. I changed her body mechanics and put a harness on her because she always wanted to run too fast. She listened to my advice, used her talent and ran very well. I only ran her in one race in 1996 before the Olympic Trials marathon. She ran well in a 10K race on a windy day. As the marathon approached I told her that no one in the USA can beat you. Before she went to run the trials in North Carolina I told her, "Don't take the lead until mile 18." I told her not to worry because they can't beat you. The TV announcers didn't know who she was until late in the race. I remember watching the race on television and thinking that the announcers should find out her name and inform the viewing audience because she is going to win. I think she took the lead near mile 15. She then proceeded to increase the pace to a 5:20 mile. From then on no one was close to her. She said she just jogged in. She ran a 2:29:54. She then went to run in the 1996 Olympic Games in Atlanta. I thought she would be one of the top two finishers, but early in the race her foot was injured and she had to drop out. She couldn't run. She had to have an operation on her foot. It was a big disappointment for me because she did not get the opportunity to show the world how well she could run in the Olympics. But she is a champion because she always ran the best that she could. Later she set the American masters record at 41. I think she ran 2:32.39. The next year she ran approximately 2:33.36. She had a few fractures this last year in her pelvis. I consider Jenny a jewel. That is the reason that many of us stay in coaching. We love to work with people who have great attitudes. That's what life is about.

The reason I'm coaching now is I have some very good women. They are Frances Santin, Kate Vermeulen from Canada (she'll be competing in the Commonwealth Games), and Maggie Vessey. They all have great attitudes. As long as the athletes I coach can make the sacrifices to be the best they can, I will continue to coach. I have been thirty-nine for thirty-two years now. Every birthday I celebrate my thirty-ninth!

Prior to starting this interview Joe went to his room and got his computer which contained

Joe Douglas, Coach, Santa Monica Track Club, 2006.

the names and entire records of the women he coached who were members of the Santa Monica Track Club. Listed below are many of them.

Carol Lewis

Michelle Finn-Burrell

Claudette Groenendaal

Miesha Marzell

Linda Heinmiller

Ellen Lyons

Jenny Spangler

Brigita Langerholc

Gail Conway

Dorianne Lambelet

Annetta Luevano Webber

Tania Fisher

Sandra Moya

Kate Vermeulen

Maggie Vessey

Jenny Adams

Delisa Walton-Floyd

Essie Washington

INTERVIEW: RAMONA PAGEL

(December 1, 1999) I began competing in high school when I was a sixteen-year-old sophomore. We actually had a class in which we learned all of the track events. At the end of the six week track class, we had a little track meet with all of the six periods. I decided that I liked that sport and wanted to try the sport. We had no girls track team but a group of us wanted to start one. We actually had to go down to the school board, this is in the late seventies, and we talked them into hiring a coach and starting a track team. Enough of us were interested that they actually did it. So, the next year they started the track team and I wanted to do everything. That's what you want to do when you're a kid.

Since I was a large girl and fairly strong, they shoved me over to the throwing events. When I started, the coach they hired didn't know very much about track. They had us throw the shot. They said, "You have to throw this." I said, "Well, how far do I have to throw it." They said, "You have to throw it 25 feet to make the team." So I said, "Okay." We started practicing and practicing and then we had a little inter-squad meet and I hit 25 feet exactly. Soon after that I found out that we were throwing the boys junior varsity shot! A ten pound shot instead of the eight pound shot. It was kind of funny at that point. It seemed like it was so heavy. We didn't even have discus that first year. We had to go through all that. You really don't think of things as obstacles at that age, you just do what you are allowed to do and no one said no, so we kept going.

The coach was there for one year as the track coach. She decided to have a family so the following year the men's coach became the head woman's coach, as well. When we got the men's head coach, Coach Bruce Vlink, he was very good. He was the throwing coach and was very excited about track.

My first conference meet that had the discus was when I was a junior and I didn't throw very well, something like 107 feet. In 1979, when I was a senior, I won! I was pleased with that and this enabled me to go on to the state meet. I was the first athlete from my high school to go to the state meet and it was a big deal, I even got my name on the marquee. However, it was a strong competitive year. We had three girls in southern California that threw the shot 50+ feet in high school. I, actually, at that time, had thrown 147 feet in the discus and I was thought of as a discus thrower. There was another girl named Leslie Deniz who had thrown 170 then, but 147 was still in the higher end of things.

At that state meet, I basically choked my brains out in the discus, you know, everyone has one of those days, and I cried and cried and cried. It was horrible. And then I came back the next day, and my coach kind of brushed me off and said, "Get back in there." I threw a PR in the shot and placed third and I think that's when I became a shot putter. I threw 46' 6½", my best. That was like a 2 foot PR for me in the state meet. That kind of carried me on and then into college.

I was on a track scholarship in college, tuition and books. Tuition was $107. I was at Cal State Long Beach for three years and then I went to San Diego State and graduated. I thought things were better at San Diego State but women's athletics were still maturing. Things have come a long way.

Ramona Pagel, 1999.

My first year in college, I think I hit 49 feet in the shot and I hit 160 in the discus. I qualified for AIAW in the discus but not the shot. Then I went to AAU Nationals and I qualified in the shot in the trials in 1980 but not the discus. So I kind of flip-flopped. My next year, I think I threw 52 and maybe 165; the following year 54/55 and I did not improve much in the discus. I red-shirted a year and actually stopped going to school for a semester; I thought I needed to work. I still trained, though. The next semester I went down to San Diego. I was traveling back and forth during the season. I wasn't competing for the team but I was going to school. That year I threw about the same in the shot, 54/55, but I improved in the discus to about 170.

My senior year I threw 58' 8" and 184 in the discus. This is 1984 and I won the NCAAs and made the 1984 Olympic team. That was the first national team that I was on and there was ¼ of an inch between fourth place and myself. It was a great year for me — really challenging and motivated me to continue throwing.

Making the Olympic team was kind of neat. I think I spent the whole night saying, "Wow, I made the Olympic team." It was really fantastic because I'm from L.A. So, in one respect, you're not going anywhere; it's not a trip. I vowed to make the most of it. I went to all of the training camps and pre–Olympic meets; Kent my husband and coach followed me around by car from city to city. It must have been hard on him but I think he enjoyed it. It was a highly guarded Olympics. I stayed in the village even though my parents lived ten minutes away. The village life was part of the experience and I wanted to soak everything in, the people, the experience, everything.

Walking into the stadium was a highlight of my career. You're the home team. Hearing the stands erupt in emotion when the team came in — it was really neat; I still get chills when I think about it today. It was a very powerful experience. I wasn't used to this and I didn't realize that you had to focus and concentrate on competing and all that other good stuff. So, it was a bit of a shock when I got on the field and everyone was yelling at me. I'm like, who do I know here? It's amazing to try to think of all that now after being so focused on it. I definitely lacked focus the first time. It was an experience that you can't duplicate any other time.

From there, I got more heavily involved. My goal the next year was to break the American record. Bonnie Dasse and I had a wonderful battle in trying to break that record, which belonged to Maren Seidler. We were both vying to hit 62' 2½". Whoever got there first would continue on. I think I won just by virtue of being stronger than her in a physical way. She was ahead most of the year partly because I was trying to finish school but Bonnie ended up with a stress fracture in her wrist. I am sure it was disappointing for her because in '84 she had a stress fracture in her back that kept her from making the team. We both were giving it our all and we couldn't have done it without each other to compete against.

So the day before graduation, I set the American record, graduated from college and had a wham-bam weekend. I was kind of sad the morning of graduation because I was so focused on throwing I had forgotten to get anything to wear for graduation. Thank goodness you have to wear those robes!

I then continued to throw the discus but I just wasn't as good at it. I was still in the 180s. In 1985, I made my first sets of teams. We went to Europe, Japan, and Australia. There was a lot of traveling that summer. I got a lot of experience doing those meets and even had some good successes.

The year after that I just kept trying to set more records. I think I set a couple of American records. I finally finished setting records in 1988.

My best throw in the shot put was 66' 2½". That day I knew I was going to throw well. I just knew I was going to throw well. I had had outstanding practices the week before; I was comfortable because it was in San Diego. I was so confident I had invited my parents to come down from L.A. They came down. I just knew, that whole week coming up to that meet that I was going to throw well. And I did. It was one of those rare moments in life when everything goes as you planned and trained for. I had this huge series between 64' 10" and 66'. Afterward, I waited for the world to change; it never did, but physically I had found my limit. I was throwing the discus that year, too, and throwing pretty far in practice. The goal being I would double at the games. Another goal accomplished, I made the Olympic team in both the shot and the discus. In the discus I tied with Connie Price but she won on second best throw — which was okay — cause, I won the shot. And the discus was first, so I was kind of worried; I wanted the shot win more than the discus. I threw 63' at the trials in Indianapolis that year, and can't remember being so nervous before. In qualifying I think I threw 53' and people would come up to me and ask me if I was okay. Fortunately, I was able to put some of my fear aside and set a trials record.

That year we went to Seoul. I was expecting huge things, of course, after setting the American record. I got some good results. I threw 61 in qualifying, which was my best in an international meet, but it was very disappointing considering how far I should have thrown. In the discus I threw better. My best was 189' at 8 in the morning. It was a whole new experience waking up before the sun and trying to qualify. It was very weird. The whole atmosphere was strange because we were in a different sociological atmosphere. It was a really good experience, because I learned so much and gained confidence.

In 1992 and 1996 I had my best Olympic finishes. They were both very good. I made the finals those two times. After 1988, basically my goal was to compete internationally. That was a big disappointment in Seoul after having thrown so far and then not being able to reproduce it at international level. One of my biggest problems was that I had a hang-up with my size. I was so small. I was very small compared to all the European throwers. Every time I'd get into a big meet, I knew I had to be perfect. Whereas they could make mistakes and still be very strong and be able to get away with things. But, I knew that I had to be perfect.

The world championship in Helsinki was a memorable meet. I think I surprised people. They considered me a good thrower but I had never made a final. I came up with a big throw on my last throw, my third throw, and I made the finals. Dwight Stones was announcing: he goes, "She's been around forever — she'll never make it. She's never done this before." Then all of a sudden I did something and you could tell in his voice that he was surprised. He's been around for so long, too. I always knew I could throw that far in that situation. It was just a matter of putting it together at the right time. You prepare and you prepare and you don't do it. You prepare and you prepare and you don't do it. Just getting the right combination of things together is hard. You get a real appreciation for people who get world records and gold medals. I have more of an appreciation for that than someone who has never tried because they don't understand all of the preparation that goes into it. They appreciate it but I know what the athletes go through to get it. That was probably the biggest meet of my life.

I retired after 1996, after four Olympic teams. I do a lot of clinics now. We do a couple of local clinics and the Dartmouth clinic and I did the junior elite clinic. You have to give back into the sport, especially in the throws. They are neglected, especially in the women's throws. It's not something you're going to get paid a lot of money for.

I run a lot actually and I try to lift four days a week, just to stay in touch. But, no masters. I knew why I was quitting: because of so many years of punishment to the body. I was lucky and never had an operation. I've had serious injury. My back has been really bad. That's my weak link. When the wrist was going, and the hips start to go — you have to use the body for the rest of your life and you can just punish it so much.

INTERVIEW: CONNIE PRICE SMITH

(June 1998, December 4, 2005) I got started in track and field in the ninth grade. A great friend of mine, my junior high coach, talked me into throwing the shot. Before that I played softball. I started playing softball when I was twelve and then I didn't get to play in organized sports until the ninth grade.

My first sport in ninth grade was volleyball. Then I went from volleyball to basketball to track and field. I played basketball all four years of high school and I did track and field for all four years also.

My senior year in high school I did all four sports: volleyball, basketball, softball and track and field. Track and field and softball overlapped each other. In Missouri, I won the state championship in track and field my junior and senior years. My sophomore year I think I got like sixth place or something. I think I threw 36 feet. My junior and senior years I threw like forty feet. I didn't throw the discus. I did the shot and the triple jump, I ran the 100 and I ran on the 4 × 100 relay.

Jackie Joyner and I played basketball, probably every year from my sophomore year. We played against each other in tournaments — usually for the Christmas tournament East St. Louis came over — and they always beat us by God knows how many points. They had an incredibly good team. I think the top seven people on their team all went to division 1 schools.

I remember the first time I watched a national championship. It was in '85. I didn't have a clue about track after NCAAs. John, my husband, took me to Indianapolis. He was actually competing so I went there to watch him. It was just really interesting and exciting to think that you could keep doing it. For me, I wasn't sure what I would really do. John kept telling me you can do this and you can do that. I went and I watched and just the energy and the atmosphere of being at the track meet was exciting enough to make me want to do it.

I competed during my fifth year in college in 1985. I finished there and went to my first TAC Nationals in Eugene, Oregon. From there I made my first international team in 1987, which was the World University Games. I made both the World University Games that year and the world championships. It was exciting and interesting. I started in 1986. I was finished with college.

In 1987, I got a contract with Nike which allowed me to keep doing it. It went from there. I made a team in '87. I made the Olympic team in '88. Then I made every international team after that up to 2000. It was a wonderful, long career.

My first Olympics in Seoul was totally nothing like what I had expected. I got there and just being in the village around people — you are just in awe. You're walking around and you're — it was hard for me because I never imagined initially, or when I was younger, being an Olympian or being in sports. So, I was just in awe of everything there. I was absolutely amazed at the number of people that were there watching, the level of people there that were competing — the intensity. It was fun though. It was fun to be in the environment.

A lot of people ask the question all the time, "What is the highlight of your career?" There are probably two that come to mind first. One was in '87 at nationals because it was all so new to me and I was in the discus You have people over here that are like, "Yea, yea, go Connie" and people over here that are like, "Who is she? What does she think she's doing? Blah, blah, blah, blah." To go in and win nationals being very, very green and not knowing what the heck I was doing and just going out there. John would always say, "A ring is a ring, go out there and just throw over

Connie Price Smith, 2005.

the line and don't worry about anything else." That's what I did. Winning that and just getting the support coming into the sport. Everybody was supportive like TAC in development and everybody wanting to help me.

The other probably was in '96 when I made the finals of the Olympic games and not having to walk off of the field after the first three throws; that was probably one of the biggest highlights for me.

Other highlights were walking into the stadium in Atlanta. It was incredible and just getting to travel.

I am the head coach now at Southern Illinois University. I have both the men's and women's programs. I do a lot with the NCAA and I do a lot with USATF. I have four assistant coaches, one of which is John, my husband [laughter]. He's good to work with. The administration is really supportive of me in trying to develop a program. I enjoy it a lot.

Everything has been really great about track and field. There's been some bad times but all the good times make up for everything that's ever happened. I've gotten to travel and see the world and meet all of the different people, which I probably wouldn't have gotten to do.

INTERVIEW: JENNY SPANGLER

(March 8, 2006) I actually got started in track and field in high school my freshman year. I grew up in Rockford, Illinois and went to Guilford High School. I actually went out for the basketball team my freshman year and got cut. I decided I wanted to do a sport and decided to give track a try. That's how I got started.

I knew when I started that I wasn't much of a sprinter just from the Presidential Physical Fitness Awards we used to have. I always had trouble with the 50 yard dash. I always did really well in the 600 yard dash. I started out with the 800. It seemed like the farther the distance I did, the better I got and the more I loved it. It just kind of took off from there.

Some of my highlights are: I went to the University of Iowa on a track and cross country scholarship. While I was there I was NCAA All American in 10,000 meters in track and also in cross country. Also while I was there, at age 19, I ran my first marathon. It was Grandma's

Marathon up in Duluth, Minnesota. That was 1983. I won the race in just over 2:33 and set the American junior record which still stands today.

I was fortunate enough, with that time, to be able to compete in the 1984 U.S. Olympic marathon trials which, of course, you know Joan Benoit won. It was quite an event. I can't remember what place I was. But, I tried out for the '84 and '88 trials and didn't make it. Then in '96 I won the U.S. women's Olympic marathon trials.

[At the time of my 1996 marathon trials victory] I was about 32. It was a time in my life where I had just recently been divorced and had taken a little bit of time off from running. I just really wanted to get back into my running again. I just kind of put all my eggs into one basket. Willie Rios began coaching me and then called Joe Douglas asking him to work with me. I started training with Joe Douglas and the Santa Monica Track Club. I had moved out to California. Actually, my qualifier for the trials, I had some difficulty in that marathon. So, going into the trials I was ranked 61st. I had been having some great workouts. I knew I was in great shape. Joe Douglas thought I was probably in around 2:30 shape. In 61st, no one really paid much attention to me [laughter], which was fine.

Just standing on the line, my goal was to have the best race of my life because I knew I had a good marathon left inside of me and I just loved the distance. I didn't believe I'd be in the top three just because there were so many other awesome women.

It was just one of those magical days. I just started off— felt great — the pace felt great — we just started clicking off the miles. All the other front runners kept talking about who was back there and all that talk. I just kept focused on what I was doing.

Somewhere shortly after the halfway mark, Joe Douglas had always told me, "If you feel like you're running too comfortably you need to pick it up" and I thought, you know, I feel like I'm running pretty easy, maybe I better pick it up a little bit. So, I threw in this 5:20 something mile which I didn't even know about and left everybody.

I started getting really scared. I'm like, "What are you doing?" [laughter] But I just felt great and I just kept hammering off the miles. I kept waiting for people to come up on me. I just kept thinking people are going to start coming up and they are going to start passing me. I get up to mile 20. I thought, you know, you've gone this far just keep going. Try to get in the top 3. Try to get in the top 3. Then by 24, I thought, wow, you can really win this thing. It was just one of the highlights of my life and running career. It was just a magical day where everything comes together and you feel great. It's just indescribable almost. I was so focused and running within myself that I kept charging ahead and just running. I wasn't paying too much attention to the chitter chatter and stuff around me. I was just trying to click off the miles.

It was funny afterwards. I heard that the press was going crazy. When you're ranked 61st they don't pay a lot of attention to you going in. They were doing whatever they could to find out stuff about me. The husband of one of my training partners happened to be standing by the press truck. I didn't know him very well. They were saying we've got to find out more information about Jenny. He said "My wife trains with her." They yanked him over to the press truck and said "Tell us about her." He's like, "All I know about her is that she went to the University of Iowa and she's currently single." [laughter] It was a lot of fun for us.

Walking into the Olympic stadium in Atlanta was incredible. I was very, very nervous. Actually, for this race I was scared because I knew my achilles wasn't right. It was early in the morning and I was just awestruck by this feat that we were about to take on — just being here in the Olympics. I remember getting on the bus at the Olympic village that morning. All of the athletes had to ride on this bus over to the stadium. No one would look at each other. It was so quiet in there. You could just hear a pin drop. We rode over in silence. It was dark outside. Just entering that — it brought tears to my eyes. It was wonderful.

I ran about seven miles. The first few laps on the track were fine. Atlanta was pretty hilly. As soon as we started getting into the hills, the achilles just was very, very painful. I tried to slow down a little bit. It was still very painful. The further I got I was afraid that I was going to rupture it or do something bad to end my running career. As much as I wanted to finish that race — in fact, I thought, why can't you just walk it? You can't do that. That was probably one of the hardest things I had to do in my life. People were out there cheering, "Go, USA" and I didn't want to drop out in front of everybody. But I knew it was something I was going to have to do. So I just held my breath at one point and stopped. Of course, I was totally devastated for a long time. But as the years have clicked by, I have a wonderful family now but it still was a horrible day in my life. But to put it all in perspective I kind of forget about it now. I was actually surprised at the number of people who dropped out of that race. I was so excited for Ann Marie Lauck to come in 10th. It was a tough course on a tough day. I had so much support down there. Years later I was giving a talk for a running club and this guy told me that he still had one of my fluid bottles that were out on the course. He actually picked it up [laughter].

After Atlanta I had some achilles surgery — took some time off — had a baby — got married and then finally, back in 2003, after baby and lots of injuries I came back and ran the LaSalle Bank Chicago Marathon in just over 2 hours 32 minutes and set, at that time, the masters record for American women in the marathon. Colleen DeReuck has since beaten it. At that time, I actually held both the junior record and the masters record for U.S. women in the marathon. It was kind of cool to do that at age 19 and then at age 40 to do that.

I'm still running and competing and coaching. Those are pretty much my highlights.

INTERVIEW: DEANNE VOCHATZER (THE 1996 OLYMPIC COACH)

(December 6, 2002) Basically I started late in track and field because I was a pre–Title IX baby and so there were no opportunities throughout high school to run. My background was in ballet. I had eighteen years of classical ballet. So, I continued to dance through the first part of my running career. I was blessed to have a very supportive family who completely backed and supported me at a time in history when it was not exactly fashionable for girls/women to compete in sports!

I was a junior in high school when the boys track coach, Mel Jones, decided that he was going to have the cheerleaders run a relay at one of the track meets. Never having been instructed in any mannerisms of running whatever, I thought it would be fun, and so against one of our rivals, their cheerleaders ran against our cheerleaders. So, that began my career. I always thought it was because I showed talent. Years later he told me it was because I was a nasty competitor. After that he asked me if I wanted to learn how to run. Again this was in 1965-66 when there weren't a lot of opportunities. So, he took me under his wing and because of my ballet background, hurdles were somewhat easy for me to do. Mel and his wife Connie became my second family and he was my rock.

I remember the first race I ever ran; as a matter of fact, it was a 400. Because it was a boys track meet it was his daughter — he made her run — and a girlfriend — there were only three of us. That was my first race. There were also some 9th grade boys in the 400 as well.

To make a long story short, I was in lane three and I didn't understand the staggers and the lanes. So, after the gun went off, I immediately cut over to lane one. My first race I won, and I ran really fast but then I found out I was disqualified. I ran a 58.5. I had a lot of learning to do. It would have been around 61 if I didn't cut in. I remember I was so embarrassed, I didn't know what to do when I found out I had to be DQed. So, my first race was not totally successful. But, it started my career.

From there I went to be tutored by Roxy Anderson and joined the Laurel Track Club, which was four hours away from Chico, in northern California. My mom drove me every Sunday. We left at 4 am down old highway 99 and drove to Balboa Stadium at San Francisco City College to work out with Irene Obera, Cherri Sherrard and Denise Pascal Smith. It was quite a group. I was very lucky to come up through the club system and I competed until I was 31. I started at 17 and competed all those years because I was a late bloomer.

I traveled throughout the country. I made my first team in 1969. I was a hurdler. I was never fortunate enough to make an Olympic team. I seemed to be injured Olympic years. I made my second United States team in 1973 with our ex-chair, Lynn Cannon, a javelin thrower.

At that time I got my degree and was going to work on my masters and the day I graduated, the president of Chico State offered me the job at Chico to begin coaching because I had caused so much trouble while I was there.

As a freshman, I got arrested for trespassing when I tried to workout on the track. A little campus policeman was going to have me removed. He said "Don't make me do this. Can't you just walk outside?" I probably could have handled the situation better but I didn't. Then he went to the president and the president told the men's track coach that he had to let me run. It was a very tumultuous three to four years while I went to school there and ran. But, I got the opportunity and had a lot of help from people like Payton Jordan, Berny Wagner and Roxy from the Laurel Track Club.

I stayed there for five years and then had a chance to finish my masters and run for the Florida Track Club. Jimmy Carnes asked me to come to Florida. He was sponsoring a women's track team. He paid for me to go to school to finish my masters and I ran for the Florida Track Club. Then sometimes fate has its way and the man upstairs had a plan. I had a very serious injury and a couple of days later the women's track coach at Florida got fired. So, I became coach of the Lady Gators for a while. That's when Brooks Johnson began working with me. We ended up marrying a few years later.

But, I decided that I was definitely going to coach — that was going to be my career. I still competed, which was a big mistake. But, at that time, you didn't have any options. There was no funding. You worked full time and then squeezed in the competition.

I stayed in Florida until 1980. Then I came back to California. Those were the AIAW days and there were all kinds of tumultuous things going on —fights and battles — and it wore you out. I needed a break. I went to the high school and was the athletic director from 1980–1987 in a high school in San Jose. I had a nun who was a kick-butt nun and she said, "You do what you need to do." We built a gym. There

Deanne Vochatzer, 2002.

were only two teams when I got there. When I left we had nine girls' sports teams. It was a great experience. During those years, I coached for the Puma Track Club. I had elite athletes like Robin Campbell and others. I decided it was time to go back to collegiate coaching.

I went to U. C. Davis. In 1991, I got offered a great position at Cal Poly, San Luis Obispo. I went there, re-married, came back and I've been at Davis for ten years.

In 1996, I was lucky enough to have my colleagues put me forth for the women's Olympic head coach and it was a life changing experience.

It was a crossover from one side to the other — to have the Olympic Games at home. I'll never forget any aspect of it. Sometimes you push a button and I just start jabbering like it was yesterday because it was such an all out assault on every one of your senses. I felt the responsibility of being a female; I won't lie about it. There's only been two women head coaches before me and I didn't want to make a mistake to cause problems for the talented women that were to come behind me, but also because it was in our country. On that team we had 55 women, 22 married and 9 moms — it was very nice. When I was competing in the 70s, 19½ was our average age compared to 29.1 for this team. The team in 2000 was 29.2 years of age. So, it's very different.

I've been very lucky to grow up through the ranks: pre–Title IX, then the club ranks, then to great mentorship by some great people, and then now and that part of my career where my goal is to keep mentoring these young women because there's a gap. There's a gap because you have to have a screw loose like I do because society has not changed that much. We have certainly made progress. But, you're still expected to have children, be in the home, have dinner on the table, and iron the shirts. You can't do that and if anyone says that it's not that way, it's very untrue. You have to have someone who is willing to take those risks and juggle that and whomever your life partner is has to be willing to come halfway. It's intriguing. I'm enjoying that part. I'm still coaching and now that U.C. Davis is going division I, that will be a whole new experience for our program.

My goal, this is my 32nd year coaching, is to coach for five more years and then move into administration. My major goal at this point is mentoring young women to step up to the plate and take the high risk, high profile position.

Some of the phenomenal moments of 1996? One was before the Games even started. Everyone always tried to figure out who was going to light the torch. So, there was all of this intrigue. The Atlanta Braves Stadium is where they got everyone together six hours before opening ceremony. They brought the United States team over last so we wouldn't have to sit out for so long. As we went up the ramp, this limo pulled up and out got Muhammad Ali — and with his advanced stage of Parkinson's — to me, to watch him stand up there and high five or shake the hands of all the American athletes and let them see his infirm body at this point, I'll never forget it. Then to watch him light the torch because there was a moment when we didn't think it was going to happen and we thought he was going to get burned — you talk about nervous — I broke into a cold sweat and the whole delegation was silent and then, thank God, five seconds later, his arm came up and the arrow went up; it was something else.

The other, I still breathe heavily when I remember. It was when the two relay teams both won gold medals — because those two relay teams represented years of sacrifice — marriages that failed and women battled through it — three of the women in both relay teams have children. We had babysitting service at relay practice and I knew what was on the line for them. I knew what pressures they were under. I remember Maicel Malone in the 4 × 4 telling me, "Coach D, just get up out front and tell me to run for my baby" [choked up] I still do that. So, that to me, to watch those women cross the finish line and win a gold medal and take the victory lap with their little kids in their arms was a big thrill. That was probably the crowning thing when people ask about what a glamorous position the Olympic coach has.

I go back to when we started out after the trials, driving vans sixteen hours to Chapel Hill and then going down to the cellar where Nike delivered all the uniforms, and unpacking probably fifteen hours in 100 degree heat and laughing, "Aren't we glamorous Olympic coaches?" We packed the fifty something bags for the athletes, and then, after the bombing, once the Games had started, the eating patterns changed. So, each night we would find out what the athletes wanted and we would go to the Safeway about 2am after drug testing — Martha Watson and I and Mamie Rallins — we'd buy yogurt and deli meats packed in ice to take in to the warm-up track and have our trainers hide it in the ice chest and take it in to eat; we had to be there so early because of the new security. So, as I said before, it was a life-changing experience.

The future for me, if I ever get my behind in gear, is to get some of these in writing — that still is a goal. At U.C. Davis, my program is still my main focus: moving it to division I. At the convention, mentoring leadership programs with Terry Crawford is a focus. In USTCA, we have planned programs to show young women how to step up and do it and the motto, "If you're not part of the solution, you're part of the problem." I believe that and I try to live that!

17

1997

The Outdoor Nationals

The USA National Outdoor Track and Field Championships were held in Indiana University Track and Field Stadium, Indianapolis, Indiana from June 11 to June 15.

---

100 meters

The *New York Times* reported, "Running into a slight head wind tonight, Jones won the 100 meters at the national championship in 10.97 seconds, having already run the previous two fastest times in the world this season, 10.98 and 10.92, in Thursday's preliminary rounds. She returned to track and field full time in March, and already she has become what many people long expected she could become — the fastest woman in the world."

1. Marion Jones, Nike International Track Club	10.97
2. Chryste Gaines, Nike International Track Club	11.19
3. Inger Miller, Nike International Track Club	11.21
4. Carlette Guidry, Team adidas	11.29
5. D'Andre Hill, Asics International Track Club	11.37
6. Celena Mondie-Milner, PowerAde Track Club	11.40
7. Sabrina Kelly, University of Texas	11.42

200 meters

"Running three days after her 25th birthday, Miller had a clear lead as the runners came off the curve, and she only increased that as she got her best legal time of the year, 22.62, well up on Cheryl Taplin (22.90)," reported *Track & Field News*.

1. Inger Miller, Nike International Track Club	22.62
2. Cheryl Taplin, Nike International Track Club	22.90
3. Zundra Feagin, Asics International Track Club	23.06
4. Jearl Miles-Clark, Reebok Racing Club	23.06
5. Carlette Guidry, Team adidas	23.14
6. LaTasha Jenkins, Ball State University	23.33
7. Tameka Roberts, University of Texas, San Antonio	23.58
8. Chryste Gaines, Nike International Track Club	27.17

400 meters

1. Jearl Miles-Clark, Reebok Racing Club	49.40	MR
2. Kim Graham, Asics International Track Club	50.65	
3. Maicel Malone-Wallace, Asics Track Club	50.74	
4. Michelle Collins, unattached	50.77	
5. Natasha Kaiser-Brown, Health South	51.21	
6. Shanelle Porter, Team U.S. West	51.22	
7. Chandra Burns, Michigan State University	51.71	
8. Jessica Hudson, LaGrange Track Club	52.23	

800 meters

The *New York Times* reported: "After the 1988 Olympic trials, Kathi Rounds shelved her running career, disgusted with the state of track and field. After an absence of six years, and the birth of a daughter, she returned to training, only to miss a spot on the 1996 Olympic team because of a competitor's late charge. Today her comeback reached a more satisfying conclusion with a national title in the women's 800-meter race.

"Today, in a slow race, Rounds positioned herself for a final move and took the lead with 200 meters remaining, winning in 2:00.45."

1. Kathleen Rounds, Nike International Track Club	2:00.45
2. Joetta Clark, Foot Locker Athletic Club	2:00.64
3. Jill McMullen, Asics International Track Club	2:00.81
4. Hazel Clark, University of Florida	2:01.42
5. Michelle DiMuro-Ave, unattached	2:03.25
6. Tanya Blake, Santa Monica Track Club	2:04.55
7. Delisa Floyd, unattached	2:07.98
8. Julian Reynolds, Georgetown University	2:08.72

1500 meters

"Already the only woman ever to win the event three times in a row, Regina Jacobs ran her 1500 streak to four, and also claimed overall title No. 6, leaving her just one behind the total tallied by Francie Larrieu-Smith between 1970 and '80," reported *Track & Field News*.

1. Regina Jacobs, Mizuno Track Club	4:03.42
2. Suzy Hamilton, Nike InternationalTrack Club	4:04.36
3. Sarah Thorsett, Nike International Track Club	4:07.34
4. Amy Wickus, Nike International Track Club	4:08.26
5. Ruth Wysocki, Nike International Track Club	4:11.58
6. Shayne Wille, University of Colorado	4:12.69
7. Juli Henner, Reebok Enclave	4:12.82
8. Kathy Franey, Nike International Track Club	4:13.06

3000m steeplechase (exhibition)

1. Melissa Teemant, Brigham Young University	10:30.90
2. Elizabeth Jackson, Brigham Young University	10:38.72
3. Grace Padilla, Reebok VO2 Max Track Club	10:44.12
4. Janet Trujillo, Auburn University	10:55.57
5. Sally Perkins, Central Massachusetts Striders	11:00.31
6. Kristin Von Teuber, Reebok VO2 Max Track Club	11:11.96
7. Erin Kelly, Butler University	11:31.44
8. Pam Allie-Morrill, Liberty Athletic Club	11:32.65

5000 meters

1. Libbie Hickman, Nike International Track Club	15:37.73	
2. Amy Rudolph, Reebok Racing Club	15:45.21	
3. Melody Fairchild, Nike International Track Club	15:45.54	
4. Elva Dryer, Nike International Track Club	15:47.90	
5. Cheri Goddard, Reebok Enclave	15:55.79	
6. Gina Procaccio, Nike International Track Club	16:02.80	
7. Kristen Ihle, Nike International Track Club	16:08.04	
8. Michele Buresh-Chalmers, Mountain West Track Club	16:09.19	

10,000 meters

1. Lynn Jennings, Nike International Track Club	32:26.41	
2. Annette Peters, Nike International Track Club	32:28.55	
3. Deena Drossin, Reebok Racing Club	32:53.18	
4. Kristin Beaney, Central Massachusetts Striders	33:00.88	
5. Jennifer Rhines, Reebok Racing Club	33:17.26	
6. Gwyn Coogan, New Balance Track Club	33:36.70	
7. Natalie Nalepa, unattached	33:47.39	
8. Rachel Sauder, Nike International Track Club	33:51.66	

10 kilometer walk

1. Debbi Lawrence, unattached	46:45.36	
2. Sara Standley, unattached	46:53.07	
3. Victoria Herazo, California Walkers	47:18.05	
4. Joanne Dow, unattached	47:22.26	
5. Jill Zenner, Cedarville College	48:10.73	
6. Debora Van Orden, unattached	48:41.70	
7. Dana Yarbrough, Athletes In Action	49:09.97	
8. Lyn Brubaker, unattached	49:19.07	

100 meter hurdles

"Morrison had established a clear lead by the second hurdle and kept inching away, even though Anjanette Kirkland and Dawn Bowles also scored lifetime bests with their 12.74 clockings," wrote *Track & Field News.*

1. Melissa Morrison, Reebok Racing Club	12.61	equals MR
2. Anjanette Kirkland, Texas A&M University	12.74	
3. Dawn Bowles, unattached	12.74	
4. Cheryl Dickey, Nike International Track Club	12.88	
5. Yolanda McCray, University of Miami	12.98	
6. Kimberly Carson, Reebok International	13.06	
7. Tiffany Lott, Brigham Young University	13.29	
8. Shandi Boyd-Pleasant, unattached	22.21	

400 meter hurdles

"Batten had a clear lead by the middle of the backstretch and just kept pouring it on," said *Track & Field News.*

1. Kim Batten, Reebok Racing Club	52.97	MR
2. Tonja Buford-Bailey, Nike International Track Club	54.05	
3. Ryan Tolbert, Vanderbilt University	54.21	
4. Rebecca Buchanan, Reebok Racing Club	54.96	
5. Trevaia Williams, Atoms Track Club	56.34	

6. Michelle Johnson, Tucson Elite Athletic Club   56.51
7. Melinda Sallins, unattached   57.37
8. Sandra Glover, unattached   58.84

High jump

"...No one had much luck at 6' 5" until, with only Aldrich left as a threat, Acuff became the height's sole conqueror on her third attempt," reported *Track & Field News*.

1. Amy Acuff, University of California, Los Angeles   6' 5"
2. Angela Bradburn-Spangler, PowerAde Track Club   6' 4"
3. Erin Aldrich, Asics International Track Club   6' 4"
4. Karol Jenkins, unattached   6' 2¼"
5. Gwen Wentland, Nike International Track Club   6' 2¼"
6. Tisha Waller, unattached   6' ½"
7. Tanya Hughes-Jones, Asics International Track Club   6' ½"
8. Clare Look-Jaeger, Beach Track Club   5' 10½"

Pole vault

While this is the first championship year for the pole vault in the United States, this event is not yet in the world outdoor program.

1. Stacy Dragila, Rocky Mt. Elite   14' 1¼" MR
2. Melissa Price, Fresno State University   13' 1½"
3. Melissa Mueller, unattached   12' 11½"
4. Kellie Suttle, Bell Athletics   12' 9½"
   and Kimberly Becker, Bell Athletics
6. Jill Nuttbrock, High Plains Track & Field   12' 1½"
7. Alexa Harz, No Limit Sports   11' 9¾"
8. Erica Hoenig, No Limit Sports   11' 9¾"

Long jump

Track & Field News reported, "By a single inch, Marion Jones stopped Jackie Joyner-Kersee's awesome streak of USATF or Olympic Trials long jump wins at 9. Jones — who was 12 when JJK began her string — led from round 1 with a windy 22' 3¾" jump."

1. Marion Jones, Nike International Track Club   22' 9"
2. Jackie Joyner-Kersee, Honda Track Club   22' 8"
3. Sharon Couch, Goldwin Track Club   22' 2½"
4. Shana Williams, Team adidas   21' 11¾"
5. Angee Henry, Reebok Racing Club   21' 6¼"
6. Shonda Swift, unattached   21' 2"
7. Marieke Veltman, Reebok Racing Club   21' 2"
8. Dawn Burrell, unattached   21' 1¾"

Triple jump

"While 9-time No. 1 U.S. ranker Sheila Hudson — recovering from injury — took only 8th at 42' 4", Niambi Dennis took a lead in round 1 at 44' 8" then stretched it to 44' 8¾" in round 4 to win her first national title at age 27," said *Track & Field News*.

1. Niambi Dennis, U.S. Army   44' 8¾"
2. Shonda Swift, unattached   44' 8"
3. Cynthea Rhodes, Reebok Racing Club   44' 5¼"
4. Vanitta Kinard, Kansas State University   44' 2"
5. Tiombé Hurd, unattached   43' 4¼"

6. Telisa Young, Reebok Racing Club	42' 9½"
7. Amy Littlepage, University of California, Berkeley	42' 4¼"
8. Sheila Hudson, Reebok Racing Club	42' 4"

Shot put

"In a weird three-peat, Connie Price-Smith won a sixth straight and 8th overall shot title by throwing the identical mark of 62' 6½" in rounds 2, 4 and 5. That's also exactly how far she threw to win in '92, only ½" longer than in '95, and just 1¼" shy of her mark of last year," reported *Track & Field News*.

1. Connie Price-Smith, Team adidas	62' 6½"
2. Valeyta Althouse, Reebok-Bruin Track Club	61' ¼"
3. Tressa Thompson, University of Nebraska	58' 2"
4. Dawn Dumble, Reebok-Bruin Track Club	57' 4¾"
5. Crystal Brownlee, University of South Carolina	56' 8⅕"
6. Amy Christiansen, unattached	55' ¼"
7. Beth Bunge, unattached	52' 2"
8. Dawn Ellerbe, unattached	50' 11½"

Discus

According to *Track & Field News*, "Throwing in warm, still air, Lacy Barnes-Mileham emerged as the U.S. discus titlist for the third time in her career, but first since '91. In the 4th round, she sailed her platter out to 200' 8", her second 200-footer of the year and a mark she matched in round 5. That took the lead from '95 champ Edie Boyer's 197' 1" opener."

1. Lacy Barnes-Mileham, Nike International Track Club	200' 8"
2. Suzy Powell, University of California, Los Angeles	198' 4"
3. Edie Boyer, unattached	197' 1"
4. Kris Kuehl, unattached	196' 10"
5. Aretha Hill, University of Washington	196' 5"
6. Dawn Dumble, Reebok-Bruin Track Club	189' 2"
7. Pamela Dukes, Reebok Racing Club	186' 6"
8. Allison Franke, unattached	179' 2"

Javelin

"Winning her first national title at 192' was good for the gold medal but not good enough to get Lynda Lipson to Athens for the world championships. Wheeler, who placed second and Carroll, the bronze medalist, will make the trip to Athens, both having already met the qualifying standard," reported *Track & Field News*.

1. Lynda Lipson, Klub Keihas	192'
2. Erica Wheeler, unattached	187' 9"
3. Nicole Carroll, Asics International Track Club	185' 3"
4. Emily Carlsten, University of North Carolina	174' 1"
5. Tiffany Lott, Brigham Young University	173' 3"
6. Donna Mayhew, South Bay Track Club	172' 8"
7. Kim Kreiner, Kent State University	168' 2"
8. Kirsten Schultz, Kansas State University	167' 5"

Hammer

"Dawn Ellerbe received a bloody cut above the eye from a flying hammer wire when Kiyomi Parish's second-round throw fouled into a cage post. The AR taped the gash and went on, though, to improve from her 205' 8" opener leader to a 206' 7" in round 6," said *Track & Field News*.

1. Dawn Ellerbe, unattached	206' 7" MR
2. Renetta Seiler, Kansas State University	199' 11"
3. Kiyomi Parish, Pomona-Pitzer College	196' 6"
4. Molly Duggan, Oregon International Track Club	194' 8"
5. Windy Dean, unattached	189' 1"
6. Anna Norgren, Boston Athletic Association	189'
7. Rachelle Noble, University of California, Los Angeles	188' 11"
8. Tara Crozier, Kutztown University	183' 8"

Heptathlon

Track & Field News reported:

Kelly Blair is a second-day heptathlete — as in, of the two first-day events she PRed in here, one was an unspectacular 43' 7" shot that really just made up for a slightly down high jump (5' 8½"). The other, a 24.13 200, led the pack, and Blair finished day 1 in 3rd behind Kym Carter and DeDee Nathan. Nobody else was remotely in the hunt.

On day 2, defending champ Blair long-jumped 21' 4¾" w to leap over Carter. Next, Blair's 169' 3" jav — best in the field by more than 20 feet — gave her a 150-point lead over Nathan. Blair's 2:15.31 in the climatic 800 lost her only 2 points from that margin, as she PRed with 6465 to become the No. 3 American ever.

1. Kelly Blair, Nike International Track Club	6465
2. DeDee Nathan, Indiana Track Club	6317
3. Kym Carter, Reebok Racing Club	6289
4. Ali McKnight, unattached	5783
5. Jamie McNeair, unattached	5762
6. Heather Sterlin, University of Colorado	5688
7. Trina Bindel, unattached	5620
8. Kristi McGihon, Beach Track Club	5568

The Indoor Nationals

The USA Indoor Track and Field Championships were held in the Georgia Dome, Atlanta, Georgia, February 28 through March 1.

A small article appeared in the *New York Times* on Saturday captioned, "Repeat in Pole-Vault."

"Stacy Dragila, the national record-holder in the pole-vault, won her second straight title in the United States Indoor Championships in Atlanta last night. She qualified for the American team that will compete in next weekend's world championships in Paris. Dragila, who owns the American indoor (14 feet 1¼ inches) and outdoor (13' 9¼") pole vault records, soared 13' 1½" to make her first international team."

Sunday's *New York Times* write-up featured Gail Devers and Mary Slaney.

Gail Devers and Mary Slaney ran the best times in the world this year in the 60-meter dash and the 1,500-meter run, respectively, to win their events today at the United States indoor track and field championships.

The two women are favorites at next weekend's world indoor track and field championships in Paris.

"My strategy was that I wanted to go out hard," said Slaney, who made the United States Olympic team in the 5,000 meters last year. "If you go back to 1984 when I fell, if I had gone out harder, that wouldn't have happened."

...For the second week in a row, Devers beat her archrival, Gwen Torrence. Although Torrence's second-place finish in 7.12 seconds qualified her for the world championships, the Atlanta native said Friday that she would not run. That gave her spot on the American team to the third-place finisher, Aleisha Latimer.

...Joetta Clark was unchallenged on her way to a victory in the women's 800-meter run, pulling away from the field easily on the backstretch of the last lap to finish in 2:00.86.

---

60 meters
1. Gail Devers, Nike Track Club   7.00
2. Gwen Torrence, unattached   7.12
3. Aleisha Latimer, Colorado Flyers   7.22

200 meters
1. Tameka Roberts, University of Texas, San Antonio   23.27
2. Michelle Brown, University of Kentucky   23.32
3. Chryste Gaines, Nike Track Club   23.40

400 meters
1. Jearl Miles-Clark, Reebok Racing Club   51.31
2. Natasha Kaiser-Brown, unattached   52.07
3. Anita Howard, Reebok Racing Club   52.61

800 meters
1. Joetta Clark, Foot Locker Athletic Club   2:00.86
2. Amy Wickus, Nike Track Club   2:02.56
3. Alisa Hill, New Balance Track Club   2:03.01

1500 meters
1. Mary Slaney, Nike Track Club   4:03.88
2. Suzy Hamilton, Nike Track Club   4:08.83
3. Sarah Thorsett, PowerAde Track Club   4:13.97

3000 meters
1. Amy Rudolph, Reebok Racing Club   9:01.27
2. Cheri Goddard, Reebok Enclave   9:01.54
3. Tracy Dahl, Asics International Track Club   9:11.55

60 meter hurdles
1. Cheryl Dickey, Nike Track Club   7.91
2. Melissa Morrison, Reebok Racing Club   7.93
3. Dawn Bowles, unattached   8.01

4 × 400 meter relay
1. University of Nebraska   3:36.98
   (LaTisha Croom, Jill Myatt, Stella Klassen, Charmane
      Burton)
2. Baylor University   3:37.39
3. Rice University   3:37.86

Distance medley relay
1. University of North Carolina   11:18.35
   (Karen Godlock, Monique Hennagan, Erin Hayes,
      Blake Phillips)
2. Cornell University   11:21.02
3. Princeton University   11:21.70

Pole vault
1. Stacy Dragila, Rocky Mountain Elite   13' 1½"
2. Melissa Price, Fresno State University   12' 9½"
3. Tiffany Smith, No Limit Sports   12' 9½"

Pentathlon (held at Manhattan, Kansas — one entry)
1. Jill Montgomery, unattached   3962

3000 meter walk
1. Debbi Lawrence, Natural Sport Walking Club   13:14.24
2. Kristen Mullaney, Park Racewalkers   13:18.69
3. Victoria Herazo, Walking Club of Georgia   13:25.37

20 lb. weight throw
1. Dawn Ellerbe, University of South Carolina   70'   ¼" MR
2. Renetta Seiler, Kansas State University   63' 11½"
3. Molly Duggan, Oregon International Track Club   61' 5½"

High jump
1. Angela Bradburn-Spangler, PowerAde Track Club   6' 3½"
2. Karol Jenkins, unattached   6' 2¼"
3. Gwen Wentland, Nike Track Club   5' 11½"

Triple jump
1. Cynthea Rhodes, Reebok Racing Club   45' 5"
2. Niambi Dennis, unattached   44' ¾"
3. Monica Cabbler, unattached   43' 7¾"

Shot put
1. Valeyta Althouse, Bruin Track Club   61' 10½"
2. Connie Price-Smith, unattached   61' 5"
3. Eileen Vanisi, Reebok Racing Club   56' 8¾"

Long jump
1. Dawn Burrell, unattached   21' 4¾"
2. Shana Williams, Team adidas   21' 3¼"
3. Marieke Veltman, Reebok Racing Club   21' ¾"

6th IAAF World Outdoor Track and Field Championships: Olympic Stadium, Athens, Greece, August 2–10

100 meters

After one false start, *Track & Field News* reported, "The next getaway was clean, with Jones quickly establishing a half-step lead over Pintusevich and Ottey. But while Jones and Pintusevich reached peak speed between 50 and 60m, Ottey was understandably spent (she ran about 50m before coming to a stop after the false start recall), and began to be picked up by the others.

"Pintusevich, meanwhile, hadn't yielded an inch to Jones since the first 10m of the race, and as they reached the last 10, Jones suddenly exhibited a shocking loss of form, her smooth style turning raggedy. Two lanes outside her, the Ukrainian forced herself across the line, sure that she had won. But it was not to be."

1. Marion Jones	10.83
5. Inger Miller	11.18
8. Chryste Gaines	11.32

200 meters
"American hope Inger Miller was lifeless in the stretch, finishing 5th in 22.52. 'My legs just felt heavy,' she said. 'I felt flat; I just didn't have it,'" reported *Track & Field News*.

| 5. Inger Miller | 22.52 |

400 meters
"...Miles-Clark stayed virtually even with Richards through the curve," stated *Track & Field News*. "Running in her fourth WC final, the American gained maybe a nose on Richards in the early homestretch, but then lost ground to the Jamaican's long steps in the last 25m."

| 3. Jearl Miles-Clark | 49.90 |

800 meters
"Running in her fifth Worlds, American vet Joetta Clark made her first final, running 2:02.05 for 7th."

| 7. Joetta Clark | 2:02.05 |

1500 meters
According to *Track & Field News*: "Lining up for the final, Jacobs appeared to be a slight favorite over Sonia O'Sullivan (the '93 silver medalist) and Carla Sacramento (the '95 bronze medalist)." While "...little happened through three laps..., Jacobs finally broke free and sprinted to the lead entering the final turn before Sacramento — near the lead the whole race but having avoided the fray — moved to the front entering the home straight and powered to a 4:04.24 victory. Jacobs held 2nd, just fending off the physical Weyermann...."

The *New York Times* added, "The United States had an inviting chance to collect a second gold medal, but a shoving incident in the final 250 meters of the women's 1,500 meters led to a three-runner pileup on the backstretch and interfered with Regina Jacobs's strong final kick. The chaos cost her the race, said Jacobs, who won the silver medal...."

| 2. Regina Jacobs | 4:04.63 |

5000 meters
Hickman's seventh place was a PR for her. She told the *New York Times* of her first ever major final, "It felt really good those last couple of laps."

| 7. Libbie Hickman | 15:11.15 |

10,000 meters
"Annette Peters, the only American to make the final, finished 13th in 32:43.38, obviously troubled by the heat," reported *Track & Field News*. "'I felt great that first 5K, then they just pulled away.'"

| 13. Annette Peters | 32:43.38 |

10 kilometer walk
No American women were in the final.

Marathon
The United States Team placed ninth with the women below making up the team.

25.	Cheryl Collins	2:43:42
36.	Julia Kirtland	2:49:43
40.	Jeanne Peterson	2:51:59

100 meter hurdles

No American women were in the final.

400 meter hurdles

Jon Hendershott wrote in *Track & Field News*: "...Hemmings tore off the line, making up the stagger on Batten by hurdle 3. Tatyana Tereshchuk and Buford-Bailey also ran strong early. By barrier 7, Hemmings and Batten were even, with Bidouane 4th behind the fading Buford-Bailey." Batten slipped back in the final straight and Hemmings led Bidouane over the final obstacle. But then Bidouane stretched out her stride, edging ahead only in the final couple of meters to beat Hemmings (53.09) by a stride. Batten (53.52) held on for 3rd....

"Batten, clearly upset by the outcome, said, 'This is a big disappointment. I pushed it hard early, but never got my stride pattern. Yet I felt both Deon and I would be well into the 52s in the final. I admit I'm surprised at Bidouane winning.'"

| 3. | Kim Batten | 53.52 |
| 6. | Tonja Buford-Bailey | 54.77 |

4 × 100 meter relay

"Three-quarters of the U.S.'s Olympic champion 4 × 100 squad combined with one newcomer to defend the world title," Jon Hendershott continued.

Despite safe passes, this win was fast: an American Record 41:47 that trails only East Germany's venerable world record of 41:37 on the all-time list.

The new face joining Chryste Gaines, Inger Miller and Gail Devers in the quartet was Marion Jones. The 100 champion stormed the backstretch in the final to lock up the title and claim the distinction of being the only woman to win a pair of golds in Athens.

...Gaines — the lone holdover from the '95 winners — kept the U.S. even with everyone else. A conservative exchange sent Jones away on her churning backstretch carry, which put the U.S. ahead for good. Jones, who had spent the early part of the evening in the long jump pit, said, "It's been a long time since I was on a relay. When you get the opportunity to run with a talented group like this, it's really nice."

Another safe pass sent Miller around the turn with about a meter's edge over Jamaica and France.

Miller and Devers made the final trade with a clear lead and the two-time Olympic century winner added another meter to the margin.

| 1. | USA | 41.47 | AR, MR |

(Chryste Gaines, Marion Jones, Inger Miller, Gail Devers)

4 × 400 meter relay

Bob Hersh reported for *Track & Field News*:

...Maicel Malone ran a strong 51.2 for the U.S. to lead Russia's Tatyana Chebykina (also 51.2) by about a foot at the handoff.... "I knew I needed to get out and be aggressive," said Malone, a gold medal winner in '93 and '96. "That's all I thought about." Olga Kotlyarova (49.8) overtook Kim Graham (50.2) coming out of the lane break and was never headed.

The American Graham said, "I just got out, tried to do the best I could and make sure I was in position for the next leg."

...Kim Batten ran a 50.51 to close the gap a bit, but was herself overtaken and all but passed by hurdle rival Deon Hemmings, whose 49.58 put Jamaica right in the thick of things. Batten said, "It was my first time to run on a big-time national relay team. I underestimated it a little; it was more painful than I thought it would be. I've got to really think if I'm going to do this again."

Sandie Richards took the baton for Jamaica and immediately passed Jearl Miles-Clark and settled in behind Tatyana Alekseyeva. Coming off the final turn, Miles-Clark swung wide, took dead aim on Jamaica and Russia and passed them both.

But on the inside, Breuer made her move at the same time. Alekseyeva, running on the outside of lane 1, left just enough room for Breuer to sneak through. "...I felt Breuer on the turn. I thought she would have to swing wide outside of me," said Miles-Clark. "I didn't think the Russian would let her through on the inside. But there was an opening and she snuck through. I felt her about 10m out. I dug deep but I couldn't come up with it. I tried my hardest, but we came out with the silver. We'll have to settle for that right now, but there's always next year."

2. USA   3:21.03
(Maicel Malone-Wallace, Kim Graham, Kim Batten, Jearl Miles-Clark)

High jump
No American women were in the final.

Long jump
"...The qualifying round was almost a disaster for the U.S., and the final wasn't much better," reported Ed Gordon for *Track & Field News*. "Two-time winner Jackie Joyner-Kersee and USATF champ Marion Jones barely made the cut as the last two, while Sharon Couch was eliminated.... Jones departed for relay preparation time after a meager 21' 9", a full foot behind her Indy effort (but still the best 10th place ever).

...Fourteen years after her first championship, Heike Drechsler was still able to post a last-attempt 22' 7¼" to take 4th and push arch-rival JJK to 5th."

The *New York Times* reported, "The end of an era came in the women's long jump as Joyner-Kersee completed her final world championship with a fifth-place finish. Joyner-Kersee achieved her best jump tonight on her first attempt...."

5. Jackie Joyner-Kersee	22' 3"
10. Marion Jones	21' 9"

Triple jump
11. Cynthea Rhodes	45' 3"

Shot put
Garry Hill reported, "...For the only time in Olympic/WC history, other than the boycott-weakened '84 Games, the U.S. had three in the final...."

5. Connie Price-Smith	62' 4"
11. Valeyta Althouse	55' 6¼"
12. Tressa Thompson	54' 1"

Discus
No American women were in the final.

Javelin
No American women were in the final.

Heptathlon
"...DeDee Nathan came within 29 points of her PR to finish as the top American, 7th at 6298. 'It's been tough, a long two days,' she said. 'Sunday was 14 hours; today was 13½ hours. I'm really excited that it's done,'" reported Garry Hill.

7. DeDee Nathan	6298
10. Kelly Blair	6253

6th IAAF World Indoor Track and Field Championships: Paris, France, March 7–9

60 meters	
1. Gail Devers	7.06
400 meters	
1. Jearl Miles-Clark	50.96
800 meters	
3. Joetta Clark	1:59.82
1500 meters	
2. Mary Slaney	4:05.22
10. Suzy Hamilton	4:10.82
3000 meters	
12. Cheri Goddard	9:04.05
60 meter hurdles	
3. Cheryl Dickey	7.84
5. Melissa Morrison	7.88
4 × 400 meter relay	
2. USA	3:27.66 AR

(Shanelle Porter, Natasha Kaiser-Brown, Anita Howard, Jearl Miles-Clark)

Pole vault	
1. Stacy Dragila	14' 5¼" equals WR
Long jump	
12. Shana Williams	20' 9¾"
Shot put	
6. Connie Price-Smith	60' 3¾"
Pentathlon	
3. Kym Carter	4627
7. DeDee Nathan	4513

U.S. Marathon Championships: Columbia, South Carolina, February 8

The *New York Times* reported: "Julia Kirtland put her local knowledge to good use in the United States women's marathon championship today, breaking away over the final 10 miles to win by nearly one and a half minutes." It was a personal best for her.

1. Julia Kirtland	2:37:46

IAAF World Cross Country Championships: Turin, Italy, March 23

26. Amy Rudolph	22:00
29. Deena Drosin	22:02
35. Elva Dryer	22:09

38. Gwyn Coogan	22:10
44. Kristin Beaney	22:12
50. Nnenna Lynch	22:19

The American women finished in sixth place.

Overall Grand Prix Standings

3. Kim Batten	91
13. Marion Jones	63
15. Amy Acuff	61

Other News and Honors

Deena Drossin won the national cross country championships.

Track & Field News: Athlete of the Year (USA and World)

Marion Jones

American and World Rankings — Track & Field News

100 meters
Marion Jones (1st in world)
Gail Devers (3rd in world)
Inger Miller (7th in world)

200 meters
Marion Jones (1st in world)
Inger Miller (3rd in world)
Cheryl Taplin

400 meters
Jearl Miles-Clark (3rd in world)
Maicel Malone
Michele Collins

800 meters
Jearl Miles-Clark (6th in world)
Joetta Clark (8th in world)
Kathi Rounds

1500 meters
1. Regina Jacobs (2nd in world)
2. Suzy Hamilton (5th in world)
3. Mary Slaney

3000 meters
Regina Jacobs
Amy Rudolph
Laren Hecox-Candaele

5000 meters
Regina Jacobs (10th in world)
Libbie Hickman
Amy Rudolph

100 meter hurdles
Melissa Morrison (4th in world)
Cheryl Dickey (5th in world)
Dawn Bowles

400 meter hurdles
Kim Batten (2nd in world)
Tonja Buford-Bailey (6th in world)
Ryan Tolbert

10 kilometer walk
Debbi Lawrence
Victoria Herazo
Sara Standley

High jump
Amy Acuff (5th in world)
Angela Bradburn-Spangler
Erin Aldrich

Pole vault
Stacy Dragila (2nd in world)
Melissa Price
Melissa Mueller

Long jump
Jackie Joyner-Kersee (7th in world)
Marion Jones
Sharon Couch

Triple jump
Cynthea Rhodes
Niambi Dennis
Shonda Swift

Shot put
Connie Price-Smith (6th in world)
Valeyta Althouse
Tressa Thompson

Discus
Suzy Powell

Seilala Sua
Lacy Barnes-Mileham

Hammer
Dawn Ellerbe
Renetta Seiler
Windy Dean

Javelin
Erica Wheeler
Lynda Lipson
Nicole Carroll

Heptathlon
Kelly Blair (9th in world)
DeDee Nathan
Kym Carter

On January 11, at Pocatello's Kibbie Dome, Stacy Dragila became the first American woman to clear 14 feet in the pole vault.

Jackie Joyner-Kersee was named the first recipient of the "Humanitarian Athlete of the Year" award on December 5. The award was created to recognize contributions outside the field of competition.

Joetta Clark, 34, ran in the Millrose Games 800 meters for the nineteenth year. She has won the 800 meters six times from 1985 to 1996.

Mary Slaney, 35, won the Millrose women's mile in 4:26.67. She won her first race in the Millrose Games 23 years ago. She now has six Millrose titles.

Evelyn Ashford was inducted into the National Track and Field Hall of Fame on December 4. The biography below is from the National Track and Field Hall of Fame website.

EVELYN ASHFORD

Inducted: 1997, athlete
Born: April 15, 1957 — Shreveport, Louisiana

Events
100 m — 10.76
200 m — 21.83

One of the greatest women's sprinters in track and field history, Evelyn Ashford ranked first in the world four times and was the top-ranked American seven times, including four in a row from 1981 to 1984. A competitor at the 1976 Olympic Games while attending UCLA, she also competed in the 1984, 1988 and 1992 Games, winning four gold medals and a silver. She set an Olympic record when she ran 10.97 to win the 100m at the 1984 Games. She was a two-time world record holder in the 100 meters, running 10.79 at Colorado Springs in 1983 and surpassing that record when she ran 10.76 in Zurich in 1984. Among her greatest achievements was her double victory at the 1979 World Cup when she defeated East Germany's dominant sprinters, beating Marlies Gohr in the 100m and world-record holder Marita Koch in the 200m. She repeated her double sprint victories in the 1981 World Cup. Overall, she was on 15 national teams during the period from 1976 to 1992, a very long career for a sprinter. She won 19 national titles, including six indoors.

Records Held
World Record: 100 m — 10.79
World Record: 100 m — 10.76 (August 22, 1984)
Olympic Record: 100 m — 10.97

Championships
1976 Olympics: 100 m (5th)
1984 Olympics: 100 m —10.97 (1st)
1984 Olympics: 400 m relay (1st)
1988 Olympics: 100 m (2nd)
1988 Olympics: 400 m relay (1st)
1992 Olympics: 400 m relay (1st)
1979 World Cup: 100 m (1st)
1979 World Cup: 200 m (1st)
1981 World Cup: 100 m (1st)
1981 World Cup: 200 m (1st)

Education
high school: Roseville (Roseville, California), 1975
undergraduate: UCLA (Los Angeles, California), 1978

Occupations
Business

INTERVIEW: JEARL MILES CLARK

(November 29, 2001) Well, how did I get started in track? I was pretty fast as a kid. I was born in Gainesville, Florida and for thirteen years I lived in a rural area called Archer, Florida, which was about seven miles out of Gainesville, Florida. I used to run up and down the dirt roads [laughter]. I was a little tomboy. I was swinging in trees beating all the boys in elementary school in football. So, I had pretty good speed then.

As I went through high school, my sister ran track. I saw my sister running track. And, me being the normal little kid, I wanted to do what my sister did. That's how I really got started in track. I got started because my sister ran and it just went from there.

In junior high school I ran one year. Then in ninth grade year we moved to Gainesville. My mother and father separated and in my tenth grade year I moved to another high school, same city, Gainesville. That's when I started, in tenth grade. I didn't run in ninth grade.

I started out as a sprinter, long jumper actually [laughter]. Of course, all I wanted to do was jump and sprint and jump and sprint. I actually tried hurdles once but my mom didn't like it and I didn't like it. I was always afraid of falling. So, that didn't materialize. It came to jumping and the short sprints. I was a sprinter until the latter part of my high school years.

I started running the 400 because somebody was missing from the team [laughter]. There was this huge trophy at the Bob Hayes Invitational in Jacksonville, Florida, right. So, I'm going to get that trophy this year, I told the head coach. I want to run the 100, 200, 400, okay, and then do the long jump. I figured if I won these four events I would win this trophy. She put me in the 400, the sprint medley relay and the long jump and maybe another relay. I didn't get those individual events. It's a good thing I wasn't in them, because the girl that won ran really fast. She broke the record in the 100 and 200 and she was on the winning 4 × 100

Jearl Miles Clark, 2001.

relay team. She got the trophy. I got the 400 [laughter]. This guy was at the high jump pit and yelled, "Run, Jearl." Basically I was just jogging the first 200 and I just ran the second 200 and I ended up winning and breaking the meet record. I broke the meet record in the long jump at the same time. Needless to say, I didn't, again, win that huge trophy.

I ran the 400 at the district meet. I won the district meet. I ran the 400 at the regional meet and won and then I won the state meet. That was my senior year. It was the first year I ran it. I would guess you'd say I was a late bloomer in the event. At the Bob Hayes relays, I ran my first 400. There was a guy from Alabama A&M University. He saw me run, he's like, "okay, I see this is untapped talent." He really started recruiting me. He was basically the only one that recruited me until after our state meet. By that time, my mom and I had really decided that I was going to Alabama A&M. I went to Alabama A&M.

In high school I preferred the long jump—less pain [laughter], unless you fell in the pit. I ended up doing that in college. I was doing my run-throughs and I missed and tripped and fell face first in the sand. It was at East Tennessee State, I think it was where the crowd is up top—so, you're down here—you're right next to them—you go down in the dirt and everyone sees you and starts laughing. That wasn't a fun day, but it was less strenuous than the 400 and I was really decent at it. I jumped 21 feet my junior year, that summer, and then 21 feet 2 inches in college, and 21 feet in the Penn relays my senior year. I jumped all through college and I stopped after-wards because I didn't have a coach for it and I just started running the 400.

In college, I was doing the 200 and 400—whenever Coach Henderson could find me for it [laughter]. It's funny because I went in thinking he was recruiting me for the long jump. I mean, I had this mentality: "I'm a long jumper and that's it. I will run a 4 × 400 one of these days." He finally persuaded me to do it. I fought him tooth and nail but he won me over. He tricked me too. I'm also SIAC, that's Southern Intercollegiate Athletic Conference, cross country champion. I am. Two years, I am. What he did was he said we've got to take the quarter milers and rotate them. One quarter miler will go one week and we'll rotate the next one. I was the first one to go. I was like the second person on the team. So, needless to say I ran for the rest of the year—cross country. But, I think, that really did help me. It gave me a lot of strength and endurance for the 400 that I would be running eventually—and the 8 [laughter]. But, at the time, I couldn't see it. Sometimes you just have to do what a coach tells you to even if you can't see it.

In college, my best time in college for the quarter was in my senior year—51.5, I think, at our Division 2 outdoor championships. I was in lane 8. I was just running [laughter]. I just stayed in first the whole way. That was in 1988. That was the Olympic year. I went from there to the Division 1 outdoor championship and I got third. Then we went to the U.S. championships, which were in Tampa. They were separate then from the Olympic trials. That was my second nationals.

Then we went to the Olympic trials. It's funny because I wasn't going to the Olympic trials and Coach Henderson said, "Do it, just go." I was just tired. I had no realization that there was any-thing beyond college track—okay—I had a sense that there was something after college; I just really couldn't grasp it. But, I went there, I ran, and you know, after I made the team, the top eight went, I didn't realize that once I came across that finish line in the semifinals, and I had made the finals, that I was going to the Olympic games. I ran and they took everyone from the finals. I signed up and I tried the uniforms on but they were always saying we're alternates. Behind my name was alternate and I didn't know I was going. I went through the training camp because they had javelin throwers. The javelin throwers were alternates, and I was there as an alternate. The javelin throwers weren't going. And then I asked Pearlie. I was like, "Well, my mom needs to know. She's like, am I going?" Because Seagram's, at the time, was sponsoring one parent or whomever you wanted to go over—they were paying and my mom needed to know to get off. "Pearlie, am I going?" "Yes, you're going." "Oh, okay, I didn't know that." "You didn't know that?" "No, I didn't know." If it wasn't for Coach Henderson, I wouldn't have been there. I would have been home [laughter]. But I learned a lot that year. I saw different athletes and I saw that you could actually make a living in the sport. From 1988 on I had a different outlook.

At the Olympic games, I was just there. I was just seeing things, seeing people. I was just absorbing everything. Wow, this is the Olympic Games. I was told that there was a good chance that I wouldn't be able to run but in the back of my mind I was like, I'm here, just let me have the experience. I needed that experience. I'm glad that I had that experience even though I didn't get to run. Even though people when they call my name and say three time Olympian—no, it's four, it's four. It was a great experience and I got to see some of the best athletes in the world. I got to travel out of the States and my mom got a chance to go with me too. She's gone to every Olympic Games. That was her first time in an airplane. Before that, she's like, "I'm not getting on an airplane." She had the opportunity and she went. It was a great experience for her as well as me. It was pretty cool. I came back to another year of school. My eligibility was done but I had to finish. So, I stayed in school. I'm trying to remember, we had just gotten a new track and I trained there — I just did whatever, I guess.

After I left there I went to Jacksonville. The guy that actually did some of the recruiting for me was in Jacksonville. That's how he saw me, at the Bob Hayes Relays Invitational. He was coaching Dannette Young at the time. I worked with him for a year.

In between all that, I met J.J. [J.J. Clark, now Jearl's coach and husband] rooming with Joetta. Joetta was supposed to have a single room at the Mobil meet in Fairfax. So she thought she was going to have a single room. She had her brother J.J. come up with her and her cousin Tony. They were going to spend the night with her in her hotel room. But, I got placed with her. She says she doesn't remember. She looks at me, she's like, "I know you don't like me but you're going to have to be my roommate anyway." I was like, "You know me, okay — whatever. I'll do whatever you say." She said, "My brother and cousin are here and they're going to stay, okay [laughter]. Like, every time people ask, how did you and J.J. meet, it's a little joke; he spent the night in my hotel room [laughter].

I did that for a year. Things didn't turn out the way we wanted with Caleb [Caleb White, Jearl's previous coach]. Some things didn't work out. Basically, J.J. had coached before at the high school level and he said, "Well, you know, you can't do any worse." I was still average, even though I was in the top ten in the United States. We thought that I could do better. So, I moved from Jacksonville back to Gainesville. I stayed with mom. He started training me and then that first outdoor season I PRed big time. I dropped down from 51.28 that I did in the Olympic trials to 51.01, or something like that. That was 1991. It was the first meet outdoors in Gainesville, the U.S. vs. the world. Lillie Leatherwood won and I was second. That year, we battled, Lillie and me. Then, at our national championships at Randall's Island, I ran 50.19, I think it was. That was like, "Oh my gosh." Then we went to the world championships in Tokyo and I ended up making finals. I was fifth. I was so happy. We were second in the relay.

My PR is 49.40 in 1997 in the U.S. championships in Indy. I was trying so hard in the 200 because my PR is 23.0. And, I'm like, I'm going to get 22 seconds. I was right there. I was in great shape to run it and I got into the blocks — false start — it wasn't me, and then the wind changed and I'm like, 23.0, give me the wind.

49.40 is pretty memorable for me. Actually in '93 when I first dropped under 50, 49.82, that was exciting — and the 1:56, the first was in Zurich in '97 — it wasn't an American record. Then I went to Brussels and I went 1:56.78 and I got it.

The future holds great things, I hope. I had two down years — last year and 2000, even though I won a relay gold medal. That topped it off. That made it all better. I think I'm in a position to be in the best shape of my life these next few years. With everything, I worked on my body. I can be physically fit and if I'm physically fit, I run fast. I think I'm better prepared mentally and I'm going to be better prepared physically for these upcoming years.

I'm looking for great things — American records indoors — American records outdoors. I'll go as fast as I can. I'm not going to put a time limit on it. I don't want a feeling there — she's going to break — I'm just going to run. If it happens, great. If it doesn't, I'm just going to give it my best shot. I get tired of people asking me when I'm going to retire. If my body still says, hey, go ahead — don't just tell me because I'm thirty-five, it's time to retire — just don't tell me that. I definitely know that I can run faster in the 800. I feel that I can run faster in the 400. I think the two complement each other. It's just a matter of working hard and going out there and getting it done. With the great coaching that I have in J.J., his coaching experience and my running experience, I think it can be done, and I'm going to have Hazel [Clark] there to push me too [laughter] in the 800. She's a fierce competitor. Sometimes it's like, I'm not working out with this crazy girl [laughter]. She will run you into the ground. That's a good competitive spirit that you need to have in track and field, especially when you go to the European meets and run against those girls. In the U.S. in the 800, the most aggressive person is Regina Jacobs. That's because she knows what it takes when you go over to Europe. She can get away with it here. When you push an

American 800 meter runner, they go, what's that? Hazel's first trip over to Europe, Zurich —
Mutola was on the inside, someone was in front of Mutola, someone was behind Mutola and
guess who's right outside within reach — Hazel! Mutola just goes bam and Hazel goes flying outside to lane four; she said, "She hit me." She's rougher than most people but you got to get used
to it. We went at it in '99 in Seville. I was happy with myself because she had done some things
to me prior to that. She's the chunkiest — she'll get to the 200 meters to go — she'll cut you off
and she'll expect you to back off. I got tired of backing off. I wasn't going to back off and we had
some little elbows going. I ended up getting fourth, she ended up second. She didn't win because
she was back fighting with me. Had she just run her race and stopped trying to fight with me,
perhaps we both would have medaled. But I felt happy with that race. I ran it the way I wanted
to run it. I didn't want anybody to think they could take advantage of me. The next time that we
get in a race, she's going to know — stay away from her [laughter]. Maybe, maybe not.

   [Sigh] I've accomplished a lot of things that I wanted to but there are a lot more things that
can be done.

18

1998

The Outdoor Nationals

The USA Outdoor Track and Field Championships were held in Tad Gormley Stadium, New Orleans, Louisiana, from June 19 through June 21.

---

100 meters

"Jones did her part, starting with a victory in the women's 100-meter final by 6 feet over Chryste Gaines. Jones's time of 10.72 seconds was the seventh fastest in history," reported the *New York Times.*

1. Marion Jones, Nike Track Club	10.72
2. Chryste Gaines, adidas USA	10.89
3. Inger Miller, Nike Track Club	11.12
4. Torri Edwards, University of Southern California	11.20
5. Cheryl Taplin, Vector Sports	11.25
6. Tameka Roberts, Nike Track Club	11.34
7. Kwajalein Butler, Louisiana State University	11.36
8. Aspen Burkett, University of Illinois	11.38

200 meters

Jones, 22, already won the 100 and long jump. "In the 200, she downshifted in the last 15 meters and still won by 6 meters in 22.24 seconds into a slight wind," reported the *New York Times.*

1. Marion Jones, Nike Track Club	22.24
2. Zundra Feagin-Alexander, Asics International Track Club	23.04
3. Cheryl Taplin, Vector Sports	23.07
and Carlette Guidry, adidas USA	
5. Celena Mondie-Milner, adidas USA	23.09
6. Tameka Roberts, Nike Track Club	23.40
7. Kwajalein Butler, Louisiana State University	23.60

400 meters

1. Kim Graham, Asics International Track Club	50.69
2. Rochelle Stevens, Rochelle Stevens Track Club	51.07

3. Monique Hennagan, University of North Carolina   51.11
4. Toya Brown, University of Texas   51.13
5. Shanelle Porter, U.S. West   51.17
6. Michele Collins, unattached   51.19
7. Natasha Kaiser-Brown, Health South   51.53
8. Maicel Malone-Wallace, Asics International Track Club   51.91

800 meters
1. Jearl Miles-Clark, Reebok Racing Club   1:58.78
2. Joetta Clark, Nike Track Club   1:59.01
3. Meredith Valmon, Reebok Enclave   1:59.29
4. Hazel Clark, University of Florida   2:00.23
5. Kathi Rounds, unattached   2:01.53
6. Michelle DiMuro-Ave, Asics International Track Club   2:02.09
7. Jenni Westphal, University of Wisconsin   2:02.57
8. Julian Reynolds, Georgetown University   2:05.73

1500 meters
1. Suzy Hamilton, Nike Track Club   4:05.28
2. Amy Wickus, Nike Track Club   4:07.95
3. Alisa Harvey, New Balance Track Club   4:08.33
4. Elva Dryer, Nike Track Club   4:10.02
5. Debbie Marshall, New Balance Track Club   4:10.32
6. Shayne Culpepper, adidas USA   4:10.77
7. Fran ten Bensel, New Balance Track Club   4:12.58
8. Sarah Thorsett, Nike Track Club   4:16.39

5000 meters
1. Regina Jacobs, Mizuno Track Club   15:32.31
2. Libbie Hickman, Nike Track Club   15:39.40
3. Amy Rudolph, Reebok Racing Club   15:41.31
4. Nnenna Lynch, Fila Track Club   15:41.56
5. Cheri Kenah, Reebok Enclave   15:42.62
6. Clare Taylor, Asics International Track Club   16:00.45
7. Tania Fischer, Santa Monica Track Club   16:02.73
8. Kristin Ihle, Nike Track Club   16:06.49

3000 meter steeplechase
1. Courtney Meldrum, Brigham Young University   10:21.00
2. Elizabeth Jackson, Brigham Young University   10:21.20
3. Lesley Lehane, Boston Athletic Association   10:25.90
4. Tara Haynes, Brigham Young University   10:27.79
5. Holly Hansen, Utah State University   10:39.79
6. Katie Meyer, University of Missouri   10:49.21
7. Misty Allison-Cohn, unattached   10:49.67
8. Kara Ormond, Brigham Young University   10:51.39

10,000 meters

Lynn Jennings won this race for the seventh time in twelve years.

1. Lynn Jennings, Nike International Track Club   34:09.86
2. Jen Rhines, adidas USA   34:10.31
3. Shelly Steely, Asics International Track Club   34:11.75

4. Kristin Beaney, Asics International
   Track Club   34:20.60
5. Jenny Crain, adidas USA   34:33.59
6. Marty Shue, Reebok Enclave   34:39.08
7. Laura LaMena-Coll, Moving Comfort
   Racing Team   34:52.17
8. Laura Mason-Byrne, adidas USA   35:03.14

100 meter hurdles
1. Cheryl Dickey, Nike Track Club   12.82
2. Angie Vaughn, University of Texas   12.88
3. Miesha McKelvy, San Diego State
   University   12.97
4. Melissa Morrison, Reebok Racing Club   12.98
5. Elisha Brewer, University of Arkansas   13.09
6. Tonya Lawson, unattached   13.11
7. Anjanette Kirkland, Nike Track Club   13.13
8. Trecia Roberts, Joe Gentry Track Troupe   13.33

Chryste Gaines.

400 meter hurdles
   This was Kim Batten's fifth consecutive win in the 400 meter hurdles.

1. Kim Batten, Reebok Racing Club   53.61
2. Michelle Johnson, Tucson Elite Athletic Club   54.80
3. Sandra Glover, unattached   55.11
4. LaTanya Sheffield, Sheffield Elite   55.77
5. Trevaia Davis, Nike Track Club   55.81
6. Tonya Williams, Asics International Track Club   57.51
7. Rosa Jolivet, Texas A&M University   58.74

10 kilometer walk (road)
1. Joanne Dow, adidas USA   47:06.5
2. Michelle Rohl, Moving Comfort Racing Team   47:32.7
3. Debbi Lawrence, unattached   48:34.4
4. Victoria Herazo, California Walkers   50:04.5
5. Susan Armenta, unattached   50:21.2
6. Cheryl Rellinger, Potomac Valley Striders Track Club   52:19.6
7. Gretchen Eastler-Fishman, unattached   52:44.1
8. Jill Zenner, Miami Valley Track Club   52:57.5

High jump
1. Tisha Waller, Nat's Athlete   6' 4¼"
2. Amy Acuff, unattached   6' 4¼"
3. Erin Aldrich, University of Texas   6' 2¾"
4. Karol Jenkins, unattached   6' 2¾"
5. Lisa Coleman, Beach Track Club   6' ¾"
6. Clare Look-Jaeger, Beach Track Club and   6' ¾"
   Angela Spangler, Asics International Track Club
8. Stacy Ann Grant, University of Illinois   6' ¾"

Pole vault
1. Kellie Suttle, Bell Athletics   14'
2. Stacy Dragila, Reebok Racing Club   13' 5¼"

3. Kim Becker, Bell Athletics   13' 5¼"
4. Melissa Price, Fresno State University   13' 5¼"
5. Melissa Mueller, Sky Athletics   13' 1½"
6. Tiffany Smith, No Limit Sports   12' 7½"
7. Alicia Warlick, Stanford University   12' 7½"
8. Kristin Quackenbush, University of West Virginia   12' 1½"
   and Mary Sauer, unattached

Long jump
Marion Jones won this event taking only two of her allotted six jumps.

1. Marion Jones, Nike International Track Club   23' 8" w
2. Shana Williams, adidas USA   22' 7¾" w
3. Dawn Burrell, U.S. Army   22' 7¾"
4. Yuan Hunt, Texas Southern University   21' 8" w
5. Sharon Couch-Jewell, Goldwin Track Club   21' 6¾" w
6. Angela Brown, George Mason University   21' 4¼"
7. Marieke Veltman, Reebok Racing Club   21' 2" w
8. Vonetta Jeffery, unattached   21' 1¼"

Triple jump
1. Sheila Hudson, unattached   45' ¼"
2. Cynthea Rhodes, Reebok Racing Club   44' 9¾"
3. Tiombé Hurd, unattached   44' 9½"
4. Stacey Bowers, Baylor University   44' 8"
5. Shonda Swift, unattached   44' 2"
6. Amanda Banks, unattached   43' 8½"
7. Nicole Gamble, University of North Carolina   43' 7¼"
8. Lisa Austin, unattached   43' 2½"

Shot put
Connie Price-Smith's victory was her seventh consecutive win in the event.

1. Connie Price-Smith, adidas USA   61' 3"
2. Teri Tunks, Southern Methodist University   59' 8½"
3. Tressa Thompson, unattached   57' 3¾"
4. Dawn Dumble, Reebok Bruin Track Club   57' ¼"
5. Crystal Brownlee, University of South Carolina   54' 10¾"
6. Dawn Ellerbe, New York Athletic Club   53' 2¾"
7. Seilala Sua, University of California, Los Angeles   53' ¼"
8. Christina Tolson, California State University, Northridge   52' 6"

Discus
1. Seilala Sua, University of California, Los Angeles   204' 2"
2. Kristin Kuehl, unattached   201'
3. Aretha Hill, University of Washington   198' 5"
4. Edie Boyer, unattached   196' 9"
5. Lacy Barnes-Mileham, Friends United   188' 9"
6. Dawn Dumble, Reebok Bruin Track Club   180' 7"
7. Erica Ahmann, Disney Sport   179' 3"
8. April Malveo, Louisiana Tech University   179' 2"

Hammer
1. Windy Dean, Southern Methodist University   210' 4"   MR
2. Amy Palmer, Brigham Young University   209'
3. Dawn Ellerbe, New York Athletic Club   208' 2"
4. Anna Norgren, Boston Athletic Association   202' 5"
5. Renetta Seiler, Kansas State University   199' 9"
6. Katie Panek, Wichita State University   198' 2"
7. Christina Tolson, California State University, Northridge   196' 1"
8. Staci Darden, Fresno State University   191' 5"

Javelin
1. Nicole Carroll, Asics International Track Club   185' 7"
2. Windy Dean, Southern Methodist University   184' 5"
3. Lynda Lipson-Blutreich, Klub Keihas   183' 10"
4. Ann Crouse, University of Virginia   178' 6"
5. Erica Wheeler, unattached   176' 1"
6. Kim Kreiner, Kent State University   172' 5"
7. Suzy Powell, Reebok Bruin Track Club   172' 5"
8. Jamie Strieter, Western Michigan University   164' 9"

Heptathlon
1. Kelly Blair-LaBounty, Reebok Racing Club   6402
2. Sheila Burrell, unattached   6294 w
3. Tiffany Lott, Brigham Young University   6123
4. Wendi Raatjes, Advanced Micro Devices   5867 w
5. Trina Bindel, unattached   5862
6. Nicole Haynes, Beach Track Club   5653
7. Tracye Lawyer, Stanford University   5616
8. Erin Narzinski, University of South Carolina   5294

Marion Jones was voted the outstanding female athlete of the meet.

The Indoor Nationals

The USA Indoor Track and Field Championships were held in the Georgia Dome, Atlanta, Georgia, on February 27 and 28.

"Waller Sets Record In High Jump," said the *New York Times* headline of a small article reporting the meet results with a photograph of Tisha Waller clearing the bar.

The article continues: "Tisha Waller, a fifth-grade teacher in Atlanta, broke one of the oldest American records, soaring 6 feet 7 inches, in the women's high jump in the USA Indoor Championships yesterday in Atlanta. Waller's leap came on her third and final attempt, and bettered the mark of 6' 6¾", set by Coleen Sommer in 1982 at Ottawa. Waller's previous indoor best was 6' 6¼", in 1996, when she won the national title."

60 meters
1. Christy Opera-Thompson, unattached   7.08
2. Carlette Guidry, Team adidas   7.15
3. Chryste Gaines, Team adidas   7.15

200 meters
1. Tameka Roberts, University of Texas, San Antonio   23.04

2. Carlette Guidry, Team adidas	23.04
3. Celena Mondie-Milner, unattached	23.33

400 meters
1. Jearl Miles-Clark, Reebok Racing Club	51.11
2. Jessica Hudson, Shore Athletic Club	52.49
3. Natasha Kaiser-Brown, Health South	53.12

800 meters
1. Joetta Clark, Nike Track Club	2:02.40
2. Michelle DiMuro-Ave, Asics International Track Club	2:04.44
3. Genesia Eddins, Boston International Athletic Club	2:06.10

Mile
1. Suzy Hamilton, Nike International Track Club	4:34.16
2. Cheri Goddard-Kenah, Reebok Enclave	4:37.49
3. Fran ten Bensel, New Balance Track Club	4:38.13

3000 meters
1. Elva Dryer, Nike International Track Club	8:58.87
2. Amy Rudolph, Reebok Racing Club	8:59.14
3. Joan Nesbit, New Balance Track Club	8:59.38

3000 meter walk
1. Michelle Rohl, Moving Comfort Racing Team	12:40.38
2. Joanne Dow, unattached	12:56.38
3. Gretchen Eastler-Fishman, unattached	13:20.38

60 meter hurdles
1. Melissa Morrison, Reebok Racing Club	7.87	MR
2. Kimberly Carson, HSI International	7.94	
3. Tonya Lawson, unattached	8.01	

4 × 400 meter relay
1. Clemson University	3:37.29
(Lashonda Cutchin, Samantha Watt, Nikkie Bouyer, Shekera Weston)	
2. George Mason University	3:39.40
3. Florida State University	3:39.58

Distance medley relay
1. Reebok Enclave	11:19.78
2. Central Massachusetts Striders	11:20.03
3. University of Tennessee, Chattanooga	11:55.89

High jump
1. Tisha Waller, unattached	6' 7"	AR
2. Angela Spangler, Asics International Track Club	6' 2¾"	
3. Amy Acuff, unattached	6' 2¾"	

Long jump
1. Dawn Burrell, U.S. Army	22' 8½"
2. Shana Williams, adidas USA	22' 3½"
3. DeDee Nathan, Nike Indiana Track Club	20' 7"

Pole vault
1. Stacy Dragila, Reebok Racing Club   14' 1¼"   MR
2. Tiffany Smith, No Limit Sports   12' 9½"
3. Melissa Mueller, unattached   12' 9½"

Triple jump
1. Niambi Dennis, U.S. Army   44' 5½"
2. Cynthea Rhodes, Reebok Racing Club   44' 2½"
3. Shonda Swift, unattached   44' ¾"

Shot put
1. Connie Price-Smith, adidas USA   60' 3¾"
2. Valeyta Althouse, Reebok Bruin Track Club   60' 3¾"
3. Tressa Thompson, unattached   57' 4¼"

20 pound weight throw
1. Dawn Ellerbe, New York Athletic Club   70' 3½"
2. Beth Burton, unattached   65' 2"
3. Anna Norgren, Boston Athletic Association   64' 2¼"

Tisha Waller was selected the outstanding woman athlete of the meet.

Los Angeles Invitational (8 women's events — more than any previous year): February 7

50 meters
1. Shakedia Jones, University of California, Los Angeles   6.36

500 yards
1. Falilat Ogunkoya, Nigeria   1:05.1

800 meters
1. Gabriela Guevara, Mexico   2:07.7

Mile
1. Becky Spies, New Balance Track Club   4:40.67

50 meter hurdles
1. Miesha McKelvy, San Diego State University   7.11

High jump
1. Lisa Coleman, unattached   6'

Long jump
1. Lisa Domico, San Diego State University   19' 1½"

Shot put
1. Valeyta Althouse, Reebok Bruin Track Club   59' 7½"

IAAF Golden League Grand Prix Final: Moscow, Russia, September 5

100 meters
1. Marion Jones   10.83
3. Inger Miller   11.15
6. Chryste Gaines   11.23

100 meter hurdles
2. Melissa Morrison   12.63
8. Angie Vaughn   13.10

Long jump
1. Marion Jones   23' 4¾"
6. Shana Williams   21' 11¾"
8. Dawn Burrell   21' 5¼"

Marion Jones was the women's overall winner of the Grand Prix.

8th IAAF World Cup: Johannesburg, South Africa, September 11–13

100 meters
1. Marion Jones   10.65   MR

200 meters
1. Marion Jones   21.62   MR

400 meters
6. Kim Graham   52.10

800 meters
4. Jearl Miles-Clark   2:01.58

1500 meters
4. Suzy Hamilton   4:12.52

3000 meters
3. Regina Jacobs   9:11.15

5000 meters
2. Regina Jacobs   16:26.24

100 meter hurdles
2. Angie Vaughn   12.67 w

400 meter hurdles
3. Kim Batten   53.17

High jump
3. Tisha Waller   6' 4"

Long jump
2. Marion Jones   22' 11¾"

Triple jump
5. Sheila Hudson   45' 1¾"

Shot put
3. Connie Price-Smith   61' 7¾"

Discus
6. Kristin Kuehl   196' 5"

Javelin
7. Windy Dean   172' 1"

4 × 100 meter relay
1. United States   42.00
      (Cheryl Taplin, Chryste Gaines, Inger Miller, Carlette Guidry)

4 × 400 meter relay
4. United States   3:25.34
      (Monique Hennagan, Rochelle Stevens, Kim Graham, Jearl Miles-Clark)

Point score
1. U.S.   96   (First team win ever)

26th IAAF World Cross Country Championships: Marrakech, Morocco, March 21

4 kilometers
  8. Elva Dryer   12:51
  9. Amy Rudolph   12:51
 25. Molly Watcke   13:11
 26. Kathy Franey   13:13
 33. Karen Candaele   13:20
 66. Fran ten Bensel   13:53

   The United States women placed third in the team scores with 68 points.

8 kilometers
 20. Deena Drossin   27:06
 30. Liz Wilson   27:23
 31. Joan Nesbit   27:24
 37. Nnenna Lynch   27:41
 52. Kristin Ihle   28:08
 66. Michele Chalmers   28:53

   The United States women placed fifth in the team scores with 118 points.

Other News and Honors

Track & Field News: Athlete of the Year

Marion Jones became the first American to rank first in three events in one year.

U.S. and World Rankings (top three) — Track & Field News

100 meters
Marion Jones (1st in world)
Inger Miller (3rd in world)
Chryste Gaines (4th in world)

400 meters
Jearl Miles-Clark (5th in world)
Kim Graham
Monique Hennagan

200 meters
Marion Jones (1st in world)
Inger Miller (6th in world)
Zundra Feagin-Alexander

800 meters
Jearl Miles-Clark (2nd in world)
Joetta Clark (4th in world)
Meredith Valmon (6th in world)

1500 meters
Suzy Hamilton
Regina Jacobs
Amy Wickus

3000 meters
Regina Jacobs
Cheri Kenah
Amy Rudolph

5000 meters
Regina Jacobs (10th in world)
Libbie Hickman
Amy Rudolph

10,000 meters
Lynn Jennings
Shelly Steely
Jen Rhines

100 meter hurdles
Melissa Morrison (3rd in world)
Angie Vaughn (4th in world)
Cheryl Dickey (10th in world)

400 meter hurdles
Kim Batten (1st in world)
Michelle Johnson
Sandra Glover

10 kilometer walk
Joanne Dow
Michelle Rohl
Debbi Lawrence

High jump
Tisha Waller (2nd in world)
Amy Acuff (5th in world)
Erin Aldrich

Pole vault
Stacy Dragila (6th in world)
Kellie Suttle
Melissa Price

Long jump
Marion Jones (1st in world)
Shana Williams (7th in world)
Dawn Burrell (9th in world)

Triple jump
Sheila Hudson
Cynthea Rhodes
Tiombé Hurd

Shot put
Connie Price-Smith (3rd in world)
Teri Tunks
Tressa Thompson

Discus
Seilala Sua
Aretha Hill
Suzy Powell

Hammer
Amy Palmer (4th in world)
Windy Dean
Dawn Ellerbe

Javelin
Nicole Carroll
Lynda Lipson-Blutreich
Windy Dean

Heptathlon
Jackie Joyner-Kersee (2nd in world)
Kelly Blair-LaBounty (7th in world)
DeDee Nathan (8th in world)

The International Amateur Athletic Federation named 1998 the "Year of Women in Athletics." A special issue of their magazine was devoted to women.

The first article was a tribute to Florence Griffith Joyner. Florence died this year at age 38, "following a seizure."

Comments from dignitaries included references to her speed, her flamboyant outfits and the time she spent helping children. The article said, "It is a cruel stroke of fate that during this Year of Women in Athletics we should lose an athlete who did so much to promote women in the sport."

The Women's Committee consists of a chairman and twelve members. The representative from the United States is Pat Rico, president of USA Track and Field. Pat has been a member of the Women's Committee since 1976. She was awarded the IAAF Veteran Pin in 1991.

The IAAF Council has two women members.

The Area Patron for North and Central America and the Caribbean was Marion Jones. She said, "My role is to explain to everyone who interviews me on the subject that the situation has changed, and that, from now on, women have an important role to play in our sport."

The IAAF awarded medals commemorating The Year of Women in Athletics to the following women:

Joan Benoit-Samuelson
Yue Ling Chen
Doris Heritage
Marion Jones
Louise Mead-Tricard
Patricia Rico
Anne Timmons

An article entitled, "The Pathfinder," written by this author and published in the *IAAF Magazine*, describes Wilma Rudolph's rise from a child with health problems raised

Deena Drossin.

in the segregated South to this country's first three time gold medalist in the Rome Olympics. Her wins encouraged and inspired the growth of women's track and field in the United States.

Jearl Miles-Clark set an American record of 1:56.43 for the 800 meters in Zurich, Switzerland on August 12.

Regina Jacobs set an American record in the 5000 meters of 14:52.49 in Brunswick, Maine on July 4.

Amy Palmer set an American record in the hammer throw of 220' 1" on April 3 in Austin, Texas.

Jim Dunaway reported for *Track & Field News*: "...The women's vault, a first for Madison Square Garden, was closer than expected. World indoor champ Stacy Dragila made 13' 9¾" on her first jump, while British record-holder Janine Whitlock needed two tries. The bar was raised to the WR height of 14' 6¼" could clear it.... All the jumpers were assisted by plenty of enthusiastic cheering and rhythmic applause."

Joetta Clark, 35, ran in her twentieth Millrose Games 800 meters in Madison Square Garden on February 13.

Track & Field News, in recognition of its 50th anniversary, selected a "50-Year All-Star Team."

100 meters	Evelyn Ashford
3000/5000 meters	Mary Slaney
Heptathlon	Jackie Joyner-Kersee

"Florence Griffith Joyner, 38, Champion Sprinter, Is Dead," read the headline on the obituary page of the *New York Times* on Tuesday, September 22. On the sports page the headline read, "Death at 38: Reviewing a Vibrant Life." William C. Rhoden wrote,

...Early in the morning, Jackie had received a phone call from home. FloJo was dead. "Jackie's brother called her and said that he was trying to wake her up this morning," Bob Kersee said from his car phone. "He couldn't wake her up; they called 911, the paramedics came out. She had passed away."

There was silence on the line. What do you say at a time like this? Florence Griffith Joyner was always alive, always fresh, always vibrant. She was also flamboyant and controversial.

Her death was attributed to suffocation from an epileptic seizure while she slept.

Florence Griffith Joyner leaves her husband Al and their seven-year-old daughter, Mary.

The U.S. Open, a Grand Prix meet, was held on July 25, at Southern Illinois University, Edwardsville and served as a farewell meet to retiring Jackie Joyner-Kersee.

Footnotes reported, "On July 11, 1998, the National Distance Running Hall of Fame was established in Utica, New York, to honor the sport of distance running. It is dedicated to honoring the athletes who have contributed fame and recognition to the sport of distance running." Two of the first group of five athletes inducted were women: Joan Benoit-Samuelson and Katherine Switzer.

Francine Larrieu Smith was inducted into the National Track and Field Hall of Fame. The biography below is from the USA Track and Field website.

Born: November 23, 1952 — Palo Alto, California

Events
1,500 m — 4:05.09
1 mi. — 4:28
3,000 m — 8:50.54
5,000 m — 15:15.20
10,000 m — 31:28.92
marathon — 2:27:15

Francie Larrieu Smith's running career spanned four decades and included 13 world indoor records and a total of 35 American records in distances ranging from 1000 meters to two miles. She began running at 13 and won the first competition she ever entered, a 660-yard race for junior girls. Competing for the San Jose Cindergals, she won the first of her 21 national titles as a 17-year-old in the 1500 meters in 1970. In 1972, she scored an unusual double, winning AAU national titles in the 1500m and cross country. She repeated in 1973, winning the mile and cross country championships. After missing most of a year with injuries, Larrieu-Smith came back in 1975 to set a world record of 4:28.5 in the mile at the USA-USSR indoor meet. Larrieu-Smith is the only female athlete to make five Olympic teams [sic]. She competed in the 1500 meters in the 1972 and 1976 Olympics and, also in the 1500m, made the team that boycotted the Olympics in 1980. She missed out on the 1984 team but ran the 10,000 at the 1988 Games, taking fifth. She moved up to the marathon for the 1992 Games, finishing 12th in Barcelona. At the 1992 Games, she carried the U.S. flag at the Opening Ceremonies. She also ran in the 1987 and 1991 World Championships in the 10,000. Selected by Runner's World magazine as "The Most Versatile Runner of the Quarter Century," Larrieu Smith has been head women's and men's cross country and track and field coach at Southwestern University since 1999. She earned a master's degree in Sports Administration from the University of Texas in 2000.

Records Held
World Record: 1 mi. — 4:29

Championships
1988 Olympics: 10,000 m (5th)
1992 Olympics: marathon (12th)
1970 AAU: 1,500 m (1st)
1972 AAU: 1,500 m (1st)
1973 AAU: 1 mi. (1st)

Education
high school: Fremont (Sunnyvale, California), 1970
undergraduate: Long Beach State (Long Beach, California), 1977

Occupations
Coach

INTERVIEW: CHERYL TAPLIN

(July 5, 2005) The funniest story for me is how I started my track career in my first year in high school. A girlfriend of mine wanted to play basketball. She said, "Why don't you come and play basketball with me?" I said "I don't want to play basketball." She said, "Okay, well, then let's run track together." I said, "Okay." I had never run before. I knew that I was fast. But I had never run before. I went out the first day. They had trials and they put me up against the fastest girl on the team. I ended up beating her [laughter]. The rest is history.

I went to Cleveland High School here in Seattle. In my freshman year I won four state titles. I'm still the only person, male or female, to have won two or more state titles in all four consecutive years. Just last year one of my records was finally broken. I still have a state meet record and another metro record left. I ended up leaving here with nineteen state titles.

I went to LSU. That was the greatest experience in my life. It's amazing. I didn't understand the process of recruiting at the time. I was recruited by everyone but my five choices were: Washington State, Texas A&M, Kansas State, LSU and UCLA. Had UCLA offered me a full scholarship, I probably would have gone there but it was just for the best that I ended up at LSU. It was just the greatest experience of my life.

We were seriously a family. Of course, at times, young ladies will not get along with each other off the track, but we always put our feelings aside and all the petty stuff went out the door when it came time to get on the track. We knew that there was an image that needed to be upheld for LSU. When I got there, they were three time national champions. At the time, we wanted to continue this. So, we worked very hard under Myrtle Ferguson. She was our coach. Pat Henry was our head coach but Myrtle coached the women. We had a huge respect for her, for each other, for our sport and for our school. We just wanted to maintain that.

Hard work paid off. I was a four time national champion at LSU and sixteen time All American. That's where I grew up. I was on my own. It was the first time I was away from home by myself. It was a great experience. I wouldn't change anything.

I made four world championship teams: '93, '97, and '99. I really enjoyed the World Cup in 1998. We got the gold medal in the 4 by 1.

One of the highlights of my career was in 1990. The Goodwill Games were held in Seattle. I had just graduated from high school, I had signed my letter of intent to LSU and I was a volunteer for track and field. I remember meeting Andre Cason. I had already met him when I went on my trip to Texas A&M. I remember meeting Leroy Burrell, Carlette Guidry, and I think Dannette Young. I remember Leroy and Carlette specifically. I was just so overwhelmed. I really didn't know much about track and field but I just knew that I was starting to get into the sport and here I am carrying their clothes, volunteering on the track in 1990. Well, in 1994, the next Goodwill Games, I got my first gold medal in the 4 by 1 relay. I got another medal in '98, Goodwill Games. I got 4th in the 200—I wanted third—I was almost there.

Just the experience of going overseas—I would never have gotten that chance if I had not been in track and field. The people that I met, the places that I went—going to Monte Carlo—just going all over and meeting different people—and learning how to live and cope—when you are over in Europe for three months during the summer. It was a great learning experience. I competed until 2000.

I would tell kids interested in the sport to be dedicated and if this is really what you want to do, the talent that you have can take you all over the world and you can make money at it too. But, you'll meet people from all over the world. You will get a chance to see the world and experience a lot of things that you probably wouldn't. This opens up a lot of opportunities. If I can do it, someone who didn't even know a thing about running track, they can. I didn't learn how to run really until I got to college. My summer track coach helped me out the most, Coach Flowers—Bob Flowers. He was the greatest. I started running summer track during my sophomore year. We would go to Spokane, Eugene and there were a few meets around here. I even got a chance in 1988 to go to the junior nationals in Tallahassee. I was in the Junior Olympics in '89 in Spokane and got second in the 100. Coach Flowers actually prepared me for college running with the South Central Athletic Association, otherwise known as SCAA. They helped cultivate my talent to get me to where I could go to the next level when I got to college.

My best times in the 100 are: 10.99w—11.07 and for the 200, 22.58.

Cheryl is a 1990 graduate of Cleveland High School, Seattle, WA and Louisiana State University, Baton Rouge in 1995. She currently resides in Seattle and works in community relations for the Seattle Mariners.

Professional Career:

Two-time Gold Medallist 1994 & 1998 Goodwill Games Team, 4 × 100m relay
Gold Medallist, 1998 World Cup Team, 4 × 100m relay
Ranked 9th in the world in the 100 meters in 1994
Ranked 4th in the U.S. in the 200 meters in 1997
Member of the USA World Championship Teams, 1993, '97 & '99
4th place, 4 × 100m relay —1999 World Championships, Seville, Spain
Runner Up, Washington State Athlete of the Year by the *Seattle Post Intelligencer*, 1994

Collegiate Career:

Four-time NCAA Outdoor Champion, LSU
Two-time NCAA Indoor Champion, LSU
Sixteen-time All-American, LSU
SEC Champion 100, 200 & 400meter relay, 1994
SEC Indoor Champion 55m, 1993 & '94
NCAA Runner Up 55m, 1993 & '94
World University Games Gold Medalist, 4 × 100m relay 1993 & '95

High School Career:

• Only athlete in Washington state to win two or more state titles all four years in high school.
• Nineteen Washington state high school titles — 55m (indoor), 100m, 200m, 4 × 100m relay & 4 × 200m relay.
• Currently holds the Washington state 200m record for Class AAA.

1999

The Outdoor Nationals

The USA Outdoor Track and Field Championships were held from June 24–27 at Hayward Field, Eugene, Oregon.

---

100 meters

Mel Watman reported for *American Track & Field*, "With Marion Jones automatically qualified, the race shaped up as a clash between Inger Miller, with 10.92w this season, and Gail Devers, whose only outdoor mark following a hamstring injury was a low-key 11.32. It proved close. Miller edged past Devers late in the race to win by 1/100th in a windy 10.96 with junior Angela Williams a good third."

1. Inger Miller, Nike Track Club	10.96 w
2. Gail Devers, Nike International Track Club	10.97 w
3. Angela Williams, Southern California Cheetahs	11.03 w
4. Torri Edwards, University of Southern California	11.05 w
5. Cheryl Taplin, Vector Sports	11.17 w
6. Carlette Guidry, adidas USA	11.18 w
7. Nanceen Perry, University of Texas, Austin	11.26 w
8. Passion Richardson, Nike Central Track Club	11.27 w

200 meters

Bob Rodman wrote for *The Register Guard*: "...'It's my favorite race,' [Jones] admitted after leading silver-medalist LaTasha Jenkins (22.36) and third-place finisher Inger Miller (22.46) to the tape. 'The 200 has sentimental value to me because it was the first race I ran as a child.' Jones led the field off the curve and was never seriously challenged."

1. Marion Jones, Nike Track Club	22.10
2. LaTasha Jenkins, Ball State University	22.36
3. Inger Miller, Nike Track Club	22.46
4. Nanceen Perry, University of Texas, Austin	22.72
5. Kelli White, University of Tennessee	22.82
6. Zundra Feagin, Asics Track Club	23.08
7. Lakeisha Backus, University of Texas, Austin	23.57
8. Chandra Burns, Nike Track Club	23.95

400 meters

1. Maicel Malone-Wallace, New Balance Track Club   51.29
2. Suziann Reid, University of Texas, Austin   51.38
3. Michelle Collins, Nike Track Club   51.45
4. Andrea Anderson, Gold Medal Track Club   52.09
5. Shanelle Porter, Team U.S. West   52.25
6. Yulanda Nelson, Baylor University   52.61
7. Kim Graham, Asics Track Club   52.95
8. Mikele Barber, University of South Carolina   53.05

800 meters

Again, Bob Rodman writes: "If there was a 1,200-meter race, Jearl Miles-Clark would own it like Nabisco owns cookies. Instead the 33-year-old, two-time Olympian has ruled the 400 and 800 in recent years, and on Sunday at Hayward Field she won her second consecutive national 800 title during the USA Outdoor Track & Field Championships. Miles-Clark finished the two-lap event in 1:59.47, well shy of her American record of 1:56.78, a mark she supplied in 1997, the same year Miles-Clark set the USA meet record of 49.40 in the 400.

"'But I finally made the World Championships in another event besides the 400,' said Miles-Clark, who has won the 400 at nationals four times."

1. Jearl Miles-Clark, Reebok Racing Club   1:59.47
2. Meredith Rainey Valmon, Reebok Enclave   2:00.36
3. Kathleen Rounds, unattached   2:00.71
4. Joetta Clark, Nike Track Club   2:00.74
5. Michelle DiMuro-Ave, Asics Track Club   2:03.40
6. Mary Jane Harrelson, Appalachian State University   2:03.85
7. Katrina de Boer, Georgetown University   2:06.36
8. Maureen Ferris, University of Tennessee   2:11.58

1500 meters

The *New York Times* said, "The most scintillating performance was Regina Jacobs's victory in the women's 1,500 in a meet record 4 minutes 2.41 seconds, the fastest in the world this year."

1. Regina Jacobs, Mizuno Track Club   4:02.41   MR
2. Stephanie Best, Asics Track Club   4:08.53
3. Shayne Culpepper, adidas USA   4:08.69
4. Marla Runyan, Moving Comfort Racing Team   4:10.02
5. Debbie Marshall, New Balance Track Club   4:13.02
6. Kathy Fleming, New Balance Track Club   4:13.57
7. Alisa Harvey, Avon/Fila Track Club   4:13.97
8. Julianne Henner, Reebok Enclave   4:14.56

5000 meters

The Register-Guard reported: "...The 35-year-old Jacobs was the meet's only double winner as she won the 5,000 meters in a time of 15:24.80 less than 24 hours after blowing away the 1,500-meter field. That double has never been accomplished before at the U.S. nationals.... Jacobs, looking fresh and strong, pulled up to Dryer's shoulder with 600 meters left, and then made her move at the bell lap, along with Rudolph and Kenah. Jacobs closed with a 29.8 over the final 200 to win easily, while Kenah held on to second and Dryer passed Rudolph by a stride at the finish line."

1. Regina Jacobs, Mizuno Track Club   15:24.80
2. Cheri Kenah, Reebok Enclave   15:26.60

Left: Jearl Miles Clark at the 1999 National Championships. *Right:* Inger Miller at the 1999 National Championships.

3. Elva Dryer, Nike Track Club	15:27.26
4. Amy Rudolph, Reebok Racing Club	15:27.27
5. Libbie Hickman, Nike Track Club	15:29.53
6. Kris Ihle, Nike Track Club	15:38.44
7. Blake Phillips, New Balance Track Club	15:47.00
8. Clare Taylor, Asics Track Club	15:55.15

10,000 meters
1. Libbie Hickman, Nike Track Club	31:41.33
2. Anne Marie Lauck, Nike Running Room	31:43.50
3. Deena Drossin, Reebok Racing Club	32:00.72
4. Jennifer Rhines, adidas USA	32:29.67
5. Shelly Steely, Asics Track Club	32:54.80
6. Lynn Jennings, Nike International Track Club	32:59.05
7. Leigh Daniel, Texas Tech University	33:02.02
8. Shelley Smathers, Vector Sports	33:08.98

3000 meter steeplechase
1. Elizabeth Jackson, Brigham Young University	10:07.23
2. Lisa Nye, Nike-Portland Track Club	10:12.66
3. Joan Nesbit, New Balance Track Club	10:18.55
4. Tonya Dodge, Syracuse Chargers	10:20.50
5. Kara Ormond, Brigham Young University	10:26.63

Gail Devers in lane 5 of the 100 meter hurdles final at the 1999 National Championships.

6.	Desiree Owen, unattached	10:33.44
7.	Katie Baloga, unattached	10:38.05
8.	Emily Mulick, Idaho State University	10:38.37

100 meter hurdles

"...On Sunday, before a crowd of 8,913 at Hayward Field, Devers blasted out of the blocks, flashed that familiar world-class form, and captured her fifth U.S. title in the 100-meter hurdles with a wind-aided time of 12.54, a meet record and the fastest this year under any conditions," said Curtis Anderson in *The Register-Guard*.

1.	Gail Devers, Nike International Track Club	12.54 w
2.	Miesha McKelvy, San Diego State University	12.67 w
3.	Andria King, Georgia Institute of Technology	12.73 w
4.	Sharon Couch-Jewell, Reebok Racing Club	12.74 w
5.	Yolanda McCray, University of Miami	12.77 w
6.	Tonya Lawson, Team Fila	12.86 w
7.	Melissa Morrison, Reebok Racing Club	14.19 w

400 meter hurdles

1.	Sandra Glover, unattached	54.95
2.	Michelle Johnson, Team Fila	55.53
3.	Joanna Hayes, Gold Medal Track Club	55.76
4.	Trevaia Williams-Davis, unattached	56.26
5.	LaTanya Sheffield, Sheffield Elite Track Club	56.96
6.	Melinda Sallins, Mizuno Track Club	57.98
7.	Yvonne Harrison, unattached	58.05

Left: Regina Jacobs at the 1999 National Championships. *Right:* Tisha Waller, 1998. Courtesy of Emily Poucan.

20 kilometer

1. Michelle Rohl, Moving Comfort Racing Team	1:33:17
2. Joanne Dow, adidas USA	1:35:01
3. Susan Armenta, Southern California Walkers	1:37:04
4. Danielle Kirk, Southern California Walkers	1:39:09
5. Jill Zenner, Miami Valley Track Club	1:39:38
6. Sara Standley, unattached	1:39:54
7. Margaret Ditchburn, Walk USA	1:41:23
8. Cheryl Rellinger, unattached	1:42:53

Pole vault

1. Stacy Dragila, Reebok Racing Club	14' 7¼"
2. Kellie Suttle, Nike Track Club	14' 1¼"
3. Melissa Price, Fresno State University	13' 9¼"
4. Kimberly Becker, Reebok Racing Club	13' 3½"
and Jill Wittenwyler, Nike Track Club	
6. Kristin Quackenbush, unattached	13' 3½"
7. Mary Sauer, Cornerstone Track Club	13' 3½"
8. Tracy O'Hara, University of California, Los Angeles	12' 9½"

High jump

Ron Bellamy reported for *The Register-Guard*, "…The 28-year-old Atlanta resident cleared 6 feet, 6¼ inches, brushing the bar just slightly, to win the women's high jump, her second consecutive national title and her third, including the Olympic Trials, in the past four years.

"The clearance broke the Hayward Field record, set by Tanya Hughes in 1992, and the national championship record, set by Jan Wohlschlag in 1988. Waller, who won the USA indoor title earlier this year, then took three cracks at the American record of 6' 8¼", but missed."

1. Tisha Waller, Nike Track Club	6' 6¼"	MR
2. Amy Acuff, Nike Track Club	6' 4"	
3. Karol Jenkins, Chattanooga Track Club	6' 4"	
4. Angela Bradburn-Spangler, Asics Track Club	6' 2¾"	
5. Gwen Wentland, Nike Track Club	6' 2¾"	
6. Ifoma Jones, University of Houston	6' ¾"	
7. Stacy Ann Grant, University of Illinois	6' ¾"	
8. Adriane Sims, St. Augustine's College	5' 10¾"	

Long jump

1. Dawn Burrell, U.S. Army	22' 10"	
2. Marion Jones, Nike Track Club	22' 3"	
3. Shana Williams, adidas USA	22' ¼"	w
4. Adrien Sawyer, T.C. Management	21' 11"	w
5. Angela Brown, Reebok Enclave	21' 1¼"	w
6. LaShonda Christopher, University of North Carolina	20' 10¾"	
7. Pamela Simpson, University of Southern California	20' 7¼"	
8. Starlie Graves, unattached	20' 4¼"	w

Triple jump

1. Stacey Bowers, Baylor University	44' 9¾"
2. Tiombé Hurd, Nike Track Club	44' 4¼"
3. Cynthea Rhodes, Reebok Racing Club	43' 8¾"
4. Monica Cabbler, Georgia Foundation	43' 1¾"
5. Shakeema Walker, Pennsylvania State University	43' ½"
6. Amanda Banks, unattached	42' 4"
7. Detrich Clariett, Texas A&M University	41' 10"
8. Niambi Dennis, U.S. Army	41' 10"

Shot put

1. Connie Price-Smith, Indiana Invaders	61' 10½"
2. Teri Tunks, Nike Track Club	61' 8¼"
3. Tressa Thompson, Nike Track Club	61' 5"
4. Dawn Dumble, Reebok-Bruin Track Club	57' 5½"
5. Jesseca Cross, unattached	57' 5"
6. Christina Tolson, Reebok-Bruin Track Club	54' 5¼"
7. Lisa Griebel, Iowa State University	52' 3¼"
8. Cheree Hicks, unattached	52' 1¾"

Discus

1. Seilala Sua, University of California, Los Angeles	203' 8"
2. Kris Kuehl, unattached	199' 9"
3. Aretha Hill, unattached	193' 10"
4. Shelly Borrman, Colorado State University	191' 4"
5. Suzy Powell, unattached	185' 2"
6. April Malveo, Louisiana Tech University	183' 1"
7. Dawn Dumble, Reebok-Bruin Track Club	176' 10"
8. Roberta Collins, Kent State University	176'

Connie Price Smith at the 1999 National Championships.

Hammer
1. Dawn Ellerbe, New York Athletic Club   212' 5" MR
2. Tamika Powell, Reebok Enclave   210' 10"
3. Windy Dean, New York Athletic Club   210' 1"
4. Leslie Coons, unattached   207'
5. Anna Norgren, Boston Athletic Association   202' 7"
6. Christina Tolson, Reebok-Bruin Track Club   200' 10"
7. Melissa Price, University of Nebraska   199' 11"
8. Renetta Seiler, Kansas State University   198' 5"

Javelin
    "...Blutreich led going into the finals and won with a toss of 182 feet, 2 inches, her best throw coming on her last," reported Ron Bellamy.

1. Lynda Blutreich, M-F Athletic   182' 2"
2. Cassie Morelock, University of Nebraska   175' 1"
3. Ann Crouse, University of Virginia   173' 8"
4. Erica Wheeler, unattached   170' 5"
5. Nicole Carroll, Asics Track Club   170'
6. Kristin Dunn, unattached   164' 5"
7. Serene Ross, Purdue University   162' 7"
8. Kim Kreiner, unattached   157' 11"

Heptathlon
1. Sheila Burrell, unattached   6101
2. Tiffany Lott-Hogan, Neways Athletics   6026
3. Nicole Haynes, unattached   5720

4. Wendi Raatjes, Advanced Micro Devices	5532
5. Robin Unger, unattached	5480
6. Tracye Lawyer, Stanford University	5469
7. Alicia Brimhall, Brigham Young University	5358
8. DeDee Nathan, Indiana Invaders Track Club	5318

The Indoor Nationals

The USA National Indoor Championships were held in the Georgia Dome, Atlanta, Georgia on February 26 and 27.

60 meters
1. Gail Devers, Nike International Track Club	7.04
2. Inger Miller, Nike Track Club	7.15
3. Cheryl Taplin, Vector Sports	7.17

200 meters
1. Zundra Feagin-Alexander, Asics Track Club	23.29
2. LaTasha Colander, Nike International Track Club	23.59
3. Juan Ball, Southern California Cheetahs Track Club	23.94

400 meters
1. Jearl Miles-Clark, Reebok Racing Club	51.97
2. Shanelle Porter, U.S. West Track Club	52.45
3. Michelle Collins, Nike Track Club	52.48

800 meters
1. Meredith Valmon, Reebok Enclave	2:00.55
2. Michelle Ave, Asics Track Club	2:01.82
3. Joetta Clark, Nike Track Club	2:02.24

1500 meters
1. Suzy Hamilton, Nike Track Club	4:13.96
2. Debbie Marshall, New Balance Track Club	4:17.51
3. Alisa Harvey, unattached	4:17.93

3000 meters
1. Regina Jacobs, Mizuno Track Club	9:06.52
2. Cheri Kenah, Reebok Enclave	9:11.82
3. Blake Phillips, Team New Balance	9:13.68

60 meter hurdles
1. Melissa Morrison, Reebok Racing Club	7.85
2. Cheryl Dickey, Nike Track Club	8.01
3. Andria King, Georgia Institute of Technology	8.03

4 × 400 meter relay
1. University of Nebraska	3:36.29
2. Baylor University	3:36.99
3. Rice University	3:38.52

Triple jump
1. Cynthea Rhodes, Reebok Racing Club   45' 4¼"
2. Sheila Hudson, unattached   45' 3¾"
3. Stacey Bowers, Baylor University   45' 2½"

20 lb. weight throw
1. Dawn Ellerbe, New York Athletic Club   74' 8¼"
2. Renetta Seiler, Kansas State University   68' 11¾"
3. Jesseca Cross, unattached   68' 1¾"

Pole vault
1. Stacy Dragila, Reebok Racing Club   14' 7¼"
2. Melissa Mueller, Nike Track Club   13' 11¼"
3. Kellie Suttle, Nike Track Club   13' 11¼"

High jump
1. Tisha Waller, unattached   6' 5"
2. Amy Acuff, Nike Track Club   6' 4"
3. Karol Jenkins, unattached   6' 2¾"

Shot put
1. Teri Tunks, adidas USA   62' ½"
2. Connie Price-Smith, Indiana Invaders Track Club   61' 1¼"
3. Tressa Thompson, Nike Track Club   60' 3"

Long jump
1. Shana Williams, unattached   21' 11¾"
2. Dawn Burrell, U.S. Army   21' 8"
3. Adrien Sawyer, unattached   21' 5½"

39th Los Angeles Invitational (5 women's events): Los Angeles, February 13

50 meters
1. Inger Miller, Nike Track Club   6.15

800 meters
1. Regina Jacobs, Mizuno Track Club   2:07.60

Mile
1. Julia Stamps, Stanford University   4:42.95

50 meter hurdles
1. Melissa Morrison, Reebok Racing Club   6.81   MR

High jump
1. Tisha Waller, Nike Track Club   6' 3½"

13th Pan American Games: Winnipeg, Canada, July 23–30

	Event	Place	Performance
Anderson, Andrea	400m	4	52.43
	4 × 400mr	2	3.27.50
Becker, Kimberly	PV	4	12' 9½"

	Event	Place	Performance
Best, Stephanie	1500m	3	4:18.44
Blutreich, Lynda Lipson	JT	5	182' 11½"
Bowers, Stacey	TJ	4	45' 9¾"
Bradburn, Angie	HJ	4	5' 10¾"
Brown, Angela	LJ	2	21' 4¼"
Burrell, Sheila	Heptathlon	2	6244
	4 × 100mr	2	43.27
Collins, Michelle	400m	2	51.21
	4 × 400mr	2	3.27.50
Crain, Jennifer	Marathon	7	2:54:19
Christopher, LaShonda	LJ	5	20' 8"
Dow, Joanne	20k road walk	5	1:36:33
Edwards, Torri	4 × 100mr	2	43.27
Ellerbe, Dawn	HT	1	214' 5"
Hayes, Joanna	400mh	5	55.90
Haynes, Nicole	Heptathlon	3	5999
Hill, Aretha	DT	2	193' 9"
Hurd, Tiombé	TJ	5	44' 10¾"
Ihle, Kristin	5000m	5	16:14.07
Jenkins, Karol	HJ	5	5' 10¾"
Johnson, Michelle	400mh	3	54.22
King, Andria	100mh	7	13.28
Kuehl, Kristin	DT	3	187' 8¼"
McKelvy, Miesha	100mh	3	12.91
Morelock, Cassie	JT	8	158' 7"
Nelson, Yulanda	4 × 400mr	2	3.27.50
Phillips, Blake	5000m	3	15:59.77
Porter, Shanelle	4 × 400mr	2	3.27.50
Powell, Tamika	HT	6	193' 2¾"
Rainey, Meredith	800m	3	2:01.51
Richardson, Passion	4 × 100mr	2	43.27
Rohl, Michelle	20k road walk	3	1:35:22
Runyan, Marla	1500m	1	4:16.86
Smathers, Shelley	10,000m	7	34:20.42
Smith, Connie Price	SP	1	62' 6¼"
Suttle, Kellie	PV	2	13' 11¼"
Steely, Shelly	10,000m	4	33:36.44
Steer, Teri	SP	3	59' 1¾"
Williams, Angela	100m	2	11.16
	4 × 100mr	2	43.27

7th IAAF World Outdoor Track and Field Championships: Seville, Spain, August 21–29

100 meters

"Jones ran fast enough to finish first: getting off to a fine start, controlling her power beautifully and crossing the finish line in 10.70 seconds, the fifth fastest time in history," reported the *New York Times*.

1. Marion Jones	10.70	MR
2. Inger Miller	10.79	
5. Gail Devers	10.95	

200 meters

Even *TV Guide* ran an article about Marion's injury in the 200m. "The fastest woman alive was about to surge ahead of the other runners in the 200-meter semifinals when a bolt of pain ripped through her back last August during the World Track and Field Championships in Seville, Spain. Coming off a turn, Marion dropped to the track, the victim of intense back spasms. Instantly, she knew her hopes to win three gold medals at the competition would go unfulfilled."

USA Track & Field reported: "...Inger Miller enjoyed the meet of her life in winning the 200 meter title in the world leading time of 21.77. Miller also captured the silver medal in the 100 meters in 10.79, a new personal record. When the smoke had cleared, Miller had run three career bests on the 100 meters, and one personal best in the 200 meters, but more importantly, she served notice that she will be a force to be reckoned with at the 2000 Olympics in Sydney."

The *New York Times* added, "...It has unquestionably been [Miller's] meet. She set three consecutive personal bests in the 100, taking the silver behind Jones, and today she set another one in the 200 by a whopping 33-hundredths of a second. More reassuringly, it was the best time of the year—Jones's best in 1999 was 21.81."

| 1. Inger Miller | 21.77 |

400 meters
No American women were in the final.

800 meters
| 4. Jearl Miles-Clark | 1:57.40 |

1500 meters
| 2. Regina Jacobs | 4:00.35 |
| 10. Marla Runyan | 4:06.45 |

5000 meters
| 11. Cheri Kenah | 15:20.12 |

10,000 meters
| 11. Deena Drossin | 32:11.14 |
| 16. Anne Marie Letko-Lauck | 32:57.07 |

100 meter hurdles

USA Track & Field reported, "...Although she hit the final hurdle with her trail leg and almost fell to the Mondo surface, two-time Olympic 100 meter champion Gail Devers turned back the clock, and turned off the critics by capturing the world 100-meter hurdles title for the third time in her remarkable career. Along with being a new American record, Devers's time of 12.37 is the world leader this season. Along with winning the world high hurdles title in 1993 and 1995, Gail captured silver in that event in 1991."

| 1. Gail Devers | 12.37 |

400 meter hurdles
| 5. Sandra Cummings-Glover | 53.65 |
| 6. Michelle Johnson | 54.23 |

20 kilometer walk
| 31. Susan Armenta | 1:40:20 |
| 38. Danielle Kirk | 1:43:27 |

Marathon

32. Marie Boyd	2:44:16
36. Mary Lynn Currier	2:48:05
37. Mimi Corcoran	2:49:21
38. Cindy Keeler	2:53:04

Pole vault

"...Stacy Dragila captured the first-ever women's outdoor world championships gold medal in the pole vault with a world record-tying leap of 15' 1". Dragila also won the first-ever women's indoor world championship back in 1997 with a world record-equaling jump of 14–5.25," reported *USA Track & Field.*

| 1. Stacy Dragila | 15' 1" | WR |
| 9. Kellie Suttle | 14' 3¼" | |

Heptathlon

| 11. Sheila Burrell | 6162 |
| 17. Nicole Haynes | 5787 |

Discus

| 6. Seilala Sua | 209' 1" |

Long jump

3. Marion Jones	22' 5"
6. Dawn Burrell	22' 1½"
12. Shana Williams	21' 4¾"

Hammer throw

| 10. Dawn Ellerbe | 208' 5" |
| 17. Amy Palmer-Christiansen | 196' 2" |

Shot put

| 9. Teri Tunks-Steer | 59' 2¼" |
| 11. Connie Price-Smith | 58' 8½" |

Javelin

No American women were in the final.

High jump

| 4. Tisha Waller | 6' 5" |
| 9. Amy Acuff | 6' 4" |

4 × 100 meter relay

| 4. USA | 42.30 |

(Cheryl Taplin, Nanceen Perry, Inger Miller, Gail Devers)

4 × 400 meter relay

| 2. USA | 3:22.09 |

(Suziann Reid, Maicel Malone-Wallace, Michele Collins, Jearl Miles-Clark)

7th IAAF World Indoor Track and Field Championships: Maebashi, Japan, March 5–7

60 meters

| 2. Gail Devers | 7.02 |
| 3. Inger Miller | 7.06 |

400 meters
3. Jearl Miles-Clark   51.45

800 meters
4. Meredith Valmon   1:59.11

3000 meters
3. Regina Jacobs   8:39.14   AR

60 meter hurdles
6. Melissa Morrison   7.97

4 × 400 meter relay
3. USA   3:27.59   AR
    (Monique Henderson, Michele Collins, Zundra Feagin-Alexander, Shanelle Porter)

High jump
3. Tisha Waller   6' 5"

Pole vault
5. Melissa Mueller   14' 3¼"
8. Stacy Dragila   14' 3¼"

Long jump
2. Shana Williams   22' 4½"
8. Dawn Burrell   21' 3½"

Shot put
3. Teri Tunks   61' 10½"
4. Connie Price-Smith   61' 9"

Pentathlon
1. DeDee Nathan   4753   AR

19th IAAF World Race Walking Cup: Mezidon-Canon, France, May 1, 2

20 kilometer walk
46. Michelle Rohl   1:36:50
53. Joanne Dow   1:38:08
58. Danielle Kirk   1:39:10
64. Jill Zenner   1:40:30
88. Margaret Ditchburn   1:46:26

The United States finished sixteenth in the team standings.

IAAF World Cross Country Championships: Belfast, Northern Ireland, March 27, 28

Short race (4.236 kilometers)
18. Elva Dryer   15:58
48. Amy Rudolph   16:39
49. Cathy Vasto   16:42

65. Becky Spies	17:00
74. Molly Watcke	17:16
78. Shane Culpepper	17:32

The United States women finished in ninth place with 180 points.

Long race (8.012 kilometers)

10. Deena Drossin	28:53
23. Jennifer Rhines	29:31
48. Carmen Troncoso	30:29
55. Joan Nesbit	30:44
57. Donna Garcia	30:47
70. Laura Baker	31:07

The United States team finished in eighth place with 136 points.

IAAF Grand Prix Final: Munich, September 11

200 meters

3. Inger Miller (tie)	22.64

800 meters

8. Meredith Valmon	2:03.40

400 meter hurdles

3. Sandra Cummings-Glover	53.83
5. Michelle Johnson	54.26

Shot put

3. Connie Price-Smith	61' 4¾"
5. Teri Tunks-Steer	59' 7½"

In the final Grand Prix standings, Inger Miller was eighth and Sandra Cummings-Glover was ninth out of the top ten.

Doris Brown-Heritage was inducted on December 4 into the United States Track Coaches Association Hall of Fame. *IAAF News* reported:

…The world's premier distance runner during the 1960s, Heritage set the first of her American records as an undergraduate of Seattle Pacific. She eventually owned every national record from 440 yards up to and including the mile. The longer the race, the more dominant she became. Unfortunately, during her career there were few, if any, women's races over 5,000 meters. Nevertheless, Heritage was often in the glow of the international spotlight. She qualified for the USA Olympic teams in 1968 and 1972, taking fifth in the 800 in the altitude of Mexico City. Her greatest achievement may have been her five consecutive World Cross Country Championships from 1967 to 1971, a feat never duplicated.

The husband and 8-year-old daughter of the late Florence Griffith Joyner helped unveil a statue in memory of the three-time Olympian gold medalist in Laguna Beach (California) on 21 May. …The statue depicts the world's fastest female sprinter with hands raised in victory as she crossed the finish line in the 100 meters at the 1988 Seoul Olympics.

Stacy Dragila set a world record of 15' 1" in the pole vault on August 21 in Seville, Spain.

Elizabeth Robinson-Schwartz died in May. She was 87 years old. At age sixteen, she was the first 100 meter gold medal winner in the 1928 Olympic Games. The *New York Times* added, "After Robinson won the gold, Douglas MacArthur, then the president of the American Olympic Committee, presented her with a small gold charm shaped like the world."

Bottom row, from left: Ed Temple, Pat Rico, Evelyn Ashford, Doris Heritage, Xerox representative Terry Dillman. *Center row, from left:* Valerie Brisco (with earrings), Willye White, Benita Fitzgerald Mosley. *Top row, from left:* Mildred McDaniel, Louise Ritter and Charlie Jones, 1999.

Regina Jacobs was inducted into the Black Sports Hall of Fame on November 12.

Nina Kuscsik and Francie Larrieu-Smith were in the second class of inductees into the National Distance Running Hall of Fame in Utica, New York on July 10.

Vince Reel, international track coach and editor and founder of *Women's Track & Field World* died. He was 85.

In conjunction with the outdoor championships, USATF celebrated the "Pioneers of Women's Track and Field — A Tribute to Athletes Who Made a Difference."

Other News and Honors

Track & Field News: Athlete of the Year

Inger Miller

The following women set American records:

800m	Jearl Miles-Clark	1:56.40	August 11
100mh	Gail Devers	12.37	August 28
HT	Dawn Ellerbe	230' 2"	May 15
3000mw	Michelle Rohl	12:47.52	June 19
20kmw	Michelle Rohl	1:33:17	June 26

The following women set indoor American records:

800m	Suzy Hamilton	1:58.92	February 7
3000m	Regina Jacobs	8:39.14	March 7
Pentathlon	DeDee Nathan	4753	March 5

INTERVIEW: JOANNA HAYES

(February 24, 2006) I got started when I was, I believe, nine. I started because my parents just told me to go out there and run [laughter]. They always said that when I was, like, two years old I would just always run. We had an apartment, we lived in New Hampshire. In the apartment I would just run back and forth from wall to wall. I would just run in front of the TV all day. I used to run away from my grandmother down the main street. So, they just figured I was fast and had a little talent.

I started doing the long jump when I was really young and I made, in '89, I'm so old, in 1989 I made two national teams; one for Arco Jesse Owens in the running long jump and I was third at nationals and Hershey Track and Field and I was fifth at nationals in the standing broad jump. So that was my start in the long jump. That was going into my seventh grade year. Then I took a year off.

I got into high school and decided that I missed track so I did the long jump and triple jump. My first jump was 36' 6" as a freshman. It was good because my dad did the triple jump and they figured I had a little natural ability. But, I never quite learned the correct way to do it. So, into my junior year I moved to North High School. I think I was going 38' 10" and 18' 1" and we decided that I'd try the hurdles in my junior year in high school. It was fun. I fell in my first two races and I have nice scars from that. My senior year I went undefeated in the 100 hurdles. I ran 13.06, wind-aided and 13.38 and 40.81 in the 300 hurdles. I got a scholarship to UCLA. So, that was high school and how I got started.

In UCLA I did both hurdles, 400 hurdles and 100 hurdles. I was PAC 10 champion in the 100 hurdles for three years straight and my fourth year I was going for a fourth title. I hit the eighth hurdle and kind of stumbled through into third. But, you know, I did both hurdles and the 400 hurdles always seemed to take precedence because in the big meets they were always first. I got hurt my sophomore and junior year at nationals. Finally in the NCAAs, my senior year, I ran the 400 hurdles and I won. I ran 55.16 and I came back and got third in the 100 hurdles. I always told everybody that if they were reversed I would have won both [laughter]. I was tired. It was really hard to do the double.

Joanna Hayes, 2006.

When I came out in 1999, that year I made the world university team in the 400 meter hurdles and I was the silver medalist. The girl who beat me went on to win the world championships at twenty-two years old from Cuba, Daimi Pernia. I was okay with her beating me after I found out that she was so good [laughter].

Let's see, after that then I made the team and didn't do so well at worlds because it was a new experience for me. I was in awe. I didn't give it my all in the first round and I got knocked out.

2000 was my heartbreak year. I missed the team by one place in the 400 hurdles and two places in the 100 hurdles. I took two years off. I came back in '03. I worked really, really hard. I had three jobs and trained like crazy and made the team in the 400 hurdles. I tried the double but the 100 hurdles were just too close. I locked up in the 100 hurdles semifinal. I didn't make the final. I kind of knocked into all of the hurdles. I was winning the race until eight and it wasn't good. But, I made the team. I got the flu. Went to Pan Ams and won that in 2003 in the 400 hurdles. I got some kind of illness in the Dominican Republic so I did not do well in the worlds, I think because my heart was really not in it. I really wanted the 100 hurdles. I pushed but not with everything in me.

So in 2004, I ran indoors for the first time since 1997 and I made the team. I was second to Gail. I just came to nationals, made the team, and went to worlds and I was fourth. Then I just decided in June that I would just do one — just one hurdle race and I picked the 100 hurdles — and thus the Olympic champion [laughter]. I just felt that it was time for me to pick the one I love with my heart. My heart led me back to the 100 hurdles and the Olympic championship and record. It was awesome.

This year hopefully I will get back on track. There's my career.

INTERVIEW: INGER MILLER

(February 26, 2004) Considering that my father is an Olympic silver and bronze medalist in the 100 meters, I didn't get started running until pretty late in life. My first year running was my sophomore year of high school. I took that through college and went to the University of Southern California and kind of broke out in '96 and made the Olympic team. I was very excited about that. But I think that one of the highlights of my career was in 1999 — the World Championships in Seville.

I don't know, it's weird. I decided to change coaching in the fall of 1998. I left my father, who was coaching me at the time, and wanted to change my manager and I was looking into coming with HSI and having the opportunity to train with the best men in the world and one of the best women in the 400 in the world, at the time. I had been training alone for so long that it seemed like it was a great idea to kind of boost my career. I thought that I was at a crossroads and needed the opportunity to kind of— either I was going to stay where I was or go on to the next level.

So, in December or late November of '98, I moved down to UCLA and started training with John Smith and Maurice Greene, Ato Boldon, Jon Drummond — all those guys. I haven't looked back since. I think it was a fantastic move. I had a really great indoor season in 1999 and moved on into the summer where it took me a really long time to master the technique that John Smith was trying to teach me — the drive phase — the notorious drive phase that everyone is trying to do now, especially.

It was weird because leading up to the world championships I did not have an inkling that I was going to run what I ran. My last 100 meter race before the world championships was in London and I ran something like 11.13 and cried. I cried. I mean Larry Wade can tell you that I cried and cried and said, "Oh my gosh, if I go to world championships running like this, I will not make it." I'm like — there's no way — and somehow that entire season of mistakes and trying to put together my race all came together at world championships.

The first round, of course, everybody runs 11.2. Blow out the cobwebs, kind of round. The second round I ran — the girl from Greece ran the race right before me and ran 10.86 — I finished running and the clock said 10.86 and I thought that it was the time from the previous race. I didn't think, you know, they changed the times and when they announced that was my time and I PRed by one tenth of a second, I was surprised. I was flabbergasted but I didn't want to reveal that to anybody because I knew that it was only a second round, and Oh my gosh, if I've PRed this much at this point — [laugh] what's going to happen? I had two more rounds to go.

So, the semifinal came — the next round came — I PRed once again. I ran 10.81. I couldn't believe that. And the final came and I ended up running — well, before that they actually charged me with a false start when they

Inger Miller, 2004.

just started with this electronic false start system. They charged me with a false start, which I know I did not commit because on the board, their machine showed that to my left in lane 2, Christine Arron had false started. But yet, they charged it to me. But that didn't stop me. I still had the fastest reaction time in the final with our race. I ended up second with 10.79, and I think that was fantastic. But, it wasn't over at that point. You know everyone — after you have a really great race — actually I had three races within two days — and it was like, wow! Where do you go from here? And now, it's like you have to run the 200. It's kind of like you go to this high and you get let down and you have to start all over again. It was rough, the couple of days in between trying to get ready for the 200 and really re-grouping myself. I remember running the first round and thinking — oh, my gosh — if it's like this and I'm going to be hurting like this — there's no way. And, you know, I went through the rounds and ran decent times. I remember running like a 22.17 or something, in the second round of semifinals. I was thinking — okay — well, it's there and I think that was in the round where Marion Jones fell out. I was thinking to myself after that — okay — well, I've got a good shot at this and then she fell out and I was upset because this was my time. This was the feeling that if I can win a major championship with Marion Jones in the race then people could stop talking [loud laughter]. I didn't have the chance to do that but the speculation is there that if she had been in the race, in the final, that she would not have won.

So, that is the best 200 meters, the best final, that I've ever run in my life. I mean, I look at that tape over and over again and it was as if, it's weird, it's as if I was running a practice in a sense, it felt so good. When you run and the 200 is controlled — and for me it's weird — I make an analogy between running the 200 and running kind of like in the movie, *Finding Nemo* when they jump in the Gulf Stream and they just kind of ride it. And, that's the kind of way that you have to find the Gulf Stream in the 200. You have to jump on that and once you find that Gulf Stream, it's easy — it's a rhythm that you have and no matter how fast or how slow you run, it doesn't hurt. You don't feel that last 50 meters where you know you just can't run anymore — kind of like the bear on your back kind of thing — you don't feel that. And, that's what it was. It was as if it were a continuous kind of — I could have gone on and on, it felt like. It was fantastic. I don't remember passing anybody but I do remember looking on the straight being by myself and looking, thinking there was someone in lane eight, next to me. I could see the crowd and I'm thinking, oh, gosh, I've got to keep running because there's someone there. No one was there [laughter] and 21.77 to finish was like 21 — what? 21! [laughter].

So — it was unbelievable — that year was unbelievable — it really was. Subsequently, I've been injury-ridden but I don't think there's any way to recapture that year. That's just an individual year and I'm hoping that other years will be like it and will have their own kind of feeling — but, it was fantastic!

20

2000: The Sydney Olympic Year

The Olympic Games were held in Sydney, Australia from September 22 to October 1.

	Event	Place	Performance
Acuff, Amy	HJ	DNQ	5' 10¾"
Aldrich, Erin	HJ	DNQ	6' ¾"
Anderson, Andrea	4 × 400mr	1	3:22.62
Barber, Mikele	4 × 400mr	DNC	
Batten, Kim	400mh	DNQ	55.73
Blutreich, Lynda	JT	DNQ	181' 3"
Bailey, Tonja Buford	400mh	DNQ	57.02
Burrell, Dawn	LJ	11	20' 11¼"
Burrell, Sheila	Heptathlon	26	5345
Chen, Yue Ling	20k walk	38	1:39:36
Clark, Christine	Marathon	19	2:31:35
Clark, Hazel	800m	7	1:58.75
Clark, Jearl Miles	4 × 400mr	1	3:22.62
	800m	DNQ	1:59.44
Clark, Joetta	800m	DNQ	2:04.12
Collins, Michelle	400m	DNQ	53.66
Cross, Jesseca	HT	DNQ	199' 7"
	SP	DNQ	56' 8"
Culpepper, Shayne	1500	DNQ	4:12.52
Damon, Karol	HJ	DNQ	6' 2¼"
Devers, Gail	100mh	DNF	
Dragila, Stacy	PV	1	15' 1"
Drossin, Deena	10,000m	DNQ	34:40.86
Dryer, Elva	5000	DNQ	15:23.99
Edwards, Torri	4 × 100mr	3	42.20
	200m	DNQ	23.06
	100m	DNQ	11.32
Ellerbe, Dawn	HT	7	219' 2"

433

	Event	Place	Performance
Gaines, Chryste	4 × 100mr	3	42.20
	100	DNQ	11.23
Gamble, Nicole	TJ	DNQ	43' 8¾"
Glover, Sandra	400mh	DNQ	54.98
Guidry, Carlette	4 × 100mr	DNC	
Hamilton, Suzy Favor	1500	12	4:23.05
Henderson, Monique	4 × 400mr	DNC	
Hennagan, Monique	4 × 400mr	1	3:22.62
	400m	DNQ	51.85
Hickman, Libbie	10,000m	16	31:56.94
Jewell, Sharon Couch	100mh	DNQ	13.00
Jones, Marion	100m	1	10.75
	200m	1	21.84
	LJ	3	22' 8½"
	4 × 100mr	3	42.20
	4 × 400mr	1	3:22.62
Kuehl, Kris	DT	DNQ	195'
LaBounty, Kelly Blair	Heptathlon	DNC	
Lauck, Anne Marie	5000	DNQ	15:47.78
Lawrence, Debbi	20k walk	44	1:47:20
Miller, Inger	100m	DNC	
	200m		
	4 × 100mr		
Morrison, Melissa	100mh	3	12.76
Mueller, Melissa	PV	DNQ	13' 11¼"
Nathan, DeDee	Heptathlon	9	6150
Palmer, Amy	HT	8	217'
Perry, Nanceen	4 × 100mr	3	42.20
	200m	DNQ	23.16
Powell, Suzy	DT	DNQ	195' 9"
Rhines, Jennifer	10,000m	DNQ	34:08.28
Richardson, LaTasha Colander	4 × 400mr	1	3:22.62
	400m	DNQ	52.07
Richardson, Passion	4 × 100mr	3	42.20
Rohl, Michelle	20k walk	17	1:34:26
Rudolph, Amy	5000m	DNQ	15:28.91
Runyan, Marla	1500m	8	4:08.30
Smith, Connie Price	SP	DNQ	57' 2"
Sua, Seilala	DT	10	196' 4"
Suttle, Kellie	PV	11	13' 1½"
Tunks, Teri	SP	DNQ	53' 7½"
Williams, Shana	LJ	DNQ	21' 1½"

USA Today captured the essence of pre–Olympic stories in Tom Weir's front page story on September 21, 2000, entitled, "All Eyes on Jones."

By now, even casual sports fans know Marion Jones has steadfastly and unabashedly promised the world she will leave Sydney with five gold medals. Should she deliver on her promise, it would be an Olympic record for a female track and field athlete at one Games and such a physical and psychological triumph that perhaps only a handful of other Olympic champions can fully appreciate its difficulty.

...Friday afternoon (Thursday night, ET), the quest begins. Jones will be competing in track and field's shortest, most explosive events, but she must also survive a marathon of 10 races and two rounds of long jumping spread over nine days.

Every time she walks into Olympic Stadium, all eyes and cameras will be focused on the 24-year-old from Apex, N.C. She will be the competitor the rest of the field targets, and at times she might feel her Olympic experience has boiled down to Marion Jones vs. the World."

As the action began, *USA Today* wrote, "...Jones, who won her first-round heat in 10.20 seconds, says she's ready for the 100: 'I think I am in the best shape of my life, and I am at the Olympic Games for the first time. And regardless of the rumors about the wind and the temperature, I think when I step on that track for the 100-meter final and 200-meter final, wonderful things are bound to happen.'"

Marion Jones at the 1999 National Championships.

The Olympic Results

100 meters. *Track & Field News* reported:

...In a no-stress 11.20 heat win, Jones made a definite impression with her smooth, controlled power. In the quarterfinals, she added speed to the power and boomed 10.83 as though to emphasize just who was in total control of the proceedings. Nobody else got under 11-flat.

Marion Jones won her first Olympic 100m crown in 10.75, also the year's fastest time. After a false start by Ekaterina Thanou (GRE), the race got cleanly underway. Tanya Lawrence (JAM) in lane 1, was leading Jones at 20 meters, with the rest of the field marginally behind. As the two raced along evenly to the halfway point, Merlene Ottey (JAM) and Thanou were also running side-by-side a meter back in third. Then in the final 50 meters, Jones drew powerfully away to build a startling four meter gap and stop the clock at 10.75, the year's fastest time.

Torri Edwards placed fifth in a quarterfinal in 11.32 and Chryste Gaines was eliminated in a semifinal finishing fifth in 11.23.

1. Marion Jones	10.75

200 meters. According to *Track & Field News*: The capacity crowd may have been roaring on Cathy Freeman to achieve an impossible double, but once Marion Jones had accelerated smoothly from her blocks, the contest was effectively over. But it was the manner in which she achieved her second gold of these Games in 21.84 that was impressive: already level with Debbie Ferguson in the lane outside her 50m into the race, Jones then accelerated smoothly to lead by three meters coming into the straight. So relaxed were her shoulders and face, that Jones gave the impression that she could have pulled away dramatically. But probably thinking of long jump and relay challenges to come, she just cruised, and still won by 0.37 sec."

The headline in the sports section of the *Poughkeepsie Journal* read, "Jones Glides to Another Gold." The Gannett News Service reported that,

"Marion Jones pulled the entire field of the women's Olympic 200 meters along with her Thursday night, but in the end no one could push the incomparable sprinter.

She ran clear to her second gold medal at the 2000 Summer Games, winning in 21.84 seconds, her fastest time this year. The entire field of eight runners set personal or seasonal bests in a valiant but vain effort to catch the 24-year-old from North Carolina.

Jones won the 100 meters last weekend, and is still on track to capture the five gold medals she set as her goal in Sydney."

Both Torri Edwards and Nanceen Perry were eliminated in semifinal two. Torri was sixth in 23.06 and Nanceen eighth in 23.16.

1. Marion Jones	21.84

400 meters. Michelle Collins was eliminated in the heats in 53.66. Monique Hennagan (51.85) and LaTasha Colander-Richardson (52.07) were eliminated in the quarterfinal round.

800 meters. "...American record holder Jearl Miles-Clark ran well enough but was impeded in the final 150m and ended up 5th in 1:59.44, less than 2m from a spot in the final. 'I'm very disappointed,'" she said, reported *Track & Field News*.

"...Hazel, at 22 the youngest member of the extended Clark clan, had scored a little noted PR and moved to No. 13 on the all-time U.S. list." Hazel was the only American to make the final.

Joetta Clark-Diggs was eliminated in the semis.

7. Hazel Clark	1:58.75

1500 meters. *Track & Field News* reported:

...At 300m, Runyan hopped to the front, and through a 70.56 first lap the field ran two and three lanes across, with only Szabo hanging back. Runyan relinquished the lead to Favor Hamilton just before two-to-go and the pace quickened.

Just before the completion of the second lap in 2:15.93, SFH visibly increased the tempo. As the pack surged to keep up, Tullett was tripped and went down.

...At 900m Sacramento challenged for the lead, but Favor Hamilton fought her off. Szekely was 3rd, well-placed. Up the homestretch, just before the bell, Sacramento took the lead, while Szekely moved to the American's shoulder in 2nd.

...With 250 to go, SFH took the lead back from Sacramento, who began to fade badly in the last 200. If her strength held, Suzy was looking primed for the U.S.'s first-ever Olympic medal at 1500.

Around the curve and into the homestretch, Favor Hamilton was digging deep. With 110m to go a surging M B pulled alongside. Maybe no American gold, but perhaps a medal? Coming off the curve, Favor Hamilton grimaced and her stride tightened. The two Poles eased by, then Szekely, then Dulecha. With about 80m to go, it became a scene from that nightmare where you're running but getting nowhere. Favor Hamilton's body completely shut down, and she fell to the track. Suzy finished 12th.

Marla Runyan finished 7th in 4:08.30. Shane Culpepper (4:12.52) was eliminated in heat three.

7. Marla Runyan	4:08.30
12. Suzy Favor-Hamilton	4:23.05

5000 meters. No American women were in the final. Elva Dryer (15:23.99), Amy Rudolph (15:28.91) and Anne Marie Lauck (15:47.78) were eliminated in the heats.

10,000 meters. The only American in the final was Libbie Hickman, who placed 16th in 31:56.94. Jen Rhines (34:08.28) and Deena Drossin (34:40.86) were eliminated in the heats.

16. Libbie Hickman	31:56.94

Marathon. The U.S.'s only entry, Dr. Christine Clark, finished nineteenth in 2:31:35, a PR and the fastest time of the year by an American.

19. Christine Clark	2:31:35

100 meter hurdles. *Track & Field News* reported, "Gail Devers went to the Sydney Games as, perhaps, as much an outstanding favorite in the sprint hurdles as Marion Jones in the 100m and 200m. With times of 12.33, 12.39 and 12.47 earlier in the season, and no distracting 100m to worry about, it seemed that Devers only had to show up to win the only Olympic gold that had eluded her. But then, after a 12.62 heat — the fastest of the day — Devers flew from the blocks in her semifinal, only to pull up with a hamstring complaint. It was a stunning surprise and threw the whole event wide open." Her heat time of 12.62 was faster than the winning time of 12.65.

"...Morrison was positively ecstatic with her bronze...." continued *Track & Field News*.

Sharon Couch Jewell was sixth in the semis in 13.00 and did not qualify for the quarterfinal round.

3. Melissa Morrison	12.76

400 meter hurdles. "...U.S. fortunes plummeted after reaching promising heights at the trials with Sandra Glover's 53.33 PR win and the return to form of '96 silver medalist Kim Batten and bronze winner Tonja Buford-Bailey," reported *Track & Field News*.

Buford-Bailey (57.02) was fourth in her heat. Kim Batten (55.73) placed sixth in her semifinal and Sandra Glover (55.76) was also sixth in a semifinal in 54.98.

20 kilometer walk. Michelle Rohl led the American women with a seventeenth place finish in 1:34:26. Yue Ling Chen placed thirty-eighth in 1:39:36 and Debbi Lawrence finished forty-fourth in 1:47:20.

17. Michelle Rohl	1:34:26
38. Yue Ling Chen	1:39:36
44. Debbi Lawrence	1:47:20

4 × 100 meter relay. Dave Johnson wrote in *Track & Field News*, "As for the Americans, figure that a relay involves eight critical components: four runners, a start and three passes. Now add up the U.S. performance: two big-name runners missing, a sluggish start, two bad passes. That's tough to overcome — so tough that even Marion Jones couldn't close enough of the ground as the U.S. ran 42.40 for the bronze."

3. United States	42.20
(Chryste Gaines, Torri Edwards, Nanceen Perry, Marion Jones)	

4 × 400 meter relay. Again, from Dave Johnson, "...The U. S. lined up with Miles-Clark — anchor for the last four WC — leading off. She was followed by Monique Hennagan, Jones and trials winner LaTasha Colander-Richardson.

"The idea behind the order-switching clearly was to get the lead on the first leg, hold it on the second, stretch it on the third, and force people to run overly fast on the anchor to close the gap. The strategy worked to perfection."

Marion's ticket on the relay was her one 400 meter race, the winning 49.59 in the Mt. Sac relays at Mount San Antonio College in April. Her third leg split on the relay was 49.40, the fastest of the race.

1. USA	3:22.62
(Jearl Miles-Clark, Monique Hennagan, Marion Jones, LaTasha Colander-Richardson)	

Pole vault. "...After missing her first two attempts at 14' 9", Dragila cleared the bar on her third try," reported Jere Longman in the *New York Times*. "She tends to get stronger the more jumps she takes, and tonight she outlasted Tatyana Grigoryeva, the Australian who moved here from Russia in 1997.... Dragila attempted to surpass her own world record of 15' 2¼", set in July at the United States Olympic trials, but she just nudged the bar off the stanchions on her third attempt at 15' 3". "'The gold medal is beyond any world record,' said Dragila, who lives in Pocatello, Idaho. 'To make history, I don't think there's anything better.... To take up the pole vault seven years ago and to be here with a gold medal tonight is unreal. I just never imagined this when I first went to the pole vault pit and tried it out. I still remember going into the air upside down, thinking to myself, What am I doing?'"

Yue Ling Chen with statue of her at the 1996 Olympic Games.

Kellie Suttle was eleventh with a vault of 13' 1½" and Mel Mueller did not qualify for the final. She cleared 13' 11¼".

This was the first pole vault event for women in Olympic competition.

1. Stacy Dragila	15' 1"
11. Kellie Suttle	13' 1½"

High jump. None of the American women qualified for the final. Karol Damon jumped 6' 2¼", Erin Aldrich 6' ¾" and Amy Acuff cleared 5' 10¾".

Long jump. Jere Longman wrote in the *New York Times*:

Marion Jones stood on the runway, blew air from her cheeks and shook her arms as if she were shivering on this hot, windy night at the Olympics. This was her sixth and final jump. She crouched and swung her arms, and then she leaned back, hopped slightly and began her final urgent sprint toward history.

Her form on the runway was awkward as usual, her strides chopped, her technique unreliable. She looked exactly what she was, a sprinter trying to master the long jump. No other woman possesses her immense speed, however, and when Jones landed with a sandy jolt she was 24 feet from the takeoff board. She had hoped for one big jump and this was it, clearly the longest of the competition. But was it legal?

Jones turned and hoped to see an official waving a white flag, but it was red and she scrunched her face in the smile that comes with incredulous defeat. Half of her foot had been planted beyond the takeoff board and the jump was a foul, her fourth of six attempts. Gone was any chance of becoming the first female track and field athlete to win five gold medals in one Olympics.

Dawn Burrell placed eleventh with a 20' 11¼" jump in the final. Shana Williams jumped 21' 1½" but did not qualify for the final.

3.	Marion Jones	22' 8½"
11.	Dawn Burrell	20' 11¼"

Triple jump. No American qualified for the final.

Nicole Gamble, the only entry for the United States, jumped 43' 8¾" in the qualifying round.

Shot put. None of the three American entries qualified for the final.

Connie Price-Smith put the shot 57' 2", Jesseca Cross 56' 8" and Teri Tunks 53' 7½".

Discus. Seilala Sua tossed the discus 196' 4" for 10th place. The other two American entries, Suzy Powell (195' 9") and Kris Kuehl (195') did not qualify for the final.

10.	Seilala Sua	196' 4"

Hammer. This was the first time that the hammer throw was on the Olympic program. Dawn Ellerbe finished in seventh place with a throw of 219' 2". Behind her in eighth place was Amy Palmer, with a throw of 217'. Jesseca Cross, 199' 7", did not qualify for the final round.

7.	Dawn Ellerbe	219' 2"
8.	Amy Palmer	217'

Stacey Dragila competing at the 2001 National Championships. Photograph by Brian J. Myers, ©www.photorun.net

Javelin. Lynda Blutreich, the U.S.'s only entry, threw 181' 3" and failed to make the final round.

Heptathlon. Track & Field News reported, "...National champ DeDee Nathan sat in 9th after the first day and remained in that slot at the end. And Sheila Burrell, competing with a 'jammed hip and a tweaked ankle,' was doomed to 26th after no-heighting in the high jump."

9.	DeDee Nathan	6150
26.	Sheila Burrell	5345

On Monday, October 2, Jere Longman wrote in the *New York Times*,

...The Games of the XXVII Olympiad closed tonight after 16 days of competition during which the late winter weather cooperated with early spring sunshine, hundreds of thousands of spectators were transported daily with minimal inconvenience and 47,000 volunteers greeted those attending the Olympics with unremitting friendliness and humor.

"I am proud and happy to proclaim that you have presented to the world the best Olympic Games ever," said Juan Antonio Samaranch, who participated in his final Games after 20 years as president of the International Olympic Committee.

The Olympic Trials

The United States Olympic Trials were held at California State University, Sacramento, California from July 14 to 23.

"It's that time of the quadrennium for fickle viewers to regain their interest in track and field after not caring a whit for it outside of Olympic years when track meets fail to attract all the sport's top stars and the few televised events generate low ratings," wrote Richard Sandomir in the *New York Times*. He continues:

"But 57 days before the opening ceremony at the Summer Olympics in Sydney, Australia, the United States track and field Olympic trials are headed into their final weekend in Sacramento, and anybody who wants to make the Olympic team has to show up.... These trials, which will be seen live in the Eastern and Central time zones, offer a schedule viewers can live by, unlike the taped Sydney Games, when events will be seen up to 15 hours after they occur."

---

100 meters

And so it started, Marion's quest for five gold medals. Said the *New York Times*, "It is a long process that will not be resolved for two and a half months, but Marion Jones took her first fleet steps on the long journey toward five gold medals tonight, cruising through the 100-meter preliminaries in 10.92 seconds at the United States Olympic track and field trials.

"Jones left the blocks smoothly with Gail Devers, the two-time Olympic champion at 100 meters, who held the lead for 50 meters. But no one has speed or power to stay with Jones in the second half of a 100-meter race. She reeled Devers in at about 60 meters and crossed the finish line first in 10.88 seconds, the second-fastest time in the world this year. It was especially impressive because she was running into a two-mile-an-hour wind."

1. Marion Jones, Nike Track Club   10.88
2. Inger Miller, Nike Track Club   11.05
3. Chryste Gaines, adidas USA   11.13
4. Torri Edwards, Nike Track Club   11.15
5. Gail Devers, Nike International Track Club   11.15
6. Nanceen Perry, Mizuno Track Club   11.18
7. Carlette Guidry, adidas USA   11.22
8. Passion Richardson, Nike Central Track Club   11.32

200 meters

Jere Longman wrote in the *New York Times*:

...Jones has not lost a race in three years. She got a brilliant start today and led comfortably off the curve. Miller made a charge from lane 7 and closed within a stride, but she could not overtake Jones, who was perhaps fatigued after dominating the 100 (10.88) and the long jump (23½) last weekend. She has put herself in encouraging position to become the first female track and field athlete to challenge for five gold medals in one Olympics.... Not since Carl Lewis in 1984 has an American won three events at the Olympic trials.

...I'm glad it's all over," Jones said Sunday after wining the women's 200 in 21.94 seconds, the fastest time in the world this year and an indication that she is in form to try to become the first female track and field athlete to win five golds in the Olympics.

1. Marion Jones, Nike Track Club   21.94
2. Inger Miller, Nike Track Club   22.09
3. Nanceen Perry, Mizuno Track Club   22.38
4. Torri Edwards, Nike Track Club   22.68
5. LaTasha Colander-Richardson, Nike Track Club   22.76

6. Michelle Collins, Nike Track Club   22.80
7. LaTasha Jenkins, Nike Track Club   22.99
8. Carlette Guidry, adidas USA   23.15

400 meters
1. LaTasha Colander-Richardson, Nike Track Club   49.87
2. Jearl Miles-Clark, Reebok Racing Club   50.23
3. Michelle Collins, Nike Track Club   50.29
4. Monique Hennagan, adidas USA   50.82
5. Mikele Barber, University of South Carolina   51.17
6. Andrea Anderson, unattached   51.32
7. Maicel Malone-Wallace, New Balance Track Club   51.39
8. Monique Henderson, unattached   51.79

800 meters

Prior to the 800 meter final, *USA Today* did a lengthy cover story entitled, "Keeping It All in the Family" about the Clark family. Tom Weir wrote,

...The three running members of Team Clark, who are coached by yet another Clark, seek to make history at the U.S. Olympic track and field trials with a 1-2-3 finish in the women's 800 meters.

Doing so in the final Sunday would make them the first family to sweep an Olympic track event. But the funny part of this potential family reunion at the 2000 Summer Olympics is that, for most of the Clarks, the mere mention of the grueling 800 meters once caused boundless dread and despair. To understand, let's begin with a roll call of the Clarks who will face first round competition Thursday.

The veteran is three-time Olympian Joetta Clark-Diggs, 37, who for 21 consecutive years has been ranked among the top 10 U.S. women in the 800. She's the only Clark who always loved the 800. The coach is J.J. Clark, 35, Joetta's brother and an All-American in middle distances at Villanova. He coaches at the University of Florida. The member by marriage is two-time Olympic medalist Jearl Miles-Clark, 33, J.J.'s wife. She holds the U.S. record in the 800. Hazel, 22, is the younger sister of Joetta and J.J. She was the 1998 NCAA champion in the 800.

The headline on the sports page of the *New York Times* on July 24 read, "Clarks Rule the Women's 800." Jere Longman wrote,

The women's 800 meters produced a rare family affair today at the United States Olympic trials as Hazel Clark finished first in 1 minute 58.97 seconds, her sister-in-law Jearl Miles-Clark took second in 1:59.12 and her half-sister Joetta Clark-Diggs slipped into third by a hundredth of a second in 1:59.49.

...All three members of the Clark family are coached by J.J. Clark, Miles-Clark's husband and the brother of Hazel and Joetta. The family is from Maplewood, N.J., although Clark and Miles-Clark now train in Gainesville, Fla. Clark-Diggs flies down from New Jersey two weeks a month to train with the group.

The family patriarch is Joe Clark, the disciplinarian high school principal depicted in the movie "Lean on Me."

Clark, a former figure skater, took a slight lead on the inside at 400 meters in 58.93. Miles-Clark, a three-time United States outdoor champion at 400 meters and a two-time champion at 800 meters, moved in front down the backstretch and held the margin through 600 meters in 1:29.2. She remained ahead down the homestretch but began tightening up, and Clark passed her.

Clark-Diggs, meanwhile, hung near the rear for 500 meters, then surged to make her fourth Olympic team at age 37, dipping inside of Meredith Rainey-Valmon with her final stride.

1. Hazel Clark, Nike Track Club   1:58.97
2. Jearl Miles-Clark, Reebok Racing Club   1:59.12
3. Joetta Clark-Diggs, Nike Track Club   1:59.49

Jearl Miles-Clark, Hazel Clark, Meredith Rainey-Valmon and Joetta Clark at the finish of the 800 meters race at the 2000 Olympic Trials. Photograph by Lisa Coniglio, ©www.photorun.net

4. Meredith Rainey-Valmon, Reebok Racing Club   1:59.50
5. Amy Ross–Schroer, U.S. Army   2:01.01
6. Mary Jane Harrelson, unattached   2:02.35
7. Elizabeth Diaz, unattached   2:03.44
8. Michelle Ave, Asics Track Club   2:05.62

1500 meters

Again, from Jere Longman in the *New York Times*:

...Regina Jacobs, a two-time silver medalist at the world championships, and Suzy Favor Hamilton, only the second American woman to breach four minutes in the 1,500, will face off Sunday at that distance in the Olympic track and field trials. While championship races are often tactical and slow, Tom Craig, who is Jacobs's coach and husband, believes Mary Slaney's 17-year-old American record of 3 minutes 57.12 seconds could be in jeopardy.

...At the University of Wisconsin, Favor Hamilton won nine collegiate titles. She has made two previous Olympic teams and only Slaney has surpassed her own personal best of 3:58.43 among American women.

...Jacobs will turn 37 before the Sydney Games begin and could be the oldest American to win an Olympic gold medal.... By age 17, Jacobs was participating in the 1980 Olympic trials as an 800-meter runner. But she never won a collegiate title while at Stanford, and it was not until the past three years that her career has reached full flower. In 1993, Jacobs was diagnosed with low levels of iron in her body, accounting for her wildly erratic performances on the track.... [She] has worked hard this season to make her own stride more sound, reaching less with her arms and striking the ground with her feet under her hips for maximum efficiency.

1. Regina Jacobs, Nike Track Club   4:01.01
2. Suzy Favor-Hamilton, Nike Track Club   4:01.81

From left: Jearl Miles-Clark, Hazel Clark and Joetta Clark at the medal presentation for the 800 meter race. Photograph by Victah Sailer, ©www.photorun.net

3. Marla Runyan, Asics Track Club	4:06.44	
4. Shayne Culpepper, adidas USA	4:08.38	
5. Mary Jane Harrelson, unattached	4:08.76	
6. Debbie Grant, New Balance Track Club	4:11.88	
7. Collette Liss, Indiana Invaders Track Club	4:13.45	
8. Karen Candaele, adidas USA	4:14.71	

3000 meter steeplechase (exhibition)

1. Elizabeth Jackson, Brigham Young University	9:57.20	AR
2. Lisa Nye, Nike Track Club	10:00.63	
3. Kara Ormond, Brigham Young University	10:03.09	
4. Courtney Meldrum, Brigham Young University	10:04.41	
5. Tara Haynes, Brigham Young University	10:04.45	
6. Tonya Dodge, Syracuse Chargers	10:13.83	
7. Desiree Owen, Nike Track Club	10:18.85	
8. Emily Mulick, Idaho State University	10:25.79	

5000 meters

USATF issued an Internet release stating, "Jacobs Smashes American Record in 5,000 Meters at Olympic Trials." It continues:

"Regina Jacobs on Friday night broke her own American Record in the 5,000 meters by more than 7 seconds, winning the U.S. Olympic Track & Field Trials in a time of 14 minutes, 45.35 seconds. Her previous record was 14:52.49, set in 1998."

1. Regina Jacobs, Nike Track Club	14:45.35	AR
2. Deena Drossin, Reebok Racing Club	15:11.55	

3. Elva Dryer, Nike Track Club	15:12.07	
4. Amy Rudolph, unattached	15:21.16	
5. Anne Marie Lauck, Nike Track Club	15:23.71	
6. Clare Taylor, Asics Track Club	15:30.44	
7. Shayne Culpepper, adidas USA	15:31.49	
8. Kara Wheeler, University of Colorado	15:34.47	

100 meter hurdles

1. Gail Devers, Nike International Track Club	12.33	AR
2. Melissa Morrison, Reebok Racing Club	12.63	
3. Sharon Jewell, adidas USA	12.69	
4. Ellakisha Williamson, University of South Carolina	12.81	
5. Joanna Hayes, unattached	12.87	
6. Tonya Lawson, Fila Track Club	12.94	
7. Jenny Adams, University of Houston	12.98	
8. Bisa Grant, unattached	13.04	

400 meter hurdles

"In the women's 400-meter hurdles, Glover started in lane 7, not generally a prime lane, but she took control of the race on the final curve. Her winning time was a full two-tenths of a second ahead of the previous world best of 53.53 this year," reported the *New York Times*.

1. Sandra Glover, Nike Track Club	53.33
2. Kim Batten, unattached	54.70
3. Tonja Buford-Bailey, Nike Track Club	54.80
4. Joanna Hayes, unattached	54.97
5. Michelle Johnson, unattached	55.63
6. Yvonne Harrison, Fila Track Club	55.67
7. Nikkie Bouyer, University of Arizona	56.52
8. Trevaia Williams-Davis, unattached	57.02

20 kilometer walk

1. Michelle Rohl, Moving Comfort Racing Team	1:32:39
2. Yue Ling Chen, unattached	1:33:40
3. Debbi Lawrence, Nike Track Club	1:33:48
4. Joanne Dow, adidas USA	1:36:17
5. Sara Stevenson, Olivet Nazarene University	1:37:36
6. Sara Standley, unattached	1:38:38
7. Jill Zenner, Miami Valley Track Club	1:38:54
8. Danielle Kirk, Southern California Walkers	1:40:49

Pole vault

In an article on Stacy Dragila's fear of no-heighting, the *New York Times* reported, "...Today, 20 of the 36 competitors in the women's pole vault failed to clear the opening height of 13 feet 2¼ inches. Dragila, 29, did not suffer the same wrenching disappointment, clearing the bar easily on her first attempt to advance to Sunday's final."

Jere Longman wrote in the *New York Times*: "...Dragila set the only world record at the trials. The woman's pole vault will be contested for the first time at the Olympics in September at the 2000 Summer Games in Sydney, Australia. Dragila, whose previous record was 15' 1¼", will now be the clear favorite for a gold medal. She has actually jumped higher, clearing 15' 5" at a beach competition earlier this season, but the mark was not ratified for a world record because the runway did not meet specifications.

"Dragila, who trains in Pocatello, Idaho, attempted 15' 5" today and nearly cleared it on her second attempt as the bar wobbled and appeared to stay in place before falling into the pit."

1. Stacy Dragila, Reebok Racing Club   15' 2¼"   AR, WR
2. Kellie Suttle, Nike Track Club   14' 6¼"
3. Melissa Mueller, Nike Track Club   14' 2½"
4. Mary Sauer, Asics Track Club   14' 2½"
5. Alexa Harz, unattached   13' 8½"
6. Alicia Warlick, Santa Monica Track Club and
     Tracy O'Hara, University of California at Los Angeles   13' 8½"
8. Melissa Price, Nike Track Club   13' 8½"

10,000 meters

USA Today reported, "If Anne Marie Lauck makes the Olympic team, no one will have run farther to earn a berth. She was third at the marathon trials but missed the team because she didn't have the Olympic qualifying time, fourth in the 10,000 and fifth in the 5,000.

"After 38.6 miles of competition, she could go in the 5,000 if Jacobs chooses the 1,500 and Deena Drossin, the 10,000 champion and 5,000 runner-up, chooses the 10,000 as expected."

1. Deena Drossin, Reebok Racing Club   31:51.05 MR
2. Jen Rhines, adidas USA   31:58.34
3. Libbie Hickman, Nike Track Club   31:58.68
4. Anne Marie Lauck, Nike Track Club   32:01.86
5. Annette Peters, Asics Track Club   32:09.49
6. Sylvia Mosqueda, unattached   32:18.36
7. Blake Russell, New Balance Track Club   32:20.26
8. Kristin Beaney, Reebok Racing Club   32:22.72

High jump

1. Karol Damon, unattached   6' 4"
2. Erin Aldrich, University of Texas, Austin   6' 4"
3. Amy Acuff, New Balance Track Club and   6' 2¾"
    Tisha Waller, Nike Track Club
    (Amy Acuff won jump-off for third place)
5. Angie Spangler, Asics Track Club   6'   ¾"
6. Stacy Ann Grant, unattached   6'   ¾"
7. Lynn Houston, unattached, Jennifer   5' 10¾"
    Engelhardt, University of Notre Dame,
    Gwen Wentland, Nike Track Club

Long jump

The *Poughkeepsie Journal* reported,

...Jones nearly missed out on making the final of the long jump in the U.S. Olympic trials Sunday, then rebounded with some pressure jumps to win the competition. That kept intact her bid to become the first track athlete to win five gold medals in one Olympics.

The 38-year-old Joyner-Kersee, the 1988 Olympic gold medalist and winner of six Olympic medals — more than any female track athlete — failed to make a record-tying fifth Olympic team.

...Jones, after fouling on her first two attempts in the preliminaries, soared 22 feet, 1¾ inches to reach the

Stacey Dragila.

final. After leaping into the lead on her fourth try with a wind-aided 22' 7", then being overtaken by Dawn Burrell at 22' 10" later in round four, Jones responded with the winning jump of 23' 0½", her best in a year.

"I've been waiting for that jump all year," Jones said. "That it came at the Olympic trials is great. I'll be ready for Sydney."

1. Marion Jones, Nike Track Club	23' ½"	
2. Dawn Burrell, U.S. Army	22' 10½"	w
3. Shana Williams, Nike Track Club	22' 6½"	w
4. Meosha Hubbard, Life College	22' 5¼"	w
5. Pam Simpson, unattached	21' 11½"	
6. Jackie Joyner-Kersee, Honda Track Club	21' 10¾"	
7. Adrien Sawyer, Nike Track Club	21' 7½"	
8. Jenny Adams, University of Houston	21' 2½"	

Triple jump
1. Nicole Gamble, Nike Track Club — 45' 9¾"
2. Sheila Hudson, unattached — 45' 8½"
3. Tiombé Hurd, Nike Track Club — 45' 7¾"
4. Stacey Bowers, Nike Track Club — 45' 4½"
5. Natasha Alleyne-Gibson, unattached — 45' 4½"
6. Vanitta Kinard, unattached — 44' 3¼"
7. Shakeema Walker, unattached — 44' 2¾"
8. Deana Simmons, unattached — 43' 4½"

Shot put
1. Connie Price-Smith, Nike Track Club — 61' 1½"
2. Jesseca Cross, New York Athletic Club — 58' 2½"
3. Dawn Dumble, Reebok Racing Club — 57' 1"
4. Teri Tunks, Nike Track Club — 56' 11¼"
5. Cheree Hicks, Syracuse University — 53' 10½"
6. Lisa Griebel, Iowa State University — 53' 5½"
7. Chaniqua Ross, Reebok Racing Club — 53' ¾"
8. Christina Tolson, Reebok Racing Club — 52' 4¾"

Discus
1. Seilala Sua, Reebok Racing Club — 216' 2"
2. Suzy Powell, Asics Track Club — 211' 10"
3. Kristin Kuehl, M-F Athletic — 202' 7"
4. Aretha Hill, Team Qwest — 199' 2"
5. Janet Hill, unattached — 195' 11"
6. Edie Boyer, unattached — 191' 6"
7. Roberta Collins, unattached — 189' 11"
8. Dawn Ellerbe, New York Athletic Club — 183' 7"

Javelin
1. Lynda Blutreich, Nike Track Club — 191' 2"
2. Kim Kreiner, unattached — 187' 2"
3. Emily Carlsten, University of Florida — 186' 11"
4. Kathryn Doyle, Texas A&M University — 179' 5"
5. Candace Mitchell, University of South Carolina — 174' 8"
6. Kathryn Polansky, South Eugene High School — 174' 2"
7. Beth Obruba, unattached — 173' 1"
8. Cassie Morelock, University of Nebraska — 168' 7"

Tiombé Hurd competing at the 2000 Olympic Trials. Photograph by Victah Sailer, ©www.photo run.net

Hammer

The *New York Times* reported, "In another event decided today, Dawn Ellerbe of Brooklyn won the women's hammer throw with a toss of 227 feet. The event will be contested for the first time at the Games in Sydney, and Ellerbe is considered a candidate for the bronze medal."

1. Dawn Ellerbe, New York Athletic Club	227'	MR
2. Amy Palmer, New York Athletic Club	217' 7"	
3. Jesseca Cross, New York Athletic Club	217' 2"	
4. Anna Norgren, SOBE Team Lizard	214' 5"	
5. Bethany Hart, University of Connecticut	204'	
6. Tamika Powell, Reebok Enclave	203' 10"	
7. Leslie Coons, unattached	201' 3"	
8. Maureen Griffin, unattached	201'	

Heptathlon

1. DeDee Nathan, Indiana Invaders Track Club	6343
2. Sheila Burrell, Nike Track Club	6339
3. Kelly Blair-LaBounty, Nike Track Club	6180
4. Tiffany Lott-Hogan, New Balance Track Club	6094
5. Nicole Haynes, unattached	6077
6. Wendi Raatjes, Asics Track Club	6041
7. Tracye Lawyer, Nike Track Club	5844
8. Gigi Miller, University of Arkansas	5607

U.S. Olympic Team Trials (Women's Marathon): Columbia, South Carolina, February 26

Women's Sports & Fitness wrote,

A slight, wavy-haired woman edged toward the starting line at the Olympic marathon trials last February, picking her way unnoticed among the famous Nike-and-Reebok-sponsored runners. She wore a simple black-and–white singlet bearing the name of her own sponsor, the Skinny Raven Sports Store, Anchorage, Alaska. Chris Clark, 37, a pathologist and mother of two, thought to herself that if she was lucky, she might be able to crack the top 10. "I never thought, if I do well, I'll go to Sydney," she says. "That would have been unrealistic."

Clark had flown 3,486 miles from her home in Anchorage to hot, muggy South Carolina to run in the trial, knowing her chances of qualifying were near to zero. Seeded 22nd, she was a virtual unknown next to favorites Libbie Hickman and Kristy Johnston; even Joan Benoit-Samuelson, winner of the first Olympic women's marathon in 1984, was trying to make a comeback.

...In South Carolina, Clark ran with the lead pack for the first 10 miles. Her months of gerbil-wheel monotony training in a heated room began to pay off as other runners wilted in the 80 degree heat. By mile 17, it was down to Clark and two others (the sportscasters asked each other, "Does anyone know anything about a Chris Clark?") Maintaining a brisk 5.51-minute-mile pace, she passes No. 10-ranked Anne Marie Lauck at mile 20. Kristy Johnson managed to overtake Lauck as well but failed to catch Clark. After 2 hours, 33 minutes and 31 seconds, Clark raised her arms in triumph as she crossed the finish line alone.

Experts call it one of the biggest upsets in marathon trials history.

1.	Christine Clark	2:33:31
2.	Kristy Johnston	2:35:36
3.	Anne Marie Lauck	2:36:05
4.	Susannah Beck	2:36:46
5.	Liz Wilson	2:37:27
6.	Ann Schafers-Coles	2:38:47
7.	Kim Pawelek	2:39:16
8.	Libbie Hickman	2:39:57
9.	Joan Benoit-Samuelson	2:39:59
10.	Jennifer Tonkin	2:40:31

The Indoor Nationals

The USA Indoor Track & Field Championships were held in Atlanta, Georgia, March 3–4.

In a tiny article, the *New York Times* reported that, "...Carlette Guidry, a two-time Olympic 400-meter relay gold medalist, took the women's 60 at 7.12, the fastest by an American in 2000."

In the pole vault, Stacy Dragila set a world record of 15' 1¾"; Tisha Waller won her fourth indoor high jump championship, and Connie Price-Smith captured her sixth title in the shot put.

60 meters	
1. Carlette Guidry, adidas USA	7.12
2. Passion Richardson, Nike Track Club	7.20
3. Torri Edwards, Nike Track Club	7.21

200 meters	
1. Nanceen Perry, Mizuno Track Club	22.65
2. Carlette Guidry, adidas USA	22.90
3. LaTasha Jenkins, Nike Track Club	23.28

400 meters
1. Suziann Reid, adidas USA — 52.20
2. Kim Graham, adidas USA — 52.74
3. Shanelle Porter, Team US West — 52.79

800 meters
1. Hazel Clark, Nike Track Club — 2:03.40
2. Michelle Ave, Asics Track Club — 2:05.57
3. Miesha Marzell, Fila Track Club — 2:05.58

Mile
1. Regina Jacobs, New York Athletic Club — 4:25.92
2. Collette Liss, Indiana Invaders Track Club — 4:33.28
3. Mary Jane Harrelson, unattached — 4:34.75

3000 meters
1. Marla Runyan, Asics Track Club — 9:01.29
2. Cheri Kenah, adidas USA — 9:01.66
3. Amy Rudolph, Reebok Racing Club — 9:03.14

60 meter hurdles
1. Melissa Morrison, Reebok Racing Club — 7.86
2. Sharon Jewell, adidas USA — 7.96
3. Miesha McKelvy, unattached — 8.07

Hazel Clark, 2004.

3000 meter race walk
1. Michelle Rohl, Moving Comfort Racing Team — 12:51.17
2. Jill Zenner, Miami Valley Track Club — 13:09.92
3. Debbi Lawrence, unattached — 13:26.06

4 × 400 meter relay
1. University of Nebraska — 3:35.49
2. University of Georgia — 3:39.21
3. University of North Carolina — 3:40.68

High jump
1. Tisha Waller, Nike Track Club — 6' 5"
2. Angela Spangler, Asics Track Club — 6' 2¾"
3. Gwen Wentland, Nike Track Club — 6' 2¾"

Pole vault
1. Stacy Dragila, Reebok Racing Club — 15' 1¾" WR
2. Melissa Mueller, Nike Track Club — 14' 6"
3. Mary Sauer, unattached — 14' 2"

Long jump
1. Adrien Sawyer, Nike Track Club — 21' 5½"
2. Shana Williams, adidas USA — 21'
3. Antoinette Wilks, University of South Carolina — 20' 2½"

Triple jump
1. Tiombé Hurd, Nike Track Club — 46' 1½"
2. Stacey Bowers, unattached — 44' 6"
3. Vanitta Kinard, unattached — 44' ¾"

Shot put
1. Connie Price-Smith, Nike Track Club   61' 4¼"
2. Tressa Thompson, Nike Track Club   60' 1"
3. Jesseca Cross, New York Athletic Club   58' 7¼"

Weight throw
1. Dawn Ellerbe, New York Athletic Club   77' 5¼"
2. Jesseca Cross, New York Athletic Club   69' 8¼"
3. Seilala Sua, University of California, Los Angeles   65' 11½"

40th Los Angeles Invitational (8 women's events): February 19

50 meters
1. Keyon Soley, University of California, Los Angeles   6.37

500 yards
1. Linetta Wilson, South Bay Track Club   1:03.2

800 meters
1. Grazyna Penc, Poland   2:07.21

Mile
1. Mardrea Hyman, Jamaica   4:37.31

50 meter hurdles
1. Bisa Grant, East Oakland Youth Development Center Track Club 7.00

High jump
1. Amy Acuff, New Balance Track Club   5' 10"

Pole vault
1. Mary Sauer, Cornerstone Track Club   14' 2"

Long jump
1. Angela Brown, Met. Rx   19' 9"

This meet celebrated its 40th year with the running of the 2000 games. It was the first meet held indoors on the West Coast. Al Franken, the meet founder, reminisced:

"...The biggest attraction we ever had was Wilma Rudolph. She won three gold medals in the 1960 Olympics in Rome and this was her first meet after that. It sold out days in advance and people broke through the east doors of the Sports Arena to get in, so we had an overcapacity crowd."

Of Rudolph, the Associated Press said, "Everybody was standing and cheering, couldn't wait to see her. She was lovely, glamorous, sort of provided a whole new image for women in sports. She won the 60-yard dash and the crowd went crazy."

During the entire forty years of the meet, only two of the years had as many as eight events for women (1998 and 2000).

World Cross Country Championships: Vilamoura, Portugal, March 18

12. Deena Drossin	26:59	
13. Jennifer Rhines	27:11	

"But the big surprise was that the United States, inspired by great runs from Deena Drossin in 12th and Jennifer Rhines in 13th, took the bronze — their first medal since Boston 1992." The United States finished with 98 points.

This account, and all of the following through the AP Female Athlete of the Year, appeared in *IAAF Magazine — Best of 2000*.

Golden Gala: Rome, Italy, June 30

"Race favorite Marion Jones powered ahead at the 50 meter mark to easily win the 100m. Relatively slow out of the blocks, Jones then steamed past Torri Edwards and Christine Arron. Ideal conditions for sprinting, with 21 degrees Celsius and a legal tailwind of 1.0 mps, combined to help Jones clock 10.91.

"Gail Devers recorded her third fastest time ever in the women's 100m hurdles to win with 12.47. Both Devers and Michelle Freeman (JAM) got away well at the start, but Devers was already pulling away at the third hurdle. Anjanette Kirkland came back strongly in the finish with Olga Shishigina (KZK), who had won the first leg of the Golden League in Paris, but neither could match Devers at the finish."

Exxon Mobil Bislett Games: Oslo, Norway, July 28

"Suzy Favor Hamilton had the Bislett crowd on its feet as she finished the women's 1500m in a new meeting record of 3:57.40, just 23 hundredths off the American record and the fastest time in the world this year by nearly 3 seconds.

"Gail Devers was superb in the women's 100m hurdles. The 33 year old, who had run a personal best of 12.33 at the U.S. Olympic Trials, was a convincing winner in Oslo with 12.56, a new meeting record."

Zurich Weltklasse: Zurich, Switzerland, August 11

"Marion Jones just edged out Inger Miller —10.95 to 10.96 in the 100m and came back to win the long jump as well."

Ivo Van Damme Memorial: Brussels, Belgium, August 25

"Marion Jones won the 100m with the time of 10.83. The bare statistics show it was the second fastest time this season — but it was achieved INTO a 1.3mps breeze. No woman — not even the late Florence Griffith-Joyner — had ever run as fast into such a strong wind. For once Jones had a good start — and from 30m she held a comfortable lead until the finish.

"Gail Devers became the first athlete to be certain of some Golden League gold after a sparkling 12.53 100m hurdles victory. She would have gone faster still but for a 0.8mps headwind."

ISTAF Berlin: Berlin, Germany, September 1

"Marion Jones took the absence of her closest rivals Inger Miller and Zhanna Pintusevich as a spur to run even faster than usual in the 100m. Reacting smoothly to the gun, her powerful acceleration helped her build up a huge lead by the 70m mark. Two meters clear of her closest rival, she crossed the finish line in 10.78, a Stadium record, and achieved with the help of a negligible 0.1 mps tail wind."

IAAF Grand Prix Final: Doha, Qatar, October 5

The final and richest meet of the season saw Gail Devers and Marion Jones win the hurdles and 100 meters respectively, pocketing $50,000 each for their victories. Marion captured the 100 meters in 11.00 with Chryste Gaines second, 11.09 and Torri Edwards in seventh, 11.54.

In the 100 meter hurdles, Gail ran 12.85 for the win followed by Melissa Morrison (13.00) in fourth and Sheila Burrell (13.23) in seventh.

In the Grand Prix standings, Jones was runner-up and won $100,000; Gail was third and won $50,000.

USA Winter Cross Country National Championships: Senior Women's 8K

1. Deena Drossin, Reebok Racing Club
2. Jen Rhines, adidas USA
3. Elva Dryer, Nike Track Club
4. Rachel Sauder, New Balance Track Club
5. Kim Fitchen, Nike Farm Team

IAAF Grand Prix Standings — Overall (in the top 10)

2. Gail Devers
3. Marion Jones

IAAF World Rankings (This is the first ever IAAF ranking)

Top ten in the world
1. Marion Jones
3. Inger Miller
5. Gail Devers

Other News and Honors

Track & Field News: **Athlete of the Year**

Marion Jones

Track & Field News: **U.S. Athlete of the Year**

Marion Jones

IAAF Female Athlete of the Year 2000

Marion Jones

"It was no great surprise when Marion Jones, winner of five Olympic medals, was given her trophy for Female Athlete of the Year by Prince Albert." The presentation was made at the World Athletics Gala 2000 on November 26 at the Salle des Etoiles of Monte-Carlo's Sporting d'Ete.

The Associated Press Female Athlete of the Year

Marion Jones

"...The 24-year-old Jones was the 10th woman track and field athlete to win the honor since the award was inaugurated in 1931, and the first since the late Florence Griffith Joyner in 1988."

Marion was on the cover of many magazines: *Women's Sports and Fitness* (September 2000), *Track & Field News* (December 2000), *Newsweek* (September 11, 2000), *Sports Illustrated* (October 2, 2000), *Sports Illustrated for Women* (September/October 2000) and *Vogue* (January 2001) to name a few. The cover of *Vogue* was the epitome of the woman track athlete. She was in a sequined red gown — obviously off the track — portrayed as the beautiful woman that she is.

The *IAAF News* of July 2000 ran an article entitled, "Jones Gets Total Exposure." According to the piece, Marion Jones's television advertising exposure "could only be described as Jordan-esque in sheer volume," as reported by Brandweek, which has analyzed the magnitude of her commercial presence. Seven different commercials featuring Jones — including a spot for GMC Envoy, three for Nike and an NBC Olympic promo — are all currently running on U.S. television."

Stacy Dragila was one of three women athletes selected to be on a Wheaties cereal box.

Pat Rico's term of office as president of USATF was completed this year.

Aeriwentha Faggs Starr (Mae Faggs), three time Olympian, died of cancer in January. The *IAAF News* reported, "Mae Faggs Starr, an Olympic sprinter and the first renowned athlete of Tennessee State University's 'Tigerbelles,' died January 27 at her home in Woodlawn, Ohio. She was 67. Faggs ran the lead leg on the gold-medal winning 4 × 100 relay at the 1952 Olympics in Helsinki, and was also a member of the bronze-medal winning foursome at the 1956 Games in Melbourne.

"In addition, Faggs captured 11 National AAU titles. She competed at the 1948 Summer Games in London (at age 16, but failed to make the 200m final). She was a 1976 inductee to the U.S. National Track & Field Hall of Fame."

When Mae qualified for the 1948 Olympic Team, she was a member of the New York City Police Athletic League Team.

Joetta Clark Diggs, 37, won the 800 meters in the Millrose Games in February. It was her seventh win in twenty-two years of competing in the meet. She first started competing in the Millrose Games when she was fourteen years old. She retired after this season.

An article in the *New York Times* about Stacy Dragila quotes her as saying, "'Until 1984, they didn't think women could run a marathon in the Olympics. Running that many miles, they thought it might do something inside your body. Pole vaulting was the same way. People used to ask me, 'Aren't you worried it's going to mess up your reproductive organs?' Now they say, 'You go, girl! Don't let anyone tell you no.' We deserve something we're good at. Certainly, as participants, it's nice to see how women can be feminine and strong. We are feminine and strong and confident with our bodies. I'm not going to look like this forever, I might as well show it while I can.'"

Chandra Cheeseborough and Maren Seidler were elected to the National Track & Field Hall of Fame. The following biographies appear on the National Track & Field Hall of Fame website.

CHANDRA CHEESEBOROUGH
Born: January 10, 1959 — Jacksonville, Florida

Events
200 m — 21.99
400 m — 49.05

Although only 16 years old, Chandra Cheeseborough broke onto the international track scene in spectacular fashion by winning two gold medals at the 1975 Pan American Games, taking the 200m in an American record time of 22.77. Earlier that year, the Jacksonville native had attended a summer track program at Tennessee State University and benefited from the tutelage of Hall of Fame coach Ed Temple. In 1976, she set an American junior record of 11.13 in winning the 100 meters at the national championships, then placed sixth in that event at the Montreal Olympics. After high school, she attended Tennessee State, where she was a member of national championship teams that set world indoor records of 1:08.9 in the 640-yard relay and 1:47.17 in the 800-yard sprint medley relay. She won the national indoor 200-yard dash in 1979, 1981, 1982 and 1983. Her breakthrough year in the 400m came in 1984, when she set two American records in the event, then placed second in the Los Angeles Olympics in a career best of 49.04. She made history at the 1984 Games when she became the first woman to win gold medals in both relays, held less than an hour apart. Cheeseborough later became a coach and returned to Tennessee State. She was named head coach of both men and women in 1999, following in Temple's footsteps. She also has served as an assistant coach for the U.S. team at the 1999 Junior Pan Am Championships.

Records Held
World Record: 640 yd. relay — 1:08.90
American Record: 200 m — 22.77

Championships
1976 Olympics: 100 m (6th)
1984 Olympics: 400 m — 49.04 (2nd)
1984 Olympics: 400 m relay (1st)
1984 Olympics: 1,600 m relay (1st)
1976 National Championships: 100 m — 11.13 (1st)
1979 National Indoor Championships: 200 yd. (1st)
1981 National Indoor Champs: 200 yd. (1st)
1982 National Indoor Champs: 200 yd. (1st)
1983 National Indoor Champs: 200 yd. (1st)
1975 Pan Am Games: 200 m — 22.77 (1st)

Education
high school: Jacksonville (Jacksonville, Florida), 1974
undergraduate: Tennessee State (Nashville, Tennessee), 1978

Occupations
Coach

MAREN SEIDLER
Born: June 11, 1951— Brooklyn, New York

Events
Shot Put — 19.09 m

For a period of 13 years, Maren Seidler totally dominated shot putting in the U.S. She won 23 national titles from 1967 to 1980, including a record-setting nine consecutive outdoor titles. Seidler was a member of four Olympic teams (1968, 1972, 1976 and 1980). She was also a member of three Pan American teams (1967, 1975 and 1979) and placed second in 1979. In all, she competed on 20 international teams. A graduate of Tufts University, Seidler was the first American woman to throw the shot more than 60 feet. In all, she broke the American shot put record 16 times, indoors and outdoors, and raised the outdoor record from 54' 9" to 62' 7¾". She was ranked first in the U.S. 11 times.

Records Held
American Record: Shot Put—19.09 m (June 15, 1979–   )

Championships
1968 Olympics: Shot Put (11th)
1976 Olympics: Shot Put (12th)

Education
undergraduate: Tufts (Medford, Massachusetts), 1973

World Indoor Records (held by American women as of March 6, 2000)

Pole vault	Stacy Dragila	15' 1¾"	March 3, 2000

American Indoor Records (February 2000)

50 yards		
Evelyn Ashford	5.74	2/14/83
50 meters		
Gail Devers	6.02	2/21/99
60 yards		
Evelyn Ashford	6.54	2/26/82
Jeanette Bolden	6.54	2/21/86
55 meters		
Gwen Torrence	6.56	3/14/87
60 meters		
Gail Devers	6.95	3/12/93
Marion Jones	6.95	3/9/98
200 meters		
Gwen Torrence	22.33	3/2/96
220 yards		
Valerie Brisco-Hooks	22.95	2/22/85
300 yards		
Angela Thacker	33.46	2/8/86
300 meters		
Alice Jackson	37.30	2/2/86
400 meters		
Diane Dixon	50.64	3/10/91
440 yards		
Diane Dixon	52.20	2/22/85
500 yards		
Jearl Miles-Clark	1:00.61	2/19/00

500 meters
Joetta Clark   1:09.75   3/2/85

600 yards
Delisa Walton-Floyd   1:17.38   3/13/82

600 meters
Delisa Walton-Floyd   1:26.56   3/14/81

800 meters
Mary Slaney   1:58.9ht   2/22/80
Suzy Hamilton   1:58.92   2/7/99

880 yards
Mary Slaney   1:59.7   2/22/80

1000 yards
Joetta Clark   2:23.5   3/9/86

1000 meters
Regina Jacobs   2:35.29   2/6/00

1500 meters
Mary Slaney   4:00.8   2/8/80

Mile
Mary Slaney   4:20.5   2/19/82

2000 meters
Mary Slaney   5:34.52   1/18/85

3000 meters
Regina Jacobs   8:39.14   3/7/99

Two miles
Lynn Jennings   9:28.15   2/28/86

Three miles
Margaret Groos   14:58.3   2/20/81

5000 meters
Lynn Jennings   15:22.64   1/7/90

50 yard hurdles
Deby LaPlante   6.37   2/10/78

50 meter hurdles
Jackie Joyner-Kersee   6.67   2/10/95

60 yard hurdles
Stephanie Hightower   7.36   2/25/83

55 meter hurdles
Tiffany Lott   7.30   2/20/97

60 meter hurdles
Jackie Joyner-Kersee   7.81   2/5/89

High jump
Tisha Waller   6' 7"   2/28/98

Pole vault
Stacy Dragila   15' 1½"   2/19/00

Long jump
Jackie Joyner-Kersee   23' 4¾"   3/8/94

Triple jump
Sheila Hudson   46' 8¼"   3/4/95

Shot put
Ramona Pagel   65' ¾"   2/20/87

20 pound weight throw
Dawn Ellerbe   75' 10"   2/4/2000

800 meter relay
National Team   1:33.24   2/12/94

880 yard relay
Morgan State University   1:36.8   3/7/81

880 yard medley relay
Colorado Gold   1:41.9   3/19/72

4 × 400 meter relay
National Team   3:27.59   3/7/99

Mile relay
Morgan State University   3:39.58   3/12/83

3200 meter relay
Villanova University   8:25.5   2/7/87

Two mile relay
National Team   8:42.0   3/17/72

Sprint medley relay
National Team   3:45.90   3/14/93

Distance medley relay
Villanova University   10:54.34   1/30/88

1500 meter walk
Debbi Lawrence   5:53.41   1/15/93

Mile walk
Debbi Lawrence   6:18.03   2/9/92

3000 meter walk
Debbi Lawrence   12:20.79   3/12/93

Pentathlon
DeDee Nathan   4753   3/5/99

World Records (held by American women as of December 2000)

100 meters	Florence Griffith-Joyner	10.49	July 16, 1988
200 meters	Florence Griffith-Joyner	21.34	Sept. 29, 1988
400 meter hurdles	Kim Batten	52.61	Aug. 11, 1995

Pole vault	Stacy Dragila	15' 2¼"	July 23, 2000
Heptathlon	Jackie Joyner-Kersee	7291	Sept. 23/24, 1988
	4 × 200 meter relay	1:27.46	April 29, 2000

(LaTasha Jenkins, LaTasha Colander-Richardson, Nanceen Perry, Marion Jones)

American Records

100 meters	10.49	Florence Griffith-Joyner
200 meters	21.34	Florence Griffith-Joyner
400 meters	48.83	Valerie Brisco-Hooks
800 meters	1:56.40	Jearl Miles-Clark
1000 meters	2:31.80	Regina Jacobs
1500 meters	3:57.12	Mary Slaney
Mile	4:16.71	Mary Slaney
2000 meters	5:32.7	Mary Slaney
3000 meters	8:25.83	Mary Slaney
3000 meter steeplechase	9:57.20	Elizabeth Jackson
5000 meters	14:45.35	Regina Jacobs
10,000 meters	31:19.89	Lynn Jennings
Marathon	2:21:21	Joan Benoit-Samuelson
100 meter hurdles	12.33	Gail Devers
400 meter hurdles	52.61	Kim Batten
4 × 100 meter relay	41.47	National Team

   (Chryste Gaines, Marion Jones, Inger Miller, Gail Devers)

4 × 200 meter relay	1:27.46	United States

   (LaTasha Jenkins, LaTasha Colander-Richardson, Nanceen Perry, Marion Jones)

4 × 400 meter relay	3:15.51	1988 Olympic Team

   (Denean Howard, Diane Dixon, Valerie Brisco, Florence Griffith-Joyner)

4 × 800 meter relay	8:19.9	National Team

   (Robin Campbell, Joetta Clark, Chris Gregorek, Essie Kelley)

Sprint medley relay	1:36.79	Wilt's Athletic Club

   (Brenda Morehead, Jeanette Bolden, Alice Brown, Arlise Emerson)

Distance medley relay	10:48.38	Villanova University

   (Kathy Franey, Michelle Bennett, Celeste Halliday, Vicki Huber)

5 kilometer walk	20:56.88	Michelle Rohl
10 kilometer walk	44:41.87	Michelle Rohl
20 kilometer walk	1:33:17	Michelle Rohl
High jump	6' 8"	Louise Ritter
Pole vault	15' 2¼"	Stacy Dragila
Long jump	24' 7"	Jackie Joyner-Kersee
Triple jump	47' 3½"	Sheila Hudson
Shot put	66' 2½"	Ramona Pagel
Discus	216' 10"	Carol Cady
Hammer throw	231' 2"	Dawn Ellerbe
Javelin (new)	188' 5"	Lynda Blutreich
Javelin (old)	227' 5"	Kate Schmidt
Heptathlon	7291	Jackie Joyner-Kersee

INTERVIEW: AMY ACUFF

(February 28, 2004) The first time I ever stepped foot on a track, I was five years old. I was tagging along to one of my brother's numerous sporting competitions. This was the first time that I was on a track and about halfway through the meet they had a special race. The announcer came on and invited all of the younger brothers and sisters to come out for a race — and it was a 400 meter race [laughter]. And so I came down and ran the race and got a pink ribbon. I can't remember what place it was but I was just so happy to get a pink ribbon. After that, I just felt really — I felt the urge to be involved and to do things. I didn't want to be a spectator. Everything that he was doing, I wanted to do after that point.

The next year, I was old enough at six to join the regular program. It was AAU summer track and they have a bantam age group, ten and under — so being six — which is really a lot younger than even the youngest group — it was so much fun — we'd go around to different meets, hop on a big yel-

Amy Acuff, 2004.

low bus and drive to these small cities in Texas and everyone had a track, it was an all-weather track. Texas has really good facilities. I was running the 100 meters, the 200 meters and I started doing the long jump. I was pretty proficient at the long jump. By the time I was ten, I had the bantam national record [laughter] and that was fourteen feet one inch and I still remember the number. It was just a great experience. I mean, I remember those long hot summers in Texas. We would go out and train at noon and it was just the perfect thing to get rid of that excess energy, because I would come back home and be so relaxed and just so tired. I would get a slurpy after practice [laughter], a big sugar ice drink, which is horrible to think of now, and I would do that after every practice, but it did taste really good. I would be at home and I'd just lie on the couch and drink that thing after practice and I really looked forward to going every day.

It was like a sense of freedom and exploring what my body could do — and so, I mean, it continued on — my career, and in junior high — in 7th grade — you start school track. That was a different experience. You are allowed to do five events and they would always encourage me to do the full five events to get more points for the team.

And that's how I started high jumping. In the first year, I'd say it was very awkward and a little bit scary to high jump. You have that triangular metal bar that you'd land on and sometimes the pits wouldn't be very big. At one point, I landed on the edge of the pit and landed on my head [laughter]. No harm done but it was scary and it hurt. I started high school and by my third year of high jumping, I jumped 6 feet. It was really a rapid improvement and seemed to be a natural thing for my body type and my physical ability. I got invited that year, my freshman year of high school, to come in the summer time to the Olympic training center. That's where I met Sue Humphrey and some of the development people. Sue Humphrey is going to be the Olympic coach in 2004. She lives in Austin and helped to guide me. There's a lot of education that has to happen at that age about what to expect and what to gear your goals towards — and things about nutrition, routine — things I hadn't really thought of— so, that was a great resource — to meet her and then to have her available to ask questions from that point on.

So, I finished out my high school season and I had jumped the high school national record my junior year. I made it to the Olympic trials. I had the third best jump going in and I just bombed. I no-heighted at the trials in '92. I felt really disappointed because there was no meet that I would jump under 6 feet in — in a whole year. I just really kind of got my head screwed on wrong about it. I decided I was going to do two a day jumping for the month before the trials, so I had all these aches and pains. I decided that I was going to switch from a single arm take off because that's what people told me — coaches would say, "Oh, you can't jump high with a single arm, you have to do a double arm."

"So, that month before I was going to switch it up — just making drastic changes and over training — I no-heighted at the meet. It was actually probably for the best. I don't know how I would have handled going to the Olympic Games as a sixteen-year-old. It was probably a blessing that I didn't make that Olympic team. Then I graduated and went to my first meet over in Europe. I had a great meet. I jumped a new high school record at 6' 4" and all the top girls were there, the people who had just come from the world championships. The three medalists were there. It was bad weather and raining but I felt really encouraged to jump that mark. The meet was in Innsbruck, Austria, a little tiny ski town up in the mountains.

After that I went to college. I really loved my time at UCLA. It just seemed like a big play fest out in the sun, staying at practice every day. I studied hard but I looked forward to coming to practice: taking a break from studying and the daily grind. I just felt so lucky to be outside, just the energy of having so many great athletes on one track. I never had a problem being excited or adrenalized about practice. Sometimes when you are alone out there and training, it can get difficult to be motivated or have the same intensity, but everyday at the track felt like a really special day. My sophomore year I jumped a collegiate record indoors and outdoors. I won some NCAA championships — five of them, including two indoors.

In '96 I made the Olympic team. That was a really neat experience because my best friend and roommate throughout college, Suzy Powell, a discus thrower, also made the Olympic team in '96, and it was just so cool because we had so much in common and we could go through this experience together. To have your best friend on the team, rooming together in close proximity, it was really fun. I was a little bit injured; it was a long collegiate season to try to do indoors, outdoors, do all those meets that are required, then go to the Olympic Games all the way at the end of the summer. So, it wasn't a great performance but that's the good thing about being young — you have more chances.

I got another chance in 2000. I just was so ecstatic to make the team, so relieved, because I had been in an auto accident the month before — on Olympic Boulevard in Los Angeles. Acupuncture saved me [laughter]. There was really no way I could have jumped without getting acupuncture. I was afraid I needed surgery, and I was not going to be on the team but I was training and hoping to make up that time in the months between the trials and the Olympic Games. Then, you know, it didn't quite work out again. Now I have my third chance coming up. I have so much more experience and knowledge under my belt that I really know how to approach things. It's just amazing how far the management of my health has come — my diet, being aware of my injuries and being preventative in my approach, going to the chiropractor on a regular basis, getting acupuncture treatment on a regular basis really helps a lot. I haven't had any injuries for several years now. Probably 2000, that car accident, was the last time I had an injury. I feel pretty good about things. My plan for this year is to really stay calm and control my environment, my emotions and not get caught up emotionally in everything and to really stay grounded. It's really easy to get carried away with all the hype of the Olympics, but the thing that I've noticed is that the more I stay calm and keep my stresses to a minimum, the better my body responds to things. I can train harder, more often. It doesn't take such a chunk out of me to go to a meet and put a lot of mental energy into it when I'm grounded like that. Sometimes, when there's a really stressful meet and you put a lot of emotion into it, you have a time when you come down from it and it can be hard to get up for the next meet if you have the next weekend in Europe. It seems like I'm managing that pretty well where I stay on a pretty even keel and I'm trying not to let my stresses deplete my body unduly.

INTERVIEW: JENNY ADAMS

(February 26, 2004) My love for track and field was first developed when I watched the 1988 Olympics. I remember watching Flo Jo compete for the United States and Carl Lewis too. I was really fascinated with Flo Jo because she was the first female athlete I had ever seen on television. That really stands out for me. I remember watching her compete and win and she just had so much energy and personal power. She, to me, personified just an independent, powerful woman and it was just exhilarating to watch her compete. I remember telling myself that that's exactly what I want to do; that is, I want to be like her. I wanted to represent the United States one day in the Olympics.

At that time, I expressed my feelings to my parents, who were very supportive. My dad actually built me a long jump pit in the back yard. It wasn't a big contraption. He just tilled up some dirt and he nailed a piece of wood down for the board. My brothers and I would just run on the grass and we would long jump against each other and measure our jumps. We just had a blast with it. The kids in the neighborhood would come over and we would have our little mini track meets. We also had some old mattresses and my dad actually created a standard so we set up a high jump pit with standards and a pole vault — and we would just race each other, too, without anything — we just loved sprinting. This was all in Tomball,

Jenny Adams, 2004.

Texas. It's not the suburbs and it's not quite the country, but it's a pretty rural area about an hour outside of Houston. Anyone that was close enough to ride their bikes to our house, we had them come down and have this awesome track meet whenever we could.

The long jump is just an event I always did. I started in seventh grade. I wasn't one of those kids who was put in summer camp. We just did our own sports in our backyards. So, I never ran summer track as a child. I didn't start track until I was in seventh grade. I long jumped and ran the 100 and 200.

When I was about a sophomore in high school and I was still running the 1 and the 2, I wasn't getting out of our regionals. I was fast. I was the fastest girl in our district, the fastest girl in my school, but I wasn't fast enough at our regionals to qualify for state and I knew, at the time, that my ultimate goal was to go to state — the Texas state track meet. So, my coach and I talked about it and we decided that it would be a good idea for me to learn how to hurdle and if I could use my speed and get some good technique with that, I would be a pretty decent hurdler. And that's kind of where the transition came. It's like, I felt that in order for me to be successful, I needed to find another event that maybe suited me a little better. It was hard because I loved being a sprinter. I still consider myself a sprinter, but I am so happy that I made that change because I know I wouldn't be anywhere near where I am today if I were still just trying to run the 100.

My favorite moment in my career is definitely just winning my high school state championship in Texas because I didn't qualify for states until I was a senior and then I went and won two events. And so, that was just such an emotional moment for me. I had jumped about from the time I was in seventh grade — so, it was like a six year journey till where I finally got it. So it was great.

In college, it was my ultimate goal going in as a freshman to be an NCAA champion in either the hurdles or long jump. I qualified in NCs as a freshman, but it wasn't until my senior year that I finally won the NCAA championships in the long jump. That was just an amazing moment. It was like a four year journey. It took me four years. And now I feel like I'm on that same path. It's like 2000, I went to the trials — made it to the finals but I wasn't in the top three — and I've been training for four years for this 2004 opportunity.

Basically, it's been a goal and a dream my entire life; every day, I've thought about it. A day hasn't gone by without me thinking about my goals for track and field. I guess it just started out as a dream to be an Olympian and I just really believed in myself, and worked hard and tried to make good decisions and focus in on what I needed to do in track in order to get better and to compete. I loved it, I had passion for it and now the dream has turned into a real goal — something that I feel is right around the corner.

So, that's pretty much how it started for me. I hope that young girls can see me as an example like Flo Jo was to me and they can learn that if you just really believe in yourself, find your passion, that there is absolutely no limit.

INTERVIEW: HAZEL CLARK

(February 26, 2004) First I was a figure skater and dancer. I wanted to skate. I didn't think that running was as glamorous as what I wanted to do. I got really tall and I had a very bad fall and I scarred my chin and had to get stitches. I kind of quit after that and realized that it wasn't good for me.

My dad had me in an all girls private school and there was no track team. So, he just told me to try to run, you don't have to do it. He put me in his Cadillac and drove me to the track meet and said, "You're a Clark, just go for it and you're going to win."

I went out really hard, as hard as I could, and I died. I didn't win and I said, "I hate this—this is not fun." So, I didn't do it any more that year.

The next year he transferred me to a public school where my sister and brother went to school. I went with their high school coach. So, I didn't start running until very late. A lot of people don't know that. I didn't start running until my junior year of high school. I just took off from there. I really enjoyed it. I was successful at it. It was pretty natural for me. It was a lot of fun. So, I went forth from there.

I went to the University of Florida with J.J. and I just kept developing. I was lucky to have two great coaches. I only had two coaches and they both have been really good.

After college, I went with Nike. I won nationals and I was pretty successful. Then I went to the Olympic trials. Going into the Olympic trials, a lot of people made comments like, you know, it would be good if you could go with your sister and sister-in-law to the Olympics. It kind of made me feel bad because I felt people always overlooked me. It was kind of that little sister syndrome where I was good but they kind of always underestimated me. That really motivated me to have a great year. I focused in and really wanted to prove people wrong—like I'm not the weakest link in the family. I mean, I'm very talented and I can make this team. I just had a quiet confidence and drive about me that year. I ended up winning the whole thing, which really shocked me. I really was just trying to get a spot on the team. The next thing you know, like, I'm in front. Am I winning? It was great that I won and definitely a highlight and it was also great, of course, that my sister and sister-in-law made it. It wouldn't have been the same if it wasn't the Clark

Hazel Clark, 2004.

team. That was just so special. No matter what happens, if I get injured or I was never able to run again, I have that to take with me. It was just the most special Olympic experience. It just felt good to do that as a family and see the pride of my dad and mom. It was just overwhelming.

Actually, that would be the highlight because then, unfortunately, after that I got injured really badly. It was a down time for me for two years. I broke my foot and gained a lot of weight. It was pretty depressing. I was upset because I just felt like it was the beginning of my career and for that to happen was hard. But I'm coming back this year. I think it's made me a lot stronger person. It's really motivated me to just kind of get my position back as one of the best. I know I can do it. I just have to think positively. Last year I had no confidence and this year I feel that confidence coming back. Then, it's once again having my sister and sister-in-law behind me. They have such encouraging things to say. Having the family I have, I think it helps to come back.

They always tease me about my Olympic experiences. I was making friends with everybody from every country. It's funny, because I ended up getting a terrible rash and their favorite joke was that it came from hugging and touching too many people in the village. I mean, I was just everywhere. I loved going to the crocodile hunter and I did everything I could do. I just met so many people. I love people anyway. I did a lot of interviews. It was quite a lot of fun. I remember after my final round, I was really proud of myself for making the final as a first time Olympian and PRed my whole way through. It was pretty hard and afterwards, I remember, I went out, I partied. I met people. I went sightseeing. I was so drained. I was so sick on the plane home. I could barely walk and Jearl was giving me tissues. I was coughing and sneezing. But I had the best experience. Then, when I got back to my house it was just the weirdest feeling — yeah, just like I dropped. I kind of felt so down because I was just so used to being in that whole village experience. I don't think I've ever had a time like that. Like I said, to be able to take my mom around and sightsee with her. I'll never forget, I had her seat moved closer to the track. She said she could not see in the first round. I remember the final. I heard her — "Peachy, go, Peachy." I couldn't believe I heard my mom in the Olympic stadium. She just kept calling my name and, hey, — enough, but to see the look on her face even though I got seventh. She understood the magnitude of what that was for me and how hard I worked to get there. It just meant so much. You'd have thought I won the gold medal to see her face.

That year was great. It was special. It was me working hard and believing in myself. Our family, all three of us, trained together and we worked hard and we motivated each other. We will always have these days to talk about — all the experiences that we shared together. My sister and I always blab about how they used to room us together all the time. We're twenty years different in age: why are you doing that? But, we had fun. We laughed in the rooms and joked. Joetta would spy on me from her room in the house and we laughed about that. She always had her eye on me. It was great.

PROFILE: TIOMBÉ J. HURD

(Information provided by Tiombé J. Hurd) I started running in recreational programs when I was a kid growing up in Seattle. My mother and father broke up when I was young and my mother moved to the east coast. I would take turns spending time with both of my parents. I went to elementary school in Seattle. Then I moved east and went to junior high and high school in Virginia. While in Seattle, I also took a liking to volleyball and played that as well. I really enjoyed the game. When I moved to Virginia I would always take part in the sporting challenges at school and enjoyed "field day" a lot. Once I entered high school, I wanted to join the volleyball team but my high school didn't have a team. I didn't bother to inquire about any other sports. I was quite happy just dressing up in cute clothes and being around boys.

During my sophomore year of high school, my World Cultures teacher (who was also the girl's head track coach), Don Beeby, asked me to try out for the team because I had long legs. It took a little convincing but I eventually joined the team. Beeby coached the distance runners so I had a different personal coach that worked with the sprinters and jumpers, Inez Bryant. That year they taught me how to triple jump. But in high school it's all about scoring points so it was normal for athletes to do four or five events. So, my main events ended up being the triple jump and 400 meters, but I also had to compete in the long jump, 4 × 100 and 4 × 400. My high school highlights include being the Virginia State champion in the triple jump and runner-up in the 400m.

Tiombé Hurd, 2005.

Although recruited mainly for the 400m, I didn't visit many colleges. I earned an academic scholarship and decided to go to James Madison University. JMU is in Harrisonburg, Virginia — just far enough to get away from home, but close enough that I could drive home when I wanted to. I joined the track team there. My coaches were surprised when I qualified for the NCAA Championships in the triple jump my freshman year. They asked me to take track & field seriously and offered me an athletic scholarship my second year. I had to turn away my academic scholarship in order to accept the offer because in those days NCAA rules didn't allow athletes to have any extra income coming in. Triple jump became my main focus and I only ran the relays or other events when needed.

My biggest memories from college include the NCAA Indoor Championships in 1993. I not only made the final but I won the bronze medal as well. In 1995 I got fourth at the NCAA Outdoor Championships, but it was my first time jumping over 44 feet, so I was excited. That year I was honored as JMU's Co-Athlete of the Year.

I graduated in three and a half years and earned a bachelor's degree in Hotel-Restaurant Management in December of 1994. I started graduate classes at JMU but I still had athletic eligibility to compete in the spring of 1995. When I left JMU, I transferred my credit to Howard University so I could be closer to home and finished my MBA work there. I competed during this time but not at a high level because of my hectic schedule.

I started working for Hyatt Hotels in 1997. While at Hyatt I worked nine hours a day and then trained at George Mason University at night. It was tiring but I soon learned how to work efficiently so I could handle a huge training workload in the three hours a day I had at GMU. I was coaching myself because I thought it would be too much to ask someone to stay and train with me until 9:30 at night every day. In 1998, GMU hired a new assistant men's coach, Robby Farias, and someone told him that I was coaching myself. We were introduced, we got along and started working together in the fall of 1998. In the spring of 1999 I jumped 14 meters for the first time. Fourteen meters is the benchmark that all female triple jumpers try to reach when they first start competing internationally.

In 2000, I earned my first U.S. title in winning the U.S. Indoor Championships in Atlanta with another 14 meter jump. That was a really exciting moment for me because I didn't expect to jump so well indoors. I thought I would be well on my way to making the Olympic team that summer. Unfortunately, I ended up third at the Olympic Trials and missed the Olympic qualifier by four inches. It was very depressing for me watching the Olympic Games on TV. A friend from another country even sent me a postcard from Sydney to tell me to keep my head up. I was depressed, and then I got angry and very determined. That fall I trained harder than I ever had and was in great shape going into the 2001 season.

In 2001, I was undefeated amongst Americans and won both the U.S. indoor and outdoor championships. I was jumping 14 meters on a consistent basis and made my first world championship team. I was invited to the Indoor World Championships in Lisbon, Portugal. I was an underdog because most of the people there had jumped further than me. But I was in good shape, I had a personal best performance, and won the bronze medal — the first time that an American woman ever won a medal in the triple jump at a major championship. That was my biggest achievement to date. The only downfall was that I missed the American indoor record by $1\frac{1}{2}$ inches. But I was still ecstatic.

That same year, my coach retired from athletics and moved back to his hometown in Texas. I started coaching myself again. However, I incurred slight injuries in 2002 and 2003 so I competed sparingly and those ended up being down years for me. I instead worked a lot of hours at the Hyatt. After the U.S. indoor championships in 2003 when I tore my hamstring, I had a long talk with my father and told him that I wanted to start training full-time. I thought the only way I would be able to make the 2004 Olympic team was if I became a full-time athlete. I needed to rehab my leg and I wouldn't be able to do it properly if I was working nine hours a day. My dad gave me his full support and told me that I would have to prepare a budget for myself. I had just bought a house nine months earlier and I had a lot of bills to pay. Three weeks later, I resigned from Hyatt Hotels.

Luckily, I qualified for the Olympic Job Opportunities Program (OJOP). OJOP allows U.S. athletes to work at Home Depot part-time while they train and compete but earn full-time pay and benefits. The program allows me the flexibility I need to get in quality training. I can even train twice a day when I need to so I can get in more training. I spend some time coaching myself at GMU as well as getting help from an English coach, Aston Moore. I travel to England every few months and stay six to eight weeks to get specialized attention. OJOP allows me the flexibility to travel and then return to work when I'm in the States.

The past two years have been an amazing transformation for me. Since I only work part-time now, I'm able to focus all of my efforts on training. I also have more hours in the day to put towards massage, physiotherapy appointments, resting, and eating healthy. When I was working full-time I was on the go a lot, ate fast food all the time, and didn't get much sleep. Those were not good conditions for someone trying to be an elite athlete. Now I can prepare nutritious meals at home and I have shed the excess pounds I was carrying. Being lighter helps me be a better jumper. Overall, because I am training full-time all aspects of my training are better; I'm faster, stronger and technically sound.

Last year was my first year completing a full year of training as a full-time athlete. It was a special year for me. I returned to being undefeated amongst Americans, I won both the U.S. indoor championships and the Olympic trials. At the trials I broke the American record and became only the second American woman to jump over 47 feet. I didn't perform well in Athens because I had trouble with my runway approach. However, I felt very good and wasn't nervous or intimidated. I felt physically able to do a personal best.

I am excited about competing this year. I hope to carry the momentum from last year and continue improving. I will have a short indoor season. My main focus is the outdoor season and I am looking forward to going to the world championships in Helsinki, Finland. I am hoping to become the first American woman to officially jump over 48 feet and then keep improving after that.

Interview: Kellie Suttle

(February 24, 2005) I started track and field when I was a sophomore in Francis Howell High School after I had quit gymnastics. I had done gymnastics at Olympiad Old Town for ten years and I decided to switch to something else. I started long jumping and sprinting in high school in St. Louis, Missouri. I always watched the pole vault and joked with my high school coaches, Jim Clark and Steve Miller, "Oh, I want to pole vault," but it just wasn't an option.

I went to Florissant Valley Junior College and Norris Stevenson was my coach. I did track in college also at Arkansas State University in Jonesboro, Arkansas. Coach Flannagen and Coach St. John were my coaches. While I was in college, I coached at a place called Allison's Gymnastics and the pole vaulters from the Bell Athletics Training Center at Arkansas State University used to come to the gym and I would help them out with things pertaining to gymnastics.

In 1995, Earl was looking to coach a female who had a long jumping, sprinting and gymnastics background and I just kinda filled the bill so to speak, you know. Jeff Hartwig was the one that recruited me. Earl didn't know me but he was just asking if anyone fit the criteria and Jeff said, "Hey, I know somebody right now who would be a good candidate." There was no question. I'm pretty much a daredevil. I'll try pretty much anything once so when Jeff approached me and asked if I wanted to come and do it, I said, "Sure." So, I went out there and I remember waiting for the guys to finish pole vaulting.

Kellie Suttle, 2005.

Then Earl introduced himself and he had me do a couple of things to see if I was strong enough even to pole vault. He's like, "Let's see if you can support yourself holding from a rope." Next thing you know, I'm pole vaulting.

I had my first competition two weeks after I started pole vaulting and I went to my first U.S. championships three weeks after I started pole vaulting. Due to injuries, I didn't pole vault again until three weeks before the outdoor U.S. championships and the same thing happened again. I went to my first outdoor championships in Sacramento.

In '96, I became a full time pole vaulter and decided that with Emma George pushing the world record all the time and with the Olympics being in Australia, there was really a good shot that the women's pole vault was going to be ratified as an official event for the 2000 Olympics.

In '97 the women were in their first indoor world championships. In '98 I jumped my first 14 footer to win my first U.S. title outdoors and made my first Goodwill Games team. I went to the Goodwill Games in Long Island, New York. '99 was the first outdoor world championship team for women, I believe, and I made that team.

In 2000 I made the first women's Olympic pole vault team. So, I went to the Olympics in 2000. It was me, Stacy Dragila and Mel Mueller representing the first U.S. women's pole vault team. It was a really great experience. I made the finals. I placed eleventh. Not exactly the best meet of my life but a really wonderful experience.

In 2001 I came back and decided to train for another four years. I thought I'd be done after making one Olympic team but I'm a sucker for punishment so I came back for four more years. In 2001 I made the indoor world championship team in Lisbon and then I got the silver medal. I think I jumped 4.50 to get the silver medal and then I became the second woman in U.S. history to jump 15 feet at the Drake Relays. It was my fifth consecutive win at the Drake Relays — then Modesto Relays my PR 15' 1" — that was a career highlight.

I went to my first Grand Prix final in 2001. After 2001 I had knee surgery and kind of never really bounced back until 2003. I felt like I was back to normal again and had some good competitions. I was in Birmingham that year and got fourth in the world championships.

I upped my PR last year to 15' 4" and then got third at the Olympic trials again and made the Olympic team in 2004 in Athens, Greece. Because of an injury I kind of restricted my success; I pulled my groin two weeks before the Olympic Games. So, it was kind of a struggle to show up and be relatively healthy, but those are my career highlights, I believe.

I've trained from the beginning to end with Earl Bell at Bell Athletics and with my teammate Jeff Hartwig. It's just been a really good opportunity. It was kind of a transitional period in my life. I'd just graduated from college and I really wasn't 100% sure exactly what avenue I wanted to take and then I started to venture out and try pole vaulting. It kind of, I don't know, it kind of just fit me. I guess it was an event just made for me. I've seen many girls come and go through the sport and I've just been really blessed to be able to keep up with it.

I've been able to travel the world — make a really good living — have a sponsor who's been really loyal to me since '98 and I don't know; from here on I'm just going to take it year by year and I'm not going to commit to another four years. Just take it year by year and if I'm competitive and healthy and enjoying it and another four years pop up then I'll compete in another Olympic trials — which I hate [laughter].

But, it's been a really good sport. It's been interesting to be a pioneer of something. It's been around for a while in the masters program but I think the first U.S. championships for women were in Knoxville, Tennessee in '94.

I've met a lot of great friends. I've had a lot of good experiences and I don't think any other opportunity at this time in my life would present what this opportunity does. It's been a really great experience and it still is — so I just hope for more to come — so, we'll see.

Halls of Fame

National Track and Field Hall of Fame Enshrinees

1981–2000

1981	Willye White
1983	Mildred McDaniel Singleton
1984	Madeline Manning Mims
1987	Martha Watson
1988	Barbara Ferrell Edmonson
	Evelyne Hall Adams
1989	Nell Jackson
	Ed Temple (Coach)
1990	Doris Brown Heritage
1991	Roxanne Andersen
1993	Jean Shiley Newhouse
1994	Lillian Copeland
	Kate Schmidt
1995	Valerie Brisco
	Florence Griffith Joyner
	Louise Ritter
1996	Cleve Abbott (Coach)
1997	Evelyn Ashford
1998	Francie Larrieu Smith
2000	Chandra Cheeseborough
	Maren Seidler

National Women's Hall of Fame

1993	Helen Stephens
1994	Wilma Rudolph

International Women's Sports Hall of Fame

1981	Wyomia Tyus
1983	Helen Stephens
1987	Madeline Manning Mims
1988	Willye White
1990	Nell Jackson (Coach Category)
1991	Alice Coachman Davis
1995	Barbara Jacket (Coach Category)
1996	Mae Faggs Starr
1997	Evelyn Ashford
1998	Florence Griffith Joyner
1999	Joan Benoit Samuelson

U.S. Olympic Hall of Fame

1983	Babe Didrikson
	Wilma Rudolph
1985	Wyomia Tyus

National Track and Field Hall of Fame
Historical Research Library

The National Track and Field Hall of Fame and the National Track and Field Hall of Fame Historical Research Library moved from Indianapolis, Indiana to the Amateur Athletic Foundation in Los Angeles, California. It is known as the National Track and Field Research Collection and is this country's most extensive, publicly accessible collection devoted to all aspects of track and field.

The National Track and Field Hall of Fame is located at the Armory Track and Field Center in New York City.

Awards

C. C. Jackson Awards

Two awards are presented each year in memory of C.C. Jackson, an early promoter of women's track and field.

	Track	Field
	Track	*Field*
1981	Evelyn Ashford	Pam Spencer
1982	Mary Decker	Coleen Sommer
1983	Mary Decker	Louise Ritter
1984	Valerie Brisco–Hooks	Jackie Joyner
1985	Mary Decker-Slaney	Jackie Joyner
1986	Evelyn Ashford	Jackie Joyner-Kersee
1987	Florence Griffith-Joyner	Jackie Joyner-Kersee
1988	Florence Griffith-Joyner	Jackie Joyner-Kersee
1989	Sandra Patrick-Farmer	Jan Wohlschlag
1990	PattiSue Plumer	Sheila Hudson
1991	Gwen Torrence	Jackie Joyner-Kersee
1992	Lynn Jennings/Gail Devers	Jackie Joyner-Kersee
1993	Gail Devers	Jackie Joyner-Kersee
1994	Gwen Torrence	Jackie Joyner-Kersee
1995	Kim Batten	Connie Price-Smith
1996	Gail Devers	Jackie Joyner-Kersee
1997	Marion Jones	Amy Acuff
1998	Marion Jones	Tisha Waller
1999	Marion Jones	Stacy Dragila
2000	Marion Jones	Stacy Dragila

Joseph Robichaux Award

This award is given to people who have made outstanding contributions to the women's track and field program in the United States.

1981	Bob Seaman
1982	Dr. Evie Dennis

1983	Doris Brown Heritage
1984	Dr. John Davis, Jr.
1985	Patricia Rico
1986	Jack Griffin
1987	Brooks Johnson
1988	Dr. Bert Lyle
1989	Fred Thompson
1990	Terry Crawford
1991	Sue Humphrey
1992	Barbara Jacket
1993	Teri Jordan
1994	Fred Wilt
1995	Karen Dennis and Jim Bibbs
1996	Martha Watson
1997	Rita Somerlot
1998	Martha Watson
1999	Dee Jensen
2000	Dee Jensen

Team Championship Award

1981	Tennessee State University
1982	Tennessee State University
1983	Athletics West
1984	Atoms Track Club
1985	Atoms Track Club
1986	Atoms Track Club
1987	Atoms Track Club
1988	Athletics West
1989	Athletics West
1990	Nike International
1991	Mazda Track Club
1992	Mazda Track Club
1993	Seton Hall University
1994	Reebok Running Club
1995	Reebok Racing Club
1996	Reebok Racing Club

Jesse Owens Award

The Jesse Owens Award was established in 1981. It is the highest accolade given by USA Track and Field and is presented to the individuals voted to be the outstanding performers for that year.

1983	Mary Decker
1984	Joan Benoit
1986	Jackie Joyner-Kersee
1987	Jackie Joyner-Kersee

1988	Florence Griffith-Joyner
1990	Lynn Jennings
1993	Gail Devers
1996	Gail Devers
1997	Marion Jones
1998	Marion Jones
1999	Inger Miller
2000	Stacy Dragila

Runner-of-the Year

Presented to the outstanding long distance runner of the year

1981	Joan Benoit
1983	Joan Benoit
1984	Joan Benoit
1985	Joan Benoit and Lisa Larsen Weidenbach
1986	Marty Cooksey
1987	Lynn Jennings
1988	Francie Larrieu-Smith
1989	Lisa Weidenbach
1990	Lynn Jennings
1991	Lynn Jennings
1992	Lynn Jennings
1993	Lynn Jennings
1994	Anne Marie Letko
1995	Olga Appell
1996	Anne Marie Lauck
1997	Libbie Hickman
1998	Libbie Hickman
1999	Libbie Hickman
2000	Christine Clark

Sullivan Award

An award given to honor America's top amateur athlete

1982	Mary Decker
1985	Joan Benoit-Samuelson
1986	Jackie Joyner-Kersee
1988	Florence Griffith-Joyner

Olympic Gold Medalists, 1984–2000

1984

Evelyn Ashford	100 meters
	400-meter relay
Joan Benoit	Marathon
Jeanette Bolden	400-meter relay
Valerie Brisco–Hooks	200 meters
	400 meters
	1600-meter relay
Alice Brown	400-meter relay
Chandra Cheeseborough	400-meter relay
	1600-meter relay
Diane Dixon	1600-meter relay
Benita Fitzgerald-Brown	100-meter hurdles
Denean Howard	1600-meter relay
Sherri Howard	1600-meter relay
Lillie Leatherwood	1600-meter relay

1988

Evelyn Ashford	400-meter relay
Alice Brown	400-meter relay
Sheila Echols	400-meter relay
Florence Griffith Joyner	100 meters
	200 meters
	400-meter relay
Jackie Joyner-Kersee	Long jump
	Heptathlon
Louise Ritter	High jump
Dannette Young	400-meter relay

1992

Evelyn Ashford	400-meter relay
Gail Devers	100 meters

472

Michelle Finn	400-meter relay
Carlette Guidry	400-meter relay
Esther Jones	400-meter relay
Jackie Joyner-Kersee	Heptathlon
Gwen Torrence	200 meters
	400-meter relay

1996
Gail Devers	100 meters
	400-meter relay
Chryste Gaines	400-meter relay
Kim Graham	1600-meter relay
Carlette Guidry	400-meter relay
Maicel Malone	1600-meter relay
Jearl Miles	1600-meter relay
Inger Miller	400-meter relay
Rochelle Stevens	1600-meter relay
Gwen Torrence	400-meter relay
Linetta Wilson	1600-meter relay

2000
Andrea Anderson	1600-meter relay
Jearl Miles Clark	1600-meter relay
Stacy Dragila	Pole vault
Monique Hennagan	1600-meter relay
Marion Jones	100 meters
	200 meters
	1600-meter relay
LaTasha Colander Richardson	1600-meter relay

Two Olympic Gold Medals
Alice Brown
Chandra Cheeseborough
Carlette Guidry
Jearl Miles Clark

Three Olympic Gold Medals
Valerie Brisco
Florence Griffith Joyner
Jackie Joyner Kersee
Gail Devers
Gwen Torrence
Marion Jones

Four Olympic Gold Medals
Evelyn Ashford

Marathon Winners

Boston Marathon

1981	Allison Roe	2:26:46
1982	Charlotte Teske	2:29:33
1983	Joan Benoit	2:22:43
1984	Lorraine Moller	2:29:28
1985	Lisa Larsen Weidenbach	2:34:06
1986	Ingrid Kristiansen	2:24:55
1987	Rosa Mota	2:25:21
1988	Rosa Mota	2:24:30
1989	Ingrid Kristiansen	2:24:33
1990	Rosa Mota	2:25:24
1991	Wanda Panfil	2:24:18
1992	Olga Markova	2:23:43
1993	Olga Markova	2:25:27
1994	Uta Pippig	2:21:45
1995	Uta Pippig	2:25:11
1996	Uta Pippig	2:27:12
1997	Fatuma Roba	2:26:23
1998	Fatuma Roba	2:23:21
1999	Fatuma Roba	2:23:25
2000	Catherine Ndereba	2:26:11

New York Marathon

			(Number of Women Participants)
1981	Allison Roe	2:25:29	(1,757)
1982	Grete Waitz	2:27:14	(1,899)
1983	Grete Waitz	2:27:00	(2,205)
1984	Grete Waitz	2:29:30	(2,395)
1985	Grete Waitz	2:28:34	(2,478)
1986	Grete Waitz	2:28:06	(3,323)
1987	Pricilla Welch	2:30:17	(3,689)

1988	Grete Waitz	2:28:06	(3,974)
1989	Ingrid Kristiansen	2:25:30	(4,688)
1990	Wanda Panfil	2:30:45	(4,500)
1991	Liz McColgan	2:27:32	(5,204)
1992	Lisa Ondieki	2:24:40	(5,441)
1993	Uta Pippig	2:26:24	(5,816)
1994	Tegla Loroupe	2:27:37	(6,977)
1995	Tegla Loroupe	2:28:06	(6,470)
1996	Anuta Catuna	2:28:18	(7,433)
1997	Franziska Roachat-Moser	2:28:43	(8413)
1998	Franca Fiacconi	2:25:17	(8952)
1999	Adriana Fernandez	2:25:17	(9160)
2000	Ludmila Petrova	2:25:45	(8332)

New York Mini Marathon

1981	Grete Waitz	32:44
1982	Grete Waitz	32:00
1983	Anne Audain	32:23
1984	Grete Waitz	31:53
1985	Francie Larrieu Smith	32:23
1986	Ingrid Kristiansen	31:45
1987	Lisa Martin	32:49
1988	Ingrid Kristiansen	31:31
1989	Lynn Williams	32:09
1990	Judi St. Hilaire	32:36
1991	Delilliah Asiago	32:24
1992	Liz McColgan	31:41
1993	Tegla Loroupe	32:30
1994	Anne Marie Letko	31:52
1995	Delilliah Asiago	31:22
1996	Tegla Loroupe	32:13
1997	Tegla Loroupe	31:45
1998	Kim Griffin	35:26
1999	Tegla Loroupe	31:48
2000	Tegla Loroupe	31:37

Bibliography

Chapter 1   (1981)

Amdur, Neil. "Coghlan Wins 3-Mile Run in 2nd Fastest Indoor Time." *New York Times*, February 28, 1981: 15, 16.

_____. "Miss Ashford, Sanford Take 100-Meter Sprints at Festival." *New York Times*, July 26, 1981: S1, 4.

Burns, John F. "Boycott Aura Persists in U.S.-Soviet Track." *New York Times*, July 10, 1981: 10, 16.

_____. "Soviet Union Tops U.S. Track Team." *New York Times*, July 12, 1981: 1, 6.

_____. "Women Give Soviet an Edge." *New York Times*, July 11, 1981: 19, 21.

"Coe and Moses Win in World Cup Track." *New York Times*, September 5, 1981: P13.

Connolly, Pat. *Coaching Evelyn*. New York: Harper Collins, 1991.

Davis, Scott S., ed. *American Athletics Annual*, 1982.

Litsky, Frank. "Amid Achievements, Maree Misses a Goal." *New York Times*, June 23, 1981: A22.

_____. "Fields Hits Detour in Comeback." *New York Times*, June 20, 1981: 16.

_____. "Injuries Don't Stop Joni Huntley." *New York Times*, February 27, 1981: A18.

_____. "Lewis Adding to Track and Field Laurels." *New York Times*, June 22, 1981: C6.

_____. "Lewis Takes Titles in Jump, 100 Meters." *New York Times*, June 21, 1981: 1, 7.

"News." The Athletics Congress of the USA, July 1981.

"News." The Athletics Congress of the USA, August 1981: 10–17.

Reel, Vince, ed. *Women's Track World*, January 1981.

_____. *Women's Track World*, June 1981.

_____. *Women's Track & Field World*, March 1982.

"Scott Takes Aim at Title in National 1,500 Meters." *New York Times*, June 19, 1981: A18.

"Summaries of Bislett Games." *New York Times*, June 28, 1981: S8.

"2 Sprint Races Won by Evelyn Ashford." *New York Times*, September 6, 1981: S3.

Chapter 2   (1982)

"Athletics for Women." *International Amateur Athletic Federation Official Handbook* 1982. London: International Amateur Athletic Federation, 1982: 7.

Davis, Scott S., ed. *American Athletics Annual, 1983*.

Litsky, Frank. "Lewis Repeats Double." *New York Times*, June 20, 1982: 1, 9.

_____. "Olson, Ripley Set U.S. Vault Mark." *New York Times*, June 21, 1982: C3.

_____. "Soviet Men, Women Rout U.S. in Track." *New York Times*, July 4, 1982: S3. "Mary Decker Sets Two Marks in Race." *New York Times*, February 7, 1982: S10.

"Mary Decker Tabb Lowers Mile Mark." *New York Times*, February 20, 1982: 17.

"Mrs. Tabb Sets World Mile Mark of 4: 18.08." *New York Times*, July 10, 1982: 31.

"News." The Athletics Congress of the USA, August 1982.

"News." The Athletics Congress of the USA, January 1983.

"Porter Is Surprise Cross-Country Victor." *New York Times*, November 29, 1982: C4.

Reel, Vince, ed. *Women's Track & Field World*. Vol. 15, No. 6, August 1982.

_____. *Women's Track & Field World*. Vol. 15. No. 7, September 1982.

Wallace, William N. "Hurdle Duel Spices National Title Meet." *New York Times*, February 26, 1982: B8.

_____. "Miss Ashford Captures 60-Yard Dash Title at Garden." *New York Times*, February 27, 1982: 17, 19.

_____. "Miss Cheeseborough's Night." *New York Times*, February 28, 1982: S3.

Weiss, Martin, ed. *USA/Mobil Indoor Track and Field Championships Official Program*. February 25, 1983.

Chapter 3   (1983)

Amdur, Neil. "Lewis Captures 2 Events." *New York Times*, February 26, 1983: 13, 15.

_____. "Lewis Takes World 100 Title." *New York Times*, August 9, 1983: B7, B9.

_____. "Lewis Wins 2nd and 3rd Gold Medals at Helsinki." *New York Times*, August 11, 1983: B9, B11.

_____. "Mrs. Waitz Takes World Marathon Title." *New York Times*, August 8, 1983: C1, C6.

_____. "Top Marathoners Ready in Helsinki." *New York Times*, August 7, 1983: S3.

_____. "U.S. Athletes Stand Out in World Track Events." *New York Times*, August 15, 1983: A1, C8.

Connolly, Pat. *Coaching Evelyn*. New York: Harper-Collins, 1991.

Davis, Scott S., ed. *American Athletics Annual 1983*.

_____. *American Athletics Annual 1984*.

"Female Runners File Suit." *New York Times*, August 12, 1983: A15, A19.

"Lewis Gains in 3 Events." *New York Times*, June 18, 1983: 14.

Litsky, Frank. "Americans Lead East Germans in Track." *New York Times*, June 26, 1983: S1, 9.

_____. "Lewis Wins Jump in 28–10 1/4." *New York Times*, June 20, 1983: C1, 5.

_____. "Lewis Wins U.S. 100 for 3rd Year in Row." *New York Times*, June 19, 1983: S3.

_____. "Smith and Miss Ashford Set World Records in 100." *New York Times*, July 4, 1983: 31, 33.

"News." The Athletics Congress of the USA, July 15, 1983.

"News." The Athletics Congress of the USA, July 1983.

"News." The Athletics Congress of the USA, September 1983.

"News." The Athletics Congress of the USA, November 1983.

Reel, Vince, ed. *Women's Track & Field World*. Vol. 16, No. 4, April 1983: 2.

_____. *Women's Track & Field World*. Vol. 15, No. 8, August/September 1983: 12.

Shah, Diane K. "The Grueling Road of Evelyn Ashford." *New York Times*, February 23, 1983: B7, 8.

"U.S. Falters in Track, Boxing." *New York Times*, August 25, 1983: B13.

"U.S. Wins 400 Run, Sweeps Basketball." *New York Times*, August 28, 1983: S10.

"U.S. Wins More Gold." *New York Times*, August 29, 1983: C5.

Weiss, Marty, ed. *The Athletics Congress of the USA — USA/Mobil Indoor Track and Field Championships Program*, February 25, 1983.

Chapter 4　　(1984)

Alfano, Peter." At 31, Francie Larrieu Still Pushes On." *New York Times*, June 21, 1984: B13, 16.

_____. "Kim Gallagher Runs with Goal." *New York Times*, June 25, 1984: C7.

_____. "Real Gold Isn't in the Medal." *New York Times*, June 23, 1984: 31, 33.

"Ashford Lowers Mark in 100." *New York Times*, August 23, 1984: B15.

Bateman, Hal, ed. *American Athletics Annual 1985*.

Benoit, Joan. *Running Tide*. New York, New York: Alfred A. Knopf, 1987.

"Final Grand Prix Standings." *New York Times*, February 26, 1984: S4.

Gaddie, Mary T., ed. *"Games of the XXIIIrd Olympiad Los Angeles 1984 Commemorative Book."* International Sport Publications, 1984.

Hendershott, Jon. *Track's Greatest Women*. Los Altos: Tafnews Press, 1987.

Hugman, Barry J. and Peter Arnold. *The Olympic Games*. New York, New York: Facts On File, 1988.

Katz, Michael. "Dennis Lewis Wins High Jump." *New York Times*, February 25, 1984: 19.

Litsky, Frank. "Bell Sets U. S. Mark in Vault." *New York Times*, June 10, 1984: S3.

_____. Brisco-Hooks and Coe Win." *New York Times*, August 12, 1984: S1, 4.

_____. "Decker Falls in 3,000 Race, Won by a Rumanian." *New York Times*, August 11, 1984: 1, 16.

_____. "Lewis in Olympics After Winning 100." *New York Times*, June 18, 1984: C1, 6.

_____. "Lewis Wins Long Jump for 2nd Gold of Games." *New York Times*, August 7, 1983: A1, A19.

_____. "Lewis Wins 200, His 4th Berth." *New York Times*, June 22, 1984: A19, 21

_____. "Miss Decker Triumphs at 3,000 Meters." *New York Times*, June 24, 1984: S1, 10.

_____. "Miss Decker Upset in 1500." *New York Times*, June 25, 1984: C1, 7.

_____. "Moses, Lewis Gain in Trials." *New York Times*, June 17, 1984: S3

_____. "Moses Wins Easily at Trials." *New York Times*, June 19, 1984: A25.

_____. "Thompson Wins His 2d Olympic Decathlon." *New York Times*, August 10, 1984: A1, A17.

_____. "Unfinished Business Begins." *New York Times*, June 16, 1984: 44.

_____. "U.S. Record Set by Jones at Trials." *New York Times*, June 20, 1984: B7, 11.

_____. "U.S. Track Team May Be Best Ever." *New York Times*, June 26, 1984: A20.

Moore, Kenny. "The Way It Must Be." *Sports Illustrated*, July 18, 1984: 42–69.

Reel, Vince, ed. "Another AR for Frederick." *Women's Track & Field World*, Vol. 17, No. 11, November 1984: 2.

_____. "TAC Championships." *Women's Track & Field World*, Vol. 17, No. 3, March 1984.

_____. "The Olympics." *Women's Track & Field World*, Vol. 17, No 9, September 1984: 3–11.

_____. "The Trials." *Women's Track & Field World*. Vol. 17, No 8, August 1984.

_____. "Track Wrap-Up." *Women's Track & Field World*, Vol. 17, No. 10, October 1984: 6–9.

Schaap, Dick. *"The 1984 Olympic Games."* New York, New York: Random House.

"USA/Mobil Outdoor Track & Field Championships." The Athletics Congress, July 10, 1984.

"United States Olympic Track and Field Trials." The Athletics Congress of the USA, July 25, 1984.

Vecsey, George. "Carol Lewis, Herself." *New York Times*, February 24, 1984: A19.

_____. "Moses and Ashford Join the Gold Medal List." *New York Times*, C1, C12, C13.

_____. "The Women's Olympics." *New York Times*, August 4, 1984: 15.

Wolff, Ted. "A Record Breaking Year." *16th Edition Vitalis/U.S. Olympic Invitational Program*, February 9, 1985.

"Women's 10,000 Added for '88." *New York Times*, July 27, 1984: A18.

Chapter 5   (1985)

Bateman, Hal, ed. *American Athletics Annual 1986*.

Dupont, Kevin. "Decker, in a Comeback, Breaks 2,000-Meter Mark." *New York Times*, January 19, 1985: 27.

Holt, John B. "Top Ten." *IAAF Magazine*, Issue No. 1 Jan/Feb 1986.

Janofsky, Michael. "Dixon Betters 440-Yard Mark Twice." *New York Times*, February 23, 1985: 19, 20.

Korytko, Paul, ed. "IVth World Cup." *1985 IAAF & International Competition Summary,* 121–128.

Litsky, Frank." Banks Triple Jumps to World Record." *New York Times*, June 17, 1985: C2, 10.

_____. "Little Urge to Compete." *New York Times*, June 15, 1985: 20, 21.

"News." The Athletics Congress of the USA, February 4, 1985.

"News." The Athletics Congress of the USA, December 1, 1985.

"News." The Athletics Congress of the USA, December 11, 1985

Reel, Vince, ed. "Championships." *Women's Track & Field World*, Vol. 18, No. 4, April 1985: 4, 16.

_____. "Reel Off." *Women's Track & Field World*, Vol. 18, No. 5, May 1985: 2.

Chapter 6   (1986)

Bastian, Ken. *Moscow '86 Goodwill Games.* Atlanta, Georgia: The Publishing Group and Turner Broadcasting System, 1986.

Bateman, Hal, ed. *American Athletics Annual 1987*.

"Bubka, At 19–5 3/4 , Defeats Olsen." *New York Times*, February 22, 1986: 43, 45.

Eskenazi, Gerald. "O'Sullivan Zeros In on Speed." *New York Times*, February 28, 1986: A23.

_____. "Bubka Achieves Another Best." *New York Times*, March 1, 1986: 47, 49.

Litsky, Frank. "Lewis Fails to Win 3d Title." *New York Times*, June 22, 1986: 6, 8.

_____. "Lewis Victorious in Two Events." *New York Times*, June 21, 1986: 47, 48.

_____. "Maturity Rewarded in Outdoor Track." *New York Times*, June 23, 1986: C9.

_____. "Olson Hits 19–5 3/4 for Vault Best." *New York Times*, February 9, 1986: S1, 6.

"100-Meter Dash to Ashford." *New York Times*, July 7, 1986: C7.

Rhoden, William C. "Houston Buoyed by Sports Festival." *New York Times*, August 5, 1986: A20.

Wigley, Jon and Paul Fraser, ed. *International Amateur Athletic Federation Magazine*, Issue No. 10, Nov.-Dec. 1986: 13, 21.

Chapter 7   (1987)

Bateman, Hal, ed., *American Athletics Annual 1988*.

Cava, Pete, ed. "Past World Indoor Championship Results." *USA Track & Field Indoor Handbook*, 1998: 60.

Eskenazi, Gerald. "Joyner Looks Up to His Little Sister." *New York Times*, February 26, 1987: B9, 13.

_____. "World Records Set in Long Jump and Triple Jump." *New York Times*, February 28, 1987: 51, 53.

Fraser, Paul and Jon Wigley, ed. *International Amateur Athletic Federation Magazine*, Vol. 11 No. 2 1987: 5, 18, 30.

Janofsky, Michael. "In Track, Roads Lead to Rome." *New York Times*, June 24, 1987: D31.

_____. "Joyner-Kersee at Record Pace." *New York Times*, September 1, 1987: A19, A20.

_____. "Joyner-Kersee First, But Misses Record." *New York Times*, June 25, 1987: D24.

_____. "Joyner-Kersee Ties World Record." *New York Times*, August 14, 1987: B11, 14.

_____. "Lewis Lengthens Long-Jump Streak." *New York Times*, June 27, 1987: 47, 51.

_____. "Long Jump Victory to Joyner-Kersee." *New York Times*, September 5, 1987: 43, 45.

_____. "Louganis Springs to Third Gold." *New York Times*, August 11, 1987: A21.

_____. "Moses Shows He's Still No. 1." *New York Times*, June 28, 1987: 4S.

_____. "Pan Am Games Begin." *New York Times*, August 9, 1987: 1, 5.

_____. "Unexpected Guests Fill Pan Am Rooms." *New York Times*, August 8, 1987: 45.

Litsky, Frank. "First World Meet for Indoor Track." *New York Times*, March 6, 1987: D19.

Nelson, Bert. ed. "World Champs Team Selected." *Track & Field News,* August 1987: 4–29.

Sexton, Joe. "Old Van Cortlandt Yields U.S. Titles." *New York Times*, November 29, 1987: S7.

Vecsey, George. "Record Attempt Blown Away." *New York Times*, August 17, 1987: C6.

Weiss, Marty, ed. *The Athletics Congress of the USA — USA/Mobil Indoor Track & Field Championships Program*, February 26, 1988.

Chapter 8   (1988)

Alfano, Peter. "Top Woman Climbs Higher." *New York Times*, September 25, 1988: S1, 2.

Bateman, Hal, ed. *American Athletics Annual 1989*.

Burfoot, Amby, Linda Villarosa, Bob Wischnia, Katy Williams. "Thrills, Chills and Spills." *Runner's World*, October, 1988: 74–96.

Denman, Elliott. *Anthology of the Olympic Games —*

Melbourne (1956) to Sydney (2000). Self published. West Long Branch, NJ.

Hollobaugh, Jeff. "Women's Trials." *Track & Field News*, June 1988: 6.

Janofsky, Michael. "Griffith Joyner Takes The 200." *New York Times*, July 24, 1988: S1, 6.

_____. "Joyner-Kersee Tops Herself, Again." *New York Times*, July 17, 1988: S6.

Litsky, Frank. "Cooper Emerging as a Threat in 100." *New York Times*, June 18, 1988: 49, 46.

_____. "Discus Throwers Fall Short on Youth." *New York Times*, June 17, 1988: B11.

_____. "Huber Has Eyes on Olympic Games." *New York Times*, June 19, 1988: S5, 9.

_____. "Pride and Frustration for the Americans." *New York Times*, October 2, 1988: S5.

_____. "Questions Abound Before Trials Start." *New York Times*, June 20, 1988.

_____. "Solid Lead in Heptathlon." *New York Times*, June 16, 1988: B17.

Moran, Malcolm. "Torrence Keeps Streak Alive." *New York Times*, February 27, 1988: 51, 53.

Nelson, Bert. ed. *Track & Field News*, July 1988.

_____. *Track & Field News*, August 1988: 13–19.

_____. *Track & Field News*, December 1988: 35.

_____. *Track & Field News*, January 1989: 13.

_____. *Track & Field News*, February 1989: 4, 7, 53.

"1988 U.S. Olympic Track and Field Team." *New York Times*, July 25, 1988: C6.

Peters, Keith, Kevin Saylors, Jim Dunaway, Roy Conrad, Tom Jordan, Sieg Lindstrom, Bert Nelson, Tom Jennings, Jeff Hollobaugh, Walt Murphy, Andrea Martoglio, Garry Hill, Ed Fox, Ed Gordon. "The Olympics." *Track & Field News*, November 1988: 52–74.

"The Games at a Glance." *New York Times*, October 1, 1988: 47.

USA T&F 1996 Marathon Media Guide, Shooting Star Media.

Wallace, William. "Joyner-Kersee Sets Mark." *New York Times*, February 14, 1988: S10.

Weiss, Marty, ed. *The Athletics Congress of the USA — USA/Mobil Indoor Track and Field Championships Program*, February 24, 1989.

_____. *U.S. Olympic Track and Field Trials Souvenir Program*, July 15–23, 1988.

Chapter 9   (1989)

Bateman, Hal. ed. *American Athletics Annual 1990.*

Cava, Pete. ed. "Past World Indoor Championship Results." *USA Track & Field*, 1998: 60.

"Full Results 1989." *IAAF World Athletic Series 1988–1991.*

"Griffith Joyner Is Honored." *New York Times*, February 22, 1989: 25.

Janofsky, Michael. "Griffith Joyner Retiring; 'Other Interests' Cited. *New York Times*, February 25, 1989: 49.

_____. "McKenzie Ends Joyner-Kersee's Streak." *New York Times*, February 25, 1989: 49, 50.

Nelson, Bert. ed. *Track & Field News*, April 1989.

_____. "TAC Lacking Many Stars." *Track & Field News*, August 1989: 4–21, 42–49.

_____. ed. "1989 Top Ten." *Track & Field News*, February 1991: 12–38.

_____. *Track & Field News*, August 1989.

"News." *The Athletic Congress of the USA*, March, 1989.

"News." *The Athletic Congress of the USA*, June, 1989.

"Record." *The Athletics Congress/USA*, Volume 11, Number 1: Winter 1990.

"Track." *New York Times*, September 11, 1989: C14.

"Track and Field." *New York Times*, September 9, 1989: 44.

Chapter 10   (1990)

Bateman, Hal, ed. *American Athletics Annual*. Indianapolis, Indiana: The Athletics Congress, 1991.

Janofsky, Michael. "Indoor Track Ends a Sluggish Season Strongly." *New York Times*, February 24, 1990: 45.

Nelson, Bert, ed. "1990's Top 10 Women." *Track & Field News*. February 1991: 12–38.

_____. "Goodwill Games." *Track & Field News*. October 1990: 6.

_____. "TAC Women." *Track & Field News*. August 1990: 28–39.

Weiss, Martin, ed. *USA/Mobil Indoor Track & Field Championships Program*, Friday, February 22, 1991.

Chapter 11   (1991)

Bateman, Hal, ed. *American Athletics Annual*. Indianapolis, Indiana: The Athletics Congress, 1992.

Bondy, Filip. "Favor Jostles Plumer En Route to a Victory." *New York Times*, June 16, 1991: S7.

_____. "For Want of a Gauge, the Records Were Lost." *New York Times*, June 13, 1991: B16.

_____. "O'Brien Is Headed for Where It Counts After Record-Setting Effort in Decathlon." *New York Times*, June 14, 1991: B16.

Cava, Pete. ed. "Past World Indoor Championship Results." *USA Track & Field*, 1998: 61.

_____. "1991's Top 10 Women." *Track & Field News*, February 1992: 10–47.

"Keeping Track of Things..." *The Newsletter of the Women's Track and Field Committee*, Volume 9, Number 1: January 1992.

Janofsky, Michael. "A June Chill? Welcome to Randalls Island." *New York Times*, June 13, 1991: B13.

_____. "Ailing Joyner-Kersee Pulls Out After Riding High in Heptathlon." *New York Times*, August 27, 1991: B8.

_____. "Dixon in a First, Is First in Seville," *New York Times*, March 11, 1991: C8.

_____. "Dixon Wins Another 400-Meter Title; Morceli Takes Mile." *New York Times*, February 23, 1991: L43.

_____. "Lewis Closes Out Meet with Dazzling Leap." *New York Times*, June 16, 1991: S1, 7.

Lindstrom, Sieg, Jed Brickner, Ed Fox, Bob Hersh, Garry Hill, Dave Johnson, Richard D. Smith, Jon Hendershott, Jeff Hollobaugh. "Athletes to the Rescue." *Track & Field News*, August 1991: 20–28.

Martinez, Michael. "Johnson Starts Off Slowly Again and Finishes 2d." *New York Times*, January 19, 1991: 52.

Story, Larry. "10K AR for Larrieu Smith." *Track & Field News*, May 1991: 14.

Chapter 12 (1992)

Davis, Scott, Dave Johnson and Howard Wilman, eds. *FAST — United States Track and Field Annual 1993*, Los Angeles, California, April 1993.

Denman, Elliott. *Anthology of the Olympic Games*. West Long Branch, N.J., 2000.

Hill, E. Garry. "A Meet Out of Synch." *Track & Field News*, November 1992: 20, 21.

_____. "Barcelona." *Track & Field News*, October 1992: 52–86.

_____. "1993 Women's World Rankings." *Track & Field News*, February 1994: 16–39.

Hollobaugh, Jeff, Jed Brickner, Rodney Staggs, Sieg Lindstrom, Mike Fanelli, John Parks, David Woods, Bob Bowman, Kevin Saylors, Tom Jordan, Roy Conrad, Ed Fox, Janet Vitu, Glen McMicken. "What a Trials." *Track & Field News*, August 1992: 28–66.

Janofsky, Michael. "A Course So Familiar Jennings Could Teach It." *New York Times*, March 21, 1992: 34.

_____. "A Glossy Olympics Hits the Finish Line." *New York Times*, August 10, 1992: A1, C5.

_____. "Jennings, in Her Own Backyard, Finds Winning as Easy as 1-2-3." *New York Times*, March 22, 1992: S2.

_____. "Johnson Has Lewis on Run in the 200." *New York Times*, June 28, 1992: S3.

_____. "U.S. Runs and Soars and Clicks Heels Over 9 Medals." *New York Times*, August 7, 1992: A1.

"Keeping Track of Things..." The *Newsletter of the Women's Track and Field Committee*, Volume 9, Number 3, November 1992: 3.

_____. *The Newsletter of the Women's Track and Field Committee*, Volume 9, Number 1: January 1992.

Lunzenfichter, Alain. *IAAF Quarterly Review*, Issue Two 1992, 13, 17.

Litsky, Frank. "Joyner-Kersee Wins and Worries." *New York Times*, June 22, 1992: C7.

_____. "Slaney, Slowed by Injury, Fails to Gain 3,000 Berth. *New York Times*, June 23, 1992: B12.

Moore, Kenny. *Sports Illustrated*, July 22, 1992, 64, 95–98.

Springer, Mark. ed. *USA/Mobil Indoor Track Championships Program*, February 26, 1993.

"Statistics." *New York Times*, June 29, 1992: C8.

Wallace, William N. "With Little Trouble Morceli Wins Mile." *New York Times*, February 29, 1992: 31, 36.

Chapter 13 (1993)

Bondy, Filip. "Tolbert's Victory Prevents a Devers Sweep." *New York Times*, June 19, 1993: L29.

_____. "Johnson Dominates in a 400 Showdown." *New York Times*, June 20, 1993: 4.

_____. "Vroom! That Was Devers Whipping By." *New York Times*, February 27, 1993: L29,32.

Cava, Pete. ed. "Past World Indoor Championship Results." *USA Track & Field*, 1998: 61, 62.

Cava, Pete. ed. "USA/Mobil Outdoor Track & Field Championships." *USA Track & Field*, 1993.

Davis, Scott S., Dave Johnson and Howard Wilman, eds. *FAST — United States Track and Field Annual 1994*. Los Angeles, California, April 1994.

Dunaway, James. "U.S. Team Has Speed to Burn in Germany." *New York Times*, June 21, 1993: C4.

Hill, E. Garry. ed. "1993's Top 10 Women." *Track & Field News*, February 1994: 8–39.

Lindstrom, Sieg. "The Best Yet?" *Track & Field News*, November 1993: 36–60.

Litsky, Frank. "American Day Tips to Joyner-Kersee." *New York Times*, August 18, 1993: B7, B10.

_____. "Controversies and Victories in the World Meet." *New York Times*, August 16, 1993: C3.

_____. "Devers Barely Defeats Ottey in 100 Meters." *New York Times*, August 17, 1993: B9, B13.

_____. "From Sub-Par to Most Enjoyed." *New York Times*, August 18, 1993: B10.

_____. "Jennings Finds Nice Dreams Finish 3rd." *New York Times*, March 14, 1993: S7.

_____. "Two for the Record, but Just One Gold." *New York Times*, August 20, 1993: B9, B12.

_____. "World Hurdles Mark Falls to Welshman." *New York Times*, August 21, 1993: 27, 31.

Price, Shawn, Bob Hersh, Ed Fox, Sean Hartnett, Sieg Lindstrom, Dave Johnson, Bob Bowman, Kevin Saylors. "Magic in the Air." *Track & Field News*, September 1993: 18–73.

Rhoden, William C. "Rudolph's Legacy: Triumphs Over Pain." *New York Times*, June 20, 1993: L7.

Springer, Mark. ed. *USA/Mobil Indoor Championships Program*, March 5, 1994.

Chapter 14 (1994)

Bateman, Hal and Kurt Freudenthal. "USA Mobil Outdoor Track & Field Championships." *News*, 1994.

Dunaway, Jim. AR LJ For JJK: 24–7." *Track & Field News*, August 1994: 41.

_____. "In 100, Devers and Mitchell Are First to the Finish Line." *New York Times*, June 17, 1994: B13.

_____. "Yes, Yes, Yes, Deal Knew It." *New York Times*, June 18, 1994: 33.

Hersh, Bob, Elliott Denman. "USATF Women." *Track & Field News*, September 1994: 38–47.

Hill, E. Garry, ed. "If You Build It..." *Track & Field News*, May 1994: 8–34.

_____. *Track & Field News*, February 1995: 10–15.

_____. *Track & Field News*, March 1994: 54.

Hollobaugh, Jeff. "Devers Runs 10.77w." *Track & Field News*, August 1994: 42.

"Huffman Up, Up, Up to U.S. Mark in Vault." *New York Times*, June 19, 1994: 14.

Litsky, Frank. "2 Records, and Joyner-Kersee, Fall." *New York Times*, March 6, 1994: S6.

_____. "Indoor Meet Gets Southern Exposure." *New York Times*, March 1, 1994: B15.

_____. "Track and Field." *New York Times*, May 23, 1994: C4.

_____. "Wilma Rudolph, Star of the 1960 Olympics, Dies at 54." *New York Times*, November 13, 1994: 53.

Chapter 15   (1995)

Cava, Pete. ed. "Past World Indoor Championship Results." *USA Track & Field*, 1998: 62.

Championships in Sacramento." *USA Track & Field Record*, Volume 16, Number 1: Spring/Summer 1995.

Cherry, Gene. "Fab Early-Season Marks." *Track & Field News*, June 1995: 43.

Conrad, Roy. "Bagging the Big Bucks." *Track & Field News*, November 1995: 6–8.

Davis, Scott. "Hot Sprint Action." *Track & Field News*, May 1995: 10–11.

Davis, Scott S., ed. *1996 FAST—Track and Field Athletics Annual*. Los Angeles, California, April 1996.

Francis, Amadeo. ed. "XII Juegos Panamericanos." *Pan Athlete*, Volume 12, No. 38: 1995.

Hill, E. Garry, ed. "1995 World Rankings." *Track & Field News*, December 1995: 37–49.

_____. "1995's Top 10 Women." *Track & Field News*, January 1996: 10–13.

_____. "USATF Women." *Track & Field News*, September 1995: 18–44.

_____. "End of an Era." *Track & Field News*, October 1995: 28–63.

Hollobaugh, Jeff. "Summer Heats Up with Action from USA Mobil Outdoor Championships in Sacramento." *USA Track & Field Record*, Volume 16, Number 1: Spring/Summer 1995.

Longman, Jere. "Cold, Wind, Danger Are 1–2–3 on Track." *New York Times*, June 16, 1995: B8.

_____. "Disqualification in 200 Stings Torrence." *New York Times*, August 11, 1995: B7.

_____. "Do You Know This Man?" *New York Times*, March 5, 1995: 1, 4.

_____. "Marsh Wins Slow, but Close, 100 Meters." *New York Times*, June 17, 1995: 32.

McMicken, Glen and Hal Bateman. "5th IAAF World Indoor Track & Field Championships." *USATF News*, March 1995.

Reel, Vince, ed. "Sunkist Invitational Another 'World Record' for Decker." *Women's Track & Field World*, Vol. 18, No. 2, February 1985: 7.

Scott, Mike. "Appell Ends Streak." *Track & Field News*, February 1995: 61.

Springer, Mark, ed. *USA/Mobil Indoor Track and Field Championships Program*, March 2, 1996.

USATF. *1995 USA Mobil Outdoor Track & Field Championships Report.*"

Chapter 16   (1996)

Cava, Pete. "XXIV IAAF World Cross Country Championships." *News*, 1996.

Davis, Scott, ed. *1997 FAST Track and Field Athletics Annual*, Los Angeles, California: April 1997.

Dunaway, Jim, Dave Johnson, John Hendershott. "Only at the Olympics." *Track & Field News*, October 1996: 6–55.

Fish, Mike. "Torrence Puts on a Show." *The Atlanta Journal-Constitution*, March 3, 1996: E1.

Hartnett, Sean. "Carolina Dreamin." *Track & Field News*, April 1996: 8.

Hill, E. Garry, ed. "Olympic Notebook." *Track & Field News*, November 1996: 29.

_____. "Devers Top U.S. Woman." *Track & Field News*, December 1996: 37.

_____. "Atlanta Part I." *Track & Field News*, September 1996: 6–55.

_____. "Atlanta, Phase I." *Track & Field News*, May 1996: 14.

_____. "Jennings Drops 'Em." *Track & Field News*, February 1997: 10.

Layden, Tim. "Thrills and Spills." *Sports Illustrated*, August 12, 1996: 36, 37.

Litsky, Frank. U.S. Triumphs Tempered by Joyner-Kersee's Pain." *New York Times*, July 28, 1996: S4.

Longman, Jere. "Americans Win Women's 4 × 100 and Both 4 × 400's." *New York Times*, August 4, 1996: S1, 5.

_____. "Bailey Sets 100 Mark; Devers in Photo Finish." *New York Times*, July 28, 1996: S1, 4.

_____. "Batten's Fast Recovery from an Injury Results in the Fastest Time of the Year." *New York Times*, June 17, 1996: C8.

_____. "Drama at Track, and Upset on Tennis Court." *New York Times*, August 3, 1996: 1, 32.

_____. "Johnson Misses His Record, But Demolishes Opponents." *New York Times*, March 3, 1996: 4

_____. "Joyner-Kersee Is Leading While Battling Ailments." *New York Times*, June 16, 1996: 30.

_____. "Lewis Fails to Qualify in the 100." *New York Times*, June 16, 1996: 1, 2.

_____. "Roba Wins Marathon, and Ethiopia's Heart." *New York Times*, July 29, 1996: C1, C7.

Matthews, Peter, ed. *Athletics 1997—The International Track and Field Annual*. SportsBooks Ltd., Surrey, United Kingdom.

McMicken, Glen, ed. "American Women's Outdoor Track & Field Records."*1996 USA Track & Field Outdoor Championships Media Guide.*"

_____. *1997 USA Track & Field Media Guide.*

"ResultsPlus." *New York Times*, December 8, 1996: S7.

Rhoden, William C. "It's Time for Changing of Guard for United States Track and Field." *New York Times*, June 17, 1996: C8.

USA Track & Field. *"A Year-End Review of USA National Teams."* 1996.

USA Track & Field Road Running Information Center. *1996 Marathon Media Guide*, Shooting Star Media, Inc. 1996.

USA Track & Field. "18th Annual Meeting Minutes." December 3–7, San Francisco, California.

Chapter 17   (1997)

Cava, Pete, ed. *Past World Indoor Championship Results, USA Track & Field*. 1998: 62, 63.

Davis, Scott, ed. *1998 FAST Track and Field Athletics Annual*, Los Angeles, California, April 1998.

Hendershott, Jon, Bob Hersh, Ed Gordon. "Athens Women." *Track & Field News*, November 1997: 57–71.

Hill, E. Garry, ed. "New Faces Dominate." *Track & Field News*, September 1997: 32–55.

_____. ed. "Women's Rankings." *Track & Field News*, January 1998: 29–46.

"Kirtland Wins Marathon Title." *New York Times*, February 9, 1997: 337.

Litsky, Frank. "In Her 19th Millrose, Clark Is Still Clicking." *New York Times*, February 4, 1997: B11.

Longman, Jere. "American Men Blunder, but Women Salvage a Relay Gold." *New York Times*, August 10, 1997: S1, 3.

_____. "Point Guard Wins the 100, But Devers Is Not in Race." *New York Times*, June 14, 1997: 32.

_____. "Redemption Plus a World Title in the 400 Meters for Johnson." *New York Times*, August 6, 1997: B9, B13.

_____. "Rounds Caps Comeback by Winning 800 Title." *New York Times*, June 15, 1997: S4.

_____. "Slaney Still Golden After 23 Years at the Millrose Games." *New York Times*, February 8, 1997: 29, 33.

"Repeat in Pole-Vault." *New York Times*, March 1, 1997: 32.

Schwartz, Jerry. "Devers and Slaney Race to '97 Bests." *New York Times*, March 2, 1997: 11.

Springer, Mark, ed. *Souvenir Program. USA Track & Field*. February 27–28, 1998.

"Tergat Leads Kenyans with Dramatic Victory." *New York Times*, March 24, 1997: C9.

Chapter 18   (1998)

Arcoleo, Laura and Nick Davies, ed. *IAAF Magazine: Year of Women in Athletics*, Volume 13, Issue 4: 1998.

Cava, Pete, ed. *26th IAAF World Cross Country Championships*. USATF, 1998: 10, 11.

Davies, Nicolas, ed. "Grand Prix Final Results." *IAAF Magazine*, Volume 13, Issue 5: 1998.

Davis, Scott, ed. *1999 FAST Track and Field Athletics Annual*, Los Angeles, California, 1999.

Dunaway, Jim. "Women's Vault a Hit." *Track & Field News*, April 1998; 18.

Hill, E. Garry, ed. "Women's World Rankings." *Track & Field News*, January 1999: 32–47.

_____. "Our 50-Year All-Star Team." *Track & Field News*, February 1998: 47.

Hart, Scotty, ed. *Footnotes*, Volume 27, Number 2: Summer 1999: 30.

IAAF News Supplement, 1998.

Litsky, Frank. "Aching Godina Still Expects Oomph in His Throw." *New York Times*, June 20, 1998: C7.

_____. "After 3d Title, Jones Contends She's Not Best. " *New York Times*, June 22, 1998: C1, C3.

_____. "Greene Pulls Out, but Jones Pulls Away Easily in the 100 and Long Jump." *New York Times*, June 21, 1998: SP3.

_____. "Wanamaker Mile Won by a Wisp of a Kenyan." *New York Times*, February 14, 1998: C8.

Longman, Jere. "Florence Griffith Joyner, 38, Champion Sprinter, Is Dead." *New York Times*, September 22, 1998: C23.

Rhoden, William C. "Death at 38: Reviewing a Vibrant Life." *New York Times*, September 22, 1998: D9.

USA Track & Field. 20th Annual Meeting Booklet, December 1998.

"Waller Sets Record in High Jump." *New York Times*, March 1, 1998: 9.

Chapter 19   (1999)

Anderson, Curtis. "Devers Puts Woes, and Field, Behind Her." *The Register-Guard*, June 28, 1999: 10B.

_____. "Jacobs Pulls Off Distance Double." *The Register-Guard*, June 28, 1999: 1B, 8B.

Bellamy, Ron. "June Also a Good Month for Waller." *The Register-Guard*, June 28, 1999: 6B.

_____. "Second title is one to savor." *The Register-Guard*, June 28, 1999: 9B.

Clarey, Christopher. "Greene and Miller Win 200-Meter Gold in Spain." *New York Times*, August 28, 1999: D1, D6.

_____. "Greene Surges as Jones Cruises to U.S. Double at 100 Meters." *New York Times*, August 23, 1999: D1, D8.

Davies, Nick, ed., *IAAF Magazine*, Volume 14, Issue 4 1999.

Eder, Larry, Mel Watman. "The 1999 American Championships," *American Track & Field*, Spring 1999.

_____. "The 1999 American Championships." *American Track & Field*, Summer 1999: 26, 27.

Geer, Jill M. and Scott Davis, eds. *2000 USA Track & Field Media Guide and FAST Annual*, Indianapolis, Indiana and Los Angeles, California, May, 2000.

"Greene Cruises in 200 Heat." *New York Times*, June 27, 1999: SP11.

"Hartwig and Griffin Set U.S. Records." *New York Times*, February 28, 1999: SP11.

Litsky, Frank. "Betty Robinson, a Pathfinder in Women's Track, Dies at 87." *New York Times*, May 21, 1999: B11.

Murphy, Mary. "Champion Spirit." *TV Guide*, December 18, 1999: 39–42.

"On the Roads," *USA Track & Field*: Volume 13, Summer 1999.

Rodman, Bob. "Jones Bounces Back to Run Off with 200." *The Register-Guard*, June 28, 1999: 9B.

_____. "Miles-Clark Adds Another U.S. Title." *The Register-Guard*, June 28, 1999: 9B.

"USA Reigns in Spain at IAAF World Championships." *USAT&F*, Volume 19, Number 7: August/September 1999.

"United States Track Coaches Association." *Hall of Fame Program*, December 4, 1999.

Volponi, Roberto, ed. "A Statue for a Myth of Women's Athletics." *IAAF News*: July 1999: 6.

Chapter 20   (2000)

Associated Press. "Jones Triumphs at Trials." *Poughkeepsie Journal*, July 17, 2000: C1.

Boeck, Greg. "Jones, Baseball Team Primed." *USA Today*, September 22, 2000: 1F.

Davies, Nick, ed. *IAAF Magazine*, Volume 15, Issue 4: 2000.

"Deal Wins Indoor Title for 12th Time." *New York Times*, March 5, 2000: 9.

Florida Today Wires. "Jones Named Top Female." *Florida Today*, December 28, 2000: 4C.

Gannett News Service. "Jones Glides to Another Gold." *Poughkeepsie Journal*, September 29, 2000: 1H.

Geer, Jill M. and Scott Davis, eds. *2001 USA Track & Field Media Guide and FAST Annual*. Indianapolis, Indiana and Los Angeles, California, April, 2001.

IAAF News, March 2000, n. 39: 12, 13.

IAAF News, July 2000, n. 43: 6, 14.

IAAF News, Sept/Oct 2000: N. 45.

"Jones, Clarks Reach Their Goals." *USA Today*, July 24, 2000: 9C.

Lindstrom, Sieg, Dave Johnson. "The Wizards of Oz." *Track & Field News*, December 2000: 40–63.

Longman, Jere. "A Fond Farewell from Australia." *New York Times*, October 2, 2000: S1.

Longman, Jere. "After Slow Start, Dragila Wins the First Women's Gold." *New York Times*, September 26, 2000: S4.

_____. "Clarks Rule the Women's 800." *New York Times*, July 24, 2000: D10.

_____. "Dragila Conquers Fear, Then Clears Opening Height." *New York Times*, July 22, 2000: D2.

_____. "Glover Sizzles to Victory in 400 Hurdles." *New York Times*, July 18, 2000: D5.

_____. "Goal Is 17 Feet in Women's Pole Vault." *New York Times*, February 6, 2000: SP6.

_____. "Greene and Jones Book a Visit to Sydney in the 100 Meters." *New York Times*, July 16, 2001: SP1, 4.

_____. "Greene Kicks Off Olympic Year with a Swift 60 Meters." *New York Times*, February 5, 2000: D1, D6.

_____. "In a Fast First Step, Jones Easily Wins Her 100-Meter Heat." *New York Times*, July 15, 2000: D1, 6.

_____. "Jones Leaps Far Enough, But Foul Costs Her Gold." *New York Times*, September 30, 2000: D1, D7.

_____. "The Focus Sharpens on Jones." *New York Times*, July 25, 2000: D1.

_____. "U.S. Women Seek a Comeback at Middle Distances." *New York Times*, July 16, 2000: Section 8, 1, 4.

"Pathological Runner Christine Clark." *Women's Sports & Fitness*, September 2000: 66.

Sandomir, Richard. "High Drama at U.S. Track Trials." *New York Times*, July 21, 2000: D4.

USATF. "Jacobs Smashes American Record in 5,000 Meters at Olympic Trials." Internet document: July 26, 2000.

Weir, Tom. "All Eyes on Jones." *USA Today*, September 21, 2000: 1A, 2A.

_____. "Keeping It All in the Family." *USA Today*, July 19, 2000: 1C, 2C.

Index of Photographs

General Index